Tom Holden
to
Coleen Smith

Couples in Conflict

Couples
in
Conflict

New Directions
in Marital Therapy

Edited by Alan S. Gurman, Ph.D.
and David G. Rice, Ph.D.

Jason Aronson, New York

ISBN: 0-87668-150-X
Library of Congress Catalog Number: 74-6951

This book is lovingly dedicated to
Gerri and Joy

CONTENTS

Part II—Treatment Issues
and Interventions

CONTRIBUTORS

MAJOR GORDON L. BOLTE, DSW
Director of Mental Hygiene
U.S. Disciplinary Barracks
Fort Leavenworth, Kansas 66027

ROBERT D. CARTER, Ph.D.
Associate Professor
School of Social Work
University of Michigan
Ann Arbor, Michigan 48104

JOAN M. CONSTANTINE
Private Practice of Family Therapy
22 Bullett Road
Acton, Massachusetts 01720

LARRY L. CONSTANTINE
Instructor
Center for Training in Family Therapy
Boston State Hospital-Tufts University School of Medicine
Boston, Massachusetts 02126

SHELDON K. EDELMAN, Ph.D.
Associate Professor
Department of Sociology
Kansas State University
Manhattan, Kansas 66502

RICHARD M. EISLER, Ph.D.
Assistant Professor
Department of Psychiatry and Human Behavior
University of Mississippi Medical Center
Jackson, Mississippi 39216

WILLIAM F. FEY, Ph.D.
Professor
Department of Psychiatry
University of Wisconsin Medical School
Madison, Wisconsin 53706

JEANNE A. FIGUREL, M.S.W.
Social Work Supervisor
Dixmont State Hospital
Pittsburgh, Pennsylvania 15143

ALAN S. GURMAN, Ph.D.
Assistant Professor
Department of Psychiatry
University of Wisconsin Medical School
Madison, Wisconsin 53706

JANET E. HARRELL, Ph.D.
Assistant Professor
Department of Individual and Family Studies
The Pennsylvania State University
University Park, Pennsylvania 16802

MICHEL HERSEN, Ph.D.
Professor of Clinical Psychiatry
Department of Psychiatry
University of Pittsburgh School of Medicine
Western Psychiatric Institute
Pittsburgh, Pennsylvania 15261

NATHAN HURVITZ, Ph.D.
Private Practice
Crenshaw Medical Arts Center
Los Angeles, California 90008

DAVID J. KASS, M.D.
Director of Psychiatry
Miriam Hospital
Providence, Rhode Island 02906

JOSEPH G. KEPECS, M.D.
Professor
Department of Psychiatry
University of Wisconsin Medical School
Madison, Wisconsin 53706

THOMAS P. LAUGHREN, M.D.
Psychiatry Service
Veterans Administration Hospital-Davis Park
Providence, Rhode Island 02908

JUDITH LONG LAWS, Ph.D.
Assistant Professor
Department of Psychology
Cornell University
Ithaca, New York 14850

ELSA LEICHTER, M.S.S.A.
Consultant in Group Therapy
Jewish Family Service
New York, New York 10023

ROBERT P. LIBERMAN, M.D.
Research Psychiatrist and Associate Clinical
    Professor of Psychiatry
Camarillo-Neuropsychiatric Institute
    (UCLA) Research Program
Camarillo, California 93010

W. CHARLES LOBITZ, M.A., C. Phil.
Psychology Fellow
Neuropsychiatric Institute
Center for the Health Sciences
University of California
Los Angeles, California 90024

JOSEPH LoPICCOLO, Ph.D.
Associate Professor
Department of Psychiatry and Behavioral Science
State University of New York
Stony Brook, New York 11791

PATRICK McNAMEE, M.S.W.
Social Worker
Catholic Social Service of Allegheny County
Pittsburgh, Pennsylvania 15219

DAVID H. OLSON, Ph.D.
Professor
Family Social Science
University of Minnesota
St. Paul, Minnesota 55101

ALAN F. RAPPAPORT, Ph.D.
Private Practice
110 East 82 Street
New York, New York 10028

DAVID G. RICE, Ph.D.
Associate Professor
Department of Psychiatry
University of Wisconsin Medical School
Madison, Wisconsin 53706

JOY K. RICE, Ph.D.
Assistant Professor and Director
of Continuing Education
University of Wisconsin
Madison, Wisconsin 53706

RICHARD B. STUART, DSW
Professor
Department of Psychiatry
School of Medicine
University of British Columbia
Vancouver 8, British Columbia

EDWIN J. THOMAS, Ph.D.
Professor
School of Social Work
    and Department of Psychology
University of Michigan
Ann Arbor, Michigan 48104

MARJORIE K. TOOMIM, Ph.D.
Private Practice
6542 Hayes Drive
Los Angeles, California 90048

RICHARD A. WELLS, M.S.W.
Associate Professor
School of Social Work
University of Pittsburgh
Pittsburgh, Pennsylvania 15260

CARL A. WHITAKER, M.D.
Professor
Department of Psychiatry
University of Wisconsin Medical School
Madison, Wisconsin 53706

Preface to the Second Printing

Couples in Conflict is written both for practicing clinicians and for marital and family therapists in training. The response to the first printing has been so positive that continuing demand for the volume has necessitated a second printing. Indeed, when *Couples in Conflict* was first published we expected that its general emphasis on innovation in the marital field, and—in contrast to most books in the area—its endorsement of an attitude of clinical empiricism, would make it especially attractive as a textbook for courses on couples therapy in a variety of professional disciplines. In fact, our own predictions in this regard have been greatly exceeded, and *Couples in Conflict* continues to be widely adopted as a classroom text. This continuing use of the book for teaching purposes confirms us in our belief that most of the material contained here, which we considered innovative four years ago, offers today a still very contemporary perspective on the field.

Since the first printing, several major events have occurred in the field of marital and family therapy. The literature of the field continues to grow at a rate that has at least matched, and perhaps surpassed, that of the field of behavior therapy. Since 1975 the *International Journal of Family Therapy*, the *Journal of Divorce*, the *Journal of Marriage and Family Counseling*, the *Journal of Sex and Marital Therapy*, *Family Therapy*, the *Journal of Family History*, and *Alternative Lifestyles* have all begun publication. In addition, a large and ever increasing number of new books and monographs appear in the field each year.

This proliferation of journals and books has been paralleled by the growth of the profession of marital-family therapy. A large number of states now either have, or are working toward establishing, regulations for the practice of marital-family therapy. In 1979, a new professional organization, the American Family Therapy Association (AFTA), will hold its first annual meeting in Chicago. The first major professional society in the field, the American Association of Marriage and Family Counselors, in 1978 changed its name to the American Association for Marital and Family Therapy (AAMFT). AAMFT's membership rolls have nearly doubled since the first publication of *Couples in Conflict* almost four years ago, and continued growth is expected.

It is in this exciting professional context of growth and enthusiasm that we are most pleased to have *Couples in Conflict* appear in its second printing.

In our original preface, we noted that many of the contributors to the book were relative newcomers to the field, and that many of their names would be unfamiliar to readers of the book. In the intervening four years, most of those 1975 "unknowns" have become widely recognized, and some now hold clearly established positions of leadership in the fields of family, marital, and sex therapy.

In sum, then, we believe we have assembled in these pages a sound, representative sample of what remain the cutting edges and frontiers of marital therapy. We are pleased at the prospect of this book's continued service to professionals and students interested in improving their therapeutic efficacy with people in troubled marital relationships.

ALAN S. GURMAN, PhD.
DAVID G. RICE, Ph.D.
Madison, Wisconsin
Nobember 1978

PREFACE

The literature of marital therapy is growing rapidly and much clearly valuable work in clinical innovation and empirical research has appeared in the last several years. Important contributions have been published in such widely varying sources, however, that few clinicians have been able to keep abreast of the most significant developments in the field. Because of the diversity of interests and professional background of marital therapists and others concerned with the nature of married life, even the most devoted student, practitioner, or researcher in this area finds it very difficult to stay up-to-date with the emerging frontiers of the field.

The primary purpose of *Couples in Conflict: New Directions in Marital Therapy* is to bring together a comprehensive yet necessarily selective collection of recent papers in the field which seem truly innovative, represent important breakthroughs in practice and research, and are likely to have enduring value. We have drawn on the writings of psychologists, psychiatrists, social workers, and sociologists in an effort to reveal the breadth of important recent contributions to the field. Since the final selection of papers for a collection of readings is inherently the result of an interaction between the works that exist and the conceptual and clinical predilections of those who do the selecting, it is inevitable that certain biases will influence the choice of material. We feel strongly that practices of marital therapists and, indeed, all psychotherapists, must increasingly become wedded to empirical evidence for their efficacy. While we recognize that there is probably a "scientific ceiling" beyond which our substantive understanding of the mechanisms of therapeutic change cannot go, it is clear to us that the field of marital therapy, to continue the metaphor, has just barely gotten off the ground in this regard. We think that our own teaching reflects such an attitude, with a concomitant concern about the proliferation of many current "fads" in psychotherapy. While we recognize that what is fad to one person may be fact to another, our ultimate concerns are twofold: that the mental health professions strive for the development of therapeutic interventions which produce demonstrable results and that we collectively foster the creation of clinical skills that are teachable.

This book is not intended to be a simple "how-to-do-it" volume, abundant in speculation and lacking in critical examination and evaluation. However, over four-fifths of the papers do have direct relevance to the actual conduct of marital therapy. This book could thus serve as a text for basic courses in couples therapy for students in clinical and counseling psychology, social work, psychiatric nursing, and psychiatry. Beyond its potential in formal training and teaching settings, we think that the experienced clinician, too, will find a great deal of practical usefulness in these pages. Indeed, a responsible and mature clinician never stops learning new ways in which to conceptualize therapeutic issues and to facilitate human change and growth. Finally, we are hopeful that researchers in the area of marital therapy will find herein the intellectual stimulation for advancing our scientific knowledge in this domain.

We would like to offer a few thoughts about the selections included in this book. As we have emphasized, and as the title of this work directly conveys, our purpose has been to bring together papers which we consider to represent *new* directions in couples therapy. For this reason, perhaps, the names of many of our contributors may also be ''new'' to a large portion of our readership. If this is so, then it is as we feel it should be. Our intent has not been to compile the views of acknowledged ''name people'' in the field, but rather, to select those papers which we think contain the most substance of an innovative sort, whether in the form of theoretical thought, modification and development of new clinical practices, or empirical research. Not at all surprisingly, some of this emerging work *has* been done by marital therapists whose names will be immediately recognized.

While the majority of the papers in this book have been reprinted from their original sources, several chapters are new and have been prepared especially for this volume. In such instances, we invited original contributions from colleagues in the field whom we felt could speak with expertise about their respective areas of interest. These contributions were solicited primarily in those areas of marital therapy in which we felt that there had been major new developments which had not yet received sufficient public exposure.

We are grateful to Dr. Jason Aronson, whose enthusiastic support for our project has been consistent and facilitating since the initial discussions of our proposal for this volume. Our thanks are also extended to the original publishers of those papers that have been reprinted herein for their cooperative granting of the privilege to use their material. We wish to thank Lynn Tobias and Cathy Beck for the invaluable help they have provided in the secretarial and clerical aspects of this project, with its many communications, text revisions, and pressing deadlines.

Last, and far from least, we thank all our authors for simply having made very important contributions to a more comprehensive and effective field of marital therapy.

ALAN S. GURMAN
DAVID G. RICE

Madison, Wisconsin

I
Historical Perspectives
and Emerging Trends

INTRODUCTION

Marital therapy has a short but burgeoning history. Facilities offering formal professional training in this field have appeared only in the last forty years. The magnitude of this development, like that in many areas of applied behavioral science, has been geometric rather than linear. Important innovations in technique and fledgling theoretical conceptualizations in marital therapy have evolved largely during the past decade. In the first chapter in Part I, Olson systematically chronicles the historical development of the field, differentiates it from the independent but related area of family therapy, and details its current meager theoretical and empirical underpinnings. Many of these albeit new-found clinical formulations and innovations offer stimulation and excitement to the practitioner, have promise as therapeutic techniques, and will hopefully spur careful empirical testing. Marital therapy is thus gaining substance as a discipline that is therapeutically autonomous yet highly related conceptually to many other fields.

The second chapter is Gurman's content-analysis study of the published works in marital therapy from pre-1940 to mid-1972. Gurman finds particular increased attention in recent writings to new modes of clinical practice, especially in the use of behavioral techniques, as well as an emphasis on conjoint treatment, often involving co-therapists. In addition, there are heartening trends toward the empirical documentation of client progress and outcome, and more vigorous attention to the therapeutic process. Gurman's analysis reinforces Olson's picture of the interdisciplinary nature and background of the field by finding that marital therapy publications have appeared in greatest frequency in journals that have a decidedly multidisciplinary character.

Given marital therapy's interdisciplinary nexus, with its strong ties to sociology and social theorizing, it is not surprising to find an increased concern with several current social movements and their impact on marriage. Two of these societal forces are examined in the last two chapters: Judith Laws presents a feminist's perspective on the marital adjustment literature and Larry and Joan Constantine and Sheldon Edelman discuss the treatment of couples in nontraditional, nondyadic marriages. The concern in both these articles is focused on the inhibitory effects in regard to personal growth of rigid, prescribed social and sex-role behaviors. Laws calls attention to the historically different social status and role expectations of husbands and wives, and the general lack of fulfillment and life satisfaction for women "wedded" to the fixed "housewife and mother" components of traditional marriage. A more detailed confirmatory exposition of this thesis can be found in Bernard's (1972) book on *The Future of Marriage*. Although Laws does not deal directly with the therapeutic implications of her findings, the message for the clinician seems clear. He or she cannot model only a traditional picture of marriage and expect to help many spouses toward the goals of mutual marital and personal satisfaction. The Constantines amplify this point, and feel that therapists (counselors) who "bring to the counseling relationship a strong bias in the direction of conventionality" will have difficulty helping individuals who are involved in new marital life-styles.

The four chapters in Part I review where marital therapy has been and expand upon where it is going. The writers of these chapters sensitize the marital therapist to an appreciation of the historically recent and highly interdisciplinary origins of the field, the lack of sound, tested formulations and therapeutic techniques, and a need for openness in regard to alternative ways of viewing, understanding, and helping couples in conflict.

REFERENCES

Bernard, J. *The Future of Marriage.* New York: World Publishing Co., 1972.

Section A

Current Status of Marital Therapy

DAVID H. OLSON

1   A Critical Overview*

This paper surveys the recently emerging fields of marital and family therapy in terms of their developments in research, theory and clinical practice. The parallel, but unrelated, developments of these two fields are described. A system framework was developed for categorizing the various clinical approaches in marital and family therapy. Neither field has yet developed a solid theoretical base nor tested their major assumptions or principles. However, both fields have recently become more concerned about conceptual and methodological issues. Several ways of bridging the professional gap between therapists and researchers are suggested. Recommendations for interdisciplinary borrowing are indicated and exemplary projects giving new direction to the fields are discussed.

Considering the fields of marital and family therapy in developmental perspective with other sciences, the physical sciences are the grandparents, the social sciences are the parents, and the fields of marital and family therapy are the youngsters. These two fields are really like fraternal twins in that they both were born within a decade of each other and are at about the same developmental stage as sciences. They were both born and nurtured by interdisciplinary parentage and they have developed along separate but parallel lines. Like the development of an individual within a family unit, professions in their infancy

* The articles in this review were primarily located through the use of the *International Bibliography of Research in Marriage and The Family*, 1900-1964, compiled by Aldous and Hill (1967). Updated materials from this bibliography system were provided by Nancy Dahl, reference librarian at the University of Minnesota Family Study Center. The writer also wishes to thank the students at the University of Maryland enrolled in the Family Counseling course who assisted in making the bibliography more complete. The constructive suggestions regarding the rough draft of this paper provided by Richard Q. Bell, Jay Haley, Craig Messersmith and Robert G. Ryder, were much appreciated.

need to learn from older and related disciplines so that some of the mistakes and pitfalls encountered by the older disciplines can be avoided or, at least, minimized once they are encountered. The purpose of this paper will, therefore, be to describe the early development of these fraternal twins as growing professions, to point out some of the developmental problems they are having and to suggest ways of facilitating their growth and development. It is hoped that if corrective measures are taken at this early stage of development, both of these professions can maximize their contributions to society.

Like the youth of today, these youngsters to the professional world are having an impact on the older helping professions and are challenging many time honored, but untested, ideas and assumptions. The system approach which they have introduced into the field of psychotherapy and to the study of the individual and his family is both refreshing and provocative, and it is causing a rapid evolution, if not revolution, in the helping professions.

Not unlike youth, however, the professions of marital and family therapy have proceeded with a great amount of vigor but without a sufficient amount of rigor. As a result, many of the visionary ideas have not been carefully enough developed or tested and are, therefore, in need of critical evaluation. In reviewing the work done in marital and family therapy to date, most of the relevant material was published after 1960. More specifically, there were only about twenty-five articles regarding marital therapy published before 1950. Approximately fifty articles were published during the 1950's and over one hundred publications appeared from 1960 to the present. A similar trend was found for the family therapy literature. Only approximately twenty articles were published before 1950 and about sixty were published during the 1950's. A rapid increase in productivity occurred during the 1960's when over 250 articles were published on family therapy. Totally, over 500 articles and 30 books on marital and family therapy were reviewed in this paper. Because of the large number of publications, primary attention was given to the articles and books since 1960, although a few articles from the late 1940's were included. While the survey is thorough, only the most salient and representative articles describing clinical techniques are discussed. There is, however, a rather comprehensive coverage of the research and evaluative studies of marital and family therapy.

Overview of Marital Therapy

In describing the field of marital therapy, it should be initially mentioned that much of the clinical work with couples has been previously referred to in the literature as marriage counseling. The term marriage counseling, however, does not adequately convey the range and variety of approaches to therapy with the marital dyad as it once did thirty years ago when it first became differentiated from other therapeutic approaches. The writer is, therefore, proposing that instead of using the global term marriage counseling to describe all the approaches now used by therapists working with the marital dyad, that the specific type of marital therapy be indicated. The major advantage of this change will be to make it possible to more clearly and accurately differentiate the specific therapeutic approach used. The various types of marital therapy are described later in the paper.

To paraphrase a pioneer in the field, David Mace, the field of marital therapy is both very old and very new. There has always been interest and concern about the intimate relationship of husbands and wives, but only in the last few decades has the need been such that a separate profession has developed to clinically treat couples who were having difficulties in their marital relationship. The first clinics in the United States to begin serving couples with problems opened in the early 1930's and they are still functioning today. The three primary centers and founders were the Marriage Consultation Center in New York founded by Abraham and Hannah Stone (1929), the American Institute of Family Relations founded by Paul Popenoe (1939), and the Marriage Council of Philadelphia founded by Emily Mudd (1932).

About the same time as the founding of these centers in the United States, David Mace and a small group of colleagues organized the National Marriage Guidance Council in England (Mace, 1945, 1970). While the Council had a series of setbacks, in 1943 it opened the first Marriage Guidance Center with David Mace as founder and director. He then helped establish over 100 centers in England which were later incorporated into a National Marriage Guidance Council and he was the Executive Director until 1949. Since then, the government has assisted the National Council financially and these centers are continuing to grow in England.

In 1942, a small group of pioneers in this field organized the American Association of Marriage Counselors (AAMC) in order to facilitate the development of this new profession. In 1967, the AAMC celebrated its twenty-fifth anniversary and published a book which generally surveys the history and development of the profession of marriage counseling (Peterson 1968a). In 1970, the AAMC expanded their focus by officially changing their name to the American Association of Marriage and Family Counselors (AAMFC) in order to include family therapists, who previously had no nationally affiliated group with which to identify. Generally, the members belonging to AAMFC come from a variety of professions including psychology (19%), social work (19%), the ministry (14%), sociology (8%) and the largest group identifying themselves as marital therapists (26%) (Peterson, 1968b). It is revealing that 75 percent of the membership do regard themselves as primarily identified with another professional group, but they do marital therapy as part of their clinical practice. These findings also demonstrate that marital therapy is slowly emerging as a separate profession as is family therapy.

The interdisciplinary composition of AAMFC has been both its greatest asset and its greatest liability. While it has enabled the organization to grow to almost 1,000 members and has helped to provide service to a greater number of clients in a variety of settings, it has retarded the development of clinical research and theory and the organization of professional training centers. This is because so many of those practicing marital therapy are primarily identified with another profession. As a result, the field has been seriously lacking in empirically tested principles and it is without a theoretically derived foundation on which to operate clinically. Even the latest books in the field (Ard and Ard, 1969; Peterson, 1968a; Silverman, 1967; Klemer, 1965; Nash *et al.,* 1964) or reviews (Sager, 1966, 1968) give little, if any, attention to theory or its systematic development, and empirical research is even a rarer commodity. Most of the published material focuses on clinical practices and techniques with considerable emphasis being given to illustrative case descriptions. Only recently are there positive signs that the profession is beginning to expand its empirical and theoretical base.

A unique and significant contribution of marital therapy has been the value and emphasis it has placed on the marital relationship *per se*. While the helping professions have until recently sought to understand and treat only the pathology within an individual, marital therapists have dogmatically emphasized the significance of the relationship while still valuing the integrity of the individuals involved. The priority attention given to the marital relationship has occurred in part because clients have come with specific complaints primarily centering around marriage. As a direct result of their interest in focusing on the marital relationship, they have made a second major contribution to the field of psychotherapy by originating and developing the technique of conjoint marital therapy. Ideally, the conjoint method in marital therapy involves seeing both spouses together during all the therapeutic sessions. In practice there is some flexibility in using both individual and joint sessions. However, marital therapists can be distinguished as a group by their emphasis on the marital relationship and their predominant use of the technique of conjoint therapy.

Overview of Family Therapy

While the field of family therapy is even more recent in development than marital therapy, it has experienced an amazingly large growth.[1] Already it has had a major impact on the fields of psychopathology and individual psychotherapy by shifting the perspective from individually oriented theory and techniques to relationship oriented ideas and procedures centering around viewing the family as a system. One of the consequences of the shift to family

---

[1] Other recent reviews of family therapy are Sporakowski and Mills (1969) and Mottola (1967).

therapy is that it blurs the distinctions between the various disciplines in the helping professions. Traditionally in the treatment of a problem child, the psychiatrist often saw the child, the psychologist did the diagnostic testing and the social worker saw the mother. The father was generally left out of the treatment plan. Now all these professional groups are doing family therapy. A recent survey of family therapists conducted by the Group for the Advancement of Psychiatry (GAP, 1970) found that forty percent of the therapists were social workers and another forty percent were psychiatrists and psychologists. As a result, the traditional distinction between these professional groups is becoming more obscured.

The pioneers in the field of family therapy have often been mavericks for psychiatry who were initially interested in treating families which contained a severely disturbed individual. The GAP report (1970) found that of the ten family therapists described by their colleagues as the authorities, six were psychiatrists. These pioneers were joined by a small, but growing number of persons from other fields who also were becoming more disillusioned with traditional individual approaches to therapy. These therapists were finding that when patients who had effectively been treated returned home, they often regressed or another member of the family began showing symptoms. As these therapists began to learn more about the families of their patients, they began to see more clearly that the patient usually came from a disturbed family. This led to the idea that a problem child was a symptom of a problem family. As a result, a few of these therapists began treating various members of the family together in private practice and they were finding some success with this approach. But they were generally afraid to report their experiences because of the strong Freudian tradition which dictated treating only the identified patient.[2]

However, like many of the significant breakthroughs in science, a misunderstanding by John Bell (1953) provided the historical precedent for seeing a family together in treatment, which he called family group therapy. He had read John Bowlby's account of experience with families and misinterpreted the report to mean the treatment of the family unit. After John Bell's report, others then began to speak more openly about their experiences with families in treatment. One of the earliest and most vigorous proponents of family therapy was Nathan Ackerman. While he had been experimenting with family treatment in the late 1940's, it was not until 1957 that the first Family Mental Health Clinic was opened in New York City and he became its first director. This later led to the founding in 1960 of an expanded national center in New York, the

---

[2] Although traditional psychoanalysis pointed out the significance of the family in the development of individual psychopathology, i.e., Oedipus complex, it has avoided contact with the patient's family because it would complicate the transference process. It seems ironic that while considering the family a significant factor in the etiology of emotional disorders, it did not include the family in the treatment of these disorders. An exception to this was the case involving Little Hans where Freud involved the father in the treatment of Hans. In general, however, the analysts in this country have played a suppresssive role regarding the development of marital and family therapy.

Family Institute. About the same time, but quite independently, other family programs and centers came into existence. In 1954, Murray Bowen, now director of a family therapy program at Georgetown University, began treating families at the National Institute of Mental Health. He invited families of schizophrenic patients to live in the hospital wards so that they could be studied and treated more effectively as a family unit. About the same time, Lyman Wynne, presently the director of the Adult Psychiatry Branch at NIMH, also began clinical work and research with families having a disturbed child. In 1957, Boszormenji-Nagy (1965) organized and directed the Family Therapy Project at the Eastern Pennsylvania Psychiatric Institute which investigated the potential of a psychoanalytic approach to family therapy. In 1958, the late Don Jackson organized and directed the Mental Research Institute in Palo Alto, which began to study and train professionals in conjoint family therapy, a term he originated (Jackson, 1959). This project was in part a byproduct of a previous project in the study of schizophrenia and family treatment directed by Gregory Bateson (1952-1962). In 1962, the Mental Research Institute of Palo Alto and the Family Institute of New York jointly founded a journal, *Family Process,* in order to facilitate research and theory regarding the family's role in the ideology and treatment of emotional disorders. Since then, the growth of the profession as measured by the number of publications and family training programs has increased rapidly in both quantity and quality.

To date, the field of family therapy has already made significant contributions to the understanding and treatment of schizophrenia and other emotional disorders. By utilizing the system approach to understanding the family, it has challenged many assumptions regarding the casual determinates of individual psychopathology and has developed innovative ways to treat such problems, as was so well stated by Jay Haley, an innovator in the family process approach:

> Psychopathology in the individual is a product of the way he deals with his intimate relations, the way they deal with him, and the way other family members involve him in their relations with each other. Further, the appearance of symptomatic behavior in an individual is necessary for the continued function of a particular family system. Therefore, changes in the individual can occur only if the family system changes, and resistance to change in the individual centers in the influence of the family as a group (1962:70).

Within this framework, the focus of therapeutic intervention has shifted from attempting to change an individual to working on altering the social environment in his family. "The problem was to change the living situation of a person, not to pluck him from that situation and try to change *him*" (Haley, 1969:151). By conceptualizing the family as a miniature but potent social system, it was necessary to develop new concepts that deal with the transaction between individuals operating within a family system. Although there has been difficulty with the conceptual and, particularly, the operational definitions of these terms, this approach has pointed out the inadequacy of psychoanalytic, personality and social theory concepts for adquately describing the dynamics of family process.

The impact of the family systems' approach has been steadily growing from its initial focus on the schizophrenic family to increasing concern with most emotional disorders. By focusing on the family as the source of pathology, this approach has also moved in the direction of the marital therapists for it has been rather consistently found in family therapy (Boszormenji-Nagy, 1962; Fry, 1962, Kohl, 1962, and MacGregor, 1962) that problem children came from homes where there were disturbed husband-wife relationships.[3] As Satir so clearly stated:

> The parents are the architects of the family and the marriage *relationship* as the key to all other family *relationships*. When there is difficulty with the marital pair, there is more than likely problems in parenting (1964:1).

As a result, the two professions of marital and family therapy are finding even more in common than was traditionally assumed since these professions have developed quite independently from each other. Although their ranks are starting to be filled with professionals from other helping professions, family therapists can still be differentiated in practice by their concern with the total family and their emphasis on concepts dealing with understanding the family process.

Parallel, but Unrelated, Developments of Marital and Family Therapy

While the two fields are moving in similar directions, their development was and continues to be parallel and generally unrelated to the other. As a result, they both seem to be having similar problems in developing an adequate empirical or theoretical base from which to organize and test their propositions derived from clinical practice.

Whereas both fields began to develop about the same time historically, the reason for their development came from very different sources. Marital therapy grew out of a social need for practitioners to deal with marital problems, while family therapists began their practice because they increasingly realized the inadequacy of exclusively using individual treatment techniques with their clients.

---

[3] In spite of the fact that few studies have directly investigated the type of husband-wife relationships where there is a problem child, it has been rather consistently found clinically that a problem child comes from a home where there either is a parent absent or the couple have a destructive or unfulfilled marital relationship. It should not be assumed from this evidence that there is a direct causal relationship between these two variables or that every such home has a problem child. However, until better evidence becomes available, it can be said that extreme marital disharmony is perhaps a necessary, but not sufficient condition alone for onset of emotional problems in a child. This perspective does place considerable emphasis on the significance of the marital relationship on a child's development and suggests that one should develop a healthy marital relationship before having children.

Whereas both fields are interdisciplinary in composition, they are represented by very different professional disciplines. Marital therapists have, to date, primarily come from interdisciplinary programs which focused on marriage and family relationships or they have been social workers or ministers with some additional training. The pioneers in family therapy were primarily psychiatrists. Social workers and psychologists have been somewhat active in both fields.

Whereas both fields are presently dominated by the pioneers in the field who were self-taught because there were no training centers, the fields were sufficiently different that none of the pioneers were recognized as innovators in both fields.

Whereas both fields have very much needed an empirical and theoretical base and neither group has had adequate training in research methodology or theory development, both groups went to different sources for guidance and assistance. Marital therapists have generally turned to the theoretical work of family sociology or clinical psychology. Family therapists have tended to utilize either psychodynamic formulations or ideas espoused by eminent family therapists. Neither group has attempted much in terms of empirical investigations.

Whereas both fields have restricted their clinical practice and investigations to problem families, they have each selected different types of families to work with. Marital therapists still work primarily with either couples on college campuses or with upper middle class suburbanites. Family therapists still spend much of their time with middle class families having a severely disturbed child. Recently, both marital and family therapists have become interested in expanding their clinical effectiveness with all types of problem families.

Whereas both fields have been primarily interested in understanding actual ongoing interaction of family members and developing techniques for therapeutic intervention into this process rather than relying entirely on self-reports by the identified patient, they have independently developed their own approaches. In actual practice, both marital and family therapists tend to disregard even what others in their own field have done and have worked at developing a unique style which they feel works for them. What both fields have in common is their focus on actual family interaction and not their techniques for therapeutic intervention.

Whereas both fields independently developed conjoint therapy, they initially had different reasons for developing this approach. Marital therapists have emphasized seeing husbands and wives conjointly because they wanted to focus directly on improving the husband-wife relationship. Family therapists have also developed conjoint family therapy but it was because they felt it was practically impossible to effectively help an individual without changing his family unit.

Whereas both fields are interested in training others in these approaches, there are practically no centers where both marital and family therapy are taught. Most marital therapists have been and continue to be trained in a few isolated interdisciplinary departments on college campuses. Family therapists, however, are primarily being trained either in non-academic centers in large urban cities which offer post-graduate training or in the psychiatry department of a few medical schools.

In spite of the many similarities of these two approaches to therapy, they have both continued to function rather autonomously. As a result of this autonomy, neither field has had the opportunity to benefit from the experiences of the other discipline and this has unfortunately retarded their mutual development. There are some indications that the two fields are beginning to merge in mutually beneficial ways. Increasingly, family therapists are beginning to focus more attention on the marital dyad *per se*. There are family therapists who often work only with the husband and wife in spite of the fact that the family was referred because of a disturbed child. Marital therapists are also beginning to involve some children in their treatment of the parents. As previously mentioned, the major professional organization or marital therapists has recently expanded under the name of the American Association of Marriage and Family Counselors (AAMFC) to include family therapists. This event, in itself, should greatly facilitate the mutual growth of both fields and, hopefully, a more cooperative spirit will develop.

System Analysis of Therapy Approaches

In an attempt to provide a conceptual scheme for the description of the various approaches used in marital and family therapy, a system analysis of these approaches was developed by the writer. Five basic system frameworks or types which are used for therapeutic intervention are postulated. These five frameworks are the intra-personal, interpersonal, quasi-interactional, interactional, and transactional.

Table 1 lists the five system frameworks and their general characteristics in terms of the therapeutic unit used, the focus of the treatment and the primary therapeutic goal. The therapeutic units used range sequentially from clients being seen individually (intra-personal) to the treatment of entire families (transactional). As one moves from the intra-personal to the transactional there is not only an increase in the number of individuals included in treatment, but also an orderly progression toward approximating the naturally occurring family unit. The focus of the treatment process also systematically changes from primary attention to intra-psychic phenomena, when using the intrapersonal framework, to primary concern with the marriage and family system within the transactional framework. The goal of all these system frameworks focuses to some extent on the improvement and growth of an individual. This goal is most pronounced in the intra-personal system and it becomes successively less prominent as one moves toward the transactional system framework where the primary goal is more the improvement of the inter-relationships of the family members. In conclusion, while the five system frameworks each represents a rather distinct approach, they are not pure types and always have some overlap with each other. Each, however, has a primary therapeutic focus and a primary therapeutic goal.

Table 2 presents a systematic analysis of the range of therapeutic approaches used in marital and family therapy. These approaches are categorized according to the system framework emphasized and the treatment unit used, i.e., the individual, the parent-child dyad, the marital dyad and the family. The empty cells in this table indicate either that the particular combination of system framework and therapeutic unit cannot be achieved or that it has not yet been attempted. The specific therapeutic approaches are described in greater detail in the section on clinical practice in marital and family therapy. The articles cited in Table 2 represent a survey of the published material on each approach. The claimed advantages and limitations of each of these therapeutic approaches are not discussed in this paper.

Each of the system frameworks and the therapeutic approaches representing each framework will now be described (Table 1). The *intra-personal system* framework contains approaches which treat only one person and focus on the conflicts and anxieties of the client, with inter-personal relationships being of secondary importance. Within this framework, the primary goal is to facilitate the improvement and growth of the client. This framework is best illustrated by most types of individual psychotherapy.

Table 1. Systems of Therapeutic Intervention

System Framework	Primary Therapeutic Unit	Major Therapeutic Focus	Primary Therapeutic Goal
Intra-personal	Individual	Intra-psychic, primary; Inter-personal, secondary	Improvement and growth of self
Inter-personal	Related individuals seen separately by same therapist or by collaborating therapists	Inter-personal, primary; Intra-psychic, secondary	Improvement of a relationship
Quasi-Interactional	Individual	Interactional skill	Improvement and alteration in modes of interaction
Interactional	Ad hoc group of unrelated or related individuals	Group process, primary; Intra-psychic, secondary	Improvement of self and relationship with others
Transactional	Natural group seen together	Marital and family system	Improvement of family inter-relations

Table 2. Systems Analysis of Therapeutic Approaches
Therapeutic Unit

Systems Framework	Individual	Parent-Child dyad	Marital Dyad	Family
Intrapersonal	Individual Psychotherapy[a]			
Interpersonal		Collaborative Parent-Child Therapy[b]	Collaborative Marital Therapy[d]	
		Concurrent Parent-Child Therapy[c]	Concurrent Marital Therapy[e]	
Quasi-Interactional		Filial Therapy[f]	Conjugal Therapy[h]	
Parent-Child	Marital Behavior			
		Behavior Modification[g]	Modification[i]	
Interactional	Group Psychotherapy[j]	Parental Group Therapy[k]	Marital Group Therapy[l]	Multiple Family Group Therapy[m]
Transactional		Conjoint Parent-Child Therapy[n]	Conjoint Maritial Therapy[o]	Conjoint Family Therapy[p]
				Multiple Impact Therapy[q]
				Kin Network Therapy[r]

Intrapersonal
[a] *Individual Psychotherapy.* Child or adult seen alone. (Studies in this field are not reviewed in this paper).
[b] *Collaborative Parent-Child Therapy.* Parent and child seen individually by different therapists who collaborate. Johnson and Fishback, 1944; Miller, 1967.
[c] *Concurrent Parent-Child Therapy.* Parent and child seen individually by same therapist. Powell, Taylor and Smith, 1967.
[d] *Collaborative Marital Therapy.* Both spouses seen individually by different therapists who collaborate. Martin and Bird, 1953; Martin, 1965.
[e] *Concurrent Marital Therapy.* Both spouses seen individually by same therapists. Greene, 1960; Greene and Solomon, 1963; Oberdorf, 1938; Solomon and Greene, 1963, 1965.
Quasi-Interactional
[f] *Filial Therapy.* Parent trained in Rogerian techniques with child. Andronico, Fidler and Guerney, 1967; Guerney, 1964; Guerney, Guerney and Andronico, 1966; Stover and Guerney, 1967.
[g] *Parental Behavior Modification.* Parent trained in behavior modification techniques with child. Hawkins, Peterson, Schweid and Bijou, 1966; Oakland and Wulbert, 1969; Patterson and Brodsky, 1966; Werry and Wollersheim, 1967.
[h] *Conjugal Therapy.* Group of couples trained in Rogerian techniques together. Ely, 1970.
[i] *Marital Behavior Modification.* Individual trained in behavior modification techniques to use with spouse. Goldstein and Francis, 1969; Liberman, 1970.
Interactional
[j] *Group Psychotherapy.* Unrelated persons in same group. Hallowitz and Stephens, 1959; Powell, Taylor and Smith, 1967.
[k] *Parental Group Therapy.* Parents (husband and wife) in group with other parents. Harley, 1962; Moe, Waal and Urdahl, 1960; Speers and Lansing, 1964; Wender, Ferrini and Gaby, 1965.

l *Marital Group Therapy.* Husband *and* wife in same group with other couples. Blinder and Kirschenbaum, 1967; Boas, 1962; Boyer, 1960; Bruniga, 1967; Burton, 1962; Burton and Kaplan, 1968; Dorfman, 1968; Flint and McLennan, 1962; Freeman 1965; Harker, 1962; Henderson, 1965; Jones, 1967; Leichter, 1962; Leichter and Schulman, 1968; Neubeck, 1954; Papanek, 1965; Perelman, 1960; Whitaker, 1958.

m *Multiple Family Group Therapy.* A group composed of several complete families seen together. Boas, 1962; Coughlin and Wimberger, 1968; Curry, 1965; Davies, Ellenson and Young, 1966; Jarvis, Etsy and Stutzman, 1969; Klimenko, 1968; Laqueur, Laburt and Morong, 1964; Laqueur, Wells and Agresti, 1969.

Transactional

n *Conjoint Parent-Child Therapy.* Parent, usually mother, and child seen together. Wertheim, 1959.

o *Conjoint Marital Therapy.* Couple seen together by one or more therapists. Anderson and Smith, 1963; Bach and Wyden, 1969; Bellville, Raths and Bellville, 1969; Brody, 1961-62; Calden, 1967; Geist and Gerber, 1960; Haley, 1963; Hoek and Wollestein, 1966; Kern, 1967; Lehrman, 1963; Leslie, 1964a, 1964b; Sager, 1967; Satir, 1964, 1965; Skidmore and Garrett, 1955; Watson, 1963; Weisberg, 1964.

p *Conjoint Family Therapy.* All family members seen together by one or more therapists. Ackerman, 1958, 1966 & 1967; Bell, 1953; Boszormenyi-Nagy and Framo, 1965; Bowen, 1961, and 1965; Dreikars, 1951; Friedman *et al.,* 1965; Jackson, 1959; Jackson, 1959, 1961; Jackson and Weakland, 1961; Kimbro, Taschman, Wylie and MacLennan, 1967; Minuchin *et al.,* 1967; Rakoff, Sigal and Epstein, 1963; Satir, 1964, 1965; Shellow, Brown and Osberg, 1963; Sonne and Lincoln, 1965; Whitaker, Felder and Warkentin, 1965; Wynne, 1965.

q *Multiple Impact Therapy.* Family members seen individually and together by several therapists. MacGregor, 1962, 1967; Richie, 1960.

r *Kin Network Therapy.* A group composed of nuclear family unit and kin network seen together. Berman, 1966; Daniels, 1967; Kafka and McDonald, 1963; Ostby, 1968; Speck and Rueveni, 1969.

The second framework postulated attempts to deal with the *inter-personal system* This system framework primarily focuses on the relationship between two particular family members. It usually centers on the mother-child or husband-wife dyad but these two people are not seen together during treatment. They either are seen individually, by two different therapists who collaborate, i.e., collaborative therapy, or they are seen individually by the same therapist, concurrent therapy. The major focus of the treatment is on the interpersonal relationship, but secondary attention is also given to the intra-psychic phenomena. The goal of the treatment is primarily the improvement of the relationship but the therapist does not directly observe the dyadic relationship and learns about it only as reported by the client.

Thirdly, one can intervene in a therapeutic way by focusing on the *quasi-interactional system.* The therapeutic goal usually involves systematically changing and improving the interaction style of the dyad. In some cases the dyad consists of the parent-child dyad, i.e., normally the mother and child, as in filial therapy and parent-child behavior modification. Sometimes it is the marital dyad as in conjugal therapy and marital behavior modification. In these approaches which aim at treating the quasi-interactional system, there are specific styles of interaction that the clients are taught. In two approaches, they are trained in groups to use Rogerian techniques with their spouse (conjugal therapy) and with their child (filial therapy). Generally both members of the dyad are present. The behavior modification programs train an individual to use systematically and apply learning principles. The other member of the dyad is not included in the training and this is the person whose behavior will hopefully be shaped. In general, all these techniques attempt to directly alter the interactional pattern in the dyad.

The fourth level of therapeutic intervention involves dealing with the *interactional system*. This system framework focuses on the individual but is mainly concerned with how the person actually interacts with others, thereby introducing the possibility of group process. Group process is the primary therapeutic focus and secondary consideration is given to intra-psychic phenomena. The goal is improvement in one's relationships with others and with one's feelings about himself. All these therapy groups are *ad hoc* because they are formed only because of the treatment process. However, these therapy groups are composed of both unrelated individuals as in traditional group psychotherapy or related individuals as in parental group therapy, marital group therapy and multiple family group therapy.

Lastly, one can therapeutically intervene by working with the *transactional system*. Whereas the interaction framework deals with person to person inter-acts, transaction deals with the process of inter-relationships in a historical and relational context.[4] Transaction also represents a higher level of abstraction from the ongoing interaction and deals with the family behavior as a totally integrated system. This family system operates in such a way that any change in one member has an impact on the whole family. Within the transactional framework, the focus is on the process of the family as a system. As a result, the family is ideally treated conjointly during most or all of the therapy sessions. The exception is multiple impact therapy (MIT) where various combinations of family members are seen by several therapists. The therapeutic approaches which represent this framework are conjoint parent-child therapy, conjoint marital therapy, conjoint family therapy and kin network therapy (Table 2).

[4] Although the terms interaction and transaction have been used rather extensively in the field of family therapy and in research on family process, they have often been used interchangeably as if they were synonymous. However, there are several important distinctions that have been discussed (Framo, 1965; Wynne, 1968) which need to be further delineated. Dewey and Bentley (1949) described three types of action orientation in organisms: self-action, interaction and transaction. Self-action occurs when an organism acts under its own initiative. Interaction becomes possible when another organism is introduced into the setting. Interaction occurs when an organism's behavior is seen as a reaction to the behavior of the other. Interaction, thereby, introduces the idea of cause-effect relationships. The stimulus-response model best illustrates the type of causal interconnection described. Transaction incorporates the interaction framework but extends the perspective to include the ongoing processes of all interactions. Transaction is a higher level of abstraction which views the total interaction process as a system so that it is no longer possible to isolate the initial causal relationships. Eric Berne's (1961) definition of transaction falls midway between the definitions of interaction and transaction described in this paper. He feels that transactions are chains of interactions such that a stimulus X triggers a response Y which, in turn, becomes the stimulus for another response, and so on. The writer proposes that while transaction does focus on interaction, it is considered in a historical and relational context. The family has both a past history and expectations regarding associations in the future. In addition each family member has a complex set of relationships with all the other family members so that reducing the family system into dyadic relations misses the total gestalt of family relationships. With such a perspective, it becomes more clear why transaction deals with system concepts and principles and why the interaction framework is less abstract and more limited in its orientation.

DEVELOPMENT OF TREATMENT APPROACHES

Clinical Practice of Marital Therapy

Marital therapy is defined as any therapeutic intervention technique which has as its major focus the alteration of marital dyad. There are a growing number of approaches being used in marital therapy and these include: collaborative marital therapy, concurrent marital therapy, marital behavior modification, marital group therapy, conjugal therapy, and conjoint marital therapy (Table 2, Marital Dyad). In general, these approaches for dealing with couples are still largely untested and need time for further development. But their existence does add support for the idea that the field of marital therapy has grown beyond what has been traditionally described as marriage counseling.

The goal of marital therapy has usually been defined as assisting a couple to better understand their reciprocal marital interaction and attempt to find ways in which their needs can be mutually satisfied so that the growth and development of each partner can be maximized in the relationship. Whereas most practicing marital therapists would agree that they are primarily concerned with the marital relationship, there is considerable debate regarding the extent to which they delve into unconscious processes or treat personality disorders in their clients. Many marital therapists do, in fact, still feel that their treatment is and should be limited to conscious processes. They are less concerned with treatment of individual problems in depth, hence the term counseling rather than therapy.[5] This idea was clearly stated by a past president of the American Association of Marriage and Family Counselors, Dr. Laidlaw, when he said:

> Marriage counseling is a form of short-term psychotherapy dealing with interpersonal relationships, in which problems related to marriage are the central factor . . . it is an approach carried out essentially at a conscious level. . . . If, as therapy progresses, unconscious factors are discovered which necessitate long and involved

---

[5] The distinction between therapy and counseling has often been rather unclear but the definitions have usually conveyed the ideas that therapy is of longer duration, deals with more severe cases of maladjustment, concentrates more on unconscious processes and is concerned with resolving and altering the personality dynamics within an individual. In spite of the many theorized distinctions between therapy and counseling, the differences become less clear in actual clinical practice. Harper (1960) and others have maintained that this distinction is primarily a defensive reaction by those who feel that a counselor's training is inferior. William Schofield (1966) has pointed out that there are major similarities between the two professions of counseling and clinical psychology. In this same regard, Paul Meehl emphasized that: "The distinction between 'counseling' and 'psychotherapy', if there is one, presents a knotty problem for our profession. Approximately one-half of the APA approved graduate programs make no curricular distinction between their clinical and counseling candidates. Protocols submitted by counseling and clinical candidates for the ABEPP diploma are remarkably similar" (1960:XV). So it appears that the differentiation of marriage counseling from other types of therapy offers less clarification than was initially assumed and it is now necessary to more clearly specify the type of therapeutic approach used in working with the marital dyad.

psychotherapeutic techniques, the case ceases to be in the field of marriage counseling (Laidlaw, 1957).

Regardless of whether or not marital therapists wish to deal with unconscious processes or with individual personality disturbances, they inevitably do deal with these factors when they work with a couple.

On the other hand, these distinctions between counseling and therapy become less meaningful when other approaches to marital therapy are considered. For example, a therapist working within the system framework would not focus on the distinction between unconscious or conscious processes but rather deal with the ongoing transactional process. In addition, he would maintain that the most effective way of changing an individual is by working with the family system within which the individual lives. Looking at this distinction between conscious and unconscious processes from the point of view of a marital therapist using behavior modification, he would also emphasize the meaninglessness of these concepts. He would maintain that change in a marital system takes place only when spouses are taught to reward desired behavior of each other and not reward or punish the undesirable behavior. In general, there appears to be a growing number and variety of approaches to treating the marital relationship and the term marriage counseling does not accurately convey the range of approaches used by therapists today.

Therapeutic approaches. In surveying the numerous articles on marital therapy, it becomes readily apparent that most of the literature in the field has been oriented toward describing the advantages of particular therapeutic approaches (Table 2 Marital Dyad) and sometimes illustrating them with case descriptions. There has only recently been some attempt to empirically assess the effectiveness of even the most frequently discussed approaches. As a result: "A body of principles have become widely accepted without these principles having been subjected to empirical test" (Leslie, 1964a:67). In addition, the number of approaches to marital therapy has been increasing as therapists have experimented with new methods for treating the marital dyad.

If there is any one technique which presently best represents the field, it is conjoint marital therapy. Conjoint marital therapy in its purest form involves seeing the couple together during all the sessions. Within the conceptual framework described in this paper, it represents the transactional system approach to treatment (Table 2). More has been written about the rationale and advantages of this technique by marital therapists than any other approach. The extent to which this technique is used by marital therapists was recently assessed by Alexander (1968) who surveyed the 1965 membership of AAMFC with mailed questionaires and received responses from two-thirds of the group. She found that marital therapists almost exclusively (85%) saw couples or families conjointly and only rarely (10%) saw clients individually without seeing the spouse. Therapists in AAMFC who did not identify themselves as marital therapists were divided in their use of conjoint therapy (53%) and individual treatment (47%). It needs to be emphasized that this study only surveyed the membership of AAMFC which represents a minority of those practicing ·marital therapy. For example, of the 1,800 licensed marital therapists in California during 1967, only 39 belonged to AAMFC (Peterson, 1968). This study does, however, indicate that those who identify themselves as marital therapists do use the conjoint method more than those who are from other professions.

There is evidence that the conjoint method has only in the last decade become used with increasing frequency by therapists. A study by Michaelson (1963) compared therapeutic techniques used in three clinics in various parts of the country during the years 1940, 1950 and 1960. While individual techniques were used at least 80 per cent of the time during this period of time, the use of the conjoint method increased from about five percent of the cases in 1940 to almost 15 percent of the cases in 1960. While this trend is small, the study did not describe the extent to which the conjoint method was used in marital therapy cases where the trend might have been most pronounced.

One of the few studies which has been undertaken to systematically describe the conjoint marital therapy technique was completed by the Family Service Association of America (Couch, 1969). While this study was not an empirical investigation of the effectiveness of the conjoint method, it was one of the first and best efforts to survey marital therapists regarding their judgment about the relative value of the conjoint approach for both diagnosis and treatment of marital problems and under what conditions it is most and least useful. The survey was sent to FSAA affiliated social work agencies and 146 agencies responded to the question about diagnosis and 59 replied to the treatment question. This major monograph clearly points out in great detail therapists' personal experiences with the technique. It reports that the respondents had very positive reactions to the conjoint method for diagnosing marital problems and saw this method as most advantageous for treating couples. Although many of the therapists combined individual and conjoint sessions in treatment, many relied exclusively on conjoint sessions.

Some of the reasons the conjoint method has proven so useful with marital problems has been well described by Leslie (1964b). He points out that the conjoint method is particularly useful in identifying and working through distortions, in minimizing transference and counter-transference, in drawing out conflict, in focusing on the current relationship, and indirectly altering patterns of marital interaction.

In conjoint therapy, increased attention is being given to the idea of using co-therapists as models for the couple. The advantages of co-therapists, especially male and female teams, have been described for both marital (Bellville *et al.*, 1969; Goodwin and Mudd, 1966; Gullerad and Harlan, 1962; Reding and Ennis, 1967) and family therapy (Boszorminji-Nagy and Framo, 1965; Rubinstein and Weiner, 1967; Sonne and Lincoln, 1965, 1966; Whitaker, 1965; and

Wynne, 1965). While most of these therapists feel it is very useful to use co-therapists, few would take as strong a position as Whitaker who said: "We have been forced to admit that family psychotherapy can be effectively undertaken only by a team of two therapists" (1965:191). Whereas in some cases there is a heterosexual co-therapy team, there are few cases where the co-therapists are husband and wife (Bellville *et al.*, 1969). The Bellville couple, in which the husband is a psychiatrist and the wife has no particular training in therapy, suggest that being married offers additional advantages over unmarried co-therapists. One might conclude that co-therapy is a particularly useful and meaningful experience for both the couples. Its usefulness is limited primarily by the additional time and cost involved in having two therapists instead of one.

Another approach to marital therapy that is coming into greater use is marital group therapy (Table 2), which is the interactional approach to therapy. While reported use of this approach by marital therapists occurred in the 1950's (Neubeck, 1954), the last five years has been a renewed interest in this approach. On the other hand, the two interpersonal approaches, collaborative and concurrent marital therapy, have seldom been used by marital therapists.

Two innovations in marital therapy have recently occurred which represent the quasi-interaction approach to treatment. One of the techniques is the adaption of behavior modification for use by husbands and wives (Goldstein and Francis, 1969; Liberman, 1970). Goldstein and Francis (1969) involved five graduate student wives in a behavior modification program which was aimed at extinguishing a particular undesirable behavior in a husband which his wife has been unsuccessful in altering previously. Wives were trained to record the behavior initially in order to establish a base rate. Then they were trained to systematically not reward or punish the undesirable behavior but to reward an alternative behavior that was desired. In the period of a few weeks, all the husbands had significantly changed their behavior in the desired direction from their initial base rates. This study, along with Liberman's (1970), demonstrates not only that the use of behavior modification within the marital dyad works, but that it can easily be learned and applied by one spouse without actively involving the other spouse in the treatment plan, as is required in conjoint marital therapy.

The second promising development is conjugal therapy which was originated by Bernard Guerney in collaboration with M. Andronico and A. Ely (Guerney, 1970). This quasi-interaction approach involves training couples in group sessions to use Rogerian client-centered techniques (Table 2). Couples were specifically trained to be more empathetic and non-judgemental listeners in order to help their spouses express and clarify their feelings. Pre- and post-testing with this technique by Ely (1970) demonstrated that couples in the conjugal groups showed significant increases in their direct expressions of feeling as compared with a matched control group. This application of training couples in Rogerian techniques is a natural outgrowth of the development of filial therapy previously developed by Guerney (1964, 1966) in which mothers of disturbed children were trained in these same techniques. Research on the effectiveness of filial therapy by Stover and Guerney (1967) also demonstrated significant changes in the verbal interaction of those being trained. As was found by Ely (1970), the number of reflective statements significantly increased in the mothers in filial therapy as compared to the control group. In general, the evidence supports the efficacy of both conjugal and filial therapy.

Another approach related to the developments of filial and conjugal therapy is the communication training of engaged couples developed jointly by Miller (1970) and Nunnally (1970). Their program consists of four weekly three-hour meetings in which a group of five engaged couples are trained in communication techniques which they practice in the group. Fortunately, this project also has been built within a research framework so that pre- and post-testing is being done using a battery of research techniques, and the study is being carried out with a matched control group.

In conclusion, it is not only encouraging to see new approaches for treating the marital dyad, but research is also being done in conjunction with the therapeutic programs to evaluate these techniques. As a result of the evidence, it appears that the innovations of marital behavior modification and conjugal therapy are procedures which should become a part of a marital therapist's repertoire.

Diagnosis in marital therapy. The idea of a diagnostic evaluation in marital therapy or premarital counseling has received little attention in the literature. Most marital therapists seem to make their diagnostic evaluations in rather unsystematic and subjective ways using unspecified criteria that they have found useful from their clinical experience. In the few cases described in the literature where they have attempted to make a diagnosis, they have relied primarily on standardized personality instruments such as the MMPI, Rorschach, the TAT and only rarely on measures more related to marriage such as the Marital Role Inventory (Hurvitz, 1965).

One reason why these therapists are not doing diagnostic evaluation is because there are presently no techniques which have been adequately tested or validated which can be used. Unfortunately, little work is currently underway to improve this condition. One study recently completed by Smith (1967) utilized the Ego-Strength (Es) Scale and K-factor Scale of the MMPI and a Homogeneity Scale, developed by Smith, to predict the clients' duration in marriage counseling. He tested 40 long-term couples and 40 short-term couples who were in marriage counseling. Whereas the K factor of the MMPI was not predictive, both the Es scale and Homogeneity scale did discriminate significantly between the short and long term cases. Although these results are useful, there is some question regarding the actual predictive validity of the two scales since the data analysis indicated that there was considerable overlap in the cases.

Another study recently completed by Olson (1969b) attempted to evaluate the relationship between three diagnostic approaches in marital therapy: diagnostic testing using the MMPI, diagnostic interviews, and participation in the SIMFAM technique. Couples were evaluated on the variables of assertiveness, dominance, support, creativity and activity level using these three diagnostic approaches. The findings indicated no relationship between any of the three types of diagnostic evaluations on any of the variables studied. This study indicates that one would obtain very different diagnostic evaluations if a therapist relied exclusively on any one of these diagnostic tools. It also demonstrates that considerable research is needed in the field before adequate methods can be developed for diagnosing marital dynamics in a valid manner which is useful to a marital therapist.

One of the potentially useful approaches to diagnosis for marital problems involves systematically measuring the actual interaction of the couple. Since marital therapists are concerned with the interaction process, this approach might provide them with the type of data which they might readily use. In this regard, Leik and Northwood suggested that: ''Controlled observation among family members *may* provide a more reliable diagnostic tool than the most extensive interviewing of individual members . . . prior to working with a particular individual or his family, the worker should ask the family to interact under controlled stimuli in a laboratory setting equipped for objective recording'' (1964:21-22). Only recently has this approach been attempted by Olson (1968) and by Ravich (1966) with couples having marital problems. Ravich utilized the Acme-Bolt trucking game developed by Morton Deutsch in his work with *ad hoc* groups. Ravich found this technique useful for diagnosis and as a measure of progress in therapy with couples.

In order to evaluate the use of another interaction technique for diagnosis of marital problems, Olson (1968) utilized the SIMFAM technique. This technique has been systematically developed and extensively used by Straus (1963, 1966, 1967) to study families from various social classes in three different societies. Not only does this technique provide objective scores on such variables as assertiveness, effective power, support and problem-solving ability, but it also enables the therapist to directly observe the couple or family in a standardized setting under varying degrees of stress. Additional advantages of this technique as a research and diagnostic instrument have been described elsewhere (Olson, 1968). In evaluating this technique, the objective scores and a brief interpretation of the scores were sent to the therapists of 24 couples who have participated in SIMFAM. In 22 of the 24 cases, therapists reported that the diagnostic report was congruent with their clinical experience with the couple and that this diagnostic information was useful to them as therapists. In conclusion, the SIMFAM technique does seem to be a promising method for obtaining marital interaction data which can be useful diagnostically to marital therapists.

The development of interaction techniques for diagnosis in marital therapy

does seem to have considerable potential but further work is needed in developing these methods. If the procedure is also administered during the course of
treatment and after the treatment is completed, it would also provide a measure
of change in the couple's interaction style.

Clinical Practice of Family Therapy

Although there was initially considerable resistance to the idea of clinically
treating more than the ''identified patient'', the pressure to conform to a
one-to-one therapeutic model has progressively diminished in the last decade.
The shift in treatment was a gradual move away from working with an individual to working with the total family unit. Now the treatment of the family as
a group is truly in the *Zeitgeist*. Because the shift from treating an individual to
treating a family is a major conceptual leap and because there were few
principles and techniques to use, considerable experimentation began to develop ways of treating families. As a result, there has become an amazing
increase in the variety of family therapy approaches, in the number of different
family groupings being used as treatment units, in the conceptual approaches
being used during treatment in the varied settings used for treatment, in the
number of therapists and the variety of ways they are involved with the same
family and the types of family problems being treated. As a pioneer in the
family therapy approach, Ackerman stated so appropriately in a recent paper on
family psychotherapy today:

> The most striking feature of our field today is the emergence of a bewildering array of
> diverse forms of family treatment. Each therapist seems to be doing 'his own thing'.
> . . . These varied methods, while overlapping, differ in the extent to which they deal
> with conscious and unconscious focus, content or affect, past or present. They differ
> further in the degree that they emphasize intrapsychic, inter-personal, and situational
> factors. They differ correspondingly in the degree to which they join the social to the
> psychological and the degree to which they rely on re-education, manipulation or the
> therapy of emotion and depth (1970:123-4).

The GAP report concluded that: ''Family therapy today is not a treatment
method in the usual sense; there is no generally-agreed-upon set of procedures
followed by practitioners who consider themselves family therapists''
(1970:572). What most family therapists do have in common is that they
assume the family is a causal factor in the etiology of individual psychopathology; therefore, the family should be directly involved in treatment in order to be
of most benefit to the family members.

Therapeutic approaches. Family therapy is defined as any therapeutic intervention technique which has as its major focus the alteration of the family
system. In surveying the field, there appears to be basically four different
approaches to family therapy (Table 2). The most frequently used therapeutic
approach, which is often used synonymously with family therapy, is conjoint

family therapy. Within the system framework described in this paper, it is a transactional approach to therapy. In the purest form, this method involves one or two therapists seeing all the members of the nuclear family during all the therapy sessions. There is naturally considerable variation around this theme but the basic format remains the same. The two other transactional approaches are multiple impact therapy (MIT) and kin network therapy. Multiple impact therapy uses a team of therapists to work with family members individually and in various combinations for intensive sessions for two to three days. Kin network therapy expands the group to include not only the nuclear family and its extended family but also includes some intimate friends and neighbors. The only interaction approach which has been utilized in family therapy is multiple family group therapy which brings several, usually three to four, families together in the same group. The major proponents of each of these approaches and the various rationales inherent in each are discussed in greater detail in the major articles listed in Table 2.

Description of family therapists and their clinical practice. In an attempt to describe the field of family therapy, the Group for the Advancement of Psychiatry (GAP, 1970) conducted a survey of family therapists. Of the 312 respondents surveyed, they found that over 40 percent were social workers and that another 40 percent were composed of psychiatrists and psychologists. The major reason these therapists gave for using family therapy was that they hoped this approach would help treat their clients more effectively. In regard to the therapeutic goals, the initial short range goals include determining how the presenting problems related to the family and which family members needed to be included in the treatment. Of the eight specific goals listed in the survey over 90 percent of the respondents considered all eight as important. The following three goals were judged by a high percentage of family therapists to be primary importance for *all* families in treatment: improved communication (85%); improved autonomy and individuation (56%); and improved empathy (56%). Of least significance as primary goals were individual symptomatic improvement (23%) and improved individual task performance (12%). These findings tend to indicate that family therapists do give greater emphasis to change in the family than change in any of the individuals.

The GAP report further differentiated two alternative orientations to therapy. One emphasized the alteration of behavior while the other focused more on altering the subjective feelings of the family members. The former approach emphasizes communication theory and objectively measures changes in behavior. The latter focuses more on each member's feelings and their reactions to family experiences. Most family therapists fall between these two positions. This dichotomy between the behavioral versus the phenomenological-existential orientations also occurs in other forms of psychotherapy.

In terms of their orientation regarding the relationship of individual psychopathology to the family, two points of view were expressed in the GAP report. Many of the therapists felt that the family orientations were useful but still emphasized the intrapsychic phenomena as central in treatment. A minority of the therapists viewed the family dysfunction as central. The later group, although small, contained the more prominent and experienced family therapists. The majority of the therapists surveyed fell between these two positions.

In studying the clinical practice of family therapists, the GAP report found that the majority of these therapists preferred treating the nuclear family. Sixty percent of them, however, sometimes included the extended kin and the same percentage sometimes focused on the marital dyad. While they generally preferred conjoint sessions, over sixty percent also saw one family member intermittently during the treatment sessions. Most of the family therapists surveyed work alone (90 per cent). While over two-thirds sometimes have a co-therapist, only a very small percentage usually have another therapist present. The most advantageous arrangement described was to have male-female co-therapists. The family therapists typically saw the families once a week and still used the 50-minute hour. About two-thirds of the therapists charged families the same rate as individuals.

In addition to the variety of approaches developed by various family therapists, they have also used a variety of settings as their treatment milieu. The GAP report (1970) found that 90 percent of the respondents usually had the family come to their office. However, over 70 percent of the family therapists visited the family at home, but only six percent regularly did so. Some of the early work in family therapy was done in a hospital setting where the identified patient lived and his parents would join him for therapy sessions (Boszormenyi-Nagy and Framo, 1965). In other cases the identified patient would be living at home and all the members would come in together for family treatment (Ackerman, 1966) or all family members would live together in the hospital for observation and treatment (Bowen, 1961; Nakhla *et al.*, 1969). There are also some family therapists who conduct sessions in the family's own home (Friedman, 1962; Levine, 1964; and Speck, 1964). These new treatment settings have been selected because of the interest in moving away from the therapists' private office in order to come closer to the natural habitat of the family.

While it has been maintained that experienced family therapists function in similar ways in actual therapy (Framo, 1969) there is no question that therapists conceptualize their work in very different ways. Beels and Ferber (1969) have been among the first to attempt the challenging task of systematically comparing what family therapists do in their therapy sessions. This task is particularly difficult because the well known family therapists operate in a variety of settings with different types of families and family problems. In addition, they are known not to be entirely consistent in their treatment approach. Considering these and other difficulties, Beels and Ferber did a commendable job. They first compared family therapy with the four common elements of individual therapy described by Ford and Urban (1963) in their book, *Systems of Psychotherapy,* and found distinct differences between the two approaches. In categorizing approaches to family therapy, the two major classifications they developed were conductors and reactors. *Conductors* act as leaders and organizers of the therapy session whereas the reactors generally let the family move more freely and are less controlling. *Reactors* are further subdivided into analysts who act in many ways like traditional psychoanalysts and system purists who operate with the systems framework and are concerned with family rules and communication processes. The conductors were Nathan Ackerman, Virginia Satir, Murray Bowen, Salvador Minuchin, Roland Tharp, Robert McGregor and Norman Paul. The reactor-analysts were Carl Whitaker, Lyman Wynne, Alfred Friedman, Ivan Boszormenyi-Nagy and the reactor-system purists were Don Jackson, Jay Haley, and Gerald Zuk. This classification is helpful in getting a general orientation to family therapy approaches and, hopefully, this accomplishment will encourage others to work along similar lines in order to clarify the process of family treatment.

In general, there has been little attention directed toward the evaluation of these various approaches to family therapy for treating different types of emotional problems. This has occurred, in part, because the range of emotional disorders treated by family therapists still centers around the more extreme forms of psychopathology. Another factor which has retarded evaluation is that these approaches are still in their early stages of development. What is occurring however, is a search for the methods of family therapy which most effectively can be applied to the various types of emotional problems. As a result, family therapy still continues to be primarily a technique that is increasingly being expanded and experimented with, without adequate validation procedures. As Framo emphasized:

> Technique in any form of treatment, when it exists independent of rational or theory, is likely to be mechanical and directionless. Since the theoretical underpinnings of family therapy are, of course, loosely constructed, the techniques we have come to develop have had to rely upon a body of findings which are confirmed only by that apologetic term 'clinical validity' (1962: 119).

Because of the eagerness and evangelistic nature of many family therapists, one could easily assume that the espoused approaches are highly developed rather than in the tenuous state which actually exists. There is, therefore, some need to caution those new to the field so that they do not unwittingly assume that the approaches are perfected. This point of view is well expressed by Weakland who said:

> . . . At present we know so little about family therapy, both theoretically and practically, that whatever we essay in treatment is bound in large measure to be only tentative and hopeful. We simply have not yet developed a well-defined concept and technique of treatment with certain known powers or limits . . . . Therefore, in practicing family treatment at present one has only

choice between being cautious in overall attitude . . . . or being more frankly exploratory (1962: 63-64).

In conclusion, it should be emphasized that family therapy is more than just another technique of treatment and those seeking to find *the* method for family treatment are putting the cart before the horse. As Haley stated:

> . . . . family therapy is not a method of treatment but a new orientation to the human dilemma. Given that orientation, any number of methods might be used. . . . As family therapists become more experienced, they often tend to avoid a method approach and become problem oriented (1969: 164).

What is needed is the coupling of the most effective method with the problem presented so that a therapist becomes more problem oriented rather than method oriented.

THEORY DEVELOPMENT

Theory in Marital Therapy

In 1957, referring to the knowns and unknowns in marital therapy, Emily Mudd stated that: "we have not verified or refuted many of our constantly applied assertions and theories" (1957:79). In 1966, Gerald Manus described marital therapy as a technique in search of a theory and concluded from his review that: "there is a clear picture of inconsistency, contradiction, and lack of a coherent theory" (1966:453). In 1967, David Mace said: "It can be said without fear of contradiction that marriage counseling is a field in which practice has far outrun theory" (1967: xxx).

In 1970, the search for *the* theory of marital therapy is slowly changing to a realization that there needs to be considerably more exploration of various theoretical approaches before a more integrated and comprehensive approach can be developed. This more realistic perspective regarding theory was reluctantly accepted by a group (Beck, 1969) which was studying the treatment of marital problems. They found that: "in the course of the project the first of the specific aims was also modified since the achievement of a 'conceptual framework for casework on marital problems,' even a 'tentative' one, was early recognized as too ambitious a goal" (Beck, 1969:1).

Fortunately, the new approaches to marital therapy are forcing therapists to understand other conceptual approaches. For example, the recent application of behavior modification to therapy with couples emphasizes the utility of learning theory. While most marital therapists were more or less aware of learning theory, their knowledge was generally very limited and rarely were attempts made to incorporate learning principles into their therapy sessions. In addition, this approach has challenged the idea that it takes the involvement of both spouses to change the marital system.

Another theoretical framework which has recently been emphasized by the work of Guerney (1966) and Ely (1970) is the Rogerian client-centered approach to marital dynamics. While many marital therapists have been using Rogerian principles in their treatment repertoire and have been concerned with changing the interaction pattern of couples, few have attempted to directly train couples to use Rogerian techniques with each other. This orientation, however, forces the therapist to re-evaluate the theoretical ideas of Rogers and the direct training of marital dynamics.

A third new area of theory is the exciting work of Haley (1963) and others (Jackson, 1961; Satir, 1964) to develop a system and communication approach to therapy. While much of their initial work was with families having a schizophrenic child, they have also utilized their approach with couples seeking treatment for marital problems. Unfortunately, their ideas still are not explicitly understood or applied by many marital therapists. Whereas this conceptual approach is having a profound effect on other fields of therapy, it seems to have had less effect on marital therapy.

Other than these recent developments in marital therapy, there has been little significant progress in theory development since the reviews of Leslie (1964b) and Manus (1966). While a few writers have attempted to apply role theory (Hurvitz, 1970; Kotlar, 1967; Lantz, 1959; Mangus, 1957; Pollak, 1965), self concepts (Johnsen, 1968), communication theory (Bolte, 1970) and a relationship typology (Gehrke and Maxom, 1962) to marital therapy, the work has been fragmented and rather superficial. In many cases there have been confusing and inappropriately used concepts. Often the same concepts have been used to mean very different things and different concepts have been used to describe very similar phenomena.

Marital therapists have generally operated under the myth that they are truly eclectics who have successfully integrated psychological and sociological concepts. Not only has there been little or no integration of the concepts from these two fields, but it is becoming increasingly clear that neither field alone or in combination can adequately describe the dynamic transactional process of marital therapy. As Vincent so well stated: "Our understanding of marital dynamics has not been greatly furthered by borrowing in one direction from the individualistically oriented concepts of psychoanalysis and psychology and in the other direction from the institutionally oriented concepts of family sociology" (1967:34). In this same regard, Leslie (1964b) emphasizes that: "neither sociological nor psychological concepts have any inherent primacy in the explanation of human behavior. Instead, they constitute equally valid explanations of different ranges of behavior. They complement one another, being, at one and the same time, dependent upon one another but not deducible to one another. . . . In theoretical terms, relationships cannot be extrapolated from the personality systems which enter them any more than personality can be reduced completely to a set of roles" (1964:926-7). For a more detailed discussion of related issues in this field one should consult the work of Leslie (1964b) and Manus (1966).

In conclusion, it is apparent that the field of marital therapy is in serious need of a theoretical base from which to operate. The past work in this area generally serves as an example of what are *not* fruitful approaches regarding theory development. There are, however, a few encouraging efforts to apply new conceptual frameworks to marital therapy and there is hope that from the adequate development of these middle-range theories that the field can eventually build a more systematic approach to therapy. This paper will later describe in greater detail the advantages and weaknesses of alternative theoretical frameworks, particularly the system approach.

Theory in Family Therapy

As was found in the field of marital therapy, there seems to be little direct connection between family theory and the clinical practice of family therapy. The GAP report (1970) concluded that: "There is . . . a striking gap between theory and practice; the conceptual approach formulated by family therapists bears only a tenuous relationship to his actual conduct of treatment" (p. 535). When family therapists were asked about the theoretical framework they used, the GAP report found that therapists generally used a psychodynamic or family theory. The three major family theorists which the respondents felt influenced their work were Satir, Ackerman and Jackson. Family therapists seldom reported using principles from learning theory, small group theory or existentialism. Unfortunately, most family therapists began their clinical practices without appropriate theoretical models to guide them. As Haley has pointed out: "Rather than family therapy and research developing because of a theory, it appears that people were struggling to find a theory to fit their practices" (1969:151).

By far the most significant contribution to the fields of psychopathology and psychotherapy is the system theory which has been developed and espoused by many family therapists. It has challenged the previous conceptions regarding the etiology and treatment of individual pathology *in vitro* and has encouraged theorists and therapists to consider dealing with the "identified patient" in his natural milieu, *in situ*. While the application of systems principles to family problems is a recent development, the general system theory approach is rather well established in other fields. Since the early 1950's this approach has been developed by scholars in various fields, and von Bertalanffy (1968) has done much of the pioneering work in this regard. The system approach was introduced into family therapy primarily by Jackson (1959, 1965), Haley (1963),

Watzlawick *et al.* (1967) and others at the Mental Research Institute in Palo Alto.

Concepts of system theory applied to therapy. The application of the system framework to therapy has introduced new concepts and ways of describing the therapeutic process. The family system therapist first of all assumes he is dealing with an individual who is considered an *open system* responsive to others within the larger family system. There is a *wholeness* characteristic of the family system such that a change in one person in the system (i.e., identified patient) will cause a change in the other parts of the system (i.e., family). Conversely, it is also true that: "an individual cannot change unless his family system changes" (Haley, 1962:85). This is because the family will resist change in any individual in the family. There is also a quality of *nonsummativity* such that a system is more than the sum of its parts. In the case of the family, this system is more than the sum of each of the individual personalities and there is an *emergent quality* which arises out of their interactions. There is also a quality of *equifinality* so that the best description of the family process is a description of the system. Considering the family as a system, it like other systems requires constant *feedback* but tends to resist drastic changes in order to maintain *homeostasis*. The idea that families have *homeostatic mechanisms* (Jackson, 1965) which act as thermostats in regulating the fluctuations in behavior of the family members has been found very useful in understanding families in treatment. Family therapists have rather consistently found that it is amazingly difficult to change the behavior of family members and if one member does change, there is considerable pressure by the family to minimize or reverse this change. The family system operates within a set of implicit and explicit *rules* which regulate much of behavior. Causality is no longer seen as linear (cause-effect) but as *circular* such that a response to a stimulus becomes a stimulus to further responses. Just looking at one stimulus response pattern between two family members tells you little about the total family system. The focus is on *transaction* within the system rather than (inter-acts) interaction, and it is concerned with the *process* rather than the product. This brief exploration of system concepts gives only the flavor of the approach, but it should be clear that this approach has added a new and provocative perspective to the social sciences.

Conceptualizing communication in families. The emphasis on family communication is intimately related to the idea of viewing the family as a system. Communication, verbal and non-verbal, is the means by which one can learn about the family system. As a result, the principles and concepts of system and communication theory are very interrelated. The focus in communication theory is on *meta-communication,* the communicating about communication. A basic principle is that *one cannot not communicate* just as one cannot not behave. In fact, family therapists have pointed out that the paradox of schizophrenia which is that schizophrenics are trying not to communicate but, in fact, that is itself a communication. There is a focus in the *transactions* between individuals rather than just their interactions.

Family therapists such as Jackson (1965) have described the communication in terms of game theory. Related work on game theory has been done by Berne (1961, 1964), Bernard (1964), Szasz (1961), and others. Jackson first assumes that the family is a *rule-governed system*. Although the family may behave in a wide variety of ways, the family system can be understood by learning the limited number of rules which the family follows. Jackson reasons that:

> Just as a relatively few rules permit games as complex as chess and bridge, so a few family rules can cover the major aspects of ongoing interpersonal relationships (1965:10).

Haley (1963) has pointed out that many family conflicts center about problems regarding what the rules are and who determines the rules. While most of a family's rules are implicit rather than explicit, one of the goals of family therapy is to make the implicit rules more explicit so that they can be dealt with more directly.

Another new conceptual approach for understanding family communication is the work of Watzlawick *et al.* (1967). They break down communication into three component parts: *syntatics, semantics,* and *pragmatics.* Syntatics focuses on the problems of transmitting information and considers problems related to the capacity and noise in the system. Semantics focuses on the meaning of communication and emphasizes that it is possible to have syntactical accuracy but still have a meaningless message. Lastly, pragmatics focuses on the behavioral effects of the communication which also involves the content and the context of the message.

Another very related way of describing communication is the classification of communication by Jackson (1965) into *report* and *command* components. The report component relates the content of the message being communicated and the command component defines the nature of the relationship between the two parties. According to Jackson, every message contains both types of information. He feels many communication problems occur because the command component, i.e., the relationship, is *not* clearly worked out. For example, if a husband asked his wife if she would like to go out to supper (report) the reason for the invitation could be interpreted many different ways by the wife, depending on the nature of their relationship at that time (command).

Major concepts in family pathology. One of the major difficulties family therapists faced when they used the system approach was the fact that there were no concepts which described the family processes, functional or dysfunctional. As a result, they began developing new concepts to describe what they observed in the communication patterns of disturbed families. One of the first concepts to be developed was that of the *double bind* (Bateson *et al.,* 1956). In the original article Bateson *et al.,* defined the three necessary conditions for creating a double bind. The characteristics are that:

The individual is involved in an intense relationship; that is, a relationship in which he feels it is vitally important that he discriminate accurately what sort of message is being communicated so that he can respond appropriately . . . (secondly) the individual is caught in a situation in which the other person in the relationship is expressing two orders of messages and one of these denies the other . . . (thirdly), the individual is unable to comment on the messages being expressed to correct his discrimination of what order of message to respond to, i.e., he cannot make a metacommunicative statement (1956:254).

When the concept was developed, it was proposed to be a causal factor in the etiology of schizophrenia. Others have described how to use double binds therapeutically. The double bind has elicited considerable interest and numerous clinical and theoretical papers have further delineated the concept (Bateson *et al.,* 1963; Watzlawick, 1963). For example, Kafka (1970) has reformulated the double bind and relates it to a more general theory of paradoxical experience. He has also de-emphasized the pathogenic qualities of the double bind and emphasized the positive growth potential it offers for creativity and individuation. In a recent review of double bind research Olson (1969c) attempted to empirically unbind the double bind. One of the most difficult, but deceptively simple tasks was to translate the theoretical concept into operational form. Mishler and Waxler (1968a) and others who attempted to investigate this concept found that it was almost impossible to operationalize and, therefore, decided not to study it. Others, however, ventured forth in generally naive ways. The review of empirical studies indicated that the research to date has not provided a very good test of the double bind. In addition to the many methodological problems, most of the studies also failed to develop a conceptual or operational scheme which accurately reflected the double bind phenomenon. So while the results are generally negative, the double bind still has not been very rigorously tested. Although the double bind was initially proposed as a theory, it really only represents a hypothesis which is need of being defined and refined.

Another concept developed about the same time by another family therapy group was *pseudo-mutuality* (Wynne *et al.,* 1958). This concept too was an attempt to describe the family patterns in families having a schizophrenic. In describing two human processes, that of relating to others and of developing a personal identity, Wynne *et al.* postulated three outcomes: mutuality, non-mutuality and pseudo-mutuality. In pseudo-mutuality, there is an overwhelming emphasis on fitting together as a family at the expense of self-differentiation.

In short, the pseudo-mutual relation involves a characteristic dilemma: divergence is perceived as leading to disruption of the relation and therefore must be avoided; but if divergence is avoided, growth of the relation is impossible (Wynne *et al.,* 1958:208).

Pseudo-mutuality, therefore, results in the absence of spontaneity, novelty, humor and zest. There is also a desperate preoccupation with family harmony and communications which might lead to divergent activities or ideas are often misinterpreted and diffused. In contrast to pseudo-mutuality, genuine mutuality assumes and permits individualism and divergence from the family. While the concept of pseudo-mutuality has clinical validity and is a useful description concept, there has been little empirical verification. This has primarily been due to the same difficulty that was encountered with the double bind concept, i.e., operationalizing the term. As Mishler stated when they attempted to investigate the concept:

> We recognized quite early in the work that we could not study pseudo-mutuality
> in the full meaning of that term since we could not state how we would know
> whether or not it was there (1967:7).

A concept closely related to pseudo-mutuality is that of *undifferentiated family ego mass* developed by another family therapist, Murray Bowen, for describing the pathological togetherness observed in families with schizophrenic offspring. Bowen (1965, 1966) describes this concept as an emotional oneness or ego fusion in the family and consequently, there is also minimal differentiation of the individuals in the family. He postulates that as children normally grow they become increasingly differentiated as individuals and still cling to the family ego mass. He has developed a "Differentiation of Self Scale" (Bowen, 1966) which makes no assumption about normality. Individuals low on the scale (0-25) are most fused to the family and those high on the scale (50-75) have high levels of self-differentiation. He has also found people lower on the scale are most religious, superstitious and rigid in their thinking. Little empirical work has been done with this concept or scale except for clinical evaluations in family therapy. His therapy sessions are in part directed at helping individual family members achieve higher levels of self-differentiation.

Another set of concepts developed to describe patterns in families with schizophrenics are the concepts of *schism* and *skew* developed by Lidz *et al.* (1957). Schism refers to families where there is chronic undercutting of the other spouse and severe marital difficulties. The husbands generally have little prestige in the family and the wives are emotionally cold and sexually aloof. In marital skew, the relationship focuses around one spouse who was severely disturbed. This other spouse is usually dependent and/or masochistic and would, therefore, support the weakness in the disturbed spouse. In general, both of these are extreme marital types and the result was that the children suffered in both cases. This conceptualization has seen little development either theoretically or empirically since it was proposed.

In summarizing the conceptual developments related to families in therapy, it is readily apparent that most of the concepts have been derived from work with families of schizophrenics and there has been little attempt to test the generality of these concepts when applied to other types of families. In addition, the writers have generally failed to deal with the common themes running through others' work. One example is the concern with the lack of individualism caused by certain types of families. Wynne *et al.,* refers to this process as pseudo-mutuality, Bowen describes it as undifferentiated family ego mass and Hess and Handel (1959) refer to it as connectiveness. None of these theorists, with the exception of Bowen, have attempted to operationalize their terminology. When others have attempted this task, most have found it so difficult that they either gave up investigating the concept or settled for an operational framework which had little relationship to the actual concept. The result has been that the concepts have not been empirically studied to even determine their validity or generality. Family process appears to be an intriguing but elusive phenomenon to adequately describe. At best, these concepts are only clinically validated and there is even some question whether another clinician could readily understand or use the concept in actual treatment. What is encouraging, however, is that there is a movement away from intrapsychic phenomena and attention is centering on the family as a system.

When family therapy was beginning to develop in the early 1960's, there was hope that a family typology and integrated theory would be developed which would help explain what was happening to families in treatment. This still appears to be too idealistic a goal for the present. Some are now suggesting that more attention needs to be given to the development of middle range theories which can be integrated into a more comprehensive family theory. Others feel that the development stage of a family and the corresponding crises period should be given greater emphasis. As Haley stated: '' . . . there is not a type of family which produces a type of patient, but a disturbance in a family at a certain stage and an external intervention which induces symptomatic behavior in one or more family members'' (1969:155). Hopefully, these and other points of view will become more fully developed so that there will become more adequate theory regarding the family.

RESEARCH DEVELOPMENT

Research in Marital Therapy

After surveying over 200 articles in the field of marital therapy, less than 20 studies were found which can be classified as research directly relating to the topic. This is an improvement, however, since Mudd (1957) reviewed the ''knowns and unknowns'' of research in this field and found no research studies to summarize. The few articles that do exist now are generally methodologically and conceptually weak and rely principally on self-report rather than behavioral data. Most of the research is also descriptive in nature and only a few studies have utilized rigorous methods or experimental designs. The most common approach used was a follow-up of marital therapy cases to investigate the effectiveness of treatment (Burton and Kaplan, 1968; Couch, 1969; Dicks, 1967; Ely, 1970; Fitzgerald, 1969; Goldstein and Francis, 1969; Hawkins, 1970). Other studies described the characteristics of individuals who become marital therapists in terms of their professional background and affiliation (Alexander, 1968; Kimber, 1967) and their MMPI profiles (Phillips, 1970). Also investigated were the types of clientele that come to a marital therapist (Green, 1963; Kimber, 1966; Levitt and Baker, 1969) and the type of therapeutic approach used (Alexander, 1968). Lastly, a few studies have been done to evaluate the methodological problems in doing research in this field (Olson, 1969a, 1969b; Phillips, 1967).

The studies which investigated the effectiveness of marital therapy used a variety of approaches. One of the earliest was done by Burton and Kaplan (1968) on the effectiveness of group marital therapy versus individual therapy for couples where one spouse was alcoholic. They administered a questionnaire to 144 clients who had received individual counseling and to 61 who received group marital counseling. A higher percentage of those receiving group counseling in contrast to those seen individually, 76 percent to 57 percent, felt they had gained something from the experience. The writers generally concluded that "group counseling was more 'successful' than individual counseling" (1968:78).

Several studies have been done in order to evaluate the efficacy of conjoint marital therapy. Fitzgerald (1969) saw a total of 57 couples conjointly. One group was composed of 31 patients who initially came to seek individual therapy and 26 came because of marital conflict. Length of treatment ranged from four to 125 hours with the average being 26 hours. At the termination of the conjoint sessions, he rated the couples on a five point scale and later contacted one or both of the spouses and again completed his ratings. About three quarters of the couples were judged to be improved in both groups at the time of termination and the follow-up indicated that these improvements were rather lasting. While this study has several serious limitations, some of which the researcher himself mentions, it does indicate one attempt by a private practitioner to evaluate his own practice. Another recent study of conjoint marital therapy was done by Dicks (1967) in which he clinically evaluated a random sample of 36 out of 100 of his cases. He concluded that there were positive changes in 64 percent of the cases, or using a less stringent criteria, 78 percent of the cases. This study is also methodologically weak, but it does represent the typical approach used to date in evaluating marital therapy.

One of the largest scale studies to investigate marital therapy was conducted by Dorothy Beck (1966) at the Family Service Association of America. This project collected responses to 60 open-ended questions from 400 case workers at 104 member agencies throughout the country. Over 9,000 pages of material were content analyzed and a major monograph entitled *Joint and Family Interviews* (Couch, 1969) has been published. Another monograph entitled *The Treatment of Marital Problems,* edited by Beck, will soon appear. While this investigation is primarily a descriptive analysis of the advantages and limitations of conjoint sessions as perceived by case workers, it is a necessary beginning step.

The following three studies represent the most rigorous and systematic approach to the evaluation of marital therapy. A study by Ely (1970) investigated the efficacy of conjugal therapy with a sample of 11 training couples and 11 control couples. The couples were trained in groups to use Rogerian techniques with their spouse. Pre- and post-training measures were obtained from both groups using pencil and paper tests and verbal role playing situations. He found significant increases in the training versus control group in the percentage of direct expressions of feelings and clarifications of feeling statements and concluded that conjugal therapy did effectively alter a couple's interaction. Another well designed study of conjoint and concurrent marital therapy is presently underway by Hawkins (1970). He is using a battery of tests which include the MMPI, the Mooney Problem Checklist, marital satisfaction data, marital role expectations and performance data and other related information. Couples in treatment and in randomly assigned control groups are currently being studied. Although this study is yet to be completed, it does represent the trend toward improved research in this field. Lastly, the research done using behavior modification with couples by Goldstein and Francis (1969) represents one of the most carefully designed and executed marital therapy studies to date. They trained wives to use various types of behavior modification with their husbands. The wives recorded the husbands' base rate behavior on some variable before treatment and then kept a record of the changes in that behavior during treatment. In every case, the wives were able to significantly change some undesirable behavior in their husbands that they had previously not been able to alter. Not only did the method prove effective, but systematic evaluation of change in the husband's behavior was also obtained. This study represents a useful approach to a marital therapy and to therapy evaluation because it simultaneously allows one to systematically evaluate the effectiveness of treatment and also measure process changes as they occur.

A *second* research area has been the description of individuals who become marital therapists. In general, all these studies are simply descriptive in nature. Alexander (1968) mailed questionnaires to members of AAMC and assessed their professional affiliation, the type of cases treated, and their methods of treatment. The results from this study have been mentioned previously. Another related study by Kimber (1967) surveyed professionals listed in the phone book of 74 major cities in 1964. He found 831 marriage counselors and 1,451 psychologists listed in these phone books and concluded that there is a high correlation (r = .92) between the number of these two groups in major cities. Phillips (1970) investigated the personality characteristics of 149 marital therapists using the MMPI. One hundred and thirty-nine could be rated high, average, or low in ability as marital therapists and the MMPI patterns were found to be different in each of these groups. He also found differences in marital therapists coming from the ministry as compared to those from other professions and he delineated the profile pattern of a typical marital therapist. These three descriptive studies are useful first steps in research in this field and primarily serve to point out further questions and issues that need further investigation.

A *third* research area has been the description of those who seek marital therapy. Green (1963) describes 500 consecutive couples with marital problems that came to the Conciliation Court of Los Angeles in 1960. He found that the majority of the couples had no previous professional therapy. They were primarily from the "middle class" and husbands and wives both complained primarily about money management. Counselors rated inadequate personality as the major problem in most of the marriages. Another descriptive study was done by Kimber (1966) in which he compared referred and un-referred clients using the MMPI. He found that the MMPI profiles of the 102 referred and 91 unreferred clients were very similar. Lastly, Levitt and Baker (1969) investigated the relative psychopathology of marital partners in order to assess whether the spouse who initially seeks treatment is more or less disturbed than the other spouse. Their subjects were 25 patients and their spouses from an Outpatient Clinic and they both completed the MMPI. Eleven judges were instructed simply to select which spouse in each couple was "sicker." The judges agreed in 19 of the 25 couples and generally they used the mean elevation of the MMPI profile in making their selections. The results indicated that in 13 of the 25 cases, the person coming to the clinic—i.e., identified patient—was judged as more disturbed. In four cases, the spouse of the patient was judged more disturbed and in six cases there was a split decision among the judges. In the remaining two cases, both partners sought treatment at the same time so neither could be described as the identified patient. These findings are somewhat confounding since 18 of the 25 cases had come to the clinic because of personal problems and the seven others came because of marital problems. There was no indication, however, if the patients having marital problems were also the ones where the spouse was judged as more disturbed than the identified patient. This distinction would clarify the analysis and indicate in marital therapy cases whether the more disturbed spouse is or is not the one who initially seeks help.

The *fourth* and least frequently studied topic is the methodological difficulties of doing research in marital therapy. Phillips (1967) investigated the relationship between therapists' ratings of a couple in terms of power and related these ratings to the couple's MMPI profiles. He selected 113 couples in marital therapy for this study and he found that the MMPI profiles did relate in systematic ways to the ratings and, therefore, could be used to assess power in the marital dyad. However, it should be mentioned that some MMPI scales, particularly Pd and Es, were among the four highest scales represented in most of the categories of power. No correlations were computed to indicate the degree of relationship or the predictive validity of the MMPI. In a related study completed by the writer (Olson, 1969b) regarding diagnostic evaluations using the MMPI, diagnostic interview, and the SIMFAM game with couples in marital therapy, the findings are somewhat conflicting with the findings of Phillips (1967). Olson found very low and nonsignificant correlations between the three diagnostic methods when they were used to measure assertiveness, effective power, support, creativity, or activity level. Another methodological study of family power by Olson (1969a; 1970) also demonstrated no relationship of three measures of power to the criteria measure of outcome power. In general, these later methodological studies serve to indicate that more methodological research is needed in this field before adequate research methods can be developed. Until that time, researchers should exercise greater caution in their use and interpretation of their findings.

Research in Family Therapy

While over 250 articles were published on family therapy during the 1960's, very few could be described as research studies. One recent survey of family therapists was conducted by the Group for the Advancement of Psychiatry (GAP, 1970) which provides basic descriptive information about the field. This study found that only three percent of those surveyed were involved in any research related to family therapy. A few studies (Schreiber, 1966; Shellow *et al.*, 1963) have described families in family therapy and attempts have been made to study the outcome of treatment (Minuchin *et al.*, 1967; Friedman *et al.*, 1965). Only one study was found which studied the process of family therapy *(Sigal et al., 1967)*. Although there has been a considerable increase in interaction oriented research on schizophrenic families since the early 1960's most of the attention has been directed toward comparing these families with a "normal" control group (Mishler and Waxler, 1968a, 1968b; Lennard and Bernstein, 1969; Winter and Ferreira, 1969). There has been some research on the processes of individual therapy with schizophrenic and neurotics (Lennard and Bernstein, 1969). But there has been very little systematic attention given to evaluating the outcome of the process of family therapy. There is still much truth in the statement by Parloff when he referred to the field of family therapy:

The relevant literature is vast, yet very little of it would be classed by the rigorous investigator as research. Most of the contributors to the area have been clinician-naturalists who, having perhaps a Freud-like vision of themselves, have made salutory advances from observations to conclusions with a maximum of vigor and a minimum of rigor (1961:39).

The GAP report (1970) on family therapy is a descriptive study of 312 family therapists. Although the questionnaire data was gathered during the winter of 1966-67 and was not a random sample of family therapists, it does provide a general overview of the field. It attempted to determine who was practicing family therapy, who the clients were, what goals the therapists had in treatment, what conceptual frameworks they used and the ethical problems they encountered. The results of the study have been reported elsewhere in this paper. The two other descriptive analyses of family therapy provide the least systematic, but nevertheless valuable, source of information. Schreiber (1966) describes 72 families treated at a Family Service Agency. Twenty-five families continued in treatment for more than three months. All showed great improvement in communication processes and in the presenting behavior with the problem child on the basis of their subjective clinical evaluations. The study of Shellow *et al.* (1963) described the 60 families they had seen in family therapy over a four year period. They also discussed in some detail the presenting problem, the duration of treatment and the reasons for termination.

In an attempt to more adequately assess the outcome of family therapy, two studies were conducted by teams of investigators, Friedman *et al.* (1965) and Minuchin *et al.* (1967). Friedman and his associates were interested in evaluating the effectiveness of conjoint family therapy conducted by co-therapists, preferably heterosexual teams, in the family's home. While they were very concerned with interaction process during their family therapy sessions, they used traditional self-report methods for evaluating the changes in the family process. The methods for evaluation included the Leary Interpersonal Check List, in which the family members individually rated the other members and also the co-therapists; a self-report method called the Family Participation Index and the Rorschach. The co-therapists and six observing therapists also completed a rating scale of the actual therapy sessions. While changes were observed in some of the measures, the emphasis was on the therapists' clinical judgment. Friedman concluded: ''It is our subjective impression that all the families who were in treatment gained something of importance from the therapeutic enterprise'' (1965:175).

The other study which investigated the outcome of conjoint family therapy was conducted by Minuchin and associates (1967). They treated 12 families with a juvenile delinquent and used a matched control group of 10 families, having no delinquent children. The treatment families had 30 conjoint sessions and were pre- and post-tested using the Family Interaction Appreciation Test (FIAT) and a Family Task. Both of these measures focus on the actual interaction of the family members and none of the traditional self-report diagnostic or personality measures were used. In addition to tape recording the sessions, systematic coding was done on the interaction patterns for therapy sessions near the beginning and end of the treatment. In general, pre-and post-testing comparisons regarding communication style and affective content from the Family Task showed little change, but the FIAT did show many predicted changes. The writers concluded that seven out of the 12 treatment families were clinically judged as improved. While this study has some methodological and conceptual weaknesses, it is a beginning attempt in the right direction.

Lastly, the most systematic study of family therapy outcome and process is the work by Sigal *et al.* (1969). In their study, 20 families received conjoint family therapy for varying lengths of time ranging from an average of five sessions in a group that terminated prematurely to an average of 25 sessions in the most permanent group. Ratings based on the family's interaction style were made by the therapist after the 2nd, 6th and 12th sessions. After every session a questionaire, Family Category Schema, was also completed by the therapist and other therapists rated these reports for change in the family. These therapists' ratings on change were later combined to measure the success (outcome) of the treatment. They found no relationship between the success of the treatment and the interaction scores at any of the three points during treatment. Also, the amount of interaction increased during the treatment but this increase was unrelated to the outcome. This study well exemplifies the shift in the direction of studying interaction processes and the improvement of methodology that is occurring.

In concluding this section, it should be emphasized that very little attention has been paid to the systematic evaluation of the process and outcome of family therapy. In addition, there has been a strong tendency to rely on traditional self-report methods which were not developed to capture the rich dynamics of family process. There is growing evidence that these self-report approaches do not relate to behavioral methods (Olson, 1969a, 1970) and are not suited for use in this type of research. In reviewing the studies which investigated the relationship between family types and schizophrenia, Fontana (1966) reached a similar conclusion: "Both the clinical observational and retrospective recall methods are judged to be inadequate. The third approach, direct observation and recording of family interaction, is concluded to be free of intrinsically disqualifying inadequacies" (1966:214). While a number of family researchers have developed interaction procedures which could be used, this resouce has yet been adequately tapped. In spite of what happens in this research area, clinical experimentation will probably continue at an ever growing rate. As Parloff emphasized: "Lack of classical research evidence has, however, never been a serious deterrent in the relentless development of psychotherapy theory or practice" (1961:446). One can only hope that this traditional disregard for research evaluation will change in order that a more systematically and empirically based approach can be developed for treating families.

RECOMMENDATIONS FOR DEVELOPING
MARITAL AND FAMILY THERAPY

Real and Ideal Relationship between
Research, Theory and Practice

Ideally, theoretical formulations should be derived from real life situations and then research should evaluate the validity of these ideas when they are applied in these situations. As McGuire (1969) recently discussed, theory-oriented research in natural settings is the best of both worlds, research and application. Unfortunately, researchers and practitioners live in two different worlds essentially unaffected and unconcerned with the other. As Sherif (1966) so succinctly stated:

> Professional meetings and professional journals can almost convince a person that those engaged in basic research and those in applied fields appear to be in different camps that wage cold war, when they are not ignoring each other completely. At times, it appears that the twain shall never meet (1966:1).

Although this is not a new problem to any field, it already is a problem in the newly emerging fields of marital and family therapy. This paper will attempt to describe the mutual benefits of integrating research, theory and practice and will later suggest some ways in which this can be accomplished.

First let us consider the *ideal* function and integration of research, theory and practice. The wise utilization of theory has greatly facilitated the rapid advances in many fields of science. Ideally, theory aids in summarizing our present knowledge by reducing phenomena to basic underlying and interrelated principles. In so doing, it enhances our explanatory power. Theory can also offer significant contributions to research and practice by directing one to yet unobserved principles or relationships which are derived deductively from the theory. In other words, theory provides testable hypotheses which might not have been formulated without theory. Once theoretically based hypotheses have been formulated, research plays the essential role of testing the postulated relationships. Such research ventures can significantly contribute to the development of more valid theory by clarifying the concepts with operational definitions, by indicating support or non-support for the hypothesized relationships and by directing one in reformulating the unsubstantiated portions of the theory. If research can be directed or guided by systematic theory, this increases the likelihood that the results will contribute to the further development and organization of that theory. In other words, theory and research should ideally be integrated, and this integration would prove mutually beneficial. Theory could stimulate research and enhance the value of the findings, whereas research could test theoretically derived postulates and facilitate the development of improved ones.

If research, in addition to being theoretically grounded, would also focus on applied problems, there would be numerous other advantages. First of all, it would greatly increase the relevance of the research and theory so that they might be used by those who are in pressing need for practical solutions to their problems. Secondly, it would increase the validity of the findings by testing them out in real life situations rather than in contrived and artificial situations. Thirdly, if the research is theoretically based, it would give a more adequate test of the theory and would enable it to have consequences in practice. Fourthly, it would increase the probability that researchers would include a greater variety of significant variables rather than relying on the same few variables repeatedly utilized by others. Lastly, it would increase the extent to which the results could be generalized and would encourage people to apply such findings rather than having the research simply remain in the journals for their colleagues to read.

In conclusion, research cannot be properly conducted without the guidance of theory, nor can theory be adequately developed or substantiated without empirical verification. If, in addition, theory-oriented research investigated real life problems, the coordinated approach would facilitate a complementary cycle of development in each area.

But, back to reality. This review has generally indicated that practitioners in the fields of marital and family therapy, while attempting to find a theoretical base for their practices, have rarely ventured into the research domain. While marital and family therapists have primarily restricted themselves to their private offices, researchers have become secluded in their laboratories. As a result, therapists do little research, take little interest in research and, generally fail to appreciate the value it might have to their practice.

Researchers, too, continue to go their own merry way and rarely ask questions that relate directly or even indirectly to practice. They have often confined themselves to problems which can be studied using existing methods, even though many of these traditional methods have numerous inadequacies. Or worse, researchers have first selected a method and then located a problem appropriate for that method. Rather than attempting to find answers to actual problems encountered by therapists and other practitioners, they have continued to turn to their same journals for problems to investigate. In discussing a similar problem in psychology, Sanford (1965) commented that, ·

> you realize that the authors have never looked at human experience, they went straight from the textbook or journal to the laboratory, and thence into print and thence into the business of getting research grants . . . . psychological researchers do not know what goes on in human beings, and their work shows it. Not only is it dull . . . . but it is often wrong (1965:192).

Emphasizing a further point about some research ventures, there has been so much concern with methodology that the situation arises where they might be "reliably wrong" (Sherif, 1966).

In those few instances when a researcher begins with a clinical variable or question, by the time it is operationalized it often bears little relationship to what the clinician was describing. As Framo aptly stated:

> that clinicians always wince when an experimental psychologist delimits a clinical concept for study, operationally defines it, creates a measuring instrument for it, and ends up measuring something that bears almost no resemblance to the original, although it does have the dubious merit of precision (1965:448).

Bridging the Gaps Between Research, Theory and Practice

While it is relatively easy to be aware and critical of the present situation, it is more difficult to propose constructive ways for improving the interrelationship between research, theory and practice. One must first of all appreciate that gaps between these approaches did not occur by accident. They never really were integrated and, consequently, each approach to reality developed more or less independently. Therefore, individuals were trained primarily in one area or may be two but rarely in all three. After their training, their paths seldom cross, even at professional meetings where the programs are neatly divided into research, theory, and clinical practice.

In proposing ways of changing the status quo, let us start with the marital and family therapists and what they could do. First, marital and family therapists need to come to some agreement regarding what are significant and relevant questions they are concerned with in their practice. Related to this, therapists need to clarify what their goals and objectives are in therapy. Is the goal to change the marital and family system, alter the interaction patterns, keep the relationship functioning, increase personal happiness, change specific behavior in one spouse, reduce role conflicts, facilitate individual development or all of these? Resolving this question regarding goals appears deceptively easy. However this is a difficult task, as Rogers found when a group of "expert" therapists attempted such an undertaking:

> the only therapists who agree on goals of therapy are those who have been strongly indoctrinated in the same dogma. Not only is there divergence in what we mean by success, but . . . . we do not agree in what constitutes failure (1964:7-8).

He also emphasized:

> The very portions of those interviews which to me seemed obviously moments of 'real' therapy, were experienced by others as non-therapeutic or even antitherapeutic. And the moments which some others regarded as clearly of a healing nature, I experienced as meaningless or ineffectual, or worse . . . I hope I have made my point that our differences as therapists do not lie simply in attaching different labels to the same phenomena. The difference runs deeper . . . . We differ at the most basic levels of our personal experience (1964:5-7).

In other words, before therapists can expect researchers to empirically investigate a phenomenon or question, it must first be clearly defined and judged by therapists to be relevant before a researcher begins.

Secondly, therapists need to clarify their concepts so that those who are not therapists can understand and perceive the phenomena. Typically, clinical concepts are very difficult to operationalize because of their abstractness. A good example of how an elusive concept has led researchers astray is the recent attempts to study the double bind (Olson, 1969c). While abstractness is a necessary component in a theoretical formulation, concepts must also have conceptual and operational relationships to natural situations to be useful. However:

> if divorced from actualities, abstraction becomes a game: it becomes abstraction for its own sake or for the impression that it may make on one's colleagues in the profession. In this case, abstraction becomes inner gymnastics for a select group of people who are 'in' on the secret and exclusive lingo (Sherif, 1966:4).

So until the time when therapists are able to clearly and concretely describe their concepts there will continue to be the difficulty in empirical studies using any clinical concept.

Thirdly, therapists need to permit and encourage researchers to learn more directly about the complexities of family interaction and therapeutic intervention. Researchers could be given the opportunity to observe therapy sessions. This experiential contact might not only stimulate their interest in this area but it would also make it more difficult for them to feel satisfied with the adequacy or relevance of traditional research questions and approaches. As Framo stated: "It will be hard for anyone who has seen families under the emotional impact of treatment to ever again do family research in the traditional ways" (1965:455).

Lastly, therapists need to be more open to the idea of cooperating with research projects. This will first of all increase the chances that the project will maintain relevancy with the clinical situation. It will also be a most advantageous way of enabling therapists to learn more directly about the excitement, difficulties and advantages of research.

There are also ways in which researchers can help bridge this professional gap. First, and most importantly, they can begin by turning away from their journals as the source of ideas and focusing on problems which practitioners have been interested in having better answers. Many times, both can find a question of mutual interest, even though it might be for very different reasons. Secondly, researchers could also assist therapists by providing normative data on marriage and family development in non-clinic families. Normative data of this type is currently being analyzed in a major longitudinal study of early marriage and family development by Ryder and Olson, (Ryder, 1970; Olson and Ryder, 1970). While relevant data by other family researchers have already been published, the findings have generally not been described in ways which are useful or meaningful to the practitioner. Thirdly, researchers need to be more creative and rigorous in developing improved research methods and designs so that they can more adequately test clinical concepts and treatment. This is particularly necessary when researchers are attempting to operationally define clinical concepts.

Researchers need to be more willing to move out of the classroom and the laboratory and more into clinics and other service agencies. It is obvious that most research in the social sciences is done with the most convenient and homogeneous samples. Psychologists have over-used college students (especially sophomores) and Norway rats, while family sociologists have too frequently concerned themselves exclusively with the self-reports of the housewife as the representative of the family. Such sampling procedures seriously restrict the extent to which the findings can be generalized and can also limit the validity of the results. Researchers should heed Festinger's statement that: "It should be stressed again that the problem of application of the results ... laboratory experiments to the real life situation is not solved by a simple extension of the results ... It is undoubtedly important that the results of laboratory experiments be tested out in real life situations'' (1953:141). The move into new settings might prove beneficial in that it would challenge their creativity to adapt innovative methods to these settings. It would also provide information regarding the validity of their findings and increase the application of these findings outside the laboratory setting.

Selective Interdisciplinary Borrowing

While the interdisciplinary composition of both the fields of marital and family therapy has been in some ways one of its handicaps, it might seem ironic to suggest that further interdisciplinary efforts might be very beneficial to the development of these fields. But marital and family therapists have not been true interdisciplinary eclectics because they have generally not shown an awareness of the fields other than the speciality in which they were trained. While it is beyond the scope of this paper to describe in adequate detail how this process of selective borrowing might be accomplished, a few illustrative examples will be given.

One field related to marital and family therapy which has not been adequately tapped is clinical psychology. Since the early 1950's, this field has placed major emphasis on developing an empirical base from which to develop theoretically and clinically. Considerable effort has been spent in developing and evaluating various methods and research designs for use in psychotherapy research. Clinical psychologists have also considered the many problems in evaluating the effectiveness or outcome of therapy. This has involved determining the criteria for evaluating the success for various types of clinical cases, developing adequate control groups, dealing with the findings on spontaneous recovery and considering various lengths and types of treatment. In addition to studying the outcome of therapy, there has also been some work on the process of therapy. In some of the research the therapist and the client's behavior are treated as separate variables and in a few studies the relationship process between them is the variable being studied. In addition to the current journals in this field, there are also some recent books which provide readily available examples of some of the better research (Goldstein and Dean, 1966; Gottschalk and Auerbach, 1966; Meltzoff and Kornreich, 1970; Stollak *et al.,* 1966).

A second area which could be of considerable assistance in theory development of marital and family therapy is the conceptual frameworks of family sociology. Probably the most relevant and highly developed conceptual framework is symbolic-interaction. The interaction approach emphasizes the focus on interaction of family members within a role theory framework. Some of the work has centered on the development and resolution of role conflict. Unfortunately, most of the concepts and theoretical formulations have not been applied or evaluated in real-life settings. If therapists were to attempt to apply these ideas, they might not only improve their skill and insight as therapists, but they would also be contributing to the development and evaluation of these theoretical formulations. More complete discussion of symbolic-interaction and the other conceptual frameworks are contained in edited reviews of the field by Nye and Bernardo (1967) and Christensen (1964). In addition, the family developmental framework would also help to put events into their proper perspective.

A third approach that has numerous conceptual and methodological value for marital and family therapists is the recent work in the area of family interaction. While those conducting family interaction research come from a variety of disciplines, their primary concern with observing and systematically measuring actual ongoing interaction of family members forms a natural link to marital and family therapy. Some of the earliest work in this area came from work of Bales and other social psychologists interested in studying group processes in *ad hoc* groups. While some theoretical formulations which applied to small *ad hoc* groups do not apply to family groups, the approach to focusing on interaction data rather than self report data was a most valuable contribution. Since the early sixties, there has been considerable interest in studying actual family interaction and developing new instruments which can be used for this purpose. Many of these techniques are modifications of the ''revealed difference format'' developed by Strodtbeck (1951). Recent reviews and descriptions of those various interaction procedures are available (Bodin, 1968b; Straus, 1969; Winter and Ferreira, 1969). Although many of the family interaction studies have focused on comparing families having problem children with control groups (Mishler and Waxler, 1968b), some recent work is also being done with more normal populations of married couples (Olson and Ryder, 1970) and families (Straus, 1967). Some work has also been done to apply interaction approaches in a diagnostic way in marital and family therapy (Olson, 1968; Ravich, 1966). Because these family interaction procedures were developed to measure actual family process, they have considerable potential for clinical application in marital and family therapy.

Promising New Directions

While this paper has rather critically reviewed the present status of the fields of marital and family therapy, there are several very encouraging trends which will, hopefully, keep developing. While some of these studies have been previously discussed, their significance warrants further emphasis. One approach that should be encouraged is treatment programs which have systematically built into them a conceptual framework and a research design for evaluation. The exemplary work that deserves mention is the behavior modification of husbands by their wives (Goldstein and Francis, 1969), the conjugal therapy project (Ely, 1970), the conjoint marital therapy project (Hawkins, 1970) and the communication training project (Miller, 1970; Nunnally, 1970). Most of these projects are still underway, but it is an encouraging trend to see.

A second innovative approach has been the introduction of video-taping of therapy sessions. This approach not only has many advantages as a therapeutic tool (Alger and Hogan, 1967, 1969; Berger, 1969; Paul, 1966), but it also provides a rather permanent record of the therapeutic process which can be used for research and for training therapists (Berger, 1969; Bodin 1969a, 1969b).

While there has been increasing interest in treating couples and families, there has been little attention given to a more preventive approach to families. As Vincent (1967) has emphasized, there needs to be more attention given to "marital health." While some therapists have been doing premarital counseling (Rutledge, 1966, 1968; Wilms, 1966), the unmarried couple has seldom been seen before marriage by most therapists. One potentially useful project for engaged couples is the sensitivity training program which is currently underway (Miller, 1970; Nunnally, 1970) which trains couples in various communication skills. Much more could be done with the training of couples to be better communicators and better marital partners and parents. Another way this could be done is to apply techniques used in conjugal and filial therapy to unmarried couples.

Lastly, there is increasing interest in training para-professionals in various capacities in the helping professions. Today there is a greater realization on the part of professionals that they can never effectively treat a fraction of those wanting and needing professional treatment. There is also the realization that there are many therapeutic roles that can be competently handled by a para-professional and that a professional can make better use of his professional time by training others. Since the effective program in training para-professionals conducted by Rioch and Associates at NIMH (Rioch, 1963) there have been numerous attempts to integrate non-professional people into working with fellow students having problems, (Phillips, 1968), with schizophrenics (Tomlinson et al., 1969), with marital therapy cases (Vincent, 1969) and in community mental health centers (Reiff and Riessman, 1965; Grosser et al., 1969). Because of the endless demand for professional marital and family therapy, there needs to be greater utilization of all available resources and the use of para-professionals seem to be an important resource.

Concluding Comments

As we described in the introduction of this paper, the fields of marital and family therapy are youngsters to the professional world. Judged by the rigorous and rigid standards used in the physical sciences, they are found to be lacking in many of the fundamentals. The professional gaps between therapists, theorists and researchers has not been effectively bridged so there is a dearth of research or empirical facts to build upon. Little is actually known about the process or effectiveness of the clinical approaches now in use. As a result the two fields are still operating with principles which are largely unverified and generally unrelated to their theoretical formulations.

But one should remember that these professions are youngsters compared to many other sciences and they should not be judged too harshly at this early stage. Viewed in a developmental perspective, there is reason for optimism because they have already completed some developmental tasks. They are already taking effective action to more clearly develop their identity as separate professions. They have also developed a theoretical scheme, the systems approach, which is challenging many of the traditional concepts of psychopathology and approaches to psychotherapy. Exciting projects are also underway which are models for bridging the gap between research, theory, and practice.

In closing, one cannot help but feel sympathetic and enthusiastic about these developing professions. Like the youth of today, they are genuinely struggling with their own self-identity and with developing their unique potentialities. Their energetic searching for new ideas, their creative adaptation of old ideas, and their relentless experimentation is their hallmark. Hopefully, with such momentium and potential, these fields will grow and mature in a way that will maximize their contribution to the sciences and society.

REFERENCES

Ackerman, N.W. (1954), "Disturbances in the Family: Some Unsolved Problems in Psychotherapy," *Psychiatry,* 17:359-369.
————(1958), *The Psychodynamics of Family Life.* New York: Basic Books.
————(1966), *Treating the Troubled Family.* New York: Basic Books.
————(1967), "The Future of Family Psychotherapy." Pp. 3-16 in N.W. Ackerman, F.L. Beatman, and S.N. Sherman (eds.), *Expanding Theory and Practice*

in Family Therapy. New York: Family Association of America.

———(1970), "Family psychotherapy today," *Family Process* 9:123-126.

Aldous, J. and Hill, R. (1967), *International Bibliography of Research in Marriage and the Family, 1900-1964.* Minneapolis: University of Minnesota Press.

Alexander, F. (1968), "The Empirical Study of the Differential Influence of Self-concept on the Professional Behavior of Marriage Counselors." Unpublished Ph.D. dissertation: University of Southern California.

Alger, I. and P. Hogan (1967), "The Use of Videotape Recordings in Conjoint Marital Therapy." *American Journal of Psychiatry,* 123:1425-1430.

———(1969), "Enduring Effects of Videotape Playback Experience on Marital and Family Relationships," *American Journal of Orthopsychiatry,* 39:86-96.

Anderson, F. and V. Smith (1963), "Conjoint Interview with Marriage Partners," *Marriage and Family Living,* 25:184-185.

Andronico, M.P., J. Fidler, B. Guerney, and L. Guerney (1967), "The combination of Didactic and Dynamic Elements in Filial Treatment," *International Journal of Group Psychotherapy,* 17:10-17.

Ard, B.N. and C.C. Ard (eds.) (1969), *Handbook of Marriage Counseling.* Palo Alto: Science and Behavior Books, Inc.

Bach, G.R. and S. Wyden (1969), *Intimate Enemy.* New York: William Morrow and Company.

Bateson, G., D.D. Jackson, J. Haley, and J. Weakland (1956), "Toward a Theory of Schizophrenia," *Behavorial Science* 1:251-264.

———(1963) "Note on the Double Bind," *Family Process* 2:154-161.

Beck, D.F. (1966), "Marital Conflict: Its Course and Treatment as Seen by Caseworkers," *Social Casework* 47:211-221.

———(1969), "Casework on Marital Problems: A Conceptual Exploration." Final project report to NIMH: Family Service Association of America.

———(1970), *Treatment of Marital Problems.* New York: Family Service Association of America.

Beels, D.C. and A. Ferber (1969), "Family Therapy: a View," *Family Process,* 8:280-318.

Bell, J.E. (1953), "Family Group Therapy as a Treatment Method," *American Psychologist,* 8:515.

———(1961), *Family Group Therapy.* Washington, D.C.: Department of Health, Education and Welfare. Public Health Monograph 64.

Bellville, T.P., O.N. Raths, and C.J. Bellville (1969), "Conjoint Marriage Therapy with a Husband-and-Wife Team." American Journal of Orthopsychiatry 39:473-483.

Berger, M.M. (1969), "Videotape Techniques in Psychiatric Training and Treatment," New York: Brunner/Mazel Publications.

Berman, K.K. (1966), "Multiple Family Therapy, Its Possibilities in Preventing Readmission," *Mental Hygiene,* 50:367-370.

Bernard, J. (1964), "The Adjustment of Married Mates." Pp. 675-739 in H.T. Christen (ed.), *Handbook of Marriage and the Family.* Chicago: Rand McNally.

Berne, E. (1961), *Transactional Analysis in Psychotherapy.* New York: Grove Press.

———(1964), *Games People Play.* New York: Grove Press.

Blinder, M.G., and M. Kirschenbaum (1967), "The Technique of Married Couple Group Therapy," *Archives of General Psychiatry,* 17:44-52.

Boas, C.V.E. (1962), "Intensive Group Psychotherapy with Married Couples," *International Journal of Group Psychotherapy,* 12:142-153.

Bodin, A.M. (1968a), "Conjoint Family Therapy." In W.E. Vicacke (ed.), *Readings in Introductory Psychology.* New York: American Book Company.
————(1968b), "Conjoint Family Assessment." In R. McReynolds (ed.), *Advances in Psychological Assessment.* Palo Alto: Science and Behavior Books.
————(1969a), "Family Therapy Training Literature: a Brief Guide," *Family Process* 8:272-279.
————(1969b), Videotape Applications in Family Therapy Training," *Journal of Nervous and Mental Disease,* 48:251-261.
Bolte, G.L. (1970), "A Communications Approach to Marital Counseling," *The Family Coordinator,* 19:32-40.
Boszormenyi-Nagy, I. (1962), "The Concept of Schizophrenia from the Perspective of Family Treatment," *Family Process,* 1:103-113.
Boszormenyi-Nagy, I. and J.L. Framo (eds.) (1965), *Intensive Family Therapy.* New York: Harper and Row.
Bowen, M. (1961), "Family Psychotherapy," *American Journal of Orthopsychiatry,* 31:41-60.
————(1965), "Family Psychotherapy with Schizophrenia in the Hospital and in Private Practice." In I. Boszormenyi-Nagy and J. Framo (eds.), *Intensive Family Therapy.* New York: Harper and Row.
————(1966), "The Use of Family Therapy in Clinical Practice," *Comprehensive Psychiatry,* 7:345-374.
Boyer, C.L. (1960), "Group Therapy with Married Couples," *Marriage and Family Living,* 22:21-24.
Bruniga, C.L. (1967), "Group Marriage Counseling in a State Hospital," *Hospital Community of Psychiatry,* 18:379-380.
Brody, S. (1961-2), "Psychotherapy of Married Couples: Preliminary Observations," *Psychoanalysis and the Psychoanalytic Review,* 48:94-107.
Burton, G. (1962), "Group Counseling with Alcoholic Husbands and Their Nonalcoholic Wives," *Marriage and Family Living* 24:56-61.
Burton, G. and H.M. Kaplan (1968), "Group Counseling in Conflicted Marriages Where Alcoholism Is Present: Clients' Evaluation of Effectiveness." *Journal of Marriage and the Family,* 30:74-79.
Calden, G. (1967), "Conjoint Marital Counseling." In H.L. Silverman (ed.), *Marital Counseling.* Springfield, Illinois: Charles C. Thomas.
Christensen, H.T. (ed.) (1964), *Handbook of Marriage and the Family.* Chicago: Rand McNally.
Couch, E.H. (1969), *Joint and Family Interviews in the Treatment of Marital Problems.* New York: Family Service Association of America.
Coughlin, F.I., and H.C. Wimberger (1968), "Group Family Therapy," *Family Process,* 7:37-50.
Curry, A.E. (1965), "Therapeutic Management of Multiple Family Groups," *International Journal of Group Psychotherapy,* 15:90-96.
Daniels, G. (1967), "Participation of Relatives in a Group Centered Program," *International Journal of Group Psychotherapy,* 17:336-341.
Davies, I.J., G. Ellenson, and R. Young (1966), "Therapy with a Group of Families in a Psychiatric Day Care Center," *American Journal of Orthopsychiatry,* 36:134-146.
Dewey, J., and A.F. Bentley (1949), *Knowing and the Known.* Boston: Beacon Press.
Dicks, H.V. (1967), *Marital Tensions.* New York: Basic Books.

.Dorfman, E. (1968), "Content-Free Study of Marital Resemblances in Group Therapy," *Journal of Abnormal Psychology,* 73:78-80.

Dreikars, R. (1951), "Family Group Therapy in the Chicago Community Child Guidance Centers," *Mental Hygiene,* 35:291-301.

Ely, A.L. (1970), "Efficacy of Training in Conjugal Therapy." Unpublished Ph.D. thesis: Rutgers University.

Festinger, L. (1953), "Laboratory Experiments." In L. Festinger and D. Katz (eds.), *Research Methods in the Behavioral Sciences.* New York: Dryden Press.

Fitzgerald, R.V. (1969), "Conjoint Marital Psychotherapy: An Outcome and Follow-up Study," *Family Process* 8: 260-271.

Flint, A.A., and B.W. McLennan (1962), "Some Dynamic Factors in Marital Group Psychotherapy," *International Journal of Group Psychotherapy.*

Fontana, A.F. (1966), "Familial Etiology of Schizophrenia," *Psychological Bulletin,* 66:214-227.

Ford, D. and H. Urban (1963), *Systems of Psychotherapy.* New York: Wiley and Son.

Framo, J.L. (1962), "The Theory of the Technique of Family Treatment of Schizophrenia," *Family Process,* 1:119-131.

————(1965), "Systematic Research on Family Dynamics." Pp. 407-462 in I. Boszormenyi-Nagy and J.L. Framo (eds.), *Intensive Family Therapy.* New York: Harper and Row.

————(1969), "Discussion of Beels and Ferber's Article on Family Therapy: A View," *Family Process,* 8:319-322.

Freeman, D. (1965), "Counseling Engaged Couples in Small Groups," *Social Work,* 10:36-42.

Friedman, A.S. (1962), "Family Therapy as Conducted in the Home," *Family Process,* 1:132-140.

Friedman, A.S., I. Boszormenyi-Nagy, J.E. Jungreis, G. Lincoln, H.E. Mitchell, J.C. Sonne, R.V. Speck, and G. Spivack (1965), *Psychotherapy for the Whole Family.* New York: Springer Publications.

Fry, W.F. (1962), "The Marital Context of an Anxiety Syndrome," *Family Process,* 1:245-252.

Gehrke, S. and J. Moxom (1962), "Diagnostic classification and treatment techniques in marriage counseling," *Family Process,* 1:253-264.

Geist, J. and N.M. Gerber (1960), "Joint Interviewing: A Treatment Technique with Marital Partners," *Social Casework,* 41:76-83.

Goldstein, A.P., and S.J. Dean (eds.) (1966), *The Investigation of Psychotherapy.* New York: John Wiley.

Goldstein, M.K., and B. Francis (1969), "Behavior Modification of Husbands by Wives." Paper presented at the National Council on Family Relations Annual Meeting, Washington D.C.

Goodwin, H.M., and E.H. Mudd (1966), "Marriage Couseling: Methods and Goals," *Comprehensive Psychiatry,* 7:450-452.

Gottschalk, L.A., and A.H. Auerbach (eds.) (1966), *Methods of Research in Psychotherapy.* New York: Appleton Century-Crofts.

Green, K.A. (1963), "The Echo of Marital Conflict," *Family Process,* 2:315-328.

Greene, B.L. (1960), "Marital Disharmony: Concurrent Analysis of Husband and Wife," *Diseases of the Nervous System,* 21:73-83.

Greene, B.L., and A.P. Solomon (1963), "Marital Disharmony: Concurrent Psychoanalytic Therapy of Husband and Wife by the Same Psychiatrist," *American Journal of Psychotherapy,* 17:443-456.

Grosser, C., W.E. Henry, and J.G. Kelly (eds.) (1969), *Nonprofessional in the Human Services.* San Francisco: Jossey-Bass.

Group for the Advancement of Psychiatry (1970), *The Field of Family Therapy.* Report No. 78:525-644.

Guerney, Jr., B. (1964), "Filial Therapy: Description and Rationale," *Journal of Consulting Psychology,* 28:304-310.

————(1970), Personal communication.

Guerney, Jr., B., L. Guerney, and M.P. Andronico (1966), "Filial Therapy." *Yale Scientific Magazine,* 40:6-14.

Gullerud, E. N., and V. L. Harlan, (1962), "Four-Way Joint Interviewing in Marital Counseling," *Social Casework,* 43:532-537.

Haley, J. (1962), "Whither Family Therapy," *Family Process,* 1:69-100.

————(1963), "Marriage Therapy," *Archives of General Psychiatry,* 8:213-224.

————(1966), Book review on "Intensive Family Therapy." *Family Process,* 5:289.

————(1969), "An Editor's Farewell," *Family Process,* 8:149-158.

Hallowitz, E., and B. Stephens, (1959), "Group Therapy with Fathers," *Social Casework,* 40:183-192.

Hansen, C.C. (1968), "An Extended Home Visit with Conjoint Family Therapy," *Family Process,* 7:67-87.

Harker, F.O. (1962), "Married Couples' Group in Therapy of Psychoneuroses," *Southern Medical Journal,* 55:401-405.

Harley, Jr., A.A. (1960), "Group Psychotherapy for Parents of Disturbed Children," *Mental Hospitals,* 14:14-19.

Harper, R.A. (1960), "Marriage Counseling as Rational Process Oriented Psychotherapy," *Journal of Individual Psychology,* 26:197-207.

Hawkins, J. (1970), Personal Communication.

Hawkins, R.P., R.F. Peterson, E. Schweid, and D. Bijou (1966), "Behavior Therapy in the Home: Amelioration of Problem Parent-Child Relations with the Parent in a Therapeutic Role," *Journal of Experimental Child Psychology,* 4:99-107.

Henderson, N.B. (1965), "Married Group Therapy: A Setting for Reducing Resistances," *Psychological Reports,* 16:347-362.

Hess, R.D., and G. Handel (1959), *Family Worlds.* Chicago: University of Chicago.

Hoek, A., and S. Wollstein, (1966), "Conjoint Psychotherapy of Married Couples: A Clinical Report," *International Journal of Social Psychiatry,* 12:209-216.

Hurvitz, N. (1965), "The Marital Roles Inventory as a Counseling Instrument," *Journal of Marriage and the Family,* 27:492-501.

————(1970),"Interaction Hypotheses in Marriage Counseling," *The Family Coordinator,* 19:64-75.

Jackson, D.D. (1959), "Family Interaction, Family Homeostasis and Some Implications for Conjoint Family Psychotherapy." Pp. 122-141 in J.H. Masserman (ed.), *Individual and Family Dynamics.* New York: Grune and Stratton, Inc.

————(1961), "Family Therapy in the Family of the Schizophrenic." Pp. 272-287 in M.I. Stein (ed.), *Contemporary Psychotherapies.* New York: The Free Press of Glencoe, Inc.

————(1965), "The Study of the Family," *Family Process,* 4:1-20.

Jackson, D.D., and J.H. Weakland, (1961), "Conjoint Family Therapy: Some Considerations on Theory, Technique and Results," *Psychiatry,* 24:30-45.

Jarvis, P., J. Esty, and L. Stutzman, (1969), "Evaluation and Treatment of Families at Fort Logan Mental Health Center," *Community Mental Health,* 5:14-19.

Johnsen, K.P. (1968), "Self-concept Validation as a Focus on Marriage Counseling," Family Coordinator, 17:174-180.

Johnson, A. M., and D. Fishback, (1944), "Analysis of a Disturbed Adolescent Girl and Collaborative Psychiatric Treatment of the Mother," American Journal of Orthopsychiatry, 14:195-203.

Jones, W.L. (1967), "The Villain and the Victim: Group Therapy for Married Couples," American Journal of Psychiatry, 124:107-110.

Kafka, J.S. (1970), "Ambiguity for Individuation: A Critique and Reformulation of Double Bind Theory," Archives of General Psychiatry, (in press).

Kafka, J.S., and J. W. McDonald, (1965), "The Latent Family in the Intensive Treatment of the Hospitalized Patient," Current Psychiatric Therapies, 5:172-177.

Kern, J. (1967), "Conjoint Marital Psychotherapy: An Interim Measure in the Treatment of Psychosis," Psychiatry, 30:283-293.

Kimber, J.A. (1966), "Referred and Unreferred Patients: A Comparison," Journal of Marriage and the Family, 28:293-295.

———(1967), "Psychologists and Marriage Counselors in the United States," American Psychologist, 22:862-865.

Kimbro, E., H., Taschman, H. Wylie, and B. MacLennan (1967), "Multiple Family Group Approach to Some Problems of Adolescence," International Journal of Group Psychotherapy, 17:18-24.

Klemer, R. H. (ed,) (1965), Counseling in Marital and Sexual Problems. Baltimore: Williams and Williams.

———(1966), "The Marriage Counselor in the Physician's Office," Journal of Marriage and the Family, 28:287-292.

Klimenko, A. (1968), "Multifamily Therapy in the Rehabilitation of Drug Addicts," Perspectives in Psychiatric Care, 6:220-223.

Kohl, R.N. (1962), "Pathological Reactions of Marital Partners to Improvement of Patients," American Journal of Psychiatry, 118:1036-1041.

Kotlar, S.L. (1967), "Role Theory in Marriage Counseling," Sociology and Social Research, 52:50-62.

Laidlaw, R.W. (1957), "The Psychiatrist as Marriage Counselor." Pp. 52-61 in C.E. Vincent (ed.), Readings in Marriage Counseling. New York: Crowell.

Lantz, H. (1959), "Sociological Theory and Marriage Counseling," Merrill-Palmer Quarterly 5:176-179.

Laqueur, H.P.. H.A. Laburt, and E. Marong, (1964), "Multiple Family Therapy: Further Developments," International Journal of Social Psychiatry (special edition), 2:70-80.

Laqueur, H.P., C. Wells, and M. Agresti (1969), "Multiple-Family Therapy in a State Hospital," Hospital and Community Psychiatry, 20:13-20.

Leader, A.L. (1969), "Current and Future Issues in Family Therapy," The Social Service Review, 43:1-11.

Lehrman, N.S. (1963), "The Joint Interview: An Aid to Psychotherapy and Family Stability," American Journal of Psychotherapy, 17:83-93.

Leichter, E. (1962), "Group Psychotherapy of Married Couples' Groups—Some Characteristic Treatment Dynamics," International Journal of Group Psychotherapy, 12:154-163.

Leichter, E., and G.L. Schulman, (1968), "Emerging Phenomena in Multi-family Group Treatment," International Journal of Group Psychotherapy, 18:59-69.

Leik, R. K., and L.K. Northwood, (1964), "Improving Family Guidance Through the Small Group Experimental Laboratory," Social Work, 9:18-25.

Lennard, H.L., and A. Bernstein, (1969), *Patterns in Human Interaction*. San Francisco: Jossey-Bass.

Leslie, G.R. (1964a), "Conjoint Therapy in Marriage Counseling," *Journal of Marriage and the Family*, 26:65-71.

———(1964b), "The Field of Marriage Counseling." Pp. 912-943 in H.T. Christensen (ed.), *Handbook of Marriage and the Family*. Chicago: Rand McNally.

Levine, R. (1964), "Treatment in the Home," *Social Work*, 9:19-28.

Levitt, H., and R. Baker, (1969), "Relative Psychopathology of Marital Partners," *Family Process*, 8:33-42.

Liberman, R. (1970), "Behavioral Approaches to Family and Couple Therapy," *American Journal of Orthopsychiatry*, 40:106-118.

Lidz, T., A.R. Cornelison, S. Fleck, and D. Terry, (1957), "Schism and Skew in Families of Schizophrenics," *American Journal of Psychiatry*, 64:241-248.

Mace, D.R. (1945), "Marriage Guidance in England," *Marriage and Family Living*, 7:1-25.

———(1967), "Introduction." in H.L. Silverman (ed.), *Marital Counseling*. Springfield, Illinois: Charles C. Thomas.

———(1970), "On Being a Family Specialist Then and Now: An Intergenerational Dialogue." Paper presented at the National Council on Family Relations, Chicago.

MacGregor, R. (1962), "Multiple Impact Psychotherapy with Families, *Family Process*, 1:15-29.

———(1967), "Progress in Multiple Impact Therapy." Pp. 47-58 in N.W. Ackerman, F.L. Beatman, and S.N. Sherman (eds.), *Expanding Theory and Practice in Family Therapy*. New York: Family Association of America.

Mangus, A.R. (1957), "Role Theory in Marriage Counseling," *Social Forces*, 35:200-209.

Manus, G.I. (1966), "Marriage Counseling: A Technique in Search of a Theory," *Journal of Marriage and the Family*, 28:449-453.

Martin, P.A. (1965), "Treatment of Marital Disharmony by Collaborative Therapy." Pp. 83-101 in B.L. Green (ed.), *The Psychotherapies of Marital Disharmony*. New York: The Free Press.

Martin, P.A., and H.W. Bird, (1953), "An Approach to the Psychotherapy of Marriage Partners: The Stereoscopic Technique," *Psychiatry*, 16:123-127.

McGuire, W.J. (1969), "Theory-Oriented Research in Natural Settings: The Best of Both Worlds for Social Psychology." In M. Sherif and C. W. Sherif (eds.), *Interdisciplinary Relations in the Social Sciences*. Chicago: Aldine Publications.

Meehl, P.E. (1960), Introduction in L.M. Brammer and E.L. Shostrom. *Therapeutic Psychology*. Englewood Cliffs, New Jersey: Prentice-Hall.

Meltzoff, J., and M. Kornreich, (1970), *Research in Psychotherapy*. New York: Atherton Press.

Michaelson, R. (1963), "An Analysis of the Changing Focus of Marriage Counseling." Ph.D. dissertation: University of Southern California.

Miller, J. (1967), "Concurrent Treatment of Marital Couples by One or Two Analysts," *American Journal of Psychoanalysis*, 27:135-139.

Miller, S. (1970), "The Effects of Communication Training Groups upon Self-disclosure and Openness of Engaged Couples' System of Interaction: A Field Experiment." Ph.D. thesis proposal: University of Minnesota.

Minuchin, S., B. Montalvo, B. G. Guerney, B.L. Rosman, and F. Schumer (1967), *Families of the Slums*. New York: Basic Books.

Mishler, E.G. (1967), "Problems of Interpretation in Research on Family Processes and Schizophrenia, or the Life, Death, and Rebirth of Clinical Concepts.
Paper presented at the Assoc. of Nervous and Mental Disease, New York.

Mishler, E.G., and N.W. Waxler, (1968a), *Interaction in Families: An Experimental Study of Family Processes and Schizophrenia.* New York: John Wiley and
Sons, Inc.

————(1968b), *Family Processes and Schizophrenia.* New York: Science
House, Inc.

Mittelman, B. (1968), "The Concurrent Analysis of Married Couples,"
Psychoanalytic Quarterly, 17:182-197.

Moe, M., N. Waal, and B. Urdahl, (1960), "Group Psychotherapy with Parents of
Psychotic and of Neurotic Children," *Acta Psychotherapeutica,* 8:136-146.

Mottola, W.C. (1967), "Family Therapy: A Review," *Psychotherapy: Theory,
Research and Practice,* 4:116-124.

Mudd, E.H. (1957), "Knowns and Unknowns in Marriage Counseling Research,"
Marriage and Family Living, 19:75-81.

————(1968), "The Impact of the Development of Marriage Counseling on the
Traditional and Related Professions." Pp. 171-188 in J.A. Peterson (ed.),
Marriage and Family Counseling, Perspective and Prospect. New York:
Association Press.

————(1969), "AAMC: The First Twenty-five Years, 1942-1967." Pp. 381-389 in
B.N. Ard, Jr., and C.C. Ard (eds.), *Handbook of Marriage Counseling.* Palo
Alto: Science and Behavior Books, Inc.

Nakhla, F.,L. Folkart, and J. Webster, (1969), "Treatment of Families as Inpatients," *Family Process,* 8:79-96.

Nash, E.M., L. Jessner, and D.W. Abse (eds.) (1964), *Marriage Counseling in
Medical Practice.* Chapel Hill: The University of North Carolina Press.

Neubeck, G. (1954), "Factors Affecting Group Psychotherapy with Married Couples," *Marriage and Family Living,* 16:216-220.

Nunnally, E. (1970), "Effects of Communication Training upon Empathic Accuracy and Upon Awareness of Dyadic Interaction of Engaged Couples: A Field
Experiment." Ph.D. thesis proposal: University of Minnesota.

Nye, F.I., and F.M. Bernardo (eds.) (1967), *Emerging Conceptual Frameworks
in Family Analysis.* New York: Macmillan.

Oakland, J.A., and M.K. Wulbert, (1969), "The Shaping of Handicapped
Children's Behavior by Mothers." Paper presented at the National Council on
Family Relations annual meeting, Washington, D.C.

Oberndorf, D.P. (1938), "Psychoanalysis of Married Couples," *Psychoanalysis
Review,* 25:453-457.

Olson, D.H. (1968), "Simulated Family Activity Measurement as a Diagnostic
Tool in Marriage Counseling." Paper presented at annual meeting of National
Council of Family Relations, New Orleans.

————(1969a), "The Measurement of Power Using Self-report and Behavioral
Methods," *Journal of Marriage and the Family,* 31:545-550.

————(1969b), "Diagnosis in Marriage Counseling Using SIMFAM, MMPI's, and
Therapists," American Association of Marriage Counselors' Newsletter.

————(1969c), "Empirically Unbinding the Double Bind." Symposium at the
annual meeting of the American Psychological Association, Washington, D.C.

Olson, D. H., and C. Rabunsky, (1970), "The Validity of Three Measures of
Family Power." Unpublished manuscript.

Olson, D.H., and R.G. Ryder, (1970), "Inventory of Marital Conflicts: an Experimental Interaction Procedure," *Journal of Marriage and the Family,* 32 (August): 443-448.

Ostby, C.H. (1968), "Conjoint Group Therapy with Prisoners and Their Families," *Family Process,* 7:184-201.

Papanek, H. (1965), "Group Psychotherapy with Married Couples." Pp. 157-163 in J. Masserman (ed.), *Current Psychiatric Therapies 5.* New York: Greene and Stratton.

Parloff, M.B. (1961), "The Family in Psychotherapy," *Archives of General Psychiatry,* 4:445-451.

Patterson, G.R., and G. Brodsky (1966), "A Behavioral Modification Programme for a Child with Multiple Problem Behaviours," *Journal of Child Psychology and Psychiatry,* 7:277-295.

Paul, N.L. (1966), "Effects of Playback on Family Members of Their Own Previously Recorded Conjoint Therapy Material," *Psychiatric Research Reports 20.*

Perelman, J.S. (1960), "Problems Encountered in Group Psychotherapy of Married Couples," *International Journal of Group Psychology,* 10:136-142.

Peterson, J.A. (ed.) (1968a), *Marriage and Family Counseling: Perspective and Prospect.* New York: Association Press.

————(1968b), "Marriage Counseling: Past, Present and Future." Pp. 130-153 in J.A. Peterson (ed.), *Marriage and Family Counseling, Perspective and Prospect.* New York: Association Press.

Phillips, C. (1967), "Measuring Power of Spouse," *Sociology and Social Research,* 52:35-49.

————(1968), "Teaching Young People to Help Each Other," *Adolescence,* 3:133-138.

————(1970), "A Study of Marriage Counselor's MMPI Profiles," *Journal Of Marriage and the Family,* 32:119-130.

Pollak, O. (1965), "Sociological and Psychoanalytic Concepts in Family Diagnosis." In B.L. Greene (ed.), *The Psychotherapies of Marital Disharmony.* New York: Free Press.

Powell, M., J. Taylor, and R. Smith, (1967), "Parents and Child in a Child Guidance Clinic: Should They Have the Same Therapists?" *International Journal of Group Psychotherapy,* 17:25-34.

Rakoff, V., J.J. Sigal, and N.B. Epstein, (1963), "Working-through in Conjoint Family Therapy," *American Journal of Psychotherapy,* 17:266-274.

Ravich, R.A. (1966), "Short-term, Intensive Treatment of Marital Discord," *Voices,* 2:42-48.

Reding, G.R., and B. Ennis (1967), "Treatment of the Couple by a Couple," *British Journal of Medical Psychology,* 37:325-330.

Reevey, W.R. (1967), "Educational and Professional Training of the Marital Counselor," In H.L. Silverman (ed.), *Marital Counseling.* Springfield, Illinois: Charles C. Thomas.

Reiff, R., and F. Riesman, (1965), "The Indigenous Nonprofessional," *Community Mental Health Journal Monograph, No. 1*

Rioch, M.J., (1963), "NIMH Study in Training Mental Health Counselors," *American Journal of Orthopsychiatry,* 33:678-679.

Ritchie, A. (1960), "Multiple Impact Therapy, and Experiment," *Social Work,* 5:13-21.

Rogers, C.R. (1964), "Psychotherapy Today—or Where Do We Go from Here?" *American Journal of Psychotherapy,* 18:5-16.

Rubenstein, D., and O.R. Weiner, (1967), "Co-therapy Teamwork Relationship in Family Psychotherapy." In G.H. Zuk and I. Boszormenyi-Nagy (eds.), *Family Therapy and Disturbed Families.* Palo Alto: Science and Behavior Books.

Rutledge, A.L. (1966), *Pre-Marital Counseling.* Cambridge: Schenkman Publishing Co. Inc.

————(1968), "An Illustrative Look at the History of Pre-Marital Counseling." Pp. 110-117 in J.A. Peterson (ed.), *Marriage and Family Counseling, Perspective and Prospect.* New York: Association Press.

Ryder, R.G. (1970), "Dimensions of early marriage," *Family Process* 9:51-68.

Sager, C.J. (1966), "The Development of Marriage Therapy: A Historical Review," *American Journal of Orthopsychiatry,* 36:458-467.

————(1967), "The Conjoint Session in Marriage Therapy," *American Journal of Psychoanalysis,* 113:1057-1067.

————(1968), "The Treatment of Married Couples," Pp. 213-224 in S. Arieti (ed.), *American Handbook of Psychiatry.* New York: Basic Books, Inc.

Sanford, N. (1965), "Will psychologists study human problems?" *American Psychologist,* 20:192-202.

Satir, V. (1964), *Conjoint Family Therapy: A Guide to Theory and Technique.* Palo Alto: Science and Behavior Books.

————(1965), "Conjoint Marital Therapy." Pp. 121-133 in B.L. Greene (ed.), *The Psychotherapy of Marital Disharmony.* New York: The Free Press.

————(1968), "Conjoint Family Therapy." Paper presented at Minnesota Workshop on Family Counseling University of Minnesota.

Schrieber, L.E. (1966), "Evaluation of Family Group Treatment in a Family Agency," *Family Process,* 5:21-29.

Schwartzberg, B., and E. Hammer (1968), "Joint Interview with Adolescent Girls and Their Mothers as a Family Treatment Tool," *The Family Coordinator,* 17:75-77.

Shellow, R.S., B.S. Brown, and J.W. Osberg (1963), "Family Group Therapy in Retrospect," *Family Process,* 2:52-66.

Sherif, M. (1966), "If Basic Research Is to Have Bearing on Actualities." Address to Fourth Annual Psi Chi Day; Pennsylvania State University.

Sigal, J.J., V. Rakoff, and N.B. Epstein, (1967), "Interaction in Early Treatment Sessions as an Indication of Therapeutic Outcome in Conjoint Family Therapy," *Family Process,* 6:215-226.

Silverman, H.L. (ed.) (1967), *Marital Counseling.* Springfield, Illinois: Charles C. Thomas.

Skidmore, R.A., and H.V. Garrett (1955), "The Joint Interview in Marriage Counseling," *Marriage and Family Living,* 17:349-354.

Smith, J.R. (1967), "Suggested Scales for Prediction of Client Movement and the Duration of Marriage Counseling," *Sociology and Social Research,* 52:63-71.

Smith, V.G., and D.H. Hepworth (1967), "Marriage and Counseling with One Marital Partner: Rationale and Clinical Implications," *Social Casework,* 48:352-359.

Solomon, A.P., and B.L. Green (1963), "Marital Disharmony: Concurrent Therapy of Husband and Wife by the same psychiatrist," *Diseases of the Nervous System,* 24:21-28.

————(1965), "Concurrent Psychoanalytic Therapy in Marital Disharmony." Pp. 103-119 in B.L. Greene (ed.), *The Psychotherapy of Marital Disharmony.* New York: The Free Press.

Sonne, J.C., and G. Lincoln, (1965), "Heterosexual Co-therapy Team Experiences During Family Therapy, *Family Process,* 4:117-195.

———(1966), "The Importance of Heterosexual Co-therapy Relationships in the Construction of a Family Image." In I.M. Cohen (ed.), *Family Structure, Dynamics and Therapy.* Psychiatric Research Report 20.

Speck, R.V. (1964), "Family Therapy in the Home," *Journal of Marriage and the Family,* 26:72-76.

———(1967), "Pscyhotherapy of the Social Network of a Schizophrenic Family," *Family Process,* 6:208-214.

Speck, R.V., and U. Rueveni, (1969), "Network Therapy—a developing concept." *Family Process* 8:182-191.

Speers, R.W., and C. Lansing, (1964), "Group Psychotherapy with Preschool Psychotic Children and Collateral Group Therapy of Their Parents: A Preliminary Report of the First Two Years," *American Journal of Orthopsychiatry,* 34:659-666.

Sporakowski, M.J., and P.R. Mills, (1969), "What's It All About? An Overview of Family Therapy," *Family Coordinator,* 18:61-69.

Stollak, G.E., B.G. Guerney, and M. Rothberg (1966), *Psychotherapy Research: Selected Readings.* Chicago: Rand McNally.

Stover, L., and B. Guerney, Jr., (1967), "The efficacy of training procedures for mothers in filial therapy." *Psychotherapy: Theory, Research and Practice* 4:110-115.

Straus, M.A. (1967), "The Influence of Sex of Child and Social Class on Instrumental and Expressive Family Roles in a Laboratory Setting," *Sociology and Social Research,* 52:7-21.

———(1968), "Communication, Creativity and Problem-Solving of Middle and Working-Class Families in Three Societies." Pp. 15-27 in M. Sussman (ed.), *Sourcebook in Marriage and the Family.* 3rd edition. Boston: Houghton Mifflin.

———(1969), *Family Measurement Techniques: Abstracts of Published Instruments, 1935-1965.* Minneapolis: University of Minnesota Press.

Straus, M.A., and I. Tallman, (1966), "SIMFAM: A Technique for Observational Measurement and Experimental Study of Families." Mimeographed working paper.

Strodtbeck, F.L. (1951), "Husband-Wife Interaction over Revealed Difference," *American Sociological Review,* 16:468-473.

Szasz, T.S. (1961), *The Myth of Mental Illness: Foundations of a Theory of Personal Conduct.* New York: Harper.

Tomlinson, T.M., R.P. Barthol, and H. Groot (1969), "Responses of Non-Professional Therapists to Chronic Schizophrenics," *Pschotherapy: Theory, Research and Practice,* 6:256-260.

Vincent, C.E. (1967), "Mental Health and the Family," *Journal of Marriage and the Family,* 29:18-38.

———(1969), "The Training of Professional and Subprofessional Personnel as Adjunctive Marriage Counselors: Opportunities and Dilemmas," *The Family Coordinator,* 3:217-221.

VonBertalanffy, L. (1968), *General Systems Theory.* New York: George Braziller.

Watson, A.S. (1963), "The Conjoint Psychotherapy of Married Partners," *American Journal of Orthopsychiatry,* 33:912-922.

Watzlawick, P. (1963), "A Review of the Double Bind Theory," *Family Process,* 2:132-153.

Watzlawick, P., J. H. Beavin, and D.D. Jackson (1967), *Pragmatics of Human Communication.* New York: W.W. Norton.

Weakland, J. (1962), "Family Therapy as a Research Arena," *Family Process* 1:63-68.

Weisberg, M. (1964), "Joint Interviewing with Marital Partners," *Social Casework,* 45:221-229.

Werry, J.S., and J.P. Wollersheim (1967), "Behavior Therapy with Children: A Broad Overview." *Journal of the American Academy of Child Psychiatry,* 6:346-370.

Wender, A. E., L. Ferrini, and G.E. Gaby, (1965), "Group Therapy with Parents of Children in a Residential Treatment Center," *Child Welfare,* 44:266-271.

Wertheim, E.S. (1959), "A Joint Interview Technique with Mother and Child," *Children,* 6:23-29.

Whitaker, C. (1958), "Psychotherapy with Couples," *American Journal of Psychotherapy,* 12:18-23.

———(1965), "Acting Out in Family Psychotherapy." In *Acting Out: Theoretical and Clinical Aspects.* New York: Greene and Stratton.

Whitaker, C., R. E. Felder, and J. Warkentin (1965), "Counter-transference in the Family Treatment of Schizophrenia," In I. Boszormenyi-Nagy and J. Framo (eds.), *Intensive Family Therapy.* New York: Harper and Row.

Wilms, J.H. (1966), "Counseling on Premarital Relationships," *Journal of American College Health Associates,* 15:67-70.

Winter, W.D., and H.J. Ferreira (eds.), (1969), *Research in Family Interaction.* Palo Alto: Science and Behavior Books.

Wynne, L.C. (1958), "Pseudo-mutuality in the Family Relations of Schizophrenics," *Psychiatry,* 21:205-220.

———(1965), "Some Indications and Contraindications for Exploratory Family Therapy." In I. Boszormenyi-Nagy and J.L. Framo (eds.), *Intensive Family Therapy.* New York: Harper and Row.

———(1968), "Methodologic and Conceptual Issues in the Study of Schizophrenics and Their Families," *Journal of Psychiatric Research,* 6:185-199.

Zelditch, M., Jr. (1955), "Role Differentiation in the Nuclear Family: A Comparative Study." In T. Parson and R. F. Bales (eds.), *Family Socialization and Interaction Process.* New York: Macmillan.

ALAN S. GURMAN

2   Emerging Trends in Research and Practice

The marital therapy literature through August, 1972, was content-analyzed to examine trends in the research and clinical practice of marital therapists. Analyses of a 415-item Marital Therapy Bibliography revealed that: (a) The literature experienced the beginning of its major growth spurt after 1960, with about half of the marital therapy publications appearing since 1967; (b) Journals contributing the most to the development of marital therapy form a heterogeneous mixture of professional disciplines, with multidisciplinary journals demonstrating the greatest impact; (c) The nature of much of marital therapy research and practice is rapidly changing, with a growing interest in empirical and methodological issues. Implications of these emerging trends in research and practice are discussed in terms of the future of marital therapy.

Marital therapy has come of age and is a viable psychotherapeutic enterprise and subspecialty. Thus, in recent years several bibliographic works (Aldous and Hill, 1967; Glick and Haley, 1971; Haley and Glick, 1965; National, 1965) have collected references to the existing literature, and a few reviews of specialized topics (Gurman, 1971; Lebedun, 1970) and of general research issue (Olson, 1970; Wells et al., 1972) in marital therapy have appeared. This maturational process has clearly spawned more effective treatments for marital problems and has served as a vehicle for awakening professional mental health interest in the family system, in particular, and in the active interpersonal nature of much of human psychological suffering, in general. Any boom in the application of a given therapeutic modality must also, so it seems historically, bear the weight of concurrent development of narrow "school" entrenchments, esoteric systems of meaning, and proselytizing dogma. Unfortunately, the practice of marital therapy has not escaped this fate in its growth.

Nevertheless, it would appear that in this decade any training program in the mental health field that does not offer guided, supervised, clinical experience with married couples is neglecting one of the most potent avenues for therapeutic change. Aside from such direct clinical experience, it is probably the professional literature that most affects the practice of any domain of therapeutic practice. It is primarily through this literature that advances in research and theory and innovations in technique are communicated to large numbers of clinicians and researchers.

The purpose of the present paper, then, is to examine the literature on marital therapy during the last forty-odd years. Through a content analysis of this literature, historical trends in the clinical and research aspects of marital therapy can be determined, several dimensions of the current status of the field can be described, and both likely and important directions for the future of marital therapy can be anticipated.

Method

Every publication on marital therapy through August, 1972, that could be located was included in this review. Four earlier bibliographic works (Aldous and Hill 1967; Glick and Haley, 1971; Haley and Glick, 1965; National, 1965) and the *Psychological Abstracts* were the major sources of references in this area. In addition, numerous personal communications from workers in the field supplemented these listings. In order to make the bibliography as complete as possible, entries were not limited to books and journal articles but also included papers presented at many professional meetings, conferences and symposia.[1] Yet even a comprehensive bibliography must be selected. Thus, material on the following topics was excluded from the listing: popular books for the lay public, material that focused on family therapy without explicit attention to marital therapy, material on pre-marital counseling, sex education, abortion counseling, and sexual dysfunction. Descriptions of marital interaction and studies of marital satisfaction and marital adjustment were excluded unless they focused on these issues in a patient population or, as in the case of analogue studies, had direct and clear relevance to marital therapy. When completed, this listing of publications on marital therapy comprised a bibliography of 415 entries.[2]

Each entry in the bibliography was assigned to one or more content areas. These categories reflect the major emphases of the material in the marital therapy literature. Following is a descriptive summary of the content areas:

Analogue: Studies whose purpose is to simulate some functional property of the practice of marital therapy.

Behavioral: Behavioral techniques in marital therapy with either one or both

---

[1] It is unlikely that any such listing can ever be absolutely complete; the author welcomes notices of any missing items so that the bibliography can be periodically updated.

spouses in treatment, e.g. operant conditioning, contingency-contracting, cognitive restructuring.

Bibliography or Review: Bibliographic materials on marital therapy; reviews of marital therapy literature and directly related literatures.

Client: Studies or papers that focus on the patient: personality characteristics, demographic characteristics, etc.

Collaborative, Concurrent, Combined or Individual Therapy: Papers dealing with the rationale, indications for use, etc. of collaborative, concurrent, combined or individual treatment of marital problems.

Conjoint Therapy: Papers focusing on the empirical study, theory, indications, etc. for the treatment of marital problems with both spouses seen together by the same therapist(s).

Comparative: Empirical studies or clinical essays comparing the processes and outcomes of different forms of marital therapy, e.g., conjoint versus concurrent, individual versus group, etc.

Client Progress, Assessment, Selection: Studies or papers focusing on criteria for patient selection in marital therapy, issues in predicting the outcome of treatment, etc.

Co-Therapy: Papers focusing on co-therapy by male and female therapists, e.g., rationale, indications, etc.

General: Articles or books dealing with non-specific aspects of marital therapy; general statements of the value and theory of marital therapy; edited books covering a variety of aspects of marital therapy.

Group Therapy: Studies or articles dealing with the theory or technique of treating married couples in couples' groups.

Method: Articles dealing with issues in research design, statistical analysis, or research strategy.

Outcome: Studies designed to assess the results of marital therapy on a pre-post comparison basis and papers reporting on treatment outcome in other forms; papers dealing with general issues in outcome evaluation.

Process: Studies and papers dealing with the in-therapy behavior of therapists and patients, such as relationship variables, content of therapeutic sessions, etc.

Special Population: Reports or papers on marital treatment where one or both partners is schizophrenic, aged, alcoholic, hospitalized, etc.; conjoint treatment of parents of "problem children," other special groups.

Therapist: Studies or papers focusing on the marital therapist's beliefs, attitudes and goals; personality characteristics of the marital therapist; conceptions of therapist's role and influence, etc.

---

[2] Copies of this bibliography, content-coded for each entry, are available from the author upon request.

Technique: Papers describing techniques used in marital therapy, e.g., use of videotape feedback, art therapy, use of dreams, interpretation, etc; behavioral versus analytic, individual versus group treatment, for example, are not construed as techniques in this classification.

Training: Techniques of training marital therapists; issues and policies related to the training of marital therapists; professional affairs relative to the practice of marital therapy, development of marital therapy as a specialty area, etc.

Results

The accumulated marital therapy bibliography was content-analyzed in three ways: (a) tabulation of the frequency of publications in given time periods; (b) listing of the primary journal sources of publications; and (c) tabulation of the frequency of publications by content areas in given time periods.

Table I shows the rate of growth of the marital therapy literature during the last forty-odd years. Through 1960 the literature had shown a rather consistent rate of increase of about a half-dozen publications from one time period to the next. The first major acceleration in the rate of publication then occurred in the period 1961-1963, during which the literature gained 16 more publications than in the preceding period 1958-1960. Since that time there has been a continual increase in the number of additions to the marital therapy literature in each time period. In the last six years, 1967-1972, the number of marital therapy publica-

Table 1. Frequency of Publications On Marital Therapy in Selected Time Periods

Time Period	Number of publications[a]		Cumulative Frequency
Pre–1940	5	(1.2)	5
1940–1948	11	(2.7)	16
1949–1951	16	(3.8)	32
1952–1953	16	(3.8)	48
1955–1957	21	(5.0)	69
1958–1960	29	(7.0)	98
1961–1963	45	(10.9)	143
1964–1966	68	(16.4)	211
1967–1969	119	(28.7)	330
1970–1972 [b]	85	(20.5)	415
Total	415	(100)	

[a] Numbers in parentheses indicate the percent of the total number of publications occurring in each time period.
[b] This time period extends through August, 1972, only; hence, the number of publications in this period will need to be adjusted upward later.

tions has doubled (211 at the end of 1966 versus 415 in August, 1972) and in the last nine years, 1964-1972, the number has nearly tripled (143 at the end of 1963 versus 415 in August, 1972). Finally, over three-quarters of these marital therapy publications have appeared since the beginning of the past decade.

The primary journal sources of marital therapy publications are presented in Table II. An arbitrary cutoff point of four or more such articles was chosen for inclusion in this table. Given this criterion, several observations are noteworthy. First, the heterogeneity of the professional disciplines, represented by these journals is striking: psychiatric, psychological, social work, and sociolog-

Table 2. Primary Journal Sources of Publications on Marital Therapy[a]

Journal	Number of Publications
American Journal of Orthopsychiatry	6
American Journal of Psychiatry	8
American Journal of Psychotherapy	5
American Journal of Psychoanalysis	4
Archives of General Psychiatry	6
British Journal of Medical Psychology	4
Comprehensive Psychiatry	4
Family Coordinator	6
Family Process	23
International Journal of Group Psychotherapy	18
International Journal of Social Psychiatry	4
Journal of Consulting and Clinical Psychology	4
Journal of Counseling Psychology	4
Journal of Marriage and the Family	41
Mental Hygiene	6
Psychiatry	6
Psychological Bulletin	4
Psychotherapy and Psychosomatics	4
Social Casework	22
Social Work	4
Sociology and Social Research	5

[a] Only journals publishing four or more articles on marital therapy are included in this table. Other journals publishing papers on marital therapy included: Acta Psyquiatria Psicologia America Alta, American Journal of Nursing, American Psychologist, Australian Psychology, Behavior Therapy, British Journal of Psychiatric Social Work, Bulletin of the Menninger Clinic, Bulletin of Kansaigakuin University, Canadian Psychiatric Association Journal, Children, Contemporary Psychoanalysis, Contemporary Psychotherapy, Diseases of the Nervous System, Eugenics Quarterly, Group Psychotherapy, Hospital and Community Psychiatry, Human Relations, Hygiene Mentale, International Journal of Sexology, Journal of Abnormal Psychology, Journal of the American Medical Association, Journal of the American Society of Psychosomatic Dentistry and Medicine, Journal of Health and Human Behavior, Journal of Heredity, Journal of the Medical Association of Georgia, Journal of Personality and Social Psychology, Journal of Religion and Health, Medical Times, Merrill-Palmer Quarterly, National Probation Parole Association Journal, New York State Journal of Medicine, North Carolina Medical Journal, Pastoral Counselor, Papers of the American Congress of General Semantics, Perspectives in Psychiatric Nursing, Praxis der Kinderpsychologie und Kinderpsychiatrie, Praxis

der Psychotherapie, Psychoanalysis and Psychoanalytic Review, Psychoanalytic Quarterly, Psychological Reports, Psychology, Psychosomatics, Psychotherapy: Theory, Research and Practice, Rational Living, Revista de Neuro-Psiquiatria, Smith College Studies in Social Work, Social Forces, Southern Medical Journal, Voices: The Art and Science of Psychotherapy, Western Journal of Surgery, Zeitzschrift fur Psychosomatische Medizin und Psychoanalyse.

ical journals are all included. Psychiatric journals dominate the list, while psychological journals are rather underrepresented. Also of note is the presence of a number of multidisciplinary journals. The foregoing observations are consistent with the reality of the cross-discipline nature of most of marital therapy practice, theory, and research. Perhaps the most historically significant observation that can be drawn from the data in Table II is that the two journals that have had the most impact on the marital therapy literature in numerical terms are journals devoted specifically to the study of marital and family interaction and therapy. This suggests that the fields of marital and family therapy have built the foundation for a discipline that draws heavily on several other more established disciplines yet is also developing its own independent identity.

Table III presents a content-analysis of marital therapy publications in selected time periods from pre-1940 through 1972 (August). The rate of the appearance of publications in several areas has either remained rather constant over the years or has changed unremarkably. On the other hand, it is clear that in terms of both raw numbers of publications and the rate of increase of publications in several other content areas there have been both rapid and recent

Table 3. Frequency of Publications on Marital Therapy by Content Areas in Selected Time Periods

Content Area	Time Period										
	Pre-1940	1940-1948	1949-1951	1952-1954	1955-1957	1958-1960	1961-1963	1964-1966	1967-1969	1970-1972	Total
Analogue	—	—	—	—	—	—	1	3	1	5	10
Behavioral	—	—	—	—	—	—	1	4	9	25	39
Bibliography/Review	—	—	—	—	—	—	1	6	2	8	17
Client	—	—	—	1	—	2	1	2	4	2	12
Collaborative, etc.	1	2	—	—	1	4	5	7	4	—	24
Conjoint	—	—	—	—	1	—	7	9	16	6	39
Comparative	—	—	—	1	—	1	2	4	5	1	14
Client Progress	2	1	3	3	2	2	10	11	14	6	54
Co-Therapy	—	—	—	—	1	1	2	2	3	5	14
General	1	4	5	2	9	9	11	19	23	13	86
Group	—	—	1	4	3	7	9	6	14	10	54
Method	—	—	1	—	2	1	—	5	4	11	24
Outcome	2	—	2	3	2	1	2	1	17	13	43
Process	—	—	4	1	—	1	—	2	12	9	29
Special	—	1	1	—	2	3	5	1	9	5	27
Therapist	—	—	2	—	—	1	1	5	15	4	29
Technique	—	1	2	3	3	2	1	6	16	16	50
Training	1	2	2	1	1	—	3	3	7	1	21

accelerations. The most striking changes have occurred in the appearance of publications on behavioral approaches to marital therapy, the development of new techniques (these two categories obviously overlap a good deal), the conjoint treatment of married couples, the assessment of client progress and outcome, and on the therapeutic process. Also, the notable increase of publications concerned with methodological issues in the empirical study of marital therapy would be expected to occur with the increasing interest in outcome evaluation. The growing interest in therapist variables in marital therapy is also consistent with an apparently greater attempt to specify salient parameters of the therapeutic change process. Two final observations of interest can be drawn from the data in Table 3: first, that interest in the treatment of married couples in groups has been significant over time and, second, that writings on collaborative, concurrent, combined, and individual treatment of marital problems have essentially disappeared from the literature.

Discussion

The growth of the marital therapy literature over the last four decades probably serves as the most compelling evidence of the continuing evolution of marital therapy as a separate area of professional therapeutic practice. On the other hand, the identity of marital therapy is uncertain, deriving as it does from several other fields, e.g., psychiatry, clinical psychology, sociology, and social work. That these other disciplines have not always been the most compatible of bedfellows would seem to present the field of marital therapy with a difficult challenge in its striving for therapeutic independence. *Professional* independence may be somewhat easier to attain than theoretical and scientific independence.

Ultimately, the major resource for uniting the multidisciplinary area of marital therapy will probably be the field's advances in research. It is tempting to compare the research developments of marital therapy with those that have occurred over the last twenty years in individual psychotherapy (Bergin and Garfield, 1971). Researchers in marital therapy can, and apparently already have, profited from the productive growing pains of individual therapy research. In concert with that field of research, it is clear that changing trends in the marital therapy literature are in the direction of an expanding empirical base, with increasing attention being paid to the specificity of treatment objectives and the development of multidimensional bases for assessing therapeutic change (Strupp and Bergin, 1969). While marital therapy must develop its own conceptual framework for evaluating change in the marital dyad *qua* dyad (Olson, 1970), a good deal of important work is yet to be done also in determining which factors influencing change in individual psychotherapy Luborsky *et. al.,* 1971 are salient and potent in treating married couples (Gurman, 1971).

Marital therapy, evolving out of clinical service needs (Olson, 1970) rather than laboratory experimentation, has sorely lacked a comprehensive, theoretical foundation. Thus, what has emerged is both an eclecticism of disciplines and an eclecticism of therapeutic techniques. It seems likely that, as advances in marital therapy research continue, there will develop even less interest in theoretical matters and more interest in the application of efficacious interventions. Indeed, the doctrine of "technical eclecticism" (Lazarus, 1971) has already entered the practice of marital therapy (Friedman, 1972). The present analysis and interpretation of emerging trends in the literature of marital therapy, then, suggest that the marital clinician of the next several years will become increasingly eclectic, pragmatic, and, hopefully, effective.

REFERENCES

Aldous, J., and R. Hill (1967), *International Bibliography of Research in Marriage and the Family: 1900–1964.* Minneapolis: University of Minnesota Press.
Bergin, A.E., and S.L. Garfield (eds.) (1971), *Handbook of Psychotherapy and Behavior Cange: An Empirical Analysis.* New York: Wiley.
Friedman, P.H. (1972), "Personalistic Family and Marital Therapy." In A.A. Lazarus (ed.) *Clinical Behavior Therapy.* New York: Brunner/Mazel.
Glick, I., and J. Haley (1971), *Family Therapy and Research: An Annotated Bibliography of Articles and Books 1950–1970.* New York: Grune and Stratton.
Gurman, A.S. (1971), "Group Marital Therapy: Clinical and Empirical Implications for Outcome Research," *International Journal of Group Psychotherapy,* 21: 174–189.
Haley, J., and I. Glick (1965), *Psychiatry and the Family: An Annotated Bibliography of Articles Published 1960–1964.* Palo Alto: Family Process.
Lazarus, A.A. (1970), *Behavior Therapy and Beyond.* New York: McGraw-Hill.
Lebedun, M. (1970), "Measuring Movement in Group Marital Counseling" *Social Casework,* 51: 35–43.
Luborsky, L., M. Chandler, A.H. Auerbach, J. Cohen, and H.M. Bachrach (1971), "Factors Influencing the Outcome of Psychotherapy: A Review of Quantitative Research," *Psychological Bulletin,* 75: 145–185.
National Clearinghouse for Mental Health Information (1965), *Family Therapy; A Selected Annotated Bibliography,* Public Health Service.
Olson, D.H. (1970), "Marital and Family Therapy: Integrative Review and Critique," *Journal of Marriage and the Family,* 32: 501–538.
Strupp, H.H., and A.E. Bergin (1969), "Some Empirical and Conceptual Bases for Coordinated Research in Psychotherapy," *International Journal of Psychiatry,* 7: 18–90.
Wells, R.A., T.C. Dilkes, and N. Trivelli (1972), "The Results of Family Therapy: A Critical Review of the Literature," *Family Process,* 11:189–207.

Section B

Marriage Styles, Roles and Satisfaction

3   A Feminist View
of Marital Adjustment

Traditional forms of marriage are seen by the author as oppressive to women. This is primarily the result of our system of socialization, with its emphasis on gender and marital role-stereotyped expectations and behaviors. Marital adjustment studies have usually evaluated the successfulness of marriages in terms of whether the partners achieved stability and compatibility along these traditional role-stereotyped lines. A relatively low level of methodological sophistication and experimenter bias has characterized research on marital adjustment. Investigation which concentrates on relating the balance of marital, occupational, and life-style options available to women (and men) and their associated life satisfactions is suggested. Such findings would be relevant and helpful for clinicians in developing new attitudes toward contemporary human relationships.

When a feminist approaches the research literature on marriage and the family, she comes prepared. Her primary interest is in women, in their potentialities, their experiences, and the institutions that shape these. She has no vested interest in marriage as such; indeed, she brings with her a feminist critique of that institution.

The feminist operates on the premise that women are persons with personal goals, who possess options, who may or may not choose to marry, and who retain their personhood if they do so choose. If marriage and maternity are not inevitable, nor sanctioned by divine (would you believe Natural) Law, then their outcomes may be evaluated in hedonistic or humanistic terms. The feminist asks, is marriage good for people? In particular, is marriage good for women? These are questions with which we shall be concerned in this paper. Specifically, we shall look to the research literature on marital satisfaction for answers.

The feminist enters the arena with a set of values and expectations. Unlike many others, she makes them explicit. While many sociologists seem to view marriage as the compleat institution (at least for women), feminists are more likely to view it as a total institution (Hoffman, 1960). We see marriage as oppressive to women, at least in its traditional forms; and make no mistake, it is the traditional forms we encounter in the marriage and family literature. Marriage is primarily a role relationship (see Wells and Christie, 1970), and as such denies the personhood of women. In the literature we examine, we will see evidence that normative definitions of marriage act to suppress female sexuality; that the child-bearing complex acts to reduce the wife's feelings of efficacy and even her relative power within the family; that damaging conflicts and powerful sanctions are set up to divorce the wife from the exercise of her talents and assertion of her personhood in the world outside the family, particularly as this takes the form of paid work.

This critique, of course, implicates the whole system of sex role socialization. The family system is not an isolated structure. Indeed, a major fault of the marriage literature (and one source of its conservatism) is the intellectual fallacy of treating the family—particularly the marital dyad—as a closed system.

Apart from its usefulness in substantiating the feminist critique of marriage, the literature on marital satisfaction or adjustment has a number of other characteristics which enter into the present evaluation. It is, besides being a source of data, a repository for conservative ideas about women, and a faithful reflection of some of the damaging stereotypes held by bigots undistinguished by graduate degrees. It is lamentable that scholars should hold the same prejudices; but there are additional negative consequences which derive from the peculiar powers academicians have. For one, bias becomes a self-fulfilling prophecy when the questions researchers ask (and omit) reflect traditional prejudices. The literature we will review in the following pages substitutes, for the most part, authoritative (not to say authoritarian) theorizing for a humble and inelegant empiricism. In such a context, it seems that only theoretical or critical papers produce any novel findings (Orden and Bradburn, 1968; Tharp, 1963; and Locke and Williamson, 1958). In addition to examining findings, then, we shall analyze the premises of this research as well.

A third focus of the critique will be on omissions—the neglect, in a literature which concerns itself with marriage and the wife role, of macrosocial forces which are bringing about changes in the objects of study. Thus, for example, the marriage literature serenely ignores new findings on female sexuality;

changing patterns of premarital sexual behavior; work force trends; the Women's Liberation Movement; the "population explosion," with its implications for childbearing as a rationale for marriage; and patterns of divorce.

There are a number of shortcomings that concern the reader of this literature, and I believe they are related. The first to be dealt with below are basic methodological errors, attributable in part to a certain credulity on the part of researchers vis a vis their subject and their subjects. The researchers seem to lack all scepticism with respect to the verbal behavior of their respondents, and not pursue the troublesome question of its validity. Those who are ambitious enough to use self-reports as a predictor to some criterion variable do not seem dissatisfied with "stability" (i.e., nondivorce) as the measure of a successful marriage. Most, however, are content to correlate other variables with self-reported marital satisfaction, and then make haste to draw causal inferences.

Many research options are not used by practitioners of this literature, perhaps because the phenomena do not appear to them to be problematic, or reactive. This lack of methodological nimbleness reflects a theoretical quiescence. Some of the dominant theories will be examined next, to prepare the reader for the kinds of data that are collected and the sorts of hypotheses that are tested.

The research findings will be reviewed under headings that reflect aspects of the wife role as it is defined in the theoretical formulations. In addition a large body of hitherto unexplained sex differences in marital satisfaction will be examined. Suggestions for expanding these conceptions and a discussion of needed future research conclude the paper.

Methodological Shortcomings

The elementary level at which research in the area of marriage remains has been noted repeatedly. A number of comments seem relevant to the corpus as a whole.

Unlike many other areas, research in marital adjustment/marital satisfaction shows substantial overlap in methods and even specific instruments used. This state of affairs might approximate that desideratum in scientific work, *cumulative investigation,* were it not for persisting weaknesses with respect to validity of the measuring instruments involved.

The most fundamental weakness lies in the conceptualization (and hence operationalization) of the criterion state, whether this be called marriage happiness, marital adjustment or marital satisfaction. Further confounding this problem is the use of stability (i.e., nontermination) as a proxy for marital success. Some discussions have recognized that many marriages may be stable in this sense without being happy (Hicks and Platt, 1970), but the practice of defining "successful" and "problem" couples with reference to this sort of stability remains common (e.g., Locke, 1951; Kotlar, 1965; Hawkins, 1966).

While it seems not unwarranted to infer that those who terminate their marriages are dissatisfied, to infer the obverse is less justifiable. Particularly when the "problem" couples are drawn from the population seeking help from various service agencies, and "successful" couples from the population of those not using such services, it seems likely that what differentiates the two samples is willingness to confront their difficulties (and perhaps greater commitment to the marriage). Clinic-going behavior has been shown to be related to social background factors (Bart, 1969); indeed, consumption of marriage counseling services appears to be related to ethnicity (Mitchell, 1962; Schaeff, 1966). In dealing with any socially stigmatized or deviant behavior, the researcher needs to be particularly sensitive to what Mills called "situated vocabularies of motives," or what categories are conceded legitimate to use or be). The reporting behavior that yields estimates of 60 to 85 percent "very happy" in marriage (Orden and Bradburn, 1968) should constitute evidence for a strong norm with regard to *claiming* marital happiness. Whether such reports are valid concerns us below, in the discussion of biases in verbal behavior; here we note merely that they appear to be mandatory.

We shall deal first with bias in self-reports, and subsequently with bias in describing another.

Among the sources of bias which remain largely uncontrolled in the research reviewed here, we find social desirability, stereotypy, and conventionalization. These tendencies toward bias may be consciously motivated, or they may be unconscious.

There are very few studies among those reviewed here whose validity is not seriously threatened by Edmonds' demonstration that the standard measures of marital adjustment correlate more than substantially with his measure of conventionalization. His approach illustrates a salutary cynicism, which more researchers in this area would do well to emulate. He starts from the uncommon premise that no one's marriage could truly be such as to rate some of the scores routinely obtained in studies employing the standard instruments. He notes that these are scored and weighted so as to exaggerate the incidence of extreme favorable responses—e.g., respondents reporting themselves "perfectly" happy score higher than those reporting more plausible degrees of ecstasy in the Locke-Wallace short form. Edmonds constructed 34 conventionalization items in such a way that the content referred to the most highly valued aspects of marriage, and the items counterbalanced universal truths that sounded undesirable and universal falsehoods that sounded desirable. These were interspersed with 16 items from the Burgess-Wallin Marital Happiness Scale. A shortened form of the conventionalization measure was found to correlate $+.63$ with the Locke-Wallace scale. The magnitude of this correlation is comparable with those found among different measures of marital satisfaction ($+.83 - +.88$, Locke, 1951).

A different strategy was adopted by Hawkins (1966) in an attempt to control for social desirability response set. Some of his procedures, unfortunately, were such as to arouse social desirability response set. The "normal" couples, for example, were contacted by means of a press release which had appeared in the local papers. No control of the incidence of marital problems among this sample was attempted; only the "problem" group (sampled from a psychiatric clinic) completed a checklist of marital problems (and admitting even one made the respondent eligible for inclusion in the deviant group). "Normal" respondents were paid more for their participation than "problem" couples; and the refusal rate was higher from the "normals."

Validity for the Locke short form is claimed on the basis that scores for the two groups (18 pairs roughly matched) differed significantly, in favor of the "normal" couples. However, the two samples differed with respect to another variable which might equally well account for the difference in marital adjustment scores: that is, the clinic population had admitted marital problems and the "normals" had not. One may note here that the unreliability of the criterion states used in the marital satisfaction literature may be absolute: in the Mitchell *et al.* (1966) study of couples who were undergoing marriage counseling compared with couples who were finalists in the All American Family Search, an independent psychiatric evaluation offered the opinion that one-third of the latter group exhibited psychopathological signs and could profit from counseling.

The major effort to control for social desirability in Hawkins' study is represented by the use of the Marlowe-Crown Social Desirability Scale. The nonoccurrence of significant correlations between the measures of marital adjustment and social desirability would be taken as evidence that the former is uncontaminated by the latter. In fact, significant correlations were obtained, higher for the wives ($+.37$, $p<.01$) than for the husbands ($+.31$, $p<.05$). These correlations are not so high that we may conclude that the Locke scale measure nothing other than social desirability, but are certainly high enough to demonstrate a substantial component of invalidity in the measure.

Hawkins reports his findings for the combined sample, obscuring the answers to some very interesting questions. If falling into the clinic rather than the "normal" sample is determined, not by how problematic one's marriage is but by differences in self-disclosing behavior, would we not expect differences in the subsamples' scores on the Marlowe-Crown? We would expect differences parallel to those reported for marital satisfaction: the "normal" sample should score higher on social desirability (or need for approval), as on reported marital satisfaction, and for the same reason.

A final consideration should be noted on the adequacy of Hawkins' strategy for assessing the contribution of social desirability to responses used to index marital adjustment. One consideration is that the Marlowe-Crown taps a generalized tendency to present the self in a socially desirable way; the content of the items is distinct from marriage. This in itself should reduce the obtained correlation between this scale and one focusing specifically on marriage. When the content of the items is similar, we observe (Edmonds, 1967) a correlation between the Locke and a measure or response conventionalization that is so high as to call into serious question whether the underlying phenomena are distinct.

A different strategy for assessing the social desirability component of a given attitudinal domain would be to obtain independent social desirability ratings for each item, and construct scales with items both positively and negatively keyed, matched on social desirability. This demanding and time-consuming strategy has not, to my knowledge, been adopted by any researcher working in this area. In view of the evidence for contamination of responses in this domain, an investment of this sort seems strongly indicated.[1]

In the absence of such assurances, the reader must regard with extreme skepticism *any* conclusions based on self-report responses to the kinds of items typically used to measure marital satisfaction.

Another sort of bias appears when a rater with a vested interest (i.e., a husband) describes another person (e.g., his wife) or tries to respond as though he were that person. This is the problem variously called "lack of realism" (Preston *et al.*, 1952), or "projection" (Hastort and Bender, 1952). The husband's description of his wife is, of course, a statement of his beliefs about her. It is often compared with her own description of herself (or her statement of beliefs about herself). One source of the observed difference is, of course, the husband's projection: the wife (in his eyes) is more like him than she is in her own eyes. One team of researchers (Hobart and Klausner, 1959) has corrected for this by crediting the spouse with empathy only on items where, in fact, there is a difference of opinion. That is, the discrepancy score we have been talking about (husband's prediction for wife—wife for self) is subtracted from the discrepancy (husband for self—wife for self).

With verbal report data so seriously compromised, what methods remain open to researchers interested in marital adjustment? An attempt to deal with a "deeper" or less defended level of response undertaken by Inselberg (1964) foundered on the problem of a criterion variable. Inselberg "validated" her sentence-completion instrument against one of the standard self-report scales! Still another approach was employed by Orden and Bradburn (1968) who measured both satisfiers and dissatisfiers in marriage. Orden and Bradburn's findings with respect to the nonunitary character of marital adjustment offers a caution with respect to accepting findings where a) only positive indicators are used as predictors, or b) items are summed without regard to their content.

---

[1] A number of researchers (Goode, 1956; Bowerman, 1964) have noted a generalized cultural tendency toward "optimism" with respect to marriage. This tendency might be expected to affect anticipation of marriage (Bowerman, 1964, p. 233), and also reporting behavior of actual spouses. The awareness of this possible source of bias has not, however, penetrated research procedures in the marital satisfaction literature.

Several reservations should be noted with regard to Orden and Bradburn's approach. First, their operations fall somewhat short of the implications of their theoretical approach, in that the latter suggests a "resultant forces" (Lewin, 1969) conceptualization of marital happiness, and their operations do not support this. Rather, their findings show that both positive and negative indicators predict to global satisfaction with marriage, in the directions one would predict. That is, the index of tensions correlates negatively with marital satisfaction and the index of satisfactions correlates positively.

Another reservation, which has a bearing on the result just cited, is that the indices of tension and satisfaction refer to different content. No information is afforded us as to the relative importance of specific content—e.g., sexual adjustment vs. sociability—in determining marital satisfaction. Moreover, we do not know whether sexual satisfaction is a potent determinant of marital happiness and/or lack of it is an important determinant of marital unhappiness. In Orden and Bradburn's research, a factor appears in one cluster only (and sexual adjustment, as a matter of fact, appears not at all). If a Marital Adjustment Balance score is to be used as a predictor of marital satisfaction, it would seem that the whole realm of factors should be included, and their status as satisfiers/dissatisfiers be made an *empirical* question.

Research approaches which focus on behavior rather then verbalization are rare but not unheard of. Some of these attempt to simulate actual decision or conflict situations which a couple may confront, while others involve more abstract tasks (Katz *et al.*, 1963). An early effort in this tradition was Strodtbeck's Technique of Revealed Differences (1951). After responding individually to a set of hypothetical situations, couples were brought together to resolve their differences, in a laboratory setting which permitted observation. More recently, Olson and Ryder (1970) exposed husband and wife to differing versions of situations. Conflict was manipulated by presenting each spouse with a version of the problem in which the other spouse was at fault. In this sample of 200 couples husband and wife prevailed in the final resolution about equally.

Such approaches are promising in providing direct data on process in marital adjustment. Their conclusions, of course, must be qualified by empirically demonstrated relationships with outcomes (e.g., "success" of the marriage). Similarly, the meaningfulness of data obtained in this way is a function of a) the saliency of the problem areas covered, and b) the importance each has in the marriage of the individual or couple.

Another technique might be used as an adjunct to laboratory simulation and observation. This is the use of an observer who reports on his own reactions to the experimental task or manipulation, as a control on the actual respondent's reporting. This technique has been developed by psychologists interested in separating real from socially induced responses of experimental subjects (Wolosin, 1968).

Models Employed (and Unemployed) by Researchers

Many of the criticisms to which this literature gives rise have both a conceptual and methodological component. We have argued that the corpus as a whole demonstrates a relatively low level of methodological sophistication. In addition, some avoidable shortcomings seem to be contributed by the inflexibility, unimaginativeness and conservatism of the theoretical (and metatheoretical) premises selected by the researchers. Thus, for example, viewing marriage as a closed system has precluded the option of viewing it rather as a Wenn diagram. Such a view would draw attention to variations among couples in how much of the individual is included in the marital transaction, as well as permitting exploration of cultural expectations that marriage subsumes more of the wife than of the husband (see Goode, 1956). Viewing marriage as a variable structure might lead to the elucidation of hitherto unexplained sex differences in the literature.

It may be noted, too, that an unexamined assumption that marriage is a relationship *sui generis* has led to the neglect of potentially fruitful perspectives on the marital dyad (e.g., Simmel; Lazarsfeld and Merton on homophily (1954); Blau, 1964). Other potentially valuable sources are the literature on interpersonal attraction and courtship, and the work of Thibaut and Kelley (1959), which might predict marital stability dissolution as a function of the Comparison Level of Alternatives of the parties. In the absence of such a framework the findings of Orden and Bradburn (1968) that satisfactions and dissatisfactions in marriage are essentially independent dimensions appear to have stimulated no further extension. Is there, one might ask, a critical ratio of satisfactions to dissatisfactions which precipitates marital rupture?

It may be argued, moreover, that narrowness of conceptualization results not only in the impoverishment of this literature but in some cases may obscure data which exist in the real world but are not dreamed of in our philosophy. Bem and Bem (1969) have argued, for example, that appropriate regulation of the marital relationship might better be based on the ''roommate model'' than on a more traditional sexual division of labor. In this model the domestic division of labor is not sexual, but reflects negotiation based on preference and agreement. Moreover, the choice of a spouse approximates a sociometric test rather than a role definition. Is the spouse, they ask, so interesting that I would have chosen him/her to be my best friend or roomate if he/she were of my own sex?[2] Evidence for a single standard for spousal adequacy has been found in at least some segments of the population (Kotlar, 1965; Levinger, 1964; Gurin *et al.*, 1960, Chilman and Meyer, 1966), but the theory appears not to have caught up

---

[2] Bem, Sandra and Bem, Daryl. Training the woman to know her place, 1969. (A revised version of this paper appears in Bem, *Beliefs, Attitudes, and Human Affairs*. Brooks/Cole: Belmont, California, 1970.)

with the facts. Some possible reasons for this theoretical myopia will be introduced below.

Another alternative model which has been neglected in the literature is Kimmel's and Haven's (1966). Their view of marriage as a mixed-motive game assumes superordinate shared goals and a dynamic process of learning and mutual identification.

In fact, however, a much narrower range of theoretical models prevails in the research on marital adjustment. The orthodox model in the marriage literature—judging by the regularity of its invocation by the faithful—is the traditional, instrumental, institutional or utilitarian marriage (Hicks and Platt, 1970). This model ascribes an instrumental (or outward-directed) role to the husband and an expressive role (directed inward toward family relations) to the wife. The model may be said to describe a traditional form of marriage in that the wife's activities are confined to the home. These marital roles are presumed to be complementary.

At the simplest level, this model may be viewed as a descriptive hypothesis. The question may then be asked of the empirical literature, to what extent do role expectations and/or role enactments of husbands and wives conform to this model?

In many cases, however, this model appears not as hypothesis but as ideology. In these instances the reader can discern a substantial load of surplus meaning. 1) Functionalism rears its battered head. Task specialization is presumed the most efficient strategy for social organization, in the family as in more complex structure (Blood and Wolfe, 1960).[3] 2) Metaphysical premises are adopted to justify a sexual division of labor. Thus Blood and Wolfe (1960) repeatedly refer to potent "bio-social factors," whose empirical referents are never introduced; but which "determine" a conservative definition of the wife role. 3) The wife role, then, is conceived as being dictated by (and very nearly limited to) women's biological capabilities in conception, childbearing and lactation. 4) These capabilities—not the observable facts of women's life cycle in the present world—are used to justify the expectation that a wife's primary concerns (and responsibilities) center around the home.

It is within this theoretical context that the marriage literature deals with phenomena associated with women's other capabilities—e.g., work, sexuality. Heavy normative loadings can be found on these treatments, as we shall see below.

Before we turn to this literature, it will be interesting to note some characteristics of the husband role in what may roughly be called the Parsonian model,

---

[3] Talcott Parsons and R. F. Bales. *Family Socialization and Interaction Process* (Glencoe, Illinois: The Free Press, 1955), 315-324. The degree of such differentiation would be important to specify. Empirical research in areas where differentiation-specialization hypothesis has been applied (e.g., complex organizations) indicates some trend toward reversal of this tendency (J. Woodward, *Industrial Organization, Theory and Practice.* London: Oxford University Press, 1965).

and to compare them with the other available model, Burgess' (1956) "companionship marriage."

The instrumental role, by definition, consists of the husband's efficacy with respect to the larger social system. Ordinarily his role enactment is indexed with reference to occupational success. His contribution to the marriage, then, consists in providing material resources, establishing the social status of the family unit and managing that unit's relations with the larger system (e.g., its financial transactions). The implication is that he is accountable only for these contributions, whereas the wife is responsible for the quality of the relationship, the morale of family members (particularly the breadwinner) and essentially anything that might be considered intrinsically rewarding in the dyadic relationship. (She is also, of course, responsible for many janitorial services, which will be detailed in later sections.)

What we observe, then, is that the husband role is essentially vacuous in this model. The husband's role enactments focus outside of the family unit, and impinge on the wife only as a *fait accompli*. They may operate as a constraint—e.g., in limiting the material resources and/or time that may be invested—but appear not to be the raw material of social interaction, or negotiation, or of emotional sharing. A much more severe constraint is imposed by the husband's lack of responsibility for expressive concerns. The wife is responsible for the quality of the relationship, yet the role prescriptions limit her to unilateral activity.

Consequently it should come as no surprise to observe that wives in fact adopt a strategy of insight cum accommodation—a line of action that may be pursued unilaterally, that requires no *mutual* adaptation, raises no conflicts, ensures harmony—and, of course, characterizes relationships of inequality. There is evidence, however, that wives are dissatisfied with this solution. Much of the data we deal with below in the discussion of sex differences refer to wives' desires to share expressive functions with their spouses.

Oddly enough, there does not seem to be much evidence that husbands are dissatisfied with this solution. Odder still that researchers, when they remark the asymmetry in marital roles, do so in sanguine phrases (Luckey, 1960). We may conclude from this that researchers in the marriage area accept this model and consider it not only adequate but appropriate. The commitment of "the herd of studious men" (Mill, 1869) to this model of marriage goes a long way to explain the selectivity regarding questions that are and are not explored in this research literature.

Burgess (1956) has made available an alternative model, and compared it with the "institutional" form of marriage. As of his writing, he believed that companionship marriage was emerging as the dominant form of that insitution in the United States. It differs from institutional marriage in being "democratic and permissive" rather than authoritative and autocratic; in relying for its power on internal feeling states (especially love and a growing mutual identification) rather than external constraints; in being innovative rather than traditional and static with respect to the design of the marital relation; in emphasizing personal happiness rather than duty and respect, self-expression rather than subordination; and assimilation rather than accommodation as a means of resolving conflict. Particularly interesting are the discussion of permissiveness and democracy, where the autonomy of the individual and mutuality in decision-making are stressed. The companionship marriage model takes as given the participants' right to be happy, acknowledging this as a basis for evaluating the success of the relationship. Again, personality development and self-actualization of the spouses is seen as a goal. A rigid separation of roles is expressly disavowed; rather, role sharing and a breakdown of role polarization are expected. Finally, companionship—a relation between persons rather than roles—is adopted as the chief objective of the marriage. It is to be noted that in this model, role definitions are essentially symmetrical or interchangeable for the two spouses.

Touchingly, Burgess throughout his paper refers to institutional marriage in the past tense. In the marriage literature, however, it clearly remains the model of choice. The expectation that marriage roles will be structured in the traditional way, and the prediction that marital satisfaction hinges on this, are clearly choices that the researchers make. Not one of the studies reviewed here uses Burgess as a theoretical model, and indeed, findings which would support such a model are overlooked or misinterpreted when they do not fit the institutional model.

The institutional model involves role separation between marriage partners, with instrumental and expressive functions assigned to different spouses. It involves, moreover, a premise of inequality, which appears most prominently when changes in marital roles are being discussed. The most flamboyant use of the premise appears in the literatures on working wives and family power. (The latter provides the inescapable context for consideration of the former, precisely because of the premise we are discussing here). Another aspect of this premise is seen in the assumption that enriching the roles of women—whether by an Equal Rights Amendment, paid employment or Women's Liberation —will mean a loss for men. If the simple-minded polarity of instrumental and expressive is retained, then the prediction is for role reversal (rather than role enrichment) to occur. A number of these features appear in the study by Kotlar (1965), reviewed below.

Kotlar expects to find marital satisfaction associated with role specialization along task/expressive lines. She expects, further, to find "role reversal" (i.e., the presence of instrumental traits in women and expressive traits in men) "indicative of marital maladjustment" (1965, p. 192). Instead, she finds (as a number of other researchers have done) that among the high marital adjustment couples both were comparatively high on expressive characteristics, and among low adjustment couples (50 marriage clinic clients) *both* were lower. Kotlar did find evidence of sex-role stereotyping regarding expectations of spousal roles: more instrumental characteristics were attributed to an Ideal Husband than to Ideal Wife, and conversely more expressive characteristics were attributed to the Ideal Wife. These stereotyped attribution behaviors, however, showed no differences by sex or marital adjustment.

Kotlar's study is an example of the way in which theoretical brainwashing can divorce the researcher from the accurate interpretation of data. She concludes the confirmation of her role reversal hypothesis, although the data show that for both spouses, functioning expressively is essential to marital adjustment.

Kotlar's paper is interesting, nevertheless, in illustrating a limitation of marriage theory at the present time. The institutional model, as developed by functionalists (e.g., Parsons and Bales), is a grotesquerie.[4] The facts of Bales' own research are forgotten: the essential diphasic nature of group (and individual) functioning, the alternation of task and social-emotional emphases. The notion of an individual's specializing in one or the other function does not preclude the presence and valuing of traits associated with the other function; yet Kotlar's role reversal hypothesis makes such an assumption. Moreover, task specialization is only one mechanism for the discharge of the equally essential functions; job rotation and role sharing are two others. The literature, nevertheless, seems dominated by a rigid, exaggerated and oversimplified model of marriage roles, neglecting the other theoretical and empirical possibilities.

Table 1 represents the contents of the various approaches to definition of marriage roles available as of this reading. The institutional model shows the familiar polarity; the companionship model shows more inclusive definitions for both spouses (though the specification of relative contributions of instrumental and expressive components to each role remains an empirical question). A third model, which for want of a better name I have called "empirical" after its source, shows the inclusion of expressive elements in the husband role.

Table 1. Models of Marriage Roles: Expectations held for Spouses

Type of Marriage	Instrumental		Expressive	
	Husband	Wife	Husband	Wife
Institutional	Yes	No	No	Yes
Companionship	Yes	Yes	Yes	Yes
Empirical	Yes	No	Yes	Yes

[4] Alice Rossi has criticized the neglect of the instrumental aspects of the wife-mother role and the assumption that the occupational role defines the content of the husband-father role, two errors which result from the simplistic instrumental-expressive dichotomy (1968, pp. 36ff).

Nowhere to date do we find evidence of the inclusion of task or instrumental concerns as part of the legitimate expectations of the wife role. On the contrary. The family power literature, to which we turn next, illustrates very clearly the evaluation attached to a wife's working, what we find might be considered a taboo on female instrumentality. This phenomenon, in the context of the marriage literature, takes its meaning from the presumption that monopolization of the paid-worker role underlies male dominance in the family (and rationalizes the husband's unavailability for the menial, repetitive work of the household). Female work force participation threatens both of these features of the traditional marriage, as well as undermining their rationalization by the biological division of labor. It is this sense of threat (and the underlying position of vested interest) that dominates the literature on working wives and family power.

An alternative approach, consistent with feminism and with the companionship marriage, would view the wife's contribution as an asset to the family, as well as a normal expression of her talents and the expected exercise of her options. This approach is not in evidence in the literature.

Family Power

Blood and Wolfe's (1960) paper is a classic in more ways than one. It sets out humbly enough as an empirical test of the hypothesis that certain household tasks are sex-typed masculine and others feminine. This argument is linked to the instrumental/expressive polarity with which we are now familiar. The pattern of polarization, here called "traditional," is put forth as the most efficient arrangement, and certain bio-social verities are invoked to explain why the wife role has not changed (although the husband role has). Thus, "Rather the same bio-social reasons which shaped to traditional family still supply differential resources which men and women bring to marriage (p. 271)." With respect to a specified set of household responsibilities, Blood and Wolfe did in fact find sexual specialization: men were far more likely to shovel the walk, mow the lawn and perform minor repairs than women, and conversely women were more likely to do the dishes, pick up the living room, and fix the husband's breakfast. The reader cannot help wondering at the sampling of tasks: all child care, heavy housecleaning, laundry, supply-getting, school-clothes- and health-related contacts are omitted.[5] Moreover, the effort distribution is of greater interest than the task distribution: those areas for which husbands take responsibility are infrequent, seasonal and, for apartment-dwellers, mostly non-existent. The authors present no data concerning the amount of work done by each spouse. Instead, they utter pieties about Miller

[5] For other criticisms of Blood and Wolfe, see Safilios-Rothchild's decade review of the family power literature (*J. Marr. Fam.* 32, 4, Nov. 1970, 539-552).

and Swanson's (1958) model of the "colleague family," in which spouses are "co-workers" 'with equal, interdependent, but distinct and mutually recognized competencies' (p. 268)."

The degree of respect and equality the authors accord the wife's contribution may be seen in their discussion of the family division of labor as it is affected by the wife's working. They note that during the "honeymoon" (childless) stage, husbands share more of the household tasks. They continue, "For most couples, the honeymoon period is followed quickly by the *retirement* of the wife from work to housewifery, enabling her to begin *specializing* despite the newness of her tasks (p. 271)." (Italics mine.) In other words, the wife's career is housewifery, and whatever she did before mere prologue. Lest the reader still be in the dark about the appropriate priorities for a wife, Blood and Wolfe declare, "For the husband to work overtime puts less strain on the traditional division of labor than for the wife to go outside the home to work (p. 270)." The logic here makes the wife's work analagous to her husband's overtime—above and beyond her "real work." Housework is clearly defined (by the authors, if not by the respondents) as the wife's primary job. One of the features of the article, of course, is that Blood and Wolfe are not asking, they're telling. Most of the assertions are not based on the data they report—i.e., they are the authors', not the respondents' beliefs.

Their normative orientation colors the discussion of "strain," potentially a straightforward sociological analysis. They insert the assumption that the fulltime housewife with a fulltime working husband is normal (p. 270). Then for the wife to work introduces "strain." Oddly enough, the authors do not treat the advent of a child as introducing strain, although in this instance the actual amount of work to be done increases. When a wife goes to work the amount of work remains the same. With the birth of children, however, the extra work is absorbed by the wife, as Blood and Wolfe's data show (and also Campbell's, 1967 and Heer's, 1958). The use of the sociological concept of strain, then, is restricted to situations where requirements on the *husband* increase. Little wonder these authors are so concerned about the "strains" in the marriage!

There is evidence, not only that men do less of the work involved in keeping up the household they share, but that they do less of the repetitive and physical work than the women do (Geiken, 1964). The relevance of Mainardi's (1968) analysis of the politics of housework is inescapable here. "Women's work" is *not* considered equally worthy of respect; it is not intrinsically rewarding, may even be demeaning. Men don't want to do it. Do women want to do it? Are women better suited to this work than men are? Are women better suited to this work than to the work the men are doing? It is a socially—not biologically —conservative response to answer these questions in the affirmative. Blood and Wolfe, in seeking a rationale for keeping women tied to these menial functions, might have selected a perfectly orthodox explanation at the sociological level—namely that, as a function of training, women have more skills relevant to housekeeping and men, to the outside world. This is Mainardi's Evasive Ploy # 1.

A number of research studies on the distribution of power or responsibility in the marital dyad find evidence of an egalitarian pattern early in marriage, particularly when the wife is working (Geiken, 1964; Blood and Wolfe, 1960). There is some evidence that with the advent of the childrearing stage a more traditional, husband-dominant pattern supplants the earlier symmetry. This is problematic for women, in ways that are developed below. However, it seems that a wife's working is problematic for men (although it is not clear whether this represents the researchers' feelings or the respondents').

Blood and Hamblin (1958) found that the balance of power "shifts" when the wife works. Such language is misleading, of course, since there is no data on change in a given family when the wife goes to work. Rather, Blood and Hamblin's findings show that in families with a working wife there is comparatively less husband domination. As with Axelson's (1963) study of the attitudes of husbands of working and non-working wives, it is not clear whether only the wives of less domineering men are "permitted" to work, or whether formerly domineering men become more democratic as a result of learning under conditions of wife employment.

Hoffman's (1960) findings suggest caution in the operationalization of the family power variable,[6] sometimes indexed by weight in family decision-making and sometimes by task participation. While Hoffman shared the customary assumption that husbands would lose power (i.e., increase task participation) when their wives worked, she found that although they took over new responsibilities when their wives worked, they also acquired the responsibility for decisions affecting these areas. Did they gain or lose power in this transition?

In Heer's (1958) study of family power we find a preference peculiar in a sociologist, for an explanation at the level of personality variables (but cf. Blood and Wolfe). Heer found that the working wife's power, in the working class couples, was significantly greater, relative to her husband's than was true in the middle class, and that regardless of social class, working wives had more power than housewives. He then tried to explain this in terms of a personality variable dominance, which would account for the wife's "assertiveness" manifested both in the marriage and in the labor force. Here, of course, Heer betrays the premise that it is deviant or problematic for a wife to work; hence the explanation must be sought in deepseated personality dispositions. Unfortunately for this hypothesis, the only differences found were by social class, not sex or wife's employment status.

Heer's study did produce a finding which, though unanticipated by him,

[6] For a more extensive exploration of issues related to the conceptualization and operationalization of family power, see Safilios-Rothschild, *Op. Cit.*

would not be so, perhaps, for us. He found an inverse relationship between the number of children and the wife's power in the marital relationship, with social class and the wife's employment status held constant. This finding, of course, is consistent with Campbell's (1967) and Blood and Wolfe's (1960) results, and further supports the contention that a wife's position as an equal in the marital relationship is undermined progressively by successive births.

In a later paper, Heer (1963) offers a reformulation of the family power problem, and the kinds of findings we have just reviewed. His argument may essentially be understood as relating the wife's power to the options or resources she might mobilize at a given point in the life cycle. Another way of putting this is to say that not only is the wife's assessment of her position a function of the Comparison Level of Alternatives (Thibaut and Kelley, 1959), but so is her husband's assessment. Here Blau's (1964) discussion of social exchange is relevant. The partner with fewer alternative opportunities, he notes, tends to be more dependent on and committed to the exchange relationship than the other (1964, p. 98). He notes, further, that established power (e.g., that of the husband) enables an individual to compel others to provide services without offering a fair return. Blau expects exploitation of this sort to be curbed by the threat of the exploited's forming coalitions (1964, p. 105). However, the isolated and privatized situation of the wife is one that militates against any collective action of this sort, as Mill (1869) has noted.

In another study, Campbell (1967) found that the younger a wife at marriage, the shorter the time before the birth of the first child, and the closer children are spaced, the less power the wife has in family decision making. He notes this "disadvantage" or "inferiority" is greatest when the wife was pregnant at marriage. Moreover, these wives carry the burden of household tasks, although this is not the case for wives who become pregnant early in the marriage. It seems that no feminist could make up data on the punitive uses of marital roles that would outdo what Campbell found.

Campbell's data extend our understanding of the relationship between family size and wife's share of the housework: He found, as had Heer (1958) and Blood and Wolfe (1960), that husbands take decreased responsibility for household work with the birth of the first child. However, the relationship is curvilinear: After the birth of the fourth child, the husband resumes some tasks.

These data on family power suggest a stronger formulation of the wife's situation than that found in the family planning literature. There is often noted that an interesting job is the most effective contraceptive; that is, women with experience of involving and rewarding options limit their childbearing. On the basis of the research reported here, it seems evident that childbearing is used as a mechanism for the suppression of women's exercise of their talents and rights to determine the conditions of their lives. Heer's analysis makes it clear that a woman is not esteemed, in the culture or in the small society of her family, in proportion to her exercise of her "glory," childbearing. On the contrary, this is the underside of the feminist analysis. If we—unlike practitioners of the more traditional perspectives on women—view the woman as a person with options, who involves herself in marriage, her options are not eclipsed or nullified (nor is her personhood). The data on working wives and on family power tell us, however, that to the extent that a woman is unable to exercise her options (e.g., working), her status is depressed. She is least able to do this when she has young children; and the more children she has, the more this is true. Completing the vicious circle, of course, is the probability that in the absence of viable alternatives the young wife decides to have yet another baby, and thereby perpetuate her powerlessness. Neal and Groat (1970) found evidence of just such a circular process.

Contribution of Children to Marital Satisfaction

Since children and childbearing loom so large in the definition of the wife role and are used to justify its constriction, we would do well to look closely at the data on their effects on wives' marital satisfaction.

LeMasters (1957) and Rossi (1968) have devoted considerable attention to the vicissitudes of transition to the roles of mother and father. Meyerowitz' (1970) findings are relevant, too, to the literature on what has come to be called "parenthood as crisis." While "crisis" in this context does not have the connotation of disaster or catastrophe, the choice of this word draws attention to the discontinuity introduced by the birth of the first child. Certainly the emphasis is at variance with a traditional view which envisions parenthood as the goal of marriage, and a wholly natural development. This more traditional view would engender in sensitivity to problems attendant on this major status transition.

LeMasters' was a retrospective study, which might tend toward under-representation of the stress involved in transition to parenthood. LeMasters' sample were survivors—parents interviewed within five years of the birth of the child, and presumably adjusted to the parent role at the time the data were collected. The respondents were couples with intact marriages, middle class husband occupation and a wife who had not been employed since the advent of the child. Eighty-three percent of LeMasters' respondents described a severe crisis in adjusting to the child. This experience was not mitigated by the couple's reporting that their marriage was successful (as 89 percent did), or that the child was planned (as 92 percent were). Mothers with professional training and work experience, however, suffered more.

LeMasters' interpretation of his findings is that parenthood, not marriage, is the real romantic complex in our culture; that, moreover, it is parenthood and not marriage that occasions discontinuities and conflicts (e.g., with the lifestyle adopted by many young couples). Certainly the institution of dating, for all its superficiality, is a rehearsal for monogamy (and consumership). In many young married households, both partners work, and a more equitable division of làbor obtains as long as they are childless.

Rossi (1968) carries the analysis of this phenomenon further. She draws attention to "underside" of motherhood, noting that marriage (in our society) is voluntary, but pregnancy may not be; and further, parenthood (unlike marriage) is irrevocable. Given the weight of cultural evaluations against self-determination for the pregnant woman, there are likely to be more unwanted births than unwanted marriages. This being so, what paths are open to the unwilling mother? Rossi (1963) has suggested the ways in which mothers take these stresses out on their children; Bardwick (1971) has asserted that they "act out" in reproductive-tract disorders; and Rheingold (1964) had advanced a model (not convincingly supported by data) of a continuing cycle of destructiveness in the relations of mothers with their daughters and these with their daughters. Here it is relevant to note Cohen's (1966) observation of regression of immature wives under the stress of motherhood, and Meyerowitz's finding (1970) of husband ambivalence about imminent parenthood. Gavron (1966) notes that the married couple may be reluctant to surrender the mutuality that is the achievement of their honeymoon phase, and may close the ranks against the intrusion of their children.

Rossi's radical inquiry into the requirements of the parental role(s) remains unanswered. Not only is training for these roles impoverished, but there is no apprenticeship: the new parent starts out abruptly on a 24-hour schedule. (And the literature we have reviewed so far tells us which parent it is that undergoes this shock.) In Rossi's analysis, the parental role requires much "instrumental," or rational and efficient behavior; much decision-making, much "executive" activity. Yet these responsibilities are assigned to the "expressive" specialist. Rossi (1963, 1966) and Cohen (1966) criticize American sex role socialization as preparing girls inadequately for their instrumental tasks and boys inadequately for their expressive tasks.

Other studies add further perspectives on the equivocality of motherhood in the life satisfaction of wives. Luckey and Bain (1970) found children most frequently mentioned in response to a question of the greatest satisfactions marriage had afforded. The respondents were 40 "Satisfied" and 40 "unsatisfied" couples. While companionship was cited as a satisfaction differentially by the two categories of married couples (by 68 percent of the satisfied and only 18 percent of the unsatisfied), this was not true for children. The proportion citing this response was the same regardless of marital adjustment. Among the unsatisfied couples, however, children were more often the only satisfaction listed (in 63 percent of the couples). The finding gives pause. Other authors (Renne, 1970) have suggested that the presence of children acts as a constraint, keeping spouses in an unsatisfying relationship which they would terminate if childless. Children in such marriages may be used in ulterior transactions which are damaging to them. The reader wonders what is the quality of the relationship between such a captive mother and her child; and again, what is the quality of life of a woman locked into a marriage which affords her no satisfaction aside from the sometimes burdensome tie to her children?

Renne (1970), in a large-N, representative sample survey, found 23 percent of women reporting marital dissatisfaction (as compared with 18 percent of the men). She found childless couples reported higher marital satisfaction than those with children, especially when the latter were actively engaged in childbearing. Those who had "problem children" reported lower marital satisfaction. Of course, no causal inference can be supported by data on covariation. While a problem child might represent a major source of tension, and sour a marriage, it is also possible that his pathology is a vehicle for the expression of preexisting conflict between the parents.

Other mediating factors are invoked by Neal and Groat (1970) and by Christiansen (1968). Neal and Groat found that the wife's alienation is directly related to family size. In a sample of Catholic wives (thereby controlling for religious values against contraception), the authors tested their hypothesis that feelings of lack of control and normlessness affect a wife's efficacy in fertility control.

Fifty-six percent of the high-alienation wives had a number of children in excess of their ideal family size at the time of the study. These findings suggest that when a wife feels powerless she falls back upon the biological inevitability of pregnancy, thereby cutting herself off from any options she might have and increasing her powerlessness; therefore her alienation, and again her fertility.

Elsewhere Christiansen (1968) has suggested that successful spacing of children contributes to marital satisfaction. In terms of Neal and Groat's variable, we would say that any form of successful family planning would yield feelings of efficacy and control over the environment, and counter the feeling of despair that leads to excess fertility.

Gray (1962), studying the "trapped housewife" phenomenon, compared three groups of mothers with young children. Some were involved in cooperative nursery schools, some in psychotherapy and some in neither. He asked what was the optimum hours per day the mothers wished to spend with their active young children. No difference was found among the groups studied; the mean, however, was six hours per day—considerably less than the expectation for the mother role as now structured. Gray's data point to a substantial overload built into the mother role, even for women voluntarily choosing it.

Hurley and Palonen (1967) found marital satisfaction inversely related to the "density" of children (i.e., ratio of number of children to number of years married).

In an extensive study of childrearing attitudes and practices, Cohler *et al.* (1962) found that 64 percent of paid volunteers revolunteering for another session had more children and higher socioeconomic status. These women appeared to be more "adaptive" with respect to labor and delivery, meeting the baby's needs, enjoying the relationship with the baby, handling the baby's body concerns, erotism and aggression. The authors suggest that women who are coping well with the demands of mothering permit themselves more activity outside the home. Interestingly, their data indicate that the coping women disagree more with attitude items keyed in a stereotyped "agree" direction than the ones who didn't revolunteer.

The findings of Cohler *et al*. converge with Dickson's observation that the persons we would want to employ for childcare (if we had standards for evaluating its quality) would be persons—educated, intelligent—who are probably already employed.

Thus the exploration of maternity, that component which conduces most toward construction of the wife role, leads us back to the conclusion of the necessity of options for women's happiness (marital and personal). We may conclude with Deutscher's (1962) observation that postparental adjustment is easier for those "deeply involved" in roles other than the parental.

Relief from the dissatisfactions associated with childcare and housework may be sought in two directions. The more radical (because it implies change in the options and activities of men) looks to the full exercise of options by women during their childbearing years. The more conservative envisions changing priorities for the wife as a function of the family life cycle. The idea of a sequence of wife roles is not well developed, but its outline may be discerned in the research on the family life cycle. The traditional idea that childcare is the primary responsibility and the primary satisfaction for a woman is not challenged in this literature, except by the data.

Research on the Family Life Cycle

The research on the family life cycle provides some interesting data on wives' satisfaction during the child-intensive years. These data are particularly significant in that motherhood is one of the traditional inducements/rationales for marriage for women. In particular, the joys of motherhood are expected to offset whatever costs are associated with the wife's giving up other sources of satisfaction during this period. The normative expectations are that the child needs continuous care by its biological mother, and women's labor force behavior demonstrates conformity with these expectations of the mother's behavior.

Bossard and Boll (1955) expected to find the 40's (the "empty nest" and menopausal periods) critical for women and the 50's (because of occupational stresses) critical for men. No statistically significant effects of age or family life cycle phase were found in their predominantly Protestant sample of persons from large families.

Rollins and Feldman (1970) found a decline in marital satisfaction from the Beginning phase (0-5 years married, no children), as had Marlowe (1968), Blood and Wolfe (1960). Rollins and Feldman found, however, that marital satisfaction declined for wives with the advent of children and leveled off at the Schoolage phase (oldest child is 6-13), and began to increase again with the Empty Nest phase. The findings are in general agreement with Bernard (1934), Terman (1938), and Gurin *et al.* (1960). Husbands' marital satisfaction in Rollins and Feldman's study varied in a way similar to the wives', but the magnitude of changes was substantially slighter for husbands. Together with Burchinal's (1961) and Davis and Luckey's (1966) findings that marital dis-satisfaction is related to husbands' occupation problems, this reminds us that marriage subsumes more of the average wife's concern than it does for the average husband. Put another way, we would expect a greater proportion of the variance in the wife's life satisfaction to be accounted for by the state of her marriage. This being so, the theory of cognitive dissonance would lead us to predict that wives will distort the evaluation of their marriage in a favorable direction more than husbands will. This was indeed the case in Mitchell's (1962) study, and Rollins and Feldman (1970) report more wives than husbands report their marriage is "perfect" at the Beginning Stage. We would like to see sex breakdowns of mean satisfaction ratings in other studies.

Burr (1970) did not find the gradual "disenchantment" curve that others have found in marital satisfaction, but did find substantial variation among phases of the life cycle. Both spouses in this study showed an abrupt decline in marital satisfaction when there are school age children in the home, and a gradual rise subsequently.

The negative effects of having school age children are felt in the several areas where marital satisfaction was assessed—handling of finances, household task, sex, companionship and relations with children (Burr, 1970).

Pineo (1961) found a drop in marital satisfaction in couples married 20 years.

Deutcher (1959) found that 49 middle class couples in the "postparental" stage rated themselves happier than when there had been children in the home. The ability of these respondents to make comparisons bolsters the interpreta-tions usually made by those involved in family cycle research. As in many other areas, cross-sectional comparisons are commonly used as an approximation or substitute for the longitudinal data which would provide a more direct test of the relationships under study.

Luckey (1966) found that spouses perceived each other less favorably as the years went on. Descriptive items of positive connotation correlated inversely with years married, while descriptors of negative connotation correlated posi-tively.

Luckey (1966) also found a negative association between number of children and marital satisfaction, though this relationship failed to reach significance.

Working Wives

In the research literature on working mothers we find the scientists investigating the disingenuous hypotheses of the laymen. The literature on working wives and working mothers, though distinct, share assumptions with which we are by now familiar. Given the premise that a woman's primary obligation/glory/identity is defined by her unique biological potential, the nature of the research hypotheses may be predicted. 1) A woman who wishes to give primacy (or equal emphasis) to some other area of concern is maladjusted, inadequate, immature, in flight from her femininity, and rejects "the" feminine role (Powell, 1961). 2) Children need the fulltime attention and care of their biological mother. If they fail to receive this care, they can be expected to exhibit the symptoms of Spitz' hospitalized sample of orphans. A working mother "orphans" her children.

In the 1950's, particularly, the scientific (as well as popular) vogue for the feminine mystique produced research which sought to substantiate the above hypothesis. So prevalent was the expectation of finding the children of working mothers damaged that Burchinal and Rossman (1961) found it necessary to state explicitly, ". . . maternal employment per se should not be conceptualized as maternal deprivation and hence, should not necessarily be a detrimental influence on the personality development of children (p. 334)." Burchinal and Rossman, in examining personality characteristics of children of working mothers, found no differences from normal controls even where the mother had worked before the child was three years of age. This finding was surprising in the context of an argument that continuous mother-child interaction is crucial for primary identification. The persistence of such a myth may be documented from anecdotal testimonials from any reader's friends and family, or from Glenn's survey of attitudes toward working wives (1959). Although no claims may be made for the representativeness of Glenn's sample (white women in a small South Georgia community) the findings sound a familiar note. The respondents allowed as how it is all right for a married woman to work for the following reasons (in order of endorsement rates):

To provide the necessities of living	(87.5%)
To pay debts	(67.6)
To help husband finish education	(63.2)
To buy needed equipment	(51.8)
To provide education for children	(51.8)
To buy a home	(46.6)
To care for dependent relatives	(46.4)
Dislikes housekeeping	(17.0)
Homemaking doesn't keep her busy or interested	(17.0)
Education wasted if not used	(15.8)
Working is more respectable	(8.5)

It is of interest that no reason was presented whose content referred to self-actualization or identity needs of the hypothetical wife. The data I have presented here refer only to women with preschool children. However, while the approval rates go up with the age of the hypothetical children (and are highest when there are no children), the rank order of acceptability of reasons is largely the same. It is important to note here, as in other places throughout this review, that conservative definitions of the wife role are held (and enforced) by women as well as men. In this study, conservatism was inversely related to social class and education; the overriding consideration, however, seemed to be the presence of young children.

Compare this evidence of what is considered proper with the desire of 33 percent of Komarovsky's (1964) sample of blue collar wives to work.

Impropriety aside, however, the proof of the maternal employment pudding seems to leave us with the empirical generalization that no ill effects are apparent. Burchinal and Rossman studied children of seventh to eleventh grade; Siegel *et al.* (1959) studied kindergarteners; Nye studied high school students. All of these studies found no differences between the children of working and nonworking mothers. Other studies show some advantage associated with maternal employment, with respect to achievement motivation (Powell, 1961), and self-esteem (Coopersmith, 1967).

Nevertheless, some authors, after reviewing data which show no association between maternal employment and delinquency, conclude:

> As more and more *enticements* in the way of financial gain, excitement and independence from the husband are offered married women to *lure* them from their domestic duties, the *problem* is becoming more widespread and acute (Glueck and Glueck, 1957). (Italics mine)

Implicit in the maternal employment = maternal deprivation hypothesis, of course, is the normative expectation that the child's "interest" shall take precedence over the mother's. Although it is not commonly conceded that a conflict between the child's (or the nuclear family's?) and the mother's interests may exist, we have already reviewed some data indicating that this may be the case.

Gray's (1962) study showed that even among the most enthusiastic mothers preferred hours-per-day to be spent with the child were far exceeded by the expectations attached to the traditional role of full-time mother. We have already cited evidence for the disapproval of "selfish" motivation in a person once defined as a mother (Glenn, 1959). And the family life cycle data have repeatedly demonstrated that the child-intensive phases are associated with lowest marital satisfaction for the wives (Rollins and Feldman, 1970; Burr, 1970).

There is another aspect of the working wife phenomenon which emerges more reluctantly. We have seen that maternal employment inflicts no observable damage on children, though the reverse cannot be said. However, there remains a punitive tone in the discussions the sense of a wrong not righted by the evidence of unblemished babies. The working mother is no problem for her child; however she remains one for her husband.

Some component of this "problem" seems to be simple misogyny, much of it bearing the mark of masculine projection or "extra-punitiveness" (Meyerowitz, 1970). Misogyny finds its way into the marital satisfaction literature as an explanation of marital unhappiness. Thus Levin (1969) attributes husbands' depression to the wife's rejection of "his masculine position" (undefined). The basis of her rejection is her "pathological attitude of narcissistic entitlement." Levin notes that the wives may deny any such rejection (but he knows better). He doesn't say what the "masculine position" consists of, or indeed, what "narcissistic entitlement" consists of, but it's pretty apparent that the former is legitimate and the latter is not.

Sillman (1966) attributed widespread misery and havoc in marriage to women's "repudiation of femininity" (i.e., their procreative role). We suspect that neither Sillman nor the wicked women are talking about procreation, but about the social complex that goes with it: "retirement," loss of power, loss of opportunities for skill utilization, increase in household work, etc. "If men will but bear in mind that they do not know the nature of women, they will not presume to dictate to women as to their proper vocation" (Mill, 1869, II, 23).

So said Mill; yet it is clear that a large part of what we are getting at is conflict over just such presumption on the part of men, and their resentment at women's resistence. A final example: Schaeffer and Bell report a psychological profile on a sample of student nurses, whom they had expected to find more nurturant, warm and "feminine" than the general run of girls. Imagine their righteous indignation, then, when they characterize them in terms of:

1. Suppression of interpersonal distance.
2. *Hostile* rejection of the homemaking role.
3. *Excessive* demand for striving.
4. *Over*possessiveness.
5. *Hostile* punitive control (Italics mine).

What these rumblings tell us, some of the empirical research confirms —namely that a woman who will not conform to a restrictive externally imposed definition of her role and accept a position of insubordination will be in trouble with her husband. Nye (1961) found greater conflict in marriages with working wife, inversely related to social class. Gover (1963) found nonworking wives better adjusted to marriage than working wives. Again the question may be raised whether it is dissatisfaction that causes women to seek employment or whether both dissatisfaction and the desire to work stem from a common source (e.g., talents that are not utilized in housekeeping). In most studies the motivational issues are not explored.

In a recent study, however, Orden and Bradburn (1968b) compared the effects of social class, choice and part-time vs. full-time work on marriage happiness. Wives who worked because they wanted to were happy, as were housebound wives who didn't want to work. The greatest marital satisfaction occurred in families where the wife worked voluntarily, but part-time.

Orden and Bradburn's study discovered some complex relations between spouses and their role concepts as a function of the wife's working. The husband's role adequacy (as he perceived it) was affected by his wife's working, inversely with his degree of education. Blood and Wolfe and Heer (1958) found that lower class men exerted less power over their working wives than middle class men, even though the latter *espoused* a more egalitarian ideology.) This seems to reflect a sense of threat on the part of these husbands. There is a hint, in this context, that lower-SES spouses collude in defining the wife's working as "out of necessity" since for her to do so out of positive (selfish) motivation would threaten his dominance. Her working out of real necessity would also be a threat, to his adequacy as a breadwinner. However, a joint pronouncement has greater legitimacy, and saves face.

Another way of softening the blow to the male ego appears to have been discovered by Hoffman's (1960) working wives. Although Hoffman had predicted a relationship between maternal employment, wife power and rejection of male-dominance ideology, she found instead a curvilinear relationship, with working wives both high and low on male dominance ideology having more power than nonworking wives; but those reporting a qualified rejection of the ideology had less power than nonworking wives. Hoffman's discussion of this finding suggest to me that the wives in the sample adopt differing strategies with respect to the conflict engendered by their working. Some "ward off the threat of disruption" of family power relations—as Hoffman puts it—by loudly proclaiming belief in male dominance. Whether this is calculated self-presentation (as in other "shuffling routines") or self-deception we cannot know. Other women challenge the doctrine of male dominance. In neither case do we have data on the effects of wives' positions on marital adjustment, and we know nothing of the determinants of these divergent adaptations. It is to be hoped that future research will follow up on Hoffman's hypothesis—i.e., that espousing male dominance is a compensatory response in a woman embarked upon deviancy (1963, p. 228).

These data give us evidence of some conflict between husband and wife over her employment. There are situations of course, in which such conflict does not seem to occur. Feld found no effect of employment on wives' marital happiness. Nye's finding was not replicated in his subsample of remarriages. Axelson's (1963) data show a greater acceptance of many aspects of women's freedom among husbands of working wives. Both these latter findings suggest that the interviewing variable is spouses' *agreement* on the nature of their contract, and suggest, moreover, that the *content* of the agreement may in these cases be non-traditional.

At this point we confront a major flaw in conceptualization which plagues the marriage literature and contributes to misleading conclusions. That is the failure to distinguish between agreement/disagreement (or congruence/non-congruence) on role definitions and the content of those definitions. For the most part, researchers in this area do not treat these as distinct dimensions and are sometimes off-base with their predictions. We can discern such results in the work based on the instrumental expressive polarity, which we have already reviewed, and in the research on similarity and complementarity, to which we turn next. Here it becomes even clearer that the predictor to marital satisfaction is *agreement,* and it is the researchers who inject the presupposition that the content of roles is traditional.

Studies of Similarity/Complementarity

There are numerous studies, in the marriage literature, which attempt to predict marital satisfaction on the basis of similarity of spouses' role concepts (referring to the self) and role expectations (referring to the partner) and/or the "empathy" partners exhibit in correctly predicting these entities as represented by the spouse. Some of these assume differentiation of marital roles (e.g., in the "instrumental/traditional" mode) and some do not.

Stuckert's (1963) study is a good example of the genre. Working within the framework of role theory, he argues that consistency of role enactments is essential for the smooth adjustment of a role relationship such as marriage. Consistency in this context has reference to the partner's expectations. Consequently, similarity of role definitions should lead to trouble-free interaction and hence marital satisfaction. Similarly, accuracy in perceiving the other's self concept and expectations for one's own role should facilitate the interaction and militate toward marital satisfaction. These two predictors appear to involve different mechanisms, and are perhaps appropriate under differing conditions. Similarity seems to assure harmony, and shortcircuit communication and negotiation about expectations and enactments. "Empathy," on the other hand, implies some strategy, some use to which the information about the other is to be put. In Stuckert's study accuracy of perception with respect to spouse was the specialty of wives, and went along with an accommodative strategy. Similarity, on the other hand, was the specialty of the husbands (i.e., for them similarity predicted to marital satisfaction, while for wives accuracy of perception of the spouse predicted marital satisfaction). Some of these are findings which we might have expected on the basis of the foregoing discussion of family power.

Stuckert's respondents (50 couples who had been married less than nine months) were asked to rank the importance of ten value areas three ways: 1) for marriage in general; 2) for their own marriage (this is presumably the measure of role concept or *self* values); and 3) from the point of view of their spouse. The content areas are interesting, in that they could apply (in an egalitarian marriage) to both parties equally, or could be seen as highly sex-typed (in the traditional model). They are:

1. Importance of love in marriage
2. Being able to confide in spouse
3. Showing affection
4. Respecting one's ideals
5. Appreciating the other's achievement
6. Understanding the other's moods
7. Helping make important decisions
8. Stimulating the other's ambition
9. Showing respect for the other
10. Giving self-confidence in relating to other people

In fact, though husbands' and wives' group rankings correlated highly, there were sex differences: husbands attributed great importance to wife's appreciating husband's achievement, and stimulating *his* ambition; wives gave greater emphasis to showing affection and *receiving* help in making decisions.

Stuckert's configurational analysis yielded three different patterns for husbands and three for wives. Overall, husband's marital satisfaction is predicted from similarity of his and his wife's expectations while wife's marital satisfaction is predicted from the accuracy of her perceiving the husband's expectations.

A different idea about what makes marriages work is Winch's (1954) still largely unsubstantiated hypothesis that successful mating is the result of the pairing of individuals with complementary (rather than similar) personality needs (e.g., a Dominant with a Submissive). Tharp (1963b) has rigorously critiqued Winch's research; most replications have produced more evidence for the similarity hypothesis than the complementarity hypotheses.

Luckey (1960, 1961) has done some interesting work on congruency of perceived self and family concepts, using Leary's Interpersonal Check List as a descriptive measure. The most interesting aspect of Luckey's study is, however, obliterated by the scoring method. Her procedure—and this flaw is general in the research on "congruency"—is to use the *absolute discrepancy* as a measure (inverse) of congruency. This method implies that the magnitude rather than the direction of a discrepancy is the significant datum. In Leary's theory of personality (from which the ICL is derived) there are eight classifications (or four bipolar dimensions) which seem to this reader to be sex-typed in a significant degree. That is to say, Managerial-autocratic behaviors will be viewed by most persons as male-appropriate, and polar characteristic, Modest-self effacing, as female-appropriate. If content does make a difference, might not "congruency" more appropriately be assessed taking account of this dimension of expectations?

In Luckey's study low marital satisfaction husbands saw their wives as more managerial than these saw themselves; *all* wives saw their husbands as more

managerial than these saw themselves; low satisfaction wives saw husbands as
more blunt-aggressive than husbands saw themselves; satisfied wives agreed
with *their* husbands' perception of themselves as Cooperative-conventional,
and saw the latter as more Responsible-overgenerous than the husbands saw
themselves. Husbands of low satisfaction wives saw themselves lower on this
dimension than did the husbands of high satisfaction wives, and their wives
perceived them even lower than this.

Overall, in Luckey's data, we find the pattern which has emerged in a
number of other studies: the wives seem more accepting of disappointment or
noncompliance with their expectations, essentially rather stoical. Satisfied and
unsatisfied wives were more similar in their discrepancy scores than were the
two husband groups.

In Luckey's data, some evidence of halo effects and sex role stereotyping
occurs. Satisfied spouses attribute more positive qualities to their spouse, and
Unsatisfied, more negative qualities. For both spouses, the father seems to have
been decisive: perceived similarity with father predicted marital satisfaction for
men, and perceived similarity of spouse with her father for women. However,
halo effect enters here too, for Unsatisfied wives reported their fathers as not
Responsible-cooperative, and their husbands less so.

Both Satisfied and Unsatisfied husbands perceived their wives as more
Cooperative than their mothers but the Satisfied husbands saw their wives as
more docile, less managerial and less responsible than their mothers, and the
Unsatisfied husbands the reverse. In other words, both groups of husbands
shared a traditional expectation for the wife role, but only the Satisfied husbands had wives whom they perceived as fitting the stereotype. Again, both
groups of husbands saw their ideal self as Competitive-exploitative and their
wives as docile and dependent.

An interesting difference in the comparison of spouse with ideal self occurred
for the wives. Unsatisfied wives saw no overlap between the two, while
satisfied wives saw their husbands as much resembling their ideal selves.

Karp *et al*. (1970) have proposed ideal-self congruency as the basis for mate
selection. They confirmed the existence of an association between the
respondent's ideal self and her perception of her prospective spouse's actual
self. These findings permit an alternative explanation, however. The reported
perceptions might equally well result from idealization of the fiance occurring
after the commitment to him is made, rather than being an antecedent of this
attraction.

Hobart and Klausner (1959), employing a number of empathy measures with
a sample of spouses, found that psychological empathy correlated with marital
adjustment but marital role empathy did not. In this study the wife's marital
adjustment was more strongly influenced by communication than the husband's
was. This suggests that communication is a mediating variable, and one to
which women are differentially sensitive. In this study, too, Hobart and

Klausner found that in a breakdown of role disagreement items into two sets referring to traditional vs. egalitarian marriage roles, a significant negative correlation was found between role disagreement on egalitarian role definition and wives' marital adjustment scores.

Tharp (1963b) has been concerned with the issue of nonrealism or projection in the responses which form the basis of empathy scores—that is, spouses' guesses about how their spouses would respond to given items. Studies such as those reviewed above consistently find that self: spouse correlations are higher that self: self correlations. That is, when the same person rates himself and his spouse, the ratings turn out to be more similar than when each party rates himself. Only rarely, however, has any correction for this effect been attemped (Hobart and Klausner, 1959).

Another generalization about this body of research is that agreement between the husband's self concept and his wife's perception of him is crucial for marital satisfaction. The content of both definitions is traditional, even stereotyped (Tharp, 1963b, p. 101). Corsini (1956) found that congruency between husband's self concept and wife's perception of him, and between his perception of her perception of him and that perception, were related to marital satisfaction. However, he found the same relationship among his random pairs, which strongly suggest that the data reflect shared norms or expectations about marital roles, rather than a couple's actual history of marital learning and encounter.

Tharp pinpoints the wife's function as a role-sender for this conventional content, and the agent of reinforcement for the relevant behaviors. In other words, although husbands clearly hold conservative role concepts when entering marriage, the wives play a role in keeping them so.

Moreover, the expectation that the wife's role is to discover the husband's expectations, and then accommodate, is clearly shared generally among married people (and at least some scholars: see Luckey, 1960). Such data as these suggest that the expectation of wife-accommodation may operate as a self-fulfilling prophecy, for it motivates behavior that is rewarded. There is evidence that an accommodative (or empathic, or considerate) spouse contributes to *anyone's* marital satisfaction (cf. Katz *et al.*, 1963; Kotlar, 1965), and the social norms decree that it shall be the wife's role.

Crouse *et al.* (1968) examined the relationship of a specific kind of congruency to marital adjustment. ''Integrative complexity'' was an intellectual attribute which the authors connected with adaptability and important social skills. As predicted, when both partners were high in integrative complexity, their marital satisfaction was higher than couples both low in integrative complexity. Contextual effects may be suspected, however, since the sample was composed of Princeton faculty couples.

Udry (1961) failed to find any relationship among empathy, agreement, family power structure and length of marriage in a sample of married college students. However, the married couples did show higher agreement than random pairs constructed from the same sample.

Blazer (1963) failed to find greater need-complementarity among married couples than among random pairs, nor did he find any relationship between degree of need-complementarity and marriage happiness.

Katz *et al*. (1963) predicted that satisfaction of basic needs in marriage would make spouses more prone to cooperation, self disclosure and influence by the spouse. In this study need satisfaction may be taken as a proxy for marital satisfaction. Katz *et al*. found the predicted relationship only for men. Men with high need satisfaction accepted more influence from their wives on a laboratory task, described their wives more favorably, and disclosed more than low need satisfaction men. The descriptions of their spouses by high need satisfaction husbands *and* wives showed a good deal of content overlap, as well as being more positive in tone, as compared with spouse-descriptions of low satisfaction husbands and wives. This suggests, as have other studies, that in successful marriages there is a breakdown of the sex-role polarization exemplified by the Parson-Bales hypothesis.

In contrast to the numerosity of studies that start from conventional views of marriage roles, we turn now to several areas in which the research data are scanty. These are topics which relate to women as individuals, rather than as role incumbents. Simply reviewing the studies of sexuality, and of options women exercise in addition to or instead of marriage, will convince the reader of how little a feminist perspective has been employed in the research on women in marriage. We will then examine data which, because of prevailing perspectives on marriage in the scholarly community, are little emphasized (conflict and divorce) or ignored (sex differences found in the marriage literature). We will conclude by discussing research directions that a feminist perspective can contribute to future research in marriage and the family.

Women's Options

With the overwhelming emphasis on the housekeeper and mother roles which we find in the marriage literature, scant attention is given to other options a wife may desire to exercise. Even more rare (to the point of nonexistence) is the study that leaves open the question of the priorities assigned to different options. Most researchers blandly assume the primacy of childcare (in spite of Gray's findings) and housekeeping (in spite of findings on the relationship of work satisfaction to marital satisfaction). This is a normative definition, however, rather than a hypothesis; and just to be on the safe side, it is never tested.

Rose's (1955) study casts some light on some of these questions. The population (from which a 50 percent response rate was obtained) consisted of the parents of university students in 1952-53, who received questionnaires.

Current life satisfaction was related to a variety of factors, with a retrospective cast. Unfortunately the study suffers from the "Pollyanna" bias we noted early in this review, imposed this time by the author. He lumped responses of Average satisfaction, Somewhat dissatisfied and Very dissatisfied in a category, "relatively dissatisfied"—thus stigmatizing those who were less than ecstatic.

Rose found that the "relatively dissatisfied" wives had married early, and regretted it; 76 percent of them now wished they had obtained more schooling; they reported spending more hours per week on housework than the relatively satisfied women, and desired to do less of it; a smaller proportion of them were employed, and at less prestigious jobs.

There was a tendency, though nonsignificant, for the more satisfied women to have married later, at 30 or later; Bressler and Kephart (1954) had found the same thing among women SSRC fellows. No relationship between marital satisfaction and age at marriage was found for men—understandably enough, in view of the asymmetry by sex of the effect of marriage on the exercise of options which contribute to life satisfaction. Rose also found that 24 percent of the satisfied women had paid servants, and that 85 percent of this group were employed. Again, 84 percent of the employed women high in life satisfaction felt they were in the right job, as compared with 52 percent of the relatively dissatisfied. (96 percent of satisfied men, and 79 percent of the relatively dissatisfied believe they are in the right job.) These findings with respect to work satisfaction are interesting because largely unanticipated in the literature. Although it is expected that marital satisfaction is contingent upon job satisfaction for men (Rollins and Feldman, 1970), the parental role is substituted for the occupational in the formulation for women. In fact, Nye (1961) and Orden and Bradburn (1969), as well as Rose, report that job satisfaction materially conditions life satisfaction for wives as well as husbands.

Rose's interpretation of his findings contains some interesting implicit premises. He does not take the various dissatisfiers reported by his respondents at face value, that is, as descriptions of negative experiences in marriage. Rather, he interprets them as inadequacies in the context of preparing the wife for *transition* to *another central* role (1955, p. 19). (Italics mine.) Here, of course, Rose reveals that he sees no problem with the traditionally defined components of the wife role; rather problems arise when those pressures decline. Thus, Rose sees nothing intrinsically unsatisfying about marrying too young—for women—but thinks it may prevent learning skills necessary to change roles. Nor does he seem to see anything intrinsically satisfying about working —though his data suggest the respondents do—but concedes its value as an "additional" role.

A different value orientation pervades the USSR, where the mother who does not work is disapproved, and sometimes referred to as a drone or parasite (Mace, 1961). Institutional innovations (public child care centers and many maternity benefits) support the choice of the Soviet wife to work, just as their absence in this country supports the other choice.

A suggestion that the status quo is reversible comes from an experimental study by Farmer and Bohn (1970). They were aware that home and work roles are presented to many women as irreconcilably in conflict. Fifty working women, half married and half single, took the Strong Vocational Interest Blank (which has showed strong sex differences) under standard instructions and then with experimental instructions which reduced the perceived conflict. As predicted, scores on career oriented scales increased after the experimental induction, and home oriented scores declined. These changes were observed both for the married and for the single woman.

Searls' (1966) was one of the few studies to include self-enrichment activities among items for respondents to report on. She found that women with household and/or childcare help reported more self-enrichment activities.

Axelson's (1963) study, to which we have referred several times, is relevant here in giving a more inclusive picture of how a life with options compares with one where major options are discouraged by the husband. The study compared attitudes of husbands with working and nonworking wives with respect to a variety of wife options. The attitudes of husbands of nonworking wives paralleled those of Glenn's conservative Georgia sample: 95 percent of these said a wife should work only in an emergency, or never. In reporting their wives' reasons for working, 24 percent of the husbands of working wives said their wives enjoyed working. Sixty-three percent of the husbands of nonworking wives said the children should have completed school before the wife works, as compared with 34 percent of husbands of employed wives. Only 49 percent of the husbands of nonworking wives believed women should receive equal pay for equal work, while 62 percent of husbands of working wives endorsed this dangerous doctrine. Again, husbands of working wives were more egalitarian with regard to sex: 68 percent of them felt that sexual relations should occur only when the wive or both spouses are interested, as compared with 50 percent of husbands of nonworking wives. Seventy percent of husbands of nonworking wives believe a working wife becomes too independent, while only 31 percent of those with that experience feel this is true.

In some analyses Axelson distinguished between husbands of wives working part time and wives working full time. He found, as had Orden and Bradburn, that marital satisfaction was highest for families where the wife worked part time; next for families with a nonworking wife, and lowest for families where the wife works full time.

In view of the consistent differences between the attitudes of the two groups of husbands in this study, it would have been interesting to have data from the wives on the nature of the marital relationship, and their valuing of work and marriage components of their lives.

From the existing literature, then, we can glean only suggestive bits and pieces about the kinds of options women exercise and their effects on marital and life satisfaction. (We should not forget, however, what we have learned from reviewing the family power and family life cycle research about lack of options and their effects on marital satisfaction.) No one has yet dared to explore the question of the balance of options and their relative contribution to life satisfaction for women. For that matter, no one has empirically demonstrated the nature of the relationship between life satisfaction and marital satisfaction for women and for men, although it is sometimes assumed that they are the same for women and distinct for men.

Inadequate attention has been given to the option of nonmarriage, in spite of findings (Gurin *et al.* 1960) that indicate greater sense of well-being among single women than married men or women or single men. Martinson (1955), in comparing married and unmarried women from the same high school cohort, found that the single women (who had been higher achievers in school) were better adjusted.

Other options which have not been explored include nonmaternity. Mothering is a traditional rationale for institutional marriage, to which researchers in the family seem wedded. Nevertheless, it seems likely that social awareness of the threat of overpopulation—and, more to the point, government initiatives and incentives for family limitation—will affect individual decision making with respect to childbearing. It is surprising, therefore, that researchers in this area have not anticipated major changes in the institution of the family, and prepared themselves to study these as they occur. Winch (1970) has speculated about changes in the forms and functions of the family, largely as a consequence of wide scale use of reliable contraception. His discussion links contemporary patterns of sexual behavior with labor force participation, seeing in combination two options which marriage and motherhood often shortcircuit. If his line of argument is correct, however, future developments are likely not only to alter the institution of marriage, but to disrupt the pattern of power relations which we have traced in this paper.

Major changes in women's fertility behavior presupposes, however, change or neutralization of the pro-natalist values which Blake (1968) has analyzed so tellingly. These, of course, are held not only by members of the population at large but by members of the profession, and perhaps account for the neglect of the nonmaternity option in the research literature.

Sexuality and Sexual Adjustment

The situation with respect to sexuality is much the same as with women's options: the evidence is for neglect, not exploration of this area in research.

When we look at the contribution of sex to marital satisfaction, we see a bifurcation between the approach to sexuality, the premises underlying its treatment in the marriage literature, and the findings, scanty as they are. Particularly regrettable is the neglect of a large literature on sexual behavior among young people in the United States (Simon, 1970; Davis, 1970; Kaats and Davis, 1970; Kinsey, 1953; Reiss, 1967). Another notable omission is the work of Masters and Johnson (1966), which has brought about substantial change in our thinking about female sexuality. The Freudian dicta about female passivity in coitus (and the characterology precariously built upon this premise) have been discredited (Laws, 1970). Victorianism lives, however, in the marriage and family literature. Throughout much of this literature, sex suffers a genteel neglect; elsewhere, hypotheses smack of a preference for sublimation (Wallin and Clark, 1964).

Orden and Bradburn (1968) defend this neglect as scruple rather than over-sight. Yet one of the most interesting findings in their study is the strong negative association between being affectionate and not showing love, in the context of largely *unrelated* clusters of satisfiers and dissatisfiers. It seems very likely that while presence of loving sex and/or sexual love is a strong satisfier, its absence is a powerful dissatisfier. The nonparallel content of two clusters does not allow us information on this question.

In the Wallin and Clark (1964) study the authors hypothesize that religiosity will mute the effect of sexual gratification or frustration on wives' marital satisfaction. Religion, in other words, is the opiate of the sexually frustrated. Similarly, an other-worldly emphasis in the devout should prevent sexual gratification from inflating marital satisfaction in an unseemly degree. Burgess and Wallin (1953) had found some consoling effects of religion: for wives reporting low sexual gratification, the marital satisfaction reported by religious women exceeded that reported by nonreligious women. No effect of religion was found for men, whatever their level of sexual gratification, or for women of high sexual gratification.

In this more recent study (utilizing the same sample) the authors engage in a discussion of the merits of various measures of sexual gratification. The earlier study used frequency of orgasm as an index of sexual gratification for women, and self-reported satisfaction for men. The present study utilized self-reported satisfaction for both spouses. The authors assert that orgasm and enjoyment of sex are imperfectly correlated for women, but neglect the possibility that they have different antecedents, and in fact refer to different aspects of female sexuality (see Bardwick, 1971).

The authors found nonsignificant differences by religiosity for the marital satisfaction of low sexual enjoyment wives, but no effect of religion among those of high enjoyment. A second analysis controlled for sex drive (i.e., preferred monthly frequency of coitus) and examined the relationship between religiosity and marital satisfaction. Here religiosity and marital satisfaction were positively correlated under low sex drive but not under high sex drive. The crucial analysis, revealing the relation between sex drive, sexual gratification, and marital satisfaction, was not performed. From the data presented, it is clear that religiosity mediates the relationship between sexuality and marital satisfaction at the low end of the distribution, whether we are looking at sexual aspiration (drive) or achievement. One suspects that the two are related. At the high end, however, religiosity has no power as a predictive variable, but the authors leave us with no alternative interpretation. Their data show that most high sex-gratified wives have high marital satisfaction, but among high sex drive wives the less religious are decidedly less satisfied with their marriages than the more religious.

These findings suggest the need for further work. It seems likely that sexual drive is a strong mediator of the sexual gratification variable, which predicts to marital satisfaction. As to the strength of sex as a determinant of marital satisfaction, relative to other determinants, future research will have to take up this question.

Quite a different approach to female sexuality in marriage is taken by Clark and Wallin (1965). Starting from the empirical observation that 20-25 percent of middle class American wives report having orgasm infrequently or never in the course of their marriage, Clark and Wallin wonder how this colors the sexual relationship. In their longitudinal study, they predicted (consistent with much of the research on female sexuality) that their quantity index (frequency of orgasm) is determined by quality (lovingness, mutuality, respect). They found both evidence of the positive effect of a satisfactory marriage on sexual responsiveness and evidence of a secular trend of increasing responsiveness regardless of the quality of the relationship. Moreover, they found some tendency for women to move from sexual responsiveness to unresponsiveness as a function of an unsatisfying experience in marriage.

Levinger (1966) reports a special case of the phenomenon of agreement in perceptions' predicting to marital satisfaction. In a study of spouses' reports of preferred frequency of coitus, Levinger found a significant relationship between perceived similarity and marital satisfaction for husbands but not for wives. When systematic distortion in reporting occurred, it seemed to be in the direction of supporting a norm of greater male sexuality—that is, most respondents reported husband wanted sex more than the wife did. Wives' preferred rate of coitus corresponded closely with the actual rate they reported, while husbands' preferred exceeded their actual (9.3 times per month vs. 6.9). Wives' actual rate, as reported, was 7.8. This discrepancy is interpreted in terms of a tendency to overestimate frequency when sexually sated and underestimate when sexually unsatisfied.

The whole question, broached in Levinger, of social determinants of subjective judgments concerning sexual satisfaction, remains to be investigated. A number of these studies suggest that differential norms concerning their own sexuality are held by the sexes. Among the unremarked and unexplained sex differences to be found in this literature are Tharp's (1963a) finding that sexual gratification is a factor distinct from intimacy for women but not for men. Another is Levinger's (1966) finding concerning the patterning of sex and social class in the complaint made by divorcing couples. Middle class husbands complained more about sexual incompatibility than lower class husbands did, while among the wives the relationship was reversed. Again, lower class husbands complained more about infidelity than middle class husbands, but middle class wives complained more about it than lower class wives.

Another largely unexplored topic is suggested by a finding of Bossard and Boll (1955). Bossard and Boll, on the basis of interview material, revised their estimate of why women in the forties might evince less marital satisfaction. They note that the process of sexual disinhibition in women coincides with a loss of powers and/or interest in the husbands (p. 4). In other words, inadequate sexual satisfaction affects marital satisfaction negatively; and this, rather than the emptying of the nest, may account for a decline in wives' marital satisfaction.

These studies, however, fail to follow up many important questions about the role of sexuality in marriage. Rapoport and Rapoport (1964) have done a valuable study on the tasks of the honeymoon—but they appear to assume, contrary to factual data, that sexual initiation occurs during this period. Neubeck and Schletzer (1962) have studied extramarital relationships, and more work clearly needs to be done. In Locke's (1951) study, 80 percent said sexual jealousy was a factor in their divorce. Particularly as the incidence of premarital coital experience increases, and female orgasm is used as the criterion of the successful sexual relationship, sexual adjustment will become more, not less, important and problematic in marriage. The marriage literature shows a substantial insensitivity to the ways in which sexual behavior and sexual standards are changing in the real world.

Conflict: Its Management and Mismanagement

This review of the literature on marital satisfaction might lead to the conclusion that the researchers are as prone to a Pollyannaish view of marriage as many respondents seem to be. So far from operating on the assumption that conflict is endemic to social interaction, researchers on the family appear to take cognizance of conflict only in the context of divorce. This is, of course, a biased sample, informing us only about irreconcilable conflicts. The literature is sadly lacking in data on conflict management as an aspect of marriage, yet surely this would be a potent predictor of ultimate outcomes—e.g., divorce, murder—and of the quality of the ongoing relationship.

We have discussed in previous sections the problems of validity associated with positively worded self reported measures of marital satisfaction. Given these cautions, researchers might do well to explore more thoroughly the predictive validity of conflict, problems and dissatisfactions. Rollins and Feldman (1970) found that their variable, Negative feelings from interaction with spouse, correlated more highly with General marital satisfaction (although inversely) than did Satisfaction with stage of the family life cycle or General life satisfaction. Orden and Bradburn found highly significant correlations (1968) between dissatisfiers or tensions and marital adjustment. Hawkins (1968) found only modest correlations between companionship and marital satisfaction, but much larger ones when hostility was correlated with marital satisfaction.

By and large, however, the literature fails to take cognizance of conflict in marriage. There is evidence of conflict, however, and evidence as well of potential conflict and of conflict channeled into ulterior transactions which seem to substitute for direct conflict.

Some of this conflict seems to bear a relation with the tradition of husband dominance, and challenges to it by the wife. In many cases we do not see evidence of direct conflict; rather, we have evidence of disagreement, and a correlated effect on marital satisfaction. Thus, in Katz et al.'s (1960) study, husbands' marital satisfaction was inversely related to their wives' autonomy and dominance. Luckey (1961) has a similar finding; and the literature on working wives makes a connection of this sort. Goode (1956) reports that 32 percent of respondents in his study of divorced wives gave conflicts over "authority" as the main cause of the divorce. By authority, in this study, is meant the degree of permissible dominance of husband over wife.

Mitchell et al. (1962), found that (100) "successful" and (200) "problem" couples reported the same areas of marital conflict and the same ordering. Finances was the most frequent area of conflict, followed by household management, personality disagreement, sexual adjustment, sharing household tasks, children, recreation, etc. Whether "successful" or "problem," couples in this study showed high agreement both as to areas of conflict and prevalence of conflict. These data suggest that it is not the incidence of conflict that affects marital satisfaction, but how it is handled.

Levinger (1966) tallied the complaints of applicants for divorce. Mental cruelty ranked first for both husbands (30 percent) and wives (40 percent), and neglect of home and children second. Twenty-six percent of husbands and 39 percent of wives made this charge. For wives, the next most frequent complaints were physical cruelty, handling of financial problems, drinking, verbal abuse, infidelity, lack of love and sexual incompatibility. For husbands, the third complaint was infidelity, then sexual incompatibility, in-laws, lack of love and the handling of financial problems. The rate of complaint for wives was 200 percent that of husbands.

These studies—and they are too few—all deal with conflict among stigmatized populations: divorced or clinic-going spouses. The reader is not in a position to know whether only these populations are willing to give researchers information about the conflict in their marriages, or whether the researchers are willing to ask only these populations about conflict. We are, however, limited to making *inferences* about conflict when we encounter data like the following.

Meyerowitz (1970), exploring the factorial structure of marital satisfaction of couples expecting their first child, notes several patterns which illustrate ulterior transactions involved in marital interaction. He observes one pattern in which the husband fears loss of self-esteem and his wife's attention as a result of the coming birth, and the wife remains quite unaware of it. In such couples (typically middle class) the husband controls the finances and looks forward to the return to dyadic intimacy with the ultimate departure—many years hence—of the children from the "nest" (1970, p. 39). This juxtaposition suggests that financial control may be exercised punitively in response to the husband's feeling an injury or intrusion.

This circle may be closed again, via another pattern observed by Meyerowitz. He notes a tendency for dissatisfaction in the couple's physical relationship, when the husband is extrapunitive, to result in the husband's criticizing his wife, and for her to turn to criticize his financial management (1970, p. 41).

In the situation where the wife is the object of an extrapunitive husband's criticism, and the husband anticipates negative consequences for himself in the neonatal period, the wife looks forward to the disruption of this dyadic relationship by the birth and does not wish to return to the dyad. The husband, in response, will anticipate a decline in his wife's adequacy as a homemaker (Meyerowitz, 1970, p. 42). This adds a new dimension to the bare facts reported by Blood and Wolfe and by Campbell: not only is the pregnant wife burdened by additional work, but she can anticipate criticism in the role of housekeeper as a function of her husband's spleen.

Further evidence of the punitive exercise of husband dominance is found in two more studies. Bossard and Boll (1955) explored the components of the crisis men encounter in their fifties. Some, who have been occupationally successful, have "outgrown" their wives and suffer conflict because of this. Others have failed in their occupations, and blame their wives for handicapping them. Such wives become scapegoats, and the husbands derive comfort from feelings of self pity and hostility toward the wife (1955, p. 14).

Preston *et al.* (1952) found an exception to the generalization that spouses tend to rate their spouses more favorably than themselves: the less satisfied husbands judged their wives more severely than themselves.

One would expect to find this picture balanced by evidence of aggression on the part of wives. Future research will perhaps correct this lack. The current review yielded only this observation from Meyerowitz: In marriages where the wife submits to a paternalistic husband, maternity provides a channel for gratifying her narcissistic urges (1970, p. 39). Its seems also a channel for covert counteraggression, for it provides a rationale for the wife's withdrawing from her husband *and* defining herself in a way that excludes him.

Unexplained Sex Differences

In the literature here reviewed, there is substantial evidence that the sexes expect different things in marriage. Langhorne and Secord's (1955) study illustrates one kind of difference. In a large sample of college students, they found no differences by region, age or marital status, only sex, in the traits desired in a mate. Girls stressed love, understanding and husband's achievement; boys stressed housekeeperliness, accommodation and the capacity to make an impression socially.

Geiken's (1964) findings illustrate another kind of difference. In a study of high school students' expectations regarding marriage, she found that the girls expected more sharing than the boys did. There are a number of studies which suggest that girls expect a relationship which is more egalitarian and more expressive than what their opposite numbers have in mind. A further complication must now be introduced. Each person has expectations regarding not only his own role but the other's. Sex differences in expectations is not, in itself, problematic, particularly if one holds a traditional or instrumental view of marriage. In this instance one expects the husband to be instrumental and the wife, expressive. As long as both spouses hold these complementary expectations, and their role enactments conform to them, the marriage should purr along. I assume that this expectation accounts for the neglect of some of the findings reported in this section.

If one prefers the egalitarian or companionship model of marriage (as I do), then sex differences are immediately problematic. The expectations of girls in Geiken's study refer to both spouses symmetrically, and they may be doomed to disappointment. Disconfirmation of expectations, in whatever model, predicts to marital nonsatisfaction. In fact, Geiken's study included a group of young married couples as well, and in these less sharing was observed than the high school girls were expecting. (Moreover, as in Blood and Wolfe, decisions were shared but the actual work implied by them was done substantially by the wife.)

With respect to marital role expectations of participants (as opposed to pedants), both an institutional and an egalitarian model are in evidence. One sex difference appears to be that men hold more institutional orientations and women more egalitarian ones. Further, there is evidence that the men get their way (Hurvitz, 1961). This suggests a paradox which should make the researcher wary: to the extent that role definitions differ and husbands are dominant, the marriage should appear traditional, but husbands should show higher marital satisfaction. In Burr's (1967) and in Renne's (1970) studies, wives did report lower marital satisfaction than men, but the hypothesis suggested here was not tested. Hobart and Klausner's (1959) study did find a negative correlation between frustration of wives' egalitarian preferences and their marital satisfaction.

On the other hand, there is evidence that egalitarian patterns of marriage result in high marital satisfaction (Lu, 1952) for both spouses. More precisely, there is evidence for a single standard of what makes a satisfactory marital partner (Gurin *et al.*, 1960; Chilman and Meyer, 1966; Levinger, 1964; Luckey, 1964b; Navran, 1967). The contents of the satisfactory spouse role are expressive rather than instrumental, emphasizing companionship and communication. The literature presently provides no answers to questions about the antecedents of such observed behavior patterns. Are men and women equally egalitarian, and if so, how did they get that way? Is there evidence of change from a traditional to a companionship model in married men?

Since evidence for two distinct styles of marriage is available in the current literature, it would be useful to know the distribution of couples into the two categories. There is some evidence that the traditional or institutional pattern is found among lower SES couples (Farber, 1957) and the companionship pattern among middle class couples. One may ask, are there differences by age or cohort as well? Are young people espousing companionship marriage—or is it rather, as Rossi suggests, that many couples go through a companionship stage and settle into the traditional model with the advent of children?

Another set of sex differences raises yet another question. From the earliest studies prediction of marital success has been better for men than for women—that is, there is more variance left unaccounted for by the variables used when it comes to wives than husbands. Similarly, there are a number of studies where the predicted relationships hold for men but not for women, perhaps as a function of the manipulations or the measuring instruments used (Katz *et al.* 1963; Olson and Ryder, 1970). It seems very likely that some crucial factors affecting women's marital satisfaction remain undiscovered. This is an area that needs development, with respect to conceptualization and research. One avenue is provided by the feminist perspective, which would start from the women as individuals, and seek to discover—rather than define—the factors that contribute to their life satisfaction, and what place among them marriage holds; which would seek to discover empirically the dimensions of the marital experience for women, and their positive and negative values.

Other sex differences remain to be explained. Comparisons of relative levels of marital satisfaction (assuming improvements in the measurement of this variable) by sex will be necessary in order to elucidate differences which have been discovered. For example, Rollins and Feldman used a variable, Negative feelings from interaction with spouse, which was a more meaningful predictor of marital satisfaction for wives than for husbands. Forty-seven percent of the wives reported having such feelings at least once a month. Moreover, this variable showed the same changes for wives as did marital satisfaction, while husbands evinced no changes over the family cycle. Similar effects have been observed with variables which may be sensitive to the "interior" of a marital relationship, particularly with events bearing emotional meaning (at least for women).

Again, although both wives and husbands report a decline in positive companionship with the advent of children, men's marital satisfaction is less affected by this than wives' (Rollins and Feldman, 1970).

In another study, Bossard and Boll (1955) found significant differences in marital satisfaction by age for women, with the highest proportion (88 percent) happy in their twenties, and the highest percent unhappy (23 percent) in their forties. For men, only the decade of the fifties was substantially lower, with only 55 percent reporting themselves happy and 27 percent reporting themselves unhappy. Findings such as these suggest that men's level of marital satisfaction is fixed (chronic, perhaps)—or responsive only to major changes in the family structure. Women's level of marital satisfaction, on the other hand, may fluctuate continuously as a function of events which do not affect their husbands. A parallel suggests itself here between the relatively fixed expectations men have of marriage, and their mode of being-in-the-marriage, and the outcome, measured in terms of marital satisfaction. By way of contrast, women's mode of being-in-the-marriage is perhaps more active and flexible, being anticipative and accommodative in the traditional marriage and emotive-communicative in the companionship marriage.

A final puzzle is represented by the finding that women are less reactive than men in terms of the relationship (usually interpreted as the *effect*) of research variables on marital satisfaction. Thus, Burr (1967) found that women appear to have a higher threshold for reflecting marital dissatisfaction as a function of the discrepancy between role expectations and role behavior. When importance of the behavior involved in the discrepancy is taken into account, wives appear to have greater tolerance for such discrepancy and marital satisfaction. We cannot say, at this point, whether the explanation of this finding lies in the relative indifference (for women) of the role discrepancy variable, or whether, as Burr suggests, women have a different threshold for reactivity. Comparisons of men's and women's levels of reported marital satisfaction would be necessary to begin to answer this question.

In concluding this section, we will review in some detail a study which is interesting not only from a substantive point of view but from a methodological stance as well. Tharp (1963) found intriguing sex differences in the factorial structure of marital satisfaction. The use of factor analysis makes this study one of the most methodologically sophisticated and least susceptible to subjective and conscious distortion. A particular methodological advance is the factor analysis of men's and women's responses separately, which permitted the discovery of the factors discussed here. Tharp warns repeatedly about the obscuring or averaging effects of combining spouses' responses (1963, p. 395). Tharp also reports the factorial structure of the joint space.

Using role theory as a theoretical framework, Tharp distinguishes between role expectations and role enactments, which are analyzed separately. For the most part, he discovered corresponding factors in the expectation and enactment structures. The factors in the husbands' expectation domain were Intimacy, Sexual gratification, Social activity, Togetherness, Social-emotional integration, Social influence, Wife-role adequacy, and Role sharing. All of these had corresponding enactment factors (except that Sexual gratification loaded on the Intimacy enactment factor for men, rather than emerging as a separate factor). Other expectation factors, for which no corresponding enactment factors emerged, were Sexual fidelity, Premarital chastity, Social-intellectual equality, and Parental adequacy. The structure for the female space was similar, except that Participation in community affairs emerged as a separate factor, as did Desire for masculine dominance. In addition to the noncorresponding expectation factors found for men, Tharp found among the women two enactment factors with no corresponding expectation factors: Understanding and Division of influence.

From examination of sex differences in factor loadings on items within the factors, some specific meanings emerge. In large part, in this study, comparable factors, with comparable items and loadings, characterize the domains for husbands and wives. Consequently the exceptions are of particular interest. Thus, in the Social-intellectual equality factor, loadings for husbands and wives on social background factors show the same expectation of equality. However, for an item, "Husbands and wives should have similar intellectual interests," the loading for men is only $+.13$, while that for women is $+.32$. Another difference is found in the structure of Togetherness. Items on the husband's sharing decisions with regard to finances, and sharing in the disciplining and training of the children, load on this factor for the wives, but constitute a separate factor for the husbands. Both of these findings suggest that wives expect more sharing of concerns both within the family and outside it than the husbands expect (or are willing to give). This asymmetry in expectations also appeared in Geiken's study.

Another factor showing sex differences is Wife adequacy. Both men and women agree on the inclusion of a clean house, orderly children and a good cook; however, husbands add the wife's home-centeredness and wife-obedience, and wives add the owning of material things.

For men, Parental adequacy emerges as a factor orthogonal to Intimacy (which taps elements of the spouse role). For wives, these items load on the same factor. Tharp notes the potential for conflict and misunderstanding at all the points where spouses' expectations (or normative definitions) diverge. A wife, for example, will expect that parental behavior "follows from" spousal behavior—as indeed it does for her, but not for her husband. Similarly, wifely deference is part of the dutiful-housewife cluster for the husband. but not for the wife.

Perhaps one of the most interesting sex differences to emerge in Tharp's study is that in the enactment (or experience) domain, Sexual gratification emerges as a separate factor for women, but not for men. This is, of course, the reverse of the cultural expectations regarding sexuality, which hold that women assimilate sex to love and affectional intimacy, whereas men experience sex independent of such concerns. In this sample the reverse was true.

Tharp concludes his discussion with a warning against the assumption that spousal roles are equivalent or complementary, and the research operations which obscure evidence that this is not so. An empirical, rather than a priori, approach is indicated in the light of Tharp's findings.

Conclusion

It would seem appropriate to make the conclusion to an overlong paper such as this the briefest possible. I will make no attempt to summarize the foregoing; the reader may judge for him/herself whether the program of the introduction has been carried out.

However, because the paper used as a starting point the empirical literature on marital "success," the discussion has been limited to certain points. That literature being what it is, no radical question arose in the course of the review. This is the point for such an analysis to be suggested.

On the basis of the evidence reviewed, it seems a case can be made that marriage is not good for women. Some question may be raised about the future of the institution itself. Its traditional rationales and associated popular premises may be briefly reviewed.

1. *Love finds its noblest expression in monogamy.* Marriage seems the unlikeliest vehicle for the preservation of romantic love, an ephemeral and dazzling phenomenon which, at all accounts (de Rougemont, 1940) relies for its value on its scarcity and the delicious inevitability of tragic loss.

2. *Sex finds its noblest expression in monogamy.* Not only the sexual practices of the young, but their sexual standards as well, have liberalized substantially in recent years (Davis, 1970). Smith and Smith (1971) point out that monogamy is at variance with the premarital sexual patterns of many young people, and predict strain on the institution as a result. Divorce is one social invention which has emerged in response to this strain (Goode, 1956). Co-marital sex (Smith and Smith, 1971) is another.

Even before the current "sexual revolution," however, premarital sex was accepted as long as marriage was the outcome (Kinsey, 1953; Reiss, 1967). Here is evidence of the unacknowledged use of sex as a lure to marriage (more perhaps for women than for men, in the presence of the double standard).

3. *Marriage serves an essential function for society in providing and socializing future citizens.* The extent to which this social imperative must change—in the interests of survival—has barely begun to be understood.

4. *Motherhood is a sacred responsibility, and creative besides.* Fertility is no guarantee of quality parenting. Indeed, if we value this responsibility so highly, why have we not established standards for its optimum discharge? Why

do we assign the job to dropouts? Is mothering a matter of talent or training? What about fathering?

5. *Marriage is the arena life provides for the achievement of intimacy and generativity.* Is this a hypothesis or a definition? If the former, where is the evidence? If the latter, does it imply (in the context of monogamy) the achievement of intimacy with no other? If the sole partner in intimacy is experienced through the screen provided by the wife role, and no other intimacy achieved, does not marriage foster misogyny?

6. *A fella needs a girl to call his own.* Wouldn't other forms of personal property be sufficient? On the other hand, what about *her* needs?

While the brevity of these comments may seem to convey flippancy, I think that from each researchable hypotheses might be drawn. The pursuit of such hypotheses might well turn the marriage literature on its ear. The mere suggestion of them may occasion outrage. To suggest here hypotheses based on a feminist critique of marriage is, however, enough to convince any reader that such hypotheses do not underlie the existing research.

A final note addresses itself to the irresistible temptation to speculate on the future of the institution of marriage. The emphasis in this review has been on the woman's participation—the investment she makes, and her return on that investment. Speculation on the future of marriage, then, might focus on the problem of recruitment. Mill, appropriately enough, has the final word:

> Men who fear to remove disabilities from women seem to think that, if women were free, they would shun the vocation of wife and mother. But if this vocation be natural to them and yet they will shun it, it must be that the vocation has been accompanied with disqualifications which violated other sides of women's nature. Render the married condition attractive to their nature, and they will be sure to marry. If, on the other hand, the law of marriage is to remain a law of despotism, men are right to leave women only Hobson's choice (this, or nothing). But, then, women should never have been educated. They should have been brought up to be domestic servants. (1869, II, p. 25.)

REFERENCES

Axelson, L. J. (1963), "The Marital Adjustment and Marital Role Definitions of Husbands of Working and Nonworking Wives," *Marriage and Family Living*, 25(2): 189–195.

Bardwick, J. M. (1971), *Psychology of Women: A Study of Bio-Cultural Conflicts.* New York: Harper and Row.

Bart, P. B. (1969), "Women's Status Changes in Middle Age: A Cross-cultural Study of the Turning of the Social Ferris Wheel," *Sociological Symposium*, 3:1–18.

Bem, Sandra, and Daryl Bem (1969), *Beliefs, Attitudes and Human Affairs.*

Benson, P. (1955), "Familism and Marital Success," *Social Forces*, 33(3):277–280.

Bernard, Jessie (1934), "Factors in the Distribution of Success in Marriage," *American Journal of Sociology*, 40:49–60.

Blake, J. (1965), "Demographic Science and the Redirection of Population Policy," *Journal of Chronic Diseases,* 18:1181–1200.

———(1968), "Are Babies Consumer Durables?" *Population Studies,* 22(1):5–25.

———(1969), *Population Policy for Americans: Is the Government Being Misled?* Population reprint series, Department of Demography, University of California, Berkeley.

Blau, Peter M. (1964), *Exchange and Power in Social Life.* New York: John Wiley and Son, Inc.

Blood, R. O. (1963), "Discussion of Socioeconomic Differential in the Relationship Between Marital Adjustment and Wife's Employment Status," *Marriage and Family Living*, 25(4):456–458.

———(1965), "Long Range Causes and Consequences of the Employment of Married Women," *Journal of Marriage and the Family,* 27(1):43–47.

———, and R. L. Hamblin (1958), "The Effects of the Wife's Employment on the Family Power Structure," *Social Forces*, 36(4):347–352.

Blood, R. O., and D. M. Wolfe (1960), *Husbands and Wives: The Dynamics of Married Living.* Glencoe: The Free Press.

———(1966), "The Division of Labor in American Families." Pp. 265–271 in R. J. Biddle and E. J. Thomas (eds.), *Role Theory.* New York: Wiley and Sons.

Bossard, J. H. S., and E. S. Boll (1955), "Marital Unhappiness in the Life Cycle of Marriage," *Marriage and Family Living*, 17:10–14.

Bowerman, C. E. (1964), "Prediction Studies." Chapter 6 in H. T. Christensen (ed.), *Handbook in Marriage and the Family.* Chicago: Rand McNally.

Bressler, M., and W. Kephart (1954), "Marriage and Family Patterns of an Academic Group," *Marriage and Family Living,* 16(2):121–127.

Buerkle, J. V. (1960), "Self Attitudes and Marital Adjustment," *Merill Palmer Quarterly*, 6:114–124.

Buerkle, J. V., and R. F. Badgley (1959), "Couple Role Taking: The Yale Marital Interaction Battery," *Marriage and Family Living,* 21(1):53–58.

Burchinal, L. G. (1961), "Correlates of Marital Satisfaction for Rural Married Couples," *Rural Sociology*, 26(3):282–289.

Burchinal, L. G., and J. Rossman (1961), "Relations Among Maternal Employment Indices and Development Characteristics of Children," *Marriage and Family Living*, 23:334–340.

Burgess, Ernest W., "Companionship Marriage in the United States," *Studies of the Family*: 69–87.

Burgess, Ernest, and Paul Wallin (1953), *Engagement and Marriage.* Philadelphia: J. B. Lippincott Co.

Burr, W. R. (1970), "Satisfaction of Various Aspects of Marriage Over the Life Cycle: A Random Middle Class Sample," *Journal of Marriage and the Family*, 32:29–37.

Campbell, Frederick L. (1967), "Demographic Factors in Family Organizations." Unpublished Ph.D. dissertation: University of Michigan.

Cattell, R. B., and J. R. Nesselroade (1967), "Likeness and Completeness Theories Examined by 16 Personality Factor Measures on Stably and Unstably Married Couples," *Journal of Personality and Social Psychology,* 7(4):351–361.

Chilman, Catherine S., and D. L. Meyer (1966), "Single and Married Undergraduates Measured Personality Needs and Self-rated Happiness," *Journal of Marriage and the Family*, 28:67–76.

Christensen, H. T. (1968), "Children in the Family: Relationship of Number and Spacing to Marital Success," *Journal of Marriage and the Family*, 30(2):283–289.

Clark, A. L., and P. Wallen (1965), "Women's Sexual Responsiveness and the Duration and Quality of Their Marriages," *American Journal of Sociology*, 71(2):187–196.

Cohen, M. B. (1966), "Personal Identity and Sexual Identity," *Psychiatry*, 29(1):1–14.

Cohler, Woolsey, *et al.*, (1962), "Childbearing Attitudes Among Mothers Volunteering and Revolunteering for Pathological Study," *Psychology Reports*, 23(2):603–612.

———(1961), "Exploratory Study of Employers Attitudes Toward Working Mothers," *Sociology and Social Research,* 45(2):145-156.

Coopersmith, Stanley (1967), *The Antecedents of Self-Esteem.* San Francisco: W. H. Freeman and Co.

Corsini, R. J. (1956), "Multiple Predictors and Marital Happiness," *Marriage and Family Living*, 18:240–242.

Crouse, B., M. Karlens, and H. Schroder (1968), "Conceptual Complexity and Marital Happiness," *Journal of Marriage and the Family,* 30(4):643–646.

Cutler, B., and W. G. Dyer (1965), "Initial Adjustment Processes in Young Married Couples," *Social Forces,* 44(2):195–201.

Dame, N.G., G. H. Finck, B. S. Reiner, and B. O. Smith (1965), "The Effect on the Marital Relationship of the Wife's Search for Identity," *Family Life Coordination*, 14(3):133–136.

Dean, D. G. (1966), "Emotional Maturity and Marital Adjustment," *Journal of Marriage and the Family*, 9(2):186–192.

———(1968), "Alienation and Marital Adjustment," *Sociological Quarterly*, 9(2):186–192.

Dentler, R. A., and P. Pineo (1960), "Sexual Adjustment, Marital Adjustment and Personality Growth of Husbands: A Panel Analysis," *Marriage and Family Living*, 22:45–48.

de Rougemont, D. (1940), *Love in the Western World.* New York: Harcourt Brace.

Deutscher, Irving (1962), "Socialization for Post Parental Life." In A.M. Rose (ed.), *Human Behavior and Social Process.* Boston: Houghton Mifflin Co.

Dyer, E. D. (1965), "Parenthood as Crisis." Pp. 312–323 in Howard J. Parad (ed.), *Crisis Intervention: Selected Readings.* New York: Family Service.

Edmonds, V. H. (1967), "Marital Conventionalization: Definition and Measurement," *Journal of Marriage and the Family*, 29(4):681–688.

Farber, B. (1957), "An Index of Marital Integration," *Sociometry,* 20(20):117–134.

Farmer, H., and M. Bohn (1970),"Home-Career Conflict Redirection and the Level of Career Interest in Women," *Journal of Counseling Psychology*, 17(3):228–232.

Gavron, H. (1966), *The Captive Wife: Conflicts of Housebound Mothers.* Humanities Press, Inc.

Geiken, K. F. (1964), "Expectation Concerning Husband-Wife Responsibilities in the Home," *Journal of Marriage and the Family*, 26(3):349–352.

Glenn, H. M. (1959), "Attitudes of Women Regarding Gainful Employment of Married Women," *Journal of Home Economics*, 51:247–252.

Glueck, Sheldon, and Eleanore Glueck (1957), "Working Mothers and Delinquency," *Mental Hygiene*, 41:327–352.

Golden, J. S., R. J. Silver, and N. Mandel (1963), "The Wives of 50 'Normal' American Men," *Archives of General Psychiatry*, 9(6):614–618.

Goode, W. J. (1956), *Women in Divorce*. New York: The Free Press.

———(1964), *The Family*. Englewood Cliffs, N.J.: Prentice Hall.

Goodrich, W., R. Ryder, and H. Rausch (1968), "Patterns of Newlywed Marriage," *Journal of Marriage and the Family*, 30:383–389.

Gover, D. (1963), "Socioeconomic Differential in the Relationship Between Marital Adjustment and Wife's Employment Status," *Marriage and Family Living*, 25(4):252–256.

Gray, H. (1962), "The Trapped Housewife," *Marriage and Family Living*, 24(2):179–182.

Gurin, G., J. Veroff, and S. Feld (1960), *Americans View Their Mental Health*. New York: Basic Books.

Hastorf, A. H., and I. E. Bender (1952), "A Caution Respecting the Measurement of Empathic Ability," *Journal of Abnormal and Social Psychology*, 47:574–576.

Hawkins, James L. (1966), "The Locke Marital Adjustment Test and Social Desirability," *Journal of Marriage and the Family*, 28(May):193–195.

———(1968), "Association Between Companionship, Hostility and Marital Satisfaction," *Journal of Marriage and the Family*, 30(4):647–650.

Hawkins, J., and K. Johnsen (1968), "Perception of Behavioral Conformity, Imputation of Consensus and Marital Satisfaction," *Journal of Marriage and the Family*, 31(3):507–511.

Heer, D. M. (1958), "Dominance and the Working Wife," *Social Forces*, 26:341–347.

Helfrich, M. L. (1961), "The Generalized Role of the Executive's Wife," *Marriage and Family Living*, 23(4):384–387.

Hewitt, L. E. (1958), "Student Perceptions of Traits Desired in Themselves as Dating and Marriage Partners," *Marriage and Family Living*, 20:344–359.

Hicks, Mary W., and Marilyn Platt (1970), "Marital Happiness and Stability: A Review of Research in the Sixties," *Journal of Marriage and the Family*, 32:553–574.

Hobart, C. W., and W. J. Klausner (1959), "Some Social Interactional Correlates of Marital Role Disagreement and Marital Adjustment," *Marriage and Family Living*, 21(3):256–263.

Hobbs, D. E., Jr., (1968), "Transition to Parenthood: A Replication and an Extension," *Journal of Marriage and the Family*, 30(3):413–417.

Hoffman, L.W. (1960), "Effects of the Employment of Mothers on Parental Power Relations and the Division of Household Tasks," *Marriage and Family Living*, 22(1):27–35.

Hurley, J. R., and D. P. Palonen (1967), "Marital Satisfaction and Child Density Among University Student Parents," *Journal of Marriage and the Family*, 29:483–484.

Hurvitz, Nathan (1961), "The Components of Marital Roles," *Sociological Social Research*, 45(3):301–309.

Inselberg, R. M. (1964), "The Sentence Completion Technique in the Measurement of Marital Satisfaction," *Journal of Marriage and the Family*, 26:339-341.

Jones, W. (1969), "Marriage: Growth or Disaster?" *American Journal of Psychiatry*, 125(8):1115–1119.

Kaats, Gilbert R., and Keith Davis (1970), "The Dynamics of Sexual Behavior of

College Students," *Journal of Marriage and the Family*, 32:390–397.

Karp, E. S., J. H. Kackson, and D. Lester (1970), "Ideal-Self Fulfillment in Mate Selection: A Corollary to the Complementary Need Theory of Mate Selection," *Journal of Marriage and the Family*, 32:269–292.

Katz, I., J. Goldston, M. Cohen, and S. Stucker (1963), "Need Satisfaction, Perception and Cooperative Interaction in Married Couples," *Marriage and Family Living*, 25(2):209–213.

Kemper, T. D. (1966), "Mate Selection and Marital Satisfaction According to Sibling Type of Husband and Wife," *Journal of Marriage and the Family*, 28(3):346–349.

Kerckhoff, A. C., and K. E. Davis (1962), "Value Consensus and Need Complementarity in Mate Selection," *American Sociological Review*, 27(3):295-303.

Kiell, N., and B. Friedman (1957), "Culture Lag and Housewifemanship: The Role of the Married Female College Graduate," *Journal of Educational Psychology*, 31(2):87–95.

Kimmel, P., and J. W. Havens (1966), "Game Theory vs. Mutual Identification: The Criteria for Assessing Marital Relationships," *Journal of Marriage and the Family*, 28(4):460-465.

Kinsey, A. C., *et al.*, (1953), *Sexual Behavior of the Human Female*. Philadelphia: W. B. Saunders.

Komarovsky, M. (1964), *Blue-Collar Marriage*. New York: Random House.

Kotlar, S. L. (1965), "Middle Class Marital Role Perceptions and Marital Adjustment," *Sociology and Social Research*, 49(3):283-293.

Lajewski, H. C. (1958), "Working Mothers and Their Arrangements for Care of Their Children," *Social Security Bulletin*: 8–13.

Langhorne, M. C., and P. F. Secord (1955), "Variations in Marital Needs with Age, Sex Marital Status and Regional Locations," *Journal of Social Psychology*, 41:19–38.

Lansing, J. J., and L. Kish (1957), "Family Life Cycle as an Independent Variable," *American Sociological Review*, 22:512–519.

Lazarsfeld, P. F., and R. K. Merton (1954), "Friendship as Social Process: A Substantive and Methodological Analysis." In Theodore Abel and Charles H. Page (eds.), *Freedom and Control in Modern Society*. New York: D. Van Nostrand Co.

LeMasters, E. E. (1957), "Parenthood as Crisis," *Marriage and Family Living*, 19(4):352–355.

Levin, S. (1969), "A Common Type of Marital Incompatibility," *Journal of the American Psychoanalytic Association*, 17(2):421–436.

Levinger, G. (1964), "Notes on Complementarity in Marriage," *Psychological Bulletin*, 61(2):153–157.

———(1964), "Task and Social Behavior in Marriage," *Sociometry*, 24(4):433-448.

———(1965), "Marital Cohesiveness and Dissolution: An Integrated Review," *Journal of Marriage and the Family*, 27(1):19–28.

———(1966), "Sources of Marital Dissatisfaction Among Applicants for Divorce," *American Journal of Orthopsychiatry*, 36(5):803–807.

———(1966), "Systemic Distortion of Preferred and Actual Sexual Behavior," *Sociometry*, 29(3):291–299.

———(1966), "Interpersonal Attraction and Agreement: A Study of Marriage Partners," *Journal of Personality and Social Psychology*, 3(4):367-372.

Lively, E. L. (1969), "Toward Concept Clarification: The Case of Marital Interaction," *Journal of Marriage and the Family*, 31(1):108–114.

Litwak, E., G. Count, and E. Haydon (1960), "Group Structure and Interpersonal Creativity as Factors Which Reduce Errors in the Prediction of Marital Adjustment," *Social Forces*, 38(4):308–315.

Locke, H. J. (1951), *Prediction Adjustment in Marriage: A Comparison of a Divorced and Happily Married Group*. New York: Holt.

Locke, H. J., and K. M. Wallace (1959), "Short Marital Adjustment and Prediction Tests: Their Reliability and Validity," *Marriage and Family Living*, 21(3):251–255.

Locke, H. J., and R. C. Williamson (1958), "Marital Adjustment: A Factor Analysis Study," *American Sociological Review*, 23(2):562–569.

Lopata, H.Z. (1966), "Life Cycle of the Social Role of Housewife," *Sociology and Social Research,* 51(1):5-22.

Lu, Y. C. (1952), "Marital Roles and Marital Adjustment," *Sociology and Social Research*, 36:364–368.

Luckey, E. B. (1960), "Marital Satisfaction and Congruent Self-Spouse Concepts," *Social Forces*, 39:153–157.

———(1961), "Perceptual Congruence of Self and Family Concepts as Related to Marital Interaction," *Sociometry*, 24:234–250.

———(1966), "Number of Years Married as Related to Personality Perception and Marital Satisfaction," *Journal of Marriage and the Family*, 28:44–48.

Luckey, E. G., and J. K. Bain (1970), "Children: A Factor in Marital Satisfaction," *Journal of Marriage and the Family*, 32:43–44.

Mace, David P. (1961), "The Employed Mother in the USSR," *Marriage and Family Living*, 23:330–333.

Mainardi, P. A. (1968), *The Politics of Housework*. Boston, Mass.

Martinson, F. M. (1955), "Ego Deficiency as a Factor in Marriage," *American Sociological Review,* 20(2):161–164.

Masters, W. H., and V. E. Johnson (1966), *Human Sexual Response*. Boston: Little, Brown Co.

Mayer, J. E. (1967), "The Invisibility of Married Life," *New Society*, 9:272–273.

Meyerowitz, J. H. (1970), "Satisfaction During Pregnancy," *Journal of Marriage and the Family*, 32:38–42.

Mill, John S. (1969), *The Subjugation of Women*. Oxford: Oxford Press.

Miller, D. R., and G. E. Swanson (1958), *The Changing American Parent*. New York: John Wiley and Sons.

Mitchell, H. E., J. W. Bullard, and E. H. Mudd (1962), "Areas of Marital Conflict in Successfully and Unsuccessfully Functioning Families," *Journal of Health and Human Behavior*, 3(2):88–93.

Murstein, B. I. (1967), "Empirical Test of Role, Complementary Needs and Homogamy Theories of Marital Choice," *Journal of Marriage and the Family*, 29(4):688–696.

———(1970), "Stimulus-Value-Role: A Theory of Marital Choice," *Journal of Marriage and the Family,* 32:465–481.

Navran, Leslie (1967), "Communication and Adjustment in Marriage," *Family Process*, 6:173–184.

Neal, A. G., and H. T. Groat (1970), "Alienation Correlates of Catholic Fertility," *American Journal of Sociology*, 76(3):460.

Neubeck, G., and V. M. Schletzer (1962), "A Study of Extramarital Relationships." *Marriage and Family Living*, 24(3):279–281.

Nye, I. (1961), "Material Employment and Marital Interaction Source Contingent Conditions," *Social Forces*, 40:113–119.

———(1963), Comments to "Socioeconomic Differential in the Relationship Between Marital Adjustment and Wife's Employment Status," *Marriage and Family Living*, 25(4):457.

Olson, D. H., and R. G. Ryder (1970), "Inventory of Marital Conflicts (IMC): An Experimental Interaction Procedure," *Journal of Marriage and the Family*, 32:443–448.

Orden, S. R., and N. M. Bradburn (1968), "Dimensions of Marriage Happiness," *American Journal of Sociology*, 73(6):715–731.

———(1969), "Working Wives and Marital Happiness," *American Journal of Sociology*, 74(4):392–407.

Paris, B. L., and E. B. Luckey (1966), "A Longitudinal Study of Marital Satisfaction," *Sociology and Social Research*, 50:212–223.

Perry, J. B., Jr., (1961), "The Mother Substitute of Employed Mothers: An Exploratory Inquiry," *Marriage and Family Living*, 23(4):362–367.

Peterson, E. T. (1961), "Impact of Maternal Employment on the Mother-Daughter Relationship," *Marriage and Family Living*, 23(4):355–36.

Pickford, J. H., E. I. Signori, and H. Rempel (1966), "The Intensity of Personality Traits in Relation to Marital Happiness," *Journal of Marriage and the Family*, 28(4):458–459.

Pineo, Peter C. (1961), "Disenchantment in the Later Years of Marriage," *Marriage and Family Living*, 23:3–11.

Powell, K. S. (1961), "Maternal Employment in Relation to Family Life," *Marriage and Family Living*, 23(4):350–355.

Preston, M. G., *et al.*, (1952), "Impressions of Personality as a Function of Marital Conflict," *Journal of Social and Abnormal Psychology*, 47:326–336.

Rapoport, Rhona and Robert Rapoport (1964), "New Light on the Honeymoon," *Human Relations*, 17(11):33–56.

Rappaport, A. F. (1970), "Perceptual Differences Between Married and Single College Women for the Concept of Self, Ideal Woman, and Man's Ideal Woman," *Journal of Marriage and the Family*, 32(3):441–442.

Reiss, Ira L. (1967), *The Social Context of Premarital and Sexual Permissiveness*. New York: Holt, Rinehart and Winston.

Renne, K. S. (1970), "Correlates of Dissatisfaction in Marriage," *Journal of Marriage and the Family*, 32:54–67.

Rheingold, J. C. (1964), *The Fear of Being a Woman: A Theory of Maternal Destructiveness*. New York: Grune and Stratton.

Reisman, D. (1919), "Permissiveness and Sex Roles," *Marriage and Family Living*, 2:211–217.

Rollins, B. C., and H. Feldman (1970), "Marital Satisfaction Over the Family Life Cycle," *Journal of Marriage and the Family*, 32:20–28.

Rose, A. M. (1915), "Factors Associated with the Life Satisfaction of Middle-Aged Persons," *Marriage and Family Living*, 17:15–19.

Rossi, A. S. (1964), "Equality Between the Sexes: An Immodest Proposal." In R. J. Lifton (ed.), *The Woman in America*. Boston: Beacon Press.

———(1968), "Transition to Parenthood," *Journal of Marriage and the Family*, 30:26–39.

Roth, J., and R. Peck (1956), "Class and Mobility Factors Related to Marital Adjustment," *American Sociological Review*, 16(4):478–488.

Ryder, R. O. (1967), "Compatibility in Marriage," *Psychological Reports*, 20(3):807–813.

Scanzoni, J. (1968), "A Social System Analysis of Dissolved and Existing Marriage," *Journal of Marriage and the Family,* 30:457–461.

Schaeffer, E. S., and R. Q. Bell (1957), "Patterns of Attitudes Toward Child Rearing and the Family," *Journal of Abnormal Psychology,* 4(3):391-395.

Scheff, T. S. (1966), "Users and Nonusers of a Student Psychiatric Clinic," *Journal of Health and Human Behavior,* 7:114-121.

Searls, L. (1966), "Leisure Role Emphasis of College Graduate Homemakers," *Journal of Marriage and the Family,* 28(1):77–82.

Siegel, Alberta E., *et al.,* (1959), "Dependence and Independence in the Children of Working Mothers," *Child Development,* 30:533-546.

Sillman, L. R. (1966), "Femininity and Paranoidism," *Journal of Nervous and Mental Disease,* 143(2):163-170.

Simon, William (1970), *Youth Cultures and Aspects of the Socialization Process.* Institute of Juvenile Research, Chicago.

Smith, J., and L. Smith (1971), "Co-marital Sex: The Incorporation of Extramarital Sex into the Marriage Relationship." Paper presented at annual meeting, American Psychopathological Association, New York.

Steinmann, A. (1963), "A Study of the Concept of the Feminine Role of 51 Middle Class American Families," *Genetic Psychology Monographs,* 67(2):275–352.

Stuckert, R. P. (1963), "Role Perception and Marital Satisfaction—a Configuration Approach," *Marriage and Family Living,* 25(4):415–419.

Sussman, M. B. (1961), "Needed Research on the Employed Mother," *Marriage and Family Living,* 23(4):368–374.

Terman, L. M. (1938), *Psychological Factors in Marital Happiness.* New York: McGraw-Hill.

Tharp, R. G. (1963a), "Dimensions of Marriage Roles," *Marriage and Family Living,* 25(4):389–404.

————(1963b), "Psychological Patterning in Marriage," *Psychological Bulletin,* 60(2):97–117.

————(1964), Reply to Levinger's note, *Psychological Bulletin,* 61(2):158–160.

————(1965), "Marriage Roles, Child Development and Family Treatment," *American Journal of Orthopsychiatry,* 35(3):531–538.

Thibaut, J. W., and H. H. Kelly (1959), *The Social Psychology of Groups.* New York: John Wiley and Sons.

Waller, W. (1938), *The Family: A Dynamic Interpretation.* New York: Gordon Company.

Wallin, P., and A. L. Clark (1964), "Religiosity, Sexual Gratification and Marital Satisfaction in the Middle Years of Marriage," *Social Forces,* 42(3):303–309.

Wells, T., and L. Christie (1970), "Living Together: An Alternative to Marriage," *The Futurist,* 50–57.

Winch, R. F. (1955), "The Theory of Complementary Needs in Mate-Selection: Final Results on the Test of General Hypotheses," *American Sociological Review,* 20:552–555.

————(1970), "Performance and Change in the History of the American Family and Some Speculations as to Its Future," *Journal of Marriage and the Family,* 32:6–16.

Winch, R., T. Ksanes, and V. Ksanes (1954), "The Theory of Complementary Needs in Mate Selection," *American Sociological Review,* 19(3):241–249.

Wolosin, R. (1968), "Self and Social Perception and the Attributions of Internal States," Unpublished doctoral dissertation, University of Michigan.

LARRY L. CONSTANTINE
JOAN M. CONSTANTINE
SHELDON K. EDELMAN

4   Counseling Implications of Alternative Marriage Styles

Counselors may expect an increasing number of marriages to include open intimate involvement with others either as an adjunct to the marriage or as an integral part of it. Some elements of these marital styles are extensions of the more conventional dyadic relationship but others appear to be relatively unique or to require a new focus. Key problem areas are noted and application to counseling situations is made.

Currently, many Americans are experimenting with alternate life styles and careers including involvement in altered forms of marriage (Constantine and Constantine, 1970a; Orleans and Wolfson, 1970; Otto, 1970a). It is not yet certain that this is an enduring trend or that it will necessarily involve large numbers of people, but it seems likely that the trend toward pluralism has not yet peaked. As more information about both the forms and outcomes of these marital experiences becomes available to more people, counselors will probably encounter an increasing number of marital situations which extend beyond the traditional form.

'Precise measurement of the number of marriages which depart significantly from the traditional monogamous model is not available. One estimate (Bartell, 1971) is that one to two million individuals have regularly exchanged partners with the knowledge and consent of their spouses. Kafka, Ryder, and Olson (1969) report that three percent of the National Institute of Mental Health panel of young marrieds advocated—at marriage—an ethos which explicitly valued comarital involvement. An interest in group marriage was reported by 25 percent of respondents to a *Psychology Today* poll. (Athenasiou, 1970) The minimum indication from these results is that non-traditional marital structures are seen as viable options by a sizable minority of couples today.

Therefore, it seems evident that counselors will be seeing clients who are concerned about and who have given thought to alternative marital structures; such clients are already beginning to appear with some frequency. Counselors who have been consulted by such clients can look upon these sessions as being both a challenge and an opportunity.

The discussion presented in this paper is based on research conducted since May, 1969 by the Multilateral Relations Study Project.[1] The Study Project has investigated the phenomenon of group marriage in the United States and has derived additional information about other marital structures (Constantine and Constantine, 1971a). While the project is not yet at a stage where precise data on counseling experiences can be reported (see Constantine and Constantine, 1971b) the evidence regarding counseling alternative marriage styles is such that a preliminary report seems indicated.

This paper is limited to comarital and multilateral relationships. Mate swapping (swinging) is included as secondary phenomenon only. Recent literature on mate swapping is available (Symonds, 1968, 1970; Smith and Smith, 1970; Bartell, 1971; O'Neill and O'Neill, 1970).

Comarital Relationships

A comarital relationship is defined as an intimate involvement, probably but not necessarily including sexual intimacy, which is an adjunct to an established dyadic marriage. Comarital relationships are distinguished from extramarital relations in being open and shared rather than covert and unshared and in being based on prior agreement within the dyadic relationship; these differences tend to render the similarities as being largely superficial. Comarital participants tend to perceive the comarital structure as being constructive to the dyadic marriage and often the additional members are perceived as having an integral role in the now expanded marriage.

Dyads may be involved in only one comarital relationship (i.e., where one spouse has developed an intimacy with one other person) or there may be multiple comarital relationships centering around a single dyad. Spouses may be involved in separate comarital relationships or they may develop relationships jointly with the same individual or couple. Where two couples are jointly involved comaritally, the situation has significant overlap with the multilateral marriage.

Comarital relationships may be isolated or part of a common pattern. Such

[1] The study is an autonomous project funded by the Constantines and by individual donations. The project serves as an information clearinghouse and referral agency for professional services in addition to performing research.

structures tend to vary considerably on such variables as intensity, length of involvement, and level of satisfaction. The various relationships may develop at differing rates, which usually leads to increased complexity and possible nonproductive complications. Relationship complexity seems to be the norm in most alternative marital structures; participants who have not developed an integral means of conflict resolution often require outside help.

Of special interest is the intimate network first described by Stoller (1970). Such a network consists of several separately domiciled families joined by intimate comarital bonds and committed to mutual working through of relationships. Because it is a simple and viable alternative to nuclearization, the network may be advantageous even to traditional families. Provided that adequate bases exist for conflict resolution, such a network can offer economic and personal stability and greater opportunities for career choice (especially among women) while losing few of the advantages of conventional marital structures. In addition, there is the possibility of providing sexual variety within the context of a supportive community.

The comarital relationship represents an intermediate position on a continuum anchored at one extreme by the traditional dyad and at the other extreme by a group marriage community. It retains many of the advantages of the dyad while providing additional resources for support and growth. Since it does not involve a commitment to an enduring structure other than the dyad, there is less strain on members at entry or exit than is true of the multilateral marriage structure.

Multilateral Marriage

The multilateral marriage is a voluntary family group of three or more persons, each of whom is committed to and maintains a relationship with more than one other person in a manner regarded by the participants as being "married." This marital form, more commonly (but less correctly) known as "group marriage," has engendered a sizable body of popular fictional accounts.[2] Participants often develop structures for sharing economic and personal resources: they tend to live together in one residence.

There are obvious advantages and disadvantages to the multilateral marriage. Four can live more cheaply than two pairs if they share living space and furniture. There is greater opportunity for variety and complexity in life style; nor can the sexual advantages be ignored. But there is also more opportunity for conflict and for problems due to differing life styles or different predilections

---

[2] Robert Rimmer, author of *Harrad Experiment* and *Proposition 31*, both dealing with multilateral family structure, has received thousands of letters from readers, some of which have been published. (Rimmer, 1970; 1971)

for conflict resolution or more basically, personality differences. Making each decision can easily become a difficult task.[3]

The decision to enter into such a relationship involves a commitment which is not easily broken. Participants believe in the advantages of their structure and feel that they can exert the effort required to make it work. Couples must put forth as much, or more, effort for the new structure than they would for the conventional dyad. One unique aspect is that both husbands and wives (and their cohusbands and cowives) *must* genuinely desire the expanded intimacy and involvement; where such involvement is perceived as undesirable or immoral, the group marriage is not likely to occur. Since there are few social pressures in favor of the group marriage, participants are likely to enter an involvement with a deep sense of commitment and a keen desire to exert the needed effort. However, it is still equivocal whether these groups can remain integrated over the long term. Some groups remain together after more than five years but the median for dissolved groups in the Study Project is nineteen months.

Viewed from a traditional perspective, comarital and multilateral structures can be termed immoral, unhealthy, unnecessary, or illegal. Such comments remain as hypotheses which are being tested by participants. Until precise data are available, alternative hypotheses carry equal probability. For some people, such structures may be more moral, healthier, and more constructive to the basic dyad than the traditional marital structure. Illegality is an omnipresent factor (Solis, 1971) but may become less relevant if the trend toward diversity in marital models becomes sufficiently popular. In the opinion of the authors, illegality in itself is insufficient to justify counselor condemnation.

The Family as the Treatment Unit

It is convenient to consider the totality of relationships as an extended family. "Family" or "group" are the terms most often used to denote the various structural forms described. Familial relationships are defined from within the client's perspective rather than by reference to social norms.

The client's family in a multilateral marriage includes not only his legal spouse and their children but also any other persons seen to be related through familial or marital ties. Theoretically, such a family may extend on a continuum from the simple dyad to an inter-related community involving many people of different ages and roles. In actuality, the preponderant majority of families encountered in the present study have consisted of four people, two men and

---

[3] Expanded families also encounter some more or less unique practical problems. For a detailed discussion, see Constantine and Constantine. (1970b)

two women (not necessarily two previously married couples). Most of these
familes have children in almost every case by their prior dyadic relationships.
Some contemplate having children in the group at a later date.

Before entering on a discussion of treatment approaches, it is necessary to
reflect upon the counselor himself. Recent literature has been outspoken in
asking the counselor to examine himself and his attitudes about race, sex, and
student roles. The family counseling required with new marital forms requires
the same sort of internal soul-searching. Some counselors seem to aspire to be
all things to each client; as in the other areas mentioned, one should not bring to
the counseling relationship a strong bias in the direction of conventionality. The
counselor's personal morality is not in question; his ability to accept the moral
posture of the client is involved in this matter.

Clients complain less of outright condemnation and moralizing (although it
has occurred) than they do of the more subtle behaviors of counselors whom
they consult. They feel that counselors seem not to understand the concept of a
family which deviates from currently acceptable social norms. Or, if counselors
do understand, clients report that there seems to be a lack of acceptance that
such deviation may imply a viable social choice rather than implying the
presence of mental illness or pathological deviance. Participants in these new
ventures are understandably quite anxious and tend to be overwhelmed at times
because they lack information about their new way of life and its possible
pitfalls. Counselors do not help these people by describing the new structure as
"acting out" or as social irresponsibility or by perceiving the "others" in the
family as necessarily detracting from the basic dyad.

Counseling Approaches

Counselors will, of course, use an approach which they find most comfortable for themselves within the context of the presenting problem. Some suggestions follow regarding successful interventions as practiced by or reported to the
authors.

Of importance is the early development of an overall perspective regarding
the many inter-relationships in these new marital structures. An initial session
with *all* participants is recommended. Often there will be no specific problem
presented in early sessions. Participants may be reacting to the anxiety of their
own choices or to the anxiety generated by novelty under conditions of low
information. Participants simply may be investigating the counselor as a resource, "just in case," or they may need to share their new venture with
someone whom they can trust to maintain confidentiality; these people will
have taken a major step in their lives, one which cannot be openly discussed
because of the legal problems involved.

Grunebaum, et al., (1969) have used conjoint family therapy along with concurrent individual sessions with good results. One of the authors[4] has also made use of this approach. In the conjoint approach, one is able to see all family members in interaction in the same session; sole reliance on this type of meeting may be disadvantageous where constraints upon the many interrelationships are of individual origin. Additional two- or three-person sessions are less frequent but sometimes useful.

The interactions within a group marriage have often been termed by members as a constant encounter group, and professional observations tend to reinforce this view. The dynamics of multiple depth relationships, along with the overt norm of open expression seem to move each family into frequent encounters, both positive and negative. This raises the question of the suitability of various forms of sensitivity training or other small group techniques. (See Otto, 1970b for discussion of "positive" experiential techniques.)

Several group marriages have conducted resident basic encounter groups as an ongoing process for building the marriage and for dealing with complex interpersonal difficulties. One of these employed a professional for the sessions; the results were favorable, although eventually the group dissolved.

Thus, the key elements in counseling are the counselor himself, the family (the totality of interrelationships), and the individual participants. No one technique or method is recommended, but emphasis is placed on treating the whole family as well as its component persons. Those theories which stress treatment of the individual apart from his network of relationships are seen as less relevant to the problems incurred specifically within the new marital forms.

Assessment

It is often useful to obtain objective data on participants. The Study Project utilizes an extension of the Edwards Personal Preference Schedule (EPPS) in its research. An essential criterion for the methodology of the Study Project is that any insights gained be shared with participants in responding groups. The EPPS seems to have value not only for understanding the structure and functional basis of a multilateral involvement, but also in providing productive stimuli for group discussion.

The EPPS is a paper-and-pencil instrument which measures the relative magnitude of fifteen normal personality needs. It has a long history of use in individual, marital, and premarital counseling (Kilgo, 1969). In his work with dyadic marriage structure, Drewery (1969) developed an additional methodology which elicits perceptions and a metaperspective of needs. The Study Project uses an adaptation of Drewery's method. This method is described here for its possible use in counseling situations.

[4] Edelman has counseled with two group marriages and provided information and informal advice to others.

Respondents complete the EPPS in the prescribed manner. They then rate what they perceive to be the level of their own needs on a ten-point scale for each of the EPPS needs; they do the same for each of the other members in the group. Finally, they record how each of the others will rate them. Special forms which include a discussion of needs and need-satisfaction and brief descriptions of each need are used for this purpose.[5] The result is a rich but manageable picture of perceptions and misperceptions, of self-insight and its absence, and of misunderstanding that is recognized and misunderstanding which is unseen.

All results, including the actual EPPS profiles, are returned to the family as the basis for facilitated, open discussion. The ensuing encounter usually results in major insights into the underlying perceptual basis for aspects of group functioning and dysfunction. One of the groups devised a possibly worthwhile adjunct in which each possible dyad met separately in an open encounter using the Edwards/Drewery profiles as a departure point for understanding some of the essentials of their relationship.

Certain prior conditions seem to be essential to the success of this type of interaction. The relationship between the family and the test administrator must be openly established. (Jourard and Resnick, 1970, have shown that examiner self-disclosure significantly affects EPPS results.) The test should be seen as an opportunity to learn, not as psychological rape. A respondent completing the schedule for his own edification tends to respond quite differently than he does when the testing is exclusively for the enlightenment of others.

The participants' belief in the validity and reasonableness of the test is also important. There is, especially among younger people a widespread distrust of and dislike for psychometric methods. It is generally believed that the methods are invalid and can always be easily and completely faked. Indeed, it is probably true that most of the college population views the testing situation as a game, the basis of which is to "figure out" the test, or to beat the system by successfully creating a false picture. Faking and validity checks are not fully sufficient to counter the psychological sophistication of the contemporary young person, who in many cases knows or can figure out approximately what checks have been built into the test.

The entire basis of the procedure can be shared with participants beforehand. This includes explaining the rationale of the EPPS and reasons for feeling that it does a fair job of measuring what it purports to measure. Reservations and known shortcomings of the test are presented. By using this approach, respondents generally enter the testing situation with a realistic attitude toward what the instrument can accomplish, and an awareness that their own willingness to be candid and realistic in their responses will in large part determine the value of the resulting information.

The EPPS/Drewery methodology has a particular advantage in assessing

---

[5] Copies of this form and directions for use are available from the Multilateral Relations Study Project.

multilateral situations in that it reveals a detailed picture of the group structure at reasonable cost to both counselor and respondent. The structure of a six-person family can be so complex that even the most elementary understanding must otherwise be extracted from protracted discussions with the group and with each individual. Although this methodology deals with only one set of dimensions relevant to group structure, the EPPS/Drewery scheme provides a good deal of insight into family relationships.

Communication

The complexity of interrelationships ensures that multilateral families are beset by problems in communication. This is likely to be an area in which counselors can make their most valuable contribution.

Most participants have elected a strong growth orientation (Constantine, 1971) and seem to strive for openness and authentic self-disclosure. The counselor is not likely to encounter resistance in convincing clients of the value of direct and honest communication.

One problem area results from the notable advantage that multilateral families have in comparison to the dyad: blockages in communications channels can be dealt with by turning to an alternative path. This seems to be a natural and frequent option taken by participants, and it often helps to work through the blockage. But this approach to communication can be abused to the point where communication through third parties becomes a substitute for direct communication.

The counselor can be helpful in two ways when third party communication is an over-utilized option. First, he can provide support and reinforcement to the norm of direct, honest communication, and assist the group in working through the blocked channels. Secondly, he can utilize his observations regarding the group's processes to instruct participants in methods for resolving its current and future problems.

Group dynamics literature tends to stress the difference between ''processed'' and ''unprocessed'' communications. A processed statement is one which includes the speaker's attempt to take into account the perceived feelings and opinions of others; the processed statement is a first-order abstraction from raw feelings, including as it does one's judgments about whether or not the feeling should exist, how it will be received, and how it should be stated. The unprocessed statement expresses the isolated, spontaneous, individual feelings of the speaker. If all group statements are of the processed variety, the group will experience difficulty in assessing the real feelings of its members and this tends to result in problems in resolving issues, reaching consensus, and simply understanding what is being communicated.

Thus, despite the norm of openness and honesty, groups experience problems in communication because of the nature of the statements which are made. They lack information regarding the basis for blockage. Dyadic marriages experience the same difficulties but the simpler structure eases the counselor's task.

One group marriage became aware of its over-use of processed statements in decision-making and when discussing sensitive issues such as sleeping arrangements. This group then gained practice in giving raw data statements. They found it essential that such statements would not be "held against anyone;" individuals could later offer processed statements during decision-making. Not being commited to unprocessed statements (except that they be honest) allowed people to vote by taking into consideration all the information, and this made the unprocessed statements easier to supply in the first place.

Another approach taken by families to resolve their communications problems is to write the messages. Where written communication represents the bulk of messages among intimates who are in daily face-to-face contact, however, this probably is symptomatic of extreme failure of communication. Written messages are, however, preferred to a total lack of information transfer.

Conclusion

In many respects, counseling marriages which include a multilateral element is merely an extension of dyadic counseling; however, the relative importance of various aspects of the relationships are shifted. The counselor may find his task confounded by the very complexity which tends to enrich the multilateral relationship.

Perhaps the goal is to utilize this complexity as a strength. The counselor can facilitate alternative paths of communication, promote the use of the supportive resources within the family and encourage productive use of group process to facilitate growth and handle difficult decision-making functions. There are many potential options in terms of restructuring the multilateral situation for specific ends.

The real promise of this era is that the creative counselor has an opportunity to help tailor the family structure to the people rather than to continue to help individuals fit a single structural option. Conventional monogyny is an efficient and workable structure, but it may not be the best for everyone. Neither should group marriage be hailed as a new panacea, as some writers have done; it is one form of marriage that some individuals will find particularly fulfilling. Both the challenge and the opportunity of genuine pluralism in marital forms are immense.

REFERENCES

Athenasiou, Robert, et al. (1970), "Sex," Psychology Today, 4(2):39–52.
Bartell, Gilbert D. (1971), Group Sex: A Scientist's Eyewitness Report of the American Way of Swinging. New York: Peter H. Wyden.
Constantine, Larry, L. (1971), "Personal Growth in Multi-person Marriages, Radical Therapist, 2(1).
———, and Joan M. Constantine (1970a), "Where is Marriage Going?" The Futurist, 4(2):44–46.
———(1970b), "Pragmatics of Group Marriage," The Modern Utopian, 4(3-4):33–37.
———(1971a), "Group and Multilateral Marriage: Definitional Notes, Glossary, and Annotated Bibliography," Family Process, 10:157–176.
_____(1971b), "Sexual Aspects of Multilateral Relations," Journal of Sex Research, 7(3):204–225.
Denfeld, Duane, and Michael Gordon (1970), "The Sociology of Mate Swapping: Or the Family That Swings Together Clings Together," Journal of Sex Research, 6:85–100.
Drewery, James (1969), "An Interpersonal Perception Technique," British Journal of Medical Psychology, 42:171–181
Grunebaum, Henry, et al. (1969), "Diagnosis and Treatment Planning for Couples," International Journal of Group Psychotherapy, 19:185–202.
Jourard, Sydney M., and Jaquelyn L. Resnick (1970), "Some Effects of Self-Disclosure Among College Women," Journal of Humanistic Psychology, 10:84–93.
Kafka, John S., et al. (1969), "A Non-conventional Pattern Within the Conventional Marriage Framework." Unpublished research report, National Institute of Mental Health.
Kilgo, Reese D. (1969), "The Use of the Edwards Personal Preference Schedule in Premarital and Marriage Counseling." Paper, National Council on Family Relations Annual Meeting, Washington, D.C.
O'Neill, George C., and Nena O'Neill (1970), "Patterns in Group Sexual Activity," Journal of Sex Research, 6:101–112.
Orleans, Myron, and Florence Wolfson (1970), "The Future of the Family," The Futurist, 4(2):48–49.
Otto, Herbert A. (1970a), The Family in Search of a Future. New York: Appleton-Century-Crofts.
Otto, Herbert A. (1970b), Group Methods to Actualize Human Potential. Beverly Hills: Holistic Press.
Rimmer, Robert H. (ed.) (1970), The Harrad Letters to Robert H. Rimmer. New York: New American Library.
Rimmer, Robert H. (1971), You and I . . . Searching for Tomorrow. New York: Signet.
Smith, James R., and Lynn G. Smith (1970), "Co-marital Sex and the Sexual Freedom Movement," Journal of Sex Research, 6:131-142.
Solis, Gary (1971), "Group Marriage and California Law." Harrad (Box 841, Boston, MA 02103), 2: (1 and 2).
Stoller, Frederick H. (1970), "The Intimate Network of Families." In Herbert A. Otto (ed.), The Family in Search of a Future. New York: Appleton-Century-Crofts.

Symonds, Carolyn (1968), "Pilot Study of the Peripheral Behavior of Sexual Mate Swappers." Unpublished Master's Thesis: University of California at Riverside.
Symonds, Carolyn.(1970), "The Utopian Aspects of Sexual Mate Swapping: In Theory and Practice." Paper, Annual Meeting, Society for the Psychological Study of Social Problems, Washington, D.C.

II
Treatment Issues and Interventions

INTRODUCTION

The Co-Therapy Relationship

The use of co-therapy teams in psychotherapy is not a new practice in itself. The value of such teams has long been recognized for many group therapy situations and, at times, even for individual therapy. In addition, co-therapy experiences often are acknowledged as having a good deal to offer in the training of clinicians. Recently, however, marital therapists in particular have begun to focus on many of the crucial value and sex-role issues that are especially salient in the treatment of married couples. Concerns about status, power, and a variety of role-structure dimensions have become increasingly relevant to the quality of both the relationship between male and female co-therapists and between therapists and their patient couples. As our culture continues to move toward and support increased flexibility in marital and family roles, marital therapists will need to expand their sensitivity to these matters in order to facilitate optimal therapeutic experiences for conflicted patient couples. The two papers in this Section by Joy and David Rice and Rice, Fey, and Kepecs offer interesting examples of some of the new experiential and empirical ways of examining and understanding the co-therapy relationship.

Marital Change in the Family and Group Context

As Olson well documented in Chapter 1, marital and family therapies have historically emerged along parallel but independent courses. Clearly, there is much overlap in the clinical practices of marital and family therapists, yet there are some very important theoretical differences between these two groups. In Chapter 7, Carl Whitaker, one of the leaders in the family therapy movement, offers a provocative view of how he differentiates between marital and family therapy. Marital clinicians, he feels, often make their therapeutic task far more difficult and less effective by tending to emphasize the primacy of the husband-wife axis too heavily, often to the extent of excluding from treatment the rest of the social unit of the family, i.e., the children. While it may not always be necessary to have the children involved in every therapy session, Whitaker feels that their inclusion, especially early in the treatment process, provides the therapist with a broader perspective of the couple's life and is of immense value in understanding their real-life and symbolic transactions with each other and with the therapist.

Some of the symbolic transferential themes elaborated by Whitaker are also discussed by Leichter (Chapter 8) in the group therapy context. For Leichter, the couples group becomes the new "family" of the husbands and wives in treatment, one in which a corrective emotional experience can occur through the encouragement and facilitation of honest expression of feelings. Leichter, although writing from a somewhat different theoretical viewpoint, actively sets herself up as the new "parent figure" for couples and she then attends to the patient's interpersonal struggles, which she sees as recapitulations of earlier childhood sibling experiences. Leichter usefully points out some of the characteristic response patterns and therapeutic themes that emerge in the group context with couples at different stages of the life cycle.

In the final selection in this Section, Gurman (Chapter 9) provides an overview of previous writings on group couples therapy. The primary purpose of Gurman's article is to propose a framework within which to evaluate marital change and to point to some of the questions in this area that are in most need of empirical study. The paper should be of interest to clinicians as well as researchers because it comprehensively surveys the many conflicting points of view around several key issues in the actual conduct of couples group therapy.

Behavioral Approaches to Marital Therapy

Behavior therapists have been in the forefront of the development of new treatment strategies for the psychological difficulties of children, adolescents, and other clinical problems which center on family life (Patterson, 1971). However, only in the last five or six years have they begun to be concerned with facilitating change in the marital relationship per se. Stuart's (1969) description of the use of operant methods for treating marital discord was the first substantive attempt to apply basic principles of human learning to the husband-wife pair. In Chapter 12, Stuart presents a more recent and extensive description of the use of operant-interpersonal techniques in couples therapy. In Chapter 13, Rappaport and Harrell provide a thorough review of the theoretical notions on which the kinds of behavioral-exchange procedures first described by Stuart are based. This chapter is preceded by Liberman's (Chapter 10) helpful discussion of the application of social learning principles with couples and families.

Behavioral marital therapies generally assume that disordered marriages are characterized by unsatisfactory rates of mutual positive reinforcement and that, conversely, marital satisfaction is at least partially a function of each spouse's performance of rewarding behaviors toward the other. Furthermore, in the behavioral or social-learning framework, dysfunctional marriages appear to be characterized by coercive process of "pain control" (Patterson and Hops, 1972), in which both spouses control, i.e., attempt to influence, each other by the use of aversive or noxious stimulation (nagging, criticism, threats, etc.).

The negative reinforcement that results from the termination of such unpleasant interchanges serves to strengthen the behavior of both spouses while simultaneously precluding the possibility of constructively working toward change in a positive direction. Behavioral marital therapies, therefore, emphasize an increase of "reciprocity" (Stuart, 1969) in the relationship, i.e., requiring desired behaviors to be positively consecrated. One form of behavioral-exchange contracting procedures for establishing such reciprocity is described by Rappaport and Harrell in Chapter 12. Conjoint behavioral approaches to couples therapy are based on (1) the increase of positive (desired) behaviors; (2) the specification of such changes in terms of concrete and observable acts; and (3) the concurrent change of behavior on the part of both spouses. Perhaps *the* distinguishing feature of behavioral interventions is the explicit focus on the specification of treatment goals, as highlighted in the paper by Hurvitz (Chapter 11). In this way, the effectiveness of therapy can be evaluated reliably by therapists and patients alike.

Treatment of Sexual Dysfunction

In the last decade, impressive gains have been made in the treatment of sexual dysfunctions that frequently are present in unsatisfactory marital relationships. The single most important work in this area has been, of course, that of Masters and Johnson (1970). While Masters and Johnson do not describe their work or explain its efficacy in the language of learning theory, it is clear that many of their methods do rest heavily on such behavioral tenets as extinction, graded exposure to fearful conditions, and stimulus substitution. Perhaps the major significance of the recent advances in the successful treatment of sexual dysfunction is that such methods appear to be consistently effective without detailed examination of unconscious wishes, fears, and desires. Thus efficacious techniques have been developed which are focused on the current behavior of clients and on the interpersonal *and* intrapersonal cognitive (private) factors that maintain unsatisfactory sexual behavior. Another important dimension of the newer behavioral techniques in this area is that it appears possible, at least under some conditions, to directly effect change in marital sexual behavior without attending to the marital relationship in its totality. However, marital relationships which are marked by extreme degrees of disturbance will usually require more broadly gauged therapy in order to ultimately deal effectively with specific problems of sexual dysfunction. The papers by Laughren and Kass and Lobitz and LoPiccolo (Chapters 14 and 15) which appear here are useful examples of the types of effective clinical treatment programs that have been developed recently. Laughren and Kass also present the first comprehensive and systematic literature review of the behavioral treatment of sexual dysfunction. Both these chapters offer detailed expositions of their treatment methods which should be of particular value to clinicians.

Facilitating Communications Skills

In the practice of couples therapy, most clinicians are not usually so fortunate as to be able to intervene efficiently and appropriately in only one sphere of the marital relationship. Most conflicted marriages seen by therapists are multi-problematic and, therefore, require intervention on several dimensions, either simultaneously or in sequence. One of the most common impediments to successful therapeutic intervention with couples is their lack of skill in effective communication. An effective communicative repertoire would seem to almost always be a necessary precondition for the implementation of other techniques of marital change.

"Communication" is not a mystical mélange of transactions but, rather, a set of specifiable verbal and nonverbal interchanges. Since marital communication is by definition a two-way process, both spouses need to learn two related but independent categories of skills. *Expressive skills* are those marked by minimal discrepancy between overt verbal statements and privately held, internal feelings. These skills are often referred to as genuineness, affective spontaneity, and "owning one's feelings." *Reactive skills* are those characterized by a person's ability to "tune in" to the subtle feeling tones of another person, i.e., to sense implicit affective meanings, and to respond to the other person nonjudgmentally. Research on the "necessary and sufficient conditions for therapeutic personality change" described almost two decades ago by Carl Rogers (1957) has rather consistently supported the salience of empathic understanding, unconditional positive regard, and genuineness in the facilitation of behavior change within the therapist-patient relationship (Truax and Mitchell, 1971). While it is unlikely that such relational styles are very often sufficient for personality change, their necessity in a wide variety of growthful human encounters seems clear.

It is upon such clinical, theoretical, and empirical bases that the communication training program of Wells, Figurel, and McNamee (Chapter 16) stands. Since such relationship qualities as they describe are probably basic to positive human interactions (Rogers, 1957), direct teaching of such skills to married couples can offer a potentially valuable method for improving the phenomenological experience of feeling understood and being accepted as a person. Chapters 17 and 18 by Bolte and Carter and Thomas propose somewhat different methods for facilitating communication skills. All three papers in this Section present material that should be instructive to practicing therapists. Despite the divergent theoretical underpinnings of the models proposed by Wells *et al.* (client-centered), Bolte (systems theory and transactional analysis), and Carter and Thomas (operant and social learning theory), all three place a common emphasis upon the therapist's role as an educator and model and share the assumption that marital communication skills can be taught directly through systematically structured learning experiences.

Crisis Intervention

Married couples at times reach a point of psychological crisis when a major real-life stress on the relationship is felt either from within or without. The birth of a first child, the leaving home of the eldest child, significant economic and vocational changes, etc., are often the precipitants of major turning points in couples' relationships. During such periods there is commonly a heightened sense of vulnerability and helplessness. Times of crisis often can offer the opportunity for genuine psychological growth as well as for resolution of immediate issues (Aguilera *et al.*, 1970). Toomim's paper in this section emphasizes that the crisis period of separation can be a time when spouses are enabled, through a guided therapeutic experience, to examine themselves as individuals, and to determine where they are going in life both as separate persons and as a pair.

The chapter by Eisler and Hersen highlights several of the characteristic dimensions of crisis intervention with couples and families. In the family context, as well as in the individual context, crisis intervention focuses on enhancing the *problem-solving* abilities of family members. Treatment is, thus, generally of short duration (four to six weeks) and is *goal-oriented*, with a high degree of therapist activity and planned therapeutic intervention. The aims of crisis intervention are to reestablish equilibrium in the marital dyad where previously employed coping mechanisms have failed, and to return each spouse to at least his/her previous level of psychological, parental, and vocational functioning. While the behavioral strategies presented by Eisler and Hersen may be quite appropriate and effective in many instances, their paper is presented not as a comprehensive technology for crisis intervention but, rather, as an example of a clearly articulated model for such work.

REFERENCES

Aguilera, D. C., J. M. Messick, and M. S. Farrell (1970), *Crisis Intervention: Theory and Methodology*. St. Louis: C. V. Mosby.

Masters, W. H., and V. E. Johnson (1970), *Human Sexual Inadequacy*. Boston: Little, Brown & Co.

Patterson G.R. (1971), "Behavioral Intervention Procedures in the Classroom and in the Home." In A. E. Bergin and S. L. Garfield (eds.), *Handbook of Psychotherapy and Behavior Change*. New York: Wiley, pp. 751-775.

————and H. Hops (1972), "Coercion, a Game for Two: Intervention Techniques for Marital Conflict." In R. Ulrich and P. Mountjoy (eds.), *The experimental Analysis of Social Behavior.* New York: Appleton-Century-Crofts, pp. 424-440.

Stuart, R.B. (1969), "Operant-Interpersonal Treatment for Marital Discord," *Journal of Consulting and Clinical Psychology,* 33:675-682.

Rogers, C.R. (1957), "The Necessary and Sufficient Conditions of Therapeutic Personality Change," *Journal of Consulting Psychology,* 21:95-103.

Truax, C.B., and K.M. Mitchell (1971), "Research on Certain Therapist Interpersonal Skills in Relation to Process and Outcome." In A.E. Bergin and S.L. Garfield (eds.), *Handbook of Psychotherapy and Behavior Change.* New York: Wiley, pp. 299-344.

Section A

The Co-Therapy Relationship

JOY K. RICE
DAVID G. RICE

5 Status and Sex Role Issues in Co-Therapy*

Traditionally, co-therapists have not taken into account the effects on their patients of therapist status differences and modeling of sex-role prescribed therapist behaviors. These characteristics are perceived both overtly and covertly by the patients, and often conflict with the stated goals of therapy, e.g., working toward a more equalitarian marital relationship, with greater acknowledgment of the worth of each individual. This chapter illustrates how such messages are communicated by the therapists, and presents guidelines for the development of greater co-therapist status equality and role flexible behaviors. Working toward status and sex role equality is seen as enhancing both treatment effectiveness and the therapists' own marital relationships.

The use of co-therapists in treating couples, families, and groups has become a popular form of psychotherapy. Clinicians increasingly advocate the treatment format of male and female co-therapists (Friedman, 1972; Reding and Ennis, 1964; Reding, et al., 1967 Sonne and Lincoln, 1966). A particularly interesting variation of co-therapy involves married professional co-therapists (Bellville, et al., 1969).

A central issue in co-therapy is the nature and quality of the relationship between the therapists. These matters have generally been dealt with in the writings referred to above, and the discussion of them by Bellville, et al., is perhaps representative. In a time-limited (16-session) format, these married

* Portions of this paper were presented as part of a symposium entitled "Married Professional Therapists as a Treatment Team" at the annual meeting of the American Psychological Association, Honolulu, Hawaii, September 2, 1972

co-therapists treated couples who presented primarily sexual problems. Their procedure consisted of "direct analysis" of intrapsychic difficulties affecting sexual performance, and was devised after consultation with William Masters, who is part (see Masters and Johnson, 1970) of perhaps the best known co-therapist team. The Bellvilles report a therapy success rate of 57 percent (26 of 44 couples) based on the therapists' subjective evaluations. Although they deal with the "tension between therapists," they state that these feelings can be worked out early, given the following assumptions: "To be able to work together a marital pair must have a functional marriage and family, with openness and no fight over control" (p. 480).

There would probably be general agreement among co-therapists as to the desirability of such a "functional" relationship (defined as one which provides relative comfort and fullfillment for each therapist) and of "openness" as prerequisites for working together. In regard to the stated objective of "no fight over control," most co-therapists would probably agree that this is important for successful therapy. A key issue would center around how such a conflict-free state is achieved. Specifically, does it occur as the result of one therapist (usually the woman) being unwilling to challenge the control of the other therapist (usually the man) from the very beginning of therapy? In this sense a "fight over control" is avoided by fiat. Therapists of comparable status who are sensitive to stereotyped role relationships, i.e., males dominant and females submissive, find that the issue of control in co-therapy is usually omnipresent, and must be acknowledged and dealt with openly. In our experience, many co-therapist relationships falter (see Rice, Fey, and Kepecs, 1972) because of the inability of the therapists to work through the issue of control and achieve a comfortable sharing of power and dominance.

The Bellvilles do not discuss the implications of possible co-therapist social and professional status differences. The absence of such considerations, especially in light of the fact that one member of their marital therapy team is an M.D. and one an M.A. is particularly notable. Our personal professional experience, and our close association with other co-therapy teams (both married and unmarried) suggests that perceived co-therapist status differences become critical factors in this treatment format. This matter has rarely been dealt with in the co-therapy literature. Few therapists (married or unmarried) seem willing to face, or are even cognizant of, the status role model they present to patients in its egalitarian or nonegalitarian forms.

This issue takes on greater contemporary importance due to the social impact of the Women's Liberation Movement. The issue of egalitarian relationships between the sexes has sensitized therapists to a greater awareness of the possible exploitation that can occur in typical therapeutic relationships, where a professional male in a dominant role prescribes for a passive female patient in a recipient role. The authors have previously discussed the implications of this social hierarchy, not only within the male therapist-female patient relationship, but also between co-therapists (Rice and Rice, 1973).

Status and sex role equality issues begin to affect treatment the moment a patient couple (or family or group) enters an office and discovers whom the office "belongs to," who owns the furniture, who sits in the padded swivel chair, and who buzzes the secretary. The matter of whose office one uses or whether one, indeed, has an office is but one of many subtle and yet not-so-subtle cues that patients and therapists respond to in order to elaborate the pecking order in the therapeutic relationship. Other perceived status and role differences concern professional degrees, who is called "Doctor" and who is not, who gets the larger fee, who sets the ground rules, and who does most of the talking. In a common therapeutic male-female team of psychiatrist or psychologist and social worker or nurse, etc., this individual is more likely to be the male co-therapist. Status differences are thus reinforced by differences in education and experience, and the inherent social structure perpetuates a dichotomy. Even when degrees and professional experience are essentially equal, patients tend to maintain the social order by addressing questions to the male therapist, paying the bills of the male therapist sooner, and other subtle recognitions of perceived status differences.

A related matter is the whole dilemma of what constitutes an equality of status between therapists. Is it inherently a matter of equal training and comparable experience? Given our status-conscious society, every credential probably helps, especially the possession of a Ph.D. or M.D. The issue is, of course, more complex: two Ph.D. psychologists in an essentially traditional marriage where role-dominance and task division are based on sex would hardly model egalitarian status, despite comparable educational and professional attainment. Similarly, regardless of differences in training, a therapist couple who was involved in a truly give-and-take "open" marriage (see O'Neill and O'Neill, 1972) on a day-to-day basis would probably inherently regard each other's importance and work with equal esteem and status and, in turn, model this type of behavior for a patient couple. Thus, the question of whether perceived equality of status is possible relates to marital attitudes and life-styles as well as to the nature and extent of professional training.

How can co-therapists deal with problems of status inequality? Given our social conditioning, with higher ascribed status and dominance for males, the initiative for changing the status quo in role perception and role behavior may likely rest with the female therapist. A variety of techniques of consciousness-raising (encounter groups, role-playing, etc.) advocated by the Women's Liberation movement are helpful in the process of achieving status equality in perception and role behavior change. Their procedures are also useful for training beginning male and female co-therapists. A by-product can be an improvement in the therapists' own marital situation as a consequence of such experiences.

Assuming that a professional married or unmarried therapist team is able to work out the complexities of equality in self- and other-perceived status, the advantages that accrue are many. Two, in particular, stand out. The first relates to the condition or environment of freedom that is created when both therapists, by virtue of their felt equality of worth, begin to participate freely and openly in all aspects of the treatment process. This is not to imply that the therapeutic process at all times will be balanced by "equal time" for each therapist. It is more like a seesaw with activity levels, participation, facilitation of decision-making, etc., varying at any given moment for each. The crucial variable is that both therapists are free to present their ideas. Their contributions, and their value to the therapy, is comparable both from their own and their patients' perspectives.

The second advantage of working toward equality of perceived status is that in this sort of situation, a very powerful force exists for modeling a democratic relationship between the sexes. Therapists are agents of social change and as such have a valuable opportunity for presenting to their patients new models of human (marital) relationships. Previous authors have dealt with the perception of co-therapists as modeling a certain relationship (or "therapeutic marriage"), but these illustrations have usually been strongly sex-role linked. For example, Sonne and Lincoln (1966) state:

> We have found it important, particularly in the early phase of treatment, for the female co-therapist to support the male therapist's aggressiveness, so that it is not mistaken for cruelty, and in the late phase of treatment it is important for the male therapist to particularly support the female therapist's femininity. (p.200)

These authors are describing treatment of schizophrenogenic families, and feel that clear gender-prescribed behaviors on the therapist's part are necessary to counteract gender confusion common in the patients' families. We would argue that *rigid* sex-role prescriptions for behavior (e.g., males are aggressive and dominant, females are passive and "feminine") are also a potentially pathogenic influence in the development of one's identity. What is needed is for the therapists (and parents) to model a healthy acceptance of these feelings and behaviors in all individuals, regardless of gender.

Younger couples in particular are struggling today with issues of changing male and female role status. The model advocated by the authors has particular appeal to such individuals. An example of this type of therapy serves to illustrate these points:

> A young professional couple entered therapy with the stated desire to "improve our communication with one another." In this marriage, the wife had been defined (largely by herself) as the "weak and helpless" member, the husband (by both partners) as the strong and capable member. Both therapists actively reinforced the wife's attempts to change her low self-esteem, and focused on how the differential role-stereotyped competence perceptions were affecting marital communication. At this point in therapy (after approximately 5 months and 15 sessions) the husband, who had verbally supported his spouse's attempts to become "a person in her own right," revealed his marked ambivalence concerning her growth and change (e.g., "she's doing her own thing and doesn't seem to need *me* anymore"). When the female therapist pointed out that he seemed to be directing these feelings, and appealing for support, primarily toward the male therapist, the husband said: "Yes, that's true. In fact, I am hardly aware of you [the female therapist] in here at

all." This perception was stated in spite of the fact that the woman therapist had been very active in supporting and interpreting both partners' attempts to restructure their relationship along greater perceived equality of participation and enhanced self-esteem. The woman co-therapist then indicated to the husband that his inability to grant the woman therapist equality of contribution in the therapy situation mirrored his ambivalence toward accepting his wife's growth and change. He was surprised at the revelation of this "blind spot" in his perception of therapy, but readily acknowledged its presence and the generalized meaning in terms of the marital relationship.

For older couples or those in "traditional" marriages, issues of marital power and changing roles can be quite threatening. The therapeutic modeling of an egalitarian relationship by the co-therapists requires more patience and sustained effort in dealing with this type of marriage. However, these couples, who feel "trapped" and unable to restructure their marital situation, yet retain a commitment to continue the marriage, can also gain potential benefit from therapy in which the co-therapists model status and role equality.

In any type of therapy, but particularly in an active, directive form such as advocated here, the possibility is increased for the therapists to foist their own values onto the patients, who may then perceive little freedom of choice but to accept that value system as a condition of therapy. Assuming therapists are aware that this can happen, it is important to clearly state relevant values and biases at the beginning of therapy and "lay them out on the table" along with stated possible advantages of such a therapeutic approach for the marital relationship. This, of course, contrasts with the historically accepted notion that psychotherapists should strive to remain "neutral" in therapy. Traditionally, this attitude has been promulgated as particularly important for marital therapy. Therapists have been advised to scrupulously refrain from "taking sides" (making value judgments) in the conflict between partners. However, openly stating values usually does not present major difficulties for therapy if the values have strong "democratic" connotations. Thus, concepts of role equality and shared distribution of power in marriage have cognitive appeal in this regard, and are usually accepted at least overtly by the marital partners. Covert resistance to these ideas can be dealt with in therapy, in the same ways that one would deal with any other resistance to therapeutic behavior change.

Couples with a genuine desire to preserve a traditional style of marriage do not usually seek out marital therapy except in extreme stress periods (e.g., the imminent possibility of divorce), because they are relatively satisfied with the status quo and have many societal role models (friends, movies, etc.) which support their arrangement. In this sense, an openness to exploring new values with probable restructuring of the marital relationship has good prognostic value for therapeutic change with the form of marital therapy advocated in this paper.

In summary, co-therapists have commonly not taken into account the effect on patient couples of therapist status differences and sex-role prescribed behaviors. The implications of modeling co-therapist status equality and role flexibility have been explored and suggestions have been presented as to how therapists can achieve these goals. Working toward status and sex-role equality is seen as benefiting both treatment and the therapists' own marital relationship.

REFERENCES

Bellville, T. P., O. N. Raths, and C. J. Bellville, (1969), "Conjoint Marriage Therapy with a Husband-and-Wife Team," *American Journal of Orthopsychiatry,* 39:373-483.

Friedman, B. (1973), "Co-therapy: A Behavioral and Attitudinal Survey of Third-Year Psychiatric Residents," *International Journal of Group Psychotherapy,* 23:228-234.

Masters, W. H., and V. E. Johnson (1970), *Human Sexual Inadequacy.* Boston: Little, Brown & Co.

O'Neill, N., and G. O'Neill (1972), *Open Marriage: A New Life Style for Couples.* New York: M. Evans & Co.

Reding, G. R., L. A. Charles, and M. B. Hoffman (1967), "Treatment of a Couple by a Couple: II. Conceptual Framework, Case Presentation, and Follow-up Study," *British Journal of Medical Psychology,* 40:243-252.

Reding, G. R., and B. Ennis (1964), "Treatment of a Couple by a Couple," *British Journal of Medical Psychology,* 37:325-330.

Rice, D. G., W. F. Fey, and J. G. Kepecs (1972), "Therapist Experience and 'Style' as Factors in Co-therapy," *Family Process,* 12:1-12.

Rice, J. K., and D. G. Rice (1973), "Implications of the Women's Liberation Movement for Psychotherapy," *American Journal of Psychiatry,* 130:191-196.

Sonne, J., and G. Lincoln (1966), "The Importance of a Heterosexual Co-therapy Relationship in the Construction of a Family Image." In Cohen, J. (ed.), *Family Structure, Dynamics, and Therapy,* Psychiatric Research Reports, No. 20, American Psychiatric Association, pp. 196-205.

DAVID G. RICE,
WILLIAM F. FEY,
JOSEPH G. KEPECS

6   Therapist Experience and "Style" in Co-therapy

Self-descriptions of general in-therapy behavior, attitudes toward co-therapy, and ratings of co-therapy effectiveness were collected from 25 experienced (E) and 25 inexperienced (IE) therapists who treated a total of 48 married couples in co-therapy. Major findings were: (a) six different therapeutic "styles" emerged via factor analysis of the therapists' self-descriptions of in-therapy behavior, (b) E and IE therapists as a group had different personal therapeutic styles and preferences as to the style desired in a co-therapist, (c) subjectively rated effectiveness of co-therapy correlated with the degree of comfort felt by the therapist in the relationship and the acceptance by the co-therapist, and (d) there was evidence of a "point of diminishing returns" in satisfaction for therapists in general, which came with increasing experience in doing co-therapy.

During the past two decades, there has been increased interest in the conjoint use of two therapists in treating individuals, groups, couples, and families. A comprehensive survey of 40 articles published between 1950 and 1970[1] finds many advocates of this procedure and relatively few detractors. Mullan and Sangiuliano (1960), to cite an example, list twenty-eight reported advantages of the use of two therapists in treatment. These center on (a) the more "valid" and objective observation and clarification of transference and countertransference, (b) the greater likelihood of a source of support for each therapist and for each

[1] Bibliography available on request.

patient, and (c) more rapid growth and knowledge of self for both the therapists and the patients as a by-product of enhanced feedback.

Most authors have stressed the importance of the relationship between the two therapists as a key determinant in the success of this method of therapy. In fact, critics of the method (Gans, 1962; Johnson, 1963; Slavson, 1950) have focused on the likelihood that two therapists do not have the flexibility, openness, and freedom from personal difficulties that would enable them to work effectively with one another for the patients' benefit. Gans (1962) concludes that there is little or no advantage for competent therapists to work together, although he feels the method might have some advantages for training therapists.

It is surprising that among the forty articles surveyed, there was not a single, careful, empirical study of co-therapy. In almost all cases, the authors discuss co-therapy from a clinical viewpoint and at most cite a small number of case studies to illustrate their points. Only three studies (Hoek and Wollstein, 1966; Rubin, 1967; Reding, et al., 1967) report samples of co-therapy cases large enough for statistical treatment. However, this was limited to some indication of the frequency of success of this procedure, either from the therapists' viewpoint, or as obtained by follow-up contact with the patients. Rabin (1967) was the only investigator to use a sizeable sample of therapists ($N = 38$) and to employ a control procedure (the feelings of the therapist about co-therapy versus his feelings about the use of only one therapist in treating groups). Rabin used descriptive statistics to present his findings, rather than statistical analysis. He found general agreement among the therapists surveyed in regard to the value of cotherapy (over regular group therapy) for groups in leading to (a) moderately more "therapeutic movement," (b) moderately more "working through," and (c) as the preferred method when a single treatment modality is used. His sample was made up of experienced group therapists, and this might limit the generalization of his findings to include inexperienced therapists or to those who do not do group therapy.

Working is a different clinical area, Masters and Johnson (1970) employ a co-therapy procedure with a specified therapeutic format to treat sexual problems. Although they do not report data from a large number of therapist pairs, their work has potential relevance for evaluating the effects of co-therapy in treating sexual problems.

In the present study, the following general predictions (stated, implied, or speculated about in previous work, but not empirically evaluated) were among those tested, using a large number of therapist pairs who treated married couples in four-way, conjoint co-therapy:

a. Experienced and inexperienced therapists will describe different patterns or "styles" of in-therapy behavior.

b. Depending upon therapeutic orientation or style, therapists may choose co-therapists with styles either similar or complementary to themselves (prediction of an interaction effect).

c. Certain factors heighten rated success of co-therapy, among them (a) felt compatibility with the co-therapist, (b) felt approval from the co-therapist, and (c) post-therapy discussion between the therapists.

Method

The Department of Psychiatry at the University of Wisconsin was surveyed. Co-therapy has been a regular and popular method of treating couples in outpatient psychotherapy at this facility since the arrival of Dr. Carl Whitaker in 1965. Each trainee (psychiatric resident or clinical psychology "fellow") and staff member (psychologist, psychiatrist, or social worker) who had participated in a recent co-therapy treatment experience filled out a questionnaire containing questions in regard to (a) his therapeutic "style" (b) the "style" of his co-therapist, (c) procedural facts about the therapy meetings, (d) his feelings about the effectiveness of the therapy, and (e) the staff and trainee members of the department he would most like to work with. The total sample contained self-descriptions of 50 therapists and included data on 40 cases as described by both co-therapists, plus 8 additional cases described by one of the original two therapists. Of the 40 cases in which data from both co-therapists was available, 17 were treated by two staff members, 8 by a staff member and a trainee, and 15 by two trainees.

Because experience has been shown to be an important variable in research on the effects of psychotherapy (Fey, 1958; Fiedler, 1950, 1951, Luborsky *et al.*, 1971; Meltzoff and Kornreich, 1971), the therapist sample was divided in 25 "experienced" (E) therapists and 25 "inexperienced" (IE) therapists. All therapists in the E group had completed their professional training and, in addition, were atively involved in the teaching and supervision of psychotherapy. The mean number of years of doing psychotherapy for the E therapists was 13.96 years ($\sigma = 6.89$) and for the IE therapists was 3.52 years ($\sigma = 3.02$), a highly significant difference between the two groups ($t = 6.96, df = 48, p < .001$). The mean number of couples seen in co-therapy for the E therapists was 9.96 ($\sigma = 19.47$) and for the IE therapists 7.76 ($\sigma = 9.39$). A t-test indicated no significant difference between the E and IE groups on this variable. The standard deviation for the experienced therapist reflects strong positive skewing and indicates that most E therapists have not seen a large number of couples in co-therapy, although they had much more experience than the IE therapists with other types of therapy (mostly individual psychotherapy). This is part a by-product of the fact that co-therapy is a recent professional innovation.

Comparisons among therapists were made via a series of self-descriptive statements, which appear in Table 1. For each of the statements the respondent marked a scale ranging from 1 ("never") to 5 ("always"). The factorial analysis of these self-descriptive statements in terms of therapist "styles" and comparison with the self-descriptions of one's preferred co-therapists formed the main body of data in the study.

Results

Therapist "Styles"

The responses of all 50 therapists to the self-descriptive items in Table 1 were intercorrelated and factor analyzed, using a principle components-varimax rotation procedure [see Cooley and Lohnes (1962)]. This yielded six principal. clusters or self-descriptive therapy factors. These six factors accounted for 57.4 per cent of the total variance in the factor matrix and were subjectively labeled as reflecting six different therapist "styles" or orientations. Each factor is orthogonal; none predicts any other.

The six "styles" of in-therapy behavior, the per cent of total *factor* variance of each, the key self-descriptive phrases (items which "load" highly on that factor) were:

    I. *Blank Screen* (20.5 per cent)--passive, unchanging, unprovocative, anonymous, and cautious.

    II. *Paternal* (16.8 per cent)—businesslike, patient, interpretive, interested in patient's history, and impartial.

    III. *Transactional* (16.6 per cent)—"here and now," casual relationship-oriented, interpretive, spontaneous.

    IV. *Authoritarian* (16.0 per cent)—theory-oriented, persistent, definite, goal-oriented, guiding, businesslike.

    V. *Maternal* (15.9 per cent)—talkative, explanatory, supportive, guiding, interpretive.

    VI. *Idiosyncratic* (14.1 per cent)—critical, unspontaneous, encourages conformity, nonprovocative, talkative.

Factor VI reflects some paradoxical features (talkative, yet nonprovocative) and is the most difficult factor to label subjectively. It could reflect a highly individualized and developed style and, therefore, was given the label "idiosyncratic." It may also suggest an "unusual" degree of honesty on the part of the therapist in terms of willingness to endorse self-descriptive items that do not have socially desirable connotations (e.g. the item, "critical, disapproving"). In this sense, the therapist whose in-therapy behavior is reflected in a high loading on Factor VI may have replied to the questionnaire with a different response "set" than the other therapists in the sample. The use of a differential "set" may also characterize other distinctive personality features in such a therapist that could perhaps contribute to a highly individualized style of in-therapy behavior.

Table 1
Self-description of Therapist's Behavior

Instructions: Let's agree that, as therapists, we vary our behavior to suit different kinds of patients, different stages with the same patient, etc.; thus, no one photo does us justice. Yet beneath these variations, you may have some sense of *your style in general*—that picture of you which a panel of observing therapists would get from watching you work, over time, with a variety of cases. Would you try to give us that sketch by responding rapidly, intuitively, to the following items? Encircle the appropriate number at left.

DEFINITELY NOT or NEVER

    Not much, not very or Rarely, occasionally

        Moderately or Cannot say; ±

            Quite a lot or Frequently, often

                DEFINITELY YES or ALWAYS

1 2 3 4 5	talkative
1 2 3 4 5	passive
1 2 3 4 5	explanatory
1 2 3 4 5	businesslike, "in charge"
1 2 3 4 5	supportive, reassuring
1 2 3 4 5	emphasizes "here-and-now" interaction
1 2 3 4 5	unchanging, consistent during hour
1 2 3 4 5	guiding, directing obliquely
1 2 3 4 5	provocative, challenging
1 2 3 4 5	guided by theory
1 2 3 4 5	anonymous, inscrutable
1 2 3 4 5	patient, willing to wait
1 2 3 4 5	interpretive, inferential
1 2 3 4 5	persistent, unyielding
1 2 3 4 5	interested in patient's history
1 2 3 4 5	casual, informal
1 2 3 4 5	critical, disapproving
1 2 3 4 5	objective, impartial
1 2 3 4 5	spontaneous, intuitive, improvising
1 2 3 4 5	working toward definite goals
1 2 3 4 5	focusing upon relationship(s)
1 2 3 4 5	encouraging conformity
1 2 3 4 5	cautious, premediated interventions

"Style" and Experience

On the basis of the above groupings, six transformed scores were obtained for each therapist, each score representing the relative prominence of that particular factor in his style. The group mean scores $(\bar{x})$ and standard deviations (σ) across the six factors for experienced and inexperienced therapists are presented in Table 2. The E therapists as a group describe themselves as highest on the Idiosyncratic factor and lowest on the Maternal factor. The IE therapists show the opposite pattern: highest on Maternal and lowest on Idiosyncratic. A rank order correlation (ρ) of 1.00 was obtained for the mean scores across factors of the E and IE therapists. This difference is highly significant ($\rho < .001$) and suggests that experienced and inexperienced therapists describe themselves and their in-therapy behavior differently.

Table 2
Means ($\bar{x}$) and Standard Deviations (σ) for Experienced and Inexperienced Therapists on Six Factors Reflecting Therapist "Style"

Factor	Label	Experienced (N=25)		Inexperienced (N=25)	
		$\bar{X}$	σ	$\bar{X}$	σ
I	Blank screen	51.00	15.06	47.76	14.83
II	Paternal	50.52	18.38	48.48	11.53
III	Transactional	48.76	16.61	50.42	13.64
IV	Authoritarian	49.40	17.46	49.68	12.96
V	Maternal	46.92	13.89	52.16	16.09
VI	Idiosyncratic	51.76	15.16	45.80	13.11

Additional documentation of this difference was attempted by a repeated measures analysis of variance (Edwards, 1960) performed on the factor scores for all therapists. This analysis yielded no significant main effect or interation; however, there was significant heterogeneity of variance in the factor scores, with E therapists showing greater variability than IE therapists ($F = 2.12$, $df = 149, 149, \rho < .001$). The implication is that E therapists as a group have both higher and lower scores on the different factors than the IE therapists, and this tends to cancel out any significance between group mean differences or interactions. In an attempt to reduce variability, a square root transformation was performed. Although the degree of heterogeneity of variance was reduced by this procedure, it remained significant ($F = 1.43$, $df = 149, 149$, $\rho < .025$), and further analysis was not undertaken. One might conclude from this finding that it reflects a more "differentiated" therapy style for the E therapists.

Co-therapist Preferences

Each therapist's factor scores were correlated with the mean factor scores determined from the self-descriptions of the six individuals he chose as "the co-therapist [he] would most like to treat a couple with." This provides some *tentative* ideas as to possible compatible and incompatible combinations of co-therapy "style." The following significant correlations and trends were obtained (see Table 3):

Table 3

Correlation of Experienced (E) and Inexperienced (IE) Therapist's "Style" Factor Scores with Mean "Style" Factor Scores of Those Individuals Preferred as Co-Therapists

Preferred Co-Therapist Factor	Therapist Factor											
	I		II		III		IV		V		VI	
	E	IE	E	IE	E	IE	E	IE	E	IE	E	IE
I	.42	−.16	.00	−.10	−.11	−.06	−.15	−.04	−.18	−.24	−.20	−.27
II	−.21	−.07	−.13	−.35*	−.23	.00	.07	−.04	−.22	−.04	.22	.00
III	−.24	.16	−.10	.15	.03	−.46§	.17	.31	−.17	−.04	.41†	−.04
IV	.02	.25	.21	.18	.34*	−.16	−.39†	.28	.12	.22	.28	.16
V	−.17	.35*	−.04	.04	−.15	−.30	.00	.47‡	.18	.50§	.13	.04
VI	−.62§	.05	.05	−.50§	−.02	.56§	.28	−.44†	.48‡	.11	.00	.04

*$p < .10$ (trend toward significance).
†$p < .05$
‡$p < .02$.
§$p < .01$.

Factor I (Blank Screen)—E therapist: wants co-therapist like himself, i.e. one who describes himself as also high on Blank Screen, (in Table 3, Factor I vs Factor I, r = .42, $\rho < .05$) and definitely doesn't want Idiosyncratic co-therapist. IE therapist: no significant preferences; some tendency to want Maternal co-therapist.

Factor II (Paternal)—E therapist: no significant preferences. IE therapist: tends not to want co-therapist like himself and definitely doesn't want Idiosyncratic co-therapist.

Factor III (Transactional)—E therapist: no significant preferences; tendency to want Authoritarian co-therapist. IE therapist: definitely doesn't want somebody like himself and definitely wants Idiosyncratic co-therapist.

Factor IV (Authoritarian)—E therapist: does not want co-therapist like himself. IE therapist: wants Maternal co-therapist and doesn't want Idiosyncratic co-therapist.

Factor V (Maternal)—E therapist: wants Idiosyncratic co-therapist. IE therapist: definitely wants co-therapist like himself.

Factor VI (Idiosyncratic)—E therapist: wants Transactional co-therapist. IE therapist: no significant preferences.

Further analysis of co-therapist preferences was performed by comparing the mean factor scores of individuals "chosen" as co-therapists by the E and IE therapist groups as a whole. Two of the six factors showed a highly significant between-group difference. E therapists preferred co-therapists who described themselves as significantly higher on Factor I (Blank Screen) and significantly lower on Factor III (Transactional) than those co-therapists chosen by IE therapists.[2] The implication is that experienced therapists as a group prefer a more "restrained" co-therapist, whereas inexperienced therapists prefer someone who will more actively join in the task with them.

Rated effectiveness of co-therapy. For each of the 40 cases reported by the therapists, both co-therapists were asked to answer independently the following 100-point rating scale item: "In your judgment, how effective was the therapy in this case?" In two instances the therapist did not respond, so a total of 78 ratings was obtained. It is important to note that this was the therapist's own subjective rating of the effectiveness of therapy and not a judgment by any external criterion. Data were available for 15 couples treated by two experienced therapists (E-E), 8 by an experienced and inexperienced co-therapy team (E-IE), and 16 by two inexperienced therapists (IE-IE). Mean effectiveness ratings were: E-E: $\bar{\chi}=54.80$ $(\sigma=20.88)$; E-IE: $\bar{\chi}=49.44$ $(\sigma=19.49)$; and IE-IE: $\bar{\chi}=56.84$ $(\sigma=18.11)$. An analysis of variance indicated no significant between-groups difference. However, the ratings for the E-IE co-therapist pairs were the lowest of the three groups, and this has implications for the hypothesis that for effective co-therapy, co-therapists should be of equal status. A definitive answer to this important co-therapy issue awaits a study using a larger number of cases than was employed here.

The following questionnaire items correlated significantly with the effectiveness of co-therapy, rated subjectively: For *both* E and IE therapists, only the item "How comfortable were you working with this co-therapist?" was significant (E: $r = .31, \rho < .05$, IE: $r = .37, \rho = .01$). One additional item: "Did you sense disapproval from your co-therapist?" was significant for the E therapists ($r = .38, \rho = .01$) and showed a trend toward significance for the IE therapists ($r=.26, \rho<.10$). These two items offer empirical confirmation of the importance in effective co-therapy of the relationship between the two therapists.

For E therapists, an additional item relating to peer group popularity (how often that individual was selected as a potential co-therapist from the group of experienced therapists) was significantly related to rated effectiveness of co-therapy ($r = .33, \rho <.05$). For IE therapists several additional items were significantly correlated with rated effectiveness:

   a. Number of months since termination ($r= -.43, \rho<.005$) ("memory is unkind").
   b. Conflict of goals between treating "marriage" and treating individuals ($r= -40, \rho<.01$).
   c. Frequent switch of therapist's loyalty from one spouse to another ($r= -.40, \rho<.01$).

[2] Factor I: $\bar{\chi}E=55.80, \sigma=5.05 \chi IE=50.80, \sigma=4.45; t=3.73, df=48, \rho>.001$;
Factor III: $\bar{\chi}E=43.44, \sigma=5.82; \chi IE=48.84, \sigma=4.69; t=3.62, df=48, \rho>.001$.

d. Felt discrepancy of goals with co-therapist ($r = -.30, p < .05$). As the latter item was not significant for the E therapists, the implication is that experienced therapists more likely choose co-therapists with similar goals or that goal discrepancy is not as important for them in determining the effectiveness of co-therapy.

e. Felt competition with co-therapist ($r = -.35, p < .02$).

f. Usefulness of post-therapy session talks with co-therapist ($r = .38, p < .01$).

g. Felt candidness in post-therapy session talks ($r = .44, p < .005$).

In summary, subjectively rated effectiveness of co-therapy was related to somewhat different variables for E and IE co-therapists. For both, a comfortable and mutually approving relationship between the therapist was important. In addition, IE therapists felt the need for compatible goals, a noncompetitive relationship, and candid, post-therapy session talks.

Attitude toward co-therapy. There were some suggestive and rather surprising findings that satisfaction from doing co-therapy for therapists *in general* may reach a point of diminishing returns with increasing amounts of co-therapy done. For E therapists, the item "Do you welcome the idea of four-way therapy?" showed a highly significant negative correlation with number of couples seen in co-therapy ($r = -.42, p = .005$). For IE therapists, the item "How comfortable were you working with your co-therapist?" also showed a significant negative relationship with number of couples seen ($r = -.34, p = .02$).

The question "How valuable to a couple is having a co-therapist?" showed a relationship with the following two items, significant for both E and IE therapists: (a) "Did you develop a feeling or 'transference' for the couple and regard them as a unit?" ($E:r = .31, p < .05$; $IE:r = .32, p < .05$) and (b) "Did you develop a feeling that you and your therapist became a unit or couple yourselves?" ($E: r = .52, p < .001$; $IE: r = .33, p = .02$). These items suggest important co-therapy parameters; however, they reflect the therapist's attitudes and values toward co-therapy and are not significantly correlated with subjectively rated effectiveness of co-therapy, discussed previously.

Discussion

The major statistically documented conclusions of this study are: (a) experienced and inexperienced therapists as a group have different personal therapeutic "styles" and different preferences as to the "style" desired in a co-therapist; (b) subjectively rated effectiveness of co-therapy is related to therapist comfortableness in the co-therapy relationship and felt acceptance by the co-therapist; and (c) there may be a "point of diminishing returns" in co-therapy satisfaction for therapists in general, which comes with increasing amounts of co-therapy done.

Other investigators (McNair and Lorr, 1962, 1964; Sundland and Barker, 1962) have attempted to measure different therapist "styles." Sundland and Barker (1962) and McNair and Lorr (1964) found that experience of the therapist was not significantly related to differential technique pattern or factor scores. The suggestive finding in the present study of a differential factor pattern for E and IE therapists would stand in contrast to these results; however, it will be recalled that the present sample of E therapists showed a significantly greater variability across factor scores and that this is perhaps the most meaningful differentiation between E and IE therapists. In addition to using different questionnaires to compare therapists, both Sundland and Barker and McNair and Lorr used therapists who had completed their training, while the IE group of the present study was composed primarily of therapists still in training. This along might account for the E-IE differences found here. To further elaborate the experience variable, an attempt is currently being made to replicate our findings using a longitudinal sample of therapists, divided into a larger number of experience levels.

A question might arise as to the differential effect of male and female co-therapists. There were six female therapists in our sample of 50, and they were all in the IE group. Thus we did not have a large enough sample of female therapists to evaluate adequately the effects of this variable beyond ascertaining that the "styles" of the female therapists did not confound the overall pattern of therapist factors for the IE group. The area of sex differences of co-therapists seems an interesting one for further study.

Perhaps the most surprising finding of the study concerns the "point of diminishing returns" in co-therapy satisfaction with increasing numbers of couples seen. The implication is that co-therapy may be the continuing "bag" for only a few therapists. A longitudinal study of co-therapy with a large number of therapists would seem helpful in further elaborating the question of a "point of diminishing returns" in co-therapy satisfaction.

REFERENCES

Cooley, W.W., and P.R. Lohnes (1962), *Multivariate Procedures for the Behavioral Sciences.* New York: John Wiley & Sons, Chap. 8.

Edwards, A.L. (1960), *Experimental Design in Psychological Research.* New York: Holt, Rinehart & Winston, pp. 227-232.

Fey, W.F. (1958), "Doctrine and Experience: Their Influence upon the Psychotherapist," *Journal of Consulting Psychology,* 22:403-409.

Fiedler, F.E. (1950), "A Comparison of Therapeutic Relationships in Psychoanalytic, Nondirective, and Adlerian Therapy," *Journal of Consulting Psychology,* 14:436-445.

———(1951), "Factor Analyses of Psychoanalytic, Nondirective, and Adlerian Therapeutic Relationships," *Journal of Consulting Psychology,* 15:32-38.

Gans, R.W. (1962), "Group Co-therapists in the Therapeutic Situation: A Critical Evaluation," *International Journal of Group Psychotherapy,* 12:82-88.

Hoek, A., and S. Wollstein (1966), "Conjoint Psychotherapy of Married Couples: A Clinical Report," *International Journal of Social Psychiatry,* 12:209-216.

Johnson, J.A. (1963), *Group Therapy: A Practical Approach.* New York: McGraw-Hill.

Luborsky, L., M. Chandler, A.H. Auerbach, J. Cohen, and H.M. Bachrach (1971), "Factors Influencing the Outcome of Psychotherapy: A Review of Quantitative Research," *Psychological Bulletin,* 75:145-185.

Masters, W.H., and V.E. Johnson (1970), *Human Sexual Inadequacy.* Boston: Little, Brown & Co.

McNair, D.M., and M. Lorr (1962), "Therapist 'Type' and Patient Response to Psychotherapy," *Journal of Consulting Psychology,* 26:425-429.

———(1964), "An Analysis of Professed Psychotherapeutic Techniques," *Journal of Consulting Psychology,* 28:265-271.

Meltzoff, J., and M. Kornreich (1970), *Research in Psychotherapy.* New York: Atherton Press, pp. 384-394.

Mullan, H. and I. Sangiuliano (1960), "Multiple Psychotherapeutic Practice: Preliminary Report," *American Journal of Psychotherapy,* 14:550-565.

Rabin, H. (1967), "How Does Co-therapy Compare with Regular Group Therapy," *American Journal of Psychotherapy,* 21:244-255.

Reding, G.R., L.A. Charles and M.B. Hoffman (1967), "Treatment of a Couple by a Couple: II. Conceptual Framework, Case Presentation, and Follow-up Study," *British Journal of Medical Psychology,* 40:243-252.

Slavson, A.R. (1950), *Analytic Group Psychotherapy.* New York: Columbia University Press.

Sundland, D.M., and E.N. Barker (1962), "The Orientation of Psychotherapists," *Journal of Consulting Psychology.* 26:201-212.

Section B

Marital Change in the Family and Group Context

CARL A. WHITAKER

7   **A Family Therapist Looks at Marital Therapy**

In this chapter an eminent family therapist responds to several issues raised by the editors with regard to the differences and similarities between marital therapy and family therapy in the framework of a systems approach to treatment. The following issues are highlighted and elaborated: (1) What is "Marital" therapy to a family therapist? (2) How do techniques differ? (3) What is the meaning of children's presence in treatment? (4) How does the husband-wife relationship change in family therapy? (5) Are the functions of marital and family therapy different? (6) How do the goals of these therapeutic approaches compare?

As soon as one begins to define forms of therapy that go beyond the one-to-one model, a good deal of clarification is needed. Many terms are used in reference to treatment within the family context: conjoint therapy ordinarily refers to the simultaneous treatment of all the family members; individual therapy refers to the treatment of only one member of the family, usually the "scapegoat," i.e., the family member who relieves the anxiety of the whole family system by taking the "blame" for its troubles. There are different types of family scapegoats, which I call the "white knight scapegoat" and the "black sheep scapegoat." The second type is more easily recognized by most therapists as the so-called "bad guy" or "villain" in the system. The "white knight," or family "hero" is what most of *us* are, the successful, achieving

*This chapter represents the distillation of discussions between the author and the editors, in response to several questions and issues posed to Dr. Whitaker by Drs. Gurman and Rice.

types who are thought of as the "healthy" one in our family. Actually, we are just as much the victim as the "black sheep" but most of us don't know it. In my work with families and couples, I usually play down the scapegoat from the very beginning and may get back to that person only much later and with a different family "set" toward him or her. Unfortunately, many therapists get seduced into using the "white knight" as their co-therapist. The mistake is that when we take on the knight as our co-therapist, we have unwittingly joined the family in its pathological efforts at subgrouping.

What Is Marital Therapy to a Family Therapist?

I define marital therapy as *the treatment of a couple who have no children*, whereas family therapy is *the treatment of a two-generational unit*. Any two-generational unit fits this definition, whether it is composed of parents and their own biological children, children by a previous marriage, or adopted children. *Treatment of the husband-wife axis within a two-generational unit, that is, treatment of the parents without their children, is probably better defined as family therapy of a subgroup*. Counseling involves a more advisory and educational sort of relationship. Therapy, on the other hand, is an experience with someone who is capable of handling symbolic levels of relating and one in which there is a more profound involvement of parent-child transference. Actually, psychotherapy of the husband-wife axis or, if you will, the father-mother axis, is really just one inefficient method of treating this subgroup as the family scapegoat, just as we used to mistakenly treat the child member because of the symptoms he or she had in defense of the whole family. Another comparison of interest is that of crisis intervention with a couple or family. This is an emergency measure and, as such, is often much less demanding of the therapist than the processes of ongoing growth-oriented therapy with the entire family, which is my special area of interest and work.

Again, I see *all* individual therapy as a method for treating the family, albeit very indirectly by way of the available scapegoat. When individual therapy has lasting beneficial effects rather than temporary relief, I assume that is because the therapy has been powerful enough so that it has altered the dynamics of the family as a whole. Similarly, one can work with the couple, or parent subgroup, and get change for the good because anything that puts stress on the system can create a pressure to get reorganized. This kind of therapy does not work well with a system that is grossly disturbed. The initial factor may be not so much a matter of who is there during the sessions, but where the therapist is at in his or her thinking, that is, the therapist's attitude toward what is going on and what it all means. Bowen, for example, will sometimes isolate one member of the family and treat him or her only, with the rest of the family just looking on or even kept out of his office.

I define all couples therapy as the treatment of a three-client unit: the husband is one patient, the wife is one patient, and the relationship is one patient. Couples therapy, then, is really the treatment of a triangle with all the aspects of that unit, i.e., teaming, collusion, mediation, and scapegoating. Family therapy, as the treatment of a two-generational unit that consists of mother, father, and children, deals with *multiple* triangles, collusions, schisms, skews, accusers, scapegoats, etc. Family therapy is the psychotherapy of the system as a whole. The objective of such therapy is an increase in groupness, along with increased individuation and flexibility of role structure. Flexibility of role structure means that roles are not rigidly fixed and can be interchanged without discomfort, such as when the children play parentlike roles to their own parents.

Bowen's (1966) and Jackson's (Watzlawick, Beavin, and Jackson, 1967) views about therapy are somewhat different from mine because both of them were influenced in their concepts of treating the family by their training in psychoanalysis. That influence is somewhat expressed in Jackson's work by his conviction that treatment is training in communication, i.e., individuals learn to talk to, rather than live with, each other. That, of course, is the basic one-to-one model. Bowen also deals largely in the couple pattern. He treats the married parent or nonparent couple as though it were the entire family. At times, he structures the therapy in a psychoanalytic manner by directing all dialogues between himself and one spouse at a time, while not allowing the husband and wife to talk to each other during the session.

Virginia Satir (1964), whose work is based to some extent on that of Jackson and Bateson, is essentially a student of communication. This approach, with its attention to "feedback," to me implies a neurotic understructure, so that I doubt that this model can be used effectively with people who are very primitively organized. On the other hand, communication training can be very useful with highly educated and intelligent people. Satir's approach to couple and family therapy goes beyond Jackson's however, in its modeling of family distortion patterns in regard to both the dynamics of power and the dynamics of communication.

In contrast to Bowen and Jackson, who both felt that the treatment of a two-generational unit was less desirable, whatever the symptoms, Nathan Ackerman (1966) and I have both operated on the basis that two generations is *the* basic unit for treatment and that three generations are preferable. Speck (Speck and Attneave, 1973) is even convinced that the best results can be obtained by getting together an even larger group, that is, a "network" of the extended family and friendship relations. A related but somewhat different approach is that of Auerswald (1968), who is more concerned with the profes-sional network from whom families having been getting help, including social and religious agencies, private practitioners, etc. Thus Auerswald tries to concentrate all of these helping efforts on the current situational family stress.

How Do Techniques Differ in Family and Couple Therapy?

Bowen's and Jackson's techniques are quite different from mine, in that they basically concentrate on the husband-wife axis. For example, in Bowen's three-couple group sessions, twenty minutes are spent for each couple in talking to Bowen, with no communication between the couples. Jackson attempted to instigate change in communication patterns, although the change may be precipitated by experiential stress as well as by educational techniques. Both Ackerman and Satir are basically power manipulators. For Satir, the theoretical ideas she follows to change the power dimensions in the family are based on her notions of the personality types of the blamer, the placator, the mediator, and the irrelevant person (Satir, 1972).

My primary technique in couples treatment is to deliberately plan to establish a triangle including myself, and to include the parents of each of the couple, preferably on their first visit and, if not then, at least at a later visit. Thus, I try to get authorization from the extended family from replacing it as the significant older generation person for the couple. I demand control of the new situation that psychotherapy is and demand the right to call the rules and their change or establishment. Having established or won this battle for structure, my next rule is that the couple or the family must take initiative for any change, that the therapist is a facilitator and an affect maximizer. In this way, I intentionally create a double-bind condition in my effort to reconstruct the original child-parent situation in the transference. I see the initial phase of family and couples therapy as political manipulation, in which I deliberately plan to help decathect the family scapegoat, whether it is the marriage, the father, the mother, or one of the children.

I also make major efforts to cathect the outside person in the group, who is usually the father, and attempt to involve him in therapy at the very beginning. I plan to set the situation so that mother is role-protected and neutralized until the midphase of the family therapy in much the same way one protects the queen in a chess game. I believe that therapy is most efficient and useful if the entire system is enfranchised and anxiety is roughly equal in each member and each subgroup and that the power for change comes from the mobilization of the total system.

I consider a couple who have no children as playing at being "mommy" and "daddy." For such couples, therapy should ideally include their parents. When the couple has their own children, there is reification of the "we-ness." The whole structure of the relationship then changes in such a way that the husband and wife become transferred to each other, replacing their transferences to their original parents.

What Is the Importance and Meaning of Including Children in Therapy?

The absence from therapy of children of any age lessens the likelihood that change will be stable and kept alive. Once the entire system has been involved in treatment, it *is* possible to continue therapy with just a subgroup, such as the father-mother pair. The relevance and power of treatment probably depends a great deal on its being sanctioned by the entire family system. My view on this issue is that the power of what happens in any interview is multiplied, depending on the number of family members present. For example, the warmth of the system is greatly increased by the presence of very small children, even babies. Anybody in the family belongs and any exclusions must be validated. For me, their inclusion is the rule. Let me offer an example of the way in which the presence of children alters the perspective of "what is the problem." Every child present in the family makes the question of divorce into two problems: a couple struggling with their pairing relationship, and two parents struggling with the problem of their projections and the power dynamics of their competition as parents. Furthermore, children will often "do the dance of their parents," so that the therapist can, for example, see that how the children relate to one another is sometimes exactly the way the husband and wife relate. With the whole family present, the therapist also has an "in" by relating to the children. By playing with the children and getting their affect, the therapist can quickly become a significant part of the family, through the real cuddling of the children, which constitutes symbolic cuddling of the mother and father.

It seems to me that the treatment of the husband-wife subgroup is a remnant of the psychoanalytic intrapsychic mythology in that it denies the power of the total family system. Certainly the husband-wife axis is central, but the entire system is under stress and, therefore, the entire system is the one that exercises control and power. I believe that both individual therapy and husband-wife axis therapy are less efficient and are often utilized by therapist and family alike to avoid the stresses present in the treatment of the whole system. If everyone is included, then a dialectic of belonging and individuating can take place. Anyone who is absent is further dissociated from the family system and may end up with severe affect hunger from the make-believe notion that this symbolic parenthood which we call psychotherapy can be a substitute for the reintegration of the family as such.

Some clinicians who work with couples find that the presence of children in the sessions creates unnecessary distraction in their work. I think this kind of feeling is likely to exist when the therapist's goals are mainly in the verbal and intellectual areas of the couple's relationship. The kinds of criteria a therapist uses to judge the effects of his work are central here. My work with families is growth-oriented and not organized around symptoms, as seen in my disregarding of the family's elected scapegoat. When a therapist sees only the parents, it is analogous in principle to treating one member of the couple without the other.

By doing so, the therapist cannot establish the complementary aspects of the system relationships, and, in effect, ends up doing two individual psychotherapies. Also, it seems to me that whether a therapist includes young children in the treatment or not probably depends on whether he or she has had professional experience with children or at least has children of his or her own. Another way of saying this is that therapists who exclude the children may not be very comfortable with children in general.

How Does the Marital Relationship Change in Family Therapy?

The marital relationship during family treatment becomes more defined as a subgroup of the extended family, with increased clarity of the generation gap and with the perspective that father and mother were children in their own families of origin and will always be so in a limited sense. This model of unity and separateness is a prototype for the relationship of husband and wife, so that each expands his individual personhood and is thereby free to mate without being caught in the bilateral adoption game or the bilateral pseudotherapy game. If the extended family roles become matters of choice, not prisons, then pairing becomes the pilot project for losing oneself in larger wholes without either symbiosis or coldness. Such freedom within the marriage makes scapegoating the children or the parents pointless. In this context, I define the normal family as one in which all roles are available to each individual depending upon the situation. For example, a six-year-old says, "Daddy, can I cut the meatloaf?" and Dad says, "Yes, and why don't you serve the potatoes and vegetables, too, and I'll sit in your place and complain"; or Mother comes home with a headache and says to her four-year-old daughter, "Would you rub my neck? I have a bad headache and I feel lousy." The daughter is thus free to be mother to her own mother, just as the son was free to be father to his own father and to his family group. Such role flexibility makes it possible not only for each member to play psychodrama games with the family situation, but also for the parents and the children to fight for the roles they want in the basic structure of the family model. If the father can play little boy, he's then more adequaté at playing Daddy, and if the son can play Daddy, he's more adequate at playing little boy. It should also be clear that if father and mother are free to play dependent games in their family, then they are less apt to play fixated dependent-child roles with each other or unhealthy fixated adult therapists or parents roles with each other.

It seems to me that therapy of the husband-wife axis tends to make believe that the two are back in adolescence trying to rechoose their mate, trying to reopen their individuation as though it had never been damaged by the years of marriage. Treatment of the husband-wife axis in the systems framework, which takes the children into account, adds the third dimension of reality, already biologically established, and makes this a fact in the therapy of the twosome. Therapy of the husband-wife axis involves, therefore, both the person-to-person relationship, the husband and wife role relationship, and the parent relationship. For example, the parents may learn from the therapist a new model for parental functioning, since the therapist is able to enjoy the children during the hour. The parents may get a new sense of their children as individuals because the therapist sensed them as ''people'' rather than as ''pests.''

Couples cannot become genuinely transferred to the therapist until each of them becomes separated from their own families. They can only get free by going back and reuniting, so that the separation is a joint project, not a pseudoseparation. They must go back into the family and take their ''senior year'' all over again so that they let their families go and their families let them go. That way, the separation is one of honor instead of a ''dishonorable discharge.'' In many older traditional marriages, people got married and individuation disappeared in the quest for ''togetherness.'' Nowadays, society seems to have moved to a ''do your own thing'' era in which only individuality is valued. Family therapy is an effort to help develop groupness *and* individuation concurrently (see Anonymous, 1972). This is the way it has to be, since you cannot have more of one than you have of the other.

In marital therapy, the parentification of therapist and the triangulation with the therapist may be therapeutic, but the process is less powerful and liable to reversal under the role expectations of the uninvolved members of the system and even more so by the demands of the system itself. Treatment of the husband-wife axis in the nuclear family seems to work like the treatment of the individual separately from the husband-wife axis. The treatment tends to augment the husband-wife split and sets up competition between the therapist-patient dyad and the husband-wife dyad. Thus, couples treatment tends to facilitate an emotional divorce between the husband-wife axis and the children, who are excluded just as the mate is excluded during individual treatment.

How Do the Functions of Marital and Family Therapists Differ?

In my opinion, marital therapy, i.e., the treatment of a couple without children, calls for less training than family therapy. This is because in marital therapy the therapist acts as a consultant to an ongoing ''bilateral impasse psychotherapy'' (see Whitaker, 1966). That is, in the typical American marriage, each spouse tries to be the therapist to the other spouse, or in Berne's terms, the parent, in order to straighten each other out. The couple seeks professional therapeutic aid when their own ''therapeutic'' attempts have failed. Since the husband and wife are already transferred to each other, the therapist does not have to carry all the symbolic transference and, therefore, can serve in a less demanding supervisory role to the couple's own self-help efforts. The therapist does not need to control the system and minimal input can often be very facilitative.

Family therapy, in contrast, must have the power to challenge the entire system. The therapist should be emotionally "separated" from his own family, had some psychotherapy, preferably family therapy, and be well trained in the strategies of group therapy and the manipulation of triangles. An individual therapist, with fairly limited training, can easily treat a couple without a child, since that is essentially a nonsymbolic transference relationship and is more easily modified. An individual with fairly limited training can do crisis intervention with a couple or with a family as he or she would do with an individual. Treating a family is easy in the beginning one, two, or three interviews, but the power of the family tends to fairly soon absorb the therapist or extrude him and he becomes impotent. He cannot model the uniting and the individuating which is necessary to bring about change. For a family therapist to be effective, it is particularly important that he be able to move into the family, to catalyze affect, and move out of the family to maintain his own separateness and to model both uniting and individuating. The danger of the single-therapist approach in family therapy is of being incorporated by the family or of picking a "co-therapist" out of the family for the therapist's own support.

The therapist must be able to get "into" the family. When he works alone with a family, he becomes vulnerable and that is when a real co-therapist is especially helpful. Therefore, co-therapy is often necessary both to protect him when he moves in and to strengthen him when it becomes essential to move back out.

The important issues in co-therapy are mostly based on the "marriage" of those therapists, but the power of the family makes the professional marriage liable to more stress. The co-therapy team working with a couple who have no children, that is, a one-generational unit, are in a very fortunate position because the stress does not have the biological identification voltage or affective investment which takes place with the arrival of children, where each spouse sees the other spouse and himself or herself reflected in the face, behavior, and affect of the child. Thus, co-therapy teams working with a couple are apt to develop a comfortable parental role and to be able to move from that to a four-person peer relationship in a fairly comfortable way.

Working with a two-generational or three-generational family unit is liable to develop multiple transferences in the therapist; he or she sees the parents in the model of his own parents and in the model of himself as a parent. The therapist may become twisted and contorted by his or her own countertransference vectors, and by affective investments. For example, it is a little easier to treat a couple without involving your own life model, moral tone, life experience, or personal life expectations, because in marital therapy one can be a sort of outside consultant. However, the treatment of a two-generational family unit necessitates that the therapist, if he goes beyond crisis intervention, put his own personhood, family style, and personal background on the line. The therapist may not need to involve these personal qualities overtly and verbally, but they are apparent, and they will be part of the therapy whether he wants them to be or not. In contrast, most of the training for individual therapy is a training in increased empathy, sensitivity, and communication, sending and receiving, and the therapist is usually the more powerful person in the setting. Family therapy, like group therapy, many times involves the therapist in the setting where he or she is not the most powerful person but where the family is the most powerful. The therapist must then operate from a framework that needs not only the sensitivity for involvement but also the toughness for withdrawal. The therapist can be made completely impotent by being absorbed into the family through its warmth. He or she can also be seduced by the family's "pseudomutual" quality or its "pseudohostile" quality and can be rendered useless by being made into a role-structured member of the family.

What Are the Goals of Marital and Family Therapy?

In general, couples treatment is more successful than family therapy since the one-generational unit is but a part of the system and tends to reestablish the bonds or go on to get a legal or emotional divorce, thus making the leap into complete individuation. Success here would be defined as "we will love each other for life, but cannot live together without too great a sacrifice of our personhood."

Success in family therapy, like success in individual therapy, is highly idiosyncratic and the outcome is quite variable. My illustration is that I'm like a piano teacher—some people come just to learn the chords, some like to stay on and play Beethoven, some have have more talent, some fit me better—and all of these variables make the outcome very different, depending upon the situation, in a much more subtle way even than in one-to-one therapy. A less intensely involved, more educationally oriented "technical" treatment of neurotics seems feasible, whereas technical treatment of psychotics is not feasible; similarly, technical treatment of couples is quite reasonable, but such treatment of families is not.

The goals of couples treatment seem to me to be: (1) to increase the affect investment of each spouse in himself; (2) to increase the available affect for each spouse to invest in some significant other, that is, the therapist, the current mate, a parent, or a sib; (3) a complete divorce from parents, siblings, or other previous pairings; and (4) an intensified relationship of each individual to the therapist, to achieve a maximum level of creativity, unity, and freedom.

The goals of family therapy would be: (1) reintegration of the family system as a whole; (2) the establishment of flexible relationships between the subgroups of the family, e.g., parents and children, male and females, triangles, pairs, and individuals; (3) equal distribution or an equal assumption of anxiety for the state of the family and for each individual's own adaptation; and (4) a freedom from fixated role demands and the availability of any role to any family member, as appropriate to the situation.

Obviously some of these goals for couple and family therapy overlap, but there are some important differences. It is often very difficult to know when these goals have been achieved. Still, many of these goals involve not so much "moving toward" highly specific end points, but rather "living in" a complex process of change.

REFERENCES

Ackerman, N. (1966), "Family Psychotherapy—Theory and Practice," *American Journal of Psychotherapy,* 20:405–414.

Anonymous (1972), "Toward the Differentiation of a Self in One's Own Family." In J.L. Framo (ed.), *Family Interaction,* New York: Springer, pp. 111-166.

Auerswald, E. H. (1968), "Interdisciplinary versus Ecological Approach," *Family Process,* 7:202-215.

Bowen, M. (1966), "The Use of Family Theory in Clinical Practice." *Comprehensive Psychiatry,* 7:345-374.

Satir, V. (1964), *Conjoint Family Therapy.* Palo Alto, Calif.: Science & Behavior Books.

———(1972), *Peoplemaking.* Palo Alto, Calif.: Science & Behavior Books.

Speck, R. V., and C. L. Attneave, (1973), *Family Networks.* New York: Random House.

Watzlawick, P., J. H., Beavin, and D. D. Jackson, (1967), *Pragmatics of Human Communication.* New York: W. W. Norton.

Whitaker, C. A. (1966), "Serial Impasses in Marriages," *Psychiatric Research Report No. 20,* American Psychiatric Association.

ELSA LEICHTER

8   Treatment of Married Couples Groups

Treatment of married couples in groups by one therapist is described. Emphasis is placed on the fact that treatment problems and process in such groups are quite different from therapy groups in which the participants are not related outside the group and on the need to differentiate between couples groups according to social and chronological stages.

For at least the last decade, the treatment of married couples groups as a therapeutic method increasingly has been used in the spectrum of marital therapy. There are still therapists—chiefly from the orthodox psychoanalytic school of thought—who work with one married partner exclusively and refuse even to talk to the spouse. Some find cooperative work by two therapists with each partner useful. However, an increasing number of therapists, whose major focus is on the marital relationship as such, treat the couple as a unit. In the treatment of married couples in groups two major categories can be found:

(1) Parents groups, often as an adjunct to therapy of the child, where the major goal is some modification of the parental functioning of the couple.

(2) Married couples groups proper in which the change of the marital relationship as such is the goal of therapy, but the treatment of the couple takes place within the structure of the group.

This article will focus on two major aspects of the treatment of married couples groups:

(1) On the fact that the process in the married couples group is largely affected by its structure: Some characteristic treatment problems and process phenomena in married couples groups are quite different from other therapy

groups in which the participants have no relationship other than in the treatment group.

(2) On the necessity to differentiate between the various married couples groups according to the social and chronological stages of the marriage. Furthermore, the approach of therapists with a family orientation to see "significant others" together with the married couple in family interviews as an occasional supplement to the treatment in the married couples group will also be touched upon.

THE SPECIAL CHARACTERISTICS AND TREATMENT PROBLEMS OF ALL MARRIED COUPLES GROUPS

A married couples group consisting of four or five couples is drastically different from other therapy groups with eight to ten participants who are strangers to each other. Each couple brings to the married couples group a joint history, a past, and they share a very powerful reality from which they come to the group session and to which they return to live with each other for a week till the next session. Thus, one can safely say that the married couples group consists of four or five subgroups which in fact must and, indeed, does have a strong impact on the developing group and treatment process.

Perhaps the most important is the expectation and hope of what group treatment will offer: Whereas in other therapy groups the expectation is some change of the self (even though wishes for magic may be at play), the couples usually are expecting change of the mate rather than of themselves. This is so in spite of the fact that in the initial treatment contract between therapist and couple there has to be a modicum of acceptance of the thought that the marital relationship needs modification, something which ought to imply that each partner has to take some responsibility for his own behavior and attitudes in the marriage.

Undoubtedly, in therapy groups of individuals there is also a good deal of projecting and blaming of outside forces for one's difficulties. However, in the married couples group, the projection is on the "present other"—the marital partner—and the demand that he or she change to meet the needs of the mate are all acted out in the group. Even though the mate is right there in the room, he or she will be "talked about" in terms of severe complaints, if not real attacks, or the marital partners will be involved repeatedly in a circular fight in which neither takes any self-responsibility. At the same time, group and therapist are not allowed to "get in."

Absences from the group have quite specific ramifications in a married couples group, since one partner's resistance or inability to attend a session often leads to the absence of the mate. This is especially true in the early phase when the couple interprets the idea of the "marital relationship being the focus of therapy.'' as meaning that in the group they must be a symbiotic unit and either be there together or not at all. This distortion, however, signifies more than just that.

If the nonattendance of the session is a reflection of resistance by one of the marital partners, there is a good chance that there will be a strong pull to keep the other, also, out of the session whether it is to punish the group, and (or) the therapist, or to prevent the mate from moving in a direction that is very upsetting. However, occasionally one partner may wish to attend a session without the mate (and then will find a way of preventing the mate from coming), in order to use such a session for the purpose of sharing with the group something about himself or herself, which he does not want the mate to know. While the accumulation of secrets between group and one of the spouses obviously is not desirable therapeutically, the one session without the mate can make it possible for the partner to test out the group's reaction in greater safety before he ventures letting the partner into the secret, if such, indeed, is at all feasible.

When more than one couple are absent from a session the group may seriously feel that its survival is threatened and the therapist (unless experienced and fairly clear about the dynamics of the absences) may easily merge with the group's anxiety and sense of abandonment instead of enabling the group to deal with its ''crisis.'' Dealing with its ''crisis'' often means talking about what happened in previous group sessions that led to the absences and, perhaps, more importantly, giving the group a chance to express feelings of dissatisfaction about treatment to each other or to the therapist, which due to their hostile nature had been censured heretofore. The more such communications are permitted in the group, the less it is probable that its participants will act out, either through absenting themselves and pulling their partners along or literally through ''sitting on their anger.''

Even if couples do not act out through absenting themselves from the group, they do have to live with each other day and night, and delayed or postponed reactions to the mate about what occurred in a given group session can be powerfully punitive and retaliative. The mate may have ventured for the first time to confront his partner with anger or hurt for what the partner has been doing to him or depriving him of. However, the partner's punitive and retaliative reaction literally can throw the mate back in his attempt to break through a pathological pattern of interaction and take some time till he recuperates and can take a chance again.

Yet, such confrontations are necessary, because in order to achieve the capacity to give, to relate, and to love, one also has to achieve the capacity to let oneself feel and where possible to express appropriate anger. Where anger goes far back into early childhood it takes usually the form of rage, a diffuse sense of hostility, and is largely irrational. In the therapy situation, the attempt is to convert rage into anger which can be expressed about a specific situation and about and, most importantly, toward a specific person. If this anger eventually is received without counterhostility, and the individual gradually learns to separate his or her childhood rage from appropriate potent anger, some of the bound-up inner energies are freed and can be used for more truly intimate relationships.

All therapy groups allow for a large range of interaction between the participants. Sometimes there is criticism that individuals are exposed to too much attacking. This may be true in some groups where ''expression of anger'' seems to become a purpose in and of itself. For a truly therapeutic group, however, the capacity to love better, rather than to hate better, is the goal.

In the married couples group, this whole issue has added a special significance, since the goal of ''learning to love better'' (if at all possible) is aimed at five dyadic highly rigidified subsystems in the group. The group as a whole gives each individual the opportunity to interact in any way with others, including the therapist and through the feedbacks he gets gradually to learn new and more appropriate patterns of relating. In essence, a married couples group tends to operate as a ''third family,'' which in the last analysis means that it gives each individual and couple another chance to come to life and to grow, whereas the real family (primary or present) has had a growth-thwarting effect. This is true of all therapy groups, but again the fact that each individual comes as part of a couple has its own significance. In a sense, the group as a whole represents the transferential mother. Wishes and expectations are directed at it, and dissatisfactions, as well as feelings of disappointments are equally directed at ''it,'' ''them,'' ''the group.'' (''They don't understand,'' ''they always interrupt me,'' ''they ignore me,'' or ''the group is wonderful, the only place where you can be real honest, etc.'')

In the early group process especially, the need to share time and attention with others tends to be experienced as deprivation or as in real families as a feeling that there is not enough to go around. Thus, sibling rivalries are stimulated in regard to ''preferred'' individuals and (or) ''preferred couples.'' Sometimes it can happen that a couple will not return to the next session because ''our marriage, or we, are not as interesting as the other couples,'' or ''we cannot be as aggressive as couple X, Y, or Z.'' Interestingly, however, sibling rivalries often develop between marital partners themselves, which may rather dramatically reflect their rivalrous relationship on the outside. Feelings such as ''he is pulling the wool over your eyes,'' ''you are always picking on me, but let her get away scot free,'' are frequently expressed. Later, when change in one of the partners occurs the spouse frequently reacts with jealousy and denial of the change. (As indicated earlier, there is almost always a reaction to the change because it upsets momentarily the marital equilibrium.)

In the group, unlike in the primary families, these feelings are allowed full expression and each individual in the group has the opportunity of finding out his own particular way of coping with such feelings. For example, in the couples group the person who, due to anger, does not come to the next session often is the husband or wife who "pack their suitcase" at the slightest provocation (and for comparable reasons: "Not getting enough"). This connection can be made particularly well within the group situation.

The therapist quite naturally at times becomes an important object of dissatisfaction, this dissatisfaction often is transferred onto the group peers—siblings, as frequently happens in families. If the messages or behavior seem to indicate such a move, redirecting of the anger for "unmet needs" onto the therapist in the presence of the group can have considerable therapeutic value. There has to be much freedom and acceptance for the irrational demand to be brought out: The "hungry" client or couple need first be "heard" and "received" on the child level and helped to get connected emotionally with that needy, but unacceptable part of themselves. Only then can they move on to some acceptance of the reality that what they are demanding nobody can give, and this most decidedly includes the marital partner. Essentially, all of this means that some shift of the transference from the partner onto the group or therapist takes place and, finally, one comes to better terms with what can be realistically expected from the spouse.

For the married couples group, the just described aspect of the group process has very specific implications. One has to distinguish between the partner and the group while one individual goes through a period of heightened anxiety. The partner often gets terribly frightened, fears the mate may fall apart, and does all he can to reassure, deny, and to censure. Often he gets quite angry at the mate, the therapist, or the group. His aim is to stop what seems to be quite a threat. The group—even though some individual in it can get almost as frightened as the marital partner—can be invaluable in supporting both partners in this difficult phase of allowing one partner to express anxiety and to live out strong feelings as painful connections are made. At the same time, the group is able to sympathize with the other partner's reaction, helping him see it for what it is and intervening in his attempts to stop his mate. If this is done in a supportive manner—and often the help of the therapist is needed there as he interprets angry interruptions as a reflection of apprehension or anxiety—the partner gradually becomes enabled to see the mate in a truly new light, namely as a person with his own needs and vulnerabilities. Equally important, he finally realizes that the group is working for rather than against him, the latter reaction being based on the threat which any shaking up of the marital equilibrium entails.

In this important process, then, each couple, almost like a pair of siblings, gradually experiences the group as the "good third family" which, different from their primary families, allows and, indeed, welcomes growth for each of them individually and for both of them as a pair. Their "joint growth" is finally most strikingly reflected in their ability and readiness to leave the group, and to take on jointly the responsibilities of marriage. However, before this commitment is made by the marital partners, they are given a chance to consider honestly the question of whether they wish to remain married. The author has observed that sometimes the final step of a desirable separation is taken very soon after the group therapy experience ends.

Married Couples Groups in Different Stages of Life Cycles

Even though there are universal themes pertaining to all married couples groups, there are significant psychosocial differences among married couples in consecutive states of the marital relationship which are reflected in the group treatment process psychodynamically as well as in terms of the actual content of the ongoing group session.

Young Married Couples

Young married couples often find themselves in a peculiar state of transition. Considering the long period of at least economic dependence on the parents, they are, during the early stages of marriage, still struggling to achieve separation from their primary families and in this struggle, dependency needs and independent strivings are in conflict with each other. Whereas in many other cultures, the continuing close tie to the primary family is most decidedly considered ''normal,'' in the American middle class culture the young married couple is expected to have achieved separation to a considerable extent. The inner conflict thus is intensified by societal expectation which is guilt-provoking and for some young couples only serves to prolong the struggle.

While there are some young couples who want treatment out of a mutual recognition of danger signals and out of a joint desire for growth so as to get ready for children and/or to make life altogether more satisfying, the majority of young couples come for help because of severe clashes from the start of the marriage which threaten to produce total breakdown. Unlike couples in later stages of marital development, these younger couples as a rule, are not yet really married except in the term's most external connotation. Their ties to their respective primary families are often extremely strong and one can rightfully state that the couple plus their parents constitute the *de facto* family. Just as in later marital stages the children are the focus of the difficulties, in this early period of marriage, parents and in-laws become object of marital strife and hostile dependency. They are in the kitchen and the bedroom of the young people, and often there is actual involvement in the occupational and working level.

It appears that two types of young couples in particular have the greatest difficulty with a relatively healthy separation from the parental family:

(1) Those who have lived in a symbiotic type of family and literally cannot cut the umbilical cord.

(2) Those who came from "undernourishing" isolated families in which a sense of great emotional deprivation was experienced, including those who due to a tragic reality situation suffered an actual loss of parenting—mothering.

Usually and unfortunately, such young people tend to pick marital partners who are equally deprived. This similarity may in the courtship period produce a pseudo-closeness and warmth which are taken for "love." As such young people enter marriage, they find it extremely difficult to make the transition from the hierarchical relationship in which the parent was the predominant emotional provider to the marital peer relationship in which the mutual give and take has to be balanced. The more deprived the marital partner is, the more he will tend to perceive the spouse as if he were a parental figure. In such cases, need clashes with need. What started as a hopeful relationship quickly deteriorates, leaving the couple bewildered and disappointed in a largely transferential relationship, making it psychologically impossible even to grasp the needs of the partner, let alone meet them. With such couples, many practitioners, are tempted to separate the marital partners and to treat them each individually, since the individual emotional disturbance is more than obvious. Yet, the reality of the marriage exists, even if it is a marriage of two immature, disturbed young people, who through their circular interaction, feed into and add to each other's pathology.

A married couples group can be an excellent medium of treatment for such couples as a wide range of content and process themes are touched off and focused on. Almost every piece of even the most specific discussion content, such as money or occupation, has psychological implications. Some aspect of the transferential relationship of the couple enters into the seemingly topical discussion. It is thus worked on in many different ways, with the hope that eventually the marital relationship may to the extent possible grow into a more adult relationship with the give and take more evenly balanced.

Some of the specific content themes in the young married couples group are in the area of money and occupation—"working as a team to get jobs done"—and sex. Discussions of parents and in-laws can be very specific in terms of actual experiences and relationships, but appear in less concrete terms in the here and now interactions and transactions of the therapy group.

Occupation and Money. One of the very powerful topics in all married couples groups is money; but for young couples this has a very distinct flavor, since the partners for the first time have to share the responsibility for money management which gets them immediately from the romantic aura of the courtship relationship into one of the "nitty-gritty" aspects of marital life. When both partners are working in the early phase of marriage, some of the difficult interactional issues may not appear in full strength. Frequently, there are intense involvements with parents and in-laws in this period. The mate may have been chosen less for his own personal attractiveness than for the family (parents) he has. The young man often actually may be working for his father, or father-in-law, and the question of how he is recompensed and treated can be fraught with tremendously intense emotions. These factors are, of course, interwoven with his sense of self-esteem which can be easily threatened and yet he is stuck in a situation which he hates. The wife, thus, can find herself between husband and primary family and more often than not will tend to side with the primary family. In other situations the wife may continue to accept regular material gifts from her family, gifts which allow for luxuries that the husband would not be able to meet. The interactional pattern in relation to this is contradictory: On one hand, the couples are in a silent pact to accept the gifts (and dependence) and, on the other hand, there is mutual resentment. The husband's sense of self-esteem is deeply threatened, since even where there may be a fairly good income, he cannot compete with the extras which the in-laws have to offer. For the wife, this constellation provides a good reason to undermine the husband and to hold him in contempt.

Usually it is not difficult for a married couples group to recognize some of the paradoxical, contradictory aspects of the marital interaction. Since the subject of money and money making is of much interest to most couples, many identifications and alliances—often men with men and women with women —take place in the married couples group. Thus, men who may be relating to their own "overdemanding" or "dissatisfied" wives with "passive withhold-ing" have a chance in the married couples group to react to other men's wives who show similar tendencies and "let them have it." This prepares the men for the eventual confrontation with their own partners. On the other hand, the men can take a man to task if they feel he lets his wife "step all over him." To give an example, it emerged in a married couples group that the wife continuously overspent and contracted debts which her husband then had to meet grudgingly. The group, especially the men, confronted the husband with his passivity which reflected itself also in his tendency to fall asleep in the group. It became clear that the wife substituted money for love since she had an absentee husband. On the other hand, it became equally clear that the wife took rather powerful, childish revenge on her husband for his neglect of her. Each of the marital partners, and occasionally both together, went through a period of strong anger with the group, including temporarily staying away from the sessions. Gradu-ally, however, the couple reached the point of courageous, open confrontation of each other. As an outcome of this, the wife went to work and helped with the repayment of accumulated debts, and the husband not only stopped sleeping during the group session but generally showed more aggressiveness and vital-ity.

The group can often prove a great reality-tester and can in some respects be more down to earth than the therapist when it comes to the reality aspects of money and income. It is quite helpful to put couples in the group who are economically and occupationally quite heterogeneous. Many fantasies can be diminished by the presence of seemingly "successful" couples, whose greater affluence obviously has not been the answer to all problems. On the other hand, the less "successful" and even less-educated couple may in the area of perception and emotional availability be quite ahead of their fantasized "superiors."

Teamwork. Literally, these young couples have to learn how to live together as a pair, to become a team that can get jobs done, rather than getting stuck in clashes around each necessary task. This involves profound emotional questions, especially the deeply unresolved dependency needs and excessive, infantile demands of each other which make teamwork impossible. One of the most poignant comments in this respect was found by the author in a psychosocial description of a young couple. "They can't get together on anything. They want to have coffee together, but argue about which room. They want to have sex, but cannot agree on a time. Therefore, neither sex nor coffee occurs."

In a couples group, such specific areas of breakdown can be dealt with in a very specific way through identifications on one hand and recognition of the irrational handling of specific situations on the other hand. Thus appropriate reactions or responses on the part of other couples, or individuals, whose own irrationality is not identical, are helpful elements in the group interaction. They can open up for other couples new insights into their own areas of functional breakdown.

Sex. In young married couples the question of "sex" naturally looms very large. Where the marital relationship is largely transferential, much of the sexual conflict between the partners has strongly oral connotations. Sex then becomes the object of demand and withholding.

In therapy groups of young couples, the sharing of sexual problems is, as a whole, fairly easy and almost "comes natural." To some extent, this serves as a defense for the group, the couple, or one of the marital partners to cover up the underlying need for parenting, or the use of sex as a binder of anxiety. These underlying needs are the real secrets because they are invested with shame and guilt and usually are kept out of awareness. Thus, group, couple or individual resistance emerges more powerfully when these connections are beginning to be made.

There are, however, real sexual secrets, which have to do with actual experience. Since the couples are young, earlier sexual experience is not as far removed in time as it may be the case for couples in the later stages of marriage. The secrets have usually to do with more or less traumatic childhood experiences, not infrequently of an incestuous nature. As all secrets, they are accompanied by a sense of shame and guilt and frequently are not known to the partner. When one individual in the group gets ready to reveal the forbidden actions of their childhood, the group experiences first anxiety and then great relief. These revelations are accompanied by either sobbing, tears, or giggling, as the group as a whole relive pieces of their childhood that had remained hidden from outside knowledge. Subsequently, many secrets of this nature come to the fore from other group members.

The whole area of sexual secrets, including the practicing of some sexual perversions, and sexual fantasies can be dealt with in a group quite effectively. The mate, while perhaps shocked at first, begins to understand and appreciate some of the partner's idiosyncracies in their sexual relationship. The constellation of the group with the "parent-therapist" who takes an uncritical attitude and in fact welcomes the bringing out of heretofore hidden material—be it fact or fantasy—and the sharing of comparable experiences and their mutual acceptance among peers has a deeply therapeutic potential. Usually, these discussions lead once more to the never ending topic of the "nonprotective" parents (primary families) who ignored and looked away from what was happening to their young children.

Primary Families. The relationships to parents is a continuing theme in the married couples group. It is a very complicated but most important subject of concentration. The complexity is due to the fact that behind each couple are two sets of parents, dead or alive. These discussions take place on many levels, but essentially the group treatment endeavors to help all group members to move from extreme, often very irrational attitudes toward, and perceptions of parents and parents-in-law to more realistic ones which eventually allows for healthy separation.

A couple's respective relations with, and feelings about parents and in-laws can create rather complicated marital interactions. For example, while there may be denial and idealization in relation to one's own parents, the in-laws may be the recipients of the projection and/or transference. This can drive the partner into a defensive position on behalf of his "attacked" primary family, which then prevents him from dealing in a realistic manner with his own feelings toward his primary family.Some mates deny their feelings of anger or rage toward in-laws as much as toward their own parents; in situations where the partner is able to express angry feelings or unhappiness about early deprivation he is criticized or censured by the mate for such unacceptable emotions. Yet, in the whole area of relations and reactions to primary family, the married couples group has the advantage that the partners often do have more realistic impressions that the spouse of the latter's parents and actually often know some significant background facts. Thus, the marital partners frequently are mutually able to debunk some of each other's distortions, but for this the help of the group is quite important: By having some added facts at its disposal, the group can support the partner's more objective perceptions of his in-laws while empathizing with the defensive reactions of the mate.

Hopefully, all group participants eventually can move from their extreme (transferential) positions to more realistic and mature ones in which neither total denial of anger nor total rage are necessary any longer and the parents are finally viewed as "people" with their "good" and their "bad" features.

Some group therapists with a family therapy orientation occasionally may invite the couples' parents into the group, allowing the group to gain a direct objective view of these people rather than being left with distortions which are often hard to unravel. In addition to the regular weekly group meetings other therapists prefer to have family interviews with the two generations from time to time, often including siblings of the younger pair. The purpose is not only diagnostic but most decidedly to give the family a chance to get more meaningfully involved with each other, where and if possible.

Couples Groups in Later Stages of Marriage

The couple who are parents are in a very different developmental stage of the marriage and the group process reflects this fact. Naturally, many of the themes discussed earlier, such as money and occupational difficulties, are also prevalent in this type of group. But often emotional and behavior patterns are more rigidified and there is more resistance and denial as character defenses are more habitual. There is often also more hopelessness with regard to the possibility of change.

On the perhaps more positive side, couples with children—except for the most disturbed families—usually have found a way of functioning and operating. Some teamwork must be there for the couple to perform the parental functions on at least a minimum level. These couples survived the early marriage, often quite well, even though if the beginning of the marital difficulty is retraced one can find with some couples that the arrival of the first child —something which always shakes up the dyadic balance and requires a readjustment on the part of both marital partners—was where the serious difficulty all started. In many cases, however, the problem could be kept "under wraps" till the children reflected some of the pathology of their parents and added to it so that eventually a full grown family pathology became evident.

Very often in married couples groups in which the couples are parents, the original presenting difficulty was a child rather than the marital relationship. In fact, children are all too often used to perpetuate the myth of the happy marriage or are blamed for the marital disturbance. In order to get such couples into a married couples group, a therapeutic process in which the whole family, i.e., the couple/parents, the disturbed child, and well siblings are seen and worked with together, has proved to be most helpful. As a result of such a process, the decision may be reached that the parents as a marital pair should use the help of a married couples group in order to concentrate on themselves and their relationship rather than exploiting a child to maintain the myth that everything else would be fine if only the child changed. What other treatment decisions are made depends on what the family needs and is prepared to do. By all means, however, even if treatment of the family is broken up into several parts, from time to time members ought to be brought together for testing of changes and for direct involvement with each other in a structured therapeutic milieu. Occasionally, after an intensive period of family therapy, couples join married couples groups as a next step in the total treatment process.

Fewer couples in this category come for help with the marriage *per se*. As with younger marriages, there may be couples who face their mutual difficulty and really are motivated toward help. They may maintain that the children are not affected, are doing well, etc. The practitioner with a family orientation still will try to meet with the whole family even if only for the purpose of arriving at a more reliable understanding of the marital disturbance. Such interviews often bring out some hidden disturbances in the children, as for example, a reversed structure in the family in which the children carry the parental function in many ways lest their family go to pieces. The family interviews thus can serve as fact finders leading where possible to preventive steps with regard to the children, who can be greatly relieved by having someone become aware of their burden.

Married couples groups thus frequently are composed roughly of those couples who originally came about a child—but were helped through a process to recognize and to take at least minimal responsibility for some underlying disturbance in their own relationship—and of those who asked for help with the marriage claiming correctly or incorrectly that the children were fine. Such a total group can be quite helpful to each of its subgroups. Those couples who acknowledge the marital difficulty and often are locked in a pattern of circular accusation without taking any real responsibility for the effect this has on the children get into a conflict situation with the subgroup whose pull continues to be in the direction of the children, with a concomitant minimization of marital difficulty. The latter subgroup often can break into the circular process of the former quite effectively through: (1) their articulated reaction of the effect on them (from feelings of exclusion to feelings of fear about the violence of the attacks) and (2) identifying with the other subgroup's children, who may well react similarly to their parents' destructive behavior.

If this process is to be productive, the arousal of guilt toward the children is necessary before these couples can begin to shift from their self-centered accusatory system toward taking more responsibility in their role of parents. On the other hand, couples in an open marital struggle sense the denial of those who pretend that "all is well in the marriage" and through their challenges bring the underlying marital difficulty into sharper focus. The conflictual interplay between the two subgroups tends to be quite dramatic. Thus the married couples group seems a particularly good medium for enabling the partners to decrease their respective areas of denial and projection.

Again, other themes which are focused on in the young married couples groups are very much in the picture here also, but with a somewhat different slant. For example, there are still unresolved ties to primary families, often highlighted by the existence of the children and their parents' feelings about being parents when they are still so much in childlike relationships to their own parents. The wish for mothering from the partner is often reflected by powerful sibling rivalries with one's own children. On the other hand, involvement with the mate (including sex) is avoided by concentration on a child or on the children.

The latter point brings to mind a couple who came for help because their fifteen-year-old son had become heavily involved with alcohol and drugs. They were also complaining about their younger eleven-year-old daughter who was not living up to potential scholastically and having trouble making friends. Initially, the family was worked with as a unit. After a period of intensive family therapy the marital partners were ready for concentration on their marriage in a married couples group. (Both children who had gained a lot in family therapy simultaneously were ready to get appropriate treatment for themselves.) The husband had been sexually totally impotent for three years, and the wife felt extremely rejected by her spouse. This difficulty fed into her long standing self-image of being unattractive as a woman. The "deadness" in the marital relationship was reflected in a family gloom and doom which had its serious impact on the children. The husband found it easier and less threatening to have a sort of love affair with his daughter than with his wife. The mother grew intensely jealous of the girl and increasingly upset about the son's use of drugs and alcohol. Her rage and fury were directed at both children but the girl, as a female rival, bore the brunt of her mother's hysterical outbursts.

In the married couples group, the problem of the couple was reenacted: There was very little interaction between the marital partners: The husband displayed a rather passive, lecturing kind of stance; he could express his seething rage only through taking little stabs at the therapist or others, chiefly because nobody could give him "answers." The wife went through periods of seeming calm in which, however, she accumulated anger, which then exploded. She would yell hysterically at the group or the therapist and run out of the room, claiming she got nothing and accusing the group and the therapist of letting themselves be seduced by her husband's "smart alecky" intellectualizations, which, in truth, was the only way in which he could cope with his sense of helplessness and impotence.

One of the major goals of the treatment process was to offer new life to this "dead" couple. The group became the third family in which they initially behaved as they had with their primary families and as they behaved with each other at home, the latter meaning that they were quite isolated from each other. The husband gradually was helped to acknowledge his seething rage within the transferential situation of the group, i.e., he learned how to recognize that his barbs, his sarcasm, his tendency to put others down—including the therapist

—were expressions of profound hostility for what felt to him like unending deprivation. With the female therapist he could get to some rather powerful feelings about his exploitative, nongiving mother. Subsequently, he went through a period of expressing anger directly at the women in the group. Especially, when the anger was appropriate, he was encouraged by the therapist, who welcomed the emergence of his "male aggressiveness." When at last he became ready to communicate directly, even though angrily, with his oversensitive wife her first reactions were typical of her: She became hysterical. Yet, she had been complaining she wanted her husband to be "a man" in more than one respect.

At that critical juncture, when the newly found male aggressiveness was still not quite integrated and could easily revert back to the old, familiar pattern, the wife was sufficiently supported by the group in her understandable reaction to her husband's anger because of many "old sins." This, in turn, left the therapist free to put out a clear challenge to the woman: "You can't have it both ways; if you want a man, you must let him be a man." At an earlier point in process, she had similarly challenged the husband: "If you want to have a wife, you cannot expect her to be your mother, who still cuts your food. You have to choose between the roles of little boy and husband. You can't have it both ways." (At an earlier point in group treatment, all wives had ganged up against the female therapist, who encouraged potent, male aggressiveness, which none of them could tolerate at first; their own fantasy about their husband's maleness actually being the wish that the husband should find a way of being a man [whatever that meant] and yet do the woman's bidding.) The couple began to have sexual intercourse again when they were able to have meaningful communication with each other, and both also had changed their respective roles as parents, moving essentially away from helplessness to some sense of mastery.

This example, although necessarily quite sketchy, was intended to bring out many of the points repeatedly made in this article. The obvious point that couples who are parents can be in quite different stages of the ongoing life process of the marriage needs to be stated firmly. It is important to take into consideration whether they are just starting parenthood and are themselves quite young or whether they are approaching middle age, biologically and emotionally (menopause!); whether they are the parents of several children; and whether one or more of these children has reached adolescence or young adulthood. When exactly did the difficulty reach the point that the family could not contain it any longer? Was it as soon as the nurturing of the first baby became an added function in family living? Was it when the child began to leave the symbiotic mother/child relationship and started "walking" away? Was it when the adolescent became an object of sexual attraction for the parent of the opposite sex? Was it when the husband and wife found themselves facing each other and old age after their children left?

While the writer so far has made a strong distinction between couples groups in the various stages of married life, in actual practice the lines of distinction cannot really be drawn so sharply. In fact, many therapists find it quite fruitful to have more heterogeneity in their married couples groups and to mix younger with older couples. It is obvious that the latter structure can heighten the transferences and the conflicts, as the young couples often tend to identify with the children of the middle aged couples, relating to the latter as if they were their parents. Yet, eventually and gradually they can learn to grasp the feelings and reactions of parents who are as vulnerable to the hurts from their children as is true the other way around.

Summary and Conclusions

It seems important to remember that the institution of marriage is now in a state of great flux. Since this is happening in the immediate present, it is not possible as yet to relate to it with a sense of perspective. The author is reminded of the time—some years ago—when the adolescent scene was beginning to change, not only leaving the parents but the whole adult generation bewildered and frightened. Today, the drug culture is making itself intensely felt in every social system that adolescents are part of, including the therapeutic systems (private practices, agencies, clinics).

The following outside developments are beginning to be reflected especially in young marriages and have begun to become part of the content in the married couples groups:

(1) The use of drugs by couples on a social level (similar to the use of alcohol).

(2) The switching of partners (swinging), often as a means of getting "turned on" for marital sex.

(3) Women's Liberation Movement; its repercussions and influence are beginning to make their imprint in married couples groups in which some of the arguments of the movement are used as a weapon in the battle between the sexes.

All of this is still only to a small extent part of the general culture of the married couples groups. It behooves married couples group therapists, however, to see some of the signs that may eventually end the traditional structure of marriage. Moreover, since therapists are a part of the total society, they tend like many others to react with shock and rather judgemental attitudes especially to the "swingers." Obviously such reactions do not serve to help the group members with their own similar attitude of strong disapproval. Therapists need to keep in mind, whatever their personal values may be, that couples engaging in drug-taking or couple mixing would not seek help if there were not some dissatisfaction with or even unhappiness about their current life situation. This, rather than their unacceptable behavior, makes it possible for the married couples group and the therapist to help the marital partners to achieve the kind of relationship which is mutually more satisfying and offers some stability and security to the next generation.

In terms of optimal treatment goals which, of course, have to be modified according to the couple's capacity to change—both partners need to become aware of and emotionally connected with some of their own unresolved infantile needs and those of the mate. They have to learn to know and to respect the partner's sensitive and vulnerable spots rather than constantly hitting the mate "below the belt." Only if this occurs can the treatment of married couples groups result in true mutual caring in the marital relationship.

REFERENCES

Arden, Flint, Jr., and Beryce W. MacLennan (1962), "Some Dynamic Factors in Marital Group Therapy," *International Journal of Group Psychotherapy*, 12:355.

Dicks, Henry V. (1967), "Marital Tensions." In *Clinical Studies Towards a Psychological Theory of Interaction*. New York: Basic Books.

Gallant, D. M., *et al.* (1970), "Group Psychotherapy with Married Couples: A Successful Technique in New Orleans Alcoholism Clinic Patients," *Journal of the Louisiana Medical Society*, 122:41-44.

Gottlieb, A., and E. M. Pattison (1966), "Married Couples Group Psychotherapy," *Archives of General Psychiatry*, 14:143-152.

Gurman, Alan S. (1971), "Group Marital Therapy: Clinical and Empirical Implications for Outcome Research," *International Journal of Group Psychotherapy*, 21:174.

Hooper, D. A. Sheldon, and A. J. R. Koumans (1968), "A Study of Group Psychotherapy with Married Couples," *International Journal of Social Psychiatry*, 15:57-68.

Kohn, Regina (1971), "Treatment of Married Couples in a Group," *Group Process*, 4:96.

Lebedun, M. (1970), "Measuring Movement in Group Marital Counseling," *Social Casework*, 51:35-43.

Leichter, Elsa (1962), "Group Psychotherapy of Married Couples Groups: Some Characteristic Treatment Dynamics," *International Journal of Group Psychotherapy*, 12:154.

——(1966), "The Interrelationship of Content and Process in Therapy Groups," *Journal of Social Casework*, 47:302.

Liberman, R. (1970), "Behavioral Approaches to Family and Couple Therapy," *American Journal of Orthopsychiatry*, 40:106-118.

Olsen, E. (1971), "The Marriage—A Basic Unit for Psychotherapy," *American Journal of Psychiatry*, 127:945-947.

Perlman, J.S. (1960), "Group Treatment of Married Couples. A symposium, I. Problems Encountered in Group Psychotherapy of Married Couples," *International Journal of Group Psychotherapy*, 10.

Reckless, J. (1969), "A Confrontation Technique Used with Married Couples in a Group Therapy Setting," *International Journal of Group Psychotherapy*, 19:203–213.

Sherman, S. (1956), "Group Counseling." In V.W. Eisenstein (ed.), *Neurotic Interaction in Marriage*. New York: Basic Books, 296-302.

Targow, J.G., and R.V. Zweber (1969), "Participants' Reactions to Treatment in a Married Couples Group," *International Journal of Group Psychotherapy*, 19:221-225.

ALAN S. GURMAN

9   **Evaluating the Outcomes
           of Couples Groups**

The clinical and empirical literature on group marital therapy is reviewed. An
overview of theoretical and clinical considerations focuses on attempts to
define the goals of group therapy and the indications for its use. After a brief
summary of published outcome studies, some basic research needs are described and a model is proposed for the evaluation of the outcomes of couples'
groups. It is concluded that psychoanalytic approaches fail to offer both a
viable group treatment approach for couples and a foundation for clinically
relevant research. While intrapersonal variables are relevant to the task of
couples' groups, it is argued that the primary focus of change in couples
groups should be on interactional dimensions.

The last fifteen years have seen a growing concern among psychologists,
psychiatrists, and social workers with the treatment of marital difficulties.
Despite the proliferation of "marital therapies" (Greene, 1965) having varying
patient-therapist composition and underlying theoretical positions, their common goal is the modification of the day-to-day encounters between husbands
and wives (Liberman, 1970). Group therapy has recently emerged as one of the
most frequently used treatment approaches to marital disharmony (Lebedun,
1970) because of both its economy in increasing the availability of professional
services and, more importantly, because of a number of theoretically based
treatment preferences. The purpose of this paper is to review the existing
literature on group therapy with married couples in an attempt to evaluate some
of the major theoretical, clinical, and empirical implications for the development of a presently nonexistent research methodology. The terms "psychoan-

alysis,'' ''psychotherapy,'' and ''counseling'' are arbitrarily grouped under the rubric ''therapy'' in this review, except where significant implications for theory, treatment, or outcome evaluation reflect their differential use. Because of the highly specific population on which this review is focused, it should be clearly differentiated from the several excellent general reviews of group therapy research (Bennis, 1960; Pattison, 1965; Shapiro and Birk, 1967; Bednar and Lewis, 1971) which have focused primarily on individual personality and behavioral change.

THEORETICAL AND CLINICAL CONSIDERATIONS

The current popularity of group therapy with married couples has only recently outweighed the objections of die-hard theoreticians who at first warned against and later condemned its very existence (Slavson, 1950; Hobbs, 1951; Hulse 1956; Sherman, 1956). Neubeck (1953, 1954) has accurately described their position as a ''therapeutic taboo'' against the inclusion of marital partners (or any two members of the same family) in the same therapy group. This taboo, espoused primarily by earlier psychoanalytic writers, is well summarized in Boas' (1962) comment that such treatment was seen by classical psychoanalytic group therapists as ''not only undesirable but contraindicated and a grievous technical fault.'' Proponents of psychoanalysis-in-the-group raised three major objections. First, it was feared that treatment of both spouses in the same group would produce complications of transference and countertransference in the resulting therapeutic triangle. Especially endangered would be the development of the essential transference neurosis because the presence of both the spouse and the analyst would lead to a dilution of transference reactions (Boas, 1962). The second objection was grounded in the view that treating both spouses in the same group would facilitate their ''acting-out'' and that the consequent expression of hostility or other strong negative feelings might be uncontrollable and, therefore, cause the ultimate destruction of an already weakened marriage (Hulse, 1956). Finally, it was argued that spouses would use the group to manipulate each other or to support each other's resistances and to strengthen each other's defenses (Slavson, 1950; Hulse, 1956).

Boas (1962), at first cautious about group marital therapy for these reasons, found that these fears were not substantiated in actual practice, although a ''complete transference'' did not develop. A. Gottlieb and Pattison (1966) have succinctly stated that, consistent with Boas' personal experience, psychoanalytic objections to group marital therapy have been based mostly on theoretical preconceptions which have not been validated by therapeutic experience. It should also be added in retrospect that these earlier analytic criticisms also had no substantive empirical base. Since the development of other models of group marital therapy, especially interpersonal-systemic-behavioral ones (Shapiro and Birk, 1967; Liberman, 1970), the dilution-of-transference issue has become essentially a moot point. Nor is the acting-out of neurotic ties or of hostilities a matter which deserves anxious concern since this is precisely what couples in conflicted marriages do all the time. Finally, the criticism of the group as an intensifier of defensive styles of marital interaction simply is inconsistent with more recent clinical experience and research.

Goals of Group Marital Therapy: Individual Personality Change or Facilitation of Marital Interaction?

These analytic misgivings about group marital therapy highlight the central theoretical and clinical issue in the treatment of marital difficulties, i.e., what are the goals of such intervention? Three major positions have been taken on this question. Hulse (1956) has maintained that the focus of group marital therapy should be on the "psychopathology of the individual" who has marital conflicts, not on the conflict itself. Therefore, he advocates the "cure or improvement of *underlying emotional illness*" (italics added) rather than the modification of disturbed interactional patterns in marriage. This view is supported by Boas (1962), who argues that symptomatic improvement in marital disharmony constitutes an insufficient therapeutic outcome since movement is not based on "real structural changes" within the individual personality. Several other writers have adhered to this viewpoint (Jackson and Grotjahn, 1958, 1959; Leichter, 1962; Westman et al., 1965), which is quite consistent with several of the psychoanalytic dictums against the treatment of spouses in the same therapy group. Unfortunately, many such clinicians treat the marital partner *in vacuo*, as it were, and appear greatly unaware of or unconcerned with the effects of psychotherapy of one spouse on his or her untreated partner (Fox, 1968).

Other writers (Burton, 1962; Beukenkamp, 1959; Blinder and Kirschenbaum, 1967; Linden et al., 1968) have seen the efficacy of group marital therapy in terms of its potential for facilitating more adaptive interpersonal behavior between marital partners as a result of increased self-understanding. Although the emphasis here is on marital interaction, proponents of this view do not militate against the development of insight; in fact, they foster it (Perelman, 1960; Papanek, 1965; Gottlieb and Pattison, 1966; Leslie, 1964). Treatment goals are primarily the improvement of the quality of human interaction, with intrapsychic growth and awareness seen as the means to this end and not as an end in itself. These writers see both insight and action (behavior) as necessary concomitants of positive therapeutic change. In contrast, those whose main concern in group marital therapy is with the remediation of individual pathology view the marital relationship and, therefore, marital disharmony, as basically irrelevant to the therapeutic task, except insofar as it accentuates the pathology of *individual* marital partners. In this sense, such therapy is not marital therapy at all.

Finally, there are those therapists who see themselves essentially as educators (Liberman, 1970), whose function is to directly treat or change those behaviors occurring within the marital relationship which have caused dissatisfaction. Here, there is no attempt at intensification or deepening of transference phenomena, and the concern is only with those factors bearing on marital interaction. Group marital therapy, then, is explicitly a learning experience in which spouses learn to modify and shape interlocking and reciprocal behaviors according to behavioral principles. Insight is largely irrelevant to the goal of the modification of marital behavior in terms of concrete, observable, and manipulatable contingencies of interpersonal reinforcement.

These divergent theoretical and clinical views appear to derive from disagreement about what can be called the *locus of marital disharmony,* which signifies the degree to which marital difficulties are seen as reflective of the interactional elements of human experience. The classical psychoanalytic position, as has been implied, does not offer a meaningful approach to the group treatment of marital disharmony since its goals cannot be differentiated from and, in fact, are exactly the same as, those of the psychoanalysis of the individual. Adherents to this view are essentially unconcerned with the nature of the marital relationship in which the individual analysand experiences dissatisfaction. Clinicians who are psychodynamically oriented prefer to see marital disharmony as the manifestation of a breakdown in the patterning of mutual gratification of the neurotic needs of both spouses. Hence, the goals of therapy involve not the restructuring of individual psyches but the restructuring of both spouses' internally based perceptions of and reactions to each other, i.e., those aspects of personality functioning which are of specific import to the marital relationship. The behavioral view espoused by Liberman (1970) is the one most explicitly concerned with the interactional bases of marital disharmony. Here, felt dissatisfaction in marriage is considered to be the result of ineffective use of social reinforcement in controlling the desired and undesired behavior of both spouses. Behavioral modification approaches to marital therapy, therefore, explicitly see the goal of treatment as the shaping of desired marital behaviors through the implementation of "behavioral principles of reinforcement and modeling in the context of ongoing interpersonal interactions" (Liberman, 1970).

As A. Gottlieb and Pattison (1966) have suggested, different models of group marital therapy lead to different conclusions about its effectiveness. The point that mediates such disagreement is that different theoretical systems, varying in the extent to which they consider marital disharmony a social-interpersonal phenomenon or an individual-intrapsychic concern, establish divergent treatment goals. Ideally, theory dictates therapeutic goals which, in turn, determine intervention strategies, the effectiveness of which are then systematically evaluated. Assessment of the outcomes of therapeutic techniques hopefully is then fed back into the theoretical system from which these techniques have been derived to make appropriate modifications of the conceptual relationships affecting clinical practice. This interaction between research and therapeutic practice will be examined below.

Indications and Contraindications for Group Marital Therapy

If the goals of group marital therapy are to be realized, there must be guidelines according to which patients are judged to be appropriate or inappropriate for such treatment. There needs to be clarification of the types of problems and the types of people for whom group therapy is the treatment of choice. It should be stated at the outset of this section that there is no existing empirical basis on which to evaluate the appropriateness of group therapy for married couples. There is, however, a good deal of speculation derived from clinical experience. While there are areas of strong disagreement, there is, fortunately, equally strong consensus along many dimensions.

1. Personality Types. It is generally agreed that outpatient group marital therapy is contraindicated when one spouse is psychotic (Papanek, 1965; Bruninga, 1967; Grunebaum et al., 1969), ostensibly because of the psychological fragility of such a marital partner and the resulting inability to deal with the stress and anxiety generated in marital group therapy. While clinical experience probably justifies this notion, it is unfortunate that more systematically gathered evidence on this point is not available.

According to Flint, and MacLennan (1962), immature and dependent couples with feelings of inadequacy and confused sexual identities often benefit from long-term group therapy. Grunebaum et al. (1969), however, argue that group treatment is contraindicated when both partners are immature and dependent, since the marital disorder is ''more an expression of mutual developmental difficulties than a marital issue per se.'' It strikes the writer that since most marital difficulties represent developmental deficiencies in one or both spouses or in the marital system, the position of Grunebaum and his co-workers may have been reached on the basis of a highly selective group marital therapy experience.

Strong disagreement also exists over the appropriateness of group therapy for couples variously described as sadomasochistic, character-disordered (Flint and MacLennan, 1962), reciprocally pathological (Carroll, 1963) or regressively collusive (Jones, 1967). While Flint and MacLennan have found that couples who engage in ''mutual provocative acting out'' rarely benefit from even long-term, intensive group therapy, the experience of Sherman (1956) and Henderson (1965) have been that such people, despite their strongly mobilized defenses against therapeutic involvement, are able to learn new modes of interaction in the group. Carroll (1963) takes the position that all forms of marital therapy are inappropriate in the absence of "reciprocal pathological interaction." It is somewhat surprising that what scant literature exists relevant to this point tends to favor the treatment of character-disordered couples in groups despite the fact that such people are generally seen as the most intractable patient subgroup with existing therapeutic methods.

2. *Interactional Styles.* The current status of knowledge or ignorance relevant to the appropriateness of group treatment for given married couples is probably most evident in the disparity which exists with regard to the necessary degree of interpersonal skill and openness requisite for treatment. While Papanek (1965) finds an inability to communicate openly and an "inability to relate to others" contraindicative for group therapy, Flint and MacLennan (1962) and Sherman (1956) feel that relatively withdrawn, noncommunicative couples with constricted social behavior are among the most likely to gain from such an experience. Logic certainly favors the former position, yet we have little more than a scattering of clinical experience (often useful in generating testable hypotheses, but too infrequently used to this end) on which to make such a determination.

3. *Chronicity of Disharmony.* What little has been said on this matter tends to further confuse. Carroll (1963) states decisively that only chronically experienced marital disharmony is appropriate for therapeutic intervention, and Grunebaum et al. (1969) echo this view with regard to group treatment in particular. These writers offer little in the way of conceptual justification for their position and absolutely nothing in the way of empirical support. Indeed, this predilection seems quite inconsistent with most research on therapeutic outcome in individual psychotherapy, which shows repeatedly that the least severely and most acutely disturbed patients benefit most from therapy (Truax and Carkhuff, 1967).

It should now be evident that the practice of group marital therapy is confounded by major theoretical differences, consequent varied therapeutic goals and techniques, and lack of consensus over the very nature of the people for whom such treatment is most, or at least minimally, appropriate. In the next section, we shall consider the contributions of empirical investigations of group marital therapy to the unraveling of the multiple inconsistencies which exist in this field of therapeutic practice.

ASSESSMENT OF OUTCOME IN GROUP MARITAL THERAPY

While the literature contains many statements regarding the criteria by which group marital treatment should be assessed, most have been speculatively derived from incidental clinical observation and there exists but a handful of research studies specifically designed to measure the effectiveness of therapy. This section will review (a) existing studies of client change in group marital therapy and (b) criteria for assessing outcome which presently lack a substantive empirical base, in an effort to delineate what appear to be meaningful outcome variables in the investigation of group marital therapy and to develop other fruitful lines of empirical inquiry into this treatment modality.

Empirical Studies

Empirical studies discussed herein are not limited to statistical, hypothesis-testing research but include all reports in which outcome evaluation through systematic observation is the primary concern. Thus, reports on change criteria or signs of change in clinical case studies are excluded except where such descriptive analysis is focused on assessing outcome.

Three studies have reported that positive change in group marital therapy is responsible for a general lessening of tensions and conflicts in (nuclear) family relations in addition to those of the spouses. Maizlish (1957), treating the parents of children being seen in a child-guidance clinic, observed that group therapy apparently facilitated in both spouses an increased regard for and respect of their children. A related study in the same clinic (Maizlish and Hurley, 1963) found that such treatment also increased the flexibility of child-control techniques used by the parents of 16 concurrently treated children. In a study in which children were not involved in direct concurrent treatment and group therapy was offered specifically to deal with husband-wife relations (Targow and Zweber, 1969), there were also reports of improved parent-child relations. Apparently, the effects of a positive group therapeutic experience, with increased acceptance of self and of spouse, generalizes beyond the marital dyad to other significant people in the couples' lives.

Some of the components of such improved spouse-spouse and parent-child relations can be tentatively specified. Dakan (1950), in a study of the effects of nondirective group marital therapy, found that group experience facilitated the clarification of self-perception and perception of the marital partner. Griffin's (1967) study of the effects of individual marriage counseling with wives offers data which may in part account for the nature of changed self- and spouse-perception in Dakan's study. He found significant pre-post treatment changes in his subjects' perceptions of self and spouse along the dimensions of empathy, congruence, regard, unconditionality of regard, and willingness to be known (Barrett-Lennard, 1962), the first three of which have received overwhelmingly positive support as effective ingredients in psychotherapy (Truax and Carkhuff, 1967). It appears that this clarification of self and of the marital partner is directly related to the lessened ambiguity of marital role-expectations as a result of group therapy (Dakan, 1950; Maizlish, 1957; Maizlish and Hurley, 1963; Gottlieb and Pattison, 1966).

Apparently, this redefinition of self and self-as-a-marriage partner is effected in the group experience not by massive intrapsychic reorganization but by an opportunity to become more aware of one's own feelings and of their effects on the marital partner. The increased willingness to express negative or rejecting feelings toward the spouse in a nonthreatening and accepting therapeutic group setting is of central importance (Dakan, 1950), since it allows group members to see themselves and others differently and to integrate these new perceptions into the marital relationship. The vaguely operationalized goals of "increased openness" and "improved communication" (Maizlish and Hurley, 1963; Burton and Kaplan, 1968; Targow and Zweber, 1969) in group marital therapy, then, can be construed as the positive behavioral consequences of an integrated re-evaluation of self and of self-as-marital-partner. As Hooper et al. (1968) have accurately concluded, "Changes occur (in group marital therapy), but are only invested with meaning when they become part of a dynamic *interaction* [italics added] between people."

There have been only three systematic investigations of client evaluation of the group marital therapy experience. Maizlish and Hurley (1963) developed a fifty-item, Likert-type questionnaire to measure changes in positive attitudes toward one's self and one's spouse. They found significant pre-post changes among 32 husbands and wives along the dimensions of interpersonal adaptability, sense of interpersonal responsibility, and psychological openness. These treatment changes, moreover, exceeded those in a no-treatment control group of parents enrolled in a college child-psychology course. Unfortunately, there was no follow-up, so that the scope and duration of therapeutic gains in this study cannot be assessed. Targow and Zweber (1969) did follow their 15 couples after treatment and found that spouses' evaluations of the benefits of group therapy tended to show a positive increase with the passage of time. Group members who perceived the experience negatively at termination of treatment also tended to view it somewhat more positively at follow-up. Whether such an increased positive evaluation of group marital therapy was due to a progressive implementation of therapeutic gains or to nonspecific, i.e., nontherapeutic, life experiences cannot be determined. The Targow and Zweber study is an important one in that it demonstrates that group marital therapy, like individual psychotherapy (Bergin, 1963), often has negative effects on its clientele—at termination five of the 30 subjects reported the experience to have been harmful to their marital relationships.

Burton and Kaplan (1968) have reported that 76 per cent of the clients (n=70) receiving group counseling saw the experience positively, and 70 per cent of Targow and Zweber's subjects reacted in this way. In both studies husbands and wives tended to benefit or not benefit from therapy concomitantly, i.e., when a spouse saw himself and his partner as having made gains, the partner tended to agree. These results suggest that, at least in nonpsychoanalytic group marital therapy, positive therapeutic change with individuals is not seen as occurring unless change is also perceived in the spouse. This supports the inference made earlier that positive evaluation of the group marital therapy experience by participants or by independent evaluators rests upon the presence of an improved marital *interaction* and is not the result of only felt or assessed individual change.

Speculative Indices of Change

Lebedun (1970) has attempted to categorize most of the terms frequently used in describing change in group marital therapy according to the degree of behavioral or operational explicitness they demonstrate. "Vague" criteria include such indices as increased insight and heightened self-esteem. "Quasi-specific" terms such as reduction of resistance and occurrence of transference, as described by Lebedun, do not appear to be any more explicit than his "vague" criteria and, in fact, can hardly be differentiated from many of his "specific" criteria (dependence on leader, discussion of dreams, etc.). He offers two viable criteria for spouses treated as inpatients: number of hospital readmissions and length of nonhospitalization. It is striking that the two "specific" criteria in his classification which are most relevant to outpatient couples, removal of symptomatic behavior and scores on psychological inventories, have, in the first case, been decried in most of the literature as insufficient indices (they fail to assess structural intrapsychic change) and, in the second case, have been totally neglected (an exception is Neubeck, 1954).

In light of the earlier discussion, it should not now be surprising that most of the speculative criteria of movement in group marital therapy have either failed to achieve empirical substantiation or have not been measured directly, since such indices, on the whole, are psychoanalytically derived and, as has been argued here, psychoanalysis is not a form of marital therapy. Intra-individual change by itself is not a meaningful index of an improved marital relationship—it is meaningful only when it constitutes an active ingredient of more effective behavior between marital partners. It is unlikely that analytically grounded change criteria will provide the necessary conceptual framework for clinically useful group marital therapy research.

Basic Research Needs and A New Model for Evaluation

Although group marital therapy is a rather recent therapeutic enterprise, its youth can be accepted as only a partial justification for the lack of relevant research. Marital therapy in general and group marital therapy in particular were born in psychiatric (child-guidance clinics) and social work (family service agencies) treatment settings; psychology, typically the discipline most active in psychotherapeutic research, has hardly yet made an impact on the group marital therapy literature (Lebedun, 1970.) Furthermore, it is striking that Pattison's (1965) exhaustive reference list of group therapy research includes not one citation of research on group marital therapy. Existing research tends to be based on clinical anecdote and unsystematic and impressionistic observation, and assessment of therapeutic effectiveness is generally based on measures which "occasionally . . . could only be inferred or were considered nonexistent" (Lebedun, 1970). The few attempts at systematic investigation of group marital therapy have been plagued by biased sampling of both therapists and patients (Rabkin, 1965), rater contamination, and questionable reliability and validity of evaluation instruments (see, for example, Hooper et al., 1968; Targow and Zweber, 1969), and the lack of no-treatment comparison groups.

Heeding Parloff's (1967) insightful and sardonic rebuke of reviewers of therapy research, who have "eschewed the presumptuous course of suggesting specific techniques and have acted on the sanguine assumption that it was sufficient merely to remind the researcher of the most primitive requirements of adequate investigation," this reviewer will attempt to outline briefly some of the basic needs of group marital therapy research and then, with sanctioned presumption, suggest a conceptual model on the basis of which such research might most fruitfully be initiated. The theoretical, clinical, and empirical considerations in earlier sections of this review support the urgent need for the following essential investigations of group marital therapy.

1. Comparative study of various group marital therapy methods (psychoanalytic, client-centered, behavioral, etc.). Conflicting opinion about the superiority of various group techniques is currently based on theoretical dogma and experientially selective confirmation of pre-established notions and does not offer the therapist a rational basis on which to choose his style of therapeutic group treatment of married couples.

It is felt by some (Bergin and Strupp, 1970) that broadly-based comparative studies of therapeutic effectiveness in which evaluation focuses on global and therefore somewhat vague orientations and "school" allegiances offer little in the way of expanding the technological efficacy of therapy. Nevertheless, the present status of empirical research on group marital therapy appears not only to justify but also to require studies of this sort before more sophisticated investigations concerned with the development of specific clinical techniques can emerge. An obvious *caveat* in such comparative studies is that researchers must make explicit efforts to select therapists with care when assigning them to experimental groups and then to assess the degree to which group leaders adhere to their stated techniques.

2. Comparative study of group and other marital therapies, e.g., conjoint, concurrent, collaborative. By applying various treatments across different diagnostic groups (e.g., psychotic partner, character-disordered, obsessive-compulsive intellectualizers) and personality types (e.g., dependent and immature, communicative, socially isolated), some empirical confirmation or refutation of current clinical preferences for assigning couples to different treatments may emerge. Especially useful would be a series of crossover studies in which, for example, a sample of patient couples might spend a time-limited period of, say, four months in a non-group treatment setting and then be transferred to group therapy.

The comparative study of group and other marital therapies will obviously be confounded by the problems raised with regard to the first recommendation. Comparative investigation of the effectivenss of various marital therapies, therefore, should probably be initiated with therapist samples with homogeneous orientations. Later study will require the multivariate assessment of patient characteristics, therapy orientation, and specific intervention strategies. For example, it can be speculated that various therapeutic orientations may be differentially effective when paired with different treatment interventions, that is, that patient change may be facilitated more with a given treatment modality administered by a therapist of orientation x than by a therapist of orientation y.

3. *Comparative study of the effects of group marital therapy through multiple evaluation.* Too often therapy research, especially nonempirical reports, are immensely biased by the singularity of the evaluators of the experience, e.g., therapists' evaluations of their own patients' progress. As Strupp and Bergin (1969) have encouraged, therapy outcome studies should ideally be simultaneously assessed by patients, therapists, and independent judges. The dangers in self-report studies have been well documented, and in the treatment of married couples there is a particularly strong need to assess the transfer of learning from the consultation room to behavior outside the group, since group marital therapy's effects have an immediate and continuous influence on its participants by virtue of their forced, as it were, interaction.

In addition, the adoption of a clinical and research perspective of marital disharmony as more reflective of active interpersonal maladjustments than of static intrapsychic conflict requires that assessment of the outcome of group and other marital therapies must include evaluation of the effects of treatment on other significant figures in a couple's lives, especially a couple's children. The effects that should be evaluated are twofold; direct, observable changes in the children's behavior both within and without the context of interaction with the parents.

4. *Investigation of primary therapist characteristics which have received support in other therapeutic researches (e.g., warmth, empathy, regard, position on the A-B scale).* For example, do the levels of the core therapeutic conditions of Rogers and his followers (Traux and Carkhuff, 1967) vary as a function of the number of therapists in a marital group? Are there differences in these conditions in interactions between same- and opposite-sex patients and

therapists? Does the A-B scale (Whitehorn and Betz, 1954) differentiate more successful from less successful therapists working with schizophrenic vs. neurotic marital groups as it does in individual psychotherapy? The major general question under this recommendation is whether those therapist characteristics that have been found to be of importance in individual therapy and counseling are of equal salience in group marital therapy or whether the nature of the problems of this patient population requires therapist attributes distinct from and not necessary in individual therapy.

5. *Investigation of the effects of group composition on therapeutic effectiveness.* Several writers point to the need for clarification of a variety of patient variables in the establishment of couples' groups (Conrad and Elkins, 1959; Gottlieb, 1960; Hastings and Runkle, 1963). For example, what effects do similarities or differences in symptomatology, personality patterns, economic and educational levels, age, and length of marriage have on outcome?

The position taken throughout this review has been that psychoanalysis, with its minimal explicit concern with the effects of group marital therapy on marital interaction, offers neither a viable treatment approach to marital disharmony nor the foundation for a clinically relevant research design. Whereas previous reviews of group therapy research (Bennis, 1960; Pattison 1965; Bednar and Lewis, 1971) have presented many valid suggestions for measuring individual personality change, they are of only minimal significance for outcome studies of *marital* group therapy. The evaluative focus of this research must be on indices of interpersonal, i.e., spouse-spouse, growth. This does not mean that measures of individual change are irrelevant. Rather, individual therapeutic gains or losses per se must be weighed against their real effectiveness in maintaining or facilitating positive interpersonal behavioral consequences. Self-report measures, for example, should be constructed for evaluation of individual partner's perceptions of their own and their spouse's changes in marital role attitudes, behavior patterns, and interactive impact on the respondent. In order that patient-reported and therapist-observed changes not be artifacts of the group setting or of the evaluation instruments themselves, independent behavioral analyses based on *in vivo* marital interaction are a necessity. In addition, the view held here on marital disharmony as indicative of an aggregate of specifiable maladaptive social behaviors necessarily implies that the effects of group marital therapy must also be assessed with explicit concern for the larger social system, i.e., the family, of which the marital pair is part. Evaluation of the effects of marital treatment will be comprehensive only when directed toward an understanding of the behaviors, thoughts, and feelings of marital partners in a series of active encounters in an ongoing social context.

REFERENCES

Barrett-Lennard, G.T. (1962), "Dimensions of Therapist Response as a Casual Factor in Therapeutic Change," *Psychological Monographs, 76 (#43*, Whole No. 562).

Bednar, R.L., and G.F. Lewis (1971), "Empirical Research in Group Psychotherapy." In A.E. Bergin and S. Garfield (eds.) *Handbook of Psychotherapy and Behavior Change.* New York: Wiley, pp. 812-838.

Bennis, W.G. (1960), "A Critique of Group Therapy Research," *International Journal of Group Psychotherapy*, 10:68–77.

Bergin, A.E. (1963), "The Effects of Psychotherapy: Negative Results Revisited," *Journal of Counseling Psychology*, 10:244-250.

————and H.H. Strupp (1970), "New Directions in Psychotherapy Research," *Journal of Abnormal Psychology*, 76:13-26.

Beukenkamp, C. (1959), "The Noncommunication Between Husbands and Wives as Revealed in Group Psychotherapy," *International Journal of Group Psychotherapy*, 9:308-313.

Blinder, M.G., and M. Kirschenbaum (1967), "The Technique of Married Couple Group Therapy," *Archives of General Psychiatry*, 17:44-52.

Boas, C.V.E. (1962), "Intensive Group Psychotherapy with Married Couples," *International Journal of Group Psychotherapy*, 12:142-153.

Bruninga, C.L. (1967), "Group Marriage Counseling in a State Hospital," *Hospital and Community Psychiatry*, 18:379-380.

Burton, G. (1962), "Group Counseling with Alcoholic Husbands and Their Nonalcoholic Wives," *Marriage & Family Living*, 24:56-61.

————and H.M. Kaplan (1968), "Group Counseling in Conflicted Marriages Where Alcoholism Is Present: Clients' Evaluation of Effectiveness," *Journal of Marriage and the Family*, 30:74-79.

Carroll, E.J. (1963), "Psychotherapy of Marital Couples," *Family Process*, 2:25-33.

Conrad, G.J. and H.K. Elkins, (1959), "The First Eighteen Months of Group Counseling in a Family Service Agency," *Social Casework*, 40:123-129.

Dakan, E.A. (1950), "Changes in Concept of Self and of Partner for Married Couples in Nondirective Group Therapy," Unpublished Ed.D. dissertation: Teachers College, Columbia University.

Flint, A.A., Jr., and B.W. MacLennan, (1962), "Some Dynamic Factors in Marital Group Psychotherapy," *International Journal of Group Psychotherapy*, 12:355-361.

Fox, R.E. (1968), "The Effect of Psychotherapy on the Spouse," *Family Process*, 7:7-16.

Gottlieb, S.B. (1960), Response of Married Couples Included in a Group of Single Patients," *International Journal of Group Psychotherapy*, 10:143-159.

Gottlieb, A., and E.M. Pattison, (1966), "Married Couples Group Psychotherapy," *Archives of General Psychiatry*, 14:143-152.

Greene, B. (ed.) (1965), *The Psychotherapies of Marital Disharmony*. New York: Free Press.

Griffin, R.W. (1967), "Change in Perception of Marital Relationship as Related to Marriage Counseling," *Dissertation Abstracts*, 27 (1-A), 3956.

Grunebaum, H., J. Christ and N. Neiberg, (1969), "Diagnosis and Treatment

Planning for Couples," *International Journal of Group Psychotherapy*, 19:185-202.

Hastings, P.R., and R.L. Runkle (1963), "An Experimental Group of Married Couples with Severe Problems," *International Journal of Group Psychotherapy*, 13:84-92.

Henderson, N.B. (1965), "Married Group Therapy: A Setting for Reducing Resistances," *Psychological Reports*, 16:347-352.

Hobbs, N. (1951), "Group-Centered Psychotherapy," In C.R. Rogers (ed.) *Client-Centered Therapy*. Boston: Houghton-Mifflin, pp. 278-319.

Hooper, D., A. Sheldon, and A.J.R. Koumans (1968), "A Study of Group Psychotherapy with Married Couples," *International Journal of Social Psychiatry*, 15:57-68.

Hulse, W.C. (1956), "Group Psychotherapy." In V.W. Eisenstein (ed.), *Neurotic Interaction in Marriage*. New York: Basic Books, pp. 290-295.

Jackson, J., and M. Grotjahn, (1958), "The Re-Enactment of the Marriage Neurosis in Group Psychotherapy," *Journal of Nervous and Mental Diseases*, 127:503-510.

————(1959), "The Efficacy of Group Therapy in a Case of Marriage Neurosis," *International Journal of Group Psychotherapy*, 9:420-428.

Jones, W.L. (1967), "The Villain and the Victim: Group Therapy for Married Couples," *American Journal of Psychiatry*, 124:351-354.

Lebedun, M. (1970), "Measuring Movement in Group Marital Counseling," *Social Casework*, 51:35-43.

Leichter, E. (1962), "Group Psychotherapy of Married Couples' Groups: Some Characteristic Treatment Dynamics," *International Journal of Group Psychotherapy*, 12:154-163.

Leslie, G.R. (1964), "The Field of Marriage Counseling," In H.T. Christensen (ed.), *Handbook of Marriage and the Family*, Chicago: Rand McNally, pp. 912-943.

Liberman, R. (1970), "Behavioral Approaches to Family and Couple Therapy," *American Journal of Orthopsychiatry*, 40:106-118.

Linden, M.E., H.M. Goodwin, and H. Resnik, (1968), "Group Psychotherapy of Couples in Marriage Counseling," *International Journal of Group Psychotherapy*, 18:313-324.

Miazlish, I.L. (1957), "Group Psychotherapy of Husband-Wife Couples in a Child Guidance Clinic," *Group Psychotherapy*, 10:169–180.

————and J.R. Hurley (1963), "Attitude Changes of Husbands and Wives in Time-Limited Group Psychotherapy," *Psychiatric Quarterly Supplement*, 37:230-249.

Neubeck, G. (1953), "Factors Affecting Group Psychotherapy with Married Couples." Unpublished Ed. D Dissertation: Teachers College, Columbia University.

————(1954), "Factors Affecting Group Psychotherapy with Married Couples," *Marriage and Family Living*, 16:216-220.

Papenek, H. (1965), "Group Psychotherapy with Married Couples." In H. Masserman (ed.), *Current Psychiatric Therapies*, Vol. 5. New York: Grune and Stratton, pp. 157-163.

Parloff, M.B. (1967), "Group Therapy Evaluation: Much to Do About Nothing," *International Journal of Psychiatry*, 4:352-358.

Pattison, E.M. (1965), "Evaluation Studies of Group Psychotherapy," *International Journal of Group Psychotherapy*, 15:382–397.

Perelman, J.S. (1960), "Problems Encountered in Group Psychotherapy of Married Couples," *International Journal of Group Psychotherapy*, 10:136-142.

Rabkin, L.Y. (1965), "The Patient's Family: Research Methods," *Family Process*, 4:105-132.

Shapiro, D., and L. Birk (1967), "Group Therapy in Experimental Perspective," *International Journal of Group Psychotherapy,* 17:211-224.

Sherman, S. (1956), "Group Counseling," In V.W. Eisenstein (ed.), *Neurotic Interaction in Marriage.* New York: Basic Books, pp. 296-302.

Slavson, S.R. (1950), *Analytic Group Psychotherapy with Children, Adolescents and Adults.* New York: Columbia University Press.

Strupp, H.H., and A.E. Bergin (1969), "Some Empirical and Conceptual Bases for Coordinated Research in Psychotherapy," *International Journal of Psychiatry,* 7:18-90.

Targow, J.G., and R.V. Zweber (1969), "Participants' Reactions to Treatment in a Married Couples' Group," *International Journal of Group Psychotherapy,* 19:221-225.

Truax, C.B., and R.R. Carkhuff (1967), *Toward Effective Counseling and Psychotherapy.* Chicago: Aldine.

Westman, J.C., D.J. Carek, and J.F. McDermott (1965), "A Comparison of Married Couples in the Same and Separate Therapy Groups," *International Journal of Group Psychotherapy,* 15:374-381.

Whitehorn, J.C., and B.J. Betz (1954), "A Study of Psychotherapeutic Relationships between Physicians and Schizophrenic Patients," *American Journal of Psychiatry,* 111:321-331.

Section C

Behavioral Approaches
to Marital Therapy

10 Behavioral Principles in Family and Couple Therapy

Behavioral approaches to family therapy specify the problems in concrete and observable terms, empirically applying principles of learning in
working toward therapeutic goals. The key to successful family therapy
can be found in the changes made in the interpersonal consequences of the
family members' behavior.

The current splurge of couple and family therapies is not simply an accident
or passing fad. These increasingly used modes of treatment for psychiatric
problems are anchored in a sound foundation and are not likely to blow away.
The foundation of these newer therapies lies in the opportunity they offer to
induce significant behavioral change in the participants by a major restructuring
of their interpersonal environments.

Couple and family therapy can be particularly potent means of behavior
modification because the interpersonal milieu that undergoes change is that of
the day-to-day, face-to-face encounter an individual experiences with the most
important people in his life—his spouse or members of his immediate family.
When these therapies are successful it is because the therapist is able to guide
the members of the couple or family into changing their modes of dealing with
each other. In behavioral or learning terms, we can translate "ways of dealing
with each other" into consequences of behavior or *contingencies of reinforcement*. Instead of rewarding maladaptive behavior with attention and concern,
the family members learn to give each other recognition and approval for
desired behavior.

Since the family is a system of interlocking, reciprocal behaviors (including affective behavior), family therapy proceeds best when each of the members learns how to change his or her responsiveness to the others. Family therapy should be a learning experience for all the members involved. For simplification, however, this paper will analyze family pathology and therapy from the point of view of the family responding to a single member.

Typically, families that come for treatment have coped with the maladaptive or deviant behavior of one member by responding to it over the years with anger, nagging, babying, conciliation, irritation, or sympathy. These responses, however punishing they might seem on the surface, have the effect of reinforcing the deviance, that is, increasing the frequency or intensity of the deviant behavior in the future. Reinforcement occurs because the attention offered is viewed and felt by the deviant member as positive concern and interest. In many families with a deviant member, there is little social interaction and the individuals tend to lead lives relatively isolated from each other. Because of this overall lack of interaction, when interaction does occur in response to a member's "abnormal" behavior, such behavior is powerfully reinforced (Patterson et al., 1967).

Verbal and nonverbal means of giving attention and recognition can be termed *social reinforcement* (as contrasted with food or sex, which are termed *primary reinforcement*). Social reinforcement represents the most important source of motivation for human behavior (Ferster, 1963; Skinner, 1953). Often massive amounts of such "concern" or social reinforcement are communicated to the deviant member, focused and contingent upon the member's maladaptive behavior. The deviant member gets the message: "So long as you continue to produce this undesirable behavior (symptoms), we will be interested and concerned in you." Learning the lesson of such messages leads to the development and maintenance of symptomatic or deviant behavior and to characterological patterns of activity and identity. Sometimes, the message of concern and interest is within the awareness of the "sick" member. Individuals with a conscious awareness of these contingencies are frequently termed "manipulative" by mental health professionals since they are adept at generating social reinforcement for their maladaptive behavior. But learning can occur without an individual's awareness or insight, in which case we view the maladaptive behavior as being unconsciously motivated.

Massive amounts of contingent social reinforcement are not necessary to maintain deviant behavior. Especially after the behavior has developed, occasional or *intermittent reinforcement* will promote very durable continuation of the behavior. Laboratory studies have shown that intermittent reinforcement produces behavior that is most resistant to extinction (Ferster, 1965).

Many family therapists (Framo, 1965; Handel, 1967; Vogel and Bell, 1960) have demonstrated that the interest and concern family members show in the deviance of one member can be in the service of their own psychological economy. Maintaining a "sick" person in the family can be gratifying (rein-forcing) to others, albeit at some cost in comfort and equanimity. Patterson and Reid (1967) describe how this reciprocal reinforcement can maintain deviant behavior by using the example of a child who demands an ice cream cone while shopping with his mother in a supermarket. The reinforcer for this "demand behavior" is compliance by the mother, but if she ignores the demand, the effect is to increase the rate or loudness of the demand. Loud demands or shrieks by a child in a supermarket are aversive to the mother; that is, her noncompliance is punished. When the mother finally buys the ice cream cone, the aversive tantrum ends. The reinforcer for the child's tantrum is the ice cream cone. The reinforcing contingency for the mother was the termination of the "scene" in the supermarket. In this reciprocal fashion, the tantrum behavior is maintained. I shall return to. this important aspect of family psychopa-thology—the mutually reinforcing or symbiotic nature of deviance—in the case studies below. Indeed, the balance between the aversive and gratifying consequences of maladaptive behavior in a member on the other family mem-bers is the crucial determinant of motivation for and response to treatment.

Changing the contingencies by which the patient gets acknowledgment and concern from other members of his family is the basic principle of learning that underlies the potency of family or couple therapy. Social reinforcement is made contingent on desired, adaptive behavior instead of maladaptive and symp-tomatic behavior. It is the task of the therapist in collaboration with the family or couple to (1) specify the maladaptive behavior, (2) choose reasonable goals which are alternative, adaptive behaviors, (3) direct and guide the family to change the contingencies of their social reinforcement patterns from maladap-tive to adaptive target behaviors.

Another principle of learning involved in the process of successful family therapy is modeling, also called imitation or identification. The model, some-times the therapist but also other members of the family, exhibits desired adaptive behavior which then is imitated by the patient. Imitation or identifica-tion occurs when the model is an esteemed person (therapist, admired family member) and when the model receives positive reinforcement (approval) for his behavior from others (Bandura and Walters, 1963). The amount of observa-tional learning will be governed by the degree to which a family member pays attention to the modeling cues, has the capacity to process and rehearse the cues, and possesses the necessary components in his behavioral experience which can be combined to reproduce the more complex, currently modeled behavior.

Imitative learning enables an individual to short-circuit the tedious and lengthy process of trial-and-error (or reward) learning while incorporating complex chains of behavior into his repertoire. Much of the behaviors which reflect the enduring part of our culture are to a large extent transmitted by repeated observation of behavior displayed by social models, particularly familial models. If performed frequently enough and rewarded in turn with approval by others, the imitated behavior will become incorporated into the patient's behavioral repertoire. The principles of imitative learning have been exploited with clinical success by researchers working with autistic children (Lovaas, 1966), phobic youngsters (Bandura *et al.*, 1967), and mute, chronic psychotics (Sherman, 1965). How modeling can be used in family therapy will be illustrated in the cases cited below.

I will limit the scope of the case examples to couples and families; however, the same principles of learning apply to group therapy (Liberman, 1970; Shapiro and Birk, 1967), and with some modification to individual psychotherapy (Krasner, 1962). Although learning theory has been associated in clinical psychiatry with its systematic and explicit application in the new behavior therapies, it should be emphasized that learning theory offers a generic and unitary explanation of the processes mediating change in all psychotherapies, including psychoanalytic ones (Alexander, 1965; Marmor, 1966).

Technique

Before getting to the case material, I would like to outline the main features of an application of behavior theory to family therapy. The three major areas of technical concern for the therapist are: (1) *creating and maintaining a positive therapeutic alliance;* (2) *making a behavioral analysis of the problem(s);* and (3) *implementing the behavioral principles of reinforcement and modeling in the context of ongoing interpersonal interactions.*

Without the positive therapeutic alliance between the therapist and those he is helping, there can be little or no successful intervention. The working alliance is the lever which stimulates change. In learning terms, the positive relationship between therapist and patient(s) permits the therapist to serve as a social reinforcer and model; in other words, to build up adaptive behaviors and allow maladaptive behaviors to extinguish. The therapist is an effective reinforcer and model for the patients to the extent that the patients value him and hold him in high regard and warm esteem.

Clinicians have described the ingredients that go into this positive therapist-patient relationship in many different ways. Terminology varies with the "school" of psychotherapy to which the clinician adheres. Psychoanalysts have contributed notions such as "positive transference" and an alliance between the therapist and the patient's "observing ego." Reality therapists call for a trusting involvement with the patient. Some clinicians have termed it a "supportive relationship" implying sympathy, respect, and concern on the part of the therapist. Recent research has labeled the critical aspects of the therapist-client relationship: nonpossessive warmth, accurate empathy, and genuine concern (Ballentine, 1968). Truax and his colleagues (1967) have been able to successfully operationalize these concepts and to teach them to selected individuals. They have further shown that therapists high on these attributes are more successful in psychotherapy than those who are not. Whatever the labels, a necessary if not sufficient condition for therapeutic change in patients is a doctor-patient relationship that is infused with mutual respect, warmth, trust, and affection.

In my experience, these qualities of the therapeutic alliance can be developed through a period of initial evaluation of the patient or family. The early therapist-family contacts, proceeding during the first few interviews, offer an opportunity to the therapist to show unconditional warmth, acceptance, and concern for the clients and their problems.

Also during the first few sessions, while the therapeutic relationship is being established, the therapist must do his "diagnostic." In a learning approach to family therapy, the diagnostic consists of a *behavioral* or *functional analysis* of the problems. In making his behavioral analysis, the therapist, in collaboration with the family, asks two major questions:

1. What behavior is maladaptive or problematic—what behavior in the designated patient should be increased or decreased? Each person, in turn, is asked, (1) what changes would you like to see in others in the family, and (2) how would you like to be different from the way you are now? Answering these questions forces the therapist to choose carefully *specific behavioral goals*.

2. What environmental and interpersonal contingencies currently support the problematic behavior—that is, what is maintaining undesirable behavior or reducing the likelihood of more adaptive responses? This is called a "functional analysis of behavior," and also can include an analysis of the development of symptomatic or maladaptive behavior, the "conditioning history" of the patient. The mutual patterns of social reinforcement in the family deserve special scrutiny in this analysis since their deciphering and clarification become central to an understanding of the case and to the formulation of therapeutic strategy.

It should be noted that the behavioral analysis of the problem doesn't end after the initial sessions, but by necessity continues throughout the course of therapy. As the problem behaviors change during treatment, so must the analysis of what maintains these behaviors. New sources of reinforcement for the patient and family members must be assessed. In this sense, the behavioral approach to family therapy is dynamic.

The third aspect of behavioral technique is the actual choice and implementation of therapeutic strategy and tactics. Which interpersonal transactions between the therapist and family members and among the family members can serve to alter the problem behavior in a more adaptive direction? The therapist acts as an educator, using his value as a social reinforcer to instruct the family or couple in changing their ways of dealing with each other. Some of the possible tactics are described in the case studies below.

A helpful way to conceptualize these tactics is to view them as "behavioral change experiments" where the therapist and family together re-program the contingencies of reinforcement operating in the family system. The behavioral change experiments consist of family members responding to each other in various ways, with the responses contingent on more desired reciprocal ways of relating. Ballentine (1968) views the behavioral change experiments, starting with small but well-defined successes, as leading to (1) a shift toward more optimistic and hopeful expectations; (2) an emphasis on doing things differently while giving the responsibility for change to each family member; (3) "encouragement of an observational outlook which forces family members to look closely at themselves and their relationships with one another, rather than looking 'inside' themselves with incessant why's and wherefores"; and (4) "the generation of empirical data which can be instrumental to further change, since they often expose sequences of family action and reaction in particularly graphic and unambiguous fashion."

The therapist also uses his importance as a model to illustrate desired modes of responding differentially to behavior that at times is maladaptive and at other times approaches more desirable form. The operant conditioning principle of "shaping" is used, whereby gradual approximations to the desired end behavior are reinforced with approval and spontaneous and genuine interest by the therapist. Through his instructions and example, the therapist teaches shaping to the members of the couple or family. Role playing or behavioral rehearsal are among the useful tactics employed in generating improved patterns of interaction among the family members.

The therapist using a behavioral model does not act like a teaching machine, devoid of emotional expression. Just as therapists using other theoretical schemas, he is most effective in his role as an educator when he expresses himself with affect in a comfortable, human style developed during his clinical training and in his life as a whole. Since intermittent reinforcement produces more durable behavior, the therapist may employ trial terminations, tapering off the frequency of the sessions prior to termination and "booster" sessions. (Alexander, 1965). The strategy and tactics of this behavioral approach to couples and families will be more clearly delineated in the case studies that follow. A more systematic and detailed outline of the behavior modification approach is presented in Table 1. The specification and implications of the items in this outline can be found in the manual by Reese (1966).

Case #1

Mrs. D. is a 35-year-old housewife and mother of three children who had a 15-year history of severe, migranous headaches. She had had frequent medical hospitalizations for her headaches (without any organic problems being found), and also a 1½-year period of intensive, psychodynamically oriented, individual

Table 1
A BEHAVIORAL MODEL FOR LEARNING
(adapted from E P. Reese, 1966)

1. Specify the final performance (therapeutic goals):
   - Identify the behavior.
   - Determine how it is to be measured.

2. Determine the current baseline rate of the desired behavior.

3. Structure a favorable situation for eliciting the desired behavior by providing cues for the appropriate behavior and removing cues for incompatible, inappropriate behavior.

4. Establish motivation by locating reinforcers, depriving the individual of reinforcers (if necessary), and withholding reinforcers for inappropriate behavior.

5. Enable the individual to become comfortable in the therapeutic setting and to become familiar with the reinforcers.

6. Shape the desired behavior:
   - Reinforce successive approximations of the therapeutic goals.
   - Raise the criterion for reinforcement gradually.
   - Present reinforcement immediately, contingent upon the behavior.

7. Fade out the specific cues in the therapeutic setting to promote generalization of acquired behavior.

8. Reinforce intermittantly to facilitate durability of the gains.

9. Keep continuous, objective records.

psychotherapy. She found relief from her headaches only after retreating to her bed for periods of days to a week with the use of narcotics.

After a brief period of evaluation by me, she again developed intractable headaches and was hospitalized. A full neurological workup revealed no neuropathology. At this time I recommended that I continue with the patient and her husband in couple therapy. It had previously become clear to me that the patient's headaches were serving an important purpose in the economy of her marital relationship: headaches and the resultant debilitation were the sure way the patient could elicit and maintain her husband's concern and interest in her. On his part, her husband was an active, action-oriented man who found it difficult to sit down and engage in conversation. He came home from work, read the newspaper, tinkered with his car, made repairs on the house, or watched TV. Mrs. D. got her husband's clear-cut attention only when she developed headaches, stopped functioning as mother and wife, and took to her bed. At these times Mr. D was very solicitous and caring. He gave her medication, stayed home to take care of the children, and called the doctor.

My analysis of the situation led me to the strategy of redirecting Mr. D's attention to the adaptive strivings and the maternal and wifely behavior of his wife. During ten 45-minute sessions, I shared my analysis of the problem with Mr. and Mrs. D and encouraged them to reciprocally restructure their marital relationship. Once involved in a trusting and confident relationship with me, Mr. D worked hard to give his wife attention and approval for her day-to-day efforts as a mother and housewife. When he came home from work, instead of burying himself in the newspaper he inquired about the day at home and discussed with his wife problems concerning the children. He occasionally rewarded his wife's homemaking efforts by taking her out to a movie or to dinner (something they had not done for years). While watching TV he had his wife sit close to him or on his lap. In return, Mrs. D. was taught to reward her husband's new efforts at intimacy with affection and appreciation. She let him know how much she liked to talk with him about the day's events. She prepared special dishes for him and kissed him warmly when he took initiative in expressing affection toward her. On the other hand, Mr. D was instructed to pay minimal attention to his wife's headaches. He was reassured that in so doing, he would be helping her decrease their frequency and severity. He was no longer to give her medication, cater to her when she was ill, or call the doctor for her. If she got a headache, she was to help herself and he was to carry on with his regular routine insofar as possible. I emphasized that *he should not, overall, decrease his attentiveness to his wife, but rather change the timing and direction of his attentiveness*. Thus the behavioral contingencies of Mr. D's attention changed from headaches to housework, from invalidism to active coping and functioning as mother and wife.

Within ten sessions, both were seriously immersed in this new approach toward each other. Their marriage was different and more satisfying to both. Their sex life improved. Their children were better behaved, as they quickly learned to apply the same reinforcement principles in reacting to the children and to reach a consensus in responding to their children's limit-testing. Mrs. D got a job as a department store clerk (a job she enjoyed and which provided her with further reinforcement—money and attention from people for "healthy" behavior). She was given recognition by her husband for her efforts to collaborate in improving the family's financial condition. She still had headaches, but they were mild and short-lived and she took care of them herself. Everyone was happier including Mrs. D's internist who no longer was receiving emergency calls from her husband.

A followup call to Mr. and Mrs. D one year later found them maintaining their progress. She has occasional headaches but has not had to retreat to bed or enter a hospital.

Case #2

Mrs S. is a 34-year-old mother of five who herself came from a family of ten siblings. She wanted very badly to equal her mother's output of children and also wanted to prove to her husband that he was potent and fertile. He had a congenital hypospadius and had been told by a physician prior to their marriage that he probably could not have children. Unfortunately Mrs. S was Rh negative and her husband Rh positive. After their fifth child she had a series of spontaneous abortions because of the Rh incompatibility. Each was followed by a severe depression. Soon the depressions ran into each other and she was given a course of 150 EST's. The EST's had the effect of making her confused and unable to function at home while not significantly lifting the depressions. She had some successful short-term supportive psychotherapy but again plunged into a depression after a hysterectomy.

Her husband, like Mr. D in the previous case, found it hard to tolerate his wife's conversation, especially since it was taken up mostly by complaints and tearfulness. He escaped from the unhappy home situation by plunging himself into his work, holding two jobs simultaneously. When he was home, he was too tired for any conversation or meaningful interaction with his wife. Their sexual interaction was nil. Although Mrs. S tried hard to maintain her household and raise her children and even hold a part-time job, she received little acknowledgment for her efforts from her husband who became more distant and peripheral as the years went by.

My behavioral analysis pointed to a lack of reinforcement from Mrs. S's husband for her adaptive strivings. Consequently her depressions, with their large hypochondriacal components, represented her desperate attempt to elicit her husband's attention and concern. Although her somatic complaints and her self-depreciating accusations were aversive for her husband, the only way he knew how to "turn them off" was to offer sympathy, reassure her of his devotion to her, and occasionally stay home from work. Naturally, his nurturing her in this manner had the effect of reinforcing the very behavior he was trying to terminate.

During five half-hour couple sessions I focused primarily on Mr. S, who was the mediating agent of reinforcement for his wife and hence the person who could potentially modify her behavior. I actively redirected his attention from his wife "the unhappy, depressed woman" to his wife "the coping woman." I forthrightly recommended to him that he drop his extra job, at least for the time being, in order to be at home in the evening to converse with his wife about the day's events, especially her approximations at successful homemaking. I showed by my own example (modeling) how to support his wife in her efforts to assert herself reasonably with her intrusive mother-in-law and an obnoxious neighbor.

A turning point came after the second session, when I received a desperate phone call from Mr. S one evening. He told me that his wife had called from her job and tearfully complained that she could not go on and that he must come and bring her home. He asked me what he should do. I indicated that this was a crucial moment, that he should call her back and briefly acknowledge her distress but at the same time emphasize the importance of her finishing the evening's work. I further suggested that he meet her as usual after work and take her out for an ice cream soda. This would get across to her his abiding interest and recognition for her positive efforts in a genuine and spontaneous way. With this support from me, he followed my suggestions and within two weeks Mrs. S's depression had completely lifted.

She was shortly thereafter given a job promotion, which served as an extrinsic reinforcement for her improved work performance and was the occasion for additional reinforcement from me and her husband during the next therapy session. We terminated after the fifth session, a time limit we had initially agreed on.

Eight months later at followup they reported being "happier together than ever before."

Case #3

Edward is a 23-year-old young man who had received much psychotherapy, special schooling, and occupational counseling and training during the past 17 years. He was diagnosed at different times as a childhood schizophrenic and as mentally subnormal. At age 6 he was evaluated by a child psychiatry clinic and given three years of psychodynamic therapy by a psychoanalyst. He had started many remedial programs and finished almost none of them. He, in fact, was a chronic failure—in schools as well as in jobs. His parents viewed him as slightly retarded despite his low normal intelligence on IQ tests. He was infantilized by his mother and largely ignored or criticized by his father. He was used by his mother, who was domineering and aggressive, as an ally against the weak and passive father. When I began seeing them in a family evaluation, Edward was in the process of failing in the most recent rehabilitation effort—an evening, adult high school.

The initial goals of the family treatment, then, were (1) to disengage Edward from the clasp of his protective mother, (2) to get his father to offer himself as a model and as a source of encouragement (reinforcement) for Edward's desires and efforts towards independence, (3) to structure Edward's life with occupational and social opportunities that he could not initiate on his own. Fortunately the Jewish Vocational Service in Boston offers an excellent rehabilitation program based on the same basic principles of learning that have been elucidated in this article. I referred Edward to it and at the same time introduced him to a social club for ex-mental patients which has a constant whirl of activities daily and on weekends.

During our weekly family sessions, I used modeling and role-playing to help Edward's parents positively reinforce his beginning efforts at the J.V.S. and the social club. After three months at the J.V.S., Edward secured a job and now after another seven months has a job tenure and membership in the union. He has been an active member of the social club and has gone on weekend trips with groups there—something he had never done before. He is now "graduating" to another social club, a singles' group in a church, and has started action on getting his driver's license.

The family sessions were not easy or without occasional storms, usually generated by Edward's mother as she from time to time felt "left out." She needed my support and interest (reinforcement) in her problems as a hardworking and unappreciated mother at these times. Because of the positive therapeutic relationship cemented over a period of nine months, Edward's parents slowly began to be able to substitute positive reinforcement for his gradually improving efforts at work and play instead of the previous blanket criticism (also, paradoxically a kind of social reinforcement) he had received from them for his failures. I encouraged the father to share openly with Edward his own experiences as a young man reaching for independence, thereby serving as a model for his son.

The parents needed constant reinforcement (approval) from me for trying out new ways of responding to Edward's behavior; for example, to eliminate the usual nagging of him to do his chores around the house (which only served to increase the lethargic slothful behavior which accrues from the attention) and to indicate instead pleasure when he mows the lawn even if he forgets to rake the grass and trim the hedge. They learned to give Edward approval when he takes the garbage out even if he doesn't do it "their" way. And they learned how to spend time listening to Edward pour out his enthusiasm for his job even if they feel he is a bit too exuberant.

Our family sessions were tapered to twice monthly and then to once a month. Termination went smoothly after one year of treatment.

Case # 4

Mr. and Mrs. F have a long history of marital strife. There was a year-long separation early in their marriage and several attempts at marriage counseling lasting three years. Mr. F has paranoid trends which are reflected in his extreme sensitivity to any lack of affection or commitment toward him by his wife. He is very jealous of her close-knit relationship with her parents. Mrs. F is a disheveled and unorganized woman who has been unable to meet her husband's expectations for an orderly and accomplished homemaker or competent manager of their five children. Their marriage has been marked by frequent mutual accusations and depreciation, angry withdrawal and sullenness.

My strategy with this couple, whom I saw for 15 sessions, was to teach them to stop reinforcing each other with attention and emotionality for undesired behavior and to begin eliciting desired behavior in each other using the principle of *shaping*. Tactically, I structured the therapy sessions with an important "ground-rule": No criticism or harping were allowed and they were to spend the time telling each other what the other had done during the past week that approached the desired behaviors. As they gave positive feedback to each other for approximations to the behavior each valued in the other, I served as an auxiliary source of positive acknowledgment, reinforcing the reinforcer.

We began by clearly delineating what specific behaviors were desired by each of them in the other and by my giving them homework assignments in making gradual efforts to approximate the behavioral goals. For instance, Mr. F incessantly complained about his wife's lack of care in handling the evening meal—the disarray of the table setting, lack of tablecloth, disorderly clearing of the dishes. Mrs. F grudgingly agreed that there was room for improvement and I instructed her to make a start by using a tablecloth nightly. Mr. F in turn was told the importance of his giving her positive and consistent attention for her effort, since this was important to him. After one week they reported that they had been able to fulfill the assignment and that the evening meal was more enjoyable. Mrs. F had increased her performance to the complete satisfaction of her husband, who meanwhile had continued to give her positive support for her progress.

A similar process occurred in another problem area. Mr. F felt that his wife should do more sewing (mending clothes, putting on missing buttons) and should iron his shirts (which he had always done himself). Mrs. F was fed up with the home they lived in, which was much too small for their expanded family. Mr. F resolutely refused to consider moving to larger quarters because he felt it would not affect the quality of his wife's homemaking performance. I instructed Mrs. F to begin to do more sewing and ironing and Mr. F to reinforce this by starting to consider moving to a new home. He was to concretize this by spending part of each Sunday reviewing the real estate section of the newspaper with his wife and to make visits to homes that were advertised for sale. He was to make clear to her that his interest in a new home was *contingent* upon her improvements as a homemaker.

Between the third and sixth sessions, Mrs. F's father—who was ill with terminal lung cancer—was admitted to the hospital and died. During this period, we emphasized the importance of Mr. F giving his wife solace and support. I positively reinforced Mr. F's efforts in this direction. He was able to help his wife over her period of sadness and mourning despite his long-standing antagonism toward her father. Mrs. F in turn, with my encouragement, responded to her husband's sympathetic behavior with affection and appreciation. Although far from having an idyllic marriage, Mr. and Mrs. F have made tangible gains in moving closer toward each other.

Discussion

There is too much confusion in the rationales and technique underlying current practices in family therapy. Although attempts to convey the method of family therapy always suffer when done through the written word, I do not share the belief that "the vital communications in all forms of psychotherapy are intuitive, felt, unspoken, and unconscious" (Framo, 1965). Although this article is not meant as a "how to do it" treatise for family therapists, I do intend it as a preliminary attempt to apply a few of the basic principles of imitative learning and operant conditioning to couple and family therapy.

Although the rationalized conceptualization of family therapy practiced by psychoanalytically oriented therapists differs from the learning and behavioral approach described here, closer examination of the actual techniques used reveals marked similarity. For example Framo (1965), in explaining the theory behind his family therapy, writes: "The overriding goal of the intensive middle phases consists in understanding and working through, often through transference to each other and to the therapists, the introjects of the parents so that the parents can see and experience how those difficulties manifested in the present family system have emerged from their unconscious attempts to perpetrate or master old conflicts arising from their families of origin. . . . The essence of the true work of family therapy is in the tracing of the vicissitudes of early object-relationships, and . . . the exceedingly intricate transformations which occur as a function of the intrapsychic and transactional blending of the old and new family systems of the parents. . . ."

Despite the use of psychoanalytic constructs, Framo describes the actual process of family therapy in ways that are very compatible within a learning framework. He writes: "Those techniques which prompt family interaction are the most productive in the long run. . . . It is especially useful to concentrate on here-and-now feelings: this method usually penetrated much deeper than dealing with feelings described in retrospect. . . . As we gained experience in working with families we became less hesitant about taking more forceful, active positions in order to help the family become unshackled from their rigid patterns."

Framo goes on to give illustrations of his work with families in which differential reinforcement for behavior considered more desirable and appropriate is given by the therapists. In dealing with angry and aggressive mothers, "we learned to avoid noticing what they did (e.g. emotional in-fighting) and pay attention to what they missed in life." Trying to activate passive fathers, "the therapists make every conscious effort to build him up during the sessions. . . . A number of techniques have been tried: forcing more interaction between the husband and wife; assigning tasks; having a female therapist give encouragement in a flattering way; occasional individual sessions with the father." Zuk (1967) describes his technique of family therapy in ways that fit into a reinforcement framework. He views the cornerstone of the technique the exploration and attempt "to shift the balance of pathogenic relating among family members so that new forms of relating become possible." Zuk further delineates the therapist's tactics as a "go-between" in which he uses his leverage to "constantly structure and direct the treatment situation."

It should be emphasized that the behavioral approach does not simplistically reduce the family system and family interaction to individualistic or dyadic mechanisms of reinforcement. The richness and complexity of family interaction is appreciated by the family therapist working within a behavioral framework. For instance, Ballentine (1968) states: ". . . behavior within a system cannot be so easily modified by focusing on the behavioral contingencies existing within any two-person subsystem, since one person's behavior in relation to a second's is often determined by behaviors of others within the system . . . the behavioral contingencies within a family system are manifold and constitute a matrix of multiple behavioral contingencies."

The complexity of family contingencies is exemplified by a transient problem which arose in Case #3. As Edward developed more independence from his parents and spent less and less time at home, his parents began to argue more angrily. Edward had served as a buffer between them—taking sides, being used as a scapegoat for their hostility, and serving as a "problem child" who required joint parental action and solidarity. With their buffer gone, the husband-wife relationship intensified and friction developed. Since the therapeutic goals were limited to Edward's emancipation from his parents and since it seemed that the parents were sufficiently symbiotic to contain a temporary eruption of hostility, the therapist's major efforts at this point were aimed at protecting Edward from backsliding in response to guilt or family pressure. The strategy worked, and within a few weeks the parents had reached a new modus vivendi with each other while Edward continued to consolidate and extend his gains.

A behavioral and learning approach to family therapy differs from a more psychoanalytic one. The therapist defines his role as an educator in collaboration with the family; therefore, the assigning of "sickness" labels to members, with its potential for moral blame, does not occur as it does under the medical model embodied in the psychoanalytic concept of underlying conflict or disease. There is no need for family members to acknowledge publicly their "weakness" or irrationality since insight per se is not considered vital.

The behavioral approach, with its more systematic and specific guidelines, makes it less likely that a therapist will adventitiously reinforce or model contradictory behavior patterns. The behavioral approach, consistently applied, is potentially more effective and faster. When patients do not respond to behavioral techniques, the therapist can use his more empirical attitude to ask why and perhaps to try another technique. The orientation is more experimental and "the patient is always right," with the burden on the therapist to devise effective interventions. In the psychoanalytic approach, the tendency has been for the therapist to decide that their failures are caused by patients who were inappropriate for the technique rather than viewing the technique as needing modification for the particular patient.

The work of behaviorally oriented family therapists is not restricted to the here-and-now of the therapy sessions. As the cases described reveal, much of the effort involves collaboration and involvement with adjunctive agencies such as schools, rehabilitation services, medication, and work settings. Family therapists are moving toward this total systems approach.

The advantages of behavioral approaches to family therapy sketched in this paper remain to be proven by systematic research. Such research is now proceeding (Dunham, 1966; Lewinsohn *et al.*; Patterson and Reid, 1967; Zeilberger *et al.*, 1968). Much work will go into demonstrating that family processes are "essentially behavioral sequences which can be sorted out, specified and measured with a fair degree of accuracy and precision" (Ballentine, 1968). Hopefully, further clinical and research progress made by behaviorally oriented therapists will challenge all family therapists, regardless of theoretical leanings, to specify more clearly their intervention, their goals, and their empirical results. If these challenges are accepted seriously, the field of family therapy will likely improve and gain stature as a scientifically grounded modality.

REFERENCES

Alexander, F. (1965), "The Dynamics of Psychotherapy in the Light of Learning Theory," *International Journal of Psychiatry*, 1:189-207.

Ballentine, R. (1968), "The Family Therapist as a Behavioral Systems Engineer . . . and a Responsible One." Paper read at Georgetown University Symposium on Family Psychotherapy. Washington.

Bandura, A., and R. Walters (1963), *Social Learning and Personality Development*. New York: Holt, Rinehart & Winston.

Bandura, A., J. Grusec, and F. Menlove (1967), "Vicarious Extinction of Avoidance Behavior," *Personality and Social Psychology*, 5:16-23.

Dunham, R. (1966), "Ex Post Facto Reconstruction of Conditioning Schedules in Family Interaction." In *Family Structure, Dynamics and Therapy*, Irvin M. Cohen, (ed.) Psychiatric Research No. 20, American Psychiatry Association., Washington. Pp. 107-114.

Ferster, C. (1963), "Essentials of a Science of Behavior." In J.I. Nurnberger, C.B. Ferster and J.P. Brady (eds.), *An Introduction to the Science of Human Behavior*, New York: Appleton-Century-Crofts.

Framo, J. (1965), "Rational and Techniques of Intensive Family Therapy."In I. Boszormenyi-Nagy and J.L. Framo (eds.), *Intensive Family Therapy*, New York: Hoeber Medical Division.

Handel, G. (ed.) (1967), *The Psychosocial Interior of the Family*. Chicago: Aldine.

Krasner, L. (1962), "The Therapist as a Social Reinforcement Machine." In *Research in Psychotherapy*, H. Strupp, and L. Luborsky (eds.), Washington: American Psychology Association.

Lewinsohn, P., M. Weinstein and D. Shaw (1969), Depression: A Clinical Research Approach. In *Proceedings, 1968 Conference,* San Francisco: Association for the Advancement of Behavioral Therapy.

Liberman, R. (1970), "A Behavioral Approach to Group Dynamics," *Behavior Therapy.* In press.

Lovaas, O., *et al.* (1966), "Acquisition of Imitative Speech by Schizophrenic Children,"*Science,* 51:705-707.

Marmor, J. (1966), "Theories of Learning and Psychotherapeutic Process," *British Journal of Psychiatry,* 112:363-366.

Patterson, G., *et al*. (1967), "Reprogramming the Social Environment," *Child Psychology and Psychiatry,* 8:181-195.

Patterson, G. and J. Reid (1967), "Reciprocity and Coercion: Two Facets of Social Systems," Paper read at 9th Annual Institute for Resource in Clinical Psychology, University of Kansas.

Reese, E. (1966), *The Analysis of Human Operant Behavior.* Dubuque, Iowa: Wm. C. Brown.

Shapiro, D. and L. Birk (1967), "Group Therapy in Experimental Perspectives," *International Journal of Group Psychotherapy,* 17:211-224.

Sherman, J. (1965),"Use of Reinforcement and Imitation to Reinstate Verbal Behavior in Mute Psychotics," *Journal of Abnormal Psychology,* 70:155-164.

Skinner, B. (1953), *Science and Human Behavior*. New York: Macmillan.

Truax, C., and R. Carkhuff (1967), *Toward Effective Counseling and Psychotherapy: Training and Practice*. Chicago: Aldine.

Vogel, E., and N. Bell (1960), "The Emotionally Disturbed Child as the Family Scapegoat." In *A Modern Introduction to the Family,* N.W. Bell, and E.F. Vogel, (eds.), New York: Free Press.

Zeilberger, J. S.Sampen, and H. Sloane (1968), "Modification of a Child's Prob-
lem Behaviors in the Home with the Mother as Therapist," *Journal of Applied
Behavior Analysis*, 1:47-53.
Zuk, G. (1967), "Family Therapy," *Archives of General Psychiatry*, 16:71-79.

NATHAN HURVITZ

11   **Interaction Hypotheses
in Marriage Counseling***

Marital partners are significant others who enable and constrain each
other's behavior in interaction. Problems arise when the spouses do not
have a common definition of the situation in which their interaction occurs;
they cannot understand each other's behavior causing their differences to
become conflicts. To maintain a common definition of the situation each
spouse offers explanatory hypotheses about his own and the other's behavior. Instrumental hypotheses interpret the spouses' behavior so problems can be solved; terminal hypotheses do not. The counselor assists the
spouses to develop instrumental hypotheses and he encourages each
spouse to behave in such a way as to enable his significant other to change
in accord with their professed goal in counseling.

Marriage counseling is generally differentiated from other types of counseling and psychotherapy on the basis of its concern with the spouses as they
interact. Despite this professed concern with the spouses' interaction, marriage
counselors do not have an interactional psychology or interactional principles
and practices which they utilize in marriage counseling. Such a psychology,
principles and practices are found in the sociological theories of symbolic
interactionism (Blumer, 1969; Manis and Meltzer, 1967; McCall and Simmons, 1966; Mead, 1934; Rose, 1962; Shibutani, 1961; Stryker, 1964) and

*This article is based upon a paper, "Instrumental and Terminal Hypotheses in Counseling the
Marital Dyad," presented at the Annual Meeting of the National Council on Family Relations, San
Francisco, California, August, 1967.

interpretive or understanding sociology (Freund, 1968; Gerth and Mills, 1958; Weber, 1947).

Applying concepts derived from symbolic interactionism to the clinical setting suggests that all counseling must be conducted in relation to the client's "significant other"—who is not the therapist or counselor (Sullivan, 1953), but the person who is most intimately involved with him in the shifting dyads of everyday life. In the marital dyad each spouse is his partner's significant other. According to the point of view presented here, the spouses' marital problems have structural and not intrapsychic causes; that is, their problems arise from their interaction as members of a social system they have formed and within which they perform the roles appropriate to this system to achieve goals associated with their values. Counseling activities are not oriented to exploring and interpreting assumed unconscious processes as is the case in traditional marital counseling, but to the use of behavior modification methods by the counselor and the spouses to change overt behavior.

Applying concepts derived from interpretive sociology to marriage counseling suggests that the counselor assists each spouse to understand and change his own and his spouse's behavior and attitudes by encouraging each spouse to interpret and explain his own and his spouse's behavior. Weber's understanding sociology is joined with Mead's symbolic interactionism for it involves the imputation of motives in the role-taking process by relating means to ends in social action. Action is social when the subjective meaning attached to it by the acting individual (or individuals) takes into account and is oriented toward the behavior of others (Weber, 1947). The counselor encourages both spouses to formulate "interaction hypotheses" so he can learn how each spouse perceives and interprets his own behavior, to determine how well each spouse can take the role of the other to "make sense" of his own behavior in relation to the other and to explain how the other spouse perceives and interprets his behavior.

Marital interaction occurs in social acts—those in which the participants take account of the other or take the role of the other—and those social acts which epitomize the spouses' characteristic interaction are called exchanges. These exchanges are transactions which aggravate or conciliate the spouses' relationship, escalate or de-escalate their differences. The counselor encourages the spouses to become aware of their exchanges, to analyze them and evaluate whether they do take account of the other and do take the role of the other. This is done to help the spouses understand their communication and to determine the recurrent and significant elements that each spouse reports or demonstrates in their exchanges.

One of the reasons the spouses' differences become problems is that each has a different picture in his head about their interaction; that is, each has a different definition of the situation in which their interaction occurs (Thomas, 1931), and each has a different perception and interpretation of his own and the other's behavior, thoughts, and feelings. One or both may imply or infer meanings and have associated feelings about information and behavior that are considerably and consistently different from the other's, from the prevailing norms of their reference groups, or from the society as a whole. When each spouse implies or infers different meanings to his own or the other's information or behavior he does not or does not want to take the role of the other. He responds on the basis of his associated feelings which are not those of his significant other. The other does not comprehend the reason for his partner's feelings which are considered inappropriate, irrational, manipulative, etc., and communication breaks down. Because marital interaction occurs within a society in which individualistic and competitive values are expressed and enacted in interpersonal attitudes, each spouse feels himself threatened. Then feelings of insecurity and inadequacy are aroused with concomitant defensive responses exacerbating the communication difficulties, further estranging the spouses and compounding their problems.

The counselor helps each spouse to regard his partner as his most significant other and his own and the other's behavior, its meanings and the associated feelings as complementary aspects of an interaction process in which they enable and constrain each other and determine the other's behavior in their marriage. He assists the spouse to clarify the meanings upon which each bases his feelings and to postulate the causes of the other's behavior, meanings, and feelings. He helps the spouses determine what each does that provokes undersirable behavior and negative attitudes in the other, how to respond to the other's present undesirable behavior and negative attitudes in order to extinguish them, and how to respond to the other's emergent desirable behavior and positive attitudes in order to reinforce them. The counselor also functions as a mediator in addition to his recognized activities as a therapist and educator (Zuk, 1966). He listens to the spouses report their exchanges, and when he considers it appropriate asks questions and makes observations that help the spouses achieve their professed goal (which in this paper is assumed to be to maintain and enhance their marriage). In this way he helps the spouses raise their differences from a descending cycle of ever greater disorganization and destruction to rational understanding and control, and to apply problem-solving concepts and procedures in their continuing interaction (Werner, 1965).

It is important for the spouses to make hypotheses about their interaction because the way a spouse behaves in a situation depends upon what the situation means to him. That is, it is not the spouse's verbal or non-verbal behavior alone that determines the other's response to him. His partner's response is also determined by his presumption of the meaning of the situation of which the behavior is a part. Determining of the situation implies achieving congruence and consensus by imputing and testing motives and intent. Therefore the counselor attempts to establish the meaning of the behavior and determine motives and intent as an aspect of his change-producing function.

The spouses report the meaning of the situation, of their behavior and feelings; and the counselor infers the veracity of this asserted meaning by his awareness of the totality of the spouses' interaction which includes statements about life values, marital goals, interactional style, etc., on the one hand, and expressive movements that reveal feelings that either confirm or deny these statements on the other. The inferences or assumptions about one's own and the other's behavior, meanings and feelings are called hypotheses because there are no objective data or criteria by which they can be irrefutably verified.

The counselor elicits the spouses' hypotheses by asking direct questions, even if they may appear naive to the spouses, to learn whether or not the spouses have a common definition of the situation. He asks, in marital situations which require such a procedure, "What is your difficulty; what are the problems?" The counselor follows up the spouse's reply about his own or the other's behavior, attitudes, etc., with further questions: "Why do you think you do that?" "Why do you think you feel that way?" "Why do you think he [she] does that?" "Why do you think he [she] feels that way?" The explanations or hypotheses are usually introduced with "Because . . . ," "It seems to me . . . ," "According to her [him] . . . ," "Could it be . . ." and similar statements. These hypotheses are of two types: terminal and instrumental:

A. Terminal Hypotheses. These hypotheses interpret behavior, meanings or feelings so that each spouse does not understand his own and the other's behavior, meanings or feelings in their exchanges in such a way that something can be done to change the existing situation. They may or may not be "true" and they may "fit" the information available but do not offer possible plans of action that can be utilized to change the relationship, and may aggravate the spouses' situation. These hypotheses are irrelevant, non-operative, non-applicable and destructive. Such hypotheses describe, include and utilize:

1. Psychodynamic interpretations:

Husband A: "She has an oral fixation."

Wife B: "He has an unresolved Oedipus complex."

2. Pseudo-scientific explanations:

Husband C: "She's a Scorpio. All Scorpios act like that. It's a proven fact."

Wife D: "It's my ESP. I don't know if you believe in ESP, a lot of psychologists do, I know that. I have this ESP feeling and that's how I know what he's been doing."

3. Psychological name-calling:

Husband E: "She's a latent lesbian."

Wife F: "He's mentally ill."

4. Assertions or accusations about one's own and/or one's spouse's inability or lack of desire to change his behavior, attitudes or values:

Husband G: "I don't think there is anything wrong with me and the way I see things, and if anyone is going to change it has to be her."

Wife H: "He says he is willing to change and he tells you he's willing to change, but I don't think he'll ever change and there is no use in trying."

5. Unchangeable factors outside the marriage which are responsible for the spouse's problems:

Husband I: "I have a responsibility to my mother and I'm going to meet that responsibility regardless of what she thinks or anyone thinks—and if she can't accept that fact then she'd better get a divorce now."

Wife J: "He complains about the pressure of work and says that he has to do it and that's why he doesn't have time for the family—but he's always accepting new assignments that make more pressure. He says it has to be that way but to me it doesn't make sense."

6. Inappropriate generalizations about innate qualities or traits that cannot be changed.

Wife K: "He's got a terrible temper—that's the way he is. When he gets like that you can't do anything with him."

Husband L: "She's got a jealous nature. She gets mad when I just talk to another woman—even someone she knows I never saw before in my life."

7. References to unchanging religious or philosophical principles, immutable natural laws, oppressive social forces, etc.:

Husband M: "The Bible says that women are inferior to men and her talk about women being the equal of men goes against the word of God."

Wife N: "I won't go so far as to call it a conspiracy, but there does appear to be an organized effort on the part of most men in high places in our society to prevent women from achieving their rightful place in higher echelons of education, for instance, and that's the way he thinks too—that women are a lower type of human life."

8. Assertions based upon presumed laws of human nature:

Husband O: "Everybody knows that if a man doesn't have sex regularly it builds up in him so he just naturally looks for an outlet."

Wife P: "He was born without will power. Anyone who drinks the way he does just doesn't have normal will power."

9. Allegations about intellectual limitations:

Husband Q: "She never could add and she can't learn how now."

Wife R: "He's stupid. He doesn't know any better and he doesn't have enough sense to know it or to care."

B. Instrumental Hypotheses. These hypotheses explain behavior, meanings or feelings so that each spouse can understand his own and the other's behavior, meanings or feelings in their exchanges in such a way that something can be done to change the existing situation. They may or may not be "true" but they "fit" the information available and offer a basis for plans of action that can be utilized to change the relationship. These hypotheses are relevant, operative, applicable, and constructive. Such hypotheses describe, include and utilize:

1. Problems arising from discontinuities in communication:

Husband S: "She says it's because I don't listen to what she says. I do. But we just don't understand each other. Maybe it's a question of semantics."

Wife T: "He tells me one thing but means something else. You know, he says he's happy but he says it in such a way that I can't believe him. I think he's depressed. I don't know what to believe."

2. Changes in the spouses' relationship following situations and experiences that disturb the spouses' reciprocity:

Husband U: "Things just haven't been the same since we visited her parents on our vacation last year. Something happened there that made her act different."

Wife V: "He's not the same man he used to be. I think our troubles started when he got that new job. Maybe it's pressure or something."

3. One's own and/or one's spouse's limitations in handling situations within and out of marriage:

Husband W: "I'm so tired after working all day that I just can't listen to her tell me the neighborhood gossip when I get home. I guess I just don't have the patience to listen to the nonsense she has to report to me."

Wife X: "He has no idea of what a little child can be expected to do—he expects too much—and then he's upset."

4. One's own and/or one's spouse's habitual behavior, attitudes and values learned in growing-up experiences:

Wife Y: "His mother never taught him to pick up after himself and so he just leaves his clothes around and expects me to clean up after him. When I tell him to pick up his clothes he says I'm complaining."

Husband Z: "Her mother had trouble with her father so she taught my wife that all men want only one thing. No wonder she's frigid."

5. Problems due to the spouses' self-feelings associated with known life experiences:

Husband AA: "My trouble is that sometimes I feel so inadequate—like I'm faking everything. I know that at work they'll discover I'm faking and fire me."

Wife BB: "The reason is that I have a guilt complex. Sometimes I try to tell myself I didn't really do wrong. But I can't fool myself. Most of the time I feel I don't deserve to live."

6. Unknown and undefinable elements in the spouses' interaction which are too transient to grasp when they occur but whose significance is understood by the spouses:

Husband CC: "I don't know what it is but she gets these blue or moody spells and she just can't get her work done. When she gets depressed that way I feel superfluous and stay out of her way."

Wife DD: "Every few months or so he gets a feeling that he has to have a drink. I don't know why he feels like that but I'm always afraid it's going to turn into a drunken siege."

When the spouses come to the counselor he reviews their situation with them and points out to them how their role performances and role expectations are not complementary (Hurvitz, 1965), how each imputes a different meaning to the same behavior and therefore has different feelings, how each one, behaving on the basis of his value system, evaluates the other from a different perspective, and how each one, in attempting to maintain and enhance his own self-esteem may do so at the expense of the other. Specifically he may point out how each one wanted the other because of the same qualities for which he now deprecates him, how each one constrains the other so he cannot function differently, how each one provokes the other to behave so he can reject him, how each uses the other as a scapegoat for his own shortcomings, and how each one gains in some way from the very behavior he complains about in the other. He shows the spouses how they are involved in several different binds or vicious circles wherein the behavior, its meanings and their feelings are contingent upon and influence the other's, and wherein their characteristic interaction compels them to interact in ways they not only cannot change, but cannot even perceive; and their own efforts to modify their situation inevitably precipitate conflict which exacerbates the problems they want to solve.

The counselor elicits and exposes these binds to the spouses so they can determine their counseling goals, understand better what is expected from them in the counseling situation, evaluate whether the counselor "understands" them, and decide whether they want to work with him. The counselor invites the spouses to offer hypotheses to explain their binds, and he also offers hypotheses. The terminal hypotheses are rejected and instrumental hypotheses accepted; and when the spouses offer instrumental hypotheses the counselor asks, "What does this explanation of your situation require of you to achieve your purpose in coming here?" The counselor attempts to couple the efforts of one spouse to those of the other, and he also helps the spouses to act on limited, specific aspects of their interaction that are amenable to change. At the same time he helps them modify their self-image and to gain greater self-esteem.

The counselor understands that each spouse comes to him with feelings of depression, hurt, etc., about himself, vindictiveness, hostility, etc. toward the other, and concern, apprehension, etc. about the counseling experience. He is aware that even if the spouses want to achieve their asserted goal each has a different definition of the situation and interprets the same behavior, meanings and feelings differently depending upon whether they are his own or the other's. Each spouse tends to interpret his own and his spouse's behavior, meanings, and feelings in ways that permit him to justify and maintain his characteristic picture of himself, to eliminate problems that are important to him but not to the other, to hold the other responsible for their problems, to blame or manipulate the other spouse in some way, to expect that not he but the other spouse will change, or to achieve a covert goal. It is only after counseling has enabled the spouse to give up his defensiveness that he will attempt to understand the spouses' interaction, accept responsiblity for his behavior, recognize his contribution to the marital problems, and commit himself to achieve a mutually desired goal. The counselor evaluates the probability of change and the spouses' achievement of their asserted goal on the basis of both spouses' commitment to this goal, the individual and joint efforts they are willing and able to exert, their individual and joint capacity to give and receive what the other requires and offers, and the limits within which they will continue to work for their goals despite the other's shortcomings and failures of omission and commission.

When the counselor invites the spouses to offer hypotheses to explain their interaction, their initial hypotheses are based solely or principally upon interpretations of their own and the other's life histories, their common knowledge of the rules followed in everyday interaction, including elements of common sense psychology (Garfinkel, 1967; Shutz, 1967), and vocal communication, usually statements of intent. However, the counselor helps them examine their vocal and other overt behavior in such a way that each becomes more aware of his own and the other's feelings which are associated with covert meanings, which are better clues to understanding each one's definition of the situation. In this way the spouses develop hypotheses which make sense of their exchanges and establish a basis upon which they can participate in a cooperative and complementary process of causing reciprocal change (this is how hypotheses differ from insights) and they conduct this process in their daily interaction at home without the counselor present.

A spouse's hypotheses present more than his perception and interpretation of his own and his spouse's information, meanings and feelings. Some spouses offer hypotheses which assume that behavior arises from within or outside the individual, and others offer hypotheses that combine the "within" and "outside" hypotheses in various ways in relation to different situations. One's spouse's consistent ascription of "guilt feelings," "enjoyment of suffering," "insecurity," "feelings of failure," "repressed hostility," etc. as the motivation for the other's behavior may tell the counselor as much about himself as it does about the spouse he is describing. The counselor may question—that is, he may invite hypotheses from one or both spouses—why a spouse ascribes these motivations to the other and why he interprets the other as he does. In this way he may elicit characteristic defenses and projections. Although a spouse may report how he learned to behave as he does, often as a defensive explanation of his present behavior, the counselor is not as interested in the presumed sources of his behavior as he is in its consequences, particularly how it is reinforced in the spouses' continuing relationship.

Whether or not a spouse is able to offer hypotheses reveals his sensitivity to people in general and to his spouse in particular. A spouse who says he is unable to offer hypotheses about himself or the other may do so because of his concern that he may inadvertently reveal more than he wants to about himself or that he has a covert goal which is different from his asserted goals. The number, variety, and relevance of his hypotheses suggests something about his intellectual capacity and his ability for creative insight, as well as his probable ability to participate in and gain from counseling. Not only does the counselor request one spouse to offer hypotheses about the other, but he also requests the spouse to offer hypotheses about why he proposed the particular hypotheses he did; and the counselor also requests one spouse to offer hypotheses about why the other spouse proposed the hypotheses about him that he did. The continuing attempts to explain their interaction, the proposal, consideration, evaluation, and choice between alternative hypotheses in individual and/or joint sessions clarifies the sources of differences and aids the spouses to achieve consensus upon which gratifying joint action can be taken. In this way self-revelation is not presumed to be an end in itself but is a means to achieve an end; and the effort to determine motivation and intent is part of the process of effecting change.

The counselor also offers hypotheses as a basis for changing the spouses' interaction in accord with their asserted counseling goal; and he informs the spouses about his hypotheses. When the counselor proposes hypotheses he may recapitulate those offered by the spouses and add others which his experience and sensitivity suggest may be relevant or significant to the spouses. He offers the spouses the opportunity to choose those which make sense to them and he pursues the spouses' choices to determine why one was chosen and another rejected. By doing so he helps each spouse define his philosophy or system for perceiving and interpreting the behavior of others in general and of his spouse in particular; and the counselor helps the spouses develop a more appropriate and real philosophy or system for understanding others.

As the counselor gets to know the spouses better and the counselor and the spouses continue to propose hypotheses, the counselor guesses and expresses their defenses and projections, their self-feelings and feelings about the other, and their fantasies and unexpressed thoughts and concerns which they have not yet been willing to acknowledge and report themselves. As interesting as this activity always is—and as fascinating as it often is—the counselor's aim is to help the spouses develop hypotheses which enable them to participate in a process of effecting mutually enhancing change. Greater awareness of oneself and sensitivity to the other in the spouses' interaction results and leads to hypotheses which can be tested. By testing their hypotheses, that is, by attempting to determine and perform appropriate behavior in accord with the spouses' expressed goal and by attempting to implement the changes implied by or required by their hypotheses, the spouses begin to think and act constructively.

The spouses' hypotheses are based upon each one's goal for the marriage, his earlier interactions with significant others from whom he learned to perceive and interpret behavior, meanings and feelings, upon his own value system which is related to his class, education, religious and ethnic identification, etc., and upon his efforts to maintain his self-esteem. When a spouse's self-esteem is threatened each one employs the common mechanisms of defense which were learned and appropriate in earlier interaction. The counselor suggests to the spouses that when they are defensive they offer terminal hypotheses which are irrational and irrelevant and deny any means for achieving their asserted goal. If necessary, he explores these hypotheses with the spouses in relation to their earlier interaction with significant others to indicate their present idiosyncratic, unusual or inappropriate perceptions and interpretations; he questions those aspects of the spouse's value system which are related to the spouses' conflict or problems; and he exposes to each spouse how he may attempt to maintain and enhance his self-esteem at the expense of the other or in other unsuitable ways. As the spouses, with the counselor's assistance, become aware of the bases and purposes of their hypotheses they reject irrational and irrelevant explanations which do not permit them to apply problem-solving thoughts and action and instead offer rational and relevant explanations which do enable and permit problem-solving thought and action to achieve their goal.

The same terminal hypothesis may be used by one spouse to attack the other and also defend himself. A husband (for instance) may claim that his wife's presumed innate quality or trait is a destructive force in their marriage and demand that she change her behavior. At the same time he also claims that he "cannot help" his behavior and his innate quality or trait must be understood and accepted by her. The counselor indicates the irrationality of such a hypothesis by restating it as though the wife offered it about her husband; or the counselor may present it about a third person. The husband may say that he has a terrible temper, that his wife knows it and she must accept his outbursts; however, he complains about her jealousy. The counselor asks whether he is as willing to accept her jealousy as he is desirous of having her accept his temper. Most spouses quickly catch on to the double standard maintained in such an attitude. Those who persist in their demand that the other accept their behavior and in their assertion that they "cannot help" it must be confronted with the contradiction between such a demand and their professed desire to maintain and enhance their marriage. Continued persistence of this double standard and refusal to accept the counselor's help in modifying the inappropriate behavior reveals that a covert goal is involved.

The counselor uses the spouses' hypotheses to determine whether the spouses have a covert goal which is different from their asserted goal, to clarify the alternatives open to the spouses, and to decide which counseling technique to apply in their situation. A spouse may assert that he wants to maintain the marriage but refuses to offer any hypotheses about his own behavior and offers only terminal hypotheses about the other spouse's. He may present psychodynamic interpretations or refer to unchanging religious or philosophical principles and insist that these are relevant despite the counselor's effort to help him understand that insisting upon such hypotheses does not help him achieve his asserted goal to maintain the marriage. The counselor may proceed in two ways. He may question whether the spouse is committed to his asserted goal or has a covert goal, and use the information he secures from both spouses to indicate that a covert goal may exist. Or he may point out to the spouse that he has three alternatives: to end the marriage, to live with the marriage as it is, or to change it. If the spouse accepts the alternative to end the marriage he reveals that he may have entered counseling with a covert goal or that he adopted a covert goal and is not committed to his asserted goal. If the spouse decides to continue the marriage as it is then he needs to learn ways and attitudes that may enable him to survive in an unsatisfying relationship. But if the spouse wants to change the marriage then he must consider instrumental hypotheses which offer a basis for change. The counselor should be aware that the consistent use of pseudo-scientific explanations, references to unchanging religious or phil- osophical principles, immutable natural laws, oppressive social forces, etc. may indicate psychosis in one or both spouses; and he should investigate this possibility and secure appropriate guidance to determine whether he can help a spouse with such a problem.

In assessing and attempting to change the spouses' interaction the counselor attempts to modify one problem that they are most likely to solve. He does this to help the spouses understand the principles by which he works, to indicate that changes can be achieved by the application of these principles, and to utilize the success achieved by solving one problem to encourage the spouse to exert further effort. This process may also require the spouses to develop a different definition of their situation and to make different assumptions about it. For instance, a wife complains that her husband does not call to let her know when he will come home from work and she says that if he did they would not have any problems. Her husband replies that this is not the real problem for even if he called as she requests she would find something else to complain about. However he does not offer any hypotheses about what the "real" problem is or why she makes an issue about his calls. The counselor may also question whether his calls are the real problem and urge the husband to offer an alternate hypothesis. The counselor says, "Let's agree that what your wife says is not the real reason she's upset. What do you think the real reason is?" When the husband suggests one or more hypotheses and these are evaluated, the counselor says, "You've offered a number of explanations of why your wife might be upset that fit the information we have better than the reason she gave. Why do you think she gave this reason?" In this way the counselor may help the husband understand that it is not the calls as such that are so important but what they represent: respect, gentility, concern, etc.; and the counselor suggests that it may be helpful for the husband to call his wife as she desires. If the calls and what they represent are the real problem then they have solved it. If the calls do not solve their problem then both the wife and the husband must acknowledge that there are more important problems and both must offer hypotheses about their interactions which explains it in such a way that their "real" problems are elicited and possible ways of solving these problems in accord with their expressed goal are proposed.

In the counseling setting the counselor asks one spouse, the husband, (for instance) in this constructed example, who complains about his wife's telephone conversations with her mother which upset her, "Why do you think your wife gets upset?" If the husband responds with a terminal hypothesis the counselor replies, "That may or may not be true. If it is true then it means you can't change things between you. You're here because you say you want to improve your marriage. What other reasons can you think of why she does that?" If the husband responds with a hypothesis that does not include himself as the agent in his wife's behavior the counselor replies, "We agree that her mother's calls upset her. But you can't control what her mother does. You still haven't shown how things can be changed." When the husband offers a hypothesis in which he is an agent the counselor asks him what the hypothesis requires of him; that is, how he can use it to change the unsatisfying or destructive relationship between himself and his wife. "You say that your wife talks to her mother even though it upsets her because she doesn't have anyone else to talk to and you don't talk to her the way you believe you should. We don't know if that's true or not, but it sounds reasonable. What can you do about it?" Once the husband develops a hypothesis in which he accepts the responsibility for his wife's behavior the counselor helps him to behave in such a way as to achieve the asserted counseling goal.

The counselor helps the spouses define their problems so that their hypotheses complement each other's. He asks the wife, "Why do you think he is so angry when you talk to your mother?" If she offers a terminal hypothesis the counselor replies, "That may or may not be true. If it is true then it means you can't change things between you. You're here because you say you want to improve your marriage. What other reasons can you think of why he does that?" If the wife responds with a hypothesis that does not include herself as the agent in her husband's behavior the counselor replies, "That also may or may not be true. Perhaps he is unhappy because his mother doesn't call you. But you can't control what your mother does. You still haven't shown how things can be changed." When the wife offers a hypothesis which complements her husbands's hypothesis the counselor asks her what her hypothesis requires of her, that is, how can she use it to change the unsatisfying or destructive relationship between herself and her husband. You say that your husband is upset when you talk to your mother because he thinks you regard your mother as more important to you than he is. We don't know if that's true or not—but it sounds reasonable. What can you do about it?" As he does with the husband, the counselor helps the wife fulfill the behavior required or assumed in her hypothesis.

The counselor helps the spouses understand, in terms of their hypotheses, which elements in their interaction each must accept responsibility for, and what behavior and attitudes are required of each to help his spouse change in the way he wants and expects—for this is the same kind of behavior and attitudes his spouse wants and expects from him. When the spouses determine the action they must take to implement their hypotheses, the counselor helps each spouse to behave in the way that will elicit the behavior and attitudes he wants in the other in accord with their asserted counseling goal. He makes an aware effort to encourage each spouse to continue this behavior until the other's desired behavior and positive attitudes become established in the spouses' continuing interaction. As each spouse responds to the supportive behavior and positive affect of his significant other, he enables his significant other to continue his supportive behavior and positive affect toward him. Each spouse, with the counselor's support and guidance, becomes a reciprocal stimulus for further encouragement and reinforcement of their positive interaction.

Since the present counseling approach is set within a learning framework which assumes that inappropriate behavior is learned in interaction in the same way as "normal" behavior is learned, hypotheses based upon intrapsychic dynamics, unconscious motivations, and early childhood experiences are considered terminal because they do not permit the formulation of hypotheses which enable the spouse to participate in reciprocal change activities. Once the counselor has elicited instrumental hypotheses which require change-effecting behavior, he teaches the spouses the appropriate change-initiating and change-supporting behavior by various verbal methods, modeling, role playing demonstrations, and suitable behavior modification practices. Clinical experiences has indicated that marriage counseling based upon the exploration of intrapsychic dynamics slows the reciprocal change process and requires involvement with one spouse in a way that causes greater conflict between the spouses (Hurvitz, 1967).

The counselor evaluates each spouse's hypotheses about the other to determine whether their hypotheses and their associated behavior are in accord with their asserted goal. If their hypotheses or behavior are not consistent with that required or implied by their goal, the counselor must confront the spouses and point this out to them. However, he does not regard the spouses' behavior as evidence of resistance which has intrapsychic sources. He considers each spouse's inappropriate behavior as the persistence of a well-learned way of responding to the world, to the effect of particular settings and/or associations which elicit characteristic feelings which are expressed in typical behavior, to the existence of significant others who constrain him in his usual behavior, to a belief that things cannot change, to a concern that the changed situation may be no better, or it may be worse, and what is more, he will be held responsible. However, the counselor must reconsider his own and the spouses' hypotheses, develop new hypotheses, confront the spouses with his new interpretation of their interaction, offer them other means of changing their behavior, suggest alternate ways of breaking their binds, and develop ways of gaining a smaller increment of change than he had originally attempted to secure with the spouses. When the spouses complain that it is too difficult to change, the counselor points out that if they want to achieve their asserted goal they must exert all the effort implied in the importance of the goal to them.

Like other counseling methods, interaction therapy, the imputing and implementing of interaction hypotheses also has its limitations. More than other counseling methods this one requires the joint participation of both spouses although it is possible to counsel with one spouse if he seriously attempts to determine the other's definition of the situation in their exchanges. The very difficulties that exist between the spouses may prevent them from thinking about their problems in interactional terms. The spouses may therefore find it difficult to offer hypotheses or their hypotheses may not be related or complementary. One spouse may offer hypotheses about their total interaction while the other may offer hypotheses about specific aspects of their interaction. Although terminal hypotheses do not offer a basis for changing the spouses' existing relationship and the instrumental hypotheses do, not all instrumental hypotheses are equally useful as a basis for changing the spouses' interaction. Since instrumental hypotheses require each spouse to change his own behavior in some way as a precondition to secure a desired reciprocal change in the other, each may say it is difficult to change because of constraining elements in their real-life situation, strongly held self-attitudes, the need for face-saving compromises, etc. Each spouse may claim that he cannot offer hypotheses about the other because the other does not behave consistently. Each may hesitate to offer hypotheses because the hypotheses require him to change his own behavior to bring about change in the other. Each may be apprehensive about behaving in accord with the requirements of his own hypotheses because he may not succeed at the new behavior and therefore have to accept responsibility for the spouses' lack of progress. Each may complain that his new behavior, based upon his hypotheses, and attempted after considerable reflection and misgivings and with great effort, does not bring about the desired and expected change in the other. And each may believe that his efforts to change are not met by the other's comparable endeavor and therefore questions whether he should continue to try.

The changes that the counselor attempts to assist the spouses to achieve are not easily made even though the spouses offer instrumental hypotheses and the counselor exerts considerable effort to encourage each other's efforts. If the spouses want to improve their marriage and the counselor recognizes that their lack of cooperation and coordination of their efforts is another manifestation of their problems, the counselor must exert all the necessary effort to help them modify their behavior to achieve their asserted goal. He helps the spouses make real life adjustments, he supports the spuses as capable and effective persons, individually and jointly, so they do not feel threatened by their own and the other's instrumental hypotheses and the effort required to attempt to change, and he suggest compromises that each can accept.

When a spouse cannot offer instrumental hypotheses the counselor suggests that it is most helpful for each spouse to offer a hypothesis which requires him to behave in a positive manner or express positive attitudes toward the other in order to bring about a desired change in the other in accord with their expressed counseling goal. The counselor will suggest to the husband (for instance) that he assume that his wife wants him to behave toward her so as to enhance her self-esteem, and that if he behaves in this way his wife will probably respond so as to enhance his self-esteem in return. Therefore, in ambiguous situations in which a spouse does not understand the behavior, its meanings and the other's associated feelings in order to offer hypotheses, the counselor suggests that if each would act or respond so as to make the other feel better about himself both will be encouraged to behave in ways and express attitudes which will enable them both to achieve their asserted goal.

Although the examples given here relate to marital interaction, involving the spouses' dyad, the method suggested is applicable in any situation in which two persons are involved as significant others. Thus, this method is applicable to family therapy since family groupings of various kinds may be seen as a series of shifting dyads or coalitions (Wolff, 1950), even though the family is different from the sum of its dyads.

REFERENCES

Blumer, Herbert (1969), *Symbolic Interactionism.* Englewood Cliffs, N.J.: Prentice-Hall.

Freund, J. (1968), *The Sociology of Max Weber,* New York: Pantheon.

Garfinkel, Harold (1967), *Studies in Ethnomethodology.* Englewood Cliffs, N.J.: Prentice-Hall.

Gerth, H.H. and C. Wright Mills (eds.) (1958), *From Max Weber: Essays in Sociology.* New York: Oxford University Press.

Hurvitz, Nathan (1965), "The Marital Roles Inventory as a Counseling Instrument," *Journal of Marriage and the Family,* 27:492-50.

Hurvitz, Nathan (1967), "Marital Problems Following Psychotherapy with One Spouse," *Journal of Consulting Psychology,* 31:38-47.

Manis, Jerome G. and Bernard N. Meltzer, (eds). (1967), *Symbolic Interaction, A Reader in Social Psychology,* Boston: Allyn & Bacon.

McCall, George J., and J.L. Simmons (1966), *Identities and Interactions.* New York: Free Press.

Mead, George Herbert, (1934), *Mind, Self and Society.* Chicago: University of Chicago Press.

Rose, Arnold M. (ed.) (1962), *Human Behavior and Social Processes,* Boston: Houghton-Mifflin.

Schutz, Alfred (1967), *The Phenomenology of the Social World.* Evanston, Ill.: Northwestern University Press.

Shibutani, Tamotsu (1961), *Society and Personality.* Englewood Cliffs, N.J.: Prentice-Hall.

Stryker, Sheldon (1964), "The Interactional and Situational Approaches." In Harold T. Christensen (ed.), *Handbook of Marriage and the Family.* Chicago: Rand McNally.

Sullivan, Harry S. (1953), *The Interpersonal Theory of Psychiatry.* New York: W.W. Norton.

Thomas, William I. (1931), *The Unadjusted Girl.* Boston: Little Brown and Co.

Weber, Max (1947), *The Theory of Social and Economic Organization.* New York: Oxford Unversity Press.

Werner, Harold D. (1965), *A Rational Approach to Social Casework.* New York: Association Press.

Wolff, Kurt H. (ed.), (1950), *The Sociology of George Simmel,* Glencoe, Ill.: Free Press.

Zuk, Gerald H. (1966), "The Go-Between Process in Family Therapy." *Family Process,* 5:162-178.

RICHARD B. STUART

12   Behavioral Remedies for Marital Ills: A Guide to the Use of Operant-Interpersonal Techniques*

Operant-interpersonal treatment of marital discord is a social learning approach which is based on a functional analysis of dyadic marital interaction, including both the antecedents and consequences of social behavior. A five-stage intervention procedure is described in detail and focuses on the development of a new interpersonal vocabulary, the shaping of new techniques of social influence, the establishment of new means of information exchange, the creation of new decision-making norms, and the building of new techniques for maintaining change. The model emphasizes the specification of problem behavior and the criteria for change, and in so doing permits the techniques to be taught to practitioners and students and provides patients with a rational and cogent system which they can potentially self-apply to improve their relationship.

Behavior modifiers have paid surprisingly little attention to the modification of marital discord despite the importance of marital success to physical and mental health (Stuart and Lederer, 1974). Goldiamond (1965) referred to the importance of controlling the concomitants of aggressive exchanges and, in an early anecdotal report, Stuart (1969a; 1969b) suggested the use of token reinforcement to monitor and facilitate the contractual exchange of behaviors. Goldstein and Francis (1969) trained wives to alter the contingencies of their husbands' behavior, Liberman (1970) suggested the sophisticated use of stimulus control techniques, Rappaport and Harrell (1972) used a slightly expanded concept of behavioral contracting and Welch and Goldstein (1972) explored the relative importance of lectures on contingency control and the counting of non-specified positive and negative behaviors. Of these reports only the last utilized an experimental design. In more recent work, however, Hunt and Azrin have experimentally evaluated the importance of marital

*Readers wishing to learn more about the approach described here may want to consult: R. B. Stuart and W. J. Lederer, *How to Make a Bad Marriage Good and a Good Marriage Better* (New York: W. W. Norton, 1974).

behavior change for modification of alcoholics' drinking behavior. Turner (1972) has evaluated the effectiveness of couple, couple group, and no treatment upon changes in marital interaction, and Patterson and Hops (1972) and Weiss, Hops, and Patterson (1973) have laid the groundwork for an extensive experimental evaluation of a complex experimental package. At this time, then, the literature concerning behavioral approaches to marital treatment contains a wealth of descriptions of potentially useful techniques with but scant validation of their effectiveness. Because there is increasing recognition of the importance of marital interaction as a mediator of adaptive or deficit functioning in other areas, because marriage breakdown has rapidly acquired public recognition as a major social problem, and because measurement and intervention techniques have reached a new level of efficiency, a rapid growth in the extent of behavioral research in the area can be anticipated.

This chapter offers a description of one approach to marital treatment based upon operant-interpersonal theory. It is the approach which is currently being tested in an experimental program at the University of Michigan and it should be carefully compared to a similar program in operation at the University of Oregon (Weiss, Hops, and Patterson, 1973). Data reflecting the preliminary evaluation of results will be contained in a paper presently being prepared for publication.

A Theoretical Basis for Marital Treatment

George Levinger (1965) suggested that the strength of a marital relationship is "a direct function of the attractions within and barriers around the marriage, and an inverse function of such attractions and barriers from other relationships" (p. 19). Therefore, any effort to modify marital behavior must utilize a theoretical approach which permits prediction of spousal interaction in the light of the relationship between spouses, between each partner and social forces outside the marriage, and between the couple as a unit and these outside forces. To be suitable for an operant interpersonal approach, this theory must also yield refutable hypotheses so that the effectiveness of intervention can be tested in light of its theoretical underpinnings.

The functional analysis of behavior provides an ideal means of understanding observational data, particularly when the analysis includes both the antecedents and consequences of social behavior (e.g., Patterson and Cobb, 1971). Exchange theory represented by the work of Thibaut and Kelley (1959), Homans (1961), and Blau (1964) provides an ideal means of predicting and explaining such behavioral observations. Thibaut and Kelley, for example, devised a way of predicting individual choices in social situations through reference to both the absolute standards by which a person evaluates the adequacy of his or her alternatives (the Comparison Level), the relative superiority of one existing alternative over another (Comparison Level), and the relative superiority of one existing alternative over another (Comparison Level of Alternatives). Thus, a functional analyst might observe that a husband spends more evening time working than with his family, being nagged by his wife to stay home, and seduced by his employers to put in more hours. The exchange theorist would then identify his absolute preference to relax at home rather than at work, and would also demonstrate that his actual experience nevertheless presents more powerful inducements for work instead of spending time with his family. The functional analyst can then formulate a hypothesis that a change in the husband's use of his evening hours can occur through an increase in the value of reinforcements mediated by the wife relative to the constant level of work-mediated reinforcements. When the theories of the communications analysts are added to this evaluation (Watzlawick, Beavin, and Jackson, 1967), an extremely effective theoretical basis for therapeutic intervention becomes available. This composite approach which reflects an ecological perspective on behavior through verifiable constructs can be characterized as the "operant-interpersonal" approach to marital and family treatment.

Goals of Intervention

Marriage counselors are typically asked to work toward one of two goals: to help spouses to improve their interaction or to help them to explore the desirability of dissolving their marriage. In order to help couples to improve their interaction, it is necessary to help them modify the contingencies which each sets for the behavior of the other. In order to help couples reach a sound decision to dissolve their marriage, it is necessary to facilitate their experiencing their relationship at its best within the limits of existing external pressures. This can be done by asking each to act "as if" the marriage were a success for a period of from three to five weeks. If this trial does lead to greater satisfaction, then consecutive trial periods can follow. Therefore, no matter which of the two major goals clients request, intervention procedures typically have a single focus.

Within the general objective of improving spousal interaction, specific change goals must be set. This is done by identifying the base rate of the occurrence of selected positive behaviors, identifying the target rate of these behaviors which can be specified on a graph, and singling out stages of progress toward these goals which can be considered successive approximations of the target. Thus, a wife might wish that her husband "respect her more." This can translate into her wishing that he assume some responsibility for arranging baby-sitters for the children since they both work, that he accommodate to the occasional demand that she work into the early evening by preparing his own and the children's dinner and that he prepare his own lunches. The husband might wish that his wife ''show some consideration for him'' by joining him on skiing trips, by helping to entertain his business associates occasionally and by sharing use of the family car. Each can be helped to achieve the goal of selected changes in the behavior of the other. When these goals are achieved it is reasonable to expect that the wife will feel more ''respected'' and the husband more ''considered'' because both of these feelings result from the way in which each behaves toward the other. The ultimate goal of marital counseling is, thus, an affective change but the means to the attainment of that goal is behavioral change.

Assessment of Marital Interaction

In 1969 Olson observed that ''considerable research is needed in the field before adequate methods can be developed for diagnosing marital dynamics in a valid manner which can be useful to a marriage counselor'' (p. 1). Since that time effort has gone into the development of direct-observation techniques for use in natural (e.g., Patterson and Cobb, 1971; Weiss, Hops, and Patterson, 1973) and laboratory (e.g., Olson and Straus, 1972; Braver and Stuart, 1974) environments. These techniques are costly, however, and the question of how reactive they may be has not yet been resolved. Effort has also been expended on the development of both indirect (e.g., Olson and Ryder, 1970) and direct (e.g., Stuart, 1972a) measures of a variety of areas of marital adequacy. These latter approaches have been designed to obtain information which overcomes the generality and conventionality (Edmonds, 1967) of the familiar indices of marital satisfaction (Burgess and Wallin, 1953; Locke and Wallace, 1959), which can be efficiently collected, and which yield data needed by clinicians for the planning and evaluation of intervention. The Stuart Marital Precounseling Inventory (1972a), for example, collects socially and self-monitored behavioral data, measures evaluative reactions to multiple areas of marital functioning, assesses commitment to the marriage, provides means of assessing the extent to which one partner concurs with and understands the views of the other in many areas, and provides data on the resources for interactional change available to the couple.

Intervention Structure

There are four issues to be resolved in the structuring of marital treatment. The first is whether the couple should be seen jointly or separately. Joint contact increases the likelihood that descriptions of interactional events occurring outside of treatment will be accurate, it creates an invaluable emphasis upon the role of both partners in generating and changing problematic behaviors, and it permits the therapists to efficiently instigate changes in the behavior of both partners simultaneously rather than having to rely upon the more costly process of having to work through one spouse to reach the other. The one dubious advantage of individual contact is that one spouse or the other might feel more comfortable about self-revelation in the other's absence. But this allows the therapist to be used as a confidant in the awkward position of having to violate a confidence or of entering into collusion with one mate against the other. Therefore, in addition to restricting treatment to joint contacts only, it is also prudent to make a formal agreement that any information given to the therapist in person, by phone, or in writing by either spouse will be treated as though it were common knowledge.

The second issue is whether the couple should be seen by one therapist or a man-woman therapist team, and whether they should be seen as a separate couple or as members of a couples group. While there is good reason to believe that therapist teams are effective in the treatment of sexual problems (LoPiccolo and Lobitz, 1973; Masters and Johnson, 1972), there is no available data which supports the use of teams in treating marital problems in which sex plays a secondary role. That is, there is no clear justification at this time to assume that the value of cross- and same-sexed models outweighs the cost of doubling therapist time. There is also no evidence currently available which would aid in making the programatic decision about couple or couple group therapy although work currently in progress (Turner, 1972) will shed light on this question.

A third issue is whether the duration of treatment should be short or long and whether treatment sessions should be frequent or more broadly timed. The psychotherapeutic finding that longer treatment programs tend to be more effective is fraught with methodological problems (Luborsky, Chandler, Auerbach, Cohen, and Bachrach, 1971). Recent research with delinquents (Adams, 1967; Stuart, Tripodi, and Jayaratne, 1972) and in social agencies (Reid and Shyne, 1969) has shown short-term treatment to be advantageous and, based upon similar findings, Meltzoff and Kornreich (1970) concluded that: "There is very little good evidence that time in therapy past some unidentified point brings commensurate additional benefits" (p. 346). Therefore, it is prudent to limit time in treatment in the service of economy and effectiveness, with six to eight sessions being a reasonable allowance. Establishing this time limit prior to the start of treatment has the advantage of allowing both the therapist and clients to organize their use of treatment time to maximum advantage.

On the question of the optimal spacing of therapeutic sessions, Lorr (1962) concluded a decade ago that: "Therapist time can be spread over more patients with fewer contacts and at less cost to patients" (p. 140). As there has been little contrary evidence adduced since that statement was made, it can be assumed that the optimal spacing of sessions might be biweekly, thereby allowing for the gradual fading in of behavior changes and for the maintenance of those changes once they have been initiated.

The degree of structure of the content of sessions is the final pretreatment issue. Structure of interview contact has been shown to be highly beneficial both because it helps to bring order to the clients' often chaotic perceptions of their problems (Frank, 1962) and because it increases the concreteness of specificity of the therapist's behavior (Lennard, Bernstein, and Hendin, 1960; Stuart, Tripodi, and Jayaratne, 1972; Truax and Carkhuff, 1964). In marital treatment, carefully designed and prestructured content of treatment interviews helps to reduce the likelihood that the clients will fruitlessly use the time to engage in the negative practice of prolonged fighting and it also facilitates the therapist's efforts to mobilize the clients' problem-solving efforts. Treatment content can be prestructured through several means. Precounseling forms (e.g., Stuart, 1972a) can be used to cue clients to state their goals positively and to provide the counselor with organized data which facilitate the immediate initiation of change efforts. Explanation of the logic of the intervention (e.g., Stuart, 1969a) gives the clients an opportunity to efficiently organize their own efforts. In addition, case records and tapes can be used as positive role models of client behavior. In addition to these client-focused structural aids, therapist recording of all instigations, and even the prestructuring of instigations (Stuart and Lott, 1974a) also facilitate the constructive use of every contact hour.

In summary, it has been suggested that all marital treatment should involve conjoint sessions only, that treatment should be time-limited with a planful timing of sessions, and that the content of each interview should be optimally structured. Use of a precounseling form as a means of anticipatorily socializing clients into treatment and use of a treatment contract such as that presented below are two effective means of achieving the necessary structure.

Marital Treatment Contract

Mr. _____ and Mrs. _____ have requested counseling to help with the improvement of their relationship. They agree to participate in ___,___ joint counseling sessions which will be held at intervals of _____ days. It is understood that any written, telephoned, or spoken messages to the counselor by either spouse will be assumed to be common knowledge. This assumption is necessary in order to assure both spouses of the impartial help of the counselor. Finally, both spouses agree to complete every behavioral assignment to which he or she agrees whether this assignment requires the completion of written forms, the graphing of changes in behavior, or changes in actions toward the other.

The counselor agrees to help both spouses equally toward the attainment of those goals to which all three parties agree. The counselor also agrees to explain to both spouses the logic of all therapeutic procedures, to evaluate the effectiveness of each of these procedures and to ask spouses to perform only those tasks which are believed essential to the attainment of their goals. Finally, the counselor agrees to be available by telephone between sessions solely to help with the avoidance of conflict.

Mr. _____ Mrs. _____ Dr. _____
Date:

Intervention Procedures

The procedures used in this intervention approach can be divided into five hierarchically ordered categories, analogous to the modules set forth by Weiss, Hops, and Patterson (1973), with the procedures at each higher level subsuming those at earlier levels. The five steps can be summarized as follows:

1. Begin by helping each spouse to identify those positive changes in his or her own behavior as well as that of the other, which would significantly increase both the individual and shared mutual enjoyment of the marriage; then,
2. Help the partners to develop a dependable means of exchanging these desirable behaviors which permits them both to maintain an adequate level of personal and mutual satisfaction while simultaneously rebuilding trust in each other;
3. Help each member of the pair to evolve an effective channel of verbal and nonverbal communication so that each has an unambiguous, readily available means of expressing his or her wishes and of communicating his satisfaction; then,
4. Help the couple to devise a strategy of decision-making which accords each partner a consensually agreed upon measure of control over the form and content of the marital interaction; and
5. Finally, develop with the couple a means of maintaining these changes in a climate of flexibility which allows them to adapt to the evolving internal and external demands upon their marriage (Stuart, 1972b, pp. 2-3).

Each of these steps leads to the development of an important skill of interpersonal competence. The first leads to the shaping of a behaviorally specific interpersonal vocabulary in which experience is described with precision in a manner stressing the individual's influence over his or her experience. The second leads to the acquisition of skill in interpersonal influence based upon positive, incremental techniques. The third leads to an increased ability in eliciting and utilizing feedback about one's own behavior and information about the other's desires. The fourth leads to the strengthening of effective norms governing the allocation of power which can replace coercion as the basis for decision-making. And the fifth leads to the development of efficient techniques for naturally cuing and maintaining all phases of interaction change. Each of these procedures will now be described in more detail, with an expanded discussion available elsewhere (Stuart and Lederer, 1974).

1. Shaping a New Interpersonal Vocabulary. Clients entering marital counseling have long histories of faulty labeling of their own behavior and that of their spouses. Hurvitz (1970) has succinctly described the problem in these labeling systems as an overdependence upon "terminal hypotheses" which "may or may not be 'true' and . . . may 'fit' the information available but do not offer possible plans of action that can be utilized to change the relationship"

(p. 66). That is, no matter how great their chance accuracy be, reliance upon terminal hypotheses such as "psychodynamic interpretations," "pseudo-scientific explanations," or "psychological name-calling," reify the problem as unchangeable. If George Kelly's assertion is correct and "a person's processes are psychologically channelized by the ways in which he anticipates events" (1955, p. 46), then maintenance of terminal hypotheses function as stimuli delta for change efforts and would weaken the likelihood of their occurrence. Therefore, the first step in this treatment program is aimed at introducing the use of "instrumental hypotheses . . . (which) explain behavior, meanings or feelings . . . in such a way that something can be done to change the existing situation" (Hurvitz, 1970, p. 67). To do this, past efforts to explain *why* problems developed (e.g., "you always come home late for dinner because you resent your mother's domination so!") are replaced with explanations of *how* desired repertoires can be established (e.g., "I will be home on time if we agree to have dinner at 6:30 each day.").

Couples are trained to use this process vocabulary in place of more static terminology, coupled with efforts to particularize general statements and relate all behavioral descriptions to the situations in which the actions take place. Each then learns to express his or her wishes for changes in their spouses' behaviors in the form of a behavioral prescription. While Weiss, Hops, and Patterson (1973) ask their couples to express their "pleases" and "dis-pleases," i.e., acceleration and deceleration change targets, the present ap-proach cues clients to state all goals in terms of positive changes. This is done for three reasons. First, the technology available for acceleration is more compatible with constructive marital interaction than the technology of be-havioral suppression. Second, couples facing marital discord typically over-stress negative scanning and a purely positive data-collection process aids in overcoming this bias (Stuart, 1969a). Third, it has been noted that: ". . . there seems to be substantial support for the proposition that negative information carries greater weight than positive information" (Kanouse, Hanson, and Reid, 1972, p. 15). Therefore, the collection of both positive and negative informa-tion carries with it the risk that the negative data will outweigh the effects of the positive. For these reasons, it seems that only the collection of positive data offers these multiple advantages.

2. Shaping New Techniques of Interpersonal Influence. It has been sug-gested elsewhere (Stuart, 1969b) that couples with marital discord are more likely to use coercion than reciprocity as a norm in their interaction. Coercion and reciprocity have been defined as the use of negative and positive reinforce-ments respectively (Patterson and Reid, 1970). While some negative rein-forcement in the form of nagging is probably inevitable in marital interaction, if nagging becomes a high-frequency strategy on the part of either or both partners, the marriage loses much of its luster for the victim. To overcome the excessive use of coercion, it is necessary to convince both partners that the exchanges which they enjoy in their marriage are privileges and not rights. A privilege is "a special prerogative which one may enjoy at the will of another person upon having performed some qualifying task" (Stuart, 1971, p. 3), in contrast to a right which implies inalienable access to a reinforcer. To earn privileges, one must reinforce the other; to enjoy rights, one need only insist upon his due. By conceptualizing preferred marital pleasures as privileges, reciprocity becomes the only means of gaining access to them, replacing coercion as the means of securing rights.

Building upon the notion of privileges, behavioral contracts provide for the equitable exchange of favors by spouses. Contracts specify the responsibilities which each must meet in order to enjoy his privileges. Contributing to the technology of contracting, Weiss, Hops, and Patterson (1973) suggest that it is probably advisable to allow each spouse to choose from among several privileges each time than an obligation has been fulfilled. Early contracts begin with very specific behavioral options (e.g., if the wife takes the garbage out by 7:30, she may either have first access to the evening paper, choose the movie, television program, or other entertainment for the evening, or have her choice of leaving the windows open or shutting them in the bedroom). Later contracts are often less specific but, nevertheless, continue to provide a broad framework for behavioral exchanges with means of monitoring all contract-governed behaviors. Contracts thus help the couple to schedule the exchanges which nondistressed couples make naturally and as with any other behavioral prosthetic, they can be faded when they are no longer needed.

3. Developing New Means of Information Exchange. While marriage counselors frequently assess their clients as having "no communication," couples seeking treatment frequently complain that their marriages include too much communication which is aversive (Bienvenu, 1970; Levinger and Senn, 1967). The effort to overcome communicational problems through this program is premised on four axioms, each of which is more fully discussed elsewhere (Stuart and Lederer, 1974). Briefly stated, they are:

1. One cannot not communicate (Watzlawick, 1964). This axiom stems from the findings of numerous studies which demonstrate a continuous flow of nonverbal communication. Thus, a husband who enters and picks up the paper without greeting his wife has very unambiguously communicated his displeasure with his wife.
2. Measured honesty is required for the enrichment of relationships. This axiom stems from the repeated requests by clients that their spouses use "selective communication" (Bienvenu, 1970, p. 28) or the "selective disclosure of feelings" (Levinger and Senn, 1967, p. 256). Thus, spouses are encouraged to ask each other only for those changes which can reasonably be granted.
3. Positive information can change relationships while negative information can only stabilize them. This axiom is based upon the logic of systems theory (von Bertalanffy, 1950) which suggests that servo-mechanisms which provide negative feedback can correct errors in func-

tioning while new, positive information is needed for system change. Thus, spouses are encouraged to use the shaping principle in their interaction, making limited and very judicious use of negative feedback.

4. Every interactional description must include the speaker's cue, the first response of the other, and the consequence which he supplies for the last response of the other. This axiom stems from the work of Watzlawick, Beavin, and Jackson (1967) who stressed the importance of "punctuation" in behavioral chains. For example, a wife might complain that her husband enters without greeting her: he entered, she waited, and he did something other than express a greeting. Her description in three units (two of her husband's behavior bracketing one of hers) makes her appear guiltless. But one cannot hear such a description without wondering whether she greeted him. Her husband's next maneuver would be quite different if it was silence following a greeting rather than silence following silence. The way in which the exchange is punctuated, i.e., in odd number of units of three or more which would bias matters to the speaker's advantage or in even number of units which would place the behavior of both in an appropriate context, would greatly influence the way in which the speaker planned his or her own next actions. Training in the proper punctuation of communication chain thus greatly increases skill in constructive information exchange.

Taken together these axioms provide the building blocks for a model of effective marital communication. The first axiom leads to the adoption of a strategy in which positive messages are communicated both verbally and nonverbally while negative messages are expressed primarily in words. The second axiom leads to the expression of requests rather than condemnations, with the requests selected with kindness. The third axiom leads to a strong emphasis upon constructive communication which is itself a reinforcer as well as being a means to the end of increasing the attractiveness of one spouse to the other (Byrne and Rhamey, 1965). The fourth leads to acceptance by each spouse of the responsibility for changing painful communication patterns. A variety of techniques are available for achieving these changes, ranging from the scheduling of a standard half-hour each evening for a quiet review of the happenings of the day, the two-question rule which requires one to ask at least two questions as an indication of his interest in what the other has to say, the use of poker chips to serve as a means of on-line signals of positive evaluation, and the tape recording of stressful exchanges to identify the problematic punctuation of events. (See Stuart and Lederer, 1974, for a full description of these and other communication change techniques.)

4. Developing New Decision-Making Norms. While there is no generally agreed-upon measure of power in a marital relationship (Olson and Rabunsky, 1972; Turk and Bell, 1972), and no common pattern for distributing power (Stuart, 1972b), power can be understood to mean the ability to control decision-making. Couples make a myriad of choices, ranging from monumentally important decisions such as whether to have children or whether to remain together, to far less momentous decisions such as whether to invite in-laws for a holiday or what color to paint the living room. Successful couples develop dependable norms to allocate the power in each of these areas at varying stages in their lives. Distressed couples fail to develop effective norms and therefore have to resort to the frank use of power to cope with recurring conflict. Successful and distressed couples can therefore be differentiated according to the proportion of areas of decision which are: (1) shared equally; (2) shared unequally by agreement; or (3) usurped by one and contested by the other. In general, the person with the least to lose in the dispute has the most to gain (Waller, 1938) but the balance of power in a relationship is far more complicated than this, since it is sensitive to a matrix of forces both within and beyond the spouses themselves.

FIGURE 1. MODELS OF UNSUCCESSFUL AND SUCCESSFUL DIVISIONS
        OF DECISION-MAKING AUTHORITY.

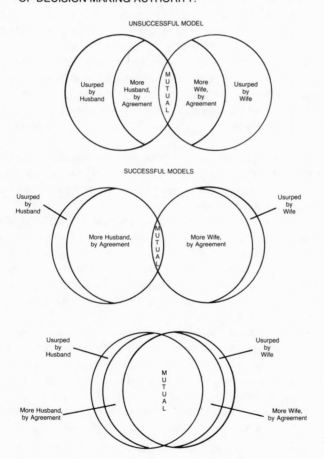

Efficiency and comfort in the marriage is certainly related to the degree to which both partners accept the existing balance of power. To improve an unsatisfactory condition, it is necessary to follow three steps. First, identify the areas in which each presently exercises power. Then, identify the areas in which each would ideally like to exercise power. This is followed by contracting for agreements governing power distribution. During these contracting sessions, the role of the therapist is that of mediator. Both spouses generally know in advance what concessions they will have to make but neither has offered to give up his claim to an area for fear of loss of face (Pruitt and Johnson, 1970). By directing both partners to change the therapist facilitates accommodation to the inevitable, leading to the development of new norms of interpersonal influence.

5. *Building Techniques for Maintaining Change*. After one person has changed his actions the new behaviors will fall under the social control of the other. But because marriages are not closed systems but rather are open to a myriad of outside influences over and above the changing demands caused by maturation of the spouses themselves, it is always necessary to protect the new behavioral balance. This can be done efficiently by developing a set of "relationship rules" for each couple which can serve as explications of norms of interaction and cues for behavior change. Stuart and Lederer (1974) offer an extensive collection of such rules. Listed here are but a few:

1. Respect the core symbols of the marriage. Following this rule protects both spouses from attacks upon their security in the relationship. It sets the limits within which arguments will occur so that the relationship is not wasted over petty disagreements.
2. Strive to end arguments, not to win them. Following this rule protects the partners from the futility of attempting to "one-up" each other. It stresses efforts to enhance rather than thwart reciprocity as a means of increasing personal satisfaction.
3. Communicate the expectation that your spouse will fulfill your wishes. Following this rule provides continuous cues for constructive behavior, while simultaneously avoiding the trap of cuing negative behaviors.
4. Encourage the behaviors which you desire in order to strengthen the chances of getting what you wish. For example, when one says, "I love you" saying "Thank you" reinforces the thought while saying "No, you don't" weakens it.

Finally, couples can also be helped to maintain changed interactional patterns by undergoing a periodic self-assessment of the strengths and targets for change in their relationship. This can be conveniently undertaken by estimating the extent to which preset goals have been achieved and by matching perceptions of the current interaction against the type of interaction to which the couple aspires. If treatment succeeded, these assessments should cue each spouse in how he or she can develop new strategies which will create the conditions for change in the other. On the other hand, treatment will have failed if each uses the assessment experience as an occasion to condemn the other.

Conclusion

This paper has set forth the rationale and a procedural guide for the operant-interpersonal treatment of marital discord. The overall design of the method is outlined in Figure 2 and reveals a series of decisions beginning with the decision of the couple to embark upon treatment and ending with the final stages of fading out intervention techniques. At each stage, the techniques and the criteria for their selection can be precisely stated. This sets the operant-interpersonal approach apart from the other systems of marital treatment (Broderick, 1971; Olson, 1971) because it permits the experimental validation of the importance of each set of procedures through factorial experimental designs (e.g., Welch and Goldstein, 1972); it permits the techniques to be taught to other practitioners and students; and it provides clients with a cogent system which they can potentially self-apply to improve upon their marriages. Therefore, while the returns are not yet in, it appears that the operant-interpersonal approach will offer the best bet yet of couples moving from poor to good and from good to better marriages.

FIGURE 2. FLOW CHART FOR OPERANT-INTERPERSONAL TREATMENT.

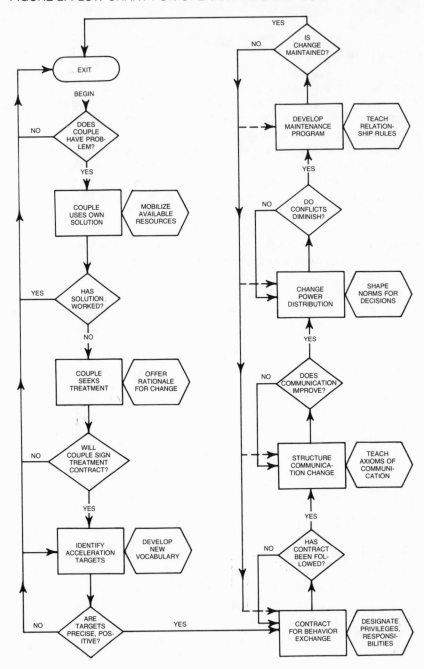

REFERENCES

Adams, S. (1967), "Some Findings from Correctional Caseload Research," *Federal Probation,* 31:48–57.

Bienvenu, M. J. (1970), "Measurement of Marital Communication," *The Family Coordinator,* 19:26–31.

Braver, J., and R. B. Stuart (1974), "Differential Reinforcement of Spouses and Strangers: An Index of Marital Satisfaction," *Family Process.* In press.

Blau, P. M. (1964), *Exchange and Power in Social Life.* New York: Wiley.

Broderick, C. B. (1971), "Beyond the Five Conceptual Frameworks: A Decade of Development in Family Theory." In C. B. Broderick (ed.), *A Decade of Family Research and Action.* Minneapolis: National Council on Family Relations.

Burgess, E. W., and P. Wallin (1953), *Engagement and Marriage.* Philadelphia: Lippincott.

Byrne, D., and R. Rhamey (1965), "Magnitude of Positive and Negative Reinforcements as a Determinant of Attraction," *Journal of Personality and Social Psychology,* 2:884–889.

Edmonds, V. H. (1967), "Marital Conventionalization: Definition and Measurement," *Journal of Marriage and the Family,* 27:681–688.

Frank, J. D. (1962), "The Role of Cognitions in Illness and Healing." In H. H. Strupp and L. Luborsky (eds.), *Research in Psychotherapy.* Washington, D. C.: American Psychological Association.

Goldiamond, I. (1966), "Self-control Procedures in Personal Behavior Problems." In R. Ulrich, T. Stachnick, and J. Mabry (eds.), *Control of Human Behavior.* Chicago: Scott, Foresman.

Goldstein, M. K., and B. Francis (1969), "Behavior Modification of Husbands by Wives." Paper presented at the annual meeting of the National Council on Family Relations, Washington, D. C.

Homans, G. C. (1961), *Social Behavior: Its Elementary Forms.* New York: Harcourt, Brace & World.

Hunt, G. M., and N. H. Azrin (0000), "A Community-reinforcement Approach to Alcoholism," *Behavior Research and Therapy.*

Hurvitz, N. (1970), "Interaction Hypotheses in Marriage Counseling," *The Family Coordinator,* 19:64–75.

Kanhouse, D. E., L. Hanson, and W. J. Reid (1972), *Negativity in Evaluations.* Morristown, N. J.: General Learning Press.

Kelly, G. A. (1955), *The Psychology of Personal Constructs;* Vol. 1. New York: W. Norton.

Lennard, H., A. Bernstein, and E. Hendin (1960), *Anatomy of Psychotherapy.* New York: Columbia University Press.

Levinger, G. (1965), "Marital Cohesiveness and Dissolution: An Integrative Review," *Journal of Marriage and the Family,* 27:1, 19–28.

Levinger, G., and D. J. Senn (1967), "Disclosure of Feelings in Marriage," *Merrill-Palmer Quarterly of Behavior and Development,* 13:252–258.

Liberman, R. (1970), "Behavioral Approaches to Family and Couple Therapy," *American Journal of Orthopsychiatry,* 40:106–118.

Locke, H. J., and K. M. Wallace (1959), "Short Marital-Adjustment and Prediction Tests: Their Reliability and Validity," *Journal of Marriage and Family Living,* 21:251–255.

LoPiccolo, J., and W. C. Lobitz (1973), "Behavior Therapy of Sexual Dysfunction." In L. A. Hamerlynck, L. C. Handy, and E. J. Mash (eds.), *Critical Issues in Behavior Modification,* Champaign, Ill.: Research Press.

Lorr, M. (1962), "Relations of Treatment Frequency and Duration to Psychotherapeutic Outcome." In H. H. Strupp and L. Luborsky (eds.), *Research in Psychotherapy.* Washington, D. C.: American Psychological Association.

Luborsky, L., M. Chandler, A. H. Auerbach, J. Cohen, and H. M. Bachrach (1971), "Factors Influencing the Outcome of Psychotherapy: A Review of Quantitative Research." *Psychological Bulletin,* 75:145–185.

Masters, W. H., and V. E. Johnson (1972), "The Rapid Treatment of Human Sexual Dysfunctions." In C. J. Sager and H. S. Kaplan (eds.), *Progress in Group and Family Therapy.* New York: Brunner/Mazel.

Meltzoff, J., and M. Kornreich (1970), *Research in Psychotherapy.* New York: Atherton Press.

Olson, D. H. (1969), "Diagnosis in Marriage Counseling Using SIMFAM, MMPI's and Therapists," *American Association of Marriage Counselors Newsletter,* Spring:1.

———(1970), "Marital and Family Therapy: Integrative Review and Critique," *Journal of Marriage and the Family,* 32:501–538.

———, and C. Rabunsky (1972), "Validity of Four Measures of Family Power," *Journal of Marriage and the Family,* 34:224–234.

Olson, D. H., and R. G. Ryder (1970), "Inventory of Marital Conflicts (IMC): An Experimental Interaction Procedure," *Journal of Marriage and the Family,* 31:433–448.

Olson, D. H., and M. A. Straus (1972), "A Diagnostic Tool for Marital and Family Therapy: The SIMFAM Technique," *The Family Coordinator,* 21:55–62.

Patterson, G. R. (1971), "Behavioral Intervention Procedures in the Classroom and in the Home." In A. E. Bergin and S. L. Garfield (eds.), *Handbook of Psychotherapy and Behavior Change: An Empirical Analysis.* New York: Wiley.

———, and J. A. Cobb (1972), "Stimulus Control for Classes of Noxious Behaviors." In J. F. Knutson (ed.), *The Control of Aggression: Implications for Basic Research.* Chicago: Aldine.

Patterson, G. R. and H. Hops (1972), "Coercion, a Game for Two: Intervention Techniques for Marital Conflict." In R. E. Ulrich and P. Montjoy (eds.), *The Experimental Analysis of Social Behavior.* New York: Appleton-Century-Crofts.

Patterson, G. R., and J. B. Reid (1970), "Reciprocity and Coercion: Two Facets of Social Systems." In C. Neuringer and J. Michael (eds.), *Behavior Modification in Clinical Psychology.* New York: Appleton-Century-Crofts.

Pruitt, D. G., and D. F. Johnson (1970), "Mediation as an Aid to Face Saving in Negotiation," *Journal of Personality and Social Psychology,* 14:239–246.

Rappaport, A. F., and J. Harrell (1972), "A Behavioral-Exchange Model for Marital Counseling," *The Family Coordinator,* 21:203–212.

Reid, W. J., and A. W. Shyne (1969), *Brief and Extended Casework.* New York: Columbia University Press.

Stuart, R. B. (1969a), "Operant-Interpersonal Treatment for Marital Discord," *Journal of Consulting and Clinical Psychology,* 33:675–682.

———(1969b), "Token Reinforcement in Marital Treatment." In R. Rubin and C. M. Franks (eds.), *Advances in Behavior Therapy.* New York: Academic Press.

———(1971), "Behavioral Contracting within the Families of Delinquents," *Journal of Behavior Therapy and Experimental Psychiatry,* 2:1–11.

————(1972a), *Marital Pre-counseling Inventory.* Champaign, Ill.: Research Press.

————(1972b), *Marital Pre-Counseling Inventory: Counselors Guide.* Champaign, Ill.: Research Press.

————, and W. J. Lederer (1974), *How to Make a Bad Marriage Good and a Good Marriage Better.* New York: W. W. Norton.

Stuart, R. B., and L. Lott (1974a), "Behavioral Contraction: A Cautionary Note," *Journal of Behavior Therapy and Experimental Psychiatry.*

————(1974b), "Fixed Treatment Methods for the Treatment of Delinquents and Their Families," *Federal Probation.*

Stuart, R. B., T. Tripodi, and S. Jayaratne (1972), "The Family and School Treatment Model of Services for Predelinquents." Paper presented at the 80th annual meeting of the American Psychological Association, Honolulu.

Thibaut, J. W., and H. H. Kelley (1959), *The Social Psychology of Groups.* New York: Wiley.

Truax, C. B., and R. R. Carkhuff (1964), "Concreteness: A Neglected Variable in Research in Psychotherapy," *Journal of Clinical Psychology,* 20:264–267.

Turk, J. L., and N. W. Bell (1972), "Measuring Power in Families," *Journal of Marriage and the Family,* 34:215–223.

Turner, A. J. (1972), "Couple and Group Treatment of Marital Discord: An Experiment." Paper presented at the fifth annual meeting of the Association for the Advancement of Behavior Therapy, New York.

von Bertalanffy, L. (1950), "An Outline of General System Theory," *British Journal of Philosophy,* 1:134–165.

Waller, W. (1938), *The Family: A Dynamic Interpretation.* New York: Gordon.

Watzlawick, P. (1964), *An Anthology of Human Communication.* Palo Alto: Science and Behavior Books.

————, J. H. Beavin, and D. D. Jackson (1967), *Pragmatics of Human Communication.* New York: W. W. Norton.

Weiss, R. L., H. Hops, and G. R. Patterson (1973), "A Framework for Conceptualizing Marital Conflict, a Technology for Altering It, Some Data for Evaluating It." In L. A. Hamerlynck, L. C. Handy, and E. J. Mash (eds.), *Critical Issues in Behavior Modification.* Champaign, Ill.: Research Press.

Welch, J. C., and M. K. Goldstein (1972), "The Differential Effects of Operant-Interpersonal Intervention." In R. D. Rubin (ed.), *Advances in Behavior Therapy,* New York: Academic Press.

ALAN F. RAPPAPORT
JANET E. HARREL

13   A Behavioral Exchange Model for Marital Counseling

The authors describe an approach to marriage counseling based on the principles of reciprocity and social exchange. Behavior modification techniques are utilized to implement this program designed to resolve marital conflict between spouses. Using an educational model throughout the program, spouses are encouraged to negotiate their own reciprocal-exchange contracts with decreasing dependency on the counselor-educator. A case study is presented to illustrate the functionality of the model.

Although most, if not all, marital counselors are concerned with the resolution of conflict in marriage, only a few of these professionals present specific techniques for the accomplishment of this goal. A review of the most recent books on marriage counseling (Ard and Ard, 1969; Greene, 1965; Silverman, 1967) indicates that a majority of experts in this field speak in terms of vague generalities, while avoiding the scientific preciseness demanded for rigorous empirical testing. Olson (1970), in a recent review of marital and family therapy, emphasized the importance of using operationally defined concepts for the future growth and development of these infant professions.

Perhaps the term ''communication'' best illustrates the dilemma. Whereas most counselors repeatedly stress the importance of *effective communication* in marriage, relatively few take the time or trouble to operationalize and thereby clarify this vague concept. Thus, the typical student is left with the impression that communication is the very heart of a sucessful marriage, without knowing much about this heart or how it operates. While some meager attempts to operationalize marital communication have been made previously, only recently has Guerney (1970) systematically presented a precise model for marital communications. Based on Rogerian psychotherapy, the model consists of teaching spouses specific "speaker" and "listener" roles for the enhancement of marital communication. Emphasis is placed on an open and direct expression of feelings and empathic listening. A recent study by Ely (1970) has documented the efficacy of training groups of married couples in these conjugal therapy techniques over an eight-week training program. Research currently in progress by Collins (1971) and Rappaport (1971) further explores relationship changes resulting from a six-month conjugal program and an intensive marathon type of conjugal therapy.

To complement the existing conjugal program, the present authors plan to operationalize another educational model for the resolution of marital conflict. This new behavioral-exchange model emphasizes the teaching of specific reciprocal exchange and bargaining skills to groups of married couples. The authors believe that most married couples can effectively utilize these cooperative bargaining skills in their relationship to reduce conflict and tension, while providing mutual gratification based on a reciprocal behavioral exchange designed to accelerate desirable behaviors. All couples are encouraged, from the start, to negotiate their own contracts and thereby decrease dependence on the therapist-educator. If the theoretical principles underlying the behavioral-exchange model can be validated empirically and utilized in conjunction with the conjugal model, marital counselors will be provided with operationally defined therapeutic programs for the enhancement of communication and resolution of conflict in marriage.

Following a brief literature review of the existing behavioral exchange approaches to marriage counseling, the authors will present the new behavioral-exchange model.[1] The paper will conclude with an actual application of this new model to a specific couple in marital counseling.

Application of Behavioral and Exchange Principles to Marital Counseling

The successful application of operant or behavioral principles to the marital dyad has recently been reported by Goldstein and Francis (1969). In this study, the researchers trained five graduate student wives to use behavior modification techniques to extinguish a particular undesirable behavior in their husbands. A few weeks after implementing these techniques in their marital relationships,

[1] A complete literature review was included in an earlier unpublished draft of this manuscript available from the authors. The introductory material presented here before the "Theoretical Overview" did not appear in the author's original article; it has been added in order to provide a more comprehensive view of the behavioral approach.

all five wives reported desirable changes in their husbands' behavior. Utilizing base rates and weekly frequency charts of specific behaviors, the researchers found statistically significant changes in all fives cases ($p < .05$).

Liberman (1970) also advocates the use of behavior modification techniques within the marital dyad. In describing the task of the marital therapist, Liberman states:

> (1) Specify the maladaptive behavior, (2) choose reasonable goals which are alternative adaptive behaviors, (3) direct and guide the family to change the contingencies of their social reinforcement patterns from maladaptive to adaptive target behavior . . . the therapist acts as an *educator* using his value as a social reinforcer to instruct the family or couple in changing their ways of dealing with each other. (pp. 108-110)

The author perceives the marital relationship as an evolving system along a developmental continuum. As with all social systems, emphasis is placed on both interactions within the marriage and transactions with other systems outside of the marriage.

A recent paper presented by Knox (1970) emphasized the application of behavioral therapy to the marital dyad. In this paper, Knox briefly presented his theoretical model and its relevance to marital unhappiness. Techniques such as selective reinforcement, assertive responses, the Premack principle, sexual responses, extinction, punishment, stop-think, systematic desensitization, modeling, emotional extremes, covert reinforcement, and cognitive dissonance were discussed in relation to marriage counseling. In a book by Knox (1971), these behavioral approaches to marital counseling receive the attention and scientific analysis they appear to warrant.

While the above discussion leaves little doubt that behavior modification can be applied successfully to discord in marriage, even these techniques are far from ideal. In the Goldstein and Francis (1969) study cited above, the counselor worked with only one spouse to modify or shape the behavior of the other spouse. Obviously, this approach is most useful when one spouse refuses to cooperate in the therapeutic process. On the other hand, it would appear more functional to work with both spouses when both were willing to cooperatively work on their marital problems. This conjoint approach allows the counselor to focus on the interaction in the particular "system" along with its situational and developmental uniqueness. Using specific behavioral techniques, the counselor can help the couple establish a reciprocal and mutually satisfying relationship. Kimmel and Havens (1966) address themselves to this important and often neglected issue:

> It is assumed that there are *learnable* skills in making marital relationships more meaningful. The willingness to examine the symbolic dimensions in issues and the capacity to evaluate anticipated outcomes in *mutual* rather than individualistic terms can be seen as a developmental skill. Success and satisfaction in conflict resolution through mutual identification should be cumulative in the same way that the build up of conflict and tension through individuated competition is

cumulative. Thus, the mutual identification criterion has the most relevance and significance . . . The task of the marriage counselor can be seen as the transformation of marital conflict from an individualistic perspective to a more satisfactory mutual identification pattern. The task is clearly more reasonable if he has both parties to the conflict available to him in conjoint therapy. (p. 465)

In a series of related articles, Tharp (1963a, 1963b, 1964, 1965) emphasized the importance of role expectations and cooperative bargaining in marital or family relationships. Tharp and Otis (1966) describe their method of teaching family members specific negotiation skills to enhance their interaction. Within this model, the therapist, serving as arbitrator, encourages family members to establish their own functional contracts (i.e., family division of labor) based on a *quid pro quo* system of "I'll change this, if you change that (p. 432)."

Lederer and Jackson (1968), in their enlightening book entitled *The Mirages of Marriage,* also elaborated on the importance of reciprocal cooperative bargaining in marriage. Using a behavioral approach similar to the one advocated by Tharp and Otis (1966), the authors carefully describe their process of implementing functional bargains of *quid pro quos* in marital relationships. Specific contracts were presented by the authors to illustrate their particular approach to marital counseling.

The best example of a structured behavioral exchange program designed to enhance marital interaction has been devised recently by Stuart (1969). In this most provocative article, the author presents his operant-interpersonal treatment for marital discord. Exchange and behavioral principles are applied systematically to specific relationship problems.

> Operant-interpersonal treatment of marital discord is premised on the assumption that successful marriages can be differentiated from unsuccessful marriages by the frequency and range of reciprocal positive reinforcements exchanged by both partners. Beginning with the clarification of behavior change objectives for each partner, a four-step treatment approach culminating in an exchange of positive responses on a reciprocal basis is suggested. (p. 675)

In his discussion contrasting successful to unsuccessful marriages, Stuart asserts that:

> In successful marriage, both partners work to maximize mutual reward while minimizing individual costs. A reciprocal exchange of potent social reinforcement is established in which each partner controls sufficient rewards to compensate the other for the rewards which are expected or received from him. In an unsuccessful marriage, both partners appear to work to minimize individual costs with little apparent expectation of mutual reward. In an effort to trim costs, few positive rewards are dispensed; positive reinforcement, as a strategy of behavioral control, is replaced by negative reinforcement (removal of an aversive event following the expected response). (p. 676)

Hence the treatment plan that Stuart developed depends upon increasing mutual positive reinforcement within the marital dyad.

While the treatment philosophy provided by Stuart appears conceptually strong, the actual illustrations presented in the article were disappointing in that they relied exclusively on a token economy. The present authors view the token system as a structured vehicle to initiate reciprocal exchange in conjugal relationships where positive reciprocity is defunct. That is, when necessary, tokens could be paired with social reinforcers with the hope of phasing out the tokens as soon as possible. With Stuart's operant-interpersonal model, the token economy is not phased out or replaced by an exchange of behaviors. Hence, while Stuart theoretically recognizes the importance of reciprocal exchange in marriage, his case studies depend on a token economy and not necessarily a reciprocal exchange of behaviors.

Another apparent weakness in the operant-interpersonal model is the implicit reliance upon the counselor to implement the program and serve as "the architect of change." It appears to the present authors that reciprocal exchange skills could be learned by married couples with the use of an educational model (Guerney, *et al.*, 1970; 1971). That is, dyads could learn to negotiate their own reciprocal exchange contracts without continued dependence on the counselor. It is with these two limitations in mind that the authors now proceed to present the behavioral-exchange approach to marital counseling.

BEHAVIORAL-EXCHANGE MODEL

Theoretical Overview

The behavioral-exchange model, presented in this section, relies heavily on the principles of social exchange and reciprocity. Within this model, both spouses are expected and, in fact, required to "give" to "get" more out of the relationship. Thus the model is feasible only when both spouses express a willingness to bargain and compromise.

Drawing implications from the research findings reported by Blood and Wolfe (1960), Heer (1963), and Levinger (1965) on power differential in marital dyads, the present authors assume that the behavioral-exchange model is best suited for those relationships in which both spouses possess resources valuable to each other. That is, the *quid pro quo* system, on which the model is founded, assumes that both spouses hold valuable resources in the relationship and that, in turn, these resources determine the power of each spouse in the marriage. When both husband and wife have equal or nearly equal power in the marriage, compromise and bargaining appear likely. When, on the other hand, one spouse has significantly more resources and power than the other spouse, compromise and bargaining do not seem as likely. For why should the powerful partner bargain or compromise with the less powerful partner when, in his eyes, he has nothing to gain by this process? In those marriages where one spouse cannot pool many resources valuable to his mate, it is unlikely that the behavioral-exchange model could be applied successfully.

Assuming that both spouses are willing and able to bargain and compromise, the counselor(s) begin the program by describing, in detail, the importance of reciprocal exchange and bargaining in marriage. The present authors agree with Stuart (1969) when he claims:

> Clients benefit from an explanation of the approach for at least two reasons. First, such explanations may help free each spouse from his inaccurate and negatively biasing prejudices. Second, when each spouse is fully aware of the logic of the treatment, he can participate more fully in effective therapeutic planning and execution. (p. 677)

Following the description, the counselors teach specific reciprocal exchange and bargaining skills to (groups of) married couples by modeling and didactic techniques. Employing this educational model, the counselors continue to teach dyads how to apply these skills to their specific relationship problems. The goal of the program is to have spouses eliminate their undesirable behaviors and replace them with desirable behaviors on a reciprocal basis. To rephrase this in behavioral terminology, the counselors seek to teach married couples specific reciprocal exchange and cooperative bargaining skills that they can use in their relationship to decelerate and extinguish undesirable behaviors while, at the same time, accelerating those target behaviors perceived to be desirable and rewarding to the marriage.

Operant principles prevalent in behavioral therapy are crucial in implementing the behavioral-exchange program. Perhaps the most important variable of all is positive reinforcement. In the present model it is assumed that when spouses substitute desirable behaviors in place of undesirable behaviors, these new behaviors, implemented on a reciprocal basis, will serve to positively reinforce both individuals and eventually lead to a more satisfying marriage.

Preparing a hierarchy of undesirable behaviors allows the couple to begin their behavior change program with relatively innocuous problems that will be easy to modify. Beginning with the least difficult target behaviors, it is important that each individual count the number of times the target behavior occurs prior to implementing any change program. These baseline data provide an accurate, objective picture to both the couple and the counselors of the nature and frequency of the problem. Counting behaviors also encourages the couple to phrase their problems in terms which facilitate modification procedures.

While counting target behaviors, the couples also observe what happens before and after the target behavior occurs. In this way, the couple can learn to identify the cues or discriminative stimuli which set the occasion for the undesirable behaviors, as well as identifying the consequences or reinforcers which maintain the behaviors. A successful behavior-exchange program can be implemented only after these behaviors are identified. Once the reinforcers which maintain an undesirable behavior are identified, the couple can remove these consequences and therefore decelerate the behaviors. If the target behaviors can be restated in positive terms, the conselors or couple can arrange positive consequences to maintain the behaviors. Thus if the couple can identify specific circumstances which foster desirable or undesirable behaviors, they can share the responsibility of encouraging or avoiding these circumstances in the future.

A recent book edited by Krumboltz and Thoresen (1969) contains a review of the research literature employing behavioral contracts for extremely deviant children. In the introduction to this review, the authors make the following comment:

> Counselors themselves need not be a party to many behavioral contracts. Frequently the counselor may serve the role only of helping to negotiate a behavior contract between two or more parties who may be having some type of misunderstanding. The potential benefits of behavior contracts in cases of marital disharmony . . . has scarcely begun to be realized. (p. 89)

The present authors, accepting this position, utilize a written behavioral contract in the behavioral-exchange program. A written contract, although extremely businesslike, provides many advantages over an oral contract. First and perhaps most importantly, a written contract provides a ready reference for all parties and therefore memory does not play a significant role. Second, when and if difficulties arise in the relationship, a written contract can be modified or renegotiated most easily. Finally, a written contract, placed on the refrigerator door, serves to constantly remind both spouses about their commitment to the program. For these reasons, the present authors have adapted a written contract which has to be agreed upon and signed by all parties involved (husband, wife, and counselor).

Proper reinforcement schedules are important in the behavioral-exchange program. Couples are encouraged to reinforce each other continuously at first while new behaviors are being shaped. After the target behaviors reach the desired frequency, the couples are instructed to gradually change from a continuous schedule of reinforcement to an intermittent schedule in order to maintain the new behaviors.

Before, during, and after the behavioral-exchange procedure is implemented, the couple is strongly encouraged to keep accurate daily records of their target behaviors. In this way, both the counselors and the couple can judge the progress and success of the program, and most importantly, assess a need for change if progress is not satisfactory.

There are many theoretical similarities between the present model and the operant-interpersonal model presented by Stuart. Both models recognize the significance of reciprocity, compromise, and operant behavior in a functional relationship. As indicated earlier, a primary difference between the two models involves the present author's use of an educational model to teach dyads reciprocal exchange skills and then allow them to establish their own contracts, with minimal dependency on the counselor. Also, the present model does not reply upon a token economy at any time during the program. Perhaps the best way to note the difference between the two models is for the reader to compare the illustration in this paper to those presented in the Stuart article.

In conclusion, the authors believe that although the two models are theoretically similar, the present program, making use of an educational model, will be most helpful for marriage counselors who desire to teach their clients specific techniques to resolve marital conflict. Additionally, the present model appears to be better adapted for use with groups of married couples.

Implementation of the Model

Before implementing the behavioral-exchange program, the counselor has the ethical obligation to inform the couple of all approaches to marriage counseling available to them in the community. After receiving a brief description of each approach, the couple will be better prepared to make the final decision regarding which approach is best suited for their particular relationship problems. If the couple chooses the behavioral-exchange program, the counselor should follow five steps to implement the model.

Step One: Applying Reciprocal Exchange Skills to Marriage Problems. After spouses are exposed to the fundamental principles of reciprocal exchange and behavior modification, they must be taught how to apply these principles to their marriage. Thus the counselors use both didactic and modeling techniques to facilitate the learning process.

First, counselors describe and then role-play a typical marital conflict that exemplifies reciprocity and cooperative bargaining. The counselors use reciprocal exchange skills to negotiate their demands. After negotiating, the counselors establish a written contract in concise behavioral terms.

Following this first step of modeling for the clients, the counselors suggest another hypothetical marital conflict, but this time the clients serve as facilitators in the negotiation process. Counselors employ positive reinforcement with the clients whenever they demonstrate a competency at reciprocal exchange.

Finally, the counselors suggest a third hypothetical marital conflict, but this time the clients use reciprocal exchange skills to establish their *own* contracts. During this phase, the counselors facilitate their learning and provide positive reinforcement whenever possible.

Step Two: Labeling Undesirable Behaviors in Spouse. The therapist starts this step by instructing both husband and wife to independently prepare lists of three *specific* undesirable behaviors manifested by spouse (1 = most undesirable; 3 = least undesirable). Following this, both spouses are instructed to prepare lists indicating their usual or typical way of responding to each of these three undesirable spousal behaviors, in order to identify the reinforcers which maintain these behaviors. With the therapist serving as arbitrator, the dyad reviews their lists conjointly, modifying or changing them based upon their direct communication. Both spouses must be satisfied with the final lists. To conclude this second stage, the therapist finalizes the lists with the dyad and elaborates on "vicious cycles" that exist within the relationship, emphasizing how they may unwittingly maintain their maladaptive system of interaction by using reciprocal reinforcement principles in a destructive manner.

Step Three: Labeling Positive or Desirable Behaviors in Spouse. Husband and wife are instructed to prepare lists of specific positive or desirable behaviors manifested by spouse (1 = most positive behavior of spouse). This list should consist of those spousal behaviors which are valued and/or rewarding to the relationship. In other words, each partner indicates those behaviors manifested by spouse that they particularly value (i.e., wife may indicate husband helping her feed the baby; husband may indicate wife actively participating in sexual intercourse).

Step Four: Implementation of Contract. Each spouse keeps a week-long record of the initial base rate of the others' undesirable behavior number three. After recording initial base rates and observing the reinforcers, spouses negotiate their own contract to reciprocally eliminate undesirable behaviors and replace them with desirable ones. The therapist, again acting as arbitrator, has the dyad start with the least threatening behaviors first. Agreement on a contract should insure reciprocity right from the beginning. If the first behavioral-exchange results in mutual satisfaction for both partners, a positive pattern will be created and the couple will most likely want to continue bargaining to further enhance their marriage. Thus, it is extremely important for the couple to start their negotiations on the least undesirable behaviors first.

The therapist should guide the couple in their bargaining and caution them about moving too quickly. It is suggested that, in most cases, no more than one contract a week be established during the early stages of the program. Also, early in the program each partner should receive a positive reinforcement from spouse (see step two) every time a desirable behavior replaces an undesirable behavior. This is changed to an intermittent schedule as soon as the behaviors reach the desired frequency. To illustrate, each time the husband helps the wife feed the baby (acceleration of a desirable behavior), he should receive verbal praise or a kiss from his spouse (a positive reinforcer). The goal, or course, is to accelerate the process of mutually rewarding behavior exchanges in the marital relationship. Once the established destructive patterns of interaction are extinguished and replaced by mutually agreed upon positive behaviors, the authors hypothesize that spouses will be happier and receive more rewards from their marriage.

Step Five: Renegotiation of Contracts. The functional marital relationship is not a stagnant homeostatic system but rather an adaptive and evolving system which continually changes during its developmental continuum. In light of various internal and external factors which serve to facilitate change within the marital dyad over the course of the family life cycle, counselors employing the behavioral-exchange model should continually emphasize the need for flexibility on the part of both spouses. That is, both spouses should realize the inevitable need to modify or renegotiate contracts as their present ones become outdated. It has become apparent to the present authors that those couples exhibiting the most flexibility in the behavior-exchange program are also the ones benefiting most from the program.

To illustrate, a newly married couple will most likely modify or completely change their hierarchies (see steps two and three) as they progress through the family life cycle. Whereas at the beginning of their marriage a couple may use reciprocal exchange skills to enhance their interpersonal adjustment, later on in the marriage they can use these same skills to negotiate child-care responsibilities and divisions of labor. To reiterate, all married couples in the behavioral-exchange program should be encouraged to continually modify their hierarchies and negotiate new contracts in light of developmental and situational changes.

To conclude, good bargains characterize a functional and satisfying marriage. A strong marriage exists only when both spouses are willing to ''give'' to ''get'' more from the relationship.

Illustrations

In this section, the authors apply the behavioral-exchange model to a specific marital counseling situation. Although the present illustration involves only one dyad, the therapeutic process employed appears adequately suited for use with groups of married couples. A male-female therapy team was utilized to assure optimal therapeutic effectiveness (Bellville et. al., 1969; Goodwin and Mudd, 1966).

Session One

Mr. and Mrs. X, a young married couple with one infant child, first came for counseling because of unsatisfying sexual relations. Early in the session, Mr. X expressed strong negative feelings about his marriage, in general, and his wife's sexual frigidity, in particular. He believed that her lack of interest in sex could be traced to guilt feelings resulting from her premarital illegal abortion at the age of sixteen. Mrs. X, on the other hand, completely rejected this rationale, claiming that her present lack of interest in sex could simply be attributed to the care and attention required by the baby. She claimed that motherhood demanded all of her time and energy, leaving little, if any, interest in sexual relations with her husband. While the X's disagreed about the cause of the problem, there was mutual agreement in that their primary problem was sexual (the husband demanding a more active and involved sex partner and the wife wanting her husband to adjust to little or no sex until the child matured and placed fewer demands on her).

At this point, the counselors carefully explained to the couple the approaches to marriage counseling available to them in the community (private marriage counseling, psychological clinic, conjugal therapy, behavioral-exchange therapy). Mr. and Mrs. X decided on the behavioral-exchange approach. The counselors then spent about a half-hour describing the program with Mr. and Mrs. X. Emphasis was placed on reciprocity, social exchange, cooperative bargaining, and compromise in relation to the marital dyad. The couple was also exposed to the basic principles underlying behavior modification and how they could apply these principles to their relationship. Finally, within an educational model, the counselors attempted to relate behavioral and exchange principles to marriage by illustrating specific examples with which the couple could identify.

After the X's demonstrated an adequate understanding of these principles, the counselors began implementation of the behavioral-exchange program. Mr. and Mrs. X were instructed to independently prepare lists, as described earlier in this paper (see "Implementation of the Model"), and bring these lists to the next counseling session scheduled for the forthcoming week. The first session lasted approximately two hours.

Session Two

The second session emphasized teaching of specific reciprocal exchange skills to the couple and having them apply these skills to their particular relationship. By using their prepared lists (Forms 1 and 2), the X's learned how to reciprocally eliminate undesirable behaviors in their marriage, while, at the same time increasing positive or desirable behaviors. Hence, each spouse agreed to eliminate an undesirable behavior (one which had negative consequences to the total relationship) and replace it with a desirable behavior if, in turn, the other spouse also agreed to the same condition (reciprocal exchange).

Form 1

Mrs. X: Prepared Lists [a]

I. Undesirable Behaviors of Spouse
   1. I dislike his constant complaining. He complains about everything.

---

[a] These lists have been modified slightly for simplicity and clarity.

2. I dislike the way he forces his ideas, wants, and desires on me. He tries to mold me and shape me to conform to his expectations.

3. I dislike the way he never compliments me without qualifications.

II. My Reaction to These Behaviors

1. I tell him that that's the way it is and he can't do anything about it. Often, I say nothing and just keep it inside.

2. I am usually hurt by this and get angry and try to say something that will hurt him in return. I also tell him that I'm sorry that I'm not what he wants me to be.

3. I respond by usually saying nothing—just keeping it inside. Just some kind of recognition would really help.

III. Desirable or Positive Behaviors of Spouse

1. It's nice when he gets excited about something we can both do.

2. I like it when he compliments me in front of other people.

3. I appreciate his doing the dishes.

Form 2

Mr. X: Prepared Lists[a]

I. Undesirable Behaviors of Spouse

1. She has no desire for sex. She laughs when kissed—shows no sexual interest at all.

2. She walks away from me when I am talking to her. She usually tells me to shut up.

3. She spends the little time we have together picking up things, taking showers, doing odd jobs, etc.

II. My Reaction to These Undesirable Behaviors

1. My first reaction was to kiss her. When I found out that this turned her off I stopped, trying not to push what obviously annoyed her.

2. I usually get mad and say things again to make sure she understands.

3. I usually sit there although sometimes I say something to her. It makes me feel as though her housework is more important than me.

III. Desirable or Positive Behaviors of Spouse

1. She is a good cook.

2. She works uncomplainingly.

3. Keeps house clean.

4. Very good mother to baby.

5. Very organized.

6. Dependable.

7. Thoughtful about many things.

---

[a] These lists have been modified slightly for simplicity and clarity.

Mr. and Mrs. X started their behavioral-exchange program with the least undesirable behaviors on their prepared lists. Mrs. X complained about not receiving unqualified compliments from her husband, while Mr. X complained about not spending enough time alone with his wife discussing pleasant activities. The counselors helped the couple rephrase these complaints into positive and desired behaviors (pinpointing target behaviors). Thus, Mrs. X indicated that what she really wanted was an increase in compliments from her husband and Mr. X indicated that what he really wanted was more time together to discuss pleasant activities (acceleration of desirable behaviors). The next step was to establish an agreeable contract in behavioral terminology. The contract stated:

> *For Mr. X:* I will increase the number of unqualified compliments to my wife *if,* in return, she agrees to spend a half-hour per day giving me her undivided attention for the discussion of pleasant activities.
>
> *For Mrs. X:* I will spend a half-hour per day giving my husband my undivided attention to discuss pleasant activities *if,* in return, he agrees to compliment me more and not place any qualifications on these compliments.

It is quite apparent that reciprocity and cooperative bargaining served as the heart of this functional contract. Both spouses were willing to "give" to "get" more out of the relationship. Following the establishment of this contract, the counselors explained the importance of keeping accurate daily records of the new behaviors (frequency counts).[2] Graph paper was distributed to the dyad and the record-keeping process was carefully described. Mrs. X was to note each unqualified compliment paid to her by her husband on a daily basis and, likewise, Mr. X was to keep a daily account of their actual time spent together discussing pleasant activities. The counselors also emphasized the importance of reinforcement of the new desirable behaviors. Mr. X was told to make the half-hour home interaction as pleasant as possible for his wife, so that she would enjoy the time spent together and want to continue with this new behavior. In a similar fashion, Mrs. X was told to show some form of gratitude or appreciation every time her husband paid her a compliment, so that this desirable behavior would become reinforcing for him as well as her. The contract was reviewed one last time and both parties agreed with all conditions stated (Form 3). The contract was to go into effect the following day.

Before the session closed, the couple was instructed to negotiate and implement a second contract, on their own, during the next ten-day period. Furthermore, this new contract was again to focus on relatively minor undesirable behaviors. If the dyad enountered difficulty with this task, they were instructed to phone one of the counselors. The meeting closed after one hour with both counselors and clients feeling satisfied with the progress made. A third session was scheduled for ten days later.

[2]Baseline data were not collected by this couple. In this instance, the counselors accepted their word that the present rate of target behaviors was zero. A more rigorous implementation of this model is suggested by the authors and would include collection of baseline data for all groups.

Form 3

Mr. and Mrs. X
Behavioral-Exchange Contract No. 1
February, 1971

CONTRACT

It is hereby agreed that:
(A) Mr. X will increase the number of unqualified compliments paid to his wife if, in return, she spends a half-hour per day with her husband. During this time Mr. X is to have his wife's undivided attention to discuss pleasant activities.
(B) Mrs. X will spend a half-hour per day providing her husband with her undivided attention for the discussion of pleasant activities if, in return, Mr. X provides her with an increase in unqualified compliments. This contract is to go into effect on (date).

Husband

Wife

Witness

Session Three

The third session started with a review of the daily frequency charts representing the implementation of the first contract (see Figures 1 and 2). The counselors immediately noted that Mr. and Mrs. X were not behaving in accord with the contract. This observation was followed by a discussion of why Mrs. X was not fulfilling her end of the contract. She indicated that although she enjoyed the time spent together with her husband, her commitments to her work and the baby did not allow for a free half-hour every evening. Mrs. X thus wanted to renegotiate for a quarter-hour per evening rather than a half-hour commitment. Mr. X, understanding the demands placed on his wife, was willing to modify the initial contact as his wife had suggested. Hence, as a result of their open communication, Mrs. X was to spend a quarter-hour per day with her husband and the contract was so amended. In spite of this limitation, Mrs. X reported that her husband had stopped all of his qualified compliments and Mr.

Number of Desired Behaviors Observed
Unqualifed Compliments

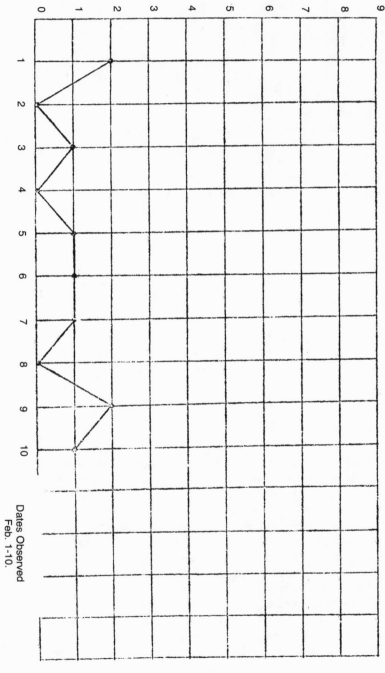

FIGURE 1. OBSERVATION RECORD   Behavioral-Exchange Contract

Target Behavior: To increase the number of unqualified compliments given to Mrs. X each day by Mr. X

Observer: Mrs. X   Observation Period: Feb. 1-10   Contract Number: 1
Phase Number: 1

Dates Observed
Feb. 1-10.

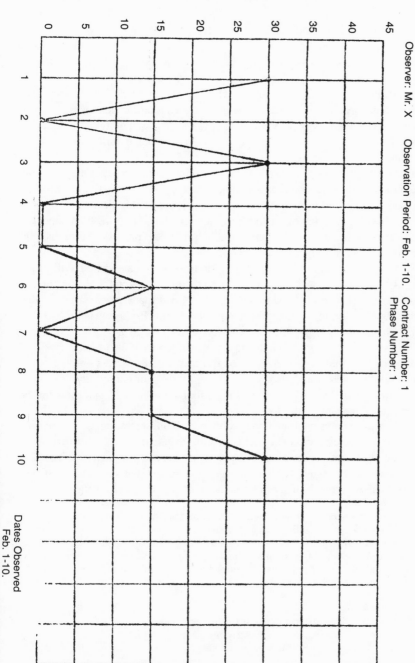

FIGURE 2. OBSERVATION RECORD. Behavioral-Exchange Contract

Target Behavior: To increase the amount of time (when she gives her undivided attention) Mrs. X spends with Mr. X during each day.

Observer: Mr. X   Observation Period: Feb. 1-10.   Contract Number: 1
Phase Number: 1

Number of Desired Behaviors Observed
Minutes Spent With Spouse

Dates Observed
Feb. 1-10.

X reported that his wife did provide her undivided attention whenever they were together (deceleration of undesirable behaviors to zero rate). It was also interesting to note the similar behavioral patterns between spouses on a daily basis as indicated in Figures 1 and 2.

Mr. and Mrs. X indicated that they were unable to find the time to negotiate a second contract, on their own, during the past ten days. The counselors listened, in a client-centered manner, while the X's explained the reasons and unfavorable circumstances accountable for their failure to establish a second contract. The counselors then expressed their mild disappointment in that the X's did not establish a second contract, as was agreed upon during the previous session.

During much of the third session, Mr. and Mrs. X explored their relationship and indicated that their problems definitely exceeded the sexual area. Mrs. X focused on husband's inability to make and stand by his decisions. Mr. X emphasized the fact that his wife rarely, if ever, lived up to his high expectations. These statements were considered helpful to the process of establishing specific behavioral modifications in the future.

Toward the end of the session, Mrs. X indicated that she wanted to discuss, with the counselors, a situation coming up the next weekend that was sure to create marital tensions. To summarize, Mr. X had made plans earlier in the week to go barhopping with another couple the coming Friday evening. Mrs. X, although not really enjoying this activity, agreed to go along. A few days previously, Mr. X expressed a desire for his wife to wear a particular dress on Friday evening that he perceived to be quite attractive. Mrs. X, on the other hand, felt this dress was "sleazy" and inappropriate for barhopping. Furthermore, she felt as if she would be making a fool out of herself, since most girls wore slacks or jeans to the local bars.

Following the presentation of the problem, the counselors suggested that Mr. and Mrs. X use their reciprocal-exchange skills to help resolve the conflict. As a first step, the counselor restated the problem in clear and precise terms. The X's negotiated on the issues for about a half-hour under the supervision of the counselors. As a result of these negotiations, two contracts resulted:

Contract One

For Mrs. X: I agree to go barhopping with my husband and his friends this Friday evening and to be an active and involved partner *if,* in return, he allows me to choose my own clothing for the evening and does not complain about it afterward.
For Mr. X: I agree not to complain about my wife not wearing a particular dress that I find attractive *if,* in return, she goes barhopping with me and tries to be an active and involved partner.

Contract Two

For Mrs. X: I agree to wear the dress my husband finds attractive *if,* in return, he takes me out to dinner at a moderately priced restaurant in about two weeks.
For Mr. X: I agree to take my wife out to dinner at a moderately priced restaurant within the next two weeks *if,* in return, she wears a dress I find particularly attractive.

These two contracts appeared to satisfactorily resolve the immediate problem for Mr. and Mrs. X. That is, both spouses felt pleased with the contracts they had established, as a result of their willingness to communicate, promise, and bargain.

The present authors conclude this section, hopeful that the reader has become more aware of the behavioral-exchange model and its applicability to marriage counseling. As of this writing, Mr. and Mrs. X were still being seen by the counselors, on a biweekly basis, and appeared to be making many positive and desirable changes in their relationship as a result of their reciprocal-exchange contracts.

Conclusion

Having presented a preliminary picture of the behaviorial-exchange model and its application to marital counseling, the present authors now focus their attention on the elaboration and refinement of this model. First, we suggest that further development of the model can best be accomplished through direct clinical experience with (groups of) married couples. That is, although the theoretical justification for this model has been clearly established, there still exists a definite need to refine and test it through continuing clinical research. We sincerely hope that other concerned researchers will join us in this task.

Second, the present authors perceive the behavioral-exchange model as only one of several possible educational models to help ameliorate marital unhappiness. The Conjugal Relationship Modification Program, devised by Dr. Bernard Guerney, emphasizes the teaching of specific communication skills to groups of married couples. The behavioral-exchange model presented herein complements the Conjugal Program by providing an optional program for those couples perceiving a need to solve specific problems after learning effective communication skills. There now exists a need for researchers and clinicians to apply these communication and behavioral-exchange techniques to such diverse marital problems as sex, decision-making, conflict resolution, money management, and others.

To conclude this presentation, the authors summarize, as objectively as possible, five potential strengths as well as five precautions for implementation of the model.

Potential Strengths of the Behavioral-Exchange Model

1. Teaches married couples reciprocal exchange and operant skills to help them resolve their present difficulties and those that will arise in their future.
2. Encourages couples to eliminate undesirable behaviors on a reciprocal basis

and replace them with more desirable behaviors (those reinforcing to the marriage).

3. Emphasizes a behavioral analysis of marital interaction.
4. Identifies the unmotivated partner in the marriage (the spouse unwilling to compromise and bargain to improve the relationship).
5. Fosters self-reliance of the couple by having *them* negotiate their own behavioral-exchange contracts (with minimal dependence on the counselor).

Precautions Associated with the Behavioral-Exchange Model

1. Not functional for those marriages where one or both spouses are unable or unwilling to compromise and bargain (large power differential).
2. Counselors must be knowledgeable as to both social exchange theory and operant learning principles.
3. Couples should be cautioned to proceed slowly in moving along their hierarchy from least undesirable to most undesirable behaviors.
4. Counselors must serve as positive reinforcers throughout the program.
5. Couples must learn and keep daily behavioral records of their progess in the program.

REFERENCES

Ard, B. N., and C. C. Ard (eds.) (1969), *Handbook of Marriage Counseling.* Palo Alto: Science & Behavior Books.
Bellville, T. P., O. N. Raths, and C. J. Bellville (1969), "Conjoint Marriage Therapy with a Husband-and-Wife Team," *American Journal of Orthopsychiatry,* 39:473-483.
Blood, R. O. and D. M. Wolfe (1960), *Husband and Wives: The Dynamics of Family Living.* Glencoe, Ill.: Free Press.
Collins, J. (1971), "Marital Adjustment and Communication Changes as a Function of a Six-Month Conjugal Therapy Program." Unpublished Ph.D.proposal: The Pennsylvania State University.
Ely, A. L. (1970), "Efficacy of Training in Conjugal Therapy." Unpublished Ph.D thesis: Rutgers University.
Goldstein, M. K., and B. Francis (1969), "Behavior Modification of Husbands by Wives." Paper presented at the Annual Meeting of the National Council on Family Relations, Washington, D.C.
Goodwin, H. M., and E. H. Mudd (1966), "Marriage Counseling: Methods and Goals," *Comprehensive Psychiatry,* 7:450-452.
Greene, B.L. (ed.) (1965), *The Psychotherapies of Marital Disharmony.* New York: Free Press.
Guerney, Jr., B. G. (1970), Personal communication.

————, G. E. Stollak, and L. Guerney (1970), "A Format For a New Mode of Psychological Practice: Or How to Escape a Zombie," *The Counseling Psychologist,* 2:97-104.

————(1971), "The Practicing Psychologist as Educator—an Alternative to the Medical Practitioner," *Professional Psychology,* in press.

Heer, D. M. (1963), "The Measurement and Bases of Family Power: An Overview," *Journal of Marriage and the Family,* 25:133-139.

Kimmel, P. R., and J. W. Havens (1966), "Game Theory versus Mutual Identification: Two Criteria for Assessing Marital Relationships," *Journal of Marriage and the Family,* 28:460-465.

Knox, D. H. (1970), "Behavior Therapy and Marriage Problems." Paper presented at Annual Meeting of the National Council on Family Relations, Chicago.

————(1971), *Marriage Happiness: A Behavioral Approach to Counseling.* Champaign, Ill.: Research Press Company.

Krumboltz, J. D., and C. E. Thoresen (eds.) (1969), *Behavioral Counseling.* New York: Holt, Rinehart, & Winston.

Lederer, W. J., and D. D. Jackson, (1968), *The Mirages of Marriage.* New York: W. W. Norton.

Levinger, G. (1965), "Marital Cohesiveness and Dissolution: An Integrative Review," *Journal of Marriage and the Family,* 27:19-28.

Liberman, R. (1970), "Behavioral Approaches to Family and Couple Therapy," *American Journal of Orthopsychiatry,* 40:106-118.

Olson, D. H. (1970), "Marital and Family Therapy: Integrative Review and Critique," *Journal of Marriage and the Family,* 32:501-538.

Rappaport, A. F. (1971), "The Effects of an Intensive Conjugal Relationship Modification Program." Unpublished Ph.D. thesis: The Pennyslvania State University.

Silverman, H. L. (ed.) (1967), *Marital Counseling.* Springfield, Ill.: Thomas.

Stuart, R. B. (1969), "Operant-Interpersonal Treatment for Marital Discord," *Journal of Consulting and Clinical Psychology,* 33:675-682.

Tharp, R. G. (1963a), "Psychological Patterning in Marriage," *Psychological Bulletin,* 60:97-117.

————(1963b), "Dimensions of Marriage Roles," *Marriage and Family Living,* 25:389-404.

————(1964), "Reply to Levinger's Note," *Psychological Bulletin,* 61:158-160.

————(1965), "Marriage Roles, Child Development and Family Treatment," *American Journal of Orthopsychiatry,* 35:531-539.

————, and G.D. Otis (1966), "Toward a Theory for Therapeutic Intervention in Families," *Journal of Consulting Psychology,* 30:426-434.

Section D

Treatment of Sexual Dysfunction

THOMAS P. LAUGHREN
DAVID J. KASS

14   # Desensitization of Sexual
        Dysfunction: The Present Status

This chapter represents the first comprehensive review of both the clinical
and empirical literature on desensitization approaches to the treatment of
sexual dysfunctions. Analysis of published studies shows both *in-vivo*
desensitization and systematic desensitization to be highly effective strategies
for these problems, with over 75% of the patients studied showing positive
outcomes. Discussion also focuses on important clinical and research issues
such as problem definition and the establishment of outcome criteria. The
second part of the paper provides a detailed procedural description of a new
desensitization model for the outpatient treatment of sexual dysfunctions.
While the model draws upon existing approaches, it proposes a new standard
method which can be systematically applied to all sexual dysfunctions. Future
clinical and empirical needs in the area are also highlighted and discussed.

Over the past decade there has been considerable progress in the treatment of
sexual dysfunction, an area which previously had been characterized by much
dogma but little data. There had been generally dismal results and poor
prognosis, with or without treatment (Cooper, 1971; Johnson, 1965). Most of
the recent therapeutic success falls within the realm of the behavior therapies.
This chapter reviews this recent behavioral literature; presents an in-vivo
desensitization program, together with a summary of recent suggestions from
the behavioral literature as an integrated and comprehensive approach to the
treatment of sexual dysfunction; and, finally, points to needed future research.

Basic Theoretical Assumptions About Sexual Dysfunction

A basic notion in our treatment program is that competing with adequate sexual responses are a variety of responses that may be broadly referred to as "discomfort." Such responses include feelings of anxiety, annoyance, shame, guilt, anger, boredom, and pressure to perform. Concomitant with these "discomfort" responses are overt physiologic responses of sexual inadequacy, including absence or loss of erection, involuntary and too-rapid ejaculation, sometimes absence of ejaculation, absence of orgastic response, vaginismus, and pain. The basic goal of our desensitization program is to help couples to extinguish "discomfort" responses in sexual encounters and to substitute "comfort" responses, including a general sense of relaxation and well-being, affection, love, desire, and pleasure. Simultaneously, it is hoped that sexually inadequate responses will be replaced with sexually adequate responses, including maintenance of erection, appropriate delay of orgasm in the male, and satisfying orgasm in both partners. The basic behavioral model for treatment of sexual dysfunction is that of desensitization, which can be viewed theoretically either as reciprocal inhibition of undesirable responses with desirable responses (Wolpe, 1969), or as simple operant extinction of undesirable responses and operant shaping of desirable responses (Evans, 1973). The actual therapeutic approaches to desensitization are categorized as either systematic or in-vivo desensitization. Systematic desensitization involves the simultaneous use of hierarchies of fearful imaginal scenes and relaxation, either self-induced by training in deep-muscle relaxation, or by administration of anxiolytic drugs (Wolpe, 1969). In-vivo desensitization involves the breaking down of a complex and fearful task into graded steps so that the fearful individual can gradually approximate the final task while maintaining a low level of anxiety.

Recent Desensitization Approaches to Sexual Dysfunction

Ten treatment series of sexual dysfunction cases will be considered in this section. Improvement rates will be compared in terms of the specific desensitization methods employed. Several additional important and controversial treatment variables will also be examined. The studies fall into the two general categories of in-vivo desensitization and systematic desensitization. The basic method in the in-vivo approaches was to assign couples gradually more intimate levels of physical encounter. They were instructed to begin with minimal exercises of touch and caressing and to proceed on to higher levels of physical encounter only as they became comfortable with lower levels. For systematic desensitization, hierarchies of gradually more intimate imaginal scenes were constructed and were presented with concomitant relaxation, either drug-induced or self-induced after deep-muscle relaxation training. Wolpe, who was the first therapist to publish treatment results of sexual desensitization, used an in-vivo desensitization paradigm (Wolpe, 1958, 1969), as has been subsequently adopted by Masters and Johnson (1970), Lobitz and Lo Piccolo (1972), and Kass (1973). Cooper (1969 b,c) also has used a method which is a variant of in-vivo desensitization. His treatment consisted of sex education, supportive psychotherapy, and training in deep-muscle relaxation, to be used by clients before and during actual sexual encounters. His clients were instructed not to have intercourse until they held strong erections for several minutes. The instructions Cooper provided his clients were clearly less specific than those of the other authors, and it is only because of his emphasis on relaxation during the actual sexual encounter, and his focus on gradual progress with comfort, that he is included in the in-vivo group. Of the systematic desensitization series, Lazarus (1961, 1963) and Obler (1973) have used self-induced deep-muscle relaxation as the antagonistic response, while Brady (1966) and Friedman (1968) have used drug-induced relaxation for deconditioning anxiety to imaginal scenes. Jones and Park (1972) have used a combination of drug-induced and deep-muscle relaxation for deconditioning anxiety. In addition to the usual hierarchies, Obler (1973) used films and slides depicting the specific sexual dysfunctions of the clients as part of their hierarchies. Both Obler and Lobitz and Lo Piccolo used role-playing and behavioral rehearsal of heterosexual social encounters. Lobitz and Lo Piccolo focused specifically on social initiation procedures preceding sexual activity. Sex education and counseling formed a part of all these therapeutic endeavors. Reported outcomes of studies of the behavioral treatment of sexual dysfunction are presented in Tables 1 and 2. Considering some important differences in population and treatment methods, it is remarkable that the overall improvement rates tend to cluster around 80%. Nevertheless, there *are* salient characteristics common to all these interventions: their de-emphasis of the intact complete sexual act, but rather, successive approximations of sexual encounter, either in fantasy or reality, and the prohibition of actual sexual encounter beyond a level with which a couple is comfortable.

Before further comparison of these studies, several issues need to be considered. There is considerable variation in the extent to which different authors provide data about their patient populations and treatment selection factors. Clearly, population differences could account for differential treatment results or could spuriously account for similar results, if, for example, treatment techniques of high and low efficacy were applied to populations of severely dysfunctional and only moderately dysfunctional couples respectively. Among the *in-vivo* studies, Masters and Johnson (1970) have used the largest sample (N=790) and provide the fullest description of their clientele. Their clients ranged in age from twenty-three to seventy-six and largely came from the upper middle class, with a disproportionate skewing toward high educational attainment and professional status. They had to have been referred by other profes-

Table 1. Improvement Rates in Studies of *In-Vivo* Desensitization of Sexual Dysfunction

Author	Date	Sexual Dysfunction	Improvement Rate
Cooper [a]	1969(b)	Premature ejaculation	
		Type 1	10% (1/10)
		Type 2	85% (6/7)
		Type 3	46.2% (6/13)
		Overall	43% (13/30)
Cooper [b]	1969(c)	Heterogeneous group of dysfunctional males	39% (19/49)
Kass [c]	1973	Heterogeneous group of dysfunctional couples	87.5% (14/16)
Lobitz and Lo Piccolo [d]	1972	1° Orgasmic dysfunction	100% (13/13)
		2° Orgasmic dysfunction	33.3% (3/9)
		Premature ejaculation	100% (6/6)
		Erective failure	66.7% (4/6)
		Overall	75% (26/34)
Masters and Johnson [e]	1970	Premature ejaculation	97.8% (182/186)
		1° Impotence	59.4% (19/32)
		2° Impotence	73.8% (157/213)
		Ejaculatory incompetence	82.4% (14/17)
		1° Orgasmic dysfunction	83.4% (162/193)
		Situational orgasmic dysfunction	77.2% (115/149)
		Masturbatory	90.9% (10/11)
		Coital	80.2% (85/106)
		Random	62.5% (20/32)
		Vaginismus	100% (29/29)
		Overall	82% (648/790)
Wolpe [f]	1969	Heterogeneous group of dysfunctional males	67.7% (21/31)
Total for All In-Vivo Desensitization Groups:			78.2% (749/950)

NOTE: The difficulties in summing data from studies which differ in population, problem definitions, treatment technique, outcome criteria, and follow-up are conceded. However, it is felt that there is some utility in doing this at this state of the art.

[a] Types 1, 2, and 3 refer respectively to chronic types with good erections, acute onset type with erectional insufficiency, and gradual onset type with concomitant insidious onset impotence.

[b] This series included both acute and insidious onset impotence, ejaculatory incompetence, and premature ejaculation; it is not stated in either this or the preceding paper (1969b), but it is possible that there is patient overlap between these two reports; as mentioned, the overall poor results for these two series might be explained either on the basis of a particularly chronic population, or on

considerable deviation in the treatment method from the other four *in-vivo* studies; if the overall improvement rate for the *in-vivo* studies is calculated without Cooper's data, the result is 82.3%.

[c] This series included cases of impotence, frigidity, and premature ejaculation. Kass's two failures were couples who did not complete the entire sequence of exercises, and if eliminated, would result in a success rate of 100%.

[d] It is significant that the three successes with secondary orgasmic dysfunction were the last three cases treated, most likely a result of the authors changing the treatment technique (McGovern and Stewart, 1972). These authors stress the importance of simultaneously resolving nonsexual marital problems while pursuing the sexual desensitization program with these couples.

[e] These improvement rates are the initial (2-week) rates rather than the 5-year follow-up rates which are not yet completed; preliminary 5-year results indicate an insignificant drop in any of the subgroups except for a 5% drop for secondarily impotent males.

[f] This series included cases of impotence and premature ejaculation; Wolpe presents a 67.7% rate of entire recovery, but an 87.1% rate of acceptable recovery.

Table 2. Improvement Rates in Studies of Systematic Desensitization of Sexual Dysfunction

Author	Date	Sexual Dysfunction	Improvement Rate
		Systematic Desensitization: Self-Induced Relaxation	
Lazarus [a]	1963	Chronic Frigidity	56.2% (9/16)
	1961	Impotence	100% (2/2)
Obler [b]	1973	Heterogeneous Group of Dysfunctional Couples	82% (18/22)
Author	Date	Sexual Dysfunction	Improvement Rate
		Systematic Desensitization: Drug-Induced Relaxation	
Brady	1966	Chronic Frigidity	80% (4/5)
Jones and Park [c]	1972	Orgasmic Dysfunction	79.7% (55/69)
		Impotence	85.7% (6/7)
		Ejaculatory Incompetence	100% (1/1)
		Overall	80.5% (62/77)
Friedman	1968	Erective Failure	80% (8/10)
		Premature Ejaculation	50% (3/6)
		Ejaculatory Incompetence	0% (0/3)
		Overall	74% (11/19)
Total for All Systematic Desensitization Groups:			75.2% (106/141)

[a] Lazarus includes among his failures those women who terminated before 6 sessions; he gives a success rate of 100% for those women who completed at least 15 sessions.

[b] This series includes cases of impotence, premature ejaculation, and orgasmic dysfunction.

[c] Jones and Park use deep-muscle relaxation training concomitantly with the drug-induced relaxation; they mention an additional 6 clients who were improved but not cured, bringing their improvement rate to 88.3%.

sionals, and the only other requirements for entering treatment were an absence of psychosis and a willingness of both spouses to cooperate in the program. It should be noted that a willingness to take two weeks off from regular activities and responsibilities, to devote this time entirely to the treatment of their sexual problem, and to pay a substantial fee ($2500), represents a high and perhaps unusual degree of motivation. Kass's (1973) clients were largely young and educated couples from a university setting, and the same appears to be true of Lobitz and Lo Piccolo's (1972) clients. Since chronicity of sexual dysfunction may be an important variable in determining response to treatment, the studies with younger couples need to be evaluated with this variable in mind. Indeed, Cooper (1969a), in his study of sexually dysfunctional males, listed among the poor prognostic factors older age, long duration of the problem, and insidious onset. In his study with premature ejaculators, Cooper (1969b) discriminated among three types based essentially on chronicity, and notes that only the acute onset type responds well to treatment. In an interesting discussion of the types of anxiety found in impotent males, Cooper (1969a) distinguishes between "early onset anxiety," (developing prior to, at the time of, or soon after the onset of potency) and "late onset anxiety" (developing months or years later). He suggests that "early onset anxiety" is a cause of the impotence in the males of this type, and that "late onset anxiety" is a consequence of impotence in the males of this second type. In any case, he provides evidence that males of the "early onset type" do significantly better in therapy than those of the "late onset type." In a later study, Cooper (1969c) dealt with a heterogeneous group of dysfunctional males, some of whom suffered from chronic dysfunctions. His overall results in this series were notably inferior to those that have been reported by other workers. Perhaps his poor results can be explained partly in terms of the chronicity issue, but it might also be argued that his treatment method is not as explicitly an *in-vivo* desensitization as are most of the other reports noted in Table 1.

The provision of population data from systematic desensitization studies is also variable. In general, the patients seem to have been drawn from either middle or upper-middle class groups. Lazarus (1963) worked with a group of chronic and persistently "frigid" women and reported an overall success rate of only 56 percent. However, he included among his failures those patients who terminated very early in treatment, and states that every patient who underwent more than fifteen sessions was cured. Brady (1966) also worked with a group of chronically frigid women and obtained an impressive improvement rate. Jones and Park's (1972) group of mixed dysfunctional couples all had at least a year of history of dysfunction, were willing to work together, had "predominantly positive relationships outside of the sexual area," and had no other psychiatric diagnosis. This raises the issue of the prognostic importance of the status of the couples' general relationship. Masters and Johnson (1970) explain a number of their failures on the basis of dysfunctional marriages, and many other authors also allude to the importance of cooperative partners. Kass (1973) also experienced some difficulty with sexually dysfunctional couples who had additional nonsexual conflicts, but notes that it is not the dysfunctional relationship *per se* that interferes with the desensitization program. Rather, it is the specific occurrences of fighting during the practice sessions that retard progress. For those couples who can learn not to argue during the practice session, the prognosis for the sex program is excellent. For those couples who continue to carry their conflict into the sexual area, the prognosis is poor. It is interesting that in their use of female surrogates for dysfunctional males without partners, Masters and Johnson were at least as successful as with self-selected couples, whether married or otherwise. This observation suggests that a neutral surrogate relationship is also conducive to the treatment of sexual dysfunction. Masters and Johnson never attempted the reverse situation of a dysfunctional female and male surrogate, and have since dropped their female surrogate program. But, apparently, there are currently some other workers successfully using both male and female surrogates.

In comparing actual treatment programs and outcomes, it is clear that several controversial treatment variables need to be critically examined. Masters and Johnson recommend an intensive two-week commitment to a sexual desensitization program, in contrast to all other reported programs, which are typically outpatient arrangements in the home community, without any major disruption or isolation from the couple's routine life. In light of comparably good results in these other programs, it is suggested that an outpatient approach is feasible. In favor of outpatient treatment in the home community is the argument that this community rather than a motel room in a distant city will become a discriminative stimulus for adequate sexual functioning. The data from other studies is often not complete regarding the number and length of sessions, and the total duration of treatment, but in surveying both the group and case studies, it appears that one might often reasonably expect good results in 12-15 outpatient visits of 45-minute duration, over a time period of 2-3 months or less. These are average figures, and certainly there will be couples who progress much slower or faster.

In all of the reported studies, a partner was available for each dysfunctional client. However, there was considerable variation in the extent to which the focus was on a dysfunctional pair. For all of the in-vivo desensitization groups, the couples were worked with as a unit. For most of the systematic desensitization groups, the couples were involved as a unit in assessing the problem, and may have been seen together several times subsequently, but the focus was primarily on desensitization of the identified dysfunctional member. In spite of this difference, the results are generally comparable between the two groups. Since in most cases of systematic desensitization the couples were asked to refrain from actual sexual encounters beyond the level of encounter reached in the hierarchy, the couples may have been indirectly engaging in an in-vivo desensitization program, while the systematic desensitization may have served as an adjunctive measure to facilitate and control this process. One final treatment variable of concern is the treatment team. Masters and Johnson (1970) feel that dual-sex therapy teams are essential, since it is easier for a female client to identify with a female therapist, and similarly for a male client and male therapist. Lobitz and Lo Piccolo (1972) have also used dual-sex therapy teams. However, none of the other in-vivo series, and none of the systematic desensitization series, were done with dual-sex therapy teams. Since the results are comparable, it would seem that dual-sex therapy teams are not an essential feature of treatment, and if so, then certainly not indicated from an economic perspective. Relevant to this conclusion is the finding that empirical support for co-therapy teams in general couples treatment is similarly lacking (Gurman, 1973).

The inadequacies of problem definition, outcome criteria, follow-up, and lack of control groups need to be examined. Considerable differences exist in the extent to which different authors have been specific in defining the individual dysfunctional syndromes and outcome criteria. Regarding problem definition, the range is from an absence of definition to the careful definitions of Masters and Johnson, which in some cases even offer quantification. The same diversity is true of outcome criteria, and the range is from general statements about "sexual adjustment" to very specific and quantified measures of outcome. In general, the more recently published studies offer more in terms of specificity of outcome measures. Obler (1973) has used several psychological tests, including a Sexual Anxiety Scale and an Anxiety Differential Scale, as well as physiological measures, including galvanic skin response and heart rate. These measures were applied before, during, and after treatment. In addition, Obler has published his results in terms of success/experience ratios, i.e., a cumulative ratio, obtained over the treatment period. This is a ratio of the total number of successful sexual encounters to the total number of sexual encounters. Obler has also provided one of the only two controlled studies of sexual dysfunction, and his results suggest a very striking advantage of desensitization therapy over traditional group therapy (82% vs. 2.5%) for the treatment of sexual dysfunction. In a much earlier controlled study of impotent males, Lazarus (1963) found that group desensitization of impotent males was more effective (2/2) than traditional group treatment (0/3). Finally, Lo Piccolo et al. (1972) have developed two sexual behavior inventories. The first of these records intercourse attempt-frequency and duration; and for each such sexual encounter, the percent of times erection is obtained; and for each time erection is obtained, the percent of times orgasm is obtained in the male and in the female; and finally, a self-rating (scale of 1 to 6) by each partner of general satisfaction of the couple's sexual relationship. In addition, an inventory of 17 heterosexual activities ranging from kissing to intercourse is rated (scale of 1 to 6 for each item) by each partner (Steger, 1972). These inventories are completed before treatment, at termination, and at 6-month follow-up. Finally, there is also much variation in the extent and thoroughness of follow-up. Most studies have done follow-up at 6 months to a year, but Masters and Johnson provide a 5-year follow-up for some of their initial couples, and it is encouraging that there is an almost insignificant drop in improvement rate. One exception is the group of secondarily impotent males, whose rate of effectiveness decreased from 73.8% to 69.1%. These data suggest that desensitization is a lasting cure in most cases, but certainly does not preclude the necessity of careful and long-term follow-up in additional studies in this area.

OUTPATIENT IN-VIVO DESENSITIZATION OF SEXUAL DYSFUNCTION

The program to be described here is similar to those previously presented by Wolpe (1969) and Masters and Johnson (1970). One problem common to both those presentations is the lack of enough detail and specificity of instructions to couples. As previously noted, the basic method in an *in-vivo* desensitization is to break down a difficult and anxiety-provoking task into very small steps so that as the fearful client gradually works through the various steps, he experiences only minimal anxiety or no anxiety at each level. Although this method is certainly inherent in both the Wolpe and Masters and Johnson programs, it is felt that the merits of the following program (developed by D. J. K.) are the specificity of the instructions at each level of encounter, the specificity of techniques for dealing with problems that arise at each level, and the specific criteria indicating when to proceed to a new level of encounter. Included within the following program will be several of the useful suggestions of Masters and Johnson (1970), as well as additional suggestions from more recent behavioral studies.

Assessment

Masters and Johnson (1970) stress the importance of taking a complete history of the individual members of the couple as well as the couple per se, including not only sexually oriented material, but also general psychosocial data and medical data. Certainly it would seem useful to gather enough information to be able to make an assessment of the status of a relationship, to have some idea of how the problem developed, to be able to rule out organic causes for sexual dysfunction, to be able to define the problem, and most important, to be able to define the specific treatment goals of the couple. It is important to obtain an assessment of the attitudes and knowledge about sexuality for each of the partners, since a necessary but not sufficient condition for success seems to be at least a healthy intellectual outlook, even if the couple is not well-equipped emotionally. Masters and Johnson (1970) present an extensive outline for history-taking which requires 10-15 hours of interviewer time. It is not at all clear that such extensive interviewing is necessary, especially since a very high success rate has been obtained by most other groups using desensitization programs and a very much abbreviated initial interviewing procedure focusing mainly on problem definition and goal-setting (approximately 1-2 hours). It is very important that possible organic causes for sexual dysfunction be ruled out. In all cases of female dyspareunia, a gynecological examination should be obtained to screen for clitoral adhesions that are being increasingly found to be a rather common cause of orgasmic dysfunction, with or without dyspareunia. It has also been suggested (Kegel, 1952) that the strength of the pubococcygeus muscle is an important parameter in determining the adequacy of orgasmic release in women. A gynecological examination would also permit the assessment of this muscle. It should be noted that for both of these problems, it is important that the examining physician be alerted to their possibility so that he can give particularattention to discovering either of these difficulties. It is also mandatory to obtain urological consultation for males with dyspareunia, but it is also important to keep in mind the variety of physical conditions that can contribute to secondary impotence. Masters and Johnson (1970, pp. 184-185) provide an extensive list.

Problem Definition and Treatment Goals

After gathering historical information from both partners, it is usually possible to define specifically the problems of sexual dysfunction. Masters and Johnson (1970) provide the most widely accepted definitions of the specific sexual dysfunction syndromes. *Premature ejaculation* is difficult to define clinically, and usually has been described in terms of an inability to delay ejaculation for a specified minimal time period of intravaginal containment. More pragmatically, Masters and Johnson consider a man a premature ejaculator if he cannot delay his ejaculation long enough for his partner to achieve orgasm in at least 50 percent of their sexual encounters, assuming that his partner is not orgasmically dysfunctional. This definition is quite arbitrary and it makes most sense to allow the couple to define their own individual goal with the therapist's assistance. Because of differences in prognosis and response to treatment, it is useful to subdivide problems of *impotence (or erectile failure)* into primary and secondary categories. Masters and Johnson define as primarily impotent a man who has never been able to achieve and/or maintain an erection quality sufficient to accomplish successful intercourse, including his orgasm. Any successful attempt, whether heterosexual or homosexual, precludes this label. Also excluded are males who for a variety of medical reasons are simply unable to obtain an erection under any circumstances. To be considered secondarily impotent, a man must have a history of at least one (and usually many) successful intromissions with ejaculation, whether with a heterosexual or homosexual partner. There then must be an episode of erective failure, and a subsequent high rate of failure to achieve successful intercourse. Masters and Johnson arbitrarily designate a failure rate of 25% as defining secondary impotence, but such definitions are probably best arrived at by the couple themselves. *Ejaculatory incompetence* is a relatively rare disorder. A man with ejaculatory incompetence rarely has difficulty in achieving or maintaining an erection quality sufficient for successful intercourse, but the difficulty involves either absolute (primary) or relative (secondary) inability to ejaculate during intercourse.

Of the sexual dysfunctions of women, *orgasmic dysfunction* is the most common. A woman is designated as having primary orgasmic dysfunction only if she reports never having achieved orgasm under any circumstances in her entire life. In order to be considered situationally nonorgasmic, a woman must have experienced at least one instance of orgasm, regardless of whether it was induced by self or by partner manipulation, developed during vaginal or rectal intercourse, or stimulated by oral-genital exchange. Further, she is said to have *masturbatory orgasmic inadequacy* if she cannot achieve orgasm by self- or partner manipulation, but functions adequately during intercourse. *Coital orgasmic inadequacy* includes those women who cannot achieve orgasm during intercourse but who can be brought to orgasm by manipulative or other stimulative techniques. The final grouping of random orgasmic inadequacy includes those women with histories of orgasmic return at least once during both masturbation and intercourse, but for whom orgasm under either of these circumstances is a rare event. *Vaginismus* is a demonstrable psychophysiologic syndrome involving spastic contraction of all components of the pelvic musculature investing the perineum and outer third of the vagina. This spastic contraction is an involuntary reflex in response to imagined, anticipated, or real attempts at vaginal penetration. Female *dyspareunia* is simply defined as pain either during intercourse or subsequent to intercourse, and is of interest in discussion of sexual dysfunction in that it is not always clear how much of the problem is secondary to definitive organic conditions (Masters and Johnson, 1970, pp. 266-294) and how much emotional and environmental variables are contributing to the pain. A sexual desensitization is relevant only in dealing with the latter variables, and it is imperative that a careful medical work-up is pursued to rule out or discover the former variables. Similarly, male dyspareunia is defined as pain associated with intercourse or subsequent to sexual encounter. Again, a sexual desensitization is relevant only in dealing with psychological variables, and a medical work-up is necessary in discovering or ruling out possible organic variables. Finally, *lack of sexual interest* can be considered a problem which usually exists simultaneous with and is related to other more specific dysfunctional syndromes. It can be conveniently defined in terms of the discrepancy between what a couple designates as their ideal frequency of sexual encounter and their actual frequency of encounter. The general sexual desensitization approach may lead to its resolution, or additional couple-oriented therapeutic maneuvers might be required. The discrepancy between the couple's ideal and actual frequency of sexual encounter might be used as one measure of the overall success of the program and would be expected to narrow with successful treatment.

It is imperative to define sexual problems in the context of the relationship and to convince the partners that they each have something to gain from treatment. This will prevent conflict for the couple about which partner is "the" client. Treatment goals should be defined as specifically as possible. It is relatively more important to define treatment goals than to define the original dysfunctional problems. The desensitization program itself serves a diagnostic function, and as will be seen later, the nature of the complaints can change as the program proceeds. Goals need not conform exactly to the accepted definitions of sexual dysfunction. For example, a couple may decide that female orgasm prior to male orgasm only 50% of the time is inadequate, and may decide that 75% is more to their liking. Or they might decide to define male performance in terms of time duration of intravaginal containment prior to his orgasm. Goals should be set within reason, but there should be flexibility. The more precisely goals are set, the easier it will be for both the therapist and the couple to assess the effects of their treatment efforts.

General Instructions

After treatment goals have been clearly defined, basic information and instructions should be given to the couple. The program requires that the couple set aside 15-minute practice sessions in bed as often as is convenient. This might range from one or two sessions per week to a maximum of two sessions per day. These should be held at a time when both partners are most likely to be relaxed and when there is a high probability for sexual interest to develop. This should include considerations of pressures from job, school, and other sources, and the program should probably not be started during a period of high stress for either partner. The times of the practice sessions should be decided in advance, preferably 24 hours or more, but with a minimum of 2 hours notice. This preplanning is important because the issue of scheduling can and often does lead to conflict and may need to be dealt with as a separate therapeutic problem. Specific instructions are given for each practice session, and the couple does not advance to the next set of instructions until they have successfully completed two sessions at the preceding level. The couple should never go beyond the level being attempted, and these sessions should be the only sexual encounters the couple engage in for the duration of the treatment program. Individual sexual activity, e.g., masturbation, outside of the sessions is permissible.

The key goal of any session is to reduce discomfort as defined earlier. The goals for level of physical encounter are secondary to the goal of both partners being comfortable. The couple should be creative in doing whatever they feel appropriate to reduce their mutual discomfort, and, of course, the methods employed by each partner will have to be acceptable in terms of not creating discomfort for the other partner. These might include in-bed activities such as listening to music, smoking, drinking, etc., or out-of-bed activities such as leaving the room, going for a walk, etc. This will at later stages of the program almost certainly include specific do's and don'ts of sexual technique. The list is endless. Part of the task, then, during the initial sessions will be for the couple to work out signaling systems by which each can signal discomfort or comfort to the other partner, and these signaling systems will have to be worked out in such a way that they will not produce discomfort in themselves. These signaling systems may be verbal and/or nonverbal and may be different for each partner, but should be consistent throughout the program. Some couples have used humming of various frequencies to indicate approval or disapproval of partner behaviors. Others have used generally neutral words with specific meanings defined by the couple. A common nonverbal communication technique has been for one partner to physically guide the other partner's hands in a manner pleasing to the original partner. Again, the primary goal should be discomfort reduction, but always with the secondary goals of attainment of each level of encounter. The attempt to attain a given level of physical encounter while remaining comfortable should be maintained for only 15 minutes at a time, but the couple may continue the session as long as they please if they wish to continue and are comfortable. It cannot be emphasized too strongly that the couple should not press on with attempting a given level of physical encounter when they are experiencing discomfort, but rather should focus on achieving comfort for both partners at a *lower* level of physical encounter.

Stages of Sexual Encounter

The following are the specific stages of physical encounter that the couple will attempt to master with comfort:

1. Nonerotic physical contact: Couple lying unclothed (or with clothes if too uncomfortable unclothed) next to one another in bed, in contact and feeling one another's warmth, but without kissing or stroking.
2. Nonbreast and genital stroking: Couple engaging in kissing and mutual stroking, but avoiding breasts and genitals.
3. Breast and genital stroking: Couple engaging in kissing and mutual stroking, including breasts and genitals.

These three initial stages are important to the couple not only in preparation for further stages, but also in the development of a consistent and workable signaling system. In all subsequent assignments to engage in more advanced stages, the couple should always begin each session by moving through these initial three stages.

Masters and Johnson's (1970) discussion of "sensate focus" exercise, including "mutual pleasuring," communicating, and restrictions on sexual arousal, is roughly similar to the material presented in this treatment program up through stage 3. Masters and Johnson's discussion focuses more specifically on the individual sensory experiences of touch, sight, smell and olfaction rather than on the level of comfort with various stages of overall physical-sensory involvement stressed in this program. They also suggest using moisturizing lotions in the mutual stroking exercises. Such lotions not only present a pleasant medium to work with but also desensitize the individual male and female partners to vaginal lubricant and seminal fluid respectively. It may also be useful to have the couple read *The Art of Erotic Massage* (Whelan and Cochran, 1973) and to introduce the use of lubricants such as K-Y surgical jelly or scented lotions to help them through these initial exercises.

4. Self-masturbation to orgasm.

5. Mutual masturbation to orgasm.

These two stages involve masturbation, both self and mutual. The self-masturbation stage might be questioned by some patients because of cultural biases, but this is an important stage to master. It is not uncommon for women with orgasmic dysfunction to have only limited or no experience masturbating. It is important for women to develop facility with masturbation in order to condition a response which previously has been occurring at a low or zero frequency. By learning self-masturbation, they are in a better position to teach their partners how to stimulate them in subsequent stages. This latter statement also applies to men, and in any case, it is useful to have both partners engaging in self-masturbation because the problem then continues to be defined as a shared couples problem. Also, it is important to obtain orgasm for both partners early in the program since this functions as a strong reinforcer and helps to maintain both partners' participation in the program.

Since masturbation is such a crucial and sometimes problematic area, special efforts may be required in getting through these stages. Couples may have difficulty masturbating in each other's presence, and so it is sometimes useful to have couples initially masturbate in different rooms and gradually move toward self-masturbation in the same room. Discussion of masturbation with the therapist and even assignment of reading material might help individual partners to develop accepting intellectual attitudes about masturbation. It may be helpful at times to have the male and female partner read, respectively, *The Sensuous Man*, ("M", 1972, pp. 45-52) or *The Sensuous Woman*, ("J", 1971, pp. 43-52). Women, in particular, may need special instructions in self-masturbation. Lobitz and Lo Piccolo (1972) have developed a program based on a graduated approach model to help women achieve masturbatory facility. The woman begins by using a hand mirror and anatomy diagrams to increase her self-awareness. She also begins Kegel's (1952) exercises for toning up the pelvic musculature. These involve simple voluntary contractions of the pelvic musculature for ten repetitions, three times daily, for several weeks. Next, she manually explores her genitals, and gradually focuses on sensitive areas that produce sexual pleasure. She is introduced to the use of lubricants and gradually increases her manipulations of responsive areas. We have found it useful to take the focus off the achievement of orgasm, and, rather, to focus on achieving comfort simultaneous with various levels of sexual arousal. McCullough and Montgomery (1972) have developed a method of rating of sexual arousal which we have used. This SUA (subjective units of arousal) scale ranges from 0 to 10. Zero equals no arousal and 10 equals orgasm. By quantifying arousal, we are able to keep the focus on comfort maintenance and yet achieve gradual increases in arousal and eventual orgasm. A vibrator may be indispensable at the self- and-mutual-masturbatory stages, and can be easily faded. Dengrove (1971) discusses the use of vibrators for masturbation, both self and mutual, and as an adjunct to arousal in actual intercourse. He describes the different types in use, both hand-held and penis-shaped, and also indicates the usefulness of an electric toothbrush with soft bristles.

In addition to problems with masturbation, some clients have problems becoming sexually aroused to their partners. It is desirable to begin resolving this problem at the stages of masturbation. Lobitz and Lo Piccolo (1972) have modified an orgasmic reconditioning technique of Davison (1968) and Marquis (1970) for use in enhancing the arousal of partners to one another. Basically, a classical conditioning paradigm is used. The partner who is to be reconditioned is asked to focus on material that has been erotically stimulating in the past, whether this involves the use of literature, pictures, fantasy, or some combination thereof. The client is then asked to masturbate to the point of orgasm and, just prior to orgasm, is asked to switch to a fantasy of sexual encounter with the other partner. A Polaroid picture of the partner engaging in sexual activity is useful for patients who have difficulty fantasizing. Subsequently, the client introduces the partner fantasies earlier in the masturbatory sequence until these fantasies themselves become erotically stimulating. This technique can be used both for self- and mutual masturbation, and subsequently during intercourse for enhancing arousal. Lo Piccolo *et al.* (1972) present a case in which they successfully used this arousal reconditioning procedure in the treatment of a homosexual male with erectile failure and ejaculatory incompetence with his heterosexual partner. Homosexual fantasies were used for initial arousal, and later in the masturbatory sequence, heterosexual fantasies involving his partner were substituted. Again, Polaroid pictures of his partner were used to aid fantasy production. This arousal reconditioning in conjuction with an *in-vivo* desensitization program was entirely successful in helping this male to perform adequately in his heterosexual encounters. This is of particular interest because of a significantly lower success rate for impotent men with histories of either religious orthodoxy or homosexual orientation. Annon (1971) provides a comprehensive review of the use of fantasies in association with masturbation, and his paper can be an additional source of ideas in working with clients who have difficulties in the area of arousal.

Lobitz and Lo Piccolo (1972) have also suggested an adjunctive technique for dealing with controlled and inhibited women who have difficulty accepting the uncontrollable movements and vocal releases that often accompany their orgastic responses. These women are asked to role-play, in the presence of their husbands, an exaggeration of their orgastic response until they are completely comfortable with this aspect of orgasm. They can then continue comfortably with the masturbatory exercises.

One additional note will be added here regarding the possible concomitant use of systematic desensitization in hastening the progress of the program. This might be useful in getting beyond *in-vivo* obstacles at any of the earlier stages already discussed, or in any of the subsequent instructions. The therapist should be aware of any heightened and recalcitrant anxiety that occurs at any stage and should not hesitate to utilize systematic desensitization techniques at this point (Wolpe, 1969). This will involve setting up hierarchies of imaginal scenes and teaching deep-muscle relaxation. The deep-muscle relaxation will not only be useful in deconditioning anxiety to the hierarchy items, but also can be used by the client prior to and during actual practice sessions. For particularly refractory clients it may be necessary and desirable to additionally use drug-induced relaxation. Friedman (1966) provides a useful protocol for this procedure.

Intercourse

At this point in the program, it is occasionally found that the specific sexual dysfunctions which the couple identified as problems have been resolved. This is not surprising in that intercourse is a complex mutual behavior consisting of individual simpler behaviors, most of which have been adequately learned in earlier stages of the program. In particular, anxiety responses which are probably the basis of the various sexual dysfunction syndromes, have been extinguished, allowing the adequate sexual responses to be coordinated by the couple into a successful intercourse experience. However, this is not always the case, and it is even possible that new problems will be uncovered at this point. An example of this would be a couple who initially define their dysfunction as premature ejaculation in the male, and then discover that even when the male is able to maintain his erection for a reasonable length of time, his female partner is not achieving orgasm. Another example would be a couple who initially defined their problem as orgasmic dysfunction in the female partner, and then need to redefine the problem as premature ejaculation in the male when, after successfully attaining orgasmic response in the female through masturbation, the focus turns to the male partner's inability to delay his orgasm for a sufficient length of time. These examples further emphasize the diagnostic value of this uniform approach. It is possible that any of the specific syndromes, or some combination, of premature ejaculation, secondary erectile failure, ejaculatory incompetence, or secondary orgasmic dysfunction might be present at this point in the program. In contrast to Masters and Johnson (1970), Kass (1973) has found that a single standard sequence of instructions is effective, whichever of these syndromes remain.

The basis of this sequence of instructions is *in-vivo* desensitization as previously described, and here entails the successive and gradual approximation of adequate intercourse behaviors and responses. As with all earlier exercises, the primary goal during these intercourse exercises should be the maintenance of comfort simultaneous with gradual advancement through the successive approximations. At no time should any sexual achievement goal take precedence over this primary goal. As with the earlier stage, the couple should advance through stages 1 to 3 before proceeding with the intercourse instructions. The rate at which the couple progresses through these intercourse exercises will be largely an individual matter and, as earlier, advancement to the next higher level should occur after two successful 15-minute practice sessions at the preceding level. If difficulty is encountered at any of these levels, it may be necessary for the therapist to further break down the goal into smaller steps for *in-vivo* desensitization or to utilize adjunctive systematic desensitization to diminish particularly strong anxiety responses. After reaching the expected goals in these intercourse practice sessions, the couple should mutually masturbate to orgasm to conclude the sessions.

The focus throughout this instructional sequence will be on a time measure for adequate erectile response in the male partner. Initially, the couple is asked to predict the length of time the male will be able to maintain an adequate erection during full insertion without ejaculating, in a nonthrusting intercourse position of the couple's choice. If this estimate is less than 15 seconds, it is best to begin with partial insertion for a time interval that the male partner is able to comfortably maintain. This partial insertion may be a very shallow penetration, or it may even be necessary to begin with the erect penis several inches away or in direct contact with the labia. The depth of penetration can then be gradually increased in succeeding sessions. During any single session, only one level and time interval of encounter should be attempted, and this may be repeated several times during the session, with mutual masturbation or even earlier levels of encounter occupying the intervening time. At any point in these intercourse exercises that the male partner begins to approach ejaculatory inevitability, he should withdraw, and the couple should return to an earlier level of encounter until the male partner is again ready for insertion.

Once the male partner is able to maintain his erection during full insertion for

15 seconds, the time interval expectation is incrementally increased. These increments can usually be 15 seconds, and again there should be several repetitions of the insertion for the expected time interval during each practice session. Once the male is able to delay his ejaculation for 60 seconds at this minimal level of encounter, the couple is asked to introduce thrusting movements along with the insertion. Initially the expectation should be for 5 seconds of thrusting followed by 55 seconds of simple insertion. The amount of thrusting should be increased by 5-second increments, until the male is comfortably able to delay his ejaculation for 60 second intervals of active thrusting. The couple can then proceed on to longer intervals of thrusting by adding 15 second increments, and usually is satisfied with a goal of 5 to 10 minutes of ejaculatory control. At this point, the couple can experiment with additional positions of intercourse, either of their own choosing, or as suggested by the therapist. Adding new positions may require initial lowering of time interval goals, and also possibly thrusting goals. It may be necessary to have additional practice sessions to achieve success comparable to that already achieved with the female-superior position. Kass (1973) found with his series that for couples who had reached the intercourse stage, this standard set of instructions was highly effective in resolving any remaining specific dysfunctions. Orgasmically dysfunctional females who had in earlier stages learned to have orgasms were now able to regularly experience orgasms during this time period. Dysfunctional males, whether with premature ejaculation, absence of ejaculation, or erectile failure, were able to maintain high-quality erections for time periods sufficient to satisfy their partners, and to then also experience orgasms themselves.

This standard set of instructions for successively approximating adequate intercourse differs from the Masters and Johnson (1970) program, which essentially suggests a different set of instructions for each specific dysfunction. Several of their specific suggestions will be reviewed here as possible adjuncts to the program described above. One problem frequently encountered by the male during the above exercises is the approach of ejaculatory inevitability during insertion. Withdrawal is usually sufficient to diminish this response, but Masters and Johnson have found the "squeeze technique" a useful adjunct. The "squeeze technique" is simply a variation of the original Seman's technique (1956) in which the female partner is instructed to stimulate her partner's penis and stop prior to orgasm. She is to continue stimulation after the point of inevitability has passed, until orgasm is again approached. By alternately starting and stopping, it is possible to train her partner to extend his control over ejaculation. Masters and Johnson's variation involves the female partner's squeezing firmly the frenulum of her partner's penis as the point of inevitability approaches, rather than just stopping. A recent additional variation, the "bulbar squeeze," involves squeezing the base of the penis, and has the advantage that it can be used during actual intercourse without withdrawing the penis. In

addition, Masters and Johnson (1970, pp. 102-105) recommend a special training position for ejaculatory control which can be used during the mutual masturbation exercises to help the male develop ejaculatory control even before attempting intercourse. Masters and Johnson (1970, pp. 310-313) recommend subsequent utilization of a lateral coital position of intercourse which they feel further facilitates ejaculatory control. For ejaculatory incompetence, Masters and Johnson suggest a sequence substantially different than that suggested in our program. Their initial goal is to obtain intravaginal orgasm and this is achieved by stimulating the male almost to the point of inevitability and rapidly following with insertion. Once this is achieved, the level of excitement prior to insertion is gradually reduced until the duration of intravaginal containment prior to male orgasm has increased to a level satisfactory to the couple. This technique might be tried if the problem cannot be resolved by the standard sequence described above. Finally, for vaginismus, Masters and Johnson recommend actual demonstration of the vaginal spasm to both partners. Graduated Hegear dilators are then provided to the couple and introduced by the husband during exercises. Masters and Johnson report a 100% success rate using this technique.

FUTURE NEEDS IN THE TREATMENT OF SEXUAL DYSFUNCTION

Remarkable progress in the treatment of sexual dysfunction has been made over the past decade, and the future is promising. One problem that still has not been addressed is that of discovering a way of meeting the treatment needs of the perhaps millions of couples in this country who are troubled by sexual dysfunction. Although the problem of reaching this very large number of dysfunctional couples has not been resolved, the problem of efficacy of available treatment techniques has been diminished. The field is approaching a level of technique refinement at which controlled studies will need to be done, not only to compare desensitization techniques in general with other proposed treatment methods, but also to sort out the usefulness or lack of usefulness of the many treatment variables discussed in this paper. These include: treatment by dual-sex team vs. individual therapist; treatment of couple vs. focus on individual vs. group treatment; use of surrogates in treating both males and females without partners; *in-vivo* desensitization vs. systematic desensitization with deep-muscle relaxation vs. systematic desensitization with anxiolytic drugs; time and intensity of the course of treatment; adjunctive therapies, such as sex education and assertive training. In order for these studies to be carried out, treated populations will have to be more carefully defined with regard to such variables as age, socioeconomic status, status of relationship with sexual partner, and problem chronicity. The sexual dysfunctions themselves will have to be more carefully defined, hopefully in quantitative terms, particularly for research purposes. Better techniques for maintaining progress in treatment programs are needed, better outcome measures need to be developed, and longer follow-ups are also necessary. Finally, newer behavioral techniques will have to be applied to the treatment of sexual dysfunction as adjuncts to desensitization. A number of these have already been discussed, but further examples can be given. Lobitz and Lo Piccolo (1972) have introduced the use of a refundable penalty deposit contingent on following their treatment program, and the loss (response cost) of the deposit for failure to carry out assignments. Also, over the course of treatment, they gradually increase the extent of participation of their clients in the planning of assignments, so that at the point of termination, their clients are able to proceed on their own. Garfield *et al.* (1969) have successfully used thought-stopping and thought-substitution in treating an impotent male who was plagued by thoughts of failing to perform adequately during intercourse. It is interesting to speculate about the possibilities of using biofeedback in the treatment of sexual dysfunction. Other autonomic responses have been brought under voluntary control, so that sexual responses may also be able to be influenced in these ways. The treatment of sexual dysfunction is presently limited only by the creativity and imagination of the therapist.

REFERENCES

Annon, J. S. (1971), "The Therapeutic Use of Masturbation in the Treatment of Sexual Disorders." Paper presented at the Fifth Annual Meeting of the Association for the Advancement of Behavior Therapy, Washington, D. C.

Brady, J.P. (1966), "Brevital-Relaxation Treatment of Frigidity," *Behavior Research and Therapy,* 4:71-77.

Cooper, A. J. (1969a), "A Clinical Study of 'Coital Anxiety' in Male Potency Disorders," *Journal of Psychosomatic Research,* 13:143–147.

———(1969b), "Clinical and Therapeutic Studies in Premature Ejaculation," *Comprehensive Psychiatry,* 10:285–295.

———(1969c), "Disorders of Sexual Potency in the Male: A Clinical and Statistical Study of Some Factors Related to Short-Term Prognosis," *British Journal of Psychiatry,* 115:709–719.

———(1969d), "Outpatient Treatment of Impotence," *Journal of Nervous and Mental Disease,* 149:360–371.

———(1971), "Treatments of Male Potency Disorders: The Present Status," *Psychosomatics,* 12:235–244.

Davison, G. S. (1968), "Elimination of a Sadistic Fantasy by a Client-Controlled Counter-Conditioning Technique," *Journal of Abnormal Psychology,* 77:84–90.

Dengrove, E. (1971), "The Mechano-therapy of Sexual Disorders," *Journal of Sex Research,* 7:1–12.

Evans, I. M. (1973), "The Logical Requirements for Explanations of Systematic Desensitization," *Behavior Therapy,* 4:506–514.

Friedman, D. (1966), "A New Technique for the Systematic Desensitization of Phobic Symptoms," *Behavior Research and Therapy,* 4:139–140.

———(1968), "The Treatment of Impotence by Brevital Relaxation Therapy," *Behavior Research and Therapy,* 6:257–261.

Garfield, Z.H., J.F. McBrearty, and M. Dichter (1969), "A Case of Impotence Successfully Treated with Desensitization Combined with *in-Vivo* Operant Training and Thought Substitution." In R. Rubin and C.M. Franks (eds.), *Advances in Behavior Therapy.* New York, Academic Press.

Gurman, A. S. (1973), "The Effects and Effectiveness of Marital Therapy: A Review of Outcome Research," *Family Process,* 12:145–170.

"J" (1971), *The Way to Become the Sensuous Woman.* New York, Dell Publishing Co.

Johnson, J. (1965), "Prognosis of Disorders of Sexual Potency in the Male," *Journal of Psychosomatic Research,* 9:195–200.

Jones, W. J., and P. M. Parks (1972), "Treatment of Single-Partner Sexual Dysfunction by Systematic Desensitization," *Obstetrics and Gynecology,* 39:411–417.

Kass, D. J. (1973), "In-Vivo Treatment of Sexual Dysfunction." Unpublished data: Brown University.

Kegel, A. H. (1952), "Sexual Functions of the Pubococcygeus Muscle," *Western Journal of Surgery, Obstetrics and Gynecology,* 60:521–524.

Lazarus, A. A. (1961), "Group Therapy of Phobic Disorders by Systematic Desensitization," *Journal of Abnormal and Social Psychology,* 63:404–410.

———(1963), "The Treatment of Chronic Frigidity by Systematic Desensitization," *Journal of Nervous and Mental Disease,* 136:272–278.

Lobitz, W. C., and J. Lo Piccolo (1972), "New Methods in the Behavioral Treatment of Sexual Dysfunction," *Journal of Behavior Therapy and Experimental Psychiatry,* 3:265–271.

Lo Piccolo, J., R. Stewart, and B. Watkins (1972), "Treatment of Erectile Failure and Ejaculatory Incompetence of Homosexual Etiology," *Journal of Behavior Therapy and Experimental Psychiatry,* 3:233–236.

"M" (1972), *The Way to Become the Sensuous Man.* New York, Dell Publishing Co.

Marquis, J. N. (1970), "Orgasmic Reconditioning: Changing Sexual Object Choice Through Controlling Masturbation Fantasies," *Journal of Behavior Therapy and Experimental Psychiatry,* 1:263–271.

Masters, W. H., and V. E. Johnson (1970), *Human Sexual Inadequacy,* Boston: Little, Brown & Co.

McGovern, K. B., and R. C. Stewart (1972), "The Secondary Orgasmic Dysfunctional Female: A Critical Analysis and Strategies for Treatment." Paper presented at the Annual Meeting of the Western Psychological Association, Portland, Ore.

McCullough, J. P., and L. E. Montgomery (1972), "A Technique for Measuring Subjective Arousal in Therapy Clients," *Behavior Therapy,* 3:627–628.

Obler, M. (1973), "Systematic Desensitization in Sexual Disorders," *Journal of Behavior Therapy and Experimental Psychiatry,* 4:93–101.

Semans, J. H. (1956), "Premature Ejaculation: A New Approach," *Southern Medical Journal,* 49:353–358.

Steger, J. (1972), "The Assessment of Sexual Function and Dysfunction." Paper presented at the Annual Meeting of the Western Psychological Association, Portland, Ore.

Whelan, S., and R. Cochran (1973), *The Art of Erotic Massage.* New York: Signet.

Wolpe, J. (1958), *Psychotherapy by Reciprocal Inhibition.* Palo Alto, Calif.: Stanford University Press.

————(1969), *The Practice of Behavior Therapy.* New York, Pergamon, pp. 72-90.

W. CHARLES LOBITZ
JOSEPH LO PICCOLO

15   New Methods in the Behavioral Treatment of Sexual Dysfunction*

For 3 years we have been treating couples for a variety of sexual dysfunctions ranging from primary orgasmic dysfunction (frigidity) in females to premature ejaculation and erectile failure in males. An "orthodox" behavioral treatment program emphasizing *in vivo* desensitization has been supplemented by several clinical methods either adapted from other psychotherapies or newly introduced. A systematic masturbation program, in combination with erotic fantasy and literature, enhances sexual responding. Role-playing orgasmic response disinhibits female orgasm. Therapist self-disclosure reduces client inhibition and anxiety and models an open acceptance of sexuality. Daily client records provide data on ongoing client sexual behavior. A refundable penalty fee deposit heightens client motivation. Clients plan their own treatment for the final stages and the months following therapy. Clinical examples and outcome statistics are given.

Since 1969 the Sex Research Program at the University of Oregon Psychology Clinic has been treating couples for a variety of sexual dysfunctions. This program, directed by Joseph LoPiccolo, is part of a doctoral training program in clinical psychology and has involved the treatment of approximately 25 couples per year by a total of 16 different male–female co-therapy teams over the last 3 years. The program has had good success in treating sexual dysfunction by a behavioral approach. Within this approach we have developed or adapted from

*Preparation of this manuscript was supported in part by a grant from the University of Oregon Office of Scientific and Scholarly Research. Portions of this paper were presented at the Fourth Annual International Conference on Behavior Modification, Banff, Alberta, Canada, March, 1972, and at the annual meetings of the Western Psychological Association, Portland, Oregon, April, 1972.

others a number of new techniques for the treatment of sexual dysfunction. This paper describes some of these techniques and presents clinical examples and outcome statistics to document their effectiveness.

BACKGROUND

The general behavioral model used is based on the procedures developed by Wolpe (1969), Hastings (1963), and Masters and Johnson (1970). In the absence of any physical pathology, sexual dysfunction is viewed as a learned phenomenon, maintained internally by performance anxiety and externally by a nonreinforcing environment, principally the partner. In addition, a lack of sexual skill, knowledge, and communication on the part of one or both partners contributes to the dysfunction.

Within this social learning model, the dysfunction is treated through training changes in the couple's sexual behavior. Both partners are involved in the therapy process. Treatment consists of 15 sessions in which a male–female co-therapy team plans tasks (''homework'') to be carried out by the dysfunctioning couple between sessions. Performance anxiety in either the totally inorgasmic female or in the male with erectile failure is treated through *in vivo* graded exposure tasks following the systematic desensitization format developed by Wolpe (1969) and refined by Masters and Johnson (1970). Premature ejaculation is treated through a retraining program advocated by Semans (1956), as modified by the use of the ''squeeze'' technique (Masters and Johnson, 1970). In the case of all dysfunctions, intercourse is temporarily prohibited while the couple's repertoire of sexual behavior is rebuilt.

On the above framework, the Sex Research Program has developed several clinical innovations designed to facilitate changes in sexual behavior. These innovations fall into one of five classes: (1) Procedures designed to allow the therapists to obtain regular data on the clients' sexual behavior and to ensure that the clients carry out the ''homework'' assignments. (2) Procedures which enhance the client's desire and arousal towards his or her partner. (3) Procedures which teach interpersonal sexual skills. (4) Procedures which disinhibit clients towards displaying their own sexual arousal and responsiveness. (5) Procedures designed to maintain treatment gains after therapy has ended.

Data on Clients' Sexual Behavior

A hallmark of behavioral approaches to treatment has been the reliance or observable, quantifiable client behavior. Most problems which lend themselves to a behavioral approach (e.g. phobic or aggressive responses) are readily observable. Home observations of client behavior have become commonplace in behavioral assessment and intervention (e.g. Lewinsohn and Shaffer, 1971; Patterson, Ray and Shaw, 1968). However, for both ethical and practical reasons neither home nor laboratory observations of client behavior is possible when treating sexual dysfunction. Yet, for our program, therapists must know exactly what the clients are doing and whether they are following the treatment procedures at home. Our clients are asked to be their own data collectors. On each day on which any sexual activity occurs, clients fill out a *daily record form* detailing their sexual behavior. For each activity, the client specifies its duration, numerical ratings of the pleasure and arousal that he obtained, and subjective comments about the activity. In addition, he specifies numerical ratings of the degree of pleasure and arousal which he perceived his partner to have obtained. Throughout treatment these daily records provide therapists with feedback. Using this data they tailor the program to the client's progress.

Client Motivation

While clients are generally motivated to carry out the program, including filling out daily record forms, at times they may find it difficult to follow the prescriptions. For example, they may be tired or busy with other activities and thus avoid engaging in the prescribed number of "homework" sessions. They may be tempted to break the prohibition on intercourse or to resist trying new sexual activities that the therapists prescribe. A *refundable penalty deposit* provides an incentive for following the program. At the beginning of treatment, the clients pay their full 15 session fee plus an equal amount as a penalty deposit. If the client does not violate any of the treatment rules, his deposit is refunded in full at the end of treatment. However, should a violation occur, 1/15th of the deposit is not refunded. On a second violation, another 2/15ths is forfeited, i.e. 3/15ths altogether. The progression continues arithmetically, so that for the fifth violation 5/15ths of the deposit is forfeited, using up the entire deposit. A sixth violation would cause the therapists to terminate treatment. Treatment rules are specified in a "penalty contract" which the clients sign at the beginning of therapy. Basically, the rules are that the clients must keep appointments, turn in the daily record forms prior to their appointment, and engage in only those sexual behaviors programmed for them by the therapists.

Although this procedure has not been systematically evaluated, the fact that more than one violation rarely occurs attests to its effectiveness in motivating the clients to follow the program rules. Over the last 19 cases treated, couples were fined an average of 0.7 times. No couple has been penalized more than three times. For some clients, the penalty deposit is a more effective motivator than for others. Younger couples, especially those in the counterculture for whom money is not a powerful reinforcer, are less apt to be influenced by the threat of losing their deposit. However, for older, middle class couples, the penalty deposit provides a powerful motivation. For example, a successful certified public accountant resisted completing his assigned "homework" sessions with his wife, complaining that he had too much office work to do. Instead of cajoling her husband, the wife quietly reminded him of the penalty fee. A quick mental calculation convinced him that it was financially worthwhile to forego his office work in favor of the session with his wife.

Enhancing Clients' Arousal

A frequent aspect of sexual dysfunction is the inability of one or both clients to become sexually aroused by the partner. In cases of sexual deviations, other therapists (Davison, 1968; Marquis, 1970) have used a *classical conditioning* procedure during masturbation to condition arousal to appropriate sexual objects. We have adapted this to raise arousal levels in dysfunctional couples. The conditioning is accomplished either through masturbation or in sexual activity with the partner.

In masturbation, the client is instructed to focus on any erotic stimuli that are currently arousing. These stimuli may consist of literature, pictures, and/or fantasy. Within our program, stimulus materials have ranged from heterosexual erotic materials to homosexual fantasies. Once aroused, the client masturbates to orgasm. Just prior to orgasm, he switches his focus to fantasies of sexual activity with his partner. The unconditioned stimuli of previously arousing fantasies and materials and the unconditioned responses of sexual arousal and orgasm are, thus, paired with the presently neutral stimulus of sexual activity with the partner. On subsequent occasions, the client is instructed to switch to fantasies of the partner at earlier points in time, until fantasies of the partner become a conditioned stimulus for sexual arousal and the artificial stimuli previously used are no longer necessary. For clients who have difficulty in fantasizing their partner we have supplied a Polaroid camera and instructed them to photograph their partner in sexual activity. They use these photographs in lieu of fantasy.

This same conditioning procedure is used in sexual activity with the partner as well as in masturbation. The client first fantasizes erotic scenes to become aroused and then switches his focus to the present reality of sexual activity with his partner. A case study detailing this procedure has been reported elsewhere (LoPiccolo, Stewart and Watkins, 1972).

In the case of women who have never experienced orgasm from any source of physical stimulation, fantasy and erotic materials alone do not enhance the arousal level enough to produce orgasm. In such cases, *a nine-step masturbation program* has proven highly successful in producing the clients' first orgasm. The use of masturbation in treating frigidity has been reported previously (Ellis, 1960; Hastings, 1963). We have incorporated it as a systematic part of our treatment for primary orgasmic dysfunction. This program is based on evidence that more women can reach orgasm through masturbation than through any other means (Kinsey *et al.*, 1953), and that masturbation produces the most intense orgasms (Masters and Johnson, 1966). The nine steps follow a graduated approach model (Wolpe, 1969) to desensitize the client to masturbation. The details of the program have been described elsewhere (Lo Piccolo and Lobitz, 1972, but can be summarized as follows:

Step 1: The client is given the assignment to increase her self-awareness by examining her nude body and appreciating its beauty. She uses a hand mirror to examine her genitals and identify the various areas with the aid of diagrams in Hastings' book *Sexual Expression in Marriage* (1966). In addition she is started on a program of Kegel's (1952) exercises for increasing tone and vascularity of the pelvic musculature.

Step 2: The client is instructed to explore her genitals tactually as well as visually. To avoid performance anxiety, she is not given any expectation to become aroused at this point.

Step 3: Tactual and visual exploration are focused on locating sensitive areas that produce feelings of pleasure when stimulated.

Step 4: The client is told to concentrate on manual stimulation of identified pleasurable areas. At this point the female therapist discusses techniques of masturbation, including the use of a lubricant.

Step 5: If orgasm does not occur during Step 4, the client is told to increase the intensity and duration of masturbation. She is told to masturbate until "something happens" or until she becomes tired or sore.

Step 6: If orgasm is not reached during Step 5, we instruct the client to purchase a vibrator of the type sold in pharmacies for facial or body massage. In our most difficult case to date, three weeks of daily 45-minute vibrator sessions were required to produce orgasm.

Step 7: Once the client has achieved orgasm through masturbation, we introduce the husband to the procedure by having him observe her. This desensitizes her to displaying arousal and orgasm in his presence and also functions as an excellent learning experience for him.

Step 8: The husband manipulates his wife in the manner she has demonstrated in Step 7.

Step 9: Once orgasm has occurred in Step 8, we instruct the couple to engage in intercourse while the husband stimulates his wife's genitals, either manually or with a vibrator.

We currently also use heterosexual erotic pictures or literature to supplement the nine-step masturbation program. The efficacy of this combination was demonstrated fortuitously when three different women in the masturbation program saw a sexually explicit film at a local x-rated cinema. They each reported masturbating to their first orgasm shortly after having viewed the film.

Teaching Interpersonal Sexual Skills

Most couples who seek treatment for sexual dysfunction have behavioral skill deficits. They may feel deep affection for each other, but have difficulty expressing their emotions, initiating and refusing sexual contact, and assertively communicating their likes and dislikes. We view these deficits not as emotional inhibitions, but primarily as lack of social skill. These deficits are overcome in therapy sessions through therapist *modeling* and client *role playing*. These techniques have achieved considerable efficacy in the treatment of social avoidance and other phobias (e.g., Bandura, 1971). We have directly adapted them to cases of sexual dysfunction.

In the Sex Research Program these techniques are used to demonstrate appropriate intiation, refusal, and emotional assertion responses, and to allow the couple to practice these in a protected environment. They are then instructed to practice these skills at home as part of their intersession "homework" assignment. For example, a female client might complain that her husband initiates sexual activity in a crude, alienating manner, that he never displays his love for her, and that he does not engage in sexual behaviors that she finds arousing. In this case a mutual failure is involved—the wife has not taught her husband what she desires. The therapy team models verbal initiation of sexual activity and verbal expression of tender emotions and has the clients practice these behaviors in the therapy session, while giving each other feedback about their performances.

Disinhibition of Sexuality

Role playing is useful not only in skill training, but also as a disinhibitor of sexual responses. Hilliard (1960) has instructed inorgasmic women to feign orgasm to satisfy their partners. She reported that in many cases this pretense became a reality. Therapists in our own program have instructed inorgasmic women to role play an orgasm, not to deceive their partner, but to disinhibit themselves about losing control and showing intense sexual arousal. Since the male partner is present when these instructions are given, deceit is avoided. This particular use of role playing is analogous to Kelly's (1955) fixed-role therapy in which the client is asked to enact the role of someone different from himself. In sex therapy the role is a different sexual response rather than an entire personality change.

Orgasmic roleplaying is useful at two points in therapy: first, for the woman who is highly aroused by masturbation but becomes apprehensive at the approaching orgasm and thus loses sexual arousal as stimulation continues; second, for the woman who masturbates to orgasm when alone but cannot achieve it if her partner is present. In either case we instruct the couple to engage in the following procedure. During sexual activity at home the woman is to role-play not just an orgasm, but a gross exaggeration of orgasm with violent convulsions and inarticulate screaming. Knowing that this orgasm is not real, the couple is free to make a game, even a parody of the response. We instruct them to repeat this until they pass from their initial anxiety and embarrassment to amusement and finally boredom with the procedure.

Orgasmic roleplaying has been especially useful with intellectual, controlled clients who are ashamed and embarrassed about the muscular contractions and involuntary noises which accompany orgasm. In three cases where the women had been unable to reach orgasm despite the use of all our other treatment procedures, this technique led to their first orgasm.

Our most common stratagem for disinhibiting clients to sexual responses is *therapist self-disclosure*. In advocating self-disclosure, Jourard (1964) has emphasized therapist spontaneity during the session but has stated that one need not tell the client about one's life outside the therapy hour (p. 71). In the Sex Research Program therapists do not only answer clients' questions, but also volunteer information about their own sexual behavior. Because the therapist has a respected position of authority in our culture, the therapists unashamedly discussing their own enjoyment of sexual activity is an acceptable and seemingly effective way of disinhibiting clients about their own sexuality. In particular, self-disclosure about masturbation and oral-genital sex facilitates change in the client's attitude towards these behaviors. However self-disclosure should be withheld until the client has gotten to know the therapist. Premature self-disclosure may alienate some clients.

Another use of therapist self-disclosure has been in reducing clients' anxiety about their "abnormality" or "inadequacy" in having a sexual dysfunction. For example, one premature ejaculator, who had made considerable progress in therapy, was concerned that he would always have to rely on the squeeze technique as part of his lovemaking. The male therapist reassured him by saying that he also used the squeeze on occasion. The female therapist, who, in this instance was the male therapist's wife, reinforced the point by stating that she encouraged the squeeze as part of their sexual repertoire because it prolonged their lovemaking.

Maintaining Treatment Gains

Regardless of a treatment program's initial success, the proof of its efficacy is the degree to which clients can maintain their gains once therapy has ended.

Our follow-up assessments 6 months after termination indicate that treatment gains have generally persisted.

This maintenance is due, in part, to *client participation in planning treatment* in the final therapy sessions. After 12 or 13 sessions of therapy, the clients have a good idea of the strategy behind their treatment. With the therapists' guidance, they now plan their own ''homework'' assignments for the next sessions. This prepares them to handle any problems which may arise after therapy has terminated. At the end of therapy the clients write out a maintenance program of specific behaviors for the months following. At this time, they also make a list of the behaviors that contributed to their problem before treatment, how these have changed, and what they plan to do should the problems recur. The clients keep these lists.

Results

Over the past 3 years the Sex Research Program has experienced generally good results in the treatment of sexual dysfunction. Applying Masters and Johnson's (1970) criterion that the female partner be satisfied ''in at least 50 per cent of their coital connections (p. 92),'' our success rate is as follows: 13 out of 13 treated cases of female primary orgasmic dysfunction, six out of six premature ejaculation cases, four out of six erectile failure cases, and three out of nine cases of secondary orgasmic dysfunction. However, with regard to the secondary orgasmic dysfunction cases, it should be noted that our three most recently treated cases are our three successes. These followed a major revision of our program for secondary orgasmic dysfunction, based on data from the first six cases. The data and the revisions are reported elsewhere (McGovern and Stewart, 1972).

To supplement Masters and Johnson's (1970) criterion for success, we have developed a measurement instrument, the Oregon Sex Inventory (LoPiccolo, 1972; Steger, 1972), for assessing pre-post treatment changes in a couple's sexual functioning. Our success rate as reflected by the scales of this inventory equals or exceeds the rate on Masters and Johnson's (1970) criterion.

We think our success is due, in part, to the clinical innovations with which we supplement a ''traditional'' behavioral treatment program. Daily client records provide data on ongoing sexual behavior. A refundable penalty fee deposit heightens motivation. Fantasy and pornography, in combination with a nine-step masturbation program, enhance sexual responsiveness. Role-playing serves to impart social-sexual skills and to disinhibit female orgasm. Therapist self-disclosure reduces client inhibition and anxiety, and models an open acceptance of sexuality. To ensure the maintenance of therapy gains, clients plan their own treatment for the final stages and for the months following therapy.

Despite our generally good success rate, the separate effectiveness of each procedure needs to be investigated. In all of the cases treated, a combination of procedures has been used, thus precluding an evaluation of any particular technique's contribution. We are currently engaged in research to evaluate the components of our program.

REFERENCES

Bandura, A. (1971), "Vicarious and Self-reinforcement Processes." In R. Glaser (ed.), *The Nature of Reinforcement,* New York, Academic Press.

Davison, G. S. (1968), "Elimination of a Sadistic Fantasy by a Client-controlled Counter-Conditioning Technique," *Journal of Abnormal Psychology,* 77:84-90.

Ellis, A. (1960), *The Art and Science of Love.* New York: Lyle Stuart.

Hastings, D.W. (1963), *Impotence and Frigidity.* Boston: Little, Brown & Co.

———(1966), *Sexual Expression in Marriage.* New York: Bantam.

Hilliard, M. (1960), *A Woman Doctor Looks at Love and Life,* New York: Permabook.

Jourard, S. M. (1964), *The Transparent Self.* Princeton, N.J.: D. Van Nostrand.

Kelly, G. A. (1955), *The Psychology of Personal Constructs.* New York: W.W. Norton.

Kegel, A. H. (1952), "Sexual Functions of the Pubococcygeus Muscle," West. J. *Sang. Obstet. Gynol. 60:521.*

Kinsey, A. C., W. B. Pomeroy, C. E. Martin, and P. H. Gebhard (1953), *Sexual Behavior in the Human Female.* Philadelphia: W. B. Saunders.

Lewinsohn, P. M., and M. Shaffer (1971), "Use of Home Observations as an Integral Part of the Treatment of Depression: Preliminary Report and Case Studies," *Journal of Consulting and Clinical Psychology,* 37:87-94.

LoPiccolo, J. (1972), "Scoring and Interpretation Manual for the Oregon Sex Inventory." University of Oregon: Unpublished manuscript.

———and W. C. Lobitz (1972), "The Role of Masturbation in the Treatment of Sexual Dysfunction," *Archives of Sexual Behavior,* (in press).

——— , R. Stewart, and B. Watkins (1972), "Case Study: Treatment of Erectile Failure and Ejaculatory Incompetence with Homosexual Etiology," *Journal of Behavior Therapy and Experimental Psychiatry,* 3:233-236.

Marquis, J. N. (1970), "Orgasmic Reconditioning: Changing Sexual Object Choice Through Controlling Masturbation Fantasies," *Journal of Behavior Therapy and Experimental Psychiatry,* 1:263-271.

Masters, W. H., and V. E. Johnson (1966), *Human Sexual Response.* Boston: Little, Brown & Co.

———(1970), *Human Sexual Inadequacy.* Boston: Little, Brown & Co.

McGovern, K. B., and R. C. Stewart (1972), "The Secondary Orgasmic Dysfunctional Female: A Critical Analysis and Strategies for Treatment," Paper presented at the Annual Meeting of the Western Psychological Association, Portland, Ore.

Patterson, G. R., R. S. Ray, and D. A. Shaw (1968), "Direct Intervention in the Families of Deviant Children," *Oregon Research Institute Research Bulletin* 8: No. 9.

Semans, J. (1956), "Premature Ejaculation: A New Approach," *Southern Medical Journal*, 46:353-357.

Steger, J. (1972), "The Assessment of Sexual Function and Dysfunction," Paper presented at the Annual Meeting of the Western Psychological Association, Portland, Ore.

Wolpe, J. (1969), *The Practice of Behavior Therapy,* New York: Pergamon Press.

Section E

Facilitating Communication Skill

RICHARD A. WELLS
JEANNE A. FIGUREL
PATRICK McNAMEE

16   Group Facilitative Training with Conflicted Marital Couples*

A structured short-term approach to the direct teaching, in a group context, of facilitative marital communication skills is described. The systematic method, derived from the interpersonal formulations of client-centered therapy and the principles of social learning theory, focuses on the training, experiencing, and communication of accurate empathy, warmth, and genuineness. The model of facilitative training specifies the stages of therapist, group, and couples interaction that must occur for emphatic communication to take place, and prescribes a number of exercises and tasks which can be used toward this end. A research project is described which emphasizes an empirical assessment of the gains achieved through this approach. Results indicate that positive changes in marital adjustment follow from such training and suggest that the approach constitutes an effective and efficient method of treating some types of marital problems.

A major conceptual and practical difficulty in marital therapy and research is the problem of making specific the relationship of particular therapist activities to the behaviors that are identified as goals for the client. The behaviors desired by the client are typically not defined operationally, and there is often no direct connection between these desired behaviors and the skills needed or used by the therapist. As a consequence much therapist activity tends to be nonspecific, at worst random, and, at best, rarely seen by both client and therapist as relevant to their stated goals.

Recent research on systematic facilitative training (and related approaches such as filial and conjugal therapy) seems to offer some solutions to the

*The research project described in this paper is being supported by Catholic Social Service of Allegheny County, Pennsylvania. We are grateful for the interest and cooperation of the Executive Director, Mr. Albert Phaneuf, and the staff of the agency.

problems noted above (Carkhuff, 1969; Ely, 1970; Guerney, *et al.*, 1971). The methodologies of these training approaches are clearly and operationally defined and their goals specific and concrete. The techniques and skills used by the therapist are clearly identified and related to the selected goals. Therapist and client time involved is short-term, client satisfaction tends to be high, and results seem to be both significant and long lasting (Carkhuff, 1971).

The present authors are engaged in a research project comparing the effects of systematic facilitative training for groups of conflicted marital couples with the effects of short-term conjoint marital counseling of such couples. This chapter is a position statement and description of the systematic training methods used in the couples groups. Later reports will detail the experimental design and the results of the total study.

Theoretical Position

The present study relies heavily on the conceptual framework of Carkhuff (1969), and on several applications of these theoretical foundations to systematic training (Carkhuff, 1971; Ely, 1970; Pierce and Drasgow, 1969). Systematic facilitative training, as a model for communication and behavior change, has evolved from several sources. The interpersonal formulation of client-centered counseling (Rogers, 1957), the findings of psychotherapy research (Bergin and Garfield, 1971; Rogers, *et al.*, 1967) and behavior modification (Bandura, 1969; Wolpe and Lazarus, 1966) have contributed theories, methods, and techniques to such training.

The elements of facilitative communication that have been clearly identified to date are accurate empathy, warmth, and genuineness. Substantial evidence indicates that the level of these qualities determines the quality of significant encounters (Carkhuff, 1969; Truax and Carkhuff, 1967; Truax and Mitchell, 1971). These findings are particularly salient in psychotherapy, where there appears to be a close relationship between the therapist's level of facilitation and both client level of self-exploration and behavioral and personality changes (Truax and Mitchell, 1971). Other studies indicate that high levels of these qualities reliably distinguish adjusted from maladjusted marriages (Navran, 1967; Quick and Jacob, 1973).

Futher studies support the position that these facilitative qualities can be developed and enhanced—whether in trainee or client populations—through specific procedures (Carkhuff, 1969; Truax and Carkhuff, 1967). The communication of conceptual content has been taught as a skill in Western culture for 2500 years in logic and rhetoric curriculums. The communication of affective content, as an interpersonal skill, is equally amenable to a systematic training approach.

The model presented here predicted that highly facilitative therapists would be able to teach affective communication skills to conflicted married couples.

It was also predicted that through clear and empathic communication the couples would enhance the quality of their relationship as well as solve particular problems they may be encountering.

The model specifies certain stages of therapist, group, and couples interaction that must occur if these changes are to take place, and prescribes a number of therapist, group, and couple tasks, which can be used as needed by the members. These stages and tasks will be described below. As a method of marital therapy it may be characterized, in Olson's terminology, as *quasi-interactional,* with goals of "systematically changing and improving the interaction style of the dyad" (Olson, 1970).

Model of Facilitiative Training

The model of systematic facilitative training was developed by Truax and Carkhuff (1967). It is a combined didactic-experiential process involving three distinct, but overlapping phases:

(1) *The didactic phase* serves as an introduction to the facilitative qualities and offers a rationale for the importance of such qualities in a marital relationship. The didactic base is added to during the training as the individuals gain more knowledge of and comfort with the skills through experience both in and out of the group.

(2) *The modeling or "shaping" phase* is that part in which the individuals are taught through a variety of step-by-step procedures how to respond in a facilitative manner to other group members and, later, their own spouses.

(3) *The group experience* itself is the third phase. Conducting the training in a group provides immense support to each individual as he attempts to develop more self-awareness and provides many natural opportunities for each individual to use these responsive skills in helping others who are struggling with similar feelings. It also permits a person to see his spouse as a person that others in the group respect and find helpful.

The groups were structured to run for a total of eight weekly two-hour sessions. The couples were aware of this time limit at the beginning of the series. In addition, each couple was allowed an option of up to three conjoint interviews (either concurrent with or subsequent to the group sessions) to handle any unique problems they were meeting in applying to their marriage skills learned in the group. Couples were informed of the expectation that, if one person was unable to attend a session, the other spouse would attend.

Description of Groups

Prior to beginning the research project, a pilot group was formed with three couples. One couple dropped out immediately before actually beginning in the group. One wife dropped out after four weeks when she separated from her husband. Thus, this pilot group consisted of one couple and one husband at the conclusion.

The project couples were randomly assigned to groups from the regular intake of the agency. The only screening criteria were that the couple be requesting marital counseling, be between eighteen and fifty years of age and be available the evening the group was meeting.

Four couples were assigned, following an initial interview, to each of two groups. One couple dropped out of each group shortly after the first meeting, while the remaining couples attended regularly. All continuing couples have been white, middle-class, at least nominally Catholic, with high school education or better.

The two groups completed at this time thus included a total of six couples. They presented a range of moderate to severe problems in marital functioning —chronic or acute communication difficulties, conflict around role and relationship expectations, infidelity, actual and threatened separation—with a mean marital adjustment score almost identical with mean scores reported elsewhere for maladjusted marital pairs (Locke and Wallace, 1959).

It was decided that the groups would be led by male and female co-therapists (R. W. and J. F.). Both therapists had previous individual experience in leading training groups for students, caseworkers, and volunteers. Since the leader in a systematic facilitative training group provides a necessary model for the group members in facilitative qualities, co-therapists would allow for broader modeling. That is, in addition to being individual models of empathic communication, they could also model such communication in an on-going relationship (Napier and Whitaker, 1972). This appeared to be an important decision because, despite the impact of women's liberation in North America, our participants, both male and female, openly expressed their belief that communication is a problem in marriage since women communicate differently than men.

Techniques of Training

The didactic phase began in the first group session after the co-therapists and group members had introduced themselves. One of the co-therapists presented material for approximately twenty minutes on attending behavior, responding behavior, and levels of empathy. A three-point scale of empathic response was defined: (1) ignoring; (2) minimizing or subtracting; and (3) interchangeable. The presentation was deliberately kept short to maintain interest and to avoid further increasing the level of anxiety of both the group members and the co-therapists. The material was largely drawn from Carkhuff's *The Art of Helping* (1972) and, in subsequent weeks, the members were given reading assignments from this monograph.

The modeling or "shaping" phase began with a listening exercise using a "round robin" format, that is to say, proceeding around the group from one individual to the next. Beginning with one of the co-therapists,[1] each person in turn told the person next to him "how he feels right now about being here" while the rest of the group listened. The person to whom he was speaking then summarized what he had heard. This exercise served two purposes. First, it began to bring into focus the material presented on attending behavior. Thus, after each summary, a short discussion would concentrate on whether the summary was accurate; that is, what others in the group heard and what nonverbal behavior indicated to the speaker that the summarizer was listening. Second, by instructing the group to talk about "how they feel right now," the group began to share such common feelings as anxiety and apprehension. This exercise provided a noticeable relief in the tension which existed at the beginning of the session. It should be noted that we structured the seating so that no individual sat beside his spouse in these early sessions.

The next exercise was designed to focus the group on feelings and the vocabulary used to describe them. Each person, proceeding around the circle again, was asked to say and complete the sentence "You feel . . ." Examples such as "You feel happy," "You feel angry," etc., were given. While everyone was expected to participate, anyone could say "Pass" at a point where he was stuck. The exercise continued around the circle with one co-therapist listing the words on a blackboard until everyone passed. Discussion following this exercise stressed the naturalness of this vocabulary and looked at the words of different intensity which describe similar feelings.

The third exercise included both the listening skills of the first exercise and the vocabulary development of the second exercise. Using the "round robin" format, one person spoke to the person next to him who then summarized what he heard. The rest of the group members and the co-therapists, however, were instructed to write down single words to describe the feelings of the speaker *as he spoke*. The discussion then focused on the summary (which was often only content-oriented) and the feelings related to this content. While the use of the "round robin" format clearly indicated our expectation that everyone would participate in the dialogues, the use of the writing involved all the other members at the same time and provided a concrete source of reference for each group member. In the discussion, each person was encouraged to direct his feeling words to the person who was the speaker and to check out whether this was what the speaker was really feeling.

The exercises can be viewed as the discrimination phase in which the group members become more familiar with the vocabulary of words used to describe different types and intensity of feeling and increased their ability to perceive affective content. In general, these exercises were completed by the second

[1] We would emphasize that the co-therapists continued to participate in the exercise throughout the training. They thus modeled both speaker and listener roles and heightened the norm of participation.

session, though work on discrimination continued throughout the eight sessions.

The next exercise began the communication phase. The speaker and listener were instructed to carry on a dialogue for about three minutes. The speaker (helpee) was to talk about anything about which he had some feeling, e.g., job, parents, children. The listener (helper) was to respond naturally, as he would in any conversation, but to focus his responses on the feelings rather than the content of the conversation. The rest of the group members were to write down the feelings as they heard them from the speaker. At the conclusion of the dialogue, the co-therapists encouraged the speaker and the listener to talk about how each felt during the dialogue, helping them to recall specific responses which were particularly helpful to the speaker or which the listener would like to rephrase. These dialogues were taped so that the group could go back to discuss individual responses. The members were encouraged to rate the responses according to the previously mentioned scale and to suggest responses they believed would be more helpful. They were instructed to direct these alternative responses to the speaker who could genuinely reflect whether that response would have been more helpful. This exercise was repeated over several sessions, permitting each individual as many opportunities as possible to be both a speaker and a listener.

After each individual had had some experience in each role, the format of the above exercise was continued with one modification—an individual began engaging in dialogues with his own spouse. Though at the end of each of the earlier group sessions couples had been instructed to attempt to practice the skills at home, this was the first point within the sessions at which they actually practiced and received assistance in communicating directly with their own spouses. While the speaker could select any topic to discuss, the co-therapists pointed out that accurate empathic communication in a close, meaningful relationship can be very difficult and encouraged them to select areas of lesser intensity to begin practicing these skills. The remaining sessions, approximately the sixth through the eighth, continued to use spouse-to-spouse dialogues which gave each couple the opportunity to practice (and receive feedback on) their facilitative skills.

Discussion of the Training Groups

The phases of facilitative training were outlined in the previous section; beyond this educational, skill-training focus we tended to keep our model of group process relatively simple. Three general guidelines were most influential in our approach to group leadership:

Facilitation. The primary task of the group leader is to offer a high and consistent level of facilitative response within the group. We have already cited evidence for the importance of these qualities to constructive human growth.

Norm-setting. The ways of behaving which will become characteristic of a particular group are most powerfully influenced by the behavior of the leaders. Thus, if the leaders hope that members will be empathic and self-disclosing with one another, then the leaders must demonstrate these behaviors themselves. In a time-limited group the leaders must set such standards as rapidly and clearly as possible.

Cohesion. Yalom reviews the data indicating that cohesive groups tend to achieve better outcomes (Yalom, 1970). Cohesion is a broad concept that, in part at least, refers to the members' sense of comfort and belonging in the group. These aspects of cohesion can be seen as related to the level of facilitation between leaders and members and among members.

Thus, these three guidelines for group leadership become interrelated: if the leaders offer high levels of facilitative response this will encourage similar responses among members, developing and increasing group cohesion.

Several factors were apparent in the process of group training and will be discussed more fully. These include: (1) the short-term nature of the groups, forcing a concentration upon change; (2) the influence of random assignment on leadership activities; (3) the appearance of certain characteristic patterns within the groups; (4) cultural norms that affected group interaction; and (5) the growth of facilitative response within the groups.

The short-term nature of the training group—eight two-hour sessions —placed pressures on both leaders and members to accomplish the desired changes within these time dimensions. However, as in most short-term therapy, the time limit was openly acknowledged and used (Phillips and Weiner, 1966; Reid and Shyne, 1967). As leaders, we were explicit in stipulating the time limit and in keeping track of how many sessions had been used and how many were left. Our expectation was clear that constructive change could take place within these time limits and we had the conviction that short-term treatment was a valid therapeutic approach.

Aside from the general criteria stated earlier, couples were randomly assigned to group treatment. This differs from approaches to group treatment where efforts are made to select clients who are regarded as especially suitable for a group approach or to compose a particular type of group. The active, direct leadership role was influenced by the random assignment to group treatment. It meant that we were confronted with an existing group and had to find out how that particular combination of people would interact. It was also our responsibility to influence group process toward constructive interaction. This was accentuated by certain general characteristics that became rather rapidly apparent in a group's response to us and to each other.

Thus, two of our couples were quick to question and challenge the idea that more empathic communication could be helpful in their marriages. In one of the initial dialogues, a husband brought out very directly his doubt that a response to feeling would work. He believed he could learn the skills but contended that they would have little application in his immediate relationships.

We could recognize, at a content level, his skepticism but most importantly, we had to respond to both his hopelessness and his desire for something better. The leaders' empathic responses to these feelings—not attempting to take them away but, simply, to fully recognize their presence—facilitated other members to share their doubts and initiated a vital dimension of human growth, self-exploration (Carkhuff, 1972).

In a follow-up session, three and a half months after the termination of this group, the same member recalled his earlier feelings. He spoke of himself as bitter and cynical, not only in relation to his marriage but also in response to a series of job disappointments. He described the group experience as helping him become more sensitive within his marriage and as also having much wider application in his life.

Another group was much more caught up in anxiety and fear. Behaviorally, they were less talkative in the sessions, and experienced great difficulty in trying out their facilitative skills in their daily lives. As these factors became apparent, the leaders had to respond to the group's growing self-understanding of their dilemma and to challenge them toward action (Carkhuff, 1972). Self-understanding centered around their longing for closeness but their fear of its consequences. They could resolve this dilemma only as the leaders confronted them with the need to act, despite their apprehensions.

Certain cultural norms were also evident within the interaction of the groups. The difficulties that many men have in acknowledging and expressing their feelings was apparent at a very early stage. A comparable problem for some of the women lay in their tendency to characteristically adopt a hurt, passive position. These difficulties may have been more apparent because the group members were randomly assigned to the training rather than being self-selected participants with high levels of interest in, or willingness to examine, their affective lives. In either case the response of the leaders was critical. We were prepared to explicitly acknowledge the fearfulness and anxiety inherent in changing one's behavior. At the same time, we were free in sharing ourselves and our own feelings, thus setting up very powerful norms counter to those within the group.

Even with the relatively brief time limit of the eight sessions, changes in individuals, and within groups, were evident. The ability of members to empathically respond to each other was particularly illustrated in an instance where a couple became extremely angry at each other as they attempted a dialogue within the group. The other members were able to respond to the feelings of each spouse and at the same time support their efforts to understand each other. In another group, a separated spouse was vehement in his bitterness and anger over the perceived futility of his situation. The group's steady facilitation of his feelings was vital in enabling him to later move beyond this impasse.

In summary, then, systematic facilitative training undoubtedly offers a defined, concrete technology for developing more effective interpersonal skills. Beyond this, the leaders' facilitation toward the members becomes a model for the members' more heightened responsiveness to each other. The group thus becomes more than a specific training workshop but assumes dimensions of a truly therapeutic and growth-producing experience.

The Use of Conjoint Interviews

The design of the project allowed for the use of maximum of three conjoint interviews per couple, either concurrent with or subsequent to the group training. The couples varied widely in their use of conjoint sessions although most used at least two of them. The co-leaders of the training group were therapists (individually) for the conjoint interviews. We tended to leave the option for conjoint sessions up to the clients but now believe that we should take more initiative in arranging at least one or two sessions for each couple because of their great usefulness in further refining their communication skills.

Three factors were apparent in the conjoint sessions: (1) Because of the relationship established between therapist and client in the training group, it was possible to move quite rapidly into highly relevant material. (2) The effects of the facilitative training were evident in these interviews, along with a marked decrease in the recriminatory blaming that many couples go through in early stages of conjoint treatment. (3) Perhaps as a consequence of these first two factors, we were able in the conjoint sessions to concentrate on specific and concrete areas of marital functioning and more easily work out mutually agreeable solutions.

Evaluation of Outcome

Empirical research in group therapy, whether process or outcome oriented, is scanty (Bednar and Lawlis, 1971). Most studies rely heavily, if not exclusively, on the therapist's own evaluation of outcome. This may be supplemented by directly or indirectly soliciting reports from clients about the effects of treatment.

The pilot group did rely upon this sort of clinical and self-report evaluation. The three members who completed the full eight sessions of the group reported that they experienced a number of positive gains in their lives in general and in their intimate relationships that they saw as stemming from the facilitative training. Our own observations were consonant with these reports. With the group, we saw definite progress in their ability to respond empathically to other group members and a similar, though more limited, gain in their ability to respond empathically to their spouses.

In the research project, we built in a number of more objective outcome measures which were administered at pre- and post-treatment points. These comprised the Wallace Marital Adjustment Test (WMAT) and two subscales, Empathic Understanding and Level of Regard, from the Barrett-Lennard Relationship Inventory (1962). In addition, we tape-recorded ten minutes of typical interaction between each couple, at the same intervals. These latter data will be reported at a later time.

The WMAT is a well-validated test of marital adjustment that has been widely used in a variety of studies (Locke and Wallace, 1959). The Barrett-Lennard subscales were selected because of their immediate relevance to the goals of facilitative training and also because of studies that have shown that the perception of these qualities in a spouse reliably distinguishes between adjusted and maladjusted marriages (Navran, 1969; Quick and Jacob, 1973).

Data from the two project groups is summarized in Table 1. In all instances, change was in the predicted direction of a more adjusted relationship. Analysis of the differences between pre- and post-treatment means on our three measures indicated that these were all significant ($p < .025$, one-tailed).

Table 1. Pre- and Post-Treatment Outcome Measures

Adjustment	Wallace Marital Test (WMAT)		Empathic Understanding		Level of Regard	
	Pre	Post	Pre	Post	Pre	Post
Mean	72.5	93.5	−0.59	0.59	0.79	1.99
S.D.	21.47	21.31	0.94	0.83	1.18	0.80

$N = 10$. One couple had not yet completed post-testing at the time of this writing.

A more detailed examination of the areas of change is of interest. On the WMAT, a major area of change was in the individual's rating of the degree of happiness or unhappiness in their marriage. However, there were also definite indications of change in methods of settling differences. Initially, couples saw one or the other spouse as having to "give in," while after treatment couples were much more likely to settle differences through a mutal give-and-take process. Finally, there were also changes toward a higher degree of agreement on sexual relations. While sexual adjustment was not a direct focus of the training groups, we would speculate that the improvement in this area was a generalized effect from the specific gains in emotional communication.

Similarly, the marked gains in the perception of regard would appear to be a generalized effect from the enhancement of empathic response between couples. In other words, an individual who experiences his spouse as more perceptive of and responsive of his feelings will also experience his spouse as more caring and respecting. We were surprised to find the change in Level of Regard as pronounced as our data indicated. This subscale had been selected as a change index because of its significant relationship to marital adjustment (Quick and Jacob, 1973), but it was certainly unexpected that such a significant gain would occur.

It was, of course, less surprising to find positive changes in Empathic Understanding since this was the direct focus of the training group. The significant gains in this area confirm our clinical impressions that we were accomplishing what we had intended to accomplish, namely, the enhancement of empathic responding.

Conclusion

We have described the use of systematic facilitative training in groups as a treatment modality for conflicted marital couples. Our data would indicate that positive changes in marital adjustments do result from such training and that this approach constitutes an effective and efficient method of treating marital problems.

REFERENCES

Bandura, A. (1969), *Principles of Behavior Modification.* New York: Holt, Rinehart & Winston.

Barrett-Lennard, G. T. (1962), "Dimensions of Therapist Response as a Casual Factor in Therapeutic Change," *Psychological Monographs,* 76 (43, Whole No. 562).

Bednar, R. L., and G. F. Lawlis (1971), "Empirical Research in Group Psychotherapy." In A. E. Gergin and S. L. Garfield (eds.), *Handbook of Psychotherapy and Behavior Change.* New York: John Wiley & Sons.

Bergin, A. E., and S. L. Garfield (1971), *Handbook of Psychotherapy and Behavior Change.* New York: Wiley & Sons.

Carkhuff, R. R. (1969), *Helping and Human Relations,* 2 vols. New York: Holt, Rinehart & Winston.

———(1971), "Training as a Preferred Mode of Treatment," *Journal of Counseling Psychology,* 18:123-131.

———(1972), *The Art of Helping.* Amherst, Mass.: Human Resources Development Press.

Ely, A. (1970), "Efficacy of Training in Conjugal Therapy." Unpublished Ph.D dissertation: Rutgers University.

Guerney, B. G., G. Stollack, and L. Guerney (1971), "The Practicing Psychologist as Educator—An Alternative to the Medical Practitioner Model," *Professional Psychology,* 2:276-282.

Locke, H. J., and K. M. Wallace (1959), "Short Marital Adjustment and Prediction Tests: Their Reliability and Validity," *Marriage and Family Living,* 21:251-255.

Napier, A., and C. Whitaker (1972), "A Conversation on Co-therapy." In A. Ferber, M. Mendelsohn, and A. Napier (eds.), *The Book of Family Therapy.* New York: Jason Aronson, Inc.

Navran, L. (1967), "Communcation and Adjustment in Marriage," *Family Process,* 6:173-184.

Olson, D. H. (1970), "Marital and Family Therapy: Integrative Review and Critique," *Journal of Marriage and the Family,* 32:501-538.

Phillips, A. L., and D. N. Weiner (1966), *Short-Term Psychotherapy and Structured Behavior Change.* New York: McGraw-Hill.

Pierce, R., and J. Drasgow (1969) "Teaching Facilitative Interpersonal Functioning to Psychiatric Inpatients," *Journal of Counseling Psychology,* 16:295-298.

Quick, E., and T. Jacob (1973), "Marital Disturbance in Relation to Role Theory and Relationship Theory," *Journal of Abnormal Psychology,* 82:309-316.

Reid, W., and A. Shyne (1967), *Brief and Extended Casework.* New York: Columbia Unversity Press.

Rogers, C. R. (1957), "The Necessary and Sufficient Conditions of Therapeutic Personality Change," *Journal of Consulting Psychology,* 21:95-103.

————, E. Gendlin, D. Kiesler, and C. B. Truax (1967), *The Therapeutic Relationship and Its Impact.* Madison, Wisc.: University of Wisconsin Press.

Truax, C. B., and R. R. Carkhuff (1967), *Towards Effective Counseling and Psychotherapy.* Chicago: Aldine.

————, and K. M. Mitchell (1971), "Research on Certain Therapist Interpersonal Skills in Relation to Process and Outcome." In A. E. Bergin and S. L. Garfield (eds.), *Handbook of Psychotherapy and Behavior Change.* New York: John Wiley & Sons.

Wolpe, J., and A. A. Lazarus (1966), *Behavior Therapy Techniques.* New York: Pergamon.

Yalom, I. D. (1970), *The Theory and Technique of Group Psychotherapy.* New York: Basic Books.

GORDON L. BOLTE

17   A Communications Approach to Marital Counseling

When the marriage counselor offers service to a marital pair conjointly, there is need for a framework within which to fit the therapeutic interventions. In the author's estimation, an approach based on communications theory provides such a framework. This article introduces some of the current theoretical considerations about communications and their relevancy to disrupted marriages and marital counseling. Sections regarding advisable cases for treatment and the intervention of the counselor will also be presented.

Introduction

As part of a self-inflicted physical conditioning program, the author was laboriously engaged in an exercise known as the "duckwalk," when to his surprise he noticed that a small group of fellow apartment dwellers were peering in through the living room window with an expression of shock written on their faces. Although he did not do so, the author felt compelled to explain his behavior to his neighbors lest they think he was in dire need of psychiatric attention.

This vignette is presented to illustrate how a phenomenon remains misunderstood until the total context in which it occurs is made lucid. Likewise, if a marital partner's behavior is studied in isolation, then emphasis is being placed on the symptom(s) to the exclusion of their effects on the spouse and inversely the spouse's involvement in them. If the contextual field is to be expanded, then a shift from symptoms to the marital relationship may be necessary. The vehicle for studying the relationship is likely to be communication, verbal and non-verbal.

Bardill states:

> Couples with marital problems tend to communicate progressively less as their conflict deepens. When communication does take place, it is often ambiguous or contradictory. Even simple tasks often result in arguments because of the nature of the ambiguous communications and on other occasions, there are contradictions between the different levels of communication. (Bardill, 1966, p. 7)

Certainly it seems true that an individual's overt behavior or verbalizations may contradict his feelings and vice versa. To eliminate these contradictions and establish clear communication is the task of the counselor. A section on therapeutic intervention will be discussed later.

The purpose of this paper is to discuss the communications approach as a vehicle for studying the marital relationship. Some of the more recent literature on the subject will be presented as related to the author's ideas and experiences. Communication is defined as "all those procedures by which one mind may affect another. This, of course, involves not only written and oral speech, but also music, the pictorial arts, the theatre, the ballet, and in fact all human behavior." (Shannon and Weaver, 1949, p. 117). It must be added that in human communications, it is virtually impossible for the receiver to distinguish the intentional from the unintentional component of a message based on the verbalized content only. The receiver must rely heavily on the previous situation, context, tone of voice, gestures and physical appearance.

By way of clarification, the interactional or communications approach is viewed in a broader sense than other similar approaches such as transactional analysis or Virginia Satir's family theory. Both of these are encompassed within communications theory, but place emphasis on various aspects of the theory. For instance, Eric Berne's Transactional Analysis stresses the "ego states" of the senders and receivers of messages while Satir's family theory emphasizes "self-esteem" as being a crucial determinant of how messages are sent and interpreted. As implied, the delineation of these various approaches is tenuous as evidenced by Dr. Roy R. Grinker's explanation of his transactional model which is seen by the author of this paper as being part and parcel of communications theory. Dr. Grinker states:

> Each [person] has an effect on the other that is specific to the situation in which they exist. One acts on the other, whose response in turn feeds back on the first. The process is reciprocal and cyclical. The setting of the system in which the transacting persons or foci exist determines and is determined by the processes going on. (Grinker, 1961, p. 200)

Indications for Advisable Cases

The advisability and inadvisability of using an interactional approach in marital counseling is difficult because the marital relationship between husband and wife includes an infinite number of factors, variables and contingencies, i.e. we do not as yet have an operational diagnostic nomenclature to guide us in the determination of what approach to employ. In lieu of such, the following indications may be helpful.

1. This approach would seem indicated when other approaches have failed. When the individual and other intrapsychic approaches have failed to correct deviant behavior of the client(s), then an approach that views relationship as a social system and attempts to manipulate it may be helpful.

2. An interactional approach might be used when a spouse is frightened by individual counseling or otherwise reticent. Whereas a marital partner may be reluctant to verbalize about his or her spouse for a myriad of reasons in individual treatment, he or she is not so likely to remain silent when confronted by the spouse in conjoint treatment.

3. As suggested by Haley, this approach may be indicated " . . . when a patient has a sudden onset of symptoms which coincides with marital conflict." (Haley, 1963, p. 118) Such reactional symptoms may be seen as a product of a change in the marital equilibrium and consequently amenable to marriage counseling.

4. Bardill indicates that:

When there is a lack of awareness of the role each partner plays in the relationship and little realization of the impact each role has on the other, conjoint interviews serve to clarify the relationship. Interview techniques may be used that force an awareness of the effect one partner has on the other. (Bardill, 1966, pp. 71-72)

5. This approach may be used when the individual egos are strong enough to endure the anxiety involved in confronting and being confronted about one's here-and-now behavior. In essence, this is to say that this approach should not be considered when the individual psychopathology of one member is so severe that further decompensation might result from such an emotionally charged experience.

In the final analysis, the treatment of choice should be determined by the individual counselor's assessment of the couple's needs and his (counselor's) security in using any given treatment model.

Theoretical Considerations

The idea that human behavior can be approached from various frames of reference is nothing new to most counselors, social workers and psychotherapists. The theoretical models employed tend to vary with the nature of the setting, the assessment of the problems, the individual academic orientation of the counselor and undoubtedly a host of other variables. The following theoretical considerations with their base in communications theory, will hopefully be an additional step in the direction of expanding the contextual field within which counselors search for supplementary tools to assist them in the enhancement of marital relationships.

Satir expresses in succinct terms what most of the communication theorists seem to be saying about this model for understanding human behavior. She states: "This theory means that any behavior that occurs between any two people is the product of both of them." She adds that: "everything can be understood once the premises from which any behavior is derived are made explicit and clear." (Satir, 1965, p. 121) It seems reasonable to assume that words or words plus grammar carry meaning in interaction and consequently are either modificatory, informative, reality testing and/or satisfying needs for self-expression. It is doubtful that any communication is just incidental or accidental noise.

Watzlawick, and others conclude that one cannot *not* communicate. (Watzlawick, Beavin, and Jackson, 1967) In terms of a marital pair, a passive husband who refuses to argue with his wife by turning away from her is communicating more than his unwillingness to quarrel. Whether he intended it or not, his wife is likely to interpret his gesture as "Get lost—I'm not going to give you the satisfaction of arguing with me." This in turn means that a receiver cannot *not* respond to a message and is thus communicating.

Watzlawick elaborates that:

Communication not only conveys information, but at the same time it imposes behavior. The report aspect of a message [verbal content only] conveys information and is, therefore, synonymous in human communication with the *content* of the message. The command aspect, on the other hand, refers to what sort of a message it is to be taken as, and, therefore, ultimately to the *relationship* between the communicants. (Watzlawick, Beavin and Jackson, 1967, p. 48)

The wife who asks her husband, "Would you like to take me to dinner?" is probably inquiring into more than her spouse's interest in taking her out to eat. She may be seeking reassurance or verification that he still loves her and desires a meaningful relationship with her. Serious conflict and hurt feelings can probably be averted so long as the husband responds favorably to at least the nonverbalized relationship aspect of the question (Do you still love me, etc.?). Hopefully, he will get additional clues (previous situation, context, tone of voice, gestures and physical appearance) to what is being asked since the verbal content of his wife's question and the relationship implications are not identical.

If this "hungry" wife is consciously or unconsciously asking a relationship question, then one or several of the following assertions may be being made:

"This is how I see myself... this is how I see you... this is how I see you seeing me..., etc." She may, for instance, be saying, "I see myself as being a faithful, lovable, worthwhile wife. I see you (husband) as having a similar evaluation of me, consequently you will prove it by taking me to dinner or by offering some response that will otherwise assure me of your feelings about me."

According to Watzlawick, the husband involved in this interaction has three possible responses he can make to his wife's relationship question:

1. Confirmation: The husband can accept (confirm) his wife's definition of self by making some response that will validate her feelings. It is entirely possible that he can do this without taking her to dinner and conversely his agreeing to take her to dinner is not necessarily confirmation since he could be doing it only out of a sense of duty.

2. Rejection: The second possible response that this husband can give in face of his wife's definition of self is to reject it. She is not likely to be pleased at his declining the dinner offer; however, his rejection presupposes at least limited recognition of what is being rejected and, therefore, does not necessarily negate wife's view of herself.

3. Disconfirmation: A response of this nature disconfirms or fails to recognize his wife's question. If he desires to destroy his wife's self-concept and eventually the marital relationship as well, the repeated use of this response may achieve that end. While rejection amounts to the message, "You are wrong," disconfirmation says in effect, "You do not exist." (Watzlawick, Beavin and Jackson, 1967) Individuals cannot emotionally tolerate a protracted period of "anomie" or "alienation" without suffering emotional conflict.

Rules. Behavioral science literature is replete with studies indicating that individual behavior becomes patterned and consequently in a given situation certain types of behavior can be predicted with a high degree of reliability. Haley attempts to apply a similar model to the interpersonal behavior of married couples when he views a couple's ability to deal with a situation as being due to the explicit or implicit rules they establish to govern their relationship. When the situation is met again, the rule established is either reinforced or changed. (Haley, 1963) A common example is the rule the couple establishes (usually implicitly) regarding the discussion of such emotionally charged areas as sexual practices, inlaws or child rearing. If a rule is broken, a norm governing the relationship has been violated and conflict may be the result.

Conflicted Communication

Many of the authors contributing to communication theory would view marital conflict as: (1) disagreements about the rules for living together; (2) disagreements about who is to set those rules, and (3) attempts to enforce rules which are incompatible with each other. Generally, couples have little difficulty resolving disagreements about which rules to follow because they can usually reach a compromise. Sharing common possessions, agreeing on recreational and social endeavors and problems of consideration for each other in various areas of living can lead to disagreements which are reasonably easy to resolve.

Conflict is likely to arise as the couple struggles with who is to make the rules and this problem is not so easily reached by compromise. For example, a wife could insist that her husband be responsible for the routine carpentry needs of the house because she does not feel her role encompasses such tasks. The husband might agree that she should not have to be a carpenter but he might disagree with her being the one that orders him to do it.

Double Binds. If marriage partners communicated at only one level, there would be little misunderstanding as to content or intent. However, this is not the case, so they often "offer each other messages which define one type of relationship at one level and an incompatible type of relationship at another." (Haley, 1963, p. 123) The wife who orders her husband to dominate her leaves the couple caught up in a network of incompatible definitions of the relationship. If the husband dominates her at her insistence, he is being dominated. This is an example of what Watzlawick defines as a "double bind": The husband is damned if he does and damned if he doesn't.

It is believed that no great harm is done so long as the double bind can be commented on and clarified. If not, this kind of paradoxical communication is lethal and it may lead to severe emotional problems.

Crossed Transactions. Eric Berne conceptualizes the breakdown of communication as being the result of "crossed transactions" rather than a misunderstanding as to the level that a message is being communicated. He indicates that:

> Individuals seem to have available a limited repertoire of ego states which are not roles, but psychological realities: (1) ego states which resemble those of parental figures (parent), (2) those which are autonomously directed toward objective appraisal of reality (adult) and (3) those which represent archaic relics, still-active ego states which are fixated in early childhood (child). (Berne, 1967, p. 23)

Communication will proceed smoothly so long as transactions are complementary, i.e., the message sent is the message received. The adult-to-adult response to "where is the toothpaste?" might be "I don't know" or "in the medicine cabinet." If the respondent becomes defensive, however, and replies, "you're always criticizing me for losing things," this is a child-parent response. The respondent is assuming a child's ego state and responding as if accused by a parent, consequently, congruent communication is broken off and a crossed transaction has occurred.

Closely akin to the concept of content vs. relationship messages is Berne's "duplex transaction" (Berne, 1967) which involves four ego states. For example: A handsome, young bachelor says "come up to my apartment and see my etchings." His attractive female companion replies, "I just love etchings. They are my favorite form of art." At the social level this is an "adult" conversation about etchings, and at the psychological level it is a "child" conversation about sex play. Superficially the "adult" seems to have the initiative, but the outcome may be determined by the "child" and the participant may be in for a surprise. Whether or not there will be a surprise and/or conflict will be determined by how aware this couple is that a crossed transaction has occurred.

Disqualification. The communication of this bachelor to his female friend provides an example of disqualification. "A disqualification enables one to say something without saying it; to take a stand for which one does not accept responsibility." (Watzlawick, Beavin and Jackson, 1967, pp. 75-76) If conflict is the outcome of this couple's conversation, either of them is in a position to claim self-righteousness and assume no responsibility for it.

Physical Symptoms. One of the most unique and controversial contributions that communication theory makes is in the area of physical symptoms. Haley indicates: "Symptoms can be seen as a product of, or a way of handling a relationship in which there are incompatible definitions of the relationship." (Haley, 1963, p. 132) For instance, the wife who develops low back pain or a headache at appropriate times can prevent sexual relations from occurring except on her own terms. The husband cannot force his will upon her without appearing inconsiderate for having done so. The problem is complicated because a symptom is something that his wife "cannot help." The wife might suggest that her husband approach her in a different manner, at which time he can do so or argue the matter. If she indicates, "I have such an excruciating headache" at a time when he is attempting to approach her, he can only withdraw in frustration, but he cannot blame her or resolve the problem. This husband is faced with incompatible messages: his behavior is circumscribed by his mate, but at the same time it is not circumscribed by the mate because the mate's behavior is "involuntary."

In summary, "communication theory conceives of a symptom as a nonverbal message: It is not I who does not (or does) want to do this, it is something outside my control, e.g., my nerves, my illness, my anxiety, my bad eyes, alcohol, my upbringing, the communists, or my wife." (Watzlawick, Beavin and Jackson, 1967, p. 80)

Intervention of the Counselor

It was suggested early in this presentation that a shift from symptoms to the marital relationship may be necessary in order to fully understand the context in which certain behavior occurs. Ruesch and Bateson seem to be alluding to this transition when they discuss the role of the therapist in the following terms:

Successful communication leads to self correction. The therapist, therefore, functions both as a teacher and an engineer who like a troubleshooter helps his patient to repair his broken-down system of communication. To implement this task he discusses only those opinions, values and habits which interfere with the patient's proper communication in hope that conscious inspection and correct use, first in the session and later at large, will exert a corrective effect. (Ruesch and Bateson, 1951, p. 132)

Ruesch and Bateson refer to the therapist's task only in relation to the individual rather than a dyad. The author believes, however, that their model lends itself to counseling with a marital pair with a minimum of alteration. Their statement includes the presumption that behavior change will occur once proper communication is *learned*. The learning will occur "first in the session and later at large." In the author's experience this type of learning occurs through the couple's repeated experience in being personally authentic and spontaneous with their spouse. Specifically, this includes their risking complete and uninhibited reporting of all they feel, think, see, and hear about themselves and their spouse. The discovery that expression of feelings does not destroy oneself or the other often frees the couple to use this problem-solving method in their relationship outside the treatment session.

Techniques and Procedures. The diversity of any given counseling situation and the unique skills of each counselor makes it difficult to specify tactics that may have any universal application. It is possible, instead, to discuss techniques and procedures which have been useful in the writer's experience, in hopes they may be of some value to others. As indicated earlier, the counselor's assessment of the partner's needs coupled with his security in using any given treatment tools should determine the tactics chosen.

The conjoint approach stands the risk of forcing too much affect too soon. The emotional instability of either marriage partner may be such that a few individual sessions may be necessary to bolster ego strengths prior to conjoint sessions. The individual sessions may also provide the counselor with "secrets" that might take a long time in being expressed in only conjoint sessions. The counselor should not betray confidence by telling a "secret"; however, the individual's awareness that the counselor knows seems to expedite the expression of it.

Once it has been decided that the conjoint method is the model of choice, the writer has found it helpful to establish a verbal contract with the couple which should specify the "ground rules" that will govern the counseling sessions. Items to be agreed upon are: time and location of sessions, number of sessions, fees, willingness to speak freely about anything one feels, sees and thinks regarding the spouse, absence of reprisal outside the counseling sessions, evaluative sessions and rules regarding sessions with an individual member. At least two of these points need clarification. The number of sessions is usually established at 10-12 with the final session being used for evaluation and the determination of whether or not to terminate treatment. A useful criterion in making this determination is when a "leveling off" of maladaptive behaviours occurs. The reaching of a plateau or practiced period of relative quiescence is often an indication that the couple has progressed as much as possible for the time being.

The second point to be clarified is the rules regarding sessions with an individual member. In general, individual sessions are to be avoided when a communications approach is used because they tend to allow a spouse to ventilate affect that should be dealt with vis-a-vis the mate and it is common for a spouse to use these sessions to attempt to align the counselor with his or her side. It is conceivable, however, that individual sessions may be used to overcome some treatment hurdle. If a counselor envisions such special problems, then a clause allowing for such should be built into treatment contract. Since free and open communication is an objective of this approach, it may be further specified that the content of individual sessions will be made available to the mate during the next conjoint session.

During the first few conjoint sessions, the counselor may wish to take an inactive role, allowing each individual to present his or her version of the problems. The diatribe that often results is seldom beneficial per se, but it should provide the counselor with valuable information regarding the communication patterns of the couple. For example, who speaks for whom, and who attributes blame or credit for his actions to someone else? How do these people get their messages across, i.e., is the verbal content consistent with the non-verbal content (tone of voice, pace, facial expression and body position)? How easily and clearly is the person heard and seen? (Hill, 1966)

As treatment progresses, it is virtually inevitable that the counselor will become more active in the therapy process in terms of exploring with the couple their interpretations of the messages they receive from the spouse in the here-and-now situation. If a verbal message is contradicted by a non-verbal message, it is often clarifying to have the receiver comment on what he or she received as a means of exposing the untenableness of the situation. The sender of the message is also provided the opportunity of "checking out" the clearness of his message which is especially important if his mate misjudged what he considered to be a straight single level message.

In cases involving extreme defensiveness, the counselor may be wise to indicate that the conflict is not a matter of "right" or "wrong" or "truth" or "falsehood" and that he (counselor) has no intention of aligning himself with either side. Instead, the focus should be placed on the *feelings* they have toward each other (in response to the here-and-now situation) because, in the final analysis, feelings rather than rational thought determine most behavior.

Extreme defensiveness is also likely to result in the flow of conversation being directed to the counselor rather than to the spouse. This is usually a clue that meaningful communication no longer exists between the pair. The counselor may request that each spouse avoid talking about the other in the third person (he or she). He may then suggest that they refer to each other in the second person (you). (Bardill, 1966, p. 77) He may also suggest that they physically turn toward each other so that as much eye-to-eye contact as possible is facilitated. Reticence to make these alterations may be overcome by the counselor talking a few minutes to demonstrate his points by role playing with one of the spouses. For example, a man who has paid little attention to his wife must sit and observe the counselor pay close attention to her remarks and encourage her to say more. In this structured situation and hopefully throughout his relationship with the couple, the counselor serves as a model of communication for the partners, which ideally will help alter the patterns they are using that lead to communication breakdown.

Finally, the counselor will occasionally, out of his own knowledge and experience, add pieces of information validated by other people. In so doing he gives the couple an opportunity to compare their experiences with those of others. (Ruesch, 1959)

Potential Pitfalls. The marriage counselor is committed to identifying *who* the clients are and avoiding identification with one member. The theoretical framework of the communications approach requires that the counselor view the marital relationship as the client. This is important because the decision has presumably already been made that it is not the intrapsychic pathology of either partner, rather their relationship, that is responsible for the conflict. This means that symptoms are viewed as interacting within the marital system and that there is no one guilty or responsible person but that both members are involved in and are influencing the production of the dilemma. (Hill, 1966)

The potential problem of the counselor aligning himself with one of the marital pair has been touched on previously but is worthy of remention because it is a common tendency when the conjoint approach is utilized. Neutrality is maintained as an ideal because siding with one member either alienates the other or identifies one as being the "sickest" and consequently in need of more attention. In either circumstance the benefits to be accrued from the communications approach are lost. While strict neutrality is impossible, the counselor should endeavor to balance his positive and negative interpretations between the partners.

Another pitfall to be avoided is the allowing of one mate to do the speaking for the other as if the other's feelings were known and accurately represented by the speaker. This may be avoided in part by ruling it out during the contract phase. However, it probably will continue because it tends to represent a life style for the couple. Helpful techniques in overcoming this problem might include reinforcing the idea that a person can "really" only speak for himself (Hill, 1966) or by the counselor asking directly for the comments and feelings of the individual spoken for. In any event, this problem will probably have to become one of the foci of the treatment process.

Still another potential pitfall involves the difficulty many couples have accepting a complementary relationship with each other and this is profoundly affected by their placing themselves in a treatment situation where the counselor "takes charge." Although the counselor is not necessarily overtly authoritarian, in fact that may not be wise or possible except in special circumstances, he is willing to offer guidance like the expert he is expected to be. As Haley states: "If a couple is to pay attention to him (counselor), he must be an authority figure, although not so omnipotent that it is necessary for the couple to topple him." (Haley, 1963, p. 139) Their ability to accept an expert has a marked influence on the treatment process and consequently on their ability to accept a complementary relationship with each other.

Critique and Summary

The appearance at the door of a marriage counselor is usually an attempt by a couple to find a more satisfying means of relating with each other. The counselor is an agent for change in a variety of ways: he encourages full and complete discussion of problem areas; he feeds back to the couple what he sees and hears and in so doing serves as a model of communication; he serves as a reasonably impartial advisor and judge; he represents an ego-ideal that can be held conjointly by the couple; he encourages a couple to examine motivations that may have been outside their awareness; and as a resource person he has knowledge of referral sources that may supplement his treatment of the couple.

In concluding this presentation of communication theory and its applicability to the treatment of marital pairs, an evaluation of its strengths and weaknesses and its advantages and disadvantages will be discussed.

One of the pragmatic strengths of the communications approach used in the conjoint treatment of a married couple is that it provides the counselor an opportunity to assess how the couple relates with each other. It provides a relatively simple framework for pointing out the fallacies inherent in verbal communication, consequently it should prove helpful in sifting out reality.

The communications approach is less threatening to the clients in some respects than other theoretical models. For example, Berne's "games analysis" provides counselors the opportunity to comment on a couple's behavior in terms of the "games they play" with each other. This sort of tangential focus on the problem areas may serve to provide some clients a degree of detachment which hopefully will reduce unnecessary anxiety by helping them understand that their behavior is "played" rather than the result of "neurotic interaction" or "intrapsychic pathology."

One of the more frequent attacks leveled at communication theory is its assiduous avoidance of intrapsychic factors and lack of concern for individual functioning. Some believe that this type of compartmentalized thinking, in which the person and the relationship are dealt with separately, sets up a peculiar form of unintended dualism that must be questioned, for each person is more than that which is reflected of him in his marriage. This concern is not without credence; however, it is doubtful that communication theory is any more compartmentalized than, for example, analytic theory or ego oriented theory with their diagnostic nomenclatures and virtual avoidance of environmental considerations involved in psychopathology.

Some argue that this theory with its focus on the relationship is superficial compared with theories that trace disturbance to its historical roots. This may be true, but the assumption that understanding the historical roots is synonymous with behavior change is highly questionable. Conversely, in the writer's experience, a minimizing of the past and the future tends to help the client feel that the counselor is with him in what he does, thinks, and feels today. The present, in all its ramifications, then becomes something the client can learn to focus upon and eventually to accept. Communication with another person about matters which are currently active becomes rewarding because the couple discovers that whatever change may occur can only occur in the present. "Manipulation of the past or the future is an illusion which prevents people from coping with their existence." (Ruesch, 1959, p. 905)

Another advantage communication theory has over more narrowly defined theories is involved in its shift from the limited intrapsychic approach to general systems theory which more nearly encompasses the life space of each marital partner. To ignore the involvement of the marital relationship in the emotional symptoms of a client, without first examining it, would be analogous to discounting the role of a brain tumor in a headache.

Some ideas for a communications approach that focuses on the relationship of a disrupted marriage have been discussed in this article. Emphasis was placed on the interactional dimension of the marital system—the driving force that determines so much of the couple's happiness together. Despite the enthusiasm portrayed for this model throughout this presentation, the author hastens to add that it should not be considered a panacea for emotional ills. Rather, it should be considered for what it is increasingly proving to be, a valuable tool to be added to the counselor's treatment repertoire, especially in those marriage counseling cases when it is deemed advantageous to see the couple conjointly.

REFERENCES

Bardill, Donald R. (1966), "A Relationship-Focused Approach to Marital Problems," *Social Work,* 2: 70-77.
Berne, Eric (1967), *Games People Play.* New York: Grove Press.
Grinker, Roy R. (1961), "A Transactional Model for Psychotherapy." In Morris I. Stein (ed.), *Contemporary Psychotherapies.* New York: The Free Press.

Haley, Jay (1963), *Strategies of Psychotherapy.* New York: Grune & Stratton.

Hill, William G. (1966), "The Family as a Treatment Unit: Differential Techniques and Procedures," *Social Work,* 2: 62-68.

Ruesch, Jurgen (1959), "General Theory of Communication." In Silvano Arieti (ed.), *Handbook of Psychiatry,* I. New York: Basic Books.

Ruesch, Jurgen, and Stanley Bateson (1951), *Communication.* New York: W. W. Norton & Co.

Satir, Virginia M. (1965), "Conjoint Family Therapy." In Bernard L. Greene (ed.), *The Psychotherapies of Marital Disharmony.* New York: The Free Press.

Shannon, C. E., and W. Weaver (1949), *The Mathematical Theory of Communication.* Urbana: University of Illinois Press.

Watzlawick, Paul, Janet H. Beavin, and Don D. Jackson (1967), *Pragmatics of Human Communication,* New York: W.W. Norton & Co.

ROBERT D. CARTER
EDWIN J. THOMAS

18 Modification of Problematic Marital Communication*

Corrective feedback and instruction (CF-I) was used as a modification technique in cases involving problematic marital communication. Exploratory analyses of two cases indicated that, in general, CF-I brought about a successful modification of problematic components of the verbal repertoires dealt with. The assessment involved the identification and measurement of inductively derived classes of verbal behavior that constituted the targets of intervention. This assessment procedure was successfully employed and, as a by-product, has led to the development of a set of provisional verbal problem categories that may be of use to researchers and practitioners who work with communication problems.

This paper reports the results of an exploratory analysis of the effects of corrective feedback and instructions on selected problems in marital communication. The assessment procedure, which may be applicable in clinical and social service settings, involved a behaviorally specific, inductive identification of problematic verbal interaction. The modification technique of corrective feedback and instructions (abbreviated as CF-I) also represents a possible addition to that body of methods now available to interpersonal helpers for the alteration of communication difficulties.

*The research upon which this report is based was supported in part by Grants SRS-CRD 425-8-286 and SRS-CRD 529-0, Social and Rehabilitation Service, Department of Health, Education and Welfare. We are indebted to Miss Marguerite M. Parrish, Executive Director, and Mrs. Margaret B. Ohlgren, Case Consultant, Catholic Social Services of Washtenaw County, Ann Arbor, Michigan, for their cooperation, encouragement, and enthusiasm in this collaborative undertaking; and to Miss Diane Ehrensaft, Mr. Art Franel, and Miss Lynn Nilles for their able assistance in data analysis.

METHOD

Overview

The research program involved a series of single-couple experiments to examine the effects of client-activated light signals on the verbal behavior of the partners. The CF-I intervention was introduced in the third of three sessions, primarily as a service to the clients for their participation in the research and to the social workers who made the referrals. It was discovered, however, that CF-I was apparently having immediate effects upon the communication behavior of several couples, so much so that a decision was made to try and measure these effects subsequent to the period of active data collection. It is this information that is provided in the present report. The electromechanical signaling apparatus is described elsewhere (Thomas, Carter, Gambrill and Butterfield, 1970; Butterfield, Thomas and Soberg, 1970), as are the possible uses of signal-mediated modification (Thomas, Carter and Gambrill, 1971).

Subjects

The host agency for the experimental project is a private, multiprogram family and children's agency. Members of the casework staff were asked to refer to the project marital couples displaying problems in their verbal interaction and who volunteered to participate in a structured series of three 1.5 hour experimental sessions. In return, the couples and their workers were to receive information on the communication problems revealed and recommendations as to how these problems might be corrected. A total of 12 couples was referred, and all were accepted. Nine of these couples completed the entire series of three experimental sessions, and data on two are presented in what follows. The sampling procedure involved in the selection of the two couples is described in the next section.

Procedure

Although specifics of the procedure varied somewhat from couple to couple, a typical three-session pattern can be described. In Session I, the couple received a description of and rationale for the experimental project. After this, they were asked to briefly discuss an innocuous practice topic. This was done to familiarize them with how to use the signaling apparatus at the same time that they were engaged in conversation with each other. Then the pair discussed for 20 minutes each of two principal topics used in this session and the next:

"Problems You Have in Your Marriage" and "Expectations of Each Other as Husband and Wife." The experimenter did not participate in these discussions. His job was to indicate the topic and then to cue the couple as to when to start and stop each discussion. As was true in all three sessions, the discussions were tape-recorded for later analysis of the verbal interaction.

Session II usually followed in 1 week. The same two topics were again discussed but with certain changes made in how the couple used the signaling apparatus. From the standpoint of the present report, Session II represented a second opportunity to gather samples of the couple's verbal interaction behavior. This information, along with that obtained in Session I, was then subjected to a prefeedback analysis that formed the basis for the CF-I intervention that was introduced during the third and final session.

The prefeedback analysis, while not perfunctory, was carried out primarily to make treatment decisions and did not have the advantage of the greater assessment sophistication we later acquired when there was time to code the tapes at a more leisurely and systematic pace. Instead, a research assistant, guided by the experimenter on hand during the sessions with the couple, listened to the tapes of the first two sessions and wrote down instances of what appeared to constitute problematic interaction. The assistant then pulled these elements together into some kind of logical categorization and provided a set of conclusions as to the central problems revealed. The experimenter, in consultation with the assistant and after himself having listened selectively to portions of the tape material, then prepared a written "Statement to Clients." This statement constituted the CF-1 intervention.

The contents of CF-1 statements varied of course with each couple, but the following components were included: (1) a brief description of the positive features observed in the couple's communication during the first two sessions; (2) a detailed explication, usually with concrete examples, of the two or three most important problems discovered during replay analysis; and (3) recommendations to the couple as to steps they might take in trying to alleviate the problems. For illustrative purposes, the following excerpts from one "Statement to Clients" are presented:

One of the primary areas of difficulty we observed in your communication has to do with your style of addressing specific problems. We can refer to this as your problem-solving style. We wish to point out certain key features of your problem-solving style that we feel are in need of improvement:

1. Not Maintaining Specificity. As a general rule, you did reveal an ability to discuss details surrounding a specific, concrete problem. For example, both of you contributed specific information that helped in clarifying the topic of whether or not one of your sets of parents should have been invited for Thanksgiving. However, the specifics of that situation were soon abandoned when the abstract issue of what holidays mean to one or the other of you was introduced. Although that particular incident is now in the past, we would suggest that when you discuss similar situations in the future you make it a rule to maintain a focus on the specifics of *the situation itself* and not allow the situation to be submerged in a discussion of abstract issues or principles. It would help if you would cue each other when you find yourselves slipping away from specifics. A statement like, "Let's get back to the specifics" might help in this connection.

2. Diverting the Focus of Discussion. This defect is related to the one just mentioned, that of not maintaining specificity, but it differs in that the problem here involves a more blatant *shift* of topics rather than the topic simply becoming more abstract. For example, in one exchange, Mrs. T said "I think when I'm trying to do something to make something for our children that you should be right there with me. They're not just my children, it's not just my responsibility. It's for us to do together for our children. . . ." Mr. T's reply was "Well when I'm cutting the grass out in the backyard or working on my truck or something like that, do you come and say 'Do you want me to help you cut the grass?' " Mrs. T then fell into the discussion of whether or not she works in the yard and how much, and the whole discussion seemed to take one giant step aside from the original topic of sharing responsibility for the children. We feel it would have been better if Mr. T had maintained a focus on the original topic, but when he did deviate from it Mrs. T could have suggested that they return to the original focus of discussion instead of allowing herself to go along with a topic shift. Mutual problems generally require the *exclusive* attention of both parties for a concentrated period of time. Too many side issues serve to dilute and weaken your problem-solving efforts.

Session III varied somewhat for different couples, but typically it involved starting off with the discussion of a new topic, "Problems You Have in Communicating with Each Other." This topic was discussed twice by most couples, once before presentation of the CF-I statement and once afterward. The statement itself was delivered by giving copies to both husband and wife and asking them to read the statement silently to themselves as the experimenter read it aloud. The clients were then permitted to solicit clarification of the contents if desired but were asked to postpone commentary until their second discussion of the Session III topic. The session ended with a more informal period of conversation in which the experimenter answered questions and, if appropriate, offered additional observations and suggestions based upon the couple's final discussion.

A sampling procedure was adopted to guide the selection of a few cases for detailed analysis of the possible effects of CF-I. A set of 14 problems was compiled at random from the array of some 23 problems that had been observed across the nine couples and designated in their written CF-I statements. Of these 14 problems, four were selected for exploratory purposes on the basis of a criterion of apparent ease of operational measurement. Each of these four involved a different case. Two of the cases are described later for illustrative purposes. It is felt that these cases best represent the experimental procedure and the mode of data analysis employed in the study.

CASE ANALYSES AND RESULTS

Case A

The problem area selected in connection with this case involved the husband's excessive question-asking and infrequent opinion-giving. The earlier, prefeedback analysis suggested that this couple displayed a remarkably consistent question-and-answer interaction pattern, with the husband (H) asking the questions and the wife (W) giving the answers. Accompanying this pattern was a low frequency of opinion-giving on the part of H, especially after the first few minutes of each discussion; W, on the other hand, expressed many opinions, mostly in response to H's questions.

The CF-I centered on the cited pattern, which was described to the couple in detail. Regarding H's behavior in particular, we advocated that he ask fewer questions and offer more opinions. To try and facilitate his opinion-giving, W was advised to ask more questions.

The analysis consisted of coding H's and W's questions and their noninterrogative utterances and comparing the frequencies in the Session III postintervention discussion with the two Session I discussions and the Session III preintervention discussion. The basis for this choice of behaviors lay in the observation that H's utterances were predominantly of a question-asking or opinion-giving type. The only other relevant utterance was an occasional short recognition response, such as "I see" or "Uh-huh." It was decided that we would ignore recognition utterances and code everything else. We coded W's noninterrogative utterances, also, because they might have changed in frequency for some unanticipated reason.

A code was developed to cover each category of utterance. A question was defined simply as a self-contained, grammatically complete, and unequivocally interrogative utterance. Noninterrogative utterances were coded in terms of what was called a *verbal unit,* which is roughly equivalent to an independent clause—a self-contained segment of speech with its own subject and predicate. Hand-operated, push-button devices were used for coding, each button activating one or another pen of a Simpson event recorder. Interrater reliability for H's questions was .96; for his noninterrogative utterance, .82.

The results are depicted in Table 1. As compared with the three preintervention, baseline discussions, H clearly increased his frequency of noninterrogative, opinion-giving utterances after intervention. There was a 39% increase over the most productive of the baseline samples, jumping from 1.55 units to 3.55 units/min. The increase over the average of the baseline discussions was 44%. However, H's question-asking did not diminish despite the intervention.

It is also clear that W did not conform to the advice to ask more questions. In fact, her level of verbal output in general declined. This over-all decline in W's output is difficult to interpret, but it seems likely that she diminished in contribution as H increased in his. H came across as much more assertive in the final discussion and he reported afterward that this was a deliberate effort on his part to comply with our recommendations. A temporal analysis of his opinion-giving in 5-min intervals revealed that whereas his opinions were concentrated in the very early portion of the preintervention discussions, they showed a gradual climb in frequency over the entire postintervention discussion.

Table 1. Number of Questions and Noninterrogative Verbal Units per Minute by Husband (H) and Wife (W) for Three Preintervention and One Postintervention Discussions for Case A[1]

	Preintervention Discussions			Postintervention Discussion
	1	2	3	
Questions				
H	1.60	.75	.67	1.39
	(32)	(15)	(10)	(22)
W	0.00	.40	.07	.07
	(0)	(8)	(1)	(1)
Noninterrog. Units				
H	.85	1.55	.73	3.55
	(17)	(31)	(11)	(56)
W	9.60	8.30	9.40	2.65
	(192)	(166)	(141)	(41)

[1] Preintervention discussions 1 and 2 were 20 min in length; preintervention 3 and the postintervention discussion were 15 min. Numbers in parentheses represent total questions or noninterrogative verbal units per discussion.

Case B

Immediately obvious upon listening to the first and second session tapes of this couple's interaction was the tendency toward abstract, debate-like and quasi-intellectual interchanges, with H taking most of the lead. Consequently, this case appeared to be a prime target for an intervention to produce greater content specificity.

In the CF-I statement, the recommendation was that the couple should avoid

COUPLES IN CONFLICT

talking about things in only vague and general ways and should keep their problem-oriented discussions specific, focused, to the point, and centered on actual (non-hypothetical) situations and events. Other suggestions were given to try and bolster the impact of this advice.

The variable of content specificity had been coded previously in another context of the research project (Thomas et al., 1971), and the relevant code category was simplified further for present purposes. The observer listened for verbal units that denoted discrete stimulus events (including behaviors), and affective events (feelings, opinions) that describe a person's reactions to or evaluations of discrete stimulus events. The same coding equipment was employed as in Case A. Both Session III discussions and one discussion from Sessions I and II were coded for specific verbal units and nonspecific verbal units of both H and W. Interrater reliability for content specificity had been established previously at a level of .85 for the original and more complex code.

Table 2. Total Number of Verbal Units, Number of Specific Verbal Units, Number of Nonspecific Verbal Units, and Percent Specific of Total Verbal Units for Couple in Three Preintervention and One Postintervention Discussions for Case C[1]

	Preintervention Discussions			Postintervention Discussion
	1	2	3	
Total Verbal Units	234	237	203	225
Specific Verbal Units	94	39	72	147
Nonspecific Verbal Units	140	198	131	78
% Specific of Total Verbal Units	40	16	35	65

[1] All discussions were 20 min in length.

The results in Table 2 indicate that the intervention to enhance content specificity appears to have been effective. The postintervention discussion was rich in specific talk—65% of all verbal units were so classified. The nearest baseline discussion was that of Session I with 40% specific talk, but it should be noted that much of that discussion was devoted to family finances. The coder was overgenerous in designating this material as specific. Actually, it seldom got much beyond references to "paying bills" and expressing concern over "credit rating." This subject matter did not come up again in any of the other coded discussions.

That the CF-I statement served to promote specificity is also indicated by a fair number of references made during the postintervention discussion to "being specific." The partners would check and question each other regarding this objective, and many concrete situational episodes were introduced throughout the interaction as a way of illustrating and clarifying a point.

VERBAL PROBLEM CATEGORIES: A PROVISIONAL LIST

Noteworthy in the approach described in this paper is the high degree of case individualization afforded by adopting an inductive stance in the selection of target problems. While some implicit categories undoubtedly guided our search during the prefeedback assessment phase of case analysis, the practice was to allow the taped interaction to suggest its own categories as much as possible. Out of these efforts there was later engendered as an unanticipated research product a set of explicit problem categories.

It can be seen that one objective in the development of these categories was to concentrate on overt behavior that can be operationalized with a minimum of inferences as to the underlying mental states of the parties involved. This noninferential approach tends to facilitate reliable coding of complex verbal behavior without losing the relevance required in clinical work.

Consistent with our own policy, it is suggested that these categories may best serve in a cueing capacity. They can aid in directing one's attention to possible problem areas in a couple's interaction. The final specification for coding purposes, however, should probably be particularized for the couple in question. In our opinion, preestablished code categories have a way of producing selections that may lack adequate correspondence with the empirical elements at hand.

The list of problem categories is as follows:

1. *Overtalk*. One interactant tends to dominate the interaction excessively in sheer verbal output. Likely measures: (a) total time spent in mere vocalization, regardless of content; (b) number of words uttered.

2. *Undertalk*. (Not necessarily a reciprocal to Overtalk.) An interactant fails to contribute much talk despite opportunities to do so (e.g., as during periods of mutual silence or when asked to respond).

3. *Fast talk*. An interactant speaks too rapidly, especially if noticed or reacted to in some discernible way by the partner.

4. *Slow talk*. An interactant speaks too slowly, especially if noticed or reacted to in some discernible way by the partner.

5. *Loud talk*. An interactant speaks too loudly, especially if noticed or reacted to in some discernible way by the partner.

6. *Quiet talk*. An interactant speaks near or at the point of inaudibility, especially if noticed or reacted to in some discernible way by the partner.

7. *Dysfluent talk*. An interactant tends to display an excess of dysfluencies in his speech (e.g., stuttering, hesitations).

8. *Affective talk*. This covers a variety of "emotional" behaviors during talk that require specification, such as crying and intense intonation.

9. *Verbal obtrusions*. An interactant too frequently emits utterances that occur during and after the onset of speech by the other. These remain as obtrusions only as long as they do not produce an immediate and apparently premature cessation of speech by the other. When the other stops speaking abruptly upon occurrences of an obtrusion, this constitutes an *interruption*.

10. *Abusive talk.* An interactant tends to engage in too frequent or too lengthy verbal criticisms of the other and in a derogatory, nonconstructive manner.

11. *Acknowledgment deficit.* An interactant fails to admit or give credit when the other is correct in a statement, or fails to express recognition of the other's point of view or assertion.

12. *Positive talk deficit.* An interactant fails to compliment or say nice things about the other as a person or about what the other says or does.

13. *Countercomplaining.* An interactant responds to a complaint with a complaint about the other, such that the initial complaint is not dealt with on its own terms.

14. *Topic avoidance.* An interactant openly refuses to discuss a particular topic or referent, or does not comply when asked to discuss it.

15. *Topic shifting.* An interactant tends to introduce new or different content that takes the focus of discussion astray prematurely.

16. *Topic persistence.* An interactant tends to dwell excessively on a given topic or referent, especially if this entails repetition of comments and little or no new information input.

17. *Poor referent specification.* An interactant fails to speak in concise, concrete, and specific terms about a referent; his speech tends to be overgeneral and abstract.

18. *Temporal remoteness.* An interactant tends to dwell excessively on referents in the fairly distant past or future, especially when these referents are tied only tenuously, if at all, to current referents.

19. *Overresponsiveness.* An interactant engages in verbal input that appears to go far beyond what was called for by a question or directive uttered by the partner (especially if the partner shows signs of impatience with the reply).

20. *Underresponsiveness.* An interactant fails to contribute as completely as a previous question or comment by the partner seems to call for (e.g., insufficient answers to questions).

21. *Excessive question-asking.* An interactant asks too many questions.

22. *Dogmatic assertion.* An interactant tends to express opinions or points of view in a categorical, unqualified, "black or white" manner.

23. *Overgeneralization.* An interactant engages in excessive stereotypic categorization of a referent as being invariably of the same type. (Look for key words like "always," "never," "every time.")

24. *Presumptive attribution.* An interactant assigns to the other nonobvious meanings, motives, feelings, especially when these inferred factors are negatively valued. ("Mind-reading," "second-guessing.")

25. *Detached utterances.* An interactant utters comments or questions that fail to show any clear semantic connection to the immediate focus of discussion, especially if these appear to confuse the partner or are not incorporated by the partner in his or her next utterance (e.g., irrelevant examples, ideas, or hypothetical situations).

26. *Excessive compliance.* An interactant overuses agreement responses, to the detriment of voicing constructive disagreements, suggestions, or qualifications in response to the partner.

27. *Opinion deficit.* An interactant fails to take an evaluative stand or voice opinions regarding referents when the interaction seems to invite same, especially when the partner is registering opinions or is asking the interactant to do so.

DISCUSSION

While admittedly exploratory, this research is suggestive of some techniques of assessment and modification that may prove useful to researchers and practitioners interested in problematic marital interaction. In assessment, the collection of a series of interaction samples prior to intervention is analogous to baselining in operant research. These samples form the basis for a later comparison to determine the extent to which the target behaviors have changed after treatment intervention. The use of an inductive, operational, and largely noninferential coding strategy in the analysis of recorded interaction may lend a degree of case-specific precision and specificity that is largely lacking in many current approaches to marital communication.

The results for the two cases reported are encouraging with respect to the efficacy of CF-I as an intervention technique. In evaluating these results, it should be noted that CF-I differs in several important respects from much of the advice-giving that frequently occurs in clinical settings. The intervention was prepared on the basis of information acquired under conditions of structured observation, with the experimenter serving primarily as a neutral task director. The CF-I statement itself was presented more or less formally and constituted explicit input for a final husband-and-wife discussion that followed immediately. Thus the couple had an opportunity to practice new ways of talking without the customary delay that follows receipt of clinical advice and its implementation in the natural environment. Also, this discussion took place under conditions of maximum surveillance by the experimenter. This very likely enhanced compliance with instructions contained in the CF-I statement. The CF-I contents were carefully worded and articulated, were behaviorally specific, and used illustrative examples drawn from the couple's own interaction. As an over-all impression, it would seem that the entire sequence of activities took on an aura of systematic precision, expertness, and credibility —all of which can serve to maximize influence and promote behavioral change.

This report should not be construed as advocating the widespread or indiscriminate use of CF-I. Instructional intervention presupposes that the requisite behaviors are already in the response repertoires of the target individuals and that verbal description and instruction are sufficient to evoke them. Obviously, this assumption would be inappropriate for many clients. In addition, it is well to consider the likelihood that CF-I would rarely be the only modification technique employed. Instructional control over new behaviors may be inadequate in maintaining the changes produced. Indeed, it is very likely that CF-I may represent only a desirable first step and that other techniques would follow for purposes of refining, expanding, and perpetuating the gains achieved. As a first step, however, its value in producing rapid and significant changes in behavior, changes that can then be capitalized upon in further treatment efforts, may be considerable.

REFERENCES

Butterfield, W. H., E. J. Thomas and R. J. Soberg (1970), "A Device for Simultaneous Feedback of Verbal and Signal Data," *Behavior Therapy,* 4: 395-401.

Thomas, E. J., R. D. Carter, and E. D. Gambrill (1971), "Some Possibilities of Behavioral Modification with Marital Problems using 'SAM' (Signal System for the Assessment and Modification of Behavior)." In R. D. Rubin, H. Fensterheim, A. A. Lazarus, and C. M. Franks (eds.), *Advances in Behavior Therapy.* New York: Academic Press, pp. 273-288.

——— and W. H. Butterfield (1970), "A Signal System for the Assessment and Modification of Behavior (SAM)," *Behavior Therapy,* 1:252-259.

Section F

Brief Therapy and Crisis Intervention

19 Structured Separation for Couples in Conflict*

A three-month trial separation with counseling is suggested as a form of crisis intervention for couples in conflict. The purpose of the counseling is to help the marital partners understand their relationship, resolve their conflicts, decide whether their future relationship will be together or apart, and grow through the separation process. A one-year follow-up was conducted with eighteen couples who completed structured separation with counseling.

Marriage counselors and psychotherapists are all too familiar with the couple who come for help stating they must either "make this marriage work or get a divorce." One partner is generally inclined to cling desperately to the marriage, willing to do almost anything to avoid divorce. The other is desirous of the marriage, but tired of trying and sees no way to go but "out." Trial separation is generally not considered a reasonable alternative. The more threatened of the two is usually afraid to let go of the semblance of control available through physical proximity. The other is looking toward complete freedom. Both may have little tolerance for the lack of structure that is implied by separation, as opposed to divorce. This paper presents a fourth alternative: a moderately structured, time-limited period of separation, with counseling.

Rationale for Structured Separation with Counseling

Separation counseling is a form of crisis intervention counseling (Parad, 1965). It is a time-limited approach that deals specifically with the immediate

*The author wishes to thank Rick Riemer for his assistance in the preparation of this paper.

crisis of family separation. The purpose of this counseling procedure is to help separating individuals understand their relationship, resolve their conflicts, decide whether their future relationship will be together or apart, and grow through the separation process.

A major assumption on which separation counseling is based is that a meaningful relationship, once established, can never be altogether lost. It can only be changed. In some cases, especially where there are children, separated partners continue to see each other and make decisions together. If they do not continue to have some tangible connection with each other, they nonetheless remain related in fantasy and imagination and memory. It is important that the couple work through the separation process carefully and thoroughly so that little unfinished business remains to interfere with their continuing separation-relationship, or in new relationships.

The techniques and methods outlined below are of particular value to separating couples, married or unmarried, and to parents and children who are separating. They may be applied by individuals with or without counseling. However, counseling is especially useful for couples having much difficulty separating, for extremely dependent individuals who are limited in emotional freedom, for those who are afraid to risk, and for those subject to severe depression.

The structured separation provides a firm time-space base within which individuals may maximize their freedom to experience and grow. It minimizes the shock of separation. It makes positive use of the separation process as an aid to development so that individuals neither deny their loss nor become victims to its pain. Respect for self and other, trust, choice, courage, honesty, emotional development, and positive growth are inherent in this method.

Conflict-laden couples who choose to separate voluntarily before their discomfort becomes intolerable gain much from openly and consciously making this choice. Manipulative and punitive maneuvers such as capricious sexual behavior, designed to force a break in the relationship are avoided. Such maneuvers often cause irreparable damage, shatter trust, and humiliate one or both mates. In separating voluntarily, the partners signify that each values himself, the other, and what they have between them enough to allow some distance. Such distance provides each with an opportunity to gain perspective and to try alternative solutions to problems. The couple may then come together again with renewed understanding and feeling, or go on to other relationships having learned a great deal from this one. Separation counseling ensures that little unfinished business remains to interfere with new experiences.

Structured separation is an excellent model for distressed families with children. These children are thus presented with parental behavior where honesty, choice, and respect are primary values. Some of the damage done by the suddenness and emotional uproar common in most divorce is mitigated. The children have both time and an open interpersonal situation in which to adapt to this major change in their lives. The children have an opportunity to discuss their feelings about the family, as it has been, and as they would like it to be. Their sense of involvement and control of their fate is considerably increased. Children's positive feelings for their parents are enhanced by seeing them cope well with conflict and crisis. In addition, parents experience less anxiety in this structured separation situation than in a comparable time negotiating for a final divorce. They thus are able to deal with their children's feelings more effectively. The separation counselor has an opportunity to help parents understand their children's reactions to the family crisis. He may then guide the parents so that they can encourage open exchange of feelings and concerns. Where necessary, the counselor may work directly with the children.

Viable relationships survive structured separation. Old patterns of thought, feeling, and behavior are broken. New patterns develop within each individual, between the couple, and even between parents and children. The couple's new relationship, whether a "together-relationship" or a "separate-relationship," is clearly based on choice rather than the force of circumstance, fear, default, or inadequacy.

The Separation Structure

The separating couple is asked to make a three-month commitment to explore themselves and the relationship. During this time both will see the counselor —optimally once a week. They are seen both individually and together. Sometimes one comes regularly and the other only as he or the therapist deems necessary.

During this time the couple is asked not to live in the same house, not to see a lawyer, and not to make any permanent financial, property, or child custody arrangements. Children remain in their own home with whichever parent is best able to care for them. Their lives are disrupted as little as possible. It is important that they maintain contact with such environmental supports as friends and school. As the couple communicate with each other while realistically assessing their needs, they resolve practical issues. Decisions are made out of the awareness of both partner's needs, not out of fear, guilt, or revenge.

Each partner agrees to be together only if, when, how, and as long as *both* are comfortable. This "choice" rule applies also to parent-child contacts. Each is free to initiate contact; each is free to end contact when he wants to, for whatever reason. The couple may have sex together only if both want to.

At the point of making the commitment to the separation structure, the couple is encouraged to express feelings about outside affairs. Freedom to explore other relationships is encouraged on the theory that such exploration maximizes choice. If the couple decides to come together again, each knows it is because he is desired over and above others. In addition, a variety of social, emotional and sexual encounters give each a more realistic view of himself interacting with others. These contacts serve to eliminate "If it weren't for you" games. They also cut throught the "I was too young and inexperienced," "Nobody else would want me," and "I had to get married" types of excuse for discontented clinging.

During these three months, the couple learns to relate to each other in terms of needs, feelings, qualities of being, defenses, and games. The process of seeing each other only by choice requires that each examine himself and the other often to decide whether or not to be together and when and how to reject the other. In this process of repeatedly accepting and rejecting, each has an extraordinary opportunity to learn to be honest with the other in communicating love, appreciation, and need, as well as hurt, fear, and anger. Each may thus learn to take responsibility for gratifying his own needs.

Honesty comes more easily during this structured separation because the couple now has little to lose. In choosing to face the ultimate loss, risks are taken which would not ordinarily be taken for fear of losing. The knowledge that one can survive financially and emotionally apart from the other and that there are alternative ways of gratifying needs breeds courage. Fears and grievances are expressed; catastrophic expectations of hurt, loss, and guilt are seldom realized. The way is cleared for the more positive feelings. One client stated after a few weeks of structured separation:

> We are talking about everything, and I feel much more free and she more loved. I also no longer feel that divorce would be such a cataclysm that I couldn't do anything that might bring it up. It feels more like a real option now, than like a threat. However, we are both trying now to see that it isn't necessary. In any case it beats lying, and suicidal fantasies, and continual frustration; and on the other hand independence no longer seems so frightening. It feels like a choice between positives now, instead of between a negative and an unknown.

A new relationship evolves out of a multitude of honest choices. This is a "let it happen" rather than a "make it happen" approach. If the couple establishes a new "together-relationship," it will be strongest if each one, being maximally himself and doing and being that which allows him most growth and satisfaction, also meets the other's needs and allows him to grow and be satisfied. Love develops when each satisfies the majority of the other's basic interpersonal needs without sacrificing his own need-satisfaction.

Separation Counseling

During the three-month time period, the separation counselor needs to attend to three major areas: (1) the individuals' response to the separation; (2) the individuals' basic quality of being; (3) the together-relationship.

Response to Separation

I have observed the following pattern among large numbers of separating people in singles groups and in clinical practice. People first experience a *shock reaction*. This is particularly obvious when the separation is sudden and unexpected. Most frequent expressions of this shock are denial and/or somatic disorder. Gastro-intestinal disturbances, headaches, changes in eating patterns, and upper respiratory infections are common. These are best attended to by a physician. The therapist's role is to use the symptom as meaningful content and help the client openly experience the pain rather than denying, avoiding, or internalizing it.

The shock reaction is generally followed by an eight-week to twelve-week *affective cycle*. The first phase of this cycle is characterized by a four-week to six-week period of depression and withdrawal or by a similar period of euphoria and activity. During the following four to six weeks, those who have been depressed and withdrawn usually begin to feel more open and become more active. They seldom go as "high" as the group who were initially euphoric. Those who have at first been euphoric and active tend to withdraw and may become somewhat depressed. Again, the "low" tends to be less intense than that experienced by those initially depressed. This counterreaction gradually shifts and stabilizes at an intermediate affective and activity level. It is on this base that the person can best either grow as a single individual or begin to establish a new dependency relationship.

One of the separation counselor's important functions is to help each client accept himself and the other as each experiences the various phases of this affective cycle. The period of withdrawal represents an unusual opportunity to introspect, to gain strength from one's own reserves, and to resist social pressure to "do something." The withdrawn period represents an opportunity to explore new directions that may be more meaningful than those followed before or during the marriage. This is a time when one may explore, in fantasy, plans to return to school, change employment, or even change careers. The excuse of "If it weren't for you and the marriage, I would have. . . ." is, at least for the moment, not valid. This is a time to confront loneliness and to explore one's own resources. The danger here is that couples will prematurely re-unite in order to avoid pain. The therapist's assurance that this is a time-limited and normal depressive reaction and his encouragement to "go with it" helps clients use this period creatively.

The period of euphoria and activity may be a natural response to the temporary freedom from conflict and the need to make an immediate final decision. People often experience genuine pleasure with their new freedom. However, euphoria may, especially if extreme, represent an avoidance of depression and grief. The individual, the partner, and the children are more accepting of this activity, if it is understood as a separation reaction. The client is encouraged to use his interactions at this time to learn about himself. As he engages in other relationships, he is better able to understand himself, the marriage, and its failure. Repressed anger may pour out during this period of activity. This is particularly true for people who have played "good guy" in the marriage and have "done everything to keep the marriage together." This may also be a time in which the individual puts all of his energies into work. He may be particularly creative at this time, exploring and investing energy in new areas of competence.

Ambivalence is inherent to separation. That the people stayed together at all indicates the existence of some positive value to the relationship. Some needs are still being gratified. The effectiveness and extent to which they gratified each other's needs may be measured by the pain experienced on threat of loss. A great deal of negativity and anger also exists, or the partners would not be separating. Most people find ambivalence difficult to sustain. It represents helplessness and loss of control. To cope with ambivalence requires the ability to tolerate non-structure, frustration, conflict, inconsistency, and simultaneous existence of opposites.

A very common way to cope with ambivalence is to focus on either the positive or negative ends of the spectrum. We find those who profess undying love and idealization of the relationship, despite a history of unhappiness and strife. More commonly, we find people who hate and malign the other and who refuse to recognize the good that was in the relationship. The polarization of attitude is often found among people who have blocked from awareness one or more feeling states. Emotions are used defensively. Thus, those who idealize often are afraid of their anger. Anger may be used to defend against tender feelings. It is often a defense against the pain of loss. Both anger and love may be used to avoid sadness, feelings of helplessness and hopelessness, or the need to face oneself. When therapist and client focus on the missing feelings, a more realistic emotional balance is attained.

Polarization of attitude in addition to being a defense against ambivalence, may also be a symptom of decision-making difficulty. When one cannot easily order data in terms of relative importance, or when one has depended on external events or people to determine one's life-pattern, there is a tendency to focus inappropriately on one aspect of a complex whole. The distorted view of the whole thus produced tends to make whatever decision one makes a necessity—a foregone conclusion.

Maintaining appropriate ambivalence puts parents in closer touch with their children. Children in a separating family generally maintain their mixed feelings. The problem of divided loyalties is minimized when parental attitudes and feelings remain balanced and realistic. Parents who can tolerate ambivalence are less prone to communicate feelings through their children or to force an emotional position on their children.

This eight-week to twelve-week affective cycle forms the basis for the three-month time period found to be necessary for effective separation counseling. Both phases of this cycle represent adaptive reactions to the situation. Decisions made during this reactive period are often the result of such factors as relief that the pain of conflict is over, or fear of the unknown, shame, and sense of failure. After the period of reaction to the past relationship and the separation situation, and after the individuals have used this time to fully assess themselves and their ways of being together, they can make decisions based on their present needs and value systems. Premature return to the marriage is avoided, as a premature and perhaps unnecessary separation.

The Individual's Basic Quality of Being

How the individual functions in general, aside from the specific separation situation, is an important area in separation counseling, as in any therapeutic system. In separation counseling, emphasis is placed on the following factors: dependency and control needs and conflicts, the range of feelings available to the individual and how they are expressed, risk-taking behavior, ways of coping with loss, reactions to freedom, value systems. Focus here is more on individual growth and development than on the relationship.

Dependency and control patterns and conflicts become quite clear when the person on whom one has depended and controlled—or has been controlled by—is gone. These patterns become increasingly apparent in the new tasks for which each partner is now responsible, the way in which each accepts responsibility for himself, and what each seeks in others to supplement or complement his own perceived inadequacies.

During these three months the counselor helps the individuals to perceive and accept dependency and control needs and to find growth promoting ways to satisfy them. The value of an equal and interdependent relationship is stressed. Manipulative maneuvers to insure security and control are discouraged; honest communication of needs and the willingness to gratify needs are encouraged.

An inability to experience and express the full range of *feelings* may have been an important factor contributing to the marital crisis. Emotional limitations will affect subsequent relationships. This time of stress is extremely valuable for opening long-closed emotional channels. Separation involves the arousal of a complex set of emotions. Some positive feeling is there, whether it be love, the memory of love, liking, or need. Sadness or grief is a natural concomitant of loss. Anger is always present as a response to the hurt and frustration of basic needs that bring people to the point of separation. Anger is a common response to the problems that accompanying adapting to new ways of living. Fear almost always accompanies risk, and risk is an essential ingredient of change. People often experience some sense of helplessness and hopelessness. Many individuals find separation especially difficult because they remain hopeful when such hope is not warranted. Feelings of guilt and shame are also generally present.

The effective separation counselor is aware of "missing" emotions. He helps individuals (a) perceive their lack, (b) understand how other feelings or thoughts are inappropriately substituted, and (c) develop an awareness of, and willingness to, in some way deal with those feelings previously repressed. Often such repression is accomplished by creating a fantasy image of oneself, the other, or the relationship. Such "defensive fantasies" do help the individual avoid certain feelings; they also prevent effective problem solving. Thus, fantasy is replaced by the awareness of the reality of the situation. With this reality as base, most problems and differences are easily resolved and the choice of leaving or maintaining the relationship is more easily made.

Risk-taking is inherent in the process of change that accompanies separation. The more risks one takes, the more opportunity for growth. This is a time for choice, change, and freedom. This is the time to "do your thing" honestly and openly: to "do nothing" during the depressed/withdrawn time; to engage the world in new ways during expansive times. This is a time when one can intensely experience every facet of existence.

Separation involves *role change*. Individuals change from marriage roles to single roles, perhaps from housewife to worker, from full-time parent to part-time parent, from accepted partner to rejected partner. Newly separated persons must cope with the loss of old roles and "trained" reciprocal role-players. They must meet new role expectations and behavior.

Sometimes people who separate change their lives so extensively that they establish new roles and new role patterns. Or, they may maintain their former role patterns but find new people or situations to play the reciprocal role (i.e. a "helper" needs someone to "help"; a dependent person needs someone to depend upon). In any event they must experience some disequilibrium while these patterns are in flux. The extent of distress experienced in making these role changes depends on the kinds of risk each takes and how gracefully and appropriately transitions are made.

Risk and change automatically involve *loss*. Each loss needs to be recognized as such and some consideration made of the meaning to the individual of the pattern and relationship lost, of his feelings about the loss, and how he goes about replacing the loss. Losses need to be mourned and thus made "finished business" (Tobin, 1971). The process by which one deals with loss is fully as important as establishing new behaviors, attitudes, roles, feelings, or relationships to replace the old. How change is accomplished is as important as what change is made. Equally important is an awareness of reluctance to change and to risk. If one does not want to risk the unknown, one can gain much by learning to accept that to which one clings.

Separation makes new *freedom* suddenly available. Freedom can be frightening. Fear of freedom and its accompanying responsibility is found especially among individuals who need an external object for support, projection, or control. Many couples separate in the belief that the other is restricting freedom to experience life fully. Others cling to a relationship to avoid this freedom. Awareness of each individual's ability to use freedom at this time is helpful in alleviating conflict, clarifying dependency and control patterns, and the limitations each individual places on himself.

Value systems change over a period of years, but the changes are often not defined. Thus, for example, a couple may begin marriage with home and children agreed upon as a primary value. One partner may change and begin to place career or money above his family. Values placed on openness vs. secrecy, flexibility vs. rigidity, monogamy vs. sexual freedom, permissive vs. authoritarian child rearing often change for one and not the other. Or, it may be that before marriage, the couple did not believe that differences in these value dimensions were important. Making the individuals' values explicit helps both understand the basis for some conflicts. It also helps individuals make decisions, take risks, and clarify life goals.

The Together-Relationship

The separation counselor attends both to the way the couple interacts during joint sessions and to the number and the quality of contacts outside the counselor's office. The counselor works with them as he would in any joint therapy situation. In addition, he remains aware of the separation process and the way in which each is coping with it. He shares his awareness with the couple so that they may understand and work with separation-related behaviors in proper context. The time-commitment structure gives the counselor, as well as the couple, the opportunity to work through situations which otherwise would very likely precipitate divorce (i.e., being open about sexual relationships with others). In the course of the three months, some couples continue to communicate, work through their differences, and learn more satisfactory patterns of mutual need gratification. By the end of the time, they choose to be together more often than they choose to be apart. They have proportionately more positive than negative interactions. These couples make a new together-relationship. Other couples spend enough time together to explore their relationship and to understand each other, and yet their time together leaves them unfulfilled. They tend to choose to be apart more often than they are together. At the end of the three-month period, they generally agree to finalize their separation. Some couples continue to be together more often than they are apart, but important conflicts remain unresolved. These couples may make a commitment to another period of structured separation, or they may structure a time-limited trial together-relationship. In the latter case, they are asked to make their own contract setting forth what each expects of the other and what each is willing to give to the other. Counseling continues until the couple are comfortable with a decision to come together or to part.

In a one-year follow-up of eighteen couples who completed structured separation with counseling six re-instated their marriage and were satisfied with the new relationship; twelve were divorced. Of these twelve, only one couple needed legal help in making a property settlement. All but one of the couples have maintained good feelings toward each other, and all felt they had made the right choice. One extremely dependent, border-line pychotic man experienced some disorganization of function for several months after finalizing the separation. The other twenty-three separating individuals had gained equilibrium as single people by the end of the time they agreed to finalize their separation.

Summary

Structured separation with counseling offers couples in conflict a method by which they can use the separation crisis to maximize growth. Couples commit themselves to a three-month period during which they agree to certain basic guidelines: to live apart; not to make any binding legal, financial, or child-custody arrangements; to be together only by *choice*. Prime importance is placed on values of choice, risk, and honesty.

By focusing on both individuals' reactions to separation, their personality structures, and their evolving together-relationship, a counselor's interventions help each partner through the various phases of the separation process.

At the end of the three-month period, people generally have a firm understanding of themselves and their relationship. The decision whether to finalize the separation or re-institute the together-relationship tends to evolve out of the time and counseling structure.

REFERENCES

Parad, J. (1965), *Crisis Intervention: Selected Readings*. New York, Family Services Association of America.
Tobin, S. (1971), "Saying Goodbye in Gestalt Therapy," *Psychotherapy*, 8:150-155.

RICHARD M. EISLER
MICHEL HERSEN

20   Behavioral Crisis Intervention Techniques

Behavioral techniques in short-term family-oriented crisis intervention treatment are examined within the context of crisis theory and behavior modification. It is noted that both approaches emphasize the importance of environmental influences in developing and maintaining maladaptive behaviors. Methods for restructuring discordant family relationships through the use of particular behavioral techniques such as feedback, modeling, behavioral rehearsal, instructions, and behavioral contracts are outlined. Three case studies are presented to illustrate the therapeutic flexibility of these techniques with crisis-prone families. Not only are families helped with presenting complaints, but a major emphasis is placed on their learning more successful problem solving skills that are to be implemented in daily interactions.

During the past decade the mental health profession has witnessed rapid development of several alternatives to purely psychodynamic formulations of behavioral maladjustment. In the traditional model the focus has been on intrapsychic abnormalities such as excessive anxiety, poor impulse control, characterological defects, etc., in understanding psychopathology. However, increasing attention is now being paid to patterns of response within the social environment in maintaining maladaptive interactive behavior.

The use of selected positive and negative environmental consequences (operant conditioning) in changing the behavior of psychiatric patients was first tested experimentally by Lindsley (1956, 1969) and Lindsley and Skinner

(1954). Principles of reinforcement derived from theories of operant conditioning were subsequently applied to clinically relevant problems by Ayllon and his associates (1963, 1965, 1968, 1962). Since then numerous other behavioral techniques have been applied to develop and maintain more desirable behavior in a broad range of psychiatric patients. Included among these techniques are feedback, instructions, behavior rehearsal, assertive training, modeling, and behavioral contracting.

Another clinical approach focusing on the relationship of adverse environmental and interpersonal stresses to development of psychopathology has been termed crisis intervention. (Eisler and Polak, 1971; Hill, 1958; Lindemann, 1944; Parad and Caplan, 1960). The goal of crisis intervention, encompassing a variety of therapeutic techniques, is to rapidly assess and treat psychological disequilibrium within the natural social environment. While treatment of the immediate social milieu typifies an approach previously utilized by family therapists of varying persuasions, crisis intervention focuses more on the immediate psychosocial precipitants of disorganization.

Concepts of Crisis

The significance of life crises related to increased vulnerability to acute impairment and enduring behavioral disorder was vividly depicted in Lindemann's[10] classic study of bereaved disaster victims whose relatives died in the tragic Coconut Grove fire in Boston. Caplan and his associates (1960, 1964, 1965) subsequently formulated a view of crisis as a transitional period during which a variety of environmental stresses (e.g., death, divorce, illness, premature birth, financial difficulty) created problems of such magnitude that the individual was unable to use his normal coping skills. Thus, the course of the individual's interaction with his natural environment at strategic points was implicated in the development of unadaptive behavioral patterns. Crisis intervention, then, according to these writers involves treatment directed towards helping the individual grapple with and overcome real life stresses.

In discussing a framework for treatment of families in crisis, previous writers have borrowed from individually oriented theories. By contrast, Atherton et al (1971) discuss functional vs. dysfunctional role behaviors within a social system in terms of how satisfying they are on a reciprocal basis to individual members. They argue that:

.... the ideal state of affairs would exist when persons live with each other in a state of mutually satisfying interdependence in which those persons are able to achieve the maximum goal attainment and personal satisfaction in their relationships with each other and their institutional systems.

With respect to crisis intervention in social systems, Jones and Polak (1968) and Polak[16] recommend confrontation of individuals within the system in terms of the mutual problems. It is also suggested that the therapist facilitate expression of emotion relative to the crisis as well as assisting family members to reorganize their roles around critical issues. In assessing inadequate crisis coping behavior, Polak (1971) underscores the failure of leadership within the system, role conflict, and the reinforcement of maladaptive behavior.

Behavioral Approaches to Crisis Intervention

From the above discussion it appears that crisis intervention, focusing on the immediate social and environmental precipitants of disturbed family functioning, might provide behaviorally oriented clinicians a useful framework within which to apply specific techniques based on social learning theory. Therefore, the remainder of this paper will be directed towards an examination of the role of behavioral techniques in family-oriented crisis intervention. The use of particular behavioral methods in the rapid restructuring of the family system will be outlined.

Three major goals of a behavioral approach to family crisis situations will be described:

1. A primary goal is to develop new problem solving or coping behavior within the family to help members resolve the precipitating problem successfully. Instead of continuing antagonistic relationships between members of the family system, the objective is to generate cooperative behavior through a program of mutual reinforcement.

2. A second goal involves the expression of both positive and negative affect with respect to the precipitating problem. Effective communication of emotion appears to be very useful in problem solving when it is expressed appropriately and in amounts relative to the eliciting stimulus.

3. A final goal is to assist the family in the application of newly developed coping skills to other conflict-ridden situations. Not only must the family deal with the immediate crisis, but family members must learn how to use their newly acquired methods of problem solving in a variety of areas. This is known as generalization or positive transfer in learning theory parlance.

In the following sections specific behavioral techniques, as they apply to the crisis intervention model, will be described in some detail.

Feedback

Feedback, or information given to patients about the nature and effects of their behavior, appears to be an important but not fully understood element in both psychodynamic and behavioral approaches to psychotherapy. The administration of feedback to patients regarding specific aspects of their behavior has proven to effect positive changes in relevant target behaviors under study (Bernhardt *et al.*, 1972; Elkin *et al.*, 1973; Leitenberg *et al.*, 1968).

With families experiencing a crisis, present clinical experience suggests that immediate feedback on their present modes of communication is often a prerequisite to changing the family's interaction patterns. Feedback in the form of therapist comments, role playing, or videotape replays of interactive sequences can all be used to give individuals information as to how their behavior affects other family members. It can also be used to show the family, as a unit, its difficulties in effective problem solving behavior. For example, some families are so conflict avoidant that they discuss everything imaginable except their most difficult problems. Other families delay problem solving attempts until so much excess emotion is aroused that effective discussion is impossible. Still other families place the entire burden of a family problem on a particular individual (often the identified patient) instead of sharing the responsibility among all members. Additionally, feedback can be used to point out confused or inconsistent communications within the family. Confusion often results when there is a discrepancy between the verbal and nonverbal aspects of a communication. The purpose of initial feedback, therefore, is to clarify precisely what is effective and what is ineffective about the family's problem solving communications.

Modeling and Role Playing

Modeling is a technique based on principles of imitative learning. When used in combination with feedback and instructions, the necessity of the individual's discovering the most effective response through trial and error is eliminated. The research literature indicates that imitating the behavior of a model has been useful in developing functional behaviors where serious deficits exist. Moreover, surplus conditioned responses have also been eliminated through modeling procedures. For example Lovaas *et. al.* (1967) used modeling in combination with reinforcement to develop language functions in autistic children. Bandura *et. al.* (1967) demonstrated the effectiveness of modeling in eliminating a maladaptive fear of dogs in young children. This was accomplished by having them observe a peer fearlessly interacting with the animals with no adverse effects.

Clinical experience with families evidencing repeated crises related to poor interpersonal functioning reveals that members are grossly deficient in their expression of affect. Either no affect is expressed or a surplus of expressed emotion is elicited by a seemingly innocuous stimulus. A further characteristic of families experiencing crises involves their rigid and stereotypic responses to one another. Often they are unable to implement alternative responses when instructed by their therapist. Rather than blaming the family for deficient motivation or ascribing the persistence of maladaptive functioning to masochistic or sadistic needs, it becomes necessary for the therapist to demonstrate alternative modes of interaction by using himself or another family member to model more adaptive responses. A number of advantages accrue as a result of using modeling techniques in dealing with a family crisis: (1) It interrupts stagnant and nonproductive forms of interaction; (2) it demonstrates precisely the verbal and nonverbal aspects of new responses; (3) family members are able to obtain some appreciation of the facilitating effects of new behaviors by observing the reactions elicited from other members; and (4) resistance to developing a different response repertoire is decreased by virtue of emulating the therapist, who presumably is a respected source of authority.

Behavioral Rehearsal

Behavioral rehearsal is a procedure whereby more desirable responses to interpersonal conflict situations are practiced under the supervision of the therapist (Lazarus, 1966). The technique is often used as an adjunct to modeling and role playing. Behavioral rehearsal is often employed in assertive training whereby both positive and negative affective responses are practiced under therapeutic direction. In the therapy of crisis situations modeling may precede the use of behavioral rehearsal. After exposure to a model's handling of crisis relevant issues, family members might be guided into a behavioral rehearsal of new modes of communication. A variety of hypothetical crisis-like situations might also be presented to the family for their solution under therapeutic guidance. Feedback in the form of commentary by the therapist is then given to family members. At times, additional modeling may be needed until effective problem solving responses are attained and become part of the family member's behavioral repertoire.

Achieving Reciprocal Reinforcement in Families

A recent study by Eisler and Polak (1971) showed that nearly one half of all patients accepted for treatment on a psychiatric crisis facility displayed severe family problems underlying their requests for admission. One third of all admissions involved separation of family members or threat of imminent separation. We have observed that problems which lead to threat of separation, divorce, child runaways, etc., occur in families that offer almost no rewards or satisfaction for participation in family life. As Stuart (1969) points out in his discussion of unsuccessful marriages: ". . . few positive rewards are dispensed; positive reinforcement as a strategy for behavioral control is replaced with negative reinforcement (removal of an aversive event following the expected response)." Given the extremely low rates of reciprocal social reinforcement occurring in crisis-prone families, the ability of family members to cope with additional stresses such as financial difficulty, illness, or natural environmental problems is extremely limited. The family's difficulty in working together to solve its common problems leads to an acceleration of aversive strategies of behavioral control (e.g., threats, criticism, withdrawal). These strategies are unlikely to succeed as they obscure present problems, generate further aversive counter-behaviors, and alienate family members. A family crisis of this nature offers the therapist a situation which is amenable to a program of positive reinforcement. His therapeutic task involves an immediate restructuring of the family system by teaching individual members methods of increasing their rates of reciprocal positive reinforcement. Techniques for achieving reciprocity will be examined in the next two sections.

Instructions

In some cases instructions to families with respect to the use of reciprocal social reinforcement has led to significant therapeutic improvement. A first step in teaching families the benefits of positive reinforcement requires an explanation as to why this method should be effective. Since the family is well practiced in aversive strategies, some examples and demonstration of the effects of reciprocal reinforcement are warranted. A next step involves the clarification of needs and expectations of discordant family members. Not only should this be stated in precise behavioral terminology, but specific rewards or reinforcers for each family member should be clearly outlined. For example, a wife might state that she would like her husband to spend one-half hour each evening chatting about the day's events instead of his reading the evening paper in total disregard of her presence. Conversely, the husband may articulate his dislike of frozen dinners and might expect a "home-cooked" meal in return for his attentiveness.

Instructions in positive strategies of behavioral control lead to improved interpersonal functioning. These kinds of instructions serve to facilitate self-observation with respect to frequency of emitting reinforcing behaviors. In the more difficult cases it is often useful for individuals to actually record frequency of reinforcers obtained and issued to others. In other cases instructions to monitor instances of reinforcing behavior may, in themselves, facilitate increased rates of reciprocal reinforcement. Instructions on reinforcement also elicit the expectation that it is possible to change the behavior of other family members by first altering one's own behavior. If family members carry out instructions to reinforce one another contingent upon performance of desirable behavior, the increases in reciprocal cooperative behavior should be apparent to them in a relatively short time. However, the ultimate goal is that naturally occurring contingencies should take over once a sufficiently high degree of reciprocity has been achieved.

Behavioral Contracts

When crises occur in families where coercive problem solving strategies are employed to the exclusion of positive incentives, behavorial contracts are useful in developing an exchange of positive reinforcement among family members. Since members of these families perceive each other with mutual distrust on the basis of past failures to perform role obligations, it becomes necessary to provide some immediate reinforcing consequences for constructive problem solving behaviors. Specifically, a behavioral contract is a negotiated agreement detailing in writing the conditions under which individual X will do something for individual Y. It therefore makes explicit the relationship between an individual's functional behavior and the social consequences for that behavior. For example, a contract might specify that if the father returns home by 6 PM and spends one-half hour helping his son with his homework, the wife will then cook his favorite meal, and the son will perform specified chores. Family contractual agreements have been described in some detail by Patterson (1971). Such contracts have been used successfully in developing reciprocal reinforcement patterns in dysfunctional marriages (Stuart, 1969), in strengthening community control over the behavior of delinquents (Stuart, 1971), and in modifying drinking behavior in an alcoholic (Miller, in press). Some contracts specify the use of points or tokens that are earned contingently upon performance of outlined behaviors. Points and tokens are then exchangeable for previously specified reinforcers at some future time.

A major advantage of behavioral contracts is that role expectations of family members are clearly applied to observable behavior. Thus, when contracts are enacted, they reduce the amount of nonproductive verbal exchanges over failure of individuals to carry out prescribed roles. Instead of a father raging at his adolescent son for being lazy and stupid while the son retorts that father is "up tight" and rigid, a negotiated contract might specify an exchange whereby the son will be allotted use of the family automobile upon achieving good grades and upon completion of specific duties. The negotiation of contracts teaches crisis prone families the principles of compromise and reciprocal positive reinforcement as being effective methods of mediating interpersonal discord. Trust and positive feelings among family members are increased when particular behaviors are reciprocally reinforced in accordance with contractual clauses. With the implementation of behavioral contracting in crisis prone families, an attempt is made to rapidly modify behavior of family members, with an expectation that attitude change will follow.

Report of Cases

The use of behavioral techniques in crisis-oriented family intervention will be illustrated in three case presentations. In each case one of us and a psychology intern served as co-therapists.

Case 1

The Jones were a middle-class couple in their early 40s. Both had been married before. The major problem originated when Tom, Mr. Jones' 16-year-old son, came to live with the couple following the death of his natural mother two years prior to our intervention. Shortly after Tom's arrival, Mrs. Jones developed symptoms of nervousness, depression, crying spells, and "hysterical" temper outbursts. She had received individual psychotherapy, tranquilizers, antidepressants, and electroconvulsive shock treatment to no avail. When the Jones came to the Medical School Clinic their marriage was near dissolution, precipitated by Mrs. Jones' ultimatum that Tom leave the house, or she would file for divorce.

During the first treatment session, the Jones were requested to reenact a typical family conflict while being videotaped. The following scene was then obtained: "Tom had failed to return home at the appointed time for supper and had not telephoned as to his whereabouts. When he finally arrived Mrs. Jones displayed a temper outburst in which she accused the boy of being selfish and inconsiderate. Tom offered a rather weak excuse that he forgot his watch, but it was delivered rather defiantly. Mr. Jones angrily denounced his wife as being an oversensitive neurotic who never gave Tom a chance to explain. Mrs. Jones then directed her rage toward Mr. Jones while Tom excused himself from the dinner table. The scene ended with Mrs. Jones in tears and Mr. Jones leaving the table complaining that he was not appreciated at home."

The family was given videotape and verbal feedback with their attention focused on the aversive series of attacks which escalated the conflict. Mrs. Jones was specifically shown how her coercive attempts to obtain cooperation from Tom and her husband eventuated in their withdrawal. Tom was shown how his passivity increased Mrs. Jones' anger. It was pointed out to Mr. Jones that his counterattack method of defending his son offered no chance of solution to the problem. Inasmuch as Mrs. Jones was unable to approach her withdrawn and negativistic stepson, and in light of Mr. Jones' inability to mediate the conflict, the therapists modeled more positive strategies designed to elicit cooperation and problem-solving behavior. One of the therapists, in the role of Mrs. Jones, portrayed a mother who, despite her irritation at her son's tardiness for dinner, was able to convey some feelings of warmth for the boy. While modeling these responses, the therapist was able to elicit some conciliatory reactions from Tom. At that point Mrs. Jones, without the aid of role playing, was able to deal more appropriately with Tom about his being late. The second therapist, role playing Mr. Jones, then modeled the part of an active mediator. He pointed out to Mrs. Jones that she had a right to expect her stepson to be home on time for dinner, but that he did not approve of her methods in coping with the problem. A solution based on reinforcement principles was then presented by the model. Tom was to notify the family of his whereabouts should he be detained. Failure to do so would result in his losing weekend privileges. Following this rather successful demonstration of problem solving techniques, the Jones were requested to tackle other potential conflict situations at home.

Towards the conclusion of ten sessions, the therapists' participation in demonstrating positive strategies of control was markedly decreased. A follow-up visit three months after termination of treatment revealed that newly developed problem solving skills were sufficiently reinforcing to all family members to be self-sustaining.

Case 2

Mr. and Mrs. Mann were an upper-middle class couple with five young sons ranging from 2 to 12 years of age. They previously underwent one year of marital counseling with little apparent success. The crisis that precipitated their referral to the Medical School Clinic was a suicide attempt by Mrs. Mann following her husband's attentiveness to an amorous divorcee at a party.

An analysis of the Manns' interaction revealed that Mrs. Mann had an endless list of complaints about her husband's lack of family involvement. During repeated interchanges it was noted that Mr. Mann displayed two types of passive-avoidance modes of reacting to her complaints. At times he agreed that she was justified in her criticisms, but failed to modify his behavior. Other times he withdrew from the discussion. However, both tactics increased Mrs. Mann's rate of complaining. Mr. Mann, on the other hand, pointed out that whenever he attempted involvement with the family (activities with the children), Mrs. Mann invariably criticized his efforts.

The preceding suggested a negative pattern of interaction involving the wife's coercive attempts to obtain positive reinforcement (attention or help with the children) from her husband. He had intermittently reinforced her aversive nagging by verbally agreeing to most of her demands while actually fulfilling very few. She however, punished his few positive attempts by being critical, thus resulting in his withdrawal and attempts to seek reinforcement outside the family. This sequence, repeated numerous times over the years, led to a relationship in which positive reinforcement from marital interaction was virtually absent. Therefore, it was decided to immediately restructure the marital relationship through a focus on specific behaviors with instructions based on principles of positive reinforcement.

In cases where there is a long history of negative expectations confirmed by deficient performance, we have found it useful to initially program the spouses to perform one or two positively reinforcing behaviors for one another. When this is accomplished on a reciprocal basis it then becomes possible to alter the chain of negative consequences. More specifically, Mr. Mann was instructed to return home at a designated time each evening. He was permitted one late night per week providing that he telephone Mrs. Mann in advance. Upon his return at home Mr. Mann was expected to spend one-half hour with his wife in conversation of a topic of her choice. In exchange, it was agreed that Mrs. Mann would prepare her husband's breakfast each morning. To ensure cooperation, the Manns were informed that continuation in treatment with us was contingent upon their performance of these homework assignments throughout the week. After this program was in effect for two weeks the bitter antagonism between the Manns had decreased to the extent that other more meaningful exchanges of reinforcing behavior could now take place.

During the course of treatment both Mr. and Mrs. Mann required brief assertive training focused on their expressing needs, expectations, and disagreements in more direct fashion. At the conclusion of eight weeks of treatment the Manns were responding more openly and more positively to each other.

Case 3

Mr. and Mrs. Roan, their 24-year-old married daughter Susan, and 16-year-old son Robert were seen in the Medical Center Clinic following an initial contact by Mr. Roan. During the course of routine history taking Mr. Roan, a 52-year-old computer programmer, described himself as being perfectionistic at work. However, he expressed concerned about the adequacy of his performance despite the fact that his supervisors were apparently satisfied with him. He felt that he had a good relationship with his family, but admitted that his son Robert was a disappointment to him. Robert apparently was only a mediocre student in high school which frustrated Mr. Roan's plans to send him to a good college.

In the first family session Mr. Roan expressed guilt feelings that he had failed in his paternal duties. Mrs. Roan was tearful throughout and evidenced an overprotective attitude towards Robert. Susan expressed her view that the family had done everything possible for Robert. Robert in turn was sullen and uncommunicative.

A rapid assessment of family interactions revealed two major problems. The first involved the family's inability to express angry feelings in a direct fashion. Unexpressed hostility was obviously compounded by Robert's recent arrest. Secondly, Robert probably had been scapegoated for other family problems which were not immediately in evidence. The initial strategy, then, was to elicit and reinforce expression of feelings related to specific events that had led to the present crisis. Some expression of anger was elicited by therapist feedback on family members' nonverbal communications of anger (e.g., Robert's pouting or Mr. Roan's sarcastic tone of voice). This was followed by Mrs. Roan and Susan expressing their feelings that Robert frequently "let the family down." In addition, they felt that Mr. Roan displayed an overly "strict" attitude toward Robert. However, at this point, the two major protagonists, Robert and Mr. Roan, were still not communicating effectively with each other. As Mr. Roan became increasingly comfortable in challenging his son, Robert withdrew or made irrelevant statements. The two therapists then modeled an interaction sequence for the two whereby both positive and negative feelings were expressed. Observation of the models resulted in a less heated dialogue between Robert and Mr. Roan. Mr. Roan was now able to express both affection and disappointment towards his son. Robert expressed a good deal of anger towards his father as being overly critical. Moreover, he pointed out to his father that he never really attended to any of his communications. Mr. Roan was surprised and apparently pleased by some of the points made by Robert, and he encouraged the boy to continue. In a later sequence, Susan was prompted and then reinforced by the therapists for mediating a conflict between her father and mother.

Six family treatment sessions were held over a three-week period. During the course of these meetings this family learned how to express both positive and negative feelings in a constructive fashion. There were indications that gains seen during treatment sessions generalized to the home situation, particularly with respect to improved communications among family members. At the conclusion of treatment Mr. Roan's symptoms had subsided and plans were being made for Robert to enter a trade school. The family was followed via telephone over the next three months, during which time they continued to make progress through their own initiatives.

Comment

With increasing attention being given to short-term crisis-oriented treatment, new and more flexible therapeutic techniques are required. Of necessity these techniques cannot be based primarily on an intense one-to-one therapeutic relationship where the development of insight and gross personality change is expected. Instead, crisis theorists and practitioners have found it more useful to concentrate therapeutic efforts toward an immediate restructuring of deficient interpersonal interactions within a designated target social system. As the family learns more effective means of functioning, therapeutic intervention is gradually diminished until the system is functioning successfully on its own.

The feasibility of using behavioral techniques within the crisis framework is of recent origin. Balson, (1971) in a case study, described the flexibility of a variety of behavioral techniques in the rapid and successful treatment of an individual "crisis" patient. In this connection, behaviorists have shown considerable ingenuity, in tailoring specific techniques to the needs of individual patients. In the last few years, there is also a growing interest in applying behavioral techniques to the more complex interactive behaviors of couples, families, and other social systems (Stuart, 1969; Stuart, 1971; Tharp and Wetzel, 1969; Liberman, 1970; Lazarus, 1971; Friedman, 1971).

As we have endeavored to point out in the case illustrations, a preliminary step in restructuring faulty interactions of a family in crisis involves a rapid behavioral assessment of current interactive difficulties. This is best accomplished through an in vivo elicitation of the family's present coping or problem solving skills. While family members are interacting around a particular issue, therapist participation should be minimal. In some cases we have observed the interactions through a one-way mirror in order to avoid influencing naturally occurring behavior. Following the elicitation of coercive, aversive, passive-avoidant, or other relatively unsuccessful modes of interaction, family members are first offered feedback with respect to their modes of dealing with one another and are taught more appropriate interactive patterns. This relearning process proceeds in a number of overlapping states, in that feedback is alternated with the teaching of new behavioral repertoires.

In this approach it is assumed that individual family members are unable to function more successfully as they do not possess requisite interactive skills. Therefore, new interactional sequences are shaped through combinations of instructions and feedback on successive performances. Imitation of therapist models facilitates development of more successful interactive responses. Verbal reinforcement from the therapist, reciprocal reinforcement from other family members, and contractual arrangements ensure the continuation of newly acquired behavioral patterns. Not only are specific issues resolved during treatment sessions, but family members learn strategies that will permit smoother resolution of additional problems that may occur in the future. Although the generalization of problem solving skills is seen to occur naturally in some families, the vast majority require both supervised practice in the office and specified assignments that are to be carried out in the home.

REFERENCES

Atherton, C.R., S.T. Mitchell, and E.B. Schein (1971), "Locating Points for Intervention," *Social Casework,* 52:131-141.
Ayllon, T. (1963), "Intensive Treatment of Psychotic Behavior by Stimulus Satiation and Food Reinforcement," *Behavior Research and Therapy,* 1:53-61.
_____and N.H. Azrin (1965), "The Measurement and Reinforcement of Behavior of Psychotics," *Journal of the Experimental Analysis of Behavior,*

8:357-383.

_____(1968), *The Token Economy: A Motivational System for Therapy and Rehabilitation*. New York: Appleton-Century-Crofts.

_____and E. Haughton (1962), "Control of the Behavior of Schizophrenic Patients by Food," *Journal of the Experimental Analysis of Behavior*, 5:343-352.

Balson, P.M. (1971), "The Use of Behavior Therapy Techniques in Crisis Intervention: A Case Report," *Journal of Behavior Therapy and Experimental Psychiatry*, 2:297-300.

Bandura, A., E.J. Grusec, and F.L. Menlove (1967), "Vicarious Extinction of Avoidance Behavior," *Journal of Personality and Social Psychology*, 5:16-23.

Bernhardt, A.J., M. Hersen, and D.H. Barlow (1972), "Measurement and Modification of Spasmodic Torticollis: An Experimental Analysis," *Behavior Therapy*, 3:294-297.

Caplan, G. (1964), *Principles of Preventive Psychiatry*. New York: Basic Books.

_____, E.A. Mason, and D.M. Kaplan (1965), "Four Studies of Crisis in Parents of Prematures," *Community Mental Health Journal*, 1:149-161.

Eisler, R.M., and P. Polak (1971), "Social Stress and Psychiatric Disorder," *Journal of Nervous and Mental Disease*, 153:227-233.

Elkin, T., *et al.* (1973), "Modification of Caloric Intake in Anorexia Nervosa: An Experimental Analysis," *Psychological Reports*, 32:75-78.

Hill, R. (1958), "Social Stresses on the Family: Generic Features of Families Under Stress," *Social Casework*, 39:139-150.

Jones, M., and P. Polak (1968), "Crisis and Confrontation," *British Journal of Psychiatry*, 25:110-117.

Lazarus, A.A. (1966), "Behavioral Research vs. Non-directive vs. Advice in Effecting Behavior Change," *Behavior Research and Therapy*, 4:209-212.

_____(1971), *Behavior Therapy and Beyond*. New York: McGraw-Hill Book Co.

Leitenberg, H., *et al.* (1968), "Feedback in Behavior Modification: An Experimental Analysis in Two Phobic Cases," *Journal of Applied Behavior Analysis*, 1:131-137.

Liberman, R.P. (1970), "Behavioral Approaches to Family and Couple Therapy," *American Journal of Orthopsychiatry*, 40:106-118.

Lindemann, E. (1944), "Symptomatology and Management of Acute Grief," *American Journal of Psychiatry*, 101:141-148.

Lindsley, O.R. (1956), "Operant Conditioning Methods Applied to Research in Chronic Schizophrenia," *Psychiatric Research Reports of the American Psychiatric Association*, 5:118-153.

_____(1960), "Characteristics of the Behavior of Chronic Psychotics as Revealed by Free Operant Conditioning Methods," *Diseases of the Nervous System*, 21:66-78.

_____and B.F. Skinner (1954), "A Method for the Experimental Analysis of the Behavior of Psychotic Patients," *American Psychologist*, 9:419-420.

Lovass, O.I., *et al.* (1967), "The Establishment of Imitation and Its Use for the Development of Complex Behavior in Schizophrenic Children," *Behavior Research and Therapy*, 5:171-181.

Miller, P.M. (in press), "The Use of Behavioral Contracting in the Treatment of Alcoholism: A Case Study," *Behavior Therapy*.

Parad, H.J., and G. Caplan (1960), "A Framework for Studying Families in Crisis," *Social Work*, 5:3-15.

Patterson, G.R. (1971), *Families: Applications of Social Learning to Family*

*Life.*Champaign, Ill.: Research Press.
Stuart, R.B. (1969), "Operant-Interpersonal Treatment for Marital Discord," *Journal of Consulting and Clinical Psychology,* 33:675-682.
_____(1971), "Behavioral Contracting Within the Families of Delinquents," *Journal of Behavior Therapy and Experimental Psychiatry,* 2:1-11.
Tharp, R.G., and R.J. Wetzel (1969), *Behavior Modification in the Natural Environment.* New York: Academic Press.

III

The Effects of Marital Therapy

INTRODUCTION

As we have seen in Part II, there have been many exciting recent technical and conceptual innovations in the clinical practice of marital therapy. These developments have been paralleled by a much-needed increased awareness of the significant value issues inherent in the description and definition of the "quality" of marital relationships (Laws, 1971; Sussman, 1972). Both of these influences appear to have stimulated applied research efforts. Part III provides an overview of research on the results, or effectiveness, of marital therapy and of some of the variables which may influence the outcome of couples therapy.

Historical Influences on the Present Status of Marital Therapy Research

As elaborated in greater detail elsewhere in this volume (Olson, Chapter 1), marital therapy has been both blessed and cursed by its multidisciplinary heritage. While the extensive interplay and exchange among psychiatrists, psychologists, sociologists, social workers, and others has been almost unique to this domain of therapeutic intervention, these disciplines have not always been the most compatible of bedfellows. Status differences between these disciplines and, at times, between subgroups within the same professional discipline, have often yielded rather arbitrary territorial prescriptions and definitions of "appropriate" role-functions which have not been in the ultimate best interests of married couples in distress. Social "casework," for example, which for a long time has involved direct service to couples in conflict, has, for all intents and purposes, never been elevated to the status of "therapeutic" intervention by most psychologists and psychiatrists. Similarly, the specialty of counseling psychology (Thompson and Super, 1964) has faced the assertions of clinical psychologists that counselors do not and, in fact, should not, practice "real" psychotherapy. Finally, the postwar conflicts between psychiatry and psychology-as-a-whole with regard to the "right" to engage in direct therapeutic service need no documentation.

Perhaps the most unfortunate result of such professional denials of the competence of "others" to do what they already do or wish to begin to do has been the underutilization of the special skills each discipline has to offer to other disciplines in fostering viable and effective approaches to dealing with marital disharmony. To date, the ultimate cost has been the failure of these many talented people to collaboratively assess and empirically examine the outcome of their marital therapy methods, which, in substance, probably have been more alike than different.

Finally, it should be noted that clinical psychology, the discipline which has had the longest and most intensive involvement in doing research in psychotherapy, has only very recently turned its attention to investigating therapeutic change in marital and family systems.

The point at issue in all of this, as we see it, is not one of *who* should do marital therapy, but one of *what* marital therapists do. The professional affiliations and disciplines of the providers of such therapeutic service is far less important than the quality of what is provided.

How Research and Practice Can Affect Each Other

The above issues notwithstanding, it is clear that empirical research in marital therapy has tremendous potential for positively influencing clinical practice. Among the major modalities of therapeutic intervention, marital and family therapies are perhaps in a unique position of not having been encumbered by many of the problems that have served to insularize other therapists and therapy researchers. In contrast to the frequent use of analogue studies in psychotherapy research (Kiesler, 1971), every study of the outcome of couples therapy to which Gurman refers in Part III has been conducted with genuine clinical populations seeking help with real problems in marital life. Thus, paradoxically, the available research in couples therapy, though *relatively* sparse, may have a high degree of clinical applicability since there is not, in this area, a long history of research findings of questionable or only oblique relevance to practice.

Researchers in marital therapy have an excellent opportunity to directly influence clinical treatment. It is incumbent upon marital therapy researchers to avoid many of the errors of their colleagues who have studied individual psychotherapy and to profit by the methodological knowledge and insight that has been gained over the last two decades (see, for example, Bergin and Strupp, 1972). It is also incumbent upon marital therapy researchers to attempt to answer the kinds of questions which *clinicians* raise about their work. Research in marital therapy can affect clinical practice substantially if researchers are willing to listen to their clinical colleagues.

Ultimately, it would seem that the most profitable route by which research can affect practice may be through the impact of marital therapy research on the *training* of clinicians. The experimental case study approach (see Bergin and Strupp, 1972; Gurman, 1973; Kiesler, 1971) is tied closely to direct therapeutic practice and offers a paradigm of experimentation and clinical service in which empirical findings have immediate and full relevance to actual treatment situations. Such an approach to clinical practice presents a viable alternative to the common distinctions and separations between clinicians and researchers and would appear to have particularly salient advantages in the teaching and training of therapists (Rice and Gurman, 1973).

In summary, there is a need for researchers and clinicians to come together in their common quests of developing more effective methods of change and understanding the mechanisms and processes that account for such change. Marital clinicians should allow researchers "into" their consulting rooms and welcome investigation of their practices by seeking the methodological aid of researchers to answer questions of major practical therapeutic importance.

Gurman has summarized these issues in Chapter 21 by noting that "Because the practice of marital therapy has not yet become ensnared in narrow, theoretical dogma, clinicians and researchers have perhaps a unique opportunity to . . . mutually influence each other and affect the growth of this field." Thus, "The quest for marital clinicians and researchers alike clearly needs to be one of disavowing unyielding adherence to therapeutic 'schools' and searching for and experimenting with interventions that produce change in couples, regardless of the treatment's 'goodness of fit' with preestablished notions."

The two chapters in Part III represent recent initial attempts to critically survey the existing research literature on the outcome of couples therapy to both determine what can be identified as factual evidence on the effects of treatment and to derive some clinically relevant propositions from these data. Hopefully, these chapters represent just the beginning of serious attempts to bridge the gap between research and practice in the field. Anticipated further interchange and mutual influence between researchers and clinicians may be among the most exciting and profitable "new directions in marital therapy."

REFERENCES

Bergin, A. E., and H. H. Strupp (1972), *Changing Frontiers in the Science of Psychotherapy.* Chicago: Aldine.

Gurman, A. S. (1973), "The Effects and Effectiveness of Marital Therapy: A Review of Outcome Research," *Family Process,* 12:145-170.

Kiesler, D. J. (1971), "Experimental Designs in Psychotherapy Research." In A. E. Bergin and S. L. Garfield (eds.), *Handbook of Psychotherapy and Behavior Change.* New York: Wiley, pp. 36-74.

Laws, J.L. (1971), "A Feminist Review of Marital Adjustment Literature: The Rape of the Locke," *Journal of Marriage and the Family,* 33:483-516.

Olson, D.H. (1970), "Marital and Family Therapy: Integrative Review and Critique," *Journal of Marriage and the Family,* 32:501-538.

Rice, D. G., and A. S. Gurman (1973), "Unresolved Issues in the Clinical Psychology Internship," *Professional Psychology,* 4:403-408.

Sussman, M. B. (ed.) (1972), *Non-Traditional Family Forms in the 1970's.* Minneapolis: National Council on Family Relations.

Thompson, A. S., and D. E. Super (eds.) (1964), *The Professional Preparation of Counseling Psychologists.* New York: Teachers College Press.

ALAN S. GURMAN

21 The Effects and Effectiveness of Marital Therapy*

The literature on outcome research in marital therapy is reviewed. Issues considered include the nature of outcome criteria, the need to establish a base line against which to measure improvement, and therapeutic effectiveness as a function of treatment type and time-in-therapy. The overall improvement rate across a heterogeneous collection of patients, therapists, and treatment modalities was 66 per cent, suggesting, conservatively, at least a moderately positive therapeutic effect in light of the judgment that "spontaneous" rates appear to be much lower in marital than in individual therapy. Evidence of deterioration in marital therapy also was discovered. No support was found for the contention that co-therapy is more effective than treatment of the couple by a single therapist. The needs of future research in the outcome of marital therapy are discussed and possible fruitful directions for such investigations suggested.

Marital therapy has emerged over the last thirty years as a clinically respected, therapeutic subspecialty. Recent general reviews by Olson (1970), and specialized reviews by Gurman (1971) and Lebedun in the marital area, however, echo one another's conclusions that relatively little about marital therapy has been established empirically and that what has been learned is based on methodologically weak studies. With the exception of the recent Wells, *et al*. (1972) critique of the results of family therapy, there have been no published reviews of the efficacy of therapy for marital problems. Furthermore,

*The author thanks Drs. Allen Bergin, Marjorie Klein, David Rice and Carl Whitaker for their helpful comments on an earlier version of this paper.

the Wells, *et al.* review included only two studies (Bellville *et al.*, 1969; Fitzgerald, 1969) of marital therapy outcome, although over two dozen such reports have now appeared (Gurman, 1973).

As Gurman (1973) noted on the basis of his content-analysis of the marital therapy literature there has been a growing trend toward experimentation and empiricism in this area in the last several years. The purpose of this review, then, is to examine both the effects and the effectiveness of marital therapy, as revealed through the research in this field.

The Nature and Scope of Marital Therapy

Gurman (1971) and Olson (1970, 1972) have noted that marital therapy is far from being a unitary treatment. For the immediate purpose of this review, marital therapy will be defined as the application of any planned, therapeutic techniques to modify the maladaptive or maladjustive relationships of married couples. Thus, the full range of theoretical treatment orientations are represented. Furthermore, the studies reviewed will focus on a wide variety of problematic marital issues including the feelings, attitudes, and behavior of the treated patients. Studies focusing on the treatment of sexual dysfunctions alone are not included here, but will be reviewed in a subsequent paper. Finally, since this review is concerned with the treatment of marital difficulties, studies of therapy with individuals that explicitly deal with marital relationships are included.

Before examining the research literature, some brief descriptions of the most frequently studied forms of marital therapy seem appropriate. *Behavioral marital therapy* (Liberman, 1970) is conducted with either both spouses or one spouse and involves the use of therapeutic techniques that are primarily of an operant conditioning nature and are based on learning theory. *Concurrent marital therapy* (Greene, 1965) may be conducted according to any theoretical position; its essence lies in the treatment of both spouses individually by the same therapist. *Conjoint marital therapy* may also be conducted with any theoretical stance; its distinguishing feature is that both spouses are seen together by one or more (cotherapy) therapists. *Conjugal marital therapy* (Ely, 1970) is based on the work of Guerney (1964) in which parents are trained in Rogerian techniques (clarification and reflection of feelings, etc.); here couples are seen conjointly in groups. *Individual marital therapy* is essentially the same as individual psychotherapy except that the patient's marital relationship is explicitly the focus of treatment; any theoretical orientation may be applied. *Group marital therapy* may be conducted according to any therapeutic persuasion and may involve a variety of specific treatment techniques; couples in group marital therapy are seen together in a group with other couples.

Method

All studies appearing in the literature through October 1972 that (a) included explicit statements of the outcome assessment procedures used and (b) involved the treatment of at least three couples (or individuals) were reviewed. These studies were of both the experimental-factorial and naturalistic kind. They focused on either therapeutic improvement rates, or correlates, and predictors of therapeutic improvement. Table 1 shows the distribution of the studies reviewed according to their time of publication. The empirical study of marital therapy outcome is a relatively recent phenomenon; over 80 per cent of these investigations have been reported in the last six years, although couples therapy had been established as an autonomous therapeutic profession as early as 1942 (Petersen, 1968).

Table 1. Distribution of Outcome Studies and Studies Reporting Improvement Rates in Marital Therapy by Time of Publication

Time Period	Number Outcome Studies	Studies Reporting Improvement Rates
1950-1954[a]	2	1
1955-1960	0	0
1961-1966	1	1
1967-1972[b]	23	13
Total	26	15

[a] Five-year interval; all others, 6 years.
[b] Through October, 1972.

Research Design and Nature of Treatment in Marital Therapy Outcome Studies

Table 2 summarizes most of the important characteristics of the research designs used in outcome studies of marital therapy. These studies have generally involved few therapists and only moderate-sized patient samples. A related point is that in almost all the studies the authors and therapists have been the same persons. This is hardly on the side of investigative objectivity. Probably a more salient issue is that less than one-third of these studies have used no-treatment control groups and that the quality of research designs used, the control group issue aside, has been numerically about equally good and poor. With regard to outcome assessment *per se,* it seems unfortunate that less than one-quarter of these studies have evaluated change in spouses both as individuals and as a dyadic (social) unit. Clearly, the assessment alone of either of these parameters of change in couples therapy is inadequate. In addition, while about three-quarters of the studies have used some form of patient self-report, a useful dimension in and of itself (Luborsky, 1971), relatively few studies have employed therapists' evaluations, independent judges' evaluations, or behavioral data, and only about half have used multidimensional assessments, now generally acknowledged as requisite of such studies (Bergin and Strupp, 1970; Strupp and Bergin, 1969). Finally, the most commonly used outcome criterion has been a global rating of change, which has many serious shortcomings (Garfield *et al.*, 1971; Mintz, 1972).

Table 2. Characteristics of Research Design in Outcome Studies of Marital Therapy

	Number of Studies		Number of Studies
Therapist Sample		Rating of Both Couples	4
Small (1-5)	16	and individuals	
Medium (6-10)	1		
Large (more than 10)	2	Outcome Rating Source	
(Not reported)	(7)	Patient Only	8
		Therapist Only	2
Patient Sample		Therapist and Patient only	4
Small (4-10)	6	Independent Judge Only	3
Medium (11-20)	3	Patient and Behavioral	6
Large (more than 20)	17	Patient and Independent Judge	2
Control Group		Therapist, Patient, and	1
Yes	8	Independent Judge	
No	18		
		Outcome Criterion	
Design Adequacy[a]		Global Rating	14
Level 1	10	Specific Change in	5
Level 2	2	Problem Behavior	
Level 3	3	General Interaction/	2
Level 4	11	Adjustment	
		Self-Concept	3
Therapist-Author Equivalence		Perception of Spouse	3
Therapists = Authors	16	Acceptance/Expression	3
Therapists ≠ Authors	3	of Feelings	
		Reconciliation or Durability	3
		Sexual Satisfaction	2
Outcome Rating Focus		Communication Skill	2
Rating of Couples	11	Positive References	1
Rating of Individuals	11	to Spouse	

Note. Sums within categories often do not agree with the total number of outcome studies reported in Table 4 because of missing information; in some cases, studies also fall within more than one subcategory.
[a]See footnote *e*, Table 4.

described in Table 3. These studies have been conducted overwhelmingly with outpatients seen in dynamically or eclectically oriented conjoint therapy. While few studies have been done on long-term treatment, the studies here are probably quite representative of the duration of most therapy practiced in outpatient clinics (Garfield, 1971).

Table 3. Characteristics of the Nature of Treatment in Outcome Studies of Marital Therapy

	Number of Studies
Therapy Type	
Concurrent	3
Conjoint	13
Individual	5
Group	11
Treatment Orientation	
Behavioral	4
Dynamically Oriented, General/Mixed	15
Client-Centered	3
Communications-Training	3
Patient Type	
General Outpatient	20
Alcoholic Involvement (1 spouse)	1
Private Practice	1
Conciliation Court	3
Child Guidance Clinic Parents	1
Treatment Length (Mean)	
Brief (1-10)	7
Moderate (11-20)	7
Long (more than 20)	3

Note. Sums within categories often do not agree with the total number of outcome studies reported in Table 4 because of missing information; in some cases, studies also fall within more than one subcategory.

Assessment of Change in Marital Therapy

Before examining available data on the efficacy of marital therapy, an overview of studies in this field will be presented. Table 4 summarizes all the marital therapy outcome studies published as of October 1972 in the 73 journals (see Gurman, 1973) that ordinarily include relevant reports. The age range of patients covered by these studies is from early twenties through mid-fifties.

Table 4
A Survey of Marital Therapy Outcome Studies Published Between 1950 and 1972

Author	Date	Therapy Type a	Patient Type b	Mean Therapy Length c	N Therapists d	N Patients	Control Group	Adequacy of Design e	Rating Source f	Outcome Criterion	Results/Conclusions
Bellville, et al.	1969	Conjoint (co-therapy)	Outpatient	16	2 (Au)	44 couples	No	1	P	General interaction, sexual satisfaction	Heterosexual co-therapy team is beneficial
Beutler	1971	Conjoint	Outpatient	12 (6-18)	10	10 couples	No	3	T, P	Global rating	Outcome related to H-W but not P-T attitude convergence
Brandreth and Pike	1967	Conjoint	Outpatient	3 couples; 2-6, 42 couples 7 or more	NR	50 couples	No	1	T, P	Global change; focal problem change	Majority of patients improved
Burton and Kaplan	1968	Group: Individual (Concurrent)	Outpatient (1 spouse alcoholic)	(1-44)	NR	61 in group; 114 in individual	No	1	P	Global rating	Group more effective than individual counseling
Cardillo	1971	Conjoint	Outpatient	5	1 (Au)	20 couples (10 treatment, 10 control)	Yes	4	P	Quality of self-concept and accuracy of perception of spouse	Communication role training affects H and W self- and-spouse perception
Dakan	1950	Group (Client-centered)	Outpatient	NR	1 (Au)	4 couples	No	2	T, P	Acceptance and expression of feelings about self and spouse	Non-directive group therapy improved views of self and spouse
Dicks	1967	Conjoint	Outpatient	13.4 (less than 10-more than 50) g	1 (Au)	36 couples	No	1	P	Global rating	Conjoint therapy is effective treatment
Ely	1970	Group (Conjugal)	Outpatient	8 2-hr. sessions	1 (Au)	11 training couples; 11 control couples	Yes	4	P, I	Expression of feelings; ability to clarify spouse's expression of feelings	Interaction quality better in training than control couples
Fitzgerald	1969	Conjoint	Outpatient (private practice)	26 (4-125)	1 (Au)	57 couples	No	1	T	Global rating	Conjoint therapy effective at termination and 2 year follow-up

Study	Year	Treatment	Setting	Duration	Sample descriptor	Sample size	Control	N	T, P, I	Outcome measure	Outcome
Freeman, et al.	1969	Mixed: Conjoint, Group, Individual	Outpatient	NR	NR	41 couples	No	1	T, P, I	Division of responsibility; relationship quality	Outcome related to: H sessions, experience level, H-W education level discrepancy; *not* related to length of therapy, type of therapy
Goldstein	1971	Behavioral (wives only)	Outpatient	NR	1 (Au)	10 (wives)	No	4	P, B	Husbands' behavior change	Significant changes in husbands' undesired behavior at termination and follow-up
Goldstein and Francis	1969	Behavioral (wives only)	Outpatient	NR	2 (Au)	5 (wives)	No	4	P, B	Husbands' behavior change	Significant changes in husbands' undesired behavior at termination and follow-up
Graham	1968	Conjoint; Conjoint plus Individual	Outpatient (conciliation court)	4 50-minute sessions (joint); 2 50-minute sessions (individual) plus 1 100-minute (joint), depending on treatment	NR	36 couples (12 per treatment)	Yes	3	I	Positive references to spouse	Treatment I increased positive mate reference more than treatment II. Both superior to control
Griffin	1967	Individual (wives only)	Outpatient	8	40 (20 experienced), 20 inexperienced	40-40 experimental (20 per treatment), 20 control	Yes	4	P	Own and spouse's empathy, warmth, & genuiness	Views of self & spouse improved more among treated than untreated Ss regardless of counselor experience level
Hickman	1970	Conjoint	Outpatient (Conciliation Court)	8	NR	30 couples (10 per two treatments, 10 control)	Yes	4	P, B	H-W "Communication"; legal reconciliation	Both treatments improved H-W attitudes; counseled group had more reconciliations than programmed text group
Hooper, et al.	1968	Group	Outpatient	24	2 (Au)	5 couples	No	1	I	Global rating	Therapy changes meaningful only in terms of H-W interaction

Study	Year	Type	Setting	Sessions/Duration	Therapists	N	Control	No.	Design	Outcome measure	Results
Kind	1968	Conjoint	Outpatient	14	NR	18 experimental couples; 25 control couples	Yes	4	P, I	Marital adjustment; communication efficiency	No significant differences between treated and control Ss
Linden, et al.	1968	Group	Outpatient	Weekly 90 min. sessions, mean NR	3 (Au) h	11 couples	No	1	P	Global rating	Group therapy is effective
Maizlish and Hurley	1963	Group	Outpatient (Child Guidance Clinic)	(12-15)	2 (Au)	32 couples (16 treatment, 16 control)	Yes	3	P, T	Attitudes toward self, spouse & children	Treated Ss changed more than untreated controls
Matanovich	1970	Group; Conjoint plus Individual	Outpatient (Conciliation Court)	6 3 hr. sessions (group); 4 1 hr. sessions (group); 1 2 hr. sessions (joint) plus 2 1 hr. individual sessions, depending on treatment	1 (Au)	40 couples (10 per treatment)	Yes	4	P, B	Legal reconciliation	Use of encounter tapes produced more reconciliations than in control Ss
Preston, et al.	1953	Concurrent	Outpatient	NR	NR	96 males 115 females	No	1	R (I)	Global rating	Movement can be judged from case records; better outcome when both spouses counseled
Reading, et al.	1967	Conjoint (co-therapy)	Outpatient	10 (2-19)	2 (Au)	15 couples	No	1	P	Global rating	Of 10 couples contacted at follow-up, 8 reported gains, 1 was divorced
Rice, et al.	1972	Conjoint (co-therapy)	Outpatient	NR	78	39 couples	No	4	T	Global rating	Therapist outcome rating related to felt comfort with co-therapist

Stuart	1969	Behavioral	Outpatient	10	1 (Au)	4 couples	No	4	P, B	Behavior change; "marital satisfaction"	Conversation time and sex frequency increased; "marital satisfaction" increased
Targow and Sweber	1969	Group	Outpatient	24 (4-more than 100)	2 groups: co-15 couples therapists (Au); 2 groups; 1 therapist (Au)		No	2	P	Global rating	Positive changes maintained at follow-up
Turner	1972	Behavioral (Group)	Outpatient	6 24 hr. sessions	2 (Au) or 1 (Au), depending on group	40 couples (10 per treatment)	No	4	P, B	Mental satisfaction; marriage durability; increase positive behaviors; decrease negative behaviors	Final data not yet available (nor follow-up data) preliminary analyses suggest significant change

Note. NR = not reported.

a All studies described in this table involved the conjoint treatment of husbands and wives except where noted as "Individual" or "Wives only"; thus, the designation "Group," for example, means that couples were treated together in a group; "Conjoint" refers to the joint treatment of a couple by themselves with their therapist(s).

b All studies described in this table were conducted with outpatients; any important descriptive characteristics of the sample are noted.

c Numbers in parentheses show the range of treatment duration where reported; numbers standing alone represent treatment length for all subjects.

d (Au) following the number of therapists indicates that the therapists were also the authors of the study.

e Adequacy of Design based on the following criteria: (a) random assignment of patients to treatments/therapists; (b) follow-up of patients; (c) inclusion of pre-post measurement of outcome; (d) research predictions stated in advance; (e) appropriate statistical analysis; (f) authors are not also the therapists in the study: 0-2 criteria met=poor (1); 3 criteria met=fair (2); 4 or 5 criteria met=good (3); 6 criteria met=very good (4).

f B = behavioral measure; I = independent judge(s); P = patient; R = case records; T = therapist.

g Dicks did not report specific treatment length data, but rather indicated number of couples per classes of treatment length, e.g., "25 to 50 interviews, 1 couple" etc.; thus this entry is based on the present author's estimates from Dicks' data.

h Two of the tree authors served as co-therapists at any given time.

Most studies have used heterogeneous samples of patients with respect to age, years married, and number of children. No outcome studies have yet been conducted with either or both spouses hospitalized. The majority of studies have dealt with outpatients seen in university clinics, family counseling and guidance centers, and other low-cost facilities. A handful of studies have been done with private practice patients and with couples seen in conciliation courts. As would be expected, most of these patients fall in the ''neurotic'' range. While a careful reading of these papers shows that a fair number of patients could reasonably be classified as borderline or schizoid, these data are not presented systematically enough to allow a precise statement of the distribution of psychiatric diagnoses. In fact, the studies are typically woefully deficient in their descriptions of patients. Such important information as age, socio-economic and educational level, diagnostic status, previous therapy, etc. are rarely all reported in a single study.

The therapists in these studies have also represented a mixed bag: psychiatrists, psychologists, social workers, marriage counselors, and others of a wide range of theoretical orientations and experience levels. The criticism of unreported (and, presumably, usually uncollected) data on relevant patient characteristics is also appropriate to the therapists in most of these studies. Detailed examination of the data in the original papers, where available, suggests that one saving characteristic of marital therapy outcome studies is that they have not used inexperienced trainee-therapists to the unfortunate extent common in most other psychotherapy research (Meltzoff and Kornreich, 1970). Other than this, however, it can be said that the only informative data on these therapists that is reported with any consistency is that they also authored the studies!

Outcome Criteria

As noted earlier, the most common outcome criterion in marital therapy research has been a global rating of the treated couples *qua* dyads or of each spouse individually. A majority of studies using such global ratings have relied heavily on patient self-report. Only rarely have these studies used independent assessment interviews such as that developed by Spitzer (1967), behavioral measures of specific symptoms (Wolpe and Lang, 1964), or evaluations of ''target complaints'' (Battle *et al.*, 1966). Other useful approaches (Strupp and Bergin, 1969), such as a standardized, psychological, paper-and-pencil test (e.g., *MMPI*), and factor-analytic batteries have almost never been used. Self- and spouse-concept ratings (Luckey, 1960; Murstein and Beck, 1972) also a promising approach, have been used infrequently.

The above criteria, it should be noted, focus entirely on the psychological functioning of *individual* patients. An alternative mode of assessing marital functioning that must be given a good deal of emphasis in future research is *interaction-testing* (Goodrich and Boomer, 1963; Olson and Ryder, 1970; Olson and Strauss, 1972; Stroatbeck, 1951), in which both spouses' behavior is observed in structured environments, allowing a variety of objective, behavioral measures of marital interaction. While a few studies surveyed here have used such procedures, their appearance on the scene is only very recent, and a great deal of work will be needed to determine which of these measures is best suited to the evaluation of specific forms of marital treatment.

A third domain likely to be important in the future assessment of the effects of marital therapy is that of role behavior, expectations, and conflict (Crago and Tharp, 1968; Tharp and Otis, 1966). This domain is clearly related to that of interaction-testing in that the focus is on patterns of behavior in the marital dyad viewed as an ongoing social system. On the other hand, discrepancies between role expectations and role enactment can be assessed via patient self-report. With few exceptions, studies in the marital therapy literature have approximated such interactive assessment only in the crudest manner, e.g., on the basis of global therapist and patient ratings of marital "quality," "happiness," "adjustment," etc.

Baseline and the Question of "Spontaneous Remission"

As in other forms of therapeutic intervention, the positive effects of marital therapy must be assessed in comparison to no-treatment. That is, to assert that marital therapy "makes a difference" the outcomes of formal, therapeutic treatment must be demonstrated to be more powerful than the facilitative effects of naturally occurring life conditions. The question of "spontaneous remission" of psychological disorders has received a great deal of attention since the appearance of Eysenck's (1952, 1966) provocative papers on the effects of psychotherapy. It is not within the province of the present review to reiterate all that has been written on this issue, yet a brief overview is needed in order to establish a framework within which to examine studies of the efficacy of marital therapy.

The rates of recovery for emotional disturbance without treatment initially used by Eysenck (1952), though often still bandied about by psychotherapy's harshest critics, have been widely criticized and are now generally considered inadequate (Bergin, 1966; Meltzkoff and Kornreich, 1970). These remission rates at two years of about 72 per cent for adult, neurotic disorders have been supplanted by more recent data reviewed by Bergin (1971). Subotnik's (1972) recent review has also questioned the adequacy of the spontaneous recovery rates for children upon which Levitt (1957) based his reviews of the results of their treatment. Though little is actually known about the natural history of psychological disorders, several important conclusions about no-treatment patients can be asserted with some confidence in their accuracy. First, there probably exists no such phenomenon as "spontaneous" remission. For example, it is clear that no-treatment subjects often do receive informal "therapeutic" contact from both professional workers and non-professionals (e.g., clergy, family physicians, friends, spouses, etc.). What has been regarded, then, as "spontaneous" change is better described as change for which the helping or facilitative sources cannot be specified. An important, related matter is that there is far less evidence than was once believed to exist that people with psychological disorders who receive no formal treatment improve as a function of the passage of time (Subotnik, 1972).

Two other conclusions about "spontaneous remission" are particularly relevant to marital therapy. A careful re-analysis of the available data by Bergin (1971) demonstrates that such recovery rates are generally substantially lower than those originally used by Eysenck (1952) and Levitt (1957). Perhaps the single most important observation in this regard is that improvement rates among no-treatment subjects vary widely from study to study and it is probably unwise to presume any specific remission rate as a comparison for treatment efficacy (Bergin, 1971; Meltzoff and Kornreich, 1970)

Finally, Bergin (1971) has demonstrated convincingly that these "spontaneous" improvement rates vary tremendously as a function of diagnosis; e.g., psychopathic and psychosomatic conditions are relatively stable, while anxieties and depressions are often quite transient and variable, offering better prognoses with or without formal treatment. In this regard, it is most disconcerting that *a thorough review of the available literature offers absolutely no empirical data on the naturally occurring ("spontaneous") rate of recovery in problematic marital relationships.* Thus, one is hard-pressed to determine a baseline against which the results of marital treatment can be compared. On the other hand, there is no *a priori* reason to predict that remission rates for marital disorders among neurotics would be any higher than the rates for adults as individuals. In fact, there are some theoretical bases (Haley, 1963) upon which one might predict such rates to be *lower* for marital difficulties.

Eysenck (1952) developed an exponential curve ($\times = 100 (1 - 10^{-0.00435N})$, where $\times$ = percentage of improvement and N the number of weeks elapsed) to predict no-treatment recovery rates as a function of time. This time-function hypothesis, as noted earlier, has been challenged (Subotnik, 1972) and Eysenck's curve was based on the questionable data in the Denker (1946) study in which, it will be recalled, no-treatment recovery rates greatly exceeded those in Bergin's (1971) more recent analyses.

Yet, if Eysenck's formula is applied to those outcome studies in Table 5 that supply treatment length data ($\bar{\chi}$ sessions = 17.45), the expected recovery rate for non-treatment couples over the same time span is 16 per cent. Note that this predicted rate errs in the direction of exaggerating the positive effects of no-treatment or, conversely, of minimizing the potency of formal treatment. Thus, if marital therapy outcomes significantly exceed even this figure, the case in behalf of their demonstrated efficacy would certainly be strengthened.

Table 5

Improvement Rates in Studies of Marital Therapy

Author	Date	N Couples	Very Much or Good Deal Improved	Somewhat Improved	Little Improved or No Change	Worse
			Outcome at Termination			
Bellville, et al.	1969	44	26 (59%)	0	18 (41%)	0
Brandreth & Pike	1967	50	31 (62%)	NR	14 (28%)	NR
Burton & Kaplan	1968	175 (HW)	111 (63%)	NR	NR	NR
Dicks	1967	36	23 (64%)	5 (14%)	NR	NR
Fitzgerald	1969	57	37 (65%)	NR	20 (35%)	0
Freeman, et al.	1969	41	24/41 (59%)	NR	17/41 (41%)	NR
Goldstein	1971	10 (W)	8 (80%)	0	2 (20%)	0
Goldstein & Francis	1969	5 (W)	5 (100%)	0	0	0
Hooper, et al.	1968	5	4 (40%)	4 (40%)	2 (20%)	0
Linden, et al.	1968	11	10 (90%)	0	1 (10%)	0
Maizlish & Hurley	1963	16	26 (80%)	0	6 (20%)	0
Preston, et al.	1953	211 (HW)	137 (65%)	0	63 (30%)	10 (5%)
Reding, et al.	1967	10	8 (80%)	0	1 (10%)	1 (10%)
Stuart	1969	4	4 (100%)	0	0	0
Tergow & Zweber	1969	15	6 (20%)	10 (33%)	5 (17%)	5 (17%)
Sub-Totals						
Couples c		253	163 (64%)	5 (2%)	71 (28%)	1(0.5%)
Individuals d		473	297 (63%)	14 (3%)	76 (16%)	15(3%)
Total		726	460 (63%)	19 (3%)	147 (20%)	16 (2%)

Note. NR = not reported.

Except where noted, couples were treated together; where spouses were not treated together, HW = husbands and wives treated separately in either group or individual setting; W = wives treated only.

Includes premature termination of treatment, as defined by given authors.

Improvement rates reported for couples *qua* couples, not for husbands and wives separately.

Improvement rates reported for spouses as individuals, not for couples *qua* couples.

One couple was divorced; therapists and patients agreed that this was a positive outcome.

Original authors supplied only verbal summaries of treatment results; improvement rates, therefore, are based on the present author's ratings of those assessments.

Original author reported that 37 of 49 couples who were "involved" in treatment (remained for minimum of four sessions) were improved at termination and follow-up; however, the present author considers the eight couples who terminated (for unspecified reasons) before the fourth session, i.e., not "involved," and thus not included in the original author's computations, to have been treatment failures as premature terminators; thus, the improvement rates in the present analysis and in the original report differ.

It is not clear from this report whether the divorce of one couple at follow-up was a positive or negative therapeutic outcome. However, since treatment apparently had been terminated mutually by both patients and therapists and since the couple had apparently entered treatment to resolve their conflicts rather than to be aided in the divorce process, it seems reasonable to classify this couple's outcome as "worse."

A Summary of Marital Therapy Outcome Studies

Despite the difficulties in marital therapy outcome assessment, there does exist a body of research on the efficacy of the treatment of marital problems.

Table 5 presents a summary of reported improvement rates in all the outcome studies of marital therapy published as of October 1972. These results were recorded as they appeared in the original papers. The categories of "Very Much or Good Deal Improved," "Somewhat Improved," "Little Improved or No Change," and "Worse" clearly represent a heterogeneity of outcome criteria across studies so that their comparability from study to study is quite tenuous. Futhermore, the number of categories per study also varied, although a majority of studies reported on more than one or two outcome classes. It is important to note that the "Somewhat Improved" category was used rarely, so that few of the "Slightly Improved" cases were likely to have been included in the former category, thus probably making estimates of improvement more certain. Obviously, in studies not reporting outcome in all categories, it is impossible to determine the distribution of outcomes for some patients. Fortunately, only three studies in Table 5 failed to report on 100 per cent of the patients.

Few of these studies indicated the number of dropouts or premature terminators from treatment. Also, as noted earlier, none of these studies supplied data on the improvement rates for couples not receiving formal marital therapy—i.e., these were all uncontrolled investigations. Patients' evaluation of treatment benefits were used in 11 of the studies, therapists' evaluation in only two studies, independent judges' evaluation in three studies. In only six studies were assessments from more than one source used. An additional note on Table 5 is that these data were culled from studies of several types of treatment: conjoint—7, group—6, individual—4, and concurrent—2. Finally, both behavioral and eclectically oriented treatments were involved in these studies.

Thus, across a variety of treatment types and therapist orientations, outcome criteria, and rater sources, the number of patients "Very Much Improved," "a Good Deal Improved," and "Somewhat Improved" is 66 per cent. This two-thirds improvement rate is almost exactly the same as that found by both Eysenck (1952) and Bergin (1971) for eclectic therapies with adult neurotics, despite differences in their analyses of the literature! Furthermore, the range of improvement rates from 53 to 100 per cent in the present analysis of marital therapy is comparable to Eysenck's range from 41 to 77 and especially comparable to Bergin's range from 42 to 87.

It should be kept in mind that these improvement rates in marital therapy are based on studies of a mean length of 17.45 sessions or roughly four and one-half months, whereas treatment duration in previous reviews has been somewhat longer. This point of comparison, and the very tentative rate of improvement predicted earlier from Eysenck's (1952) formula for no-treatment patients over the same time period, may lead many to conclude that there is strong evidence for the efficacy of marital therapy. However, the writer believes that a more cautious and conservative estimate of the efficacy of marital therapy should be placed on these findings because (a) no satisfactory base line of improvement for untreated marital problems has been established yet and (b) the heterogeneity of patient types and patient problems in the marital area probably mask differential "spontaneous recovery" rates (and, hence, differential prognostic treatment outcomes). Yet, despite differences in patient and therapist characteristics, treatment focus and manner of intervention, and inconsistent improvement criteria and assessment methods among the studies, it is clear that there are potent change-inducing elements active in the marital therapies. However, clinically relevant assessments of the specifics of the change process in marital therapy are still to be conducted. This issue will be dealt with further below.

Further Observations on Marital Therapy Outcomes

Additional analyses of the studies listed in Table 5 in terms of therapist experience level and patient diagnosis (Luborsky, 1971) were non-productive because of the insufficiency of these data in most of the papers. Assessment of improvement rates according to treatment method yielded the following: group, 71 per cent; conjoint (behavioral and non-behavioral combined), 74 per cent; conjoint (non-behavioral), 68 per cent; behavioral only, 93 per cent. The meaning of these differences is unclear. Inclinations to assert the apparent superiority of behavioral treatments must be tempered because of the small number ($n = 19$) of cases treated by these methods.

Analysis of improvement rate as a function of treatment length, however, produced a most provocative finding. When the nine studies in Table 5 in which treatment duration could be identified were ranked according to improvement rate, a Spearman *rho* of $-.57$ was obtained. Though this correlation only approaches conventional statistical significance levels ($.075>p>.05$), the tentative implication that the shorter the treatment the better the outcome is surprising, if not startling, in terms of both common clinical experience and empirical research (Luborsky, 1971). Interpretations of this finding must be made cautiously, yet one possibility is rather appealing: If treatment length is a function of pathology, then acute marital problems may seem to be more effectively treated. Thus, fast and major changes may occur in the least or most acutely distressed couples. Therefore, a crisis-intervention model may be especially relevant to the treatment of marital conflicts.[1]

Marital Therapy May Make Some Patients Worse!

Bergin (1966, 1971) has carefully documented the existence of a "deterioration effect" in individual therapy with adults, i.e., that some patients get worse as a result of apparently inept psychotherapy. This phenomenon, unfortunately,

[1] The author thanks Drs. Allen Bergin and Marjorie Klein for suggesting this interpretation.

has also been reported in three (Preston *et al.*, 1953; Reding *et al.*, 1967; Targow and Zweber, 1969) of the 15 studies of marital therapy in Table 5. Although the deterioration rate (2 per cent) across these studies is lower than that for individual therapy (10 per cent), it is even more striking that deterioration was observed in over one-quarter (3 of 11) of the investigations that included a distinguishable "worse" category. Several studies lumped together "No Change or Worse," so that it is impossible to determine the extent of deterioration from these reports. As with "Improvement" rates, no data are available on the frequency of deterioration in control couples. Furthermore, the criteria of deterioration in these studies have been unclear. It must also be noted that just as single spontaneous remission rates mask variability of remission across cases and outcome criteria, a single deterioration rate such as the 2 per cent figure used here also lacks sufficient specificity. Answers to questions such as what causes deterioration in marital therapy and the incidence of the phenomenon, like much else in the area, must await the results of future research.

One Therapist or Two? Addendum on the Co-Therapy Treatment of Couples

Some writers (Ferber *et al.*, 1972) have argued in favor of the use of co-therapists in marital and family therapy. A review of the issues involved in this approach is beyond the scope of this paper. Suffice it to say that at the time of this writing no controlled studies comparing the effectiveness of these forms of intervention exist. However, indirect evidence bearing on this question can be culled from the literature and is presented in Table 6. While co-therapy studies of marital therapy fare somewhat better than single-therapist studies (73 per cent vs. 65 per cent improvement), this difference is probably non-significant. Contrary to the notions of those who advocate co-therapy, it can be said that, on the basis of the limited data available, the null hypothesis (i.e., no outcome difference as a function of the number of therapists) is still to be accepted. These data do not "prove" that treatment by one and two therapists are equally effective, but merely that there is insufficient evidence that a difference exists.

Follow-up of Marital Therapy Outcomes

Few outcome studies of marital therapy have provided follow-up data on their patients' functioning at some point in time after the termination of treatment. Those studies that report on follow-up (Fitzgerald, 1969; Goldstein, 1971; Linden *et al.*, 1968; Stuart, 1969; Targow and Zweber, 1969) all show slight post-termination increases in improvement rates. Luborsky *et al.* (1971)

Table 6

Improvement Rates in Studies of Conjoint Marital Therapy Conducted by Co-Therapists and Single Therapists

Author	Co-Therapist Treatment			Author	Single-Therapist Treatment		
	Date	Improved[a]	No Change[a]		Date	Improved[a]	No Change[a]
Bellville et al.[b]	1969	26/44(59%)	18/44(41%)	Brandreth & Pike[b]	1967	31/50(62%)	14/50(28%)
Hooper et al.[c]	1968	8/10(80%)	2/10(20%)	Dicks[b, e]	1967	28/36(78%)	8/36(22%)
Linden et al.[b]	1968	10/11(90%)	1/11(10%)	Fitzgerald[b]	1969	37/57(65%)	20/57(35%)
Maizlish & Hurley[c]	1963	26/32(80%)	6/32(20%)	Stuart[b]	1969	4/4(100%)	0/4(0%)
Reding et al.	1967	8/10(80%)	1/10(10%)				
Total[d]							
Couples		44/65(67%)	20/65(30%)			95/147(65%)	42/147(28%)
Individuals		34/42(83%)	8/42(19%)			—	—
Couples & Individuals Combined		78/107(73%)	28/107(26%)			95/147(65%)e	42/147(28%)

Note. "Single Therapist" refers to the conjoint treatment of a couple by one therapist.

a Improved = combined data on patients rated "very much improved" and "good deal improved"; No Change = data on patients rated "little improved" and "no improvement."

b Outcome based on ratings of couples qua couples, not for husbands and wives separately.

c Outcome based on ratings of spouses as individuals, not for couples qua couples.

d Couples = summed improvement rates in studies based on ratings of change of the couple qua couple; Individuals = summed improvement rates in studies based on ratings of change of spouses as individuals; Couples & Individuals Combined = summed improvement rates in studies based on ratings of change of both couples qua couples and of spouses as individuals.

e Total based on the inclusion of Fitzgerald's premature terminators; if these early dropouts are excluded, the improvement rate in single-therapist treatment becomes 70 per cent.

note that the lack of adequate follow-up studies is not a serious problem because of the high correlations between assessments at termination and follow-up. Nevertheless, such data would still be of immense value in the field of marital therapy, since they might be a starting point for studying the natural history of problems treated by marital therapy.

The Future of Outcome Research in Marital Therapy

This section will present a brief overview of the current needs of research in marital therapy outcome. The points outlined below follow logically from the research literature that has been reviewed.

Controlled Comparative Studies

Bergin and Strupp (1970), among others, have argued that broadly based comparative studies of therapeutic effectiveness in which evaluation focuses on criteria of global change produced by therapists of vague "school" allegiances offer little in the way of improving the potency of our therapeutic interventions. With the exception of the small number of studies that have appeared to date, the field of marital therapy, because of the recency of its concern with empirical matters, hopefully will be spared many years of research with limited direct clinical applicability. Gross questions such as, "Is marital group therapy more effective than conjoint therapy?" must be avoided. There is a place for such investigative efforts in marital therapy, but it is certainly at least several years away. The verification or confirmation stage of research must follow the discovery stage, which has only recently been arrived at in this field. Comparative studies such as that being done by Crowe (1972) at the Maudsley Hospital in London may, nevertheless, finally supply much needed data on marital change in no-treatment (attention-placebo) groups. The quest for marital clinicians and researchers alike clearly needs to be one of disavowing unyielding adherence to therapeutic "schools" and searching for and experimenting with interventions that produce change in couples, regardless of the treatment's "goodness of fit" with pre-established notions.

The $n=1$ Experimental Case Study

The planned, systematic, and objectified study of single cases (Bergin and Strupp, 1970; Chassan, 1967; Lazarus and Davison, 1971) has received increasing attention in the psychotherapy literature of the last few years. This development is understandable in light of the limited effects of research on clinical practice. The $n=1$ approach, especially that based on the repeated, single-case design (Bergin and Strupp, 1970), is closely tied to direct therapeutic work and offers what is perhaps the only currently available route for decreasing the distinction between clinician and researcher, thereby yielding benefits to both. It is unlikely that marital therapies of enduring value will derive from "pure" laboratory experimentation or from theoretical abstractions *per se*. Clinicians, not experimentalists, have been responsible for the creation of most of our useful therapeutic innovations. Quantitative, experimental case studies are more valuable to both clinicians and researchers than traditional case reports. The empirical study of single cases in marital therapy (Sherwin and Toepfer, 1972) has much to recommend it.

Technique-Building and Specificity

Closely related to the points made above is the issue that the field of marital therapy, like all forms of psychological treatment, suffers at present from a lack of specific techniques for specific problems. "Marital therapy" is not a unitary phenomenon, nor is "marital disharmony." Paul's (1967, p. 111) notion that outcome research must attempt to ask (and answer) the question, "*what* treatment, by *whom*, is most effective for *this* individual with that specific problem and under *which* set of circumstances," must be the jumping-off point for future marital therapy outcome research. As Bergin (1971, p. 254) has so crisply stated, "Clearly, more specific approaches lend themselves more readily to less ambiguous tests of effectiveness."

Multidimensional Evaluation of Marital Therapy Outcomes

It is clear that the process of change in marital therapy is multidimensional. Our earlier analysis of the domains that already have been tapped and those still needing to be tapped in assessing change in the treatment of couples underscores the complexity of these phenomena. As multifactorial as are the changes occurring in individual psychotherapy (Bergin, 1971; Bergin and Strupp, 1970), they are even more so in the study of an active, ongoing, interpersonal system (Olson, 1970). Thus, future studies might simultaneously assess such relevant dimensions as symptom relief, observable behavioral change, social and vocational functioning, etc. This area of criterion development is probably the most challenging within the province of marital therapy and will, no doubt, attract the attention of researchers for some time to come. At least one study in this area is now near completion (Gurman, 1972).

The Study of Marital Therapy as Presently Practiced

Lest the proverbial baby be discarded with the bath water, it is emphasized here that the studies of primary therapist characteristics (e.g., empathic ability, experience, etc.) and patient characteristics (adequacy of functioning, motivation, educational and social assets), which have received support as predictors of outcome in individual psychotherapy, not be abandoned. While on an intuitive basis one would expect these factors to be salient in the treatment of marital difficulties as well, *a priori* hunches must not supplant empirical verification. One such study (Dormont, 1972) is already underway. Finally, it should be added that although "process" research (as it is often arbitrarily distinguished from "outcome" research) has fallen into disrepute in some circles in recent years, the complexity of a three-way or four-way therapeutic encounter is so intriguingly different from one-to-one therapy that it deserves much intensive study.

Conclusions

Although the practice of marital therapy has been with us for some time, the empirical investigation of this important area of clinical service is still at the earliest stages of development. Because the practice of marital therapy has not yet become ensnared in narrow, theoretical dogma, clinicians and researchers have perhaps a unique opportunity to choose among a wealth of "psychotherapies" to mutually influence each other and affect the growth of this field. There is already reason to believe that marital therapy as now practiced has at least moderately positive effects on its consumers. The door is wide open for the development of even more potent change processes.

REFERENCES

Battle, C. C., S. D. Imber, R. Hoehn-Saric, A. R. Stone, E. H. Nash, and J. D. Frank (1966), "Target Complaints as Criteria of Improvement," *American Journal of Psychotherapy*, 20:184-192.

Bellville, T. P., O. N. Raths, and C. J. Bellville (1969), "Conjoint Marriage Therapy with a Husband-and-Wife Team," *American Journal of Orthopsychiatry*, 39:473-483.

Bergin, A. E. (1966), "Some Implications of Psychotherapy Research for Therapeutic Practice," *Journal of Abnormal Psychology*, 71:235-246.

———(1971), "The Evaluation of Therapeutic Outcomes." In A. E. Bergin and S. L. Garfield (eds.), *Handbook of Psychotherapy and Behavior Change: An Empirical Analysis*. New York: Wiley.

Bergin, A. E., and H. H. Strupp (1970), "New Directions in Psychotherapy Research," *Journal of Abnormal Psychology*, 76:13-26.

———(1972), *Changing Frontiers in the Science of Psychotherapy*. Chicago: Aldine.

Beuter, L. E. (1971), "Attitude Similarity in Marital Therapy," *Journal of Consulting and Clinical Psychology*, 37:298-301.

Brandreth, A., and R. Pike (1967), "Assessment of Marriage Counseling in a Small Family Agency," *Social Work*, 12:34-39.

Burton, G., and H. M. Kaplan (1968), "Group Counseling in Conflicted Marriages Where Alcoholism Is Present: Clients' Evaluation of Effectiveness," *Journal of Marriage and the Family*, 30:74-79.

Cardillo, J. P. (1971), "The Effects of Teaching Communication Roles in Interpersonal Perception and Self-Concept in Disturbed Marriages," *Proceedings of the 77th Annual Convention of the American Psychological Association*," pp. 441-442.

Chassan, J. B. (1967), *Research Design in Clinical Psychology and Psychiatry*, New York: Appleton-Century-Crofts.

Crago, M., and R. G. Tharp, (1968), "Psychopathology and Marital Role Disturbance: A Test of the Tharp-Otis Descriptive Hypothesis," *Journal of Consulting and Clinical Psychology*, 32:338-341.

Crowe, M. (1972), Personal communication on "Effective Variables in Conjoint Marital Psychotherapy," study in progress, Maudsley Hospital, University of London.

Dakan, E. A. (1950), "Changes in Concept of Self and of Partner for Married Couples in Nondirective Group Therapy." Unpublished Ph. D. thesis: Teachers College, Columbia University.

Denker, P. G. (1946), "Results of Treatment of Psychoneuroses by the General Practitioner — A Follow-up of 500 Cases," *New York State Journal of Medicine*, 46:2164-2166.

Dicks, H. V. (1967), *Marital Tensions: Clinical Studies Toward A Psychological Theory of Interaction*, New York: Basic Books.

Dormont, P. (1972), Personal communication.

Ely, A. L. (1970), "Efficacy of Training in Conjugal Therapy." Unpublished Ph. D. thesis: Rutgers University.

Eysenck, H. (1952), "The Effects of Psychotherapy: An Evaluation," *Journal of Consulting Psychology*, 16:319-324.

——— (1966), *The Effects of Psychotherapy*. New York: International Science Press.

Ferber, A., M. Mendelsohn, and A. Napier, *The Book of Family Therapy*. New York: Jason Aronson, Inc.

Fitzgerald, R. V. (1969), "Conjoint Marital Psychotherapy: An Outcome and Follow-Up Study," *Family Process*, 8:260-271.

Freeman, S. J. J., E. J. Leavens, and D. J. McCulloch (1969), "Factors Associated with Success or Failure in Marital Counseling," *Family Coordinator* 18:125-128.

Garfield, S. L. (1971), "Research on Client Variables in Psychotherapy." In A. E. Bergin and S. L. Garfield (eds.), *Handbook of Psychotherapy and Behavior Change*. New York: Wiley.

Garfield, S. L., A. E. Bergin, and R. A. Prager (1971), "Evaluation of Outcome in Psychotherapy," *Journal of Consulting and Clinical Psychology*, 37:307-313.

Goldstein, M. K. (1971), "Behavior Rate Changes in Marriages: Training Wives to Modify Husbands' Behavior," *Dissertation Abstracts International*, 32(1-B):559.

———, and B. Francis (1969), "Behavior Modification of Husbands by Wives." Paper presented at the National Council on Family Relations, Washington, D.C.

Goodrich, D. W., and D. S. Boomer (1963), "Experimental Assessment of Modes of Conflict Resolution," *Family Process*, 2:15-24.

Graham, J. A. (1968), "The Effect of the Use of Counselor Positive Responses to Positive Perceptions of Mate in Marriage Counseling," *Dissertation Abstracts International*, 28(9-A):3504.

Greene, B. L. (1965), *The Psychotherapies of Marital Disharmony*. New York: Free Press.

Griffin, R. W. (1967), "Change in Perception of Marital Relationship as Related to Marriage Counseling," *Dissertation Abstracts International*, 27(1-A):3956.

Guerney, B. L. (1964), "Filial Therapy: Description and Rationale," *Journal of Consulting Psychology*, 28:304-310.

Gurman, A. S. (1971), "Group Marital Therapy: Clinical and Empirical Implications for Outcome Research," *International Journal of Group Psychotherapy*, 21:174-189.

——— (1973), "Marital Therapy: Emerging Trends in Research and Practice," *Family Process*, 12:45-54.

——— (1972), "Evaluation of Outcome in Marital Therapy," in preparation.

Haley, J. (1963), *Strategies of Psychotherapy*. New York: Grune & Stratton.

Hickman, M. E. (1970), "Facilitation Techniques in Counseling Married Couples Toward More Effective Communication," *Dissertation Abstracts International*, 31(5-A):2107.

Hooper, D., A. Sheldon, and A. J. R. Koumans (1968), "A Study of Group Psychotherapy With Married Couples," *International Journal of Social Psychiatry*, 15:57-68.

Kind, J. (1968), "The Relationship of Communication Efficiency to Marital Happiness and An Evaluation of Short-Term Training in Interpersonal Communication with Married Couples," *Dissertation Abstracts International*, 29(3-B):1173.

Lazarus, A. A., and G. C. Davison (1971), "Clinical Innovation in Research and Practice." In A. E. Bergin and S. L. Garfield (eds.), *Handbook of Psychotherapy and Behavior Change*. New York: Wiley.

Lebedun, M. (1970), "Measuring Movement in Group Marital Counseling," *Social Casework*, 51:35-43.

Levitt, E. (1957), "The Results of Psychotherapy with Children: An Evaluation," *Journal of Consulting Psychology*, 21:189-196.

——— "Psychotherapy with Children: A Further Evaluation," *Behavior Research and Therapy*, 1:45-51.

Liberman, R. P. (1970), "Behavioral Approaches to Family and Couple Therapy," *American Journal of Orthopsychiatry*, 40:106-118.

Linden, M. E., H. M. Goodwin. and H. Resnik (1968), "Group Psychotherapy of Couples in Marriage Counseling," *International Journal of Group Psychotherapy*, 18:313-324.

Luborsky, L. (1971), "Perennial Mystery of Poor Agreement Among Criteria for Psychotherapy Outcome," *Journal of Consulting Clinical Psychology*, 37:316-319.

—— M. Chandler, A. H. Auerbach, J. Cohen, and H. M. Bachrach (1971), "Factors Influencing the Outcome of Psychotherapy: A Review of Quantitative Research," *Psychological Bulletin*, 75:145-185.

Luckey, E. B. (1960), "Marital Satisfaction and Congruent Self-Spouse Concepts," *Social Forces*, 39:153-157.

Maizlish, I. L., and Hurley, J. P. (1963), "Attitude Changes of Husbands and Wives in Time-Limited Group Psychotherapy," *Psychiatric Quarterly Supplement*, 37:230-249.

Matanovich, J. P. (1970), "The Effects of Short-Term Group Counseling Upon Positive Perceptions of Mate in Marital Counseling," *Dissertation Abstracts International*, 31(6-A):2688.

Meltzoff, J., and M. Kornreich (1970), *Research in Psychotherapy*. Chicago: Aldine.

Mintz, J. (1972), "What is 'Success' in Psychotherapy?", *Journal of Abnormal Psychology*, 80:11-19.

Murstein, B. I., and G. D. Beck (1972), "Person Perception, Marriage Adjustment, and Social Desirability," *Journal of Consulting and Clinical Psychology*, in press.

Olson, D. H. (1970), "Marital and Family Therapy: Integrative Review and Critique," *Journal of Marriage and the Family*, 32:501-538.

—— (1972), "Behavior Modification Research with Couples and Families: A System Analysis, Review and Critique." Paper presented at the Sixth Annual Meeting of the Association for the Advancement of Behavior Therapy, New York.

——, and R. G. Ryder (1970), "Inventory of Marital Conflicts (IMC): An Experimental Interaction Procedure," *Journal of Marriage and the Family*, 32:443-448.

Olson, D. H., and M. A. Strauss (1972), "A Diagnostic Tool for Marital and Family Therapy: The SIMFAM Technique," *Family Coordinator*, 21:251-258.

Paul, G. L. (1967), "Strategy of Outcome Research in Psychotherapy," *Journal of Consulting Psychology*, 31:109-118.

Peterson, J. A. (ed.) (1968), *Marriage and Family Counseling: Perspective and Prospect*. New York: Association Press.

Preston, M. G., E. H. Mudd, and H. B. Froscher (1953), "Factors Affecting Movement in Casework," *Social Casework*, 34:103-111.

Reding, G. R., L. A. Charles, and M. B. Hoffman (1967), "Treatment of the Couple by a Couple II. Conceptual Framework, Case Presentation and Follow-up of Study," *British Journal of Medical Psychology*, 40:243-251.

Rice, D. G., W. F. Fey, and J. G. Kepecs (1972), "Therapist Experience and 'Style' as Factors in Co-Therapy," *Family Process*, 11:1-12.

Sherwin, N., and C. T. Toepfer (1972), "Marital Behavior Modification: A Case Report." Unpublished manuscript: Slippery Rock State College.

Spitzer, R. L., J. Endicott, and G. Cohen (1967), "The Psychiatric Status Schedule: Technique for Evaluating Social and Role Functioning and Mental Status," N.Y. State Psychiatric Institute and Biometrics Research.

Strodtbeck, F. L. (1951), "Husband-Wife Interaction over Revealed Differences," *American Sociological Review*, 16:468-473.

Strupp, H. H., and A. E. Bergin (1969), "Some Empirical and Conceptual Bases for Coordinated Research in Psychotherapy," *International Journal of Psychiatry*, 7:18-90.

Stuart, R. B. (1969), "Operant-Interpersonal Treatment for Marital Discord," *Journal of Consulting and Clinical Psychology*, 33:675-682.

Subotnik, L. (1972), "Spontaneous Remission: Fact or Artifact?", *Psychological Bulletin*, 77:32-48.

Targow, J. G., and R. V. Zweber (1969), "Participants' Reactions to Treatment in a Married Couples' Group," *International Journal of Group Psychotherapy*, 19:221-225.

Tharp, R. G., and G. D. Otis (1966), "Toward a Theory for Therapeutic Intervention in Families," *Journal of Consulting Psychology*, 30:426-434.

Turner, J. (1972), "Couple and Group Treatment of Marital Discord." Paper presented at the Sixth Annual Meeting of the Association for the Advancement of Behavior Therapy, New York.

Wells, R. A., T. C. Dilkes, and N. Trivelli (1972), "The Results of Family Therapy: A Critical Review of the Literature," *Family Process*, 11:189-207.

Wolpe, J. W., and P. J. Lang (1964), "A Fear Survey Schedule for Use in Behavior Therapy," *Behavior Research and Therapy*, 2:27-30.

ALAN S. GURMAN

22   Some Therapeutic Implications of Marital Therapy Research*

Empirical evaluations of controlled and comparative studies of marital therapy outcome are first reviewed and it is concluded that no single type of treatment has yet been demonstrated to produce effects superior to other approaches, although some models for the direct teaching of marital communication skills appear particularly promising. Studies of relevant therapist, patient, and treatment variables are also examined and discussed. On the basis of the foregoing analyses of the existing research literature, several implications are derived for clinical practice, focusing on patient selection and therapy process, the therapist's contribution, the use of co-therapists, and the application of selected treatment strategies.

The rapid evolution of marital therapy during the last three decades is evident on many fronts. Increasing attention is being paid to the training of clinicians in the area (Ferber and Mendelsohn, 1969; Ferber, Mendelsohn, and Napier, 1972; Napier and Whitaker, 1973) and it is probably true that all but the most unyieldingly traditional training programs in psychiatry and clinical psychology now offer at least some exposure to marital treatment. Social work has for a long time, of course, been keenly aware of the reciprocal ways in which marital interaction both influences and is influenced by the individual partners in the marital dyad. In addition, training in the treatment of marital problems is being introduced into new programs in family practice medicine such as the one at the University of Wisconsin. As the helping professions become increasingly involved in community intervention and the conceptualization of maladaptive

*Based in part on a paper presented at the Fourth Annual Meeting of the Society for Psychotherapy Research, Philadelphia, June, 1973.

human behavior in social learning and interaction modes (Peterson, 1968; Tharp and Wetzel, 1969), it is likely that even more training will be oriented toward intervention in ongoing social systems.

This increased emphasis in clinical training has paralleled the burgeoning literature on couples therapy. Gurman (1973a,b) has documented the almost linear increase in number of published works in this area between 1940 and 1972. Fully 49 percent of the literature in this domain of psychotherapy has appeared since 1967 and there is no apparent reason to predict that there will be a leveling-off of this trend. Gurman's analysis of the marital therapy literature also makes it clear that the nature of clinical *practice* is changing profoundly, with a growing concern for the development of demonstrably effective therapeutic techniques. This interest in the creation and application of change-producing interventions may be the most profitable avenue for the continued growth of marital therapy.

Unfortunately research in psychotherapy has generally had little impact on the day-to-day practices of mental health workers (Bergin and Strupp, 1972). This paper is a first attempt, within the marital therapy field, to translate recent research findings on the outcome of couples therapy into some clinically relevant conclusions. Marital therapists may, in this way, begin to see the potential applicability of research to their daily clinical practice. The observations and tentative propositions put forth in this analysis may also elicit the applied research interest of workers in the area.

After presenting a brief overview of the effectiveness of marital therapy, the following dimensions of marital therapy outcome research will be emphasized: comparative treatment effects, treatment factors influencing outcome, and patient and therapist variables affecting treatment outcome. The paper will conclude with a summary of practical clinical implications derived from the review.

THE EFFECTIVENESS OF MARITAL THERAPY REVISITED

Examination of variables affecting treatment outcome would be largely irrelevant to clinical practice if it could not first be determined with some degree of confidence that couples therapy in its many forms is, in fact, beneficial for its consumers. What follows in this section is a summary of the conclusions about this issue reached in this author's (1973c) review of the results of couples therapy. The reader is referred to this author's earlier chapter in this volume for a more detailed consideration of issues involved in the assessment of change in marital therapy and the nature and appropriateness of various outcome criteria used in the research which has been reported to date.

In order to assert that marital therapy "makes a difference," the outcomes of formal therapeutic interventions must be demonstrated to produce significantly more change than that which occurs "spontaneously," i.e., as a result of naturally occurring "therapeutic" events (Bergin, 1971; Subotnik, 1972). Neither as the result of controlled studies of outcome in marital therapy nor the result of epidemiological research on the natural history of psychological disorders, can any statement be made as to the baseline rate of spontaneous (no-treatment) remission of problematic marital behavior. Thus, it is logically and scientifically difficult to attribute the reported effects of treatment to particular therapeutic interventions. Without such baseline data, one is justified in concluding only very tentatively that treatment effects exceed those that might have emerged in what Bergin (1971) calls "the psychotherapy of every-day life." There would seem to be no a priori reason to assume or predict that remission rates for marital disorders would be any higher than the rates for (neurotic) adults as individuals. In fact, there are at least some clinical and theoretical bases (Ackerman, 1967; Haley, 1963; Laing and Esterson, 1970) upon which one might predict such rates to be *lower* for marital difficulties and for psychological dysfunction in any ongoing social system such as the family, its subunits, and extensions (Speck and Attneave, 1973).

Based on this theoretically based assumption that spontaneous remission of dyadic relationship dysfunctions in all likelihood do not exceed the correspond-ing rate for individuals, the present author (1973c) concluded that the 66 percent improvement rate found across the marital therapy studies he reviewed attested to the probable effectiveness of couples-therapy-on-the-average. This observed improvement rate was noted to be strikingly similar to those reported in both Eysenck's (1966) classic paper on the effect of (individual) psycho-therapy and in Bergin's (1971) more careful reanalysis of Eysenck's data and review of more recent evidence. Nevertheless, I urged (1973c) that a cautious and conservative conclusion about the efficacy of couples therapy be placed on my findings because of the lack of adequate data on improvement rates among untreated couples and because of the heterogeneity of patient types and prob-lems, therapist characteristics, treatment strategies, etc., which characterize the studies in that review. An updated summary of the improvement rates reported in studies of marital therapy appears in Table 1.

CONTROLLED STUDIES OF OUTCOME

It is important to note that only two of the studies in Table 1 (Maizlish and Hurley, 1963; Most, 1964) included no-treatment control groups. Disappoint-ingly, few such reports have appeared in the couples therapy literature of psychiatry, psychology, and social work (Gurman, 1973b). The results of the eleven studies published to date which have used control groups are sum-marized in Table 2. While the appropriateness of the "control groups" in some of these studies (e.g., Most, 1964) is highly questionable because these groups,

TABLE 1. Summary of Improvement Rates in Studies of Marital Therapy

Author	Date	N Couples [a]	Very Much or Good Deal Improved	Somewhat Improved	Little Improved or No Change [b]	Worse
			Outcome at Termination			
Bellville et al. [c]	1969	44	26 (59%)	0	18 (41%)	0
Brandreth & Pike [c]	1967	50	31 (62%)	NR	14 (28%)	NR
Burton & Kaplan [d]	1968	175 (HW)	111 (63%)	NR	NR	NR
Dicks c	1967	36	23 (65%)	5 (14%)	NR	NR
Fitzgerald [c]	1969	49	37 (76%)	NR	12 (24%)	0
Freeman et al. [c]	1969	41	24 (59%)	NR	17 (41%)	NR
Goldstein d	1971	10 (W)	8 (80%)	0	2 (20%)	0
Goldstein & Francis [d]	1969	5 (W)	5 (100%)	0	0	0
Gurman [c, i]	1973d	12	5 (42%)	4 (33%)	3 (25%)	0
Hardcastle [d]	1972	4 h	3 (43%)	0	2 (28%)	2 (28%)
Hooper et al. [d, f]	1968	5	4 (40%)	4 (40%)	2 (20%)	0
Linden et al. [c]	1969	11	10 (90%) [e]	0	1 (10%)	0
Maizlish & Hurley [d]	1963	16	26 (80%)	0	6 (20%)	0
Most [d]	1964	20 (W)	16 (80%)	0	0	4 (20%)
Preston et al. [d]	1953	211 (HW)	137 (65%)	0	63 (30%)	10 (5%)
Reding et al. [c]	1967	10	8 (80%)	0	1 (10%)	1 (10%)
Stuart c	1969	4	4 (100%)	0	0	0
Targow & Zweber [d]	1969	15	6 (20%)	10 (33%)	5 (17%)	5 (17%)
Subtotals						
Couples		257	168 (65%)	9 (4%)	66 (26%)	1 (0.4%)
Individuals		501	316 (63%)	14 (3%)	78 (16%)	21 (4%)
Total j		758	484 (64%)	23 (3%)	144 (19%)	22 (3%)

Note: NR = not reported. This table represents an updating of the data originally reported in Gurman, 1973c.

[a] Except where noted, couples were treated together; where spouses were not treated together, HW = husbands and wives treated separately in either group or individual setting; W = wives treated only.

[b] Includes premature termination of treatment as defined by given authors, when authors were able to summon evidence that early dropouts should be considered treatment failures.

[c] Improvement rates reported for couples qua couples, not for husbands and wives separately.

[d] Improved rates reported for spouses as individuals, not for couples qua couples.

[e] One couple was divorced; therapists and patients agreed that this was a positive outcome.

[f] Original authors supplied only verbal summaries of treatment results; improved rates, therefore, are based on the present author's ratings of those assessments.

[g] It is not clear from this report whether the divorce of one couple at follow-up was a positive or negative therapeutic outcome. However, since treatment apparently had been terminated mutually by both patients and therapist and since the couple had apparently entered treatment to resolve their conflicts rather than to be aided in the divorce process, it seems reasonable to classify this couple's outcome as "worse."

[h] Pre-post data obtained for only 7 of the 8 patients.

[i] Represents mean ratings of improvement across both spouses and both co-therapists.

[j] Total percentages do not equal 100% because of incomplete data reports in the studies noted.

in fact, did receive some professional attention, the majority of these investigations did employ random assignment of patients to treatment and no-treatment conditions and the quality of the research design of most of these studies is at least adequate (Gurman, 1973c). Thus, it is encouraging to learn that ten of the eleven studies using no-treatment groups have found a variety of interventions producing significant therapeutic change.

Six of the ten positive outcome studies have explored the efficacy of direct,

Table 2. Results of Controlled Studies of Marital Therapy Outcome [a]

Author	Date	Nature of Treatment(s)	Treatment Outcome Compared to Control
Cardillo	1971	Communication role training	Treatment superior to control
Ely	1970	"Conjugal"—communication training based on teaching of client-centered inter- personal "conditions"	Treatment superior to control
Graham	1968	Conjoint therapy; conjoint plus individual therapy	Both treatments superior to control
Griffin	1967	Individual treatment (wives only)	Treatment superior to control
Hickman and Baldwin	1971	Conjoint counseling; programmed text	Both treatments superior to control
Kind	1968	Brief interpersonal com- munication training	No difference between treatment and control
Maizlish and Hurley	1963	Group therapy	Treatment superior to control
Matanovich	1970	Conjoint plus individual counseling; encounter tapes	Encounter treatment superior to control
Most	1964	Individual treatment (wives only)	Treatment superior to control
Pierce	1973	Group communications training based on teaching of client-centered interpersonal "conditions"	Treatment superior to control
Weiman	1973	Conjugal therapy; recipro- cal reinforcement therapy	Both treatments superior to control
		SUMMARY	Treatment superior to control in 10 of 11 studies reviewed

[a] For details regarding design, therapists, patients, change, criteria, etc., see Gurman, 1973c. This table focuses only on outcome of treatment vs. controls; see Table 3 for details regarding comparative effects of different treatments.

teaching-based models for improving marital communication skills. The most commonly used skill-training methods have involved variations of "Conjugal Therapy" based on Guerney's (1964) early work with mothers and their children. In essence, Conjugal Therapy is a direct application of the work of Rogers (1957) and Truax and Carkhuff (1967), in which couples are taught facilitative interpersonal relationship skills such as empathic listening and responding, unconditional positive regard (acceptance, warmth), and genuineness and spontaneity of expression. These reports and others (Miller, 1971; Nunnally, 1971; Wells, Figurel, and McNamee, 1974), plus studies (Griffin, 1967; Gurman, 1973d) in which naturalistic change in these relationship dimensions during therapy has been found to be related to positive marital growth, support the salience of these dimensions of husband-wife interaction (Navran, 1967; Quick and Jacob, 1973).

Summary Comment on the Efficacy of Couples Therapy

While research on the effectiveness of marital therapy has been appearing much more frequently the past few years, it is clear that the field is behind related research in individual psychotherapy (Bergin, 1971; Bergin and Strupp, 1972), group therapy (Bednar and Lawlis, 1971; Lieberman, Yalom, and Miles, 1973), and behavior therapy (Franks and Wilson, 1973, Yates, 1971) in terms of both the number of studies and their methodological sophistication. Nevertheless, the concerns expressed earlier regarding the lack of base-rate data for no-treatment patients can be reasonably attenuated somewhat because of the evidence slowly being adduced in controlled studies of the outcome of couples therapy. As the present author (1973c) has emphasized, however, a great deal of further work in the area will be needed in an effort to accumulate data on specific treatment strategies for focalized marital difficulties. Treatment outcomes will need to be compared to no-treatment changes with respect to very clearly identified marital disturbances. For example, there are many forms of communicative dysfunction in marriage and it might be expected that independent treatments will be developed for each of these interactional patterns. Furthermore, disharmony arising out of power imbalances, lack of problem-solving skills, and noncomplementary role-functions may well call for different modes of intervention. It is highly improbable that any one clinical method will prove to be superior to all other methods for all types of marital disturbance. A technique-based clinical taxonomy of marital disorder will probably prove to be the applied frontier in working with couples in conflict.

Comparative Results in Marital Therapy

Luborsky (1972) has presented a thorough summary of all the controlled comparative studies of psychotherapy (marital and family therapies excluded) available at the time. On the basis of the emerging "box scores," he concluded that comparisons of group vs. individual therapy, client-centered vs. other therapies, behavior therapy vs. other therapies, and time-unlimited vs. time-limited therapies showed no clear differential effects for one modality vs. others. Therefore, he suggested, in the spirit of the dodo bird in *Alice in Wonderland*, "All have won, so all shall have prizes."

The results of the studies on the comparative effectiveness of several major methods of marital therapy are summarized in Table 3. It is important to point out that "marital therapy" is not, of course, a unitary phenomenon. At least six major formats and strategies in the area can be identified: conjoint therapy, concurrent therapy, individual therapy, group therapy, conjugal therapy, and

Table 3. Outcomes of Comparative Studies of Marital Therapy Methods

Author	Date	Treatment Methods Compared	Outcome
Burton & Kaplan	1968	Concurrent group vs. concurrent individual	Group superior
Cookerly	1973	Group and "interview" forms of concurrent, conjoint, and individual, i.e., 6 methods	Both conjoint treatments superior to other 4 methods; divorce rate lower in each "interview" form than in corresponding group form
Freeman et al.	1969	Conjoint vs. groups vs. individual	No differences among treatments
Graham	1968	Conjoint only vs. conjoint plus individual	Conjoint only superior
Hickman & Baldwin	1970	Conjoint vs. programmed communication training	Conjoint superior
Matanovich	1970	Encounter tapes vs. individual plus conjoint therapy	Encounter method
Pierce	1973	Communication training vs. insight therapy	Communication training superior
Reid & Shyne	1969	Brief vs. open-ended casework	Brief superior to open on some dimensions
Weiman	1973	Conjugal therapy vs. reciprocal reinforcement therapy	No difference between treatments

behavior therapy. These categories are far from being mutually exclusive, since the first four denote who (which marital partners) is present during treatment, while the latter two imply the nature of the intervention mode per se. Thus, for example, all conjugal therapy is conjoint, some is conducted in groups, etc. Behavioral treatment can likewise occur in conjoint fashion, in individual sessions, in groups, etc. Keeping this overlap issue in mind is crucial in attempting to draw inferences from the data in Table 3. That is, in none of those studies were all treatment interventions "pure," i.e., nonoverlapping with other modes or strategies. When an author's method is described as "group therapy," for example, one is uncertain as to whether salient elements of other treatments were also being applied, either by (research) design or naturalistic emergence.

With these interpretive caveats in mind, what tentative conclusions may be drawn from the available research on the comparative effectiveness of the marital therapies? Each of the six primary forms of couples therapy has been studied in at least one report; yet none has appeared in more than two. Some *very tentative* conclusions and observations can be put forth about the major marital therapy methods. *Conjoint therapy* (nonbehavioral) has been found superior to conjoint plus individual therapy, programmed communication-enhancing methods, group therapy, concurrent therapy, and individual therapy. While the studies on the comparative effects of conjoint vs. other marital therapies are still few in number, the consistent finding of the greater efficacy of conjoint methods is a striking one in a literature which, as will be seen below, has generally failed to amass converging research results. It will be particularly interesting to determine whether conjoint therapies of different modes produce differential effects and rates of improvement; one such project (Crowe, 1973) is now in progress at the Maudsley Hospital in London. Limited evidence suggests that *group couples therapy* is superior to individual and concurrent treatment. Group therapy generally retains the conjoint nature of treatment, so that it is still to be determined whether the salient elements in couples groups derive from spouses' being seen together or from the group experience *per se*. Another useful comparison in this form of therapy would be between broadly based group approaches and more structured and focused ones, such as conjugal therapy. *Conjugal therapy* has been examined in only two comparative studies (Pierce, 1972; Weiman, 1973). Still, several reports with good-quality research designs (Ely, 1970; Miller, 1971; Nunnally, 1971; Wells *et al.*, 1974) have marshaled evidence for the utility of this strategy for the enhancement of dyadic communication. Further research is likely to summon greater support for this model of teaching facilitative marital relationship skills. In the only available comparative study of *behavioral marital therapy* (Weiman, 1973), reciprocal reinforcement therapy (Rappaport and Harrell, 1972; Stuart, 1969) produced positive therapeutic effects essentially equivalent to those of conjugal therapy. A growing series of carefully documented empirical reports (Knox, 1973; Patterson, Hops, and Weiss, 1972; Rappaport and Harrell, 1972; Stuart, 1969; Turner, 1972; Weiman *et al.*, 1973; Weiss *et al.*, 1973; Welch and Goldstein, 1972) predict a promising future for behavioral models based on reciprocal reinforcement, contractual negotiation, and other methods borrowed from social learning theory and social exchange theory (Thibaut and Kelley, 1959). *Concurrent therapy*, in which spouses are seen individually but in the same period of time by the same therapist, is definitely on the wane in clinical practice (Gurman, 1973b). Individual therapy for marital problems similarly has fallen into general disrepute (Hurvitz, 1967) for obvious reasons about the essential dyadic or systems nature of marital discord, although its use may be justified clinically (e.g., Goldstein, 1971; Goldstein and Francis, 1969) when one spouse refuses to participate in treatment *and* when the problematic behavior of the reluctant spouse is relatively undramatic.

Comparative Improvement Rates of the Marital Therapies

Another approach to tentatively assessing the comparative efficacy of different methods of marital therapy is to compare the reported improvement rates for each modality. Table 4 presents such data. All the comments made up to this point regarding the overlap of treatment interventions, the tenuous baseline data

TABLE 4. COMPARATIVE IMPROVEMENT RATES OF MARITAL THERAPY METHODS [a]

Treatment Method	Very Much or Good Deal Improved	Somewhat Improved	Little Improved or No Change	Worse
Group Therapy [b]	54%	16%	18%	8%
Conjoint Therapy: All Types [c]	63%	4%	26%	.005%
Conjoint Therapy: Behavioral [d]	100%	0	0	0
Conjoint Therapy: Non-Behavioral [e]	62%	4%	27%	.005%
Behavioral Therapy: All Types [f]	89%	0	11%	0

[a] All improvement rates percentages are based on total samples reported in each study, not on percent improved, to account for differences in sample sizes. Studies (Burton & Kaplan, 1968; Freeman *et al.*, 1969; Preston *et al.*, 1953) not reporting improvement rates according to treatment type are excluded.
[b] Includes studies of couples seen in groups only, although treatment was conjoint in that partners were treated in same therapy groups (Hardcastle, 1972; Hooper *et al.*, 1968; Linden *et al.*, 1968; Maizlish & Hurley, 1963; Targow & Zweber, 1969). Total *N*=90.
[c] Excluding studies of group therapy. Includes studies by Bellville *et al.*, 1969; Brandreth & Pike, 1967; Dicks, 1967; Fitzgerald, 1969; Gurman, 1973c; Stuart, 1969. Total *N*=213.
[d] Includes only the study by Stuart (1969). *N*=4 couples.
[e] Includes studies by Bellville *et al.*, 1969; Brandreth & Pike, 1967; Dicks, 1967; Fitzgerald, 1969; Gurman, 1973d. Total *N*=209.
[f] Includes studies by Goldstein, 1971; Goldstein & Francis, 1969; Stuart, 1969; Total *N*=19.

for untreated couples, etc., need to be kept in mind in such an analysis. Finally, as noted in tablenotes b through f, the total subject pools across studies are *extremely* small, so that generalizations based on these data may be quite hazardous in that the treatment results obtained may, to an indeterminate extent, be particular to the treatment settings in which the studies noted were conducted. Nevertheless, what emerges quite clearly from these data is, not surprisingly, fully consistent in principle with the conclusion reached earlier, i.e., that different marital therapies yet have not been adequately demonstrated to produce significant differential treatment outcomes.

THERAPIST, PATIENT, AND TREATMENT FACTORS INFLUENCING THE OUTCOME OF MARITAL THERAPY

Our final approach to examining the empirical literature on marital therapy focuses on therapist, patient, and treatment factors (excluding modality types) which have been studied in relation to treatment outcome. Although there is a substantial literature in this realm in other psychotherapies (see, for example, Bergin and Garfield, 1971; Luborsky *et al.*, 1971), this domain has been essentially untapped by marital therapy researchers. Nevertheless, both the existing findings *and* the absence of relevant research offer some useful implications for clinical practice.

The Therapist's Contribution

The only therapist characteristic that has been studied in relation to patient change is that of experience level. Two reports have shown that more experienced therapists, working singly, have produced better treatment outcomes than inexperienced therapists (see Table 5). This finding is fully consistent with the data emerging from Luborsky *et al.*'s (1971) analysis of factors affecting outcome in individual psychotherapy. Unfortunately, there is still little empirical understanding of the mechanisms or processes by which experience facilitates change. Increased diagnostic acumen, comfort-with-self as a healing agent, greater self-awareness, etc., are among the likely explanatory candidates, based on *clinical* inference. A forthcoming analysis of this area (Auerbach and Johnson, in preparation) will offer the first thorough consideration of the dimensions of therapist experience which influence therapeutic change.

In addition, two studies (see Table 5) have found that discrepancies between therapists' experience levels in co-therapy are *negatively* related to outcome, i.e., the less alike co-therapists are in terms of their amount of clinical experience, the poorer are the results of their treatment efforts. These findings are probably explicable in terms of the associated status differences of co-therapists and the resulting interaction dynamics and perceptions in four-way couples

TABLE 5. THERAPIST, PATIENT AND TREATMENT FACTORS AFFECTING
THE OUTCOME OF MARITAL THERAPY

Author	Date	Variable	Results or Relationship to Outcome
		Therapist Factors	
Freeman et al.	1969	Therapist experience level	Positive
Griffin	1967	Therapist experience level	Positive
Gurman	1973e	Co-therapist experience level difference	Negative
Rice et al.	1972	Co-therapist experience level difference	Negative
		Patient Factors	
Griffin	1967	Change in own and spouse's empathy, warmth, & genuineness	Positive
Gurman	1973e	Age (husband, wife, and average)	None
		Previous therapy	None
		Years married	None
Gurman	1973d	Change in spouse-spouse interpersonal facilitative skill (empathy, warmth, genuineness)	Positive
Freeman et al.	1969	Age	None
		Previous therapy	None
		Years married	None
Preston et al.	1953	Both spouses involved in treatment (vs. one spouse involved)	Positive
		Therapist-Patient Interactive Factors	
Beutler	1971	Patient-therapist attitude convergence	None
		Spouse-spouse attitude convergence	Positive
Gurman	1973f	Patient-co-therapist attitude convergence	Positive (varies according to P-T pair)
		Spouse-spouse attitude convergence	Positive
		Treatment Factors	
Freeman et al.	1969	Treatment length	None
Gurman	1973e	Treatment length	Positive
Reid & Shyne	1969	Brief vs. extended casework	Brief superior on some dimensions
Turner	1972	Increasing positive behaviors vs. decreasing negative behaviors	Increasing positive yielded superior results

therapy. Such issues are discussed in detail in two other chapters (Rice, Fey and Kepecs, 1972; Rice and Rice, 1974) in this volume.

Considering the abundance of research (Gurman and Razin, in preparation) on the therapist's contribution to psychotherapy outcome, the lack of work in this area specific to marital therapy is surprising. Given this situation, marital therapists may, unfortunately, be likely to *assume* that those therapist variables which are salient in individual therapy are equally potent in couples treatment. While this *may* be the case, and both reason and clinical intuition would suggest it to be so, only sound empirical study can verify this assumption.

The Patient's Contribution

There exists little empirical knowledge of the ways in which patients contribute to the outcome of couples therapy, either in terms of those characteristics they "bring with them" to treatment or those that are assessed in the process of the therapeutic encounter. None of the patient variables (absence of psychotic trends, amount of motivation, high levels of initial anxiety or other affects, intellectual capacity, likability) which seem rather certain to be predictive of the outcome of individual psychotherapy (Luborsky *et al.*, 1971), have yet been investigated systematically in the practice of marital therapy. There is a great deal of *clinical* lore available about what couples are responsive to therapy, but little empirical documentation of what patient variables influence therapy outcome. It appears, tentatively, that patient changes attributable to the *process* of couples therapy may be relevant to these issues, e.g., couples whose attitudes converge over the course of treatment and couples whose quality of facilitative dyadic interpersonal skill improves appear to derive substantial benefit from treatment (see Table 5).

Treatment Factors Influencing Marital Change

Apart from matters of treatment modality (e.g., group, individual) and orientation (e.g., client-centered, behavioral) per se, *the* most consistent finding in individual therapy research with regard to treatment variables is that treatment length is positively related to treatment outcome (Luborsky *et al.*, 1971). Why this relationship should obtain is uncertain. Luborsky *et al.* offer the suggestions that if patients are getting useful treatment, they may remain in treatment longer and that therapists, the most common raters of outcome, may overestimate positive change in those patients who have remained in therapy longer. In addition, many therapists are convinced that some minimum number of sessions are required for any "real" change to occur, so that patients who leave therapy early tend to receive poor outcome ratings.

As noted in Table 5, only two marital therapy studies have examined the relationship between treatment length and outcome in time-unlimited therapy, yielding one positive and one negative finding. Gurman's (1973c) earlier review of the results of marital therapy found a *negative* relationship ($ms = .57$, $.075 > p > .05$) approaching statistical significance between the rate (percent) of improvement in marital therapy and the length of treatment in the nine studies which provided such data. An updated calculation of this relationship, based on those studies ($N = 10$) appearing in Table 1 which either report average treatment length or from which such data can be determined, yields (1) a Spearman *rho* of $-.48$ ($.075 > p > .05$) between length and the percent of patients judged to be "very much or a good deal improved" and (2) a *rho* of $-.79$ ($p < .01$) between length and the percent of patients rated "very much or a good deal improved" or "somewhat improved." These findings may suggest that, at least in some situations, treatment length may be negatively related to treatment outcome with married couples. It should be kept in mind, however, that these data reflect the relationship between treatment length and *percent* of couples showing improvement and that, therefore, a different relationship may exist between the number of treatment sessions specific couples receive and the extent to which they themselves improve.

Still, it is notable that across those studies in Table 1 in which treatment length data could be found, 61 percent of the couples were "very much or a good deal improved" and 76 percent were "very much or a good deal improved" or "somewhat improved" after an average treatment length of only 16.68 sessions! Thus, while the relationship between the length of therapy and the outcome of therapy on a case-by-case basis is uncertain, a great many couples appear to be deriving a great deal of benefit from a modest amount of actual therapeutic contact.

Co-Therapists vs. A Single Therapist

At the time this chapter was being prepared, no controlled studies existed on the comparative effectiveness of co-therapists vs. single therapists in the therapy of married couples. Some indirect evidence bearing on this very important question has been presented by Gurman (1973c) and an updated analysis of the data relevant to this matter is presented in Table 6. Clinical and theoretical assertions notwithstanding, it is evident that, on the basis of improvement rates across studies wherein the number of therapists per couple could be determined, there is no firm evidence of outcome differences between treatments conducted by single therapists and co-therapist teams. It is worth noting, however, that couples treated in groups do appear to derive more benefit from the co-therapy arrangement than couples seen by themselves (see note e, Table 6).

TABLE 6. IMPROVEMENT RATES IN STUDIES OF CONJOINT MARITAL THERAPY CONDUCTED BY CO-THERAPISTS AND SINGLE THERAPISTS

Co-Therapist Treatment				Single-Therapist Treatment			
Author	Date	Improved[a]	No Change[a]	Author	Date	Improved[a]	No Change[a]
Bellville et al.[b]	1969	26/44 (59%)	18/44 (41%)	Brandreth & Pike[b]	1967	31/50 (62%)	14/50 (28%)
Gurman[b]	1973d	9/12 (75%)	3/12 (25%)	Dicks[b,e]	1967	28/36 (78%)	8/36 (22%)
Hardcastle[c]	1972	3/7 (43%)	4/7 (57%)	Fitzgerald[b]	1969	37/57 (65%)	20/57 (35%)
Hooper et al.[c]	1968	8/10 (80%)	2/10 (20%)	Stuart[b]	1969	4/4 (100%)	0/4 (0%)
Linden et al.[b]	1968	10/11 (90%)	1/11 (10%)				
Maizlish & Hurley[c]	1963	26/32 (80%)	6/32 (20%)				
Reding et al.[c]	1967	8/10 (80%)	1/10 (10%)				
Total[d]				Total[d]			
Couples		53/77 (70%)	23/77 (30%)	Couples		95/147 (65%)	42/147 (28%)
Individuals		37/49 (74%)	12/49 (24%)	Individuals		—	—
Couples & individuals Combined		90/126 (71%)	35/126 (28%)	Couples & Individuals		95/139 (72%)	34/139 (24%)

Note: "Single therapist" refers to the conjoint treatment of a couple by one therapist. This table represents an updating of the data originally reported in Gurman, 1973c.

a Improved=combined data on patients rated "very much improved" and "good deal improved"; No Change=data on patients rated "little improved" and "no improvement."

b Outcome based on ratings of couples qua couples, not for husbands and wives separately.

c Outcome based on ratings of spouses as individuals, not for couples qua couples.

d Couples=summed improvement rates in studies based on ratings of change of the couple qua couple; Individuals = summed improvement rates in studies based on ratings of change of spouses as individuals; Couples & Individuals Combined = summed improvement rates in studies based on ratings of change of both couples qua couples and of spouses as individuals. Total percentages do not equal 100% because of incomplete data reports in the studies noted in Table 1.

e It is interesting to note that when group co-therapy and regular co-therapy are analyzed separately, the improvement-no change percentages become: group, 83% and 17%; regular, 67% and 33%.

SOME IMPLICATIONS FOR MARITAL THERAPY PRACTICE

This review concludes with presentation of several propositions for marital therapy practice which seem to follow from the research literature that has been considered. Whenever attempts are made to derive practical implications of psychotherapy research there is a danger of going beyond the data. In the case of marital therapy, the lack of well-designed research means that such errors in generalization are almost inherently guaranteed. Nevertheless, the existing research literature does appear to have some useful and important messages for the practicing clinician. The critical reader who may want to apply existing empirical work to his practice would, however, be well advised as he reads this section, to bear in mind the many issues that have been raised earlier in this chapter with regard to methodological deficiencies of the marital therapy literature.

The Impact of Marital Therapy

1. *Marital therapy has been demonstrated to produce at least a moderately positive therapeutic effect across a heterogeneous collection of patients, therapists, and treatment modalities.* Thus, marital therapy, as currently practiced, seems to facilitate change to a clinically significant extent. However, it must be added that, from an empirical point of reference, relatively little can be said about the mechanisms or processes by which such change takes place, except, to some extent, in the case of behavioral methods. Clinically, it is necessary to remember that there is no one treatment strategy which is superior for all the varieties of marital disharmony. This issue is developed in greater detail below.

2. *Almost all studies of marital therapy have dealt with therapies of short duration. Thus, the finding of a 76 percent improvement rate over an average of roughly four months of treatment suggests that noteworthy clinical gains may often be observed with a relatively modest investment of professional time and at rather reasonable expense to patients.* A corollary of this observation is that we have absolutely no research evidence on the effects of long-term couples therapy. This does not necessarily imply that some couples may not require extended therapy but, rather, that the burden of proof of what additional gains may be found in therapy of long duration rests with those clinicians who would advocate such practices.

3. *Marital therapy is not always beneficial or merely nonchange-producing; at times marital therapy may make patients worse.* If an intervention into human behavior is potent enough to produce positive change, under some conditions it may yield a change for the worse. Data gleaned from Table 1 leads

to the following observations about "deterioration" in couples therapy. Across those studies which included a "Worse" outcome category, 5 percent of the couples were rated as having changed in the negative direction. This figure is consistent with observed "deterioration" rates for individual psychotherapy (Bergin, 1966, 1971). Furthermore, deterioration was noted in five of the fourteen (36 percent) studies which included a "Worse" category. In addition, several studies lumped together the categories of "No Change" and "Worse," so that it is probable that the incidence of deterioration in these studies was somewhat higher than the 5 percent figure noted above, perhaps as high as 10 percent.

The causes of deterioration in psychotherapy are not without controversy. Bergin (1971) has proposed three likely explanatory schemes. He suggests that deterioration may occur (1) when an already deteriorating patient enters treatment in a process which cannot be reversed, (2) when patients who are deteriorating yet could be helped are matched with therapists who lack the skills to prevent further negative change or to reverse the direction of change, and (3) when a patient's neurotic equilibrium or resolution is undone by the therapist's interventions. It seems likely that some of the specific therapist characteristics (Bergin, 1971) likely to produce deterioration in individual therapy may also obtain in the treatment of married couples.

PATIENT SELECTION AND THERAPY PROCESS

1. *Despite much experiential clinical lore about which couples are likely to be responsive to couples therapy, many of these beliefs are paradoxical and, in addition, lack consensus among clinicians. The available research in this regard has failed to delineate what couple characteristics suggest positive treatment prognoses.* Gurman (1971), for example, has noted that some workers in group marital therapy espouse that an inability to relate openly to others is an important indication *for* referral to a couples group, while others argue that such an inability contraindicates such treatment. Furthermore, patient characteristics such as duration of marriage, ages of and presence or absence of children, extent of previous therapy, either individual or marital, etc., have not yet been demonstrated to predict couples' responses to therapy. In fact, even the degree of individual or shared (dyadic) pathology has not been examined in relation to outcome. Those patients who are most likely to benefit from treatment are assumed to be those who are least disturbed, i.e., "healthier." Still, this is an inference and has not yet achieved the status of empirical fact. The major practical implication of these points is that it may be a gross clinical error, at this point in the development of marital therapies, to initially exclude from treatment those couples who only intuitively appear to be potentially unresponsive.

2. *The qualitative process changes that occur in couples therapy, such as increased attitudinal similarity and ability to understand and respond effectively to a spouse's feelings, are probably rather good predictors of treatment outcome, even when resolution of differences in beliefs and values and the development of more efficient modes of communication are not themselves the major therapeutic targets.* It seems likely that the enhancement of effective communicative styles frequently is a necessary condition for the achievement of any treatment goals. If spouses are unable to tune in to each other's feelings, subtly expressed or manifest needs and wishes, it would appear difficult to facilitate other dimensions of interaction, whether these involve sexual behavior, child-rearing practices, the establishment of rules or meta-rules (Haley, 1963) about the division of labor in the family, decision-making powers and responsibilities, etc.

The Therapist's Contribution: The Use of Co-Therapists

1. *There is, at present, no substantive empirical basis for the necessity of using co-therapy teams in marital therapy.* Available data do not "prove" that treatment by one and two therapists is equally effective, but merely that there is insufficient evidence that a difference exists. Nor does this observation suggest that co-therapy should not be used, especially in training situations, where the confusion and discomfort of neophyte marital therapists may pose serious problems in terms of patient welfare. The complexity of the four-way interaction (see, for example, Rice and Rice, 1974) is such that under some circumstances in which co-therapist differences cannot be resolved couples may lose rather than gain by disruptive co-therapist modeling.

2. *Tentative evidence suggests that co-therapist teams may be of special value when couples are treated in groups.* Since couples in groups are likely to engage in multiple collusions both across- and within-gender, a second therapist may be particularly useful in untangling such collaborative resistances.

The Conduct of Marital Therapy: Application of Selected Treatment Strategies

1. *Since treatment length may be, to a significant extent, a function of the depth or breadth of dyadic marital pathology, an expedient model for dealing with disturbed marital relationships might usefully highlight the special value of intervention during acute marital crises in generally nondysfunctional marital relationships.* Chronically dysfunctional patterns of marital interaction may not respond well to couples therapy, especially therapy of short duration.

2. *Many long-standing marital difficulties may have become relatively autonomous from their original sources, so that behavioral disturbances may exist with relatively little attendant affect. In such cases, the marital therapist may need to intentionally precipitate a crisis in the marital relationship in order to arouse sufficient affect so that change becomes possible.* Obviously, such crisis-arousal should not endanger the patients' lives, and should be done under controlled therapeutic conditions. Stimulation of unexpressed fantasy material, provocative therapist exaggeration of characterological "styles," etc., may be useful in this regard.

3. *Conjoint therapy, in which couples are seen together, is almost always the preferred mode of intervention in dealing with marital difficulties.* While therapeutic work with individuals only may be necessary and at times sufficient for genuine change, the dangers inherent in treating only one member of the dyad (Hurvitz, 1967) are many. In addition, the available research evidence consistently favors joint treatment over both individual treatment and concurrent treatment.

4. *Structured therapeutic encounters, in which direct teaching models are operative, hold out great promise for the marital therapies and have thus far received some empirical support for their efficacy.* If one views a disturbed marital relationship as the consequence of inappropriate learning experiences which result in ineffective means of positive interactional influence (Patterson *et al.*, 1972; Weiss *et al.*, 1973; Welch and Goldstein, 1972), then clinical methods which deal directly with displeasing marital exchanges would seem to offer the most efficient and expedient model for restructuring dysfunctional marriages. Treatment based on basic principles of social learning theory would seem to be highly recommended, especially for situations in which highly specific marital difficulties exist or when a couple's initially vague complaints of dissatisfaction can be translated into clearly operationalized and publicly observable behaviors. While it is unlikely that the models developed by behavioral marital therapists will be relevant to the full range of marital dysfunctions, behavioral intervention is certainly the most attractive modality for a variety of marital distresses, especially those marked by an excessive use of spouses' aversive means of interpersonal influence, with a concomitant lack of reciprocity of positive reinforcement (Patterson *et al.*, 1972).

Efficient and effective methods for improving marital communication now exist. Conjugal therapy methods, which view husband-wife "communication" as a set of *skills* which can be learned through structured and systematic role-playing and modeling experiences, are clearly preferable to other existing approaches either when treatment is focused specifically on "improving communication" or when communicative styles need to be refined in order to facilitate work on other treatment goals.

5. *Marital therapists should work toward the development of new tech-*

niques which facilitate marital happiness in specific ways. While it is clear that the current practices of marital therapists produce at least moderate therapeutic gains on-the-average, the future of marital therapy, in both the office and the laboratory, is certain to be highlighted by an evolving technological taxonomy of marital interventions. In this regard, we do not advocate an "anything goes" attitude, but rather the adoption of a working sense of both freedom to innovate and critical skepticism to evaluate. Paul's (1967) challenging question, *"What* treatment, by *whom,* is most effective for *this* individual with *that* specific problem and under *which* set of circumstances?" though originally directed toward researchers, is an important one for clinicians as well. The practicing marital therapist would be well-advised to work toward specification of treatment goals at all times. Such specificity does not inherently require the use of a "behavioral" approach, as might be believed by some readers. Any treatment goals that are decided upon mutually by therapist and patient and for which a reasonable index of measurement or assessment is available or can be developed would meet this criterion. Since no one technique is equally applicable to all marital difficulties, it is clear that the field of marital therapy will need to foster the development of goal-relevant intervention procedures. Since changes in marital relationships can occur on many dimensions and since the assessment of change in such dyadic relationships is far more complex than change within an individual (Gurman, 1973c), marital therapists and their patients should work toward specifying treatment goals. As the expression has it, "If you don't know where you're going, you probably won't get there."

6. *The most important message of recent marital therapy outcome research for the practicing clinician is to avoid getting stuck in a unidimensional theoretical or technical rut. The marital therapist who feels comfortable doing* only *behavior therapy, or who* only *believes in teaching couples how to communicate effectively, or who belives that a spouse should* never *be seen alone for marital problems, etc., is ill-equipped for dealing with the complexities of disturbed marital relationships.* Advocacy of "technical eclecticism" in marital therapy (Friedman, 1972) seems to be the most desirable "orientation" and attitude in a field in which genuinely creative and clinically useful innovations are being evolved with increasing frequency. Each married couple is unique. The means for changing unsatisfying marital relationships into satisfying relationships or for facilitating a "de-coupling" process must then, in this sense, always have unique components. Therefore, a marital clinician should be able to respond therapeutically with a wide armamentarium of clinical skills geared toward the unique needs and desires of specific couples in conflict.

REFERENCES

Ackerman, N. W. (1967), *Treating the Troubled Family.* New York: Basic Books.

Auerbach, A. H., and M. Johnson (1975), "Research on the Therapist's Level of Experience." In A. S. Gurman and A. M. Razin (eds.), *The Therapist's Contribution to Effective Psychotherapy.* New York: Pergamon Press, in press.

Bednar, R. L., and G. F. Lawlis (1971), "Empirical Research in Group Psychotherapy." In A. E. Bergin and S. L. Garfield (eds.), *Handbook of Psychotherapy and Behavior Change.* New York: Wiley, pp. 812-838.

Bellville, T. P., O. N. Raths, and C. J. Bellville (1969), "Conjoint Marriage Therapy with a Husband-and-Wife Team," *American Journal of Orthopsychiatry,* 39:473-483.

Bergin, A. E. (1966), "Some Implications of Psychotherapy Research for Therapeutic Practice," *Journal of Abnormal Psychology,* 71:235-246.

———(1971), "Evaluation of Outcome in Psychotherapy." In A. E. Bergin and S. L. Garfield (eds.), *Handbook of Psychotherapy and Behavior Change.* New York: Wiley, pp 217-270.

———and H. H. Strupp (1972), *Changing Frontiers in the Science of Psychotherapy.* Chicago: Aldine.

Beutler, L. E. (1971), "Attitude Similarity in Marital Therapy," *Journal of Consulting and Clinical Psychology,* 37:298-301.

Brandreth, A., and R. Pike (1967), "Assessment of Marriage Counseling in a Small Family Agency," *Social Work,* 12:34-39.

Burton, G., and H. M. Kaplan (1968), "Group Counseling in Conflicted Marriages Where Alcoholism Is Present: Clients' Evaluation of Effectiveness," *Journal of Marriage and the Family,* 30:74-79.

Cardillo, J. P. (1971), "The Effects of Teaching Communication Roles in Interpersonal Perception and Self-concept in Disturbed Marriages." *Proceedings of the 77th Annual Convention of the American Psychological Association,* pp. 441-442.

Cookerly, J. R. (1973), "The Outcome of the Six Major Forms of Marriage Counseling Compared: A Pilot Study," *Journal of Marriage and the Family.*

Crowe, M. (1973), Personal communication.

Dicks, H. V. (1967), *Marital Tensions: Clinical Studies Toward a Psychological Theory of Interaction.* New York: Basic Books.

Ely, A. L. (1970), "Efficacy of Training in Conjugal Therapy." Unpublished Ph.D. diss.: Rutgers University.

Eysenck, H. (1966), *The Effects of Psychotherapy.* New York: International Science Press.

Ferber, A., and M. Mendelsohn (1969), "Training for Family Therapy," *Family Process,* 8:25-32.

——— and A. Napier (1972), *The Book of Family Therapy.* New York: Jason Aronson, Inc.

Fitzgerald, R. V. (1969), "Conjoint Marital Psychotherapy: An Outcome and Follow-up Study," *Family Process,* 8:260-271.

Franks, C. M., and G. T. Wilson, (eds.) (1973), *Annual Review of Behavior Therapy Theory and Practice 1973.* New York: Brunner/Mazel.

Freeman, S. J. J., E. J. Leavens, and D. J. McCulloch (1969), "Factors Associated with Success or Failure in Marital Counseling," *Family Coordinator,* 18:125-128.

Friedman, P. H. (1972), "Personalistic Family and Marital Therapy." In A. A. Lazarus (ed.), *Clinical Behavior Therapy*. New York: Brunner/Mazel.

Goldstein, M. K. (1971), "Behavior Rate Change in Marriages: Training Wives to Modify Husbands' Behavior," *Dissertation Abstracts International*, 32(1-B):559.

———and B. Francis, (1969), "Behavior Modification of Husbands by Wives." Paper presented at the Annual Meeting of the National Council on Family Relations, Washington, D. C.

Graham, J. A. (1968), "The Effect of the Use of Counselor Positive Responses to Positive Perceptions of Mate in Marriage Counseling," *Dissertation Abstracts International*, 28(9-A):3504.

Griffin, R. W. (1967), "Change in Perception of Marital Relationship as Related to Marriage Counseling," *Dissertation Abstracts International*, 27(1-A):3956.

Guerney, B.L. (1964), "Filial Therapy: Description and Rationale," *Journal of Consulting Psychology*, 28:304-310.

Gurman, A.S. (1971), "Group Marital Therapy: Clinical and Empirical Implications for Outcome Research," *International Journal of Group Psychotherapy*, 21:174-189.

———(1973a), "Marital Therapy: A Content-Coded Bibliography, 1928-1972," JSAS *Catalog of Selected Documents in Psychology*, 3:55-56.

———(1973b), "Marital Therapy: Emerging Trends in Research and Practice," *Family Process*, 12:45-54.

———(1973c), "The Effects and Effectiveness of Marital Therapy: A Review of Outcome Research," *Family Process*, 12:145-170.

———(1973d), "Married Couples' Interpersonal Facilitativeness and Outcome in Conjoint Therapy." Unpublished manuscript: University of Wisconsin Medical School.

———(1973e), "Therapist, Patient and Treatment Factors Influencing the Outcome of Marital Therapy." Unpublished manuscript: University of Wisconsin Medical School.

———(1973f), "Attitude Change in Marital Co-therapy," *Journal of Family Counseling*, in press.

———and A. M. Razin, (eds.), (1975), *The Therapist's Contribution to Effective Psychotherapy: An Empirical Assessment*. New York: Pergamon Press, in press.

Haley, J. (1963), *Strategies of Psychotherapy*. New York: Grune & Stratton.

Hardcastle, D. R. (1972), "Measuring Effectiveness in Group Marital Counseling," *Family Coordinator*, 21:213-218.

Hickman, M. E., and B. A. Baldwin (1971), "Use of Programmed Instruction to Improve Communication in Marriage," *Family Coordinator*, 20:121-125.

Hooper, D., A. Sheldon, and A. J. R. Koumans (1968), "A Study of Group Psychotherapy with Married Couples," *International Journal of Social Psychiatry*, 15:57-68.

Hurvitz, N. (1967), "Marital Problems Following Psychotherapy with Spouse," *Journal of Consulting Psychology*, 31:38-47.

Kind, J. (1968), "The Relationship of Communication Efficiency to Marital Happiness and an Evaluation of Short-Term Training in Interpersonal Communication with Married Couples," *Dissertation Abstracts International*, 29:(3-B):1173.

Knox, D. (1973), "Behavior Contracts in Marriage Counseling," *Journal of Family Counseling*, 1:22-28.

Laing, R. D., and A. Esterson (1970), *Sanity, Madness, and the Family*. Baltimore: Penguin.

Linden, M. E., H. M. Goodwin, and and H. Resnik (1968), "Group Psychotherapy of Couples in Marriage Counseling," *International Journal of Group Psychotherapy,* 18:313-324.

Luborsky, L. B. (1972), "Which Psychotherapies Do Best for Whom? The Essence of What We Know from 35 Controlled Comparative Studies." Paper presented at the Third Annual Meeting of the Society for Psychotherapy Research, Nashville.

————, M. Chandler, A. H. Auerbach, J. Cohen, and H. M. Bachrach (1971), "Factors Influencing the Outcome of Psychotherapy: A Review of Quantitative Research," *Psychological Bulletin,* 75:145-185.

Lieberman, M. A., I. D. Yalom, and M. B. Miles (1973), *Encounter Groups: First Facts.* New York: Basic Books.

Matanovich, J. P. (1970), "The Effects of Short-Term Group Counseling upon Positive Perceptions of Mate in Marital Counseling," *Dissertation Abstracts International,* 31:(6-A):2688.

Maizlish, I. L., and J. P. Hurley, (1963), "Attitude Changes of Husbands and Wives in Time-Limited Group Psychotherapy," *Psychiatric Quarterly Supplement,* 37:230-249.

Miller, S. L. (1071), "The Effects of Communication Training in Small Groups upon Self-Disclosure and Openness in Engaged Couples' Systems of Interaction: A Field Experiment." Unpublished Ph.D. diss.: Department of Sociology University of Minnesota.

Most, E. (1964), "Measuring Change in Marital Satisfaction," *Social Work,* 9:64-70.

Napier, A., and C. A. Whitaker (1973), "Problems of the Beginning Family Therapist," *Seminars in Psychiatry,* 5:229-241.

Navran, L. (1967), "Communication and Adjustment in Marriage," *Family Process,* 6:173-184.

Nunnally, E. W. (1971), "Effects of Communication Training upon Interaction Awareness and Empathic Accuracy of Engaged Couples: A Field Experiment." Unpublished Ph.D. diss.: Department of Sociology, University of Minnesota.

Patterson, G. R., H. Hops, and R. Weiss (1972), "A Social Learning Approach to Reducing Rates of Marital Conflict." Paper presented at the Sixth Annual Meeting of the Association for the Advancement of Behavior Therapy, New York.

Paul, G. L. (1967), "Strategy of Outcome Research in Psychotherapy," *Journal of Consulting Psychology,* 31:109-118.

Peterson, D. R. (1968), *The Clinical Study of Social Behavior.* New York: Appleton-Century-Crofts.

Pierce, R. M. (1973), "Training in Interpersonal Communication Skills with the Partners of Deteriorated Marriages," *Family Coordinator,* 22:223-227.

Preston, M. G., E. H. Mudd, and H. B. Froscher, (1953), "Factors Affecting Movement in Casework," *Social Casework,* 34:103-111.

Quick, E., and T. Jacob (1973), "Marital Disturbances in Relation to Role Theory and Relationship Theory," *Journal of Abnormal Psychology,* 82:309-316.

Rappaport, A. F., and J. Harrell (1972), "A Behavioral-Exchange Model for Marital Counseling," *Family Coordinator,* 21:203-212.

Reding, G. R., L.A. Charles, and M. B. Hoffman (1967), "Treatment of a Couple by a Couple, II: Conceptual Framework, Case Presentation and Follow-up Study," *British Journal of Medical Psychology,* 40:243-251.

Reid, W. J., and A. W. Shyne (1969), *Brief and Extended Casework.* New York: Columbia University Press.

Rice, D. G., W. F. Fey, and J. G. Kepecs (1972), "Therapist Experience and 'Style' as Factors In Co-therapy," *Family Process,* 11:1-12.
Rice, J. K., and D. G. Rice (1974), "Status and Sex-Role Issues in Co-therapy." In A. S. Gurman and D. G. Rice (eds.), *Couples in Conflict: New Directions in Marital Therapy.* New York: Jason Aronson, Inc.
Rogers, C. R. (1957), "The Necessary and Sufficient Conditions of Therapeutic Personality Change," *Journal of Consulting Psychology,* 21:95-103.
Speck, R. V. and C. L. Attneave (1973), *Family Networks.* New York: Pantheon.
Stuart, R. B. (1969), "Operant-Interpersonal Treatment for Marital Discord," *Journal of Consulting and Clinical Psychology,* 33:675-682.
————(1972), "Behavioral Remedies for Marital Ills: A Guide to the Use of Operant-Interpersonal Techniques." Paper presented at the International Symposium on Behavior Modification, Minneapolis.
Subotnik, L. (1972), "Spontaneous Remission: Fact or Artifact?" *Psychological Bulletin,* 77:32-48.
Targow, J. G., and R. V. Zweber (1969), "Participants' Reactions to Treatment in a Married Couple's Group," *International Journal of Group Psychotherapy,* 19:221-225.
Tharp, R. G., and R. J. Wetzel (1969), *Behavior Modification in the Natural Environment.* New York: Academic Press.
Thibaut, J. W., and H. H. Kelley (1959), *The Social Psychology of Groups.* New York: John Wiley & Sons.
Truax, C. B., and R. R. Carkhuff (1967), *Toward Effective Counseling and Psychotherapy.* Chicago: Aldine.
Turner, A. J. (1972), "Couple and Group Treatment of Marital Discord." Paper presented at the Sixth Annual Meeting of the Assocation for the Advancement of Behavior Therapy, New York.
Weiman, R. J. (1973), "Conjugal Relationship Modification and Reciprocal Reinforcement: A Comparison of Treatments for Marital Discord." Unpublished Ph.D. diss.: Pennsylvania State University.
————, D. I. Shoulders, and J. H. Farr (1973), "Reciprocal Reinforcement in Marital Therapy." Unpublished manuscript: Pennsylvania State University.
Weiss, R., H. Hops, and G. R. Patterson (1973), "A Framework for Conceptualizing Marital Conflict, a Technology for Altering It, Some Data for Evaluating It." In L. A. Hamerlynck, L. C. Handy, and E. J. Mash (eds.), *Behavior Change: Methodology, Concepts and Practice.* Champaign, Ill.: Research Press, pp. 309-342.
Welch, J. C., and M. K. Goldstein (1972), "The Differential Effects of Operant-Interpersonal Intervention." Paper presented at the Sixth Annual Meeting of the Association for the Advancement of Behavior Therapy, New York.
Wells, R. A., J. A. Figurel, and P. McNamee (1974), "Group Training with Conflicted Marital Couples." In A. S. Gurman and D. G. Rice (eds.), *Couples in Conflict: New Directions in Marital Therapy.* New York: Jason Aronson, Inc.
Yates, A. J. (1970), *Behavior Therapy.* New York: Wiley.

CHAPTER SOURCES

CHAPTER 1
"Marital and Family Therapy: Integrative Review and Critique," *Journal of Marriage and the Family*, 1970, Vol. 32, 501–538. Copyright 1970 by the National Council on Family Relations and reprinted by permission.

CHAPTER 2
"Marital Therapy: Emerging Trends in Research and Practice," *Family Process*, 1973, Vol. 12, 45–54. Reprinted by permission.

CHAPTER 3
"A Feminist Review of Marital Adjustment Literature: The Rape of the Locke," *Journal of Marriage and the Family,* 1971, Vol. 33, 483-516. Copyright 1971 by the National Council on Family Relations and reprinted by permission.

CHAPTER 4
"Counseling Implications of Comarital and Multilateral Relations," *The Family Coordinator*, 1972, Vol. 21, 267–273. Copyright 1972 by the National Council on Family Relations and reprinted by permission.

CHAPTER 5
(Original chapter prepared for this book.)

CHAPTER 6
"Therapist Experience and 'Style' as Factors in Co-Therapy," *Family Process*, 1972, Vol. 11, 1–12. Reprinted by permission.

CHAPTER 7
(Original chapter prepared for this book.)

CHAPTER 8
Copyright 1973 by the National Council on Family Relations and reprinted by permission. From *The Family Coordinator*, Vol. 22, 31–42.

CHAPTER 9
"Group Marital Therapy: Clinical and Empirical Implications for Outcome Research," *International Journal of Group Psychotherapy*, 1971, Vol. 21,

174–189. Copyright 1971 by International Universities Press and reprinted by permission.

CHAPTER 10

"Behavioral Approaches to Family and Couple Therapy," *American Journal of Orthopsychiatry*, 1970, Vol. 40, 106–118. Copyright 1970 by the American Orthopsychiatric Association and reprinted by permission.

CHAPTER 11

Copyright 1970 by the National Council on Family Relations and reprinted by permission. From *The Family Coordinator*, Vol. 19, 64–75.

CHAPTER 12

Paper presented at the International Symposium on Behavior Modification, Minneapolis, Minnesota, October 5, 1972. Copyright 1972 by Richard B. Stuart and reprinted by permission.

CHAPTER 13

Copyright 1972 by the National Council on Family Relations and reprinted by permission. From *The Family Coordinator*, Vol. 21, 203–212.

CHAPTER 14

(Original chapter prepared for this book.)

CHAPTER 15

Copyright 1972 by Pergamon Press and reprinted by permission. From the *Journal of Behavior Therapy and Experimental Psychiatry*, Vol. 3, 265–271.

CHAPTER 16

(Original chapter prepared for this book.)

CHAPTER 17

Copyright 1970 by the National Council on Family Relations and reprinted by permission. From *The Family Coordinator*, Vol. 19, 32–40.

CHAPTER 18

"Modification of Problematic Marital Communication Using Corrective Feedback and Instruction," *Behavior Therapy*, 1973, Vol. 4, 100–109. Copyright 1973 by Academic Press and reprinted by permission.

CHAPTER 19

"Structured Separation with Counseling: A Therapeutic Approach for Couples in Conflict," *Family Process*, 1972, Vol. 11, 299–310. Reprinted by permission.

CHAPTER 20

"Behavioral Techniques in Family-Oriented Crisis Intervention," *Archives of General Psychiatry*, 1973, Vol. 28, 111–116. Copyright 1973 by the American Medical Association and reprinted by permission.

CHAPTER 21

"The Effects and Effectiveness of Marital Therapy: A Review of Outcome Research," *Family Process*, 1973, Vol. 12, 145–170. Reprinted by permission.

CHAPTER 22

(Original chapter prepared for this book.)

Index

functional analysis (*see* behavioral analysis)

game theory, 34
generation gap, 170
Group for the Advancement of Psychiatry (GAP), 11, 26, 27
group marriage (*see* multilateral marriage)

husband rating wife, 78, 110, 227-30, 234-37
husband's expectations in marriage, 111-15, 243-44
husband's role, 81-82, 85-89, 111-15, 170-71
  and conflict management, 109
  and first child, 110

impotence, 290, 297-98, 303
integration of research, theory and practice, 44-48
interaction therapy, 15-19, 225-39
intercourse, 296-99, 305
intermittent reinforcement, 210
interpersonal therapy approach, 15-18
intra-personal therapy approach, 15-18
in-vivo desensitization, 282-86, 289-300, 303

kin network therapy, 27

lack of realism (*see* projection)
lack of sexual interest, 267-76, 291-92
learning approach, *see also* behavioral approach
  in family therapy, 209-22
  in marital therapy, 241-53, 258-76
life cycles, 92-93, 180-89
literature of marital therapy, 63-70, 379-81, 383-402, 407-25
Locke-Wallace Scale, 76

male dominance in family, 85, 97, 111
marital adjustment, 73, 123
  on basis of similarity, 98-102
  after childbirth, 80-93
  and children, 89-92, 93, 113
  and conflict management, 108-10, 328-38
  and married couples group therapy, 198-200, 324-25
  research in, 75-79

and role expectations, 111-12
and role reversal, 83-84
and sex differences, 111-15
and sexuality, 105-08, 114
stability as proxy for success, 75-76
and working wives, 94-98
Marital Adjustment Balance Score, 79
marital models, 80-85
marital relationship change (*see* change in marital relationship)
marital satisfaction (*see* marital adjustment)
marital therapist, functions of, 171-73
marital therapy, *see also* marriage counseling, married couples group therapy and behavioral approach, 138-39, 241-53
  birth of, 7-8
  change in, 387-92
  clinical practice of, 20-26
  and communication, 140-41, 197, 199, 315-25, 327-38, 340-50
  comparative results of, 412-16
  and co-therapy teams, 137-41, 145-46
  and crisis intervention, 141, 353-74
  definition of, 20, 166-67
  development of, 13-15, 407-08
  diagnosis in, 24-26
  effectiveness of, 401, 408-12, 421-22
  goals of, 173-74
  historical influences of research in, 379-80
  improvement rates, 395-97, 399, 410, 415-16, 420
  overview, 8-10
  relationship of research and practice of, 380-81
  research in, 37-41, 383-402, 407-25
  research needs of, 201-02, 400-02
  and sexual dysfunction, 281-300, 303-11
  techniques of, 168
  theory in, 30-32
  therapeutic approaches in, 20-24
marital treatment contract, 246, 258-59, 266-76
Marlowe-Crown Social Desirability Scale, 77
marriage, *see also* marital adjustment, marital therapy
  bias in research in, 74-75, 76, 78
  as closed system, 80